International Archives of the History of Ideas
Archives internationales d'histoire des idées

Founding Editors
Paul Dibon
Jeremy Popkin

Volume 242

International Archives of the History of Ideas/Archives internationales d'histoire des idées is a series which publishes scholarly works on the history of ideas in the widest sense of the word. It covers history of philosophy, science, political and religious thought and other areas in the domain of intellectual history. The chronological scope of the series extends from the Renaissance to the Post-Enlightenment. Founded in 1963 by R.H. Popkin and Paul Dibon, the International Archives of the History of Ideas/Archives internationales d'histoire des idées publishes, edits and translates sources that have been either unknown hitherto, or unavailable, and publishes new research in intellectual history, and new approaches within the field. The range of recent volumes in the series includes studies on skepticism, astrobiology in the early modern period, as well as translations and editions of original texts, such as the *Treatise of the Hypochondriack and Hysterick Diseases* (1730) by Bernard Mandeville. All books to be published in this Series will be fully peer-reviewed before final acceptance.

Joshua P. Hochschild • Turner C. Nevitt
Adam Wood • Gábor Borbély

Editors

Metaphysics Through Semantics: The Philosophical Recovery of the Medieval Mind

Essays in Honor of Gyula Klima

 Springer

Editors
Joshua P. Hochschild
Mount St. Mary's University
Emmitsburg, MD, USA

Turner C. Nevitt
University of San Diego
San Diego, CA, USA

Adam Wood
Wheaton College
Wheaton, IL, USA

Gábor Borbély
Eötvös Loránd University
Budapest, Hungary

ISSN 0066-6610 ISSN 2215-0307 (electronic)
International Archives of the History of Ideas Archives internationales d'histoire des idées
ISBN 978-3-031-15025-8 ISBN 978-3-031-15026-5 (eBook)
https://doi.org/10.1007/978-3-031-15026-5

This Springer imprint is published by the registered company Springer Nature Switzerland AG
The registered company address is: Gewerbestrasse 11, 6330 Cham, Switzerland

Preface

Gyula Klima's distinctive work recovering medieval philosophy has inspired a generation of scholars. Klima's attention to the distinctive terms, problems, and assumptions that constitute alternative historical conceptual frameworks has informed work in philosophy of language and logic, cognition and philosophical psychology, and metaphysics and theology.

This volume celebrates Klima's project by collecting new essays by colleagues, collaborators, and former students. Covering a wide range of thinkers (Plotinus, Anselm, Aquinas, Buridan, Ockham, and others) and various specific questions (e.g., about language, cognition, the soul, and God), it is unified by a common interest in applying historically sensitive, hermeneutically sophisticated, and logically rigorous philosophical interpretation to recover, and appreciate, lost perspectives.

Each chapter is published with a proper abstract, but for another reason, we forgo a conventional introduction summarizing the volume's contents: it would feel artificial. As a celebratory volume, collecting works from diverse scholars with varying points of contact with Klima's rich body of work, the collection is eclectic in style and content. Some individual chapters engage Klima's thought directly, others draw on his work explicitly or implicitly, still others don't reference him but address topics in one or another of many overlapping spheres of interest. What unifies the set of contributions is nothing more nor less than the inspiration of Klima's general "historical-analytical" intention, the concern to intelligibly reconstruct difficult fundamental ideas in the history of philosophy.

The volume is framed by two pieces which more directly expound and interpret the significance of Klima's intellectual project. At the beginning, a more personal and general appreciation of Klima's character as a person and scholar; at the end, a more detailed exposition of his record of scholarship, effectively an extended (though by no means comprehensive) bibliographic essay. By both we hope not only to introduce new readers to Klima's legacy but to honor the man who produced it.

Credit for conceiving this volume is impossible to give. Thankfully, while parallel lines don't meet, parallel conceptions can converge, and a critical mass of grateful scholars and former students eventually came to a common understanding and decided to execute. Some specific impetus deserves recognition. Gyula has been blessed with first one, and then another, devoted companion in life—devoted enough to travel to conferences with him and share in his friendships with students and colleagues. Making sure we were planning ahead for an appropriate landmark birthday, crucial encouragements and providential intercessions came first from Klima's late wife, Judit, before she died, and then later from Klima's second wife, Agnes.

As for the named editors, our work was shared but not the same. The overwhelming majority of editing individual papers was undertaken by Wood and Nevitt. Borbely secured and supported participation from key Hungarian scholars. Hochschild primarily organized and coordinated between authors and with the press. All took great pleasure in the chance to honor their teacher and friend.

Emmitsburg, MD, USA   Joshua P. Hochschild

San Diego, CA, USA   Turner C. Nevitt

Wheaton, IL, USA   Adam Wood

Budapest, Hungary   Gábor Borbély

Contents

Contributors

Guido Alt is Postdoctoral Fellow at the Department of Philosophy of Stockholm University.

Fabrizio Amerini is Associate Professor of History of Medieval Philosophy at the University of Parma (Italy).

Jacob Archambault researches the history and philosophy of logic and works as a full stack C# .NET developer in Louisville, Kentucky.

István Bodnár teaches ancient philosophy at Eötvös Loránd University (ELTE), Budapest, and Central European University (CEU), Vienna.

Gábor Borbély is Associate Professor of Philosophy at Eötvös Loránd University (ELTE), Budapest.

Laurent Cesalli is Professor of Medieval Philosophy at the University of Geneva.

Richard Cross is John A. O'Brien Professor of Philosophy at the University of Notre Dame.

Robert J. Dobie is Professor of Philosophy and Chair of the Department of Philosophy at La Salle University (Philadelphia, Pennsylvania).

Ariane Economos is Associate Professor of Philosophy and Director of the School of Humanities at Marymount University (Virginia).

Edward Feser is Professor of Philosophy at Pasadena City College (California).

Giacomo Fornasieri is a postdoctoral fellow at Lumsa University in Rome.

Joshua P. Hochschild is Professor of Philosophy at Mount St. Mary's University (Maryland).

Peter King is Professor of Philosophy at the University of Toronto.

Martin Klein is a lecturer in Philosophy at the University of Würzburg, Germany.

Fr. Daniel Patrick Moloney, a priest of the Archdiocese of Boston, is Assistant Professor at St. John Vianney Theological Seminary (Denver).

Turner C. Nevitt is Associate Professor of Philosophy at the University of San Diego.

Calvin G. Normore is Professor of Philosophy at the University of California Los Angeles.

Claude Panaccio is Emeritus Professor in the Department of Philosophy of the University of Quebec at Montreal and a fellow of the Royal Society of Canada.

Giorgio Pini is Professor of Philosophy at Fordham University (New York).

Peter G. Sobol is an honorary fellow in the History of Science Department at the University of Wisconsin.

Giovanni Ventimiglia is Professor of Philosophy and Vice Dean of the Faculty of Theology at the University of Lucerne.

Adam Wood is Associate Professor of Philosophy at Wheaton College (Illinois).

Introduction: In Appreciation of Gyula Klima

Joshua P. Hochschild

> Évezred hanyatlik, évezred kel újra,
> Míg egy földi álom e világba téved,
> Hogy a *hitlen* ember imádni tanulja
> A köd oszlopában rejlő Istenséget.

—János Arany, "Dante" (1852)

> One millennium sets and one millennium rises,
> Till a mortal's dream into that world will stray,
> Till the unbelieving person recognizes
> That mist-hidden Godhead to which he must pray.

(trans. David Hill, 2010)

What began as a peaceful student protest in Budapest on October 23, 1956 quickly turned violent. Soon many strategically placed buildings had become staging grounds for confrontation between communist and populist forces. Within days, a Soviet tank had driven through the maternity ward at Saint Margaret Hospital in Óbuda. So it was that on October 30, in the midst of the Hungarian Uprising, a midwife was called to a modest house on Bercsényi Street, and Gyula Klima was born at home.

Klima would pursue all his schooling in Hungary, completing his PhD in 1986 at Eötvös Lóránd University. In 1986 and 1987, conference presentations outside of Hungary impressed established scholars (most notably Stephen Read, Simo Knuuttila, Sten Ebbesen, and Calvin Normore), leading to fellowship offers in Finland (1989–90, and 1991), Scotland (1990) and Denmark (1991), followed by successive faculty positions at three major American universities: Yale (1991–1995), Notre Dame (1995–1999), and Fordham (1999 to the present). Keeping the last position part-time, Klima has recently returned to Budapest, now with an international network of appreciative scholarly colleagues, former students, and friends. His external accomplishments are a matter of a long publishing record and attested, directly and indirectly, in this celebratory volume, with contributions from many who have been privileged to engage with his person and work.

Invited to recount his own early career, Klima is remarkably humble and bemused by the series of accidents, chance meetings, and good fortune that set him on such a distinguished and enviable, perhaps charmed, trajectory. So it seems not inappropriate to focus on the coincidences at the very beginning—the philosopher's home-birth during a world-historic political confrontation—and draw from them three defining threads, woven through his subsequent work: the characteristic Hungarian temper of resilient, independent, and creative traditionalism; attention to the practical implications of first principles; and lastly, midwifery—at least in the Socratic sense, which is to say, the service of dialectic.

The three threads intertwine, yet each in turn can serve more dominantly: the first, to highlight some general features of Klima's style; the second, to summarize his scholarly project; and the third to highlight the animating spirit of his work.

A Magyar Mind

It is not uncommon to suggest that there is a characteristically Hungarian temperament, often traced, at least in part, to the distinctiveness of the Hungarian language. The historian John Lukacs (who emigrated from Budapest to the United States in 1946 at the age of 22) noted "the loneliness of the Magyar language," having "no relative among the great families of European languages" (Lukacs 1988, 65). Not only vocabulary, but grammar and syntax, isolates Hungarian from Germanic and Romance languages. Its structure is "agglutinative," which linguists also call "synthetic": a syntax strictly rule-based and conspicuous through added syllables rather than by inflections and prepositions. Lukacs links this to "the frequent linguistic abilities of Hungarians" (and we might conjecture that such a mother tongue would offer advantageous perspective in studying both Latin and formal logic).

Its grammar and syntax also gives Hungarian speech a distinctive sound. In appropriately musical English, Patrick Leigh Fermor described how in Hungarian "changes of sense are conveyed by a concatenation of syllables stuck on behind the first; all the vowel sounds imitate their leader, and the invariable ictus on the leading syllable sets up a kind of dactylic or anapaestic canter which, to a new ear, gives Magyar a wild and most unfamiliar ring" (Fermor 1986, 31).

Lukacs describes the language as strongly "declarative… rational rather than mystical, lyrical rather than metaphorical," which he takes to explain why "there is little that is sly and secretive in the national character" (Lukacs 1988, 110). The Hungarian literary scholar Antal Szerb, linking language to the style of the nation's parliamentary politics, said the Hungarian mind "tends to monologue, rather than to dialogue" (quoted in Lukacs 1988, 109).

These historical and cultural reflections are relevant because language is central to Klima's philosophical project, not only as an object of study, but for its range of persuasive power—a range that somewhat confirms, and somewhat challenges, Lukacs's comments on Magyar rhetorical habits. Klima's own writing moves comfortably between technical formalization and elegant, often poetic, composition.

And anyone who has heard him speak knows his playfulness with language, his love of elegant turns of phrase and vivid metaphor, and his careful enthusiasm, perfectly fluent in English but taking on a rushing intensity when speaking in his native tongue.

The "loneliness" of the Magyar tongue has also inspired an almost unsharable pride in national literature, especially poets. It was a reading of Sándor Petőfi's 1848 "National Song," an anthem for freedom asserting independence from Austria, that also roused students to begin what became the 1956 Uprising. Klima's personal favorites include Miklós Radnóti and János Arany, modern poets who yet confirm the Hungarian habit of preserving and persisting through suffering, mixing piety and melancholy, nostalgia and hope. "Many of the most enduring achievements of the nation consist of conservative efforts of recovery and rebuilding after its worst disasters" (Lukacs 1988, 110). Lukacs finds that spiritually, Hungarians are more conscious of "that blending of major and minor, of optimism and pessimism, of light and darkness that is, after all, the inevitable human condition, and also the condition of any culture that is worthwhile" (Lukacs 1988, 24). Preserving culture involves not only protecting against threats but also assimilating valuable contributions from outside.

Klima's work reflects this creative traditionalism. One of the first things one notices as his student is that he does not treat medieval thinkers as part of a past age, a lost curiosity. He once remarked that, as far as intellectual culture is concerned, the Middle Ages lasted in Hungary well into the nineteenth century. Latin was Hungary's official language until 1844, still spoken in the halls of Parliament even after that. And again linguistic and philosophical effects are linked: "[T]he Enlightenment, the Century of Reason, the French Revolution hardly touched Hungary" (Lukacs 1988, 114).

There is no denying the specifically Christian dimension of Hungary's extended medievalism. "The Magyars were a people raised to the dignity of a kingdom by Rome itself," Frederick Wilhelmsen wrote in the days following the 1956 Uprising; and the Sacred Crown of St. Stephen, signifying Hungary's 1000-year sovereign destiny, is capped by a symbol of that destiny's resilient source: a Cross, bent but not broken (Wilhelmsen 1980). While Klima has always embraced modern developments with agility—for instance, as an early adopter of the internet for sharing his work, and in his creative use of new technological examples to illustrate classical concepts—his mind draws strength from contexts usually thought long past, and he comfortably treats medieval thinkers, and their concerns, as contemporary.

This transcending of categories, or creative traditionalism, is reflected in a label some might attach to Klima's work in philosophy: "Analytic Thomism." The contested title can cover a variety of approaches, from Thomists seeking to engage analytic thinkers or using analytic approaches, to analytic philosophers willing to draw Thomistic arguments into contemporary discussions. Yet Klima stands apart in his ability to use resources from both contemporary analytic and medieval thinkers to illuminate each other, bringing both into genuine dialogue to highlight the limitations of each, without compromising the insights available in either.

For that matter *qua* "Thomist" Klima is rare among his contemporaries in not being primarily trained within one of the dominant twentieth-century "schools" (Existential, Laval, Transcendental, Lublin), whose particular preoccupations, and sometimes idiosyncratic jargon, therefore seem less significant to Klima's students. Klima acknowledges several influential teachers from his formation in Budapest, but none of them Thomists: in high school, a chemist, philologist, and polymath, Dr. György Bánhegyi; for training in formal semantics, Imre Ruzsa; and as a model of analytic philosophy, Ferenc Altrichter. From János Kelemen Klima learned more history of philosophy, as well as an appreciation of Dante, and Katalin Vidrányi was a special influence in Catholicism and scholasticism.

This background suggests a culture of rigorous philosophy, philology, intellectual history, and historically informed faith, but not of Thomism *per se*. Studying Aquinas more or less on his own—and only somewhat surreptitiously, under Hungary's softening "goulash communism" that didn't end until 1989—Klima was formed not by any school of *Thomism*, but by *Thomas*, the philosophical saint treated on his own terms and as capable of dialogue with the most prominent contemporary thinkers, Catholic or otherwise.

Although he has criticized Peter Geach in some important particulars (Klima 2015), Klima was inspired early on by Geach's confidence in Christian theology's power to keep logic honest, and by his ambition to reconstruct a pre-modern conceptual schema. As an epigraph to the third essay ("General Terms in their Referring Function") in his early volume *Ars Artium*, Klima quoted Geach's hope (articulated in his essay "History of the Corruption of Logic") to achieve the "Paradise Regained" of reconstructing an Aristotelian semantic framework (Klima 1988, 44).

In this underlying hope of recapturing a lost classical framework, Klima has something in common with another philosopher known for bringing Aquinas into very different contemporary philosophical conversations. Alasdair MacIntyre's *After Virtue* taught many to think of our moral discourse as a collection of confusing scraps and fragments; ethics is more coherent, MacIntyre proposed, if its questions are reformulated in terms of a once fundamental, but now abandoned, teleological framework. Where MacIntyre attempted to recapture lost concepts of practical reason through an alternative narration of the history of ethics, Klima seeks to recapture lost concepts of theoretical reason by bringing them into dialogue with whatever displaced them—confident that, if they were ever intelligible, a judicious application of analysis and argumentation can make them intelligible once again.

If for MacIntyre in *After Virtue* the most important tool for renewing the intelligibility of a tradition is narrative, for Klima it is logic. More specifically, Klima's project commits him to dialectic, applied to semantics. It is in these terms that we can review more properly some of his particular contributions to philosophy and philosophical scholarship.

Contributions to Metaphysics Through Semantics

One can certainly find in Klima a hint of the tragic story of decline and loss with the transition from medieval to modern philosophy, the "vanishing of substance," as he puts it in the culmination of his series of undergraduate lectures—a virtual monograph introducing the history of philosophy—delivered for Yale's Directed Studies program (Klima 1993). But this is complemented by a confident hope in anticipation of recapturing these lost ideas. Hume, and his positivist heirs, have not had the final say in modern philosophy—certainly not in eliminating metaphysics!—and Klima finds in contemporary analytic philosophy a revival of interest in fundamental principles of reality that often approaches (although rarely in such terms) medieval concepts and arguments about essences, individuation, analogy, and formal causality.

So, a recurring, explicit intention of Klima's work is to make classical metaphysical ideas available again by reconstructing and defending the coherence of the kind of discourse in which those ideas could be intelligible. As he writes at the end of his article comparing the different "essentialisms" of contemporary analytic philosophy and the Aristotelian tradition, "the time is ripe for a radical recovery of our lost metaphysical tradition, yet this is possible only through recovering the language in which it is properly conveyed, uniting the formal rigor of contemporary logical techniques with the metaphysical vigor of the pre-modern tradition" (Klima 2002a). And he begins his major paper on Aquinas's semantics of "being," announcing that he is motivated by the fact that "the very *form of discourse* within which the substantive claims of that literature [viz. Thomistic literature about the analogy of being] as well as Aquinas's own claims are formulated is radically different from that of contemporary philosophical discussions" (Klima 1996).

Still, different forms of discourse are also present *within* scholasticism, and a central theme of Klima's scholarship is the historical shift from *via antiqua* to *via moderna* semantics, which he sees as neither unmitigated progress nor an incoherent disaster, but a set of technically sophisticated innovations which nonetheless often led to confusion, with interlocutors talking past each other rather than engaging in fruitful argument. To make sense of this, Klima's strategy has been to disentangle the metaphysical shifts from the semantic developments—and so a major contribution has been to highlight the metaphysical neutrality of the different semantic frameworks, allowing for a metaphysical nominalism within the *via antiqua* and a metaphysical realism within the *via moderna* (Klima 1991).

Thus Klima's work often involves developing traditional Aristotelian or Thomistic ideas in light of later insights and tools (for instance, scholastic supposition theory or modern formal logic), as well as developing the modern insights and tools in order to reconstruct pre-modern ideas (for instance, the existential quantifier, logical formalizations of supposition theory, and clarifications of the square of opposition). For this project of making different conceptual frameworks intelligible to each other, Klima has variously cited Kuhn (on "straddling different paradigms"), Gadamer (on seeking a "fusion of horizons"), and Wittgenstein (on learning to play different "language games"), all in favor of what can also be described as a revival of "scholasticism," that is,

> a new conceptual synthesis, comparable to the scholastic synthesis, namely, one which is modern without any anachronism, and yet an authentic, organic continuation of the traditional discourse, and which therefore is able to present the breakdown of this discourse over the past few centuries as a (conceptually) merely contingent historical episode (Klima 1997).

Thus in his various projects we find Klima comfortably engaging a variety of approaches, and it is no wonder that his network of colleagues and collaborators exhibits a diverse range of commitments, interests, and styles.

This synthesizing perspective also explains what might otherwise appear the paradox, or irony, of a philosopher with Thomist sympathies devoting so much attention to a late scholastic nominalist, John Buridan. Attention to supposition theory and its novelty in relation to "realist" semantics is, on the face of it, a challenging test case for bringing rival conceptual frameworks into fruitful conversation. Klima not only meets the challenge, he finds in supposition theory resources for a revised articulation of realist semantics, capable of being brought into discourse with modern formal semantics; and this, in turn, informs engagement with topics in medieval and contemporary philosophy beyond logic and language: theories of cognition, philosophy of mind, the idea of mental language, theological discourse, and of course metaphysics.

Klima often adopts a semantic focus that does not presume metaphysical conviction, not so much to avoid but to make possible metaphysical reflection. Thus, far from construing questions of "being" as linguistic or conceptual rather than ontological, Klima's strategy of focusing on semantics helps identify where there is metaphysical disagreement and how it can be intelligibly formulated. So, for instance, he shows particular appreciation for the relation of semantics and metaphysics in his reflections on the function of the copula (Klima 2002b; here he might enjoy another Hungarian advantage: the function of the copula is less likely to be taken for granted in the Magyar tongue, where it is rarely used).

But as this example shows, even in focusing on semantics, Klima is able to shed light on traditional (and sometimes apparently intractable) metaphysical topics even within Thomism (for instance on analogy, causality, and participation; the real distinction between being and essence and divine simplicity; the soul, illumination and abstraction), avoiding the ruts of established Thomistic arguments by focusing his efforts on making novel concepts intelligible—in themselves, and as part of an overall coherent framework—independently of and as propaedeutic to the development of arguments that could defend traditional theses as true.

More recently Klima has come to refer to this strategy as "historical-analytic metaphysics" (as he has named a recent book series), and he has become increasingly explicit that, at the center of his work to recover the intelligibility of lost classical notions is attention to the role of the notion of "form." Resisting translation into the implicitly static modern notions of "objects" and "properties," form is an active principle of intelligibility and being, and plays a crucial role not only in physics or metaphysics but in cognition and thus semantics. Form thus once helped integrate philosophical inquiry, and without it we cannot properly comprehend medieval arguments and theses. As Klima described it in a recent lecture, the notion of form is a kind of "conceptual keystone" holding together the elaborate scholastic "cathedral of thought" (Klima 2021).

In this respect, Klima's project with form in medieval thought is not only parallel to or proportional with MacIntyre's project on virtue in classical ethics, but more radical and fundamental. Klima himself embraces the MacIntyre comparison, even extending and transforming it:

> Indeed, I'm following in [MacIntyre's] footsteps, while paradoxically walking ahead of him, which is after all possible if we are both walking backwards, as we are, *in history*. So, just to bore you with one more metaphor, in this strange scenario I can do two things he could not: I can *deepen his footprints*, while also *fixing my eyes on our present horizon*. I intend to *deepen* MacIntyre's footprints by digging deeper down to the roots of our contemporary predicaments, identifying the *historical-metaphysical* roots of the dismal scenario he identified in modern moral discourse. And I am *fixing my sight* on our current horizon both by taking into account recent welcome developments in the recovery of some aspects of the scholastic tradition, *and* by identifying what I think we can gain by a *full* recovery of this tradition, something that points us *beyond* this horizon… (Klima 2021, 2).

Intellectual Midwifery

Klima's strategy of facilitating metaphysical reflection through semantic clarification points to another crucial dimension of logic in his work: the role of dialectic. I earlier suggested that what narrative is to ethics in *After Virtue*—the means of reconstructing (without recourse to metaphysics!) a "teleological" alternative to modern confusion—dialectic is to metaphysics in Klima's overall project: the means of making intelligible a lost conceptual framework. As we have seen, Klima's aim in reconstruction is not so much to assert victory over other alternatives, but to learn to enter into, to occupy, and even to enrich, alternative frameworks.

Even more, dialectic trusts that, under the right conditions, we can find those alternative frameworks already within ourselves. The Platonic contrast of *mythos* and *logos* is not between supernatural and natural explanations, but between modes of persuasion. The storyteller is invitational, calling one to trust a vision proposed; the dialectician is maieutic, assisting one to recognize intelligibility in and from one's own participation in reasoning. It was thus not only an act of humility, nor as plausible deniability for the accusation of "teaching," that Socrates compared himself to a midwife. It was part of his understanding of human reason, as containing within it forgotten truths, or (in more Aristotelian terms) potencies waiting to be actualized.

In its Platonic development, dialectical exercise of *logos* even points to spiritual heights more mystical than conventional *mythos*: ideas themselves are grasped as traces of an original intelligibility, a transcendent Truth and Goodness and Being inarticulable in words, but the source and end of our participatory intellectual activity.

One might not know it from his most technical papers in medieval Aristotelian semantics, but Klima has a deep and sincere affection for Plato (and for the Platonist tradition, as in Augustine, and even the integration of neo-Platonic metaphysics in St. Thomas). Without compromising his commitment to hylomorphic anthropology, Klima admires the film *Shawshank Redemption*, which he interprets as an overt allegory of the Platonic soul's struggle for emergence into freedom from the oppression of embodied suffering. A favorite Hungarian film, *Testről és lélekről* ("On Souls and Bodies," Ildikó Enyedi, 2017), depicts ennobling *eros* in the context of a dismal slaughter-house; its two main characters suffer potentially isolating physical limitations—his mechanical, hers emotional—but are inspired by a shared, and apparently supernatural, vision of spiritual union.

What Klima admires about Socrates is precisely what Plato always tried to depict in his dialogues: a rationality seeking communion with others. Argument is an act of friendship, not competition. Not every philosopher who loves to argue is as committed to the Socratic principle that we should be as glad when shown wrong as when shown right: either way we end up closer to the truth.

If for Klima *form* is scholasticism's keystone concept, *dialectic* is its architectonic practice: hence dialectic as the "art of arts" is a recurring theme of Klima's work (starting with the title of his first book), and he finds it especially well articulated by Buridan:

> [W]e should note that dialectic (that is, logic) is rightly said to be the art of arts, by reason of a certain superiority it has over other arts, [namely], in virtue of its utility and the generality of its application to all other arts and sciences. Due to this generality, which it shares with metaphysics, it has access to disputations that concern not only the conclusions, but also the principles of all sciences (quoted in Klima 2009, 8).

This vision of dialectic offers to unify intellectual pursuits, not in the reductionist way imagined by positivists and rationalists—by translating complex ideas into a simple conceptual framework—but by making ideas intelligible in and across conceptual frameworks. Dialectic is what makes it possible to evaluate different frameworks, not by translating one into another in order to eliminate it, but to understand and inhabit both and move between them, and beyond them, ever closer to the truth. The Gadamerian "fusion of horizons" does not resolve one framework into another, but brings them into genuine conversation—making them capable of enriching each other and thus transcending their own limitations.

So understanding dialectic as *ars artium* suggests more than that it is a foundation for all the sciences; it is also the foundation of society and friendship. Dialectic is a common pursuit of truth, not competitive manipulation. This view has a Socratic and Platonic heritage, and is reinforced by traditional Christian theology, but for even this function of dialectic Klima has drawn inspiration from the nominalist arts master Buridan:

> Dialectic, when applied in speculative matters or utilized in a speculative manner, is directed toward opinion; for both disputants aim at acquiring an opinion about the point of the discussion; they take contradictory stances, and each of them should produce probable arguments for his position, if he has any. He should also solve his opponents' arguments, if they also have probable solutions—and not in a litigious manner, just in order to win, but in order that both of them should assent, in agreement with each other, to the position that they have seen to have been supported in the disputation by more probable and less soluble arguments; and if they do otherwise, then they slip into a sophistic disputation, which often happens (*Summulae de dialectica*, 7.1.4; in Buridan 2001, 499).

Teasing out the political and spiritual stakes of this conception of dialectic, Klima glossed this passage from Buridan in remarks introducing a recent conference he organized on "The Metaphysics and Theology of the Eucharist" (Budapest, September 2021):

> [T]he point is that *a dialectical disputation is not a zero-sum game*. It is all too often that we see the deterioration of such worthy discussions into petty quarrels, indeed, we shall see historical examples of how they can turn into something worse: fights, schisms, even wars (in which we know truth is the first victim), all for winning by vanquishing the opposing party. But a dialectical discussion is not for vanquishing one's opponent: it is a win-win encounter for both parties, from which both come away with the prize of *deeper understanding*.

At stake in dialectic's maieutic persistence is this commitment to the common good, the principle of friendship and justice—an implicit awareness of which permeates not only Klima's philosophical project, but his generosity to students and his dedication to colleagues and peers. It would be hard to ignore the role of community-building in Klima's career. From founding formal societies (the Society for Medieval Logic and Metaphysics in 2000, and more recently the Society for the European History of Ideas in 2021) and establishing book series, to organizing international work groups, conferences and conference sessions, Klima has fostered networks of scholars not only in philosophy but in fields such as theology, cognitive science and artificial intelligence.

The good of dialectic points not only to political but to spiritual communion. No wonder then that even in sober technical papers Klima does not shy away from gesturing to the more mystical implications of Thomistic metaphysics, and its ascent to a simple God who transcends discursive reason. Indeed, only upon directly contemplating the divine essence would dialectic lose its utility, as even St. Thomas judged his own work to be mere straw compared to what he had glimpsed of God in mystical experience.

Until we are given such experience, dialectic rightly pursued can continue to help lead us to truth, Divine and otherwise, and to improve the human condition by fostering productive harmony between minds and hearts. Klima's career testifies to the power of philosophy to overcome cultural, political, and spiritual isolation. Born in the midst of fragmentation and devastation from twentieth-century ideology and technocratic violence, Klima's pursuit of truth has animated a spiritual quest, cultivating coherence and conversation across disciplines, across nations, and across intellectual history. In his noble persistence in dialectic, Klima's efforts have not only left impressive and lasting scholarly resources, they have helped to build up a community of grateful fellow wisdom-lovers, friends inspired and humbled to join him in pursuit of ever-greater understanding of life-giving truth.

Bibliography

Buridan, John. 2001. *Summulae de Dialectica: An annotated translation, with phil-osophical introduction, by Gyula Klima*. New Haven: Yale University Press.

Fermor, Patrick Leigh. 1986. *Between the woods and the water*. New York: Viking Press. Reprinted 2005. New York: NYRB Classics.

Klima, Gyula. 1988. *Ars artium: Essays in philosophical semantics, medieval and modern*. Budapest: Institute of Philosophy, Hungarian Academy of Sciences.

———. 1991. Ontological alternatives vs. alternative semantics in medieval phi-losophy. *S: European Journal for Semiotic Studies* 3 (4): 587–618.

———. 1993. The Yale Lectures. https://faculty.fordham.edu/klima/lectures.htm.

———. 1996. The semantic principles underlying St. Thomas Aquinas's metaphys-ics of being. *Medieval Philosophy and Theology* 5 (1): 87–144.

———. 1997. What can a scholastic do in the 21st century? *Budapest Review of Books* (English Edition) 7: 167–169. https://faculty.fordham.edu/klima/21ST.HTM.

———. 2002a. Contemporary 'essentialism' vs. Aristotelian essentialism. In *Mind, metaphysics, and value in the Thomistic and analytic traditions*, ed. John Haldane, 175–194. Notre Dame: Notre Dame University Press.

———. 2002b. Aquinas' theory of the copula and the analogy of being. *Logical Analysis and History of Philosophy* 5: 159–176.

———. 2009. *John Buridan*. Oxford: Oxford University Press.

———. 2015. Geach's three most inspiring errors concerning medieval logic. *Philosophical Investigations* 38 (1–2): 34–51.

———. 2021. Historical-analytic metaphysics *or* what *should* a scholastic do in the 21st century? (Keynote lecture for "Second Scholasticism, Analytical Metaphysics, Christian Apologetics: A Conference in Honour of Professor Stanislav Sousedík's 90th birthday," October 27–29, Prague, Czech Republic.) http://www.skaut.org/s-conf/downloads.php.

Lukacs, John. 1988. *Budapest 1900: A historical portrait of a city and its culture*. New York: Grove Press.

Wilhelmsen, Frederick D. 1980. "Hungary Speaks." *Citizen of Rome: Reflections from the life of a Roman Catholic*, 3–6. La Salle, Illinois: Sherwood Sudgeon & Company.

Chapter 1
Pythagoras, the Philosopher and Grammar Teacher (Br. Lib. Add. MS 37516 *recto*)

István Bodnár

To Kornél Steiger, for all the years[*]

Keywords Pythagoras · Ancient grammarians on morphology · Epic language · *chreia* · Classroom exercises · Jokes · Autonymy · Mention and use · Vegetarianism

This paper is about a writing tablet.[1] It was acquisitioned in 1907 by the British Museum.[2] It is from Egypt, but we know nothing more about its provenience. It has been dated to the third century C.E., based on its lettering. This dating, which

[*]This piece has been long in the making. I first gave a talk on the basis of a first draft as the Annual Lecture of the Hungarian Classical Society in 2010, and at the close of the talk I marked the 65th birthday of Kornél Steiger. Then I presented a second draft in the Cambridge B-Club in October 2014. Now I am pleased that I can publish it here, with the original dedication to Steiger, the teacher who fundamentally shaped my approach and sensibilities, in a volume dedicated to Gyula Klíma, in remembrance of the years when we studied logic together under the guidance of Professor Imre Ruzsa

[1]I am grateful to Dr. Cillian O'Hogan, Curator of Classical and Byzantine Studies at the British Library at that time, for making the writing tablet accessible to me on 21 October 2014 and on 30 May 2015. I am also grateful to Professor David Sedley, whose comments on a penultimate draft saved me from quite a few errors. Needless to say, whatever errors remain are solely my responsibility. And, even more importantly, I would like to stress how much this piece owes to his fundamental insights in Sedley 1998a, b. As the continuous chain of references in this piece amply attest, Sedley's two papers served as the starting point for this piece; without them I don't think I would have gotten the joke of the *chreia*.

[2]1907 is given as the date of acquisition in Painter 1967, 110.

I. Bodnár (✉)
Eötvös Loránd University (ELTE), Budapest, Hungary

Central European University (CEU), Vienna, Austria
e-mail: bodnar.istvan@btk.elte.hu

Kenyon gave in the first publication about the tablet, remained unchallenged for quite a while.[3] Only recently did Guido Bastianini and Manfredo Manfredi date the tablet to one century later (accepted by Sedley 1998a, 167 n. 1 and 1998b, 122; Andorlini and Linguiti 1999, 681; Bastianini 2003, 169; and Piano 2015, 381 and 382). As we shall see, however, the different dates assigned do not bear on the interpretation of the contents of the tablet.

The tablet is 415 by 135 mm; it is painted white on both sides; and both sides are ruled, or rather lines for both rows and columns are scratched into the two sides. After these rows and columns had been in place—in modern parlance: after formatting—the tablet split into two, and the two broken parts were joined together with dowels. These tablets were no throwaway items. Even if they suffered serious damage, it was worthwhile to repair them, and continue to use them even with the added inconvenience caused by the fault line that—as in this case—did not run along the rows of the tablet.

Both sides of the tablet contain grammatical school exercises. The horizontal lineation of the two sides is identical. Both sides were lined by hand, without a ruler, to contain 18 lines. The vertical lineation, however, conforms to the type of exercise on the two sides. On one side, which has been dubbed the *verso* by Kenyon,[4] there is an exercise of conjugation. Here the tablet is divided into six columns, leaving the third of the tablet on the right side empty. The other side contains the declension of a specimen sentence. Here the tablet has two vertical margins scratched in.

Accordingly, the two sides are already distinguished by the formatting. It had a word manipulation side, with six columns, and a sentence manipulation side, without this articulation into columns. Needless to say, this distinction could be overruled on occasion. Just as the fault line could not prevent further use of the tablet, one could write whole sentences across the columns, or if someone needed columns on the other side as well, these could be supplied in ink on occasion. Some such versatility is also evidenced in the case of our writing tablet. Even though both sides have 18 lines scratched onto the surface, the word manipulation side is written much denser: the pupil included 32 lines of exercises on these 18 lines.

The types of exercises on both sides are well known from ancient educational practice. Greek conjugation must be learnt so that the forms come automatically without effort. Anybody who has studied Greek (or for that matter, Latin) will remember those months of tedious rote of practicing all these tables. The other side,

---

[3] Kenyon 1909, 29–30. The tablet was dated to the 3rd c. also by Cribiore in her extensive study of school exercises. See Cribiore 1996, 264 f. (item **364** in the Catalogue, a photo of the tablet features on Table LXI).

[4] Actually the order of writing these two sides may well have been the other way around: Sedley 1998a, 167 and 1998b, 122 show that "the tablet had already been repaired before the [*chreia*] was written on it," whereas Piano 2015, 381 f. observes that the side containing the conjugation of the verb νικᾶν in the optative and its participles in the nominative may have been written before the tablet was broken and repaired, because part of one of the conjugated forms apparently was located over the area where the tablet was fractured.

the one Kenyon dubbed the *recto*,[5] contains a *klisis*, a specimen of a well-known type of the *progymnasmata,* or preparatory exercises of rhetorical schooling. This is an exercise of sentence manipulation, going through the declension of a *chreia*, consisting in producing the declensional forms of the nominal group at the head of the *chreia* and the other parts of speech in the sentence co-ordinated with it, in all three numbers, and in all five cases (the vocative included) in these three numbers. A *chreia* is a single sentence that sets out a significant utterance or deed of someone that is characteristic of this person. Therefore, some of those declensions almost inevitably will produce rather bizarre outcomes—just as in our case, a sentence about Pythagoras. When we get to the sentence in the dual, it will mention the two Pythagorases. In the plural, there will be a multiplicity of Pythagorases. The aim of this exercise is not direct use of these sentences, but rather that the pupil should be able to produce without effort, and without morphological errors, nominal phrases embedded in complex syntactical structures.[6]

Apparently, as anyone can see from the transcript of Piano 2015 in Table 1.1,[7] the pupil writing here is still quite far from this proficiency. We should pass over in silence his typos, where he uses by mistake some other letter than the required one. The lack of the augment may also be assessed as such a simple mistake of lettering. The numerous minor mistakes in the dual forms should also surprise no one.

Even so, it certainly is over the top that in line 15, in the plural dative of the sentence, we read διδασκοντοις instead of the elementary grammar form διδάσκουσι. Line 5, the vocative singular, is teeming with errors. The pupil could not guess the vocative of the name Pythagoras correctly; the way he tried to put the two participles after the name into the vocative was not a high point of Greek grammatical education. At any rate, even if he could not suppress this urge, the vocative of διδάσκων is definitely not διδασκον. Furthermore, it is downright astonishing that in the singular vocative he employs—instead of the second person singular

---

[5] Note that Cribiore 1996, *loc. cit.* exchanges the order of the sides without citing a reason, and calls the conjugation side the first one, and the declension side the second one. Hock and O'Neil – perhaps under the somewhat confusing interference between Kenyon and Cribiore – locate the declension of the *chreia* first on the *recto*, and then on the *verso* (Hock and O'Neil 2002, 62 and 64).

[6] This can be true for the singular and the plural forms of the exercise. There was not much point to possessing the same dexterity with the dual. The exercise, at least in these lines, must have been meant "to show who is boss… by humiliating it [the *chreia*] into total submission," as Sedley 1998b, 128 stresses.

[7] In Table 1.1 I reproduce Piano's transcription with changes in the apparatus as follows: The remarks are in philologese Latin, and also in English. Piano's first apparatus is sorted out into two lists, a first one describing the readings of the tablet, and a second one correcting for the grammatical and clerical errors of the pupil. Here I also include Sedley's and Wouters's correction (Sedley 1998b, 125 and Wouters 2007, 150) for the incorrect vocative of Pythagoras's name in line 5. Furthermore, in the third apparatus, listing the different readings of modern editors, I included only the conjecture of line 5 from Wouters 2007, 150 f. I am extremely grateful to Valeria Piano for help and advice about the readings of the tablet, and for further comments on this paper.

Table 1.1 Br. Libr. Add Ms 37516, 1: transcription and apparatus from Piano 2015, 384 f. (from Wouters including only the conjecture of line 5)

1 ʾόˊ Πυθαγόρας φιλόσοφος ἀποβὰς καὶ γράμματα διδάσκων συνεβούλευεν τοῖς ἑαυτοῦ μαθηταῖς ἐναιμόνων ἀπέχεσθαι

2 τοῦ Πυθαγόρου φιλοσόφου ἀποβάντες καὶ γράμματα διδάσκοντος λόγος ἀπομνημονεύεται συνβουλεύοντος τοῖς ἑαυτοῦ μαθηταῖς ἐναιμόνων ἀπ[έ]ˋχεσθαιˊ

3 τῷ Πυθαγόρᾳ φιλοσόφῳ ἀποβάντι καὶ γράμματα διδάσκοντιˋ ἔδοξενˊσυνβουλεῦσαι τοῖς ἑαυτοῦ μαθηταῖς ἐναιμόνων ἀπέχεσθαι

4 τὸν Πυθαγόραν φιλόσοφον ἀποβάντα καὶ γράμματα διδάσκοντά φασιν συνβουλεῦσαι τοῖς ἑαυτοῦ μαθηταῖς ἐναιμόνων ἀπέχεσθαι

5 ὦ Πυθαγόρε φιλόσοφε ἀποβὰς καὶ γράμματα διδάσκον σύ ποτε συνεβουλεύσατοˋνˊ τοῖς ἑαυτοῦ μαθηταῖς ἐναιμόνων ἀπέχεσθαι

6 καὶ δυκῶς

7 τὼ Πυθαγόρα φιλοσόφω ἀποβάντην καὶ γράμματα διδάσκοντε συνβουλευέτην τοῖς ἑαυτοῦ μαθηταῖς ἐναιμόνων ἀπέχεσθαι

8 τοῖν Πυθαγόροιν φιλοσόφοιν ἀποβάντοιν καὶ γράμματα διδασκόντοιν λόγος ἀπομνημονεύεται συνβουλευόντοιν τοῖς ἑαυτοῦ μαθηταῖς ἐναιμόνω[ν] ˋἀπέχεσθαιˊ

9 τοῖν Πυθαγόροιν φιλοσόφοιν ἀποβάντοιν καὶ γράμματα διδασκόντοιν ἔδοξεν συνβουλεῦσαι τοῖς ἑαυτοῦ μαθηταῖς ἐναιμόνων ἀπέχεσθαι

10 τὼ Πυθαγόρα φιλοσόφω ἀποβάντην καὶ γράμματα διδάσκοντέ φασιν συνβουλεῦσαι τοῖς ἑαυτοῦ μαθηταῖς ἐναιμόνων ἀπέχεσθαι

11 ὦ Πυθαγόρα φιλοσόφω ἀποβάντην καὶ γράμματα διδάσκοντε σφώ ποτε συνβουλευσάτην τοῖς ἑαυτοῦ μαθηταῖς ἐναιμόνων ἀπέχεσθαι

12 καὶ πληθυντικῶς

13 οἱ Πυθαγόραι φιλόσοφοι ἀποβάντες καὶ γράμματα διδάσκοντες συνεβουλεύσθην τοῖς ἑαυτοῦ μαθηταῖς ἐναιμόνων ἀπέχεσθαι

14 τῶν Πυθαγορῶν φιλοσόφων ἀποβάντων καὶ γράμματα διδασκόντων λόγος ἀπομνημονεύεται συνβουλευσάντων τοῖς ἑαυτοῦ μαθηταῖς ἐναιμόνων ἀπέˋχεσθαιˊ

15 τοῖς Πυθαγόραις φιλοσόφοις ἀποβᾶσι καὶ γράμματα διδασκόντοις ἔδοξεν συνβουλεῦσαι τοῖς ἑαυτοῦ μαθηταῖς ἐναιμόνων ἀπέχεσθαι

16 τοὺς Πυθαγόρας φιλοσόφους ἀποβάντας καὶ γράμματα διδάσκοντάς φασιν συνβουλεῦσαι τοῖς ἑαυτοῦ μαθηταῖς ἐναιμόνων ἀπέχεσθαι

17 ὦ Πυθαγόραι φιλόσοφοι ἀποβάντες καὶ γράμματα διδάσκοντες ὑμεῖς ποτε συνβουλευετιν τοῖς ἑαυτοῦ μαθηταῖς ἐναιμόνων ἀπέχεσθαι

Readings of the tablet: 2 cυνβουλευοντοc *corr. ex* cυνβουλευcαντοc 3 cυνβουλευcαι *corr. ex* cυνβουλευcθαι 7 *an* αποβαντην *ex* αποβαιντην *corr.?* 8 cυνβουλευοντοιν *corr. ex,* cυνβουλευcαντοιν 15 αποβαcι *ex* αποβαντοιc *dubitanter leg.* Kenyon; *sigma fortasse ex* το *corr.* (after the second *alpha* traces of a *nu*, apparently neither corrected nor washed)

Correction of errors: 2 ἀποβάντος ‖ συμβουλευ- *hic et passim* 5 Πυθαγόρα ‖ διδάσκων ‖ συνεβούλευσας *vel* συνεβούλευες 6 δυϊκῶς 7 ἀποβάντε ‖ συνεβουλευέτην *vel* συνεβουλευσάτην 10 ἀποβάντε 11 ἀποβάντε ‖ συνεβουλεύσατον *vel* συνεβουλεύετον 13 συνεβούλευον *vel* συνεβούλευσαν 15 διδάσκουσιν 17 συνεβουλεύετε *vel* συνεβουλεύσατε

Readings/conjectures of modern editors: 5 συνεβούλευες *coni.* Wouters, *probante* Lapini 11 συνεβουλευσάτην *perperam* Hock – O'Neil 14 συνεβουλευσάντων *lapsu* Sedley 15 διδασκόντοις *lapsu* Hock – O'Neil (erroneously printed in 'corrected' text) 17 συνβουλεύετιν Sedley, συνβουλεύετιν Lapini (as a lapse of the student for συνβουλευέτην).

συνεβούλευσας—a form, συνεβουλευσατον, which with all its air of affectation happens to be a second person *dual* aorist. But the fact that we have a form that would be in order elsewhere does not mean that the pupil will employ it on that other occasion. Indeed, when it comes to the dual vocative form, the pupil has συνβουλευσατην instead, a form with the third person ending and without the augment. The third instance of the vocative, the plural one, is no better either: here, in the last line, we have a blurred συνβουλευτιν, again without the augment, and with a deeply troubling ending—instead of the second person plural συνεβουλεύετε or συνεβουλεύσατε.

Small wonder that the lack of linguistic and morphological competence on the part of the pupil gave rise to assessments, first in a summary way by Cribiore (*loc. cit.*), and then in more detail by Sedley 1998a, b, that our pupil may not have been a native speaker of Greek.[8] I leave the assessment of the competence of upper primary school pupils in third- or fourth-century Egypt to others. What I would nevertheless submit, already at the start, is that even a late fourth-century dating, and the somewhat limited morphological proficiency of the pupil, will not necessarily allow for the further claim, that one should correct the wording of the first line, because the pupil would also be liable to such elementary clerical errors of botching up his copying while writing down the specimen sentence itself. Instead, in what follows I will try to construe the *chreia* in the version as we have it throughout this writing tablet.

After this quick glance at the morphological dexterity of the pupil it is time we turned to the *chreia* itself. The text of the *chreia* is:

ὁ᾽ Πυθαγόρας φιλόσοφος ἀποβὰς καὶ γράμματα διδάσκων συνεβούλευεν τοῖς ἑαυτοῦ μαθηταῖς ἐναιμόνων ἀπέχεσθαι.

Every reader of this *chreia* could take it for granted that the advice or injunction of the second half of the sentence refers to the Pythagorean ban on eating meat, a direct consequence of Pythagoras's signature doctrine of the transmigration of souls. Hock and O'Neil, accordingly, translate the sentence as:

Pythagoras, the philosopher, once he had disembarked and was teaching writings, used to counsel his students to abstain from red meat (*Chreia* 55 in Hock and O'Neil 1986, 335 f.).

---

[8] Nevertheless, the debate about the native language and the proficiency of the pupil, between Sedley 1998a, 170 and 173 f. and 1998b, 125 and 129; and Luzzatto 2004, 174 f. with n. 45 (arguing that the native language could just as well have been Greek, and that compared to the intricacy of the exercise, the performance of the pupil is by no means so abysmal) is summarized by Piano 2015, 382. (Note, however, that Sedley 1998b expressly speaks about "the standards of comparable output from Egyptian schoolrooms," by which the student's accomplishment "may seem high-quality work." It is "by any absolute standard" that "it is not at all distinguished." Sedley 1998b, 125).

This translation was later revised, without further comment, into:

Pythagoras, the philosopher, when he had disembarked and was teaching letters, used to advise his pupils to abstain from red meat (Text 15 in Hock and O'Neil 2002, 65).

Two remarks are immediately in order about these interpretations. In the case of the first, it is somewhat strange to suggest that Pythagoras, after disembarking in Southern Italy, started to teach writings—that is, his very own writings, as Hock and O'Neil suggest in their first translation (Hock and O'Neil 1986). First of all, as for the writings of Pythagoras, there need not have been any. But let us assume for a moment that a late *chreia* might be intent, nevertheless, to attribute the teaching of Pythagorean writings to Pythagoras. This would also imply that this late *chreia* does away with the fundamental distinction between *akousmatikoi* and *mathēmatikoi* among the disciples of Pythagoras. Fundamental to this distinction is that those disciples who were supposed to observe the Pythagorean way of life were introduced to this way of life through oral precepts, which they *heard.* Pythagoras did not need to recite these precepts from a written document for these disciples.

Perhaps such considerations—and the fact that the expression γράμματα διδάσκειν does not really mean the activity of inculcating one's own, or for that matter anybody else's, writings—could lead to the revised translation where Hock and O'Neil submit that "Pythagoras, the philosopher, when he... was teaching letters, used to advise his pupils to abstain from red meat." An additional minor point about both translations would be that Pythagoras did not admonish against the eating of *red* meat, but rather against eating the meat of blooded creatures—fish and poultry included.

Sedley's two seminal papers have eliminated these problems, when he submitted the translation

The philosopher Pythagoras, when he had gone away and was teaching letters, used to advise his own pupils to abstain from blooded creatures (Sedley 1998a, 169 and 1998b, 124)

or even—after a discussion of the meaning of the adjective ἐναίμονες, which could not be captured in the translation above—the translation

The philosopher Pythagoras, went off and became a grammar teacher, and used to advise his pupils to abstain from ἐναίμονες (Sedley 1998a, 176 and 1998b., 132).

We lack any specific indication where Pythagoras could have gone off, at the close of his career as a philosopher, or as a journey to a destination where his philosophical activities were suspended for a time.[9] What Sedley rightly calls attention to is that this *chreia*—like so many others—turns on the ambiguity of a phrase, or in this case on the ambiguity of two different uses of the same phrase. Pythagoras, while

---

[9] There are indeed some indications about Pythagoras's comings and goings. E.g. Chreia 54 in Hock and O'Neil 1986, 334 f., when Pythagoras, "being asked how long human life is, went up (ἀναβάς) to his bedroom and peeked in for a short time," or somewhat more hopefully, Aristotle fr. 191 Rose (Apollonius *mirab.* 6): "Pythagoras foretold to the Pythagoreans the coming political strife; that is why he departed (ἀπῆρεν) to Metapontum unobserved by anyone" (where, however, there is no hint about Pythagoras's taking up a different line of activity like teaching grammar).

pursuing the career of a *grammatistēs*, however briefly, still lived up to his previous renown. Just as he used to advise his students against the use—the consumption—of the meat of blooded creatures, here, during his life as an instructor of proper Greek usage, he advised against the use of the adjectival form ἐναίμων, –ονος instead of the correct form, ἔναιμος, –ου.

The crucial next step in formulating an interpretation of this *chreia* is to delineate the immediate intellectual niche giving rise to this saying. Hock and O'Neil in their interpretation do not introduce such considerations; they just refer to the Pythagorean injunction against eating meat. Before turning to Sedley's considerations, as an intermediate step I would like to consider an intermediary proposal. This is the proposal by Isabella Andorlini and Alessandro Linguiti, which is a sort of hybrid of the interpretations by Hock and O'Neil and by Sedley:

> Pythagoras, the philosopher, having gone away and acting as a teacher, gave counsel to his disciples to abstain from blooded animals.[10]

Accordingly, Andorlini and Linguiti accept that Pythagoras left the place of his philosophical activities, and it was elsewhere that he became an instructor, or a master of pupils. Or, more precisely, they suggest that the second half of the *chreia* submits that in this new place of his activities, as a good schoolmaster he revised his original *dictum* in the light of common linguistic usage. In this new formulation he spoke about a ban on the consumption of blooded animals, and not on the consumption of ensouled beings.

After this Andorlini and Linguiti turn to a discussion of where we find the presence of soul so strictly tied to blood, and submit that—although there are signs of such a connection in the *Pythagoras Vita* of Diogenes Laertius, where we read that "soul nourishes itself from blood"[11]—a passage in Leviticus in the Septuagint, and another in Philo's *De vita contemplative* attest that this connection between blood and soul is a characteristic of the Judeo-Christian conception of the soul.[12] In light of this, according to them, the *chreia* sets in sharp relief how the original Pythagorean precept was reformulated in the matrix of a new cultural environment.

Before formulating an alternative proposal, I should turn now to the intellectual environment as charted by Sedley for his reading. To some extent this is in accordance with what Andorlini and Linguiti submit: Philo describes, on several occasions, the purest and most distinguished human diet—vegetarianism—as

---

[10] Andorlini and Linguiti 1999, text **91** (the translation is on p. 682): "Il filosofo Pitagora andato via e facendo il maestro consigliava ai propri discepoli di astenersi da animali sanguigni."

[11] τρέφεσθαί τε τὴν ψυχὴν ἀπὸ τοῦ αἵματος· (D.L. VIII 30).

[12] Philo, *De vita contemplativa* 73, quoted by Andorlini and Linguiti 1999, 684, pointing to Leviticus 17:11 within the section 17:10–16, establishing the exclusive connection between blood and soul and establishing the ultimate ground for the ban against eating blood. Note, however, that this connection is not exclusive to the Judeo-Christian tradition. We can find a—temporary—injunction to abstain from the consumption of blooded creatures in magical papyri: Προαγνεύσας ζ΄ ἡμέρας τοῦ τὴν σελήνην πα[ν]σέληνον γενέσθαι ἐναίμων καὶ ἀνεψε[τῶν] ἀπεχόμενος, ἀφ᾽ ὧν ἐσθίεις, μέρος ἥμι[σ]υ κ[α]τὰ ἴσον καταλιμπάνων ἐπὶ τὰς προκειμέν[ας] ἡμέρας ἐν ἀγγείῳ καλλαΐνῳ, ἐφ᾽ οὗ καὶ σὺ ἐσ[θίεις, ο]ἴνου ἀπεχόμενος... (*Papyri magicae* 4.52–57).

abstinence from blooded animals.[13] This, however, is just one of the prerequisites for the effect of the *chreia*. Apart from this doctrinal prerequisite there is another one: Pythagoras, as the stalwart of linguistic purity, should be entitled to ban his pupils from using the adjective ἐναίμων, –ονος. This ban is well grounded in actual linguistic usage. According to the *TLG* this form of the adjective features only in the Hippocratic Corpus, in the work *On the nature of bones (De ossium natura)*.[14] Accordingly, Sedley contends that the point of origin, the original intellectual environment of the *chreia*, could have been the lexicographical studies into medical terminology of the third century B.C.E., starting with Herophilus, about which our most important testimony is the collection of Hippocratic words of Erotianus from the first century C.E.

As Sedley puts it:

> The unique form ἐναίμονες will have been identified by the lexicographers as an irregular one, which should be avoided in favour of the standard ἔναιμοι. If Pythagoras had been a grammar teacher, they may have quipped, he would have advised his pupils "to abstain from ἐναίμονες". This then became the anecdote on our writing tablet… (Sedley 1998a, 176 and 1998b, 131).

This could be the case indeed, unless—as I will claim—a more straightforward intellectual niche can be found for ἐναιμόνων.[15]

As so many other things in Greek culture, the somewhat eccentric wording of the *chreia*, on my proposal, will start out from the *Iliad*. In the crowning achievement of his *aristeia*, Diomedes in Book V meets Aphrodite in combat, and wounds the immortal goddess, who is not accustomed to the din of war. Aphrodite's *ichōr* flows from her wound—her *ichōr*, because gods do not have blood.

---

[13] Sedley 1998a, 181 n. 26 and 1998b, 137 n. 31 quote also Philo, *De spec. legg.* . I 255: ἡ δ᾿ ἀπαρχὴ πρέπουσα ἱερεῦσιν ἀπ᾿ οὐδενὸς τῶν ἐναίμων, ἀλλ᾿ ἀπὸ τοῦ καθαρωτάτου τῆς ἀνθρωπίνης τροφῆς.

[14] *De ossium natura* 19: αἱ δὲ [sc. φλέβες] ἐναίμονες ἐοῦσαι ὑπ᾿ αὐτὸν ἐξοχετεύονται ἐς αὐτόν. Here the adjective refers to arteries "full of blood" (and not to blooded animals). It is important to remark that *De ossium natura*, in the same sense, employs also several times the alternative form of the adjective ἔναιμος.

[15] Note that any such proposal about the intellectual niche where using this adjective could make sense has to reject the contention of Zhmud 2019, 115. He—indeed "the former school teacher and headmaster in [him]"—goes for the more mundane variant ἐναίμων ἀπέχεσθαι and sternly rejects the reading ἐναιμόνων ἀπέχεσθαι, which would involve "too exquisite a linguistic joke even for a witty grammar teacher, let alone his audience," suggesting that the reading ἐναιμόνων "is a mistake made by the student, who made a lot of mistakes in both exercises. He could have easily misheard or misunderstood the rare and bookish word ἔναιμος, which occurs predominantly in medical or philosophical texts, and duplicated the syllable *on*, as o and ω were regularly interchanged at that time in Egypt…."

This suggestion, however, would rob us of the grammatical or philological point inculcated by Pythagoras. All one could say is that "Pythagoras… became a philosopher, and teaching grammar, advised his students to abstain from ensouled creatures, which incidentally was his most famous tenet" (Zhmud 2019, 114). The activity of the grammar teacher implied in the *chreia* accordingly will turn out to be nothing more than Pythagoras's continued philosophical proselytizing while he was teaching grammar, perhaps even using his signature philosophical injunction as a specimen sentence in grammatical instruction.

> And the immortal blood of the goddess was flowing –
> the *ichōr*, such as flows in blessed gods,
> for neither do they eat wheat, nor do they drink fiery wine,
> therefore they are <u>bloodless /unblooded</u>, and are called immortal[16]

The word for bloodless/unblooded is ἀναίμονες here, and although it occurs in Homer only here, once a word features even a single time in Homer, it is bound to have a history. Some other authors might pick it up, and grammarians will have to treat it. This is exactly what happened with ἀναίμονες. It does have occurrences in Nonnus's *Dionysiaca*, and in Oppian's *Haleutica*, and Plutarch also uses it on one occasion, when he calls—not without mock loftiness—red wine not-bloodless or not-unblooded.[17]

What is even more important, however, is that the word occurs regularly in grammarians. It is a prime example for the rule that in those adjectives and nouns ending in an unaccented –ων that derive from compound nouns or adjectives ending in -ος, the ω of the last syllable will change to o in the oblique cases,[18] and the triplet αἷμα – ἄναιμος – ἀναίμων is quoted regularly.[19] Furthermore, apart from ἀναίμων, Herodotus and poetic texts, and the scholia, lexicons etc. to them, often use the words ὁμαίμων, ξυνομαίμων, συναίμων, αὐθαίμων, describing kinship relations. Moreover, there are the adjectives ὑφαίμων, ὀλιγαίμων, πολυαίμων, ἐξαίμων, closely connected to the meaning of ἀναίμων.[20] Naturally, the morphological rule illustrated with the word ἀναίμων also holds in their case.

All in all, I would submit that there is no need to find a specific narrow cultural niche for the connection between blood and soul. The fact that the *Iliad* calls the gods ἀναίμονες, bloodless or unblooded, in contrast to mortals—connecting mortal existence with the mundane facts that we eat wheat, drink wine (and not *ambrosia*),

---

[16] ῥέε δ' ἄμβροτον αἷμα θεοῖο
  ἰχώρ, οἷός πέρ τε ῥέει μακάρεσσι θεοῖσιν·
  οὐ γὰρ σῖτον ἔδουσ', οὐ πίνουσ' αἴθοπα οἶνον,
  τοὔνεκ' <u>ἀναίμονές</u> εἰσι καὶ ἀθάνατοι καλέονται. (V 339–342)

[17] Nonnus, *Dionysiaca* III 311, XVII 386, XXXVI 39, XXXVII 755; Oppianus, *Haleutica* I 638 f.; Plutarch, *Quaestiones convivales* 692ε7.

[18] This is in contrast to those nouns or adjectives ending in –ων that are derived from an uncompounded noun or adjective ending in -ος, which retain the ω in the oblique cases, and like those other instances that are derived from verbs: they also change the ω of the ending to o in the oblique cases. See Herodian, *De declinatione* II 725, 16–25.

[19] See Herodian, *De declinatione* II 725, 25–29, where line 27 quotes the occurrence of ἀναίμονες in the *Iliad*. See also *De paronymis* II 851, 4–8, and furthermore *De prosodia catholica* I 24,12–14, regulating the accentuation of these derivatives.

[20] Of these Lapini 2013, 16 lists αὐθαίμων, συναίμων, ὁμαίμων, πολυαίμων, indicating also the occurrence of ἀναίμων in the *Iliad* and in P. Berol. 21,154 1.10 (see Maehler 1970, 154 and 157). He, however, argues from these in the opposite direction against Sedley: the presence of these forms in the corpus of Greek literature suggests that there is nothing irregular in these adjectives; the sole reason ἐναίμων is used in the *chreia* can be the wish to include yet another different declinational pattern. This, however, is very much doubtful: the adjective ἐναίμων is not the object of declination in the *chreia*; it just has to be copied from line to line, so its different declinational pattern does not add any difficulty to the exercise.

and have blood—will already be a suitable starting point. This word and its cognates called for grammatical rules. Seeing this, a grammarian came to formulate this joking *chreia*. What he needed to notice is that while the otherwise rare word ἀναίμων regularly features in his profession, its opposite, ἐναίμων never, or hardly ever occurs[21] and so should be avoided. This observation, that ἐναίμων is to be avoided is perfectly within the remit of grammatical writers, and as *gesunkenes Kulturgut* is also at home in the classroom of a grammar teacher. Small wonder then that this could be connected, tongue in cheek, with the Pythagorean injunction.[22]

It is time for us to address the issue of where Pythagoras disembarked, or what destination he left for. Alternatively—provided that he did not do so—the issue will be why such a *chreia* with *double entendre* speaks about Pythagoras in these terms.

I have already mentioned Hock and O'Neil's suggestion, that the *chreia* was meant to be understood as relating Pythagoras's intentions at the time of his arrival in southern Italy. With this, however, they took the *chreia* to speak about Pythagoras's philosophical activity, when he founded his own school or sect. Sedley speaks about Pythagoras's going away, and compares the *chreia* to a passage where Cicero reports that

> Dionysus the tyrant, when he was expelled from Syracuse was instructing boys in Corinth –
> to such extent was he unable to live without exerting authority.[23]

I admit that this line of Cicero sheds light on the motivational basis of ancient education (in crucial ways comparable to that of education just a few generations ago; see Zazie's tirade in *Zazie dans le métro*, giving her reasons why she wants to be an elementary school teacher[24]), but I fail to see here any specific connection with Pythagoras.

But perhaps we do not need to find the destination or aim of Pythagoras's journey. What we need to keep in mind is that almost all the previous translations rest

---

[21] For this the grammarians did not need to rest their case on a detailed examination of medical terminology. It was sufficient if they knew that the word ἐναίμων—if it occurs somewhere at all, like in medical terminology—will remain an isolated phenomenon, and will not have the same impact on Greek literature as the ἀναίμονες of *Iliad* V 342.

[22] Note, however, that as Luzzatto 2004, 176 n. 49 suggests, most probably this is one of those professors' jokes that only teachers delight in and poor pupils, lost in the traps of morphology, are in no position to appreciate.

[23] Sedley 1998a, 176 n. 17 and 1998b, 132. n. 21: Dionysius quidem tyrannus Syracusis expulsus Corinthi pueros docebat: usque eo imperio carere non poterat. (Cicero, *Tusc.* III 27).

[24] Oui, dit Zazie, je veux être institutrice. …
– Alors, pourquoi tu veux l'être, institutrice?
– Pour faire chier les mômes, répondit Zazie. Ceux qu'auront mon âge dans dix ans, dans vingt ans, dans cinquante ans, dans cent ans, dans mille ans, toujours des gosses à emmerder.
– Eh bien, dit Gabriel.
– Je serai vache comme tout avec elles. Je leur ferai lécher le parquet. Je leur ferai manger l'éponge du tableau noir. Je leur enforcerai des compas dans le derrière. Je leur botterai les fesses. Parce que je porterai des bottes. En hiver. Hautes comme ça (geste). Avec des grands éperons pour leur larder la chair du derche. (Queneau 1959, 29 0f).

on a tacit or explicit emendation: the article at the head of the sentence is moved one slot to the right.[25] Sedley is the only one to provide an argument for the emendation. He adduces several considerations. First, that with this minimal rearrangement we arrive at the standard *chreia*-structure. In a standardly formulated *chreia* the nominal phrase at the head of the sentence often includes after the proper name an additional specification which helps to identify unambiguously the protagonist of the *chreia*. Just by way of examples: Diogenes, the Cynic, Isocrates, the orator, Plato, the philosopher, or on a different occasion, Pythagoras, the philosopher.[26]

As a further consideration, Sedley calls attention to the very dubious morphological proficiency of the pupil writing the tablet, and submits that

> The mediocre standard of his [the pupil's] Greek will prove significant shortly, when we turn to another curious feature, namely the recurrently unorthodox order of the anecdote's first three words.[27]

The alleged rearrangement of the sentence is also further corroborated by the fact that in the first line the pupil originally started the sentence with the name Pythagoras and inserted the article only later. As a result, this article is halfway off the white writing surface of the tablet.

These considerations, however, do not prove the point. Morphological proficiency is completely different, and the difficulties involved exceed by far what is required for correctly writing out a specimen sentence. The fact that the pupil originally did not manage to write out the specimen sentence correctly does not mean that on correction—and this correction might as well have rested on the instructions of the teacher—he would have inserted the article at the wrong place.[28] If anything, rather the opposite is more plausible.

When someone copies a somewhat non-standardly formulated *chreia*, or writes down one presented orally, if it starts with article plus proper name, followed by bare noun, without an article—instead of the usual triplet, proper name – article – noun (or adjective)—it would be a quite common error to drop the unexpected article at the head of the sentence, which then later could be inserted, as a correction, where it belongs. To botch the sentence twice over, against the usual template, certainly is the less likely course of events.

Hence before rearranging the sentence on the writing tablet we should attempt an interpretation of the formulation found there, even if that formulation does not match exactly the standard *chreia* template. Interestingly, such an interpretation had been mentioned for quite some time in the literature: David Sedley reports that

---

[25] A notable exception: Luzzatto 2004, 174 (but without providing a translation).

[26] Sedley 1998a, 173 and 1998b, 128 f. This Pythagoras *chreia* goes as follows in the version given by Theon: Πυθαγόρας ὁ φιλόσοφος ἐρωτηθεὶς πόσος ἐστὶν ὁ τῶν ἀνθρώπων βίος, ἀναβὰς ἐπὶ τὸ δωμάτιον παρέκυψεν ὀλίγον, δηλῶν διὰ τούτου τὴν βραχύτητα (Theon, *Progymnasmata* 99.6–9).

[27] Sedley 1998a, 170 and 1998b, 125.

[28] Cf. the insertion of the missing word ἔδοξεν above line 3: that insertion is executed exactly where the sentence frame requires it.

Manfredo Manfredi had suggested to him that in the phrase ὁ Πυθαγόρας φιλόσοφος ἀποβάς the verb ἀποβαίνω need not refer to embarking, or leaving a place; this participle construction can also introduce a claim that Pythagoras as he came to be, or proved to be a philosopher, engaged in the activity that the *chreia* reports about.[29]

Manfredi's suggestion is explicitly rejected by Sedley in favour of the standard *chreia* structure, and then, in his wake by several interpreters.[30] This is so, although both in the case of Sedley's and Andorlini and Linguiti's translation of the *chreia*, this phrase could be taken to mean "having become—or even: having previously become—a philosopher" and could have been integrated into the interpretations they proposed. If Pythagoras were to launch himself as an instructor of grammar, after leaving a place—as on Sedley's interpretation—or if he were to take current usage on board in formulating his injunction after leaving a place—as on Andorlini and Linguiti's interpretation—one could also say that these later Pythagorean activities took place after Pythagoras had become, or had proved himself to be, a philosopher in a previous phase of his career.

But we need not even stop at this point. Although it is quite natural to take the aorist participle ἀποβάς as expressing that there is a temporal sequence between Pythagoras's two activities—one, of proving himself a philosopher, and the other, of teaching grammar—the aorist need not be parsed this way. It can also express that the first activity of Pythagoras proving himself a philosopher was a single and complete act, as contrasted to the continuous chore of teaching grammar, aptly rendered with the imperfect participle διδάσκων. This will also imply some sort of sequence, but not a sequence of two separate activities in a person's life. On this understanding of φιλόσοφος ἀποβάς we can translate the *chreia* accordingly

> Pythagoras, having proved himself a philosopher, and teaching grammar, kept on advising his pupils to abstain from blooded ones.

Not only have we saved Pythagoras from a superfluous journey with this suggestion, we can also discard the need for two different types of activities. What the *chreia* says is exactly that the Pythagorean injunction "Abstain from blooded ones" is the mark of a profound philosopher, and at the same time it is a concise command to correct linguistic use.

---

[29] Sedley 1998a, 173 n. 11 and 1998b, 129 n. 15. Cf., nevertheless, *LSJ*, ἀποβαίνω II. 4: of persons, with an Adj., *turn out, prove to be* so and so, ἀ. οὐ κοινοί *prove* partial, Th. 3.53; ἀ. χείρους Pl. *Lg*.952b; φρενιτικοὶ ἀ. Hp. *Coac*.405; τύραννος ἐκ βασιλέως ἀ. Plb. 7.13.7; also of a wound, ἰάσιμον ἀ. Pl. *Lg*. 878c.

It is important to note that although *LSJ* speaks about constructions of ἀποβαίνω + adjective, the specimen sentence in Polybius—similar to the *chreia*—contains an ἀποβαίνω + noun construction. To these examples Zhmud 2019, 113 n. 22 adds, among other instances, Arist. fr. 611 Rose (ποιητὴς ἀπέβη), Clem. Al. *Strom*. 2.7.35 (σοφὸς ἀπέβη).

[30] The notable exceptions are Lapini 2013, 12–15 and Zhmud 2019, 113 f.

At this point, we need to return, for a last time, to an evaluation of the drill written by the pupil. This is because one way of trying to decide whether the *chreia* is to be taken the way previous interpreters have tried to read it, with the emendation, or along the lines I have suggested, taking the noun φιλόσοφος as embedded in the construction φιλόσοφος ἀποβάς as the predicative complement of the participle ἀποβάς, would be to look at the singular vocative of the specimen sentence. On the interpretation of most of the previous interpreters, one would expect that both Πυθαγόρας and φιλόσοφος will stand in vocative form, as parts of the single phrase referring to the protagonist, whereas on my interpretation only Πυθαγόρας should be in the vocative. Admittedly, then, what we find on the writing tablet will be decisive about how the pupil, and perhaps also how his instructor, parsed the sentence.

For this purpose, however, we should have had access to the writing tablet of a much more stellar pupil. I have already mentioned that in the fifth line, in the singular vocative case there were three errors, one among them being that the pupil could not resist the urge to put the participle διδάσκων in the vocative, with the incorrect form διδάσκον. Accordingly, the fact that the pupil has φιλόσοφε, in the vocative, in this line, cannot settle the issue in either direction. This is because our pupil did not stop at putting φιλόσοφος in the vocative. He tried—at best on the analogy of the noun γέρων—to form the vocative of διδάσκων, not coinciding with the nominative form.[31] This means that he tried to put *all* the nominal phrases coordinated with the subject noun of the sentence into the vocative. Therefore, we have no clue whatsoever whether he saw any division of labour in the function of these nominal phrases. Maybe he did not much care what the sentence means in the first place. But even if he had some grasp of the structure of this part of the sentence— whether Sedleyan, or Manfredian—it is practically certain that through the maze of the linguistic exercise he completely lost sight of this syntactical detail and was concentrating exclusively on the morphological difficulties at hand.[32]

In this case, however, we cannot claim to have an indication from the execution of the exercise itself about the syntactical structure of the *chreia*. We are left to our own devices. In this case that should mean that we assess the available evidence— which I hope I presented properly above—and then exercise the principle of charity. In a one-liner like this, I presume charity should mean that we opt for the best, most loaded quip available, which however does not introduce unattested and unnecessary events into the historical record, like Pythagoras's putative journeys.

---

[31] Cf. the claim of Zhmud 2019, 115 that this is just a slip on the student's part, because "o and ω were regularly interchanged at that time in Egypt." This, however, disregards the fact that this would be the single occasion for such a slip on the pupil's part, so it is easier to suppose that here this is the exact—incorrect—form the pupil intended to put into writing.

[32] Corroborating the point Luzzatto 2004, 176 n. 49 makes. See n. 23 above.

Two further issues remain to be tackled. One, whether it is admissible to take the phrase τῶν ἐναιμόνων ἀπέχεθαι in Pythagoras's injunction to be ambiguous and expressing also an admonishment against the use of a word. Sedley 1998a, 177 and 1998b, 132 pointed out that "the standard Greek formula for mentioning the word without using it would here be τοῦ ἐναίμονες ἀπέχεσθαι; That would have made the meaning clear, but also of course ruined the joke."[33]

The answer to this query is supplied by Jonathan Barnes's magisterial commentary on Porphyry's *Eisagōgē*. There Barnes (Barnes 2003, 68 f., and 319–322, the Additional Note, C: Talking of Expressions) tackles in detail the autonymous use of expressions.[34] One way of autonymously integrating a word in a sentence is to embed it in a nominal phrase, like "the connector μέν," "the noun ἄνθρωπος," "the verb τρέχει," "the expression X" or "the sentence Y." From these phrases the noun governing the expression can be dropped, but the article retains its gender (connector – masculine, noun and verb – neuter, expression or sentence – feminine) irrespective of the gender of the embedded word. Then there is the other standard use mentioned by Sedley, that of using the neuter article τό before the word irrespective of its gender (or before a phrase, which does not have a gender of its own). "Moreover – Barnes adds –, when X is a noun and has a gender, authors will sometimes use the article not in the neuter but in the gender of X itself" (*op. cit.*, 320).[35] This last use matches what we have in the *chreia*, with two exceptions: ἐναιμόνων is not a noun, but an adjective used substantively; and, more importantly, it is not in the singular, as autonymously used nominal phrases typically are, but in the plural. About the first of these, I am confident that in principle τοῦ ἐναίμονος ἀπέχεσθαι can be taken both as avoiding the adjective ἐναίμων, or as avoiding an item that can be referred to by this adjective.

What is peculiar in the formulation of this *chreia* is the use of the plural. As far as autonymous use is concerned, the singular already expresses generality. If the injunction is τοῦ ἐναίμονος ἀπέχεσθαι, it is not only the forms in singular that have to be avoided. It is clear that the use of the plural, τῶν ἐναιμόνων ἀπέχεσθαι is conditioned by the actual Pythagorean precept, τῶν ἐμψύχων ἀπέχεσθαι, which is always rendered in the sources, without exception, in the plural. The author of the *chreia* intended to add a twist to that phrasal frame, and consequently was obliged

---

[33] The issue is even more acute for my interpretation. What Sedley wants is an unambiguous statement on the part of a grammar teacher, which is verbally exactly identical to the Pythagorean injunction against eating meat, whereas my interpretation needs an ambiguous injunction, which has then two different domains of application.

[34] These are occurrences in which they refer to themselves—but not necessarily to a single occurrence of the word or phrase. They may refer generally to any occurrence of the word or phrase. Otherwise, they would not be suitable for formulating grammatical rules, which are meant to apply to all (suitable) occurrences of the word or phrase.

[35] Note that the use of such conventions does not presuppose or require a theoretical account about autonymy or quotation. For a detailed recent discussion of the theoretical take of Augustine and other ancient authors on the phenomenon, see Nawar 2021.

to insert ἐναιμόνων in the plural. This, without doubt, risked the *double entendre* that is the point of the *chreia*. But construing the *chreia* as introducing a ban against using the affected, longer form of the adjective ἐναίμων, −ον is guaranteed by another framing device. Once the *chreia* mentions that Pythagoras gave advice as a teacher of grammar, we should expect that the following phrase should have some application also in that context. That expectation, then, will spot the adjective within the phrase, τῶν ἐναιμόνων ἀπέχεθαι, so that the occurrence of the adjective will serve as a trigger. Even though it is in the plural, it will fix our attention on a "grammar teacher" reading, where the injunction is about language use, formulating a blanket ban on the use of the two-ending adjective ἐναίμων, −ον, and not only on the use of its plural forms. At the same time, the other frame mentioned at the head of the *chreia*, that Phythagoras cut a philosopher by the advice he gave to his students, will also guarantee that alongside this "grammar teacher" reading, the other "philosopher" reading is also available. And in that context, the phrase τῶν ἐναιμόνων ἀπέχεθαι will serve as a different trigger, calling to mind the signature precept of vegetarianism in a Pythagorean life.

In closing I should add a few words about the evidential value of the *chreia*, and about some of the salient stereotypes on which this *chreia* rests. It should be clear by now that here it is not Pythagoras or the Pythagoreans speaking; rather, the instructors of grammar attribute this twisted version of the ban on eating meat to Pythagoras. Accordingly, the *chreia* need not have any evidential value as far as Pythagoras or later Pythagoreans are concerned. Instead, I think one should connect the *chreia* to the widespread prejudices about philosophers, and about the way philosophers employ language. We, philosophers—ancient and modern alike—not only talk about abstruse and incomprehensible things, but for this purpose we also employ bloated and strange idioms. If, for just a single example, we turn to Lucianus's *Sale of creeds* (*Vitarum auctio*), we find there a Pythagoras speaking in a bombastic idiom full of idiosyncratic riddles. The *chreia*'s key step of reformulating the ban on eating meat with an obsolete word is an instance of deploying this same *topos*.

But there is more to the *chreia* than the popular aversion or antipathy against those snooty philosophers. This is the condescension of those in charge of proper usage against those who speak some non-standard idiom. When some people—like the Pythagoras of the *chreia*—use their improper words in injunctions, they happen to speak almost like someone educated in proper usage would. They become colleagues, or at least involuntary allies of the grammarian. In these special cases philosophical speech turns upon itself.

Condescension, however, is appropriate also from the other party, those of us, philosophers and non-philosophers alike, who do not pursue proper usage as our most distinguished aim.[36] From this angle the way these guardians of language

---

[36] For a detailed—and hilarious—discussion of common accusations as part of the public perception of grammarians, see Sluiter 1988.

speak should also appear quite paradoxical. In order to proscribe it, they cannot avoid lapsing into the kind of speech they most vehemently censure. Something similar, inadvertently, happens in this *chreia* to Pythagoras, the grammar teacher: he has to say what shouldn't be said, but I do not think our *chreia* would have particularly intended to call attention to the paradoxical nature of this typical instance of an utterance about improper use, attributed to Pythagoras by a witty grammarian.

Bibliography

Andorlini, Isabella and Alessandro Linguiti. 1999. Pythagoras 2T. In *Corpus dei papiri filosofici greci e latini,* Testi e lessico nei papiri di cultura greca e latina, Parte I: Autori noti, Vol. I***, 681–684. Florence: Olschki.

Bastianini, Guido. 2003. Testi gnomici di ambito scolastico. In *Aspetti di letteratura gnomica nel mondo antico, I*, ed. Maria Serena Funghi, 167–175. Florence: Olschki.

Cribiore, Raffaella. 1996. *Writing, teachers and students in Graeco-Roman Egypt*. Atlanta: Scholars Press.

Hock, Ronald F. and Edward N. O'Neil. 1986. *The chreia in ancient rhetoric*, Vol. 1: The Progymnasmata. Atlanta: Scholars Press.

———. 2002. *The chreia in ancient rhetoric*, Vol. 2: Classroom exercises. Atlanta: Society of Biblical Literature.

Kenyon, F.G. 1909. Two Greek school-tablets. *Journal of Hellenic Studies* 29: 29–40.

Lapini, Walter. 2013. Pitagora maestro di scuola (P. Br. Libr. Add. MS 37516.1). In Testi fragmentari e critica del testo: Problemi di filologia filosofica greca, 3–22. Roma: Edizioni di storia e letteratura.

Luzzatto, Maria Tanja. 2004. L'impiego della chreia filosofica nell'educazione antica, in *Aspetti di letteratura gnomica nel mondo antico. II*, ed. Maria Serena Funghi, 157–187. Florence: Olschki.

Maehler, H. 1970. Neue Hexameter-Fragmente auf Papyrus. *Zeitschrift für Papyrologie und Epigraphik* 6: 152–170.

Nawar, Tamer. 2021. Every word is a name: Autonymy and quotation in Augustine. *Mind* 130: 595–616. https://doi.org/10.1093/mind/fzaa043.

Painter, K. 1967. A Roman writing tablet from London. *The British Museum Quarterly* 31: 101–110.

Piano, Valeria. 2015. CHR 4. In *Corpus dei papiri filosofici greci e latini: Testi e lessico nei papiri di cultura greca e latina.* Parte II.2: Sentenze di autori noti e «chreiai», 381–390. Florence: Olschki.

Queneau, Raymond. 1959. *Zazie dans le métro*. Paris: Gallimard.

Sedley, David. 1998a. Pythagoras the grammar teacher (PBrLibr Add Ms 37516, 1). In *Papiri filosofici: Miscellanea di Studi* II (Studi e testi per il *Corpus dei papiri filosofici greci e latini*, 9), 164–181. Florence: Olschki.

———. 1998b. Pythagoras the grammar teacher and Didymon the adulterer. *Hyperboreus* 4: 122–138.

Sluiter, Ineke. 1988. Perversa subtilitas. De kwade roep van de Grammaticus. *Lampas: Tijdschrift voor Nederlandse classici* 21: 41–65.

Wouters, A. 2007. Between the grammarian and the rhetorician: The κλίσις χρείας. In *Bezugsfelder: Festschrift für Gerhard Petersmann zum 65 Geburtstag*, ed. V. Oberparleiter, I. Hohenwallner, and R. E. Kritzer (*Grazer Beiträge: Zeitschrift für die Klassische Altertumswissenschaft*, Supplementband XI), 137–154. Salzburg-Horn: Berger.

Zhmud, Leonid. 2019. The papyrological tradition on Pythagoras and the Pythagoreans. In *Presocratics and papyrological tradition: A philosophical reappraisal of the sources (Proceedings of the International Workshop held at the University of Trier, 22–24 September 2016)*, ed. Christian Vassallo, 111–146. Berlin/New York: De Gruyter.

Chapter 2
Abelard on Existential Inference

Peter King

Keywords Peter Abelard · Existential import · Square of opposition · Semantics

Peter Abelard (1079–1142) has lately acquired the reputation of being the first philosopher/logician to recognize and bring to the fore what we now call "the problem of existential import."[1] This reputation is presumably based on passages such as the following (*dial.* 176.16–26):[2]

> Likewise, in categorical sentences the only proper contradiction to a given affirmation seems to be the one that destroys the whole of its meaning by a prefixed negation. For instance, the contradictory to "Every man is man" is "Not every man is man" and not "Some man is not man," for the latter will perhaps be false along with the former: when no man exists at all, what "Every man is man" says is not true, nor is what "Some man is not man" proposes...

True, Abelard is talking about contradictory negation in this passage rather than diagnosing a problem with existential import, but the insight that won him his reputation as discoverer of the problem of existential import is on display: the particular sentences that follow from universal sentences—whether they follow indirectly as

---

[1] So says Wikipedia (!) in its entry on the Square of Opposition (2021). See also Parsons [1997], Uckelman [2008], and Seuren [2010].

[2] Sic quoque in categoricis propositionibus ea tantum propria contradictio ac recte diuidens cuilibet affirmationi uidetur quae negatione praeposita totam eius sententiam destruit, ut eius quae est: *Omnis homo est homo* ea quae est: *Non omnis homo est homo*, non ea quae est: *Quidam homo non est homo*; haec enim fortasse simul erit falsa cum ea. Re enim hominis prorsus non existente neque ea uera est quae ait: *Omnis homo est homo* nec ea quae proponit: *Quidam homo non est homo...*
All translations are mine. For the works cited and their abbreviations, see the Bibliography.

P. King (✉)
University of Toronto, Toronto, Canada
e-mail: peter.king@utoronto.ca

© The Author(s), under exclusive license to Springer Nature Switzerland AG 2023
J. P. Hochschild et al. (eds.), *Metaphysics Through Semantics: The Philosophical Recovery of the Medieval Mind*, International Archives of the History of Ideas Archives internationales d'histoire des idées 242, https://doi.org/10.1007/978-3-031-15026-5_2

in the case of contradictory pairs here, or directly as in the case of subalternation—
may be false not only if what their predicate-terms express fail to apply to their
subjects, but also if their subject-terms are empty. Hence the traditional Square of
Opposition, and the logic for which it stands, makes a deep and formally indefensible assumption about the nonemptiness of its subject-terms, or, equivalently, about
the existential plenitude of its domain. Abelard therefore is credited with recognizing the problem.[3]

Much as I hate to blacken Abelard's recent reputation, it isn't clear that he
deserves the credit he has been awarded. Even in the passage from his *Dialectica*
cited above, Abelard doesn't seem to recognize that existential import poses a philosophical or logical difficulty. In particular, Abelard doesn't say that there is a problem with traditional logic *qua* formal system, or indeed that there is any problem
posed by the fact that a s subject-term might be empty. Instead, he uses the possible
emptiness of subject-terms as grounds to argue for his account of sentential negation over and against 'traditional' term-negation.[4] If there is any problem at issue in
his remarks, it is the nature of negation rather than existential import. Abelard does
deserve credit for recognizing that sentential negation differs sharply from term-
negation, but that insight, momentous as it was for the history of logic, doesn't
obviously have anything to do with existential import.

Nor is this the only reason for hesitation about granting Abelard credit. For if
Abelard thought that universal sentences carried existential import in a straightforward way, then, as Uckelman [2008] reasons, categorical sentences like "Every S is
P" would have the logical form of a conjunction: "There are Ss and every one of
them is P," $(\forall x)(Sx \rightarrow Px)$ & $(\exists x)(Sx)$. Yet Abelard insists that such universal categorical sentences are logically simple rather than compound (*multiplex*)—roughly
speaking, that they say something about something, having noncomplex subject-
predicate form rather than conjunctive, disjunctive, or conditional form.

On closer inspection it turns out that Abelard's views surrounding existential
import are complex. For while Abelard does talk about empty terms, and about
subalternation and quantification and related matters, his discussion addresses many
subtle nuances of the "problem" of existential import—or, as I shall call it to highlight its perhaps unproblematic nature and Abelard's more general interest in it,
existential inference.

The best way to begin, I think, is to take a step back from the texts and the contemporary discussion to see what is involved in existential inference of the sort at

---

[3] See Seuren [2010] for an attempt to salvage "traditional" logic along Abelardian lines.

[4] Abelard also notes that contrapositive conversion may fail in assertoric sentences when one of the
negated terms is empty: "The same error in conversion [by contraposition] happens for the same
reason in simple sentences as it does in modal sentences, namely because terms that contain all
things are part of the mixture. For instance, if I were to say 'Every non-human is non-rose' when
roses have been destroyed, 'non-rose' contains all things, and so the converse [contrapositive of
'Every non-human is non-rose', namely 'Some rose is human'], doesn't preserve the truth-
value…" (*in Per.* 400.239–401.243, cited in Binini [2018]). Yet here too Abelard is not pointing to
a general logical problem but to a specific failure of conversion due to a specific cause.

issue (§1), and then to see what Abelard has to say about it from the ground up: the distinction of the logical and grammatical parts of the simple categorical sentence (§2), his views about the nature of existential commitment (§3), and the role of quantifiers (§4). In the end, things are rather messy, and a good deal the more interesting for it.

2.1   The Problem with the Problem of Existential Import

The reasoning that supposedly lies behind the problem of existential import seems to be as follows. Begin with a universal sentence:

(1) Every S is P

In its modern guise, this is canonically represented by a universally quantified closed formula:

(1*) $(\forall x)(Sx \rightarrow Px)$

Now by subalternate entailment and a dose of common sense, a universal claim should also hold of a more limited less-than-universal range, and so from (1) we are entitled to infer the particular sentence:

(2) Some S is P

The usual formal representation of (2) takes it to be an existential quantification:

(2*) $(\exists x)(Sx \& Px)$

We may already be in trouble at this point, because while (1) arguably entails (2), (1*) doesn't entail (2*), since (1*) is compatible with $\neg(\exists x)(Sx \& Px)$ but (2*) is not. This is thought to lay bare the existential assumption behind the move from (1) to (2).[5]

But does (2), as opposed to (2*), actually land us in trouble? That is, does it make the existential assumption at issue? Well, it's worth noting that (2) is a particular sentence which might, or might not, be taken to make an ontological commitment. As it stands it isn't obviously equivalent to a sentence that explicitly makes such a commitment, such as "An S exists" or "There is an S (one that in fact is also P)." Even (2*), like (2), does not commit to any particular existent despite being existential in its logical form; it only says that there is at least one S, out of everything that is S, which is also P. For this reason, modern as well as mediaeval logicians hold that the truth of (2) or (2*) requires, and perhaps depends upon, some true singular

---

[5]A minor wrinkle: (2*) says more than a mere existential commitment to a nonempty subject-term warrants; it also declares that the S that exists is also P. It would be equally falsified by an empty predicate-term, or even the failure of any S to be P. Simplification on the complex formula does yield $(\exists x)(Sx)$, as noted below, but doesn't address the wrinkle.

sentence even though (2) and (2*) are themselves indeterminate with respect to what they are talking about.

Hence for (2) there must be some further true singular sentence such as:

(3) Socrates is P

Roughly, we have to switch from talking about kinds of things, namely things that are S (which is a general term), to making a claim about a given thing. The contemporary counterpart of (3) is the variable-free formula we arrive at by instantiating (2*), making its existential commitment explicit:

(3*) *Sa & Pa*

which must hold for some *a*. More exactly, $(\exists x)(Sx \& Px) \rightarrow (Sa \& Pa)$, for some *a*, is a logical truth. This is precisely existential instantiation of the closed formula for some element(s) of the domain. In short, we have to move from a common noun to a proper noun (mediaeval) or from a quantified to an unquantified sentence (contemporary). Since the difference between a common noun and a proper noun is just how many things the noun applies to, which is in some sense a matter of its 'quantity', the reasoning on both the medieval and the contemporary sides might be thought to be the same at bottom.

Yet even (3) is a step removed from explicit ontological commitment. On the one hand, it says more than it has to, since in addition to saying something about *S* it further incorporates a claim about (what is) *P*. On the other hand, (3) arguably says less than it needs to, since it does not make an explicit declaration of existence:

(4) Socrates is [OR: Socrates exists]

It is a substantive thesis—one that, as we shall see, Abelard rejects—to hold that (3) entails (4); true predicative claims need not assert, or even presuppose, the nonemptiness of their subject-terms; think of sentences like "Sherlock Holmes is fictional." By contrast the contemporary version, (3*), is unproblematic; it gives us the appropriate corresponding sentence:

(4*) *Sa*

by simplification, since (3*) does on its own make an existential claim (or perhaps two existential claims), following the existential commitment present in (2*).

Put all the pieces together. From a general claim we can reasonably infer a particular (though not definite) claim; such particular claims might be taken to involve an existential commitment, at a minimum requiring there to be at least one appropriately-related singular existential claim that is true. On the traditional reading, it is said, (2) requires the truth of some singular sentence like (3), which in turn entails (4), leading to the conclusion that (1) is true only if some singular existential claim like (4) is true. On the contemporary reading, (1*) doesn't entail (2*), so the blurring of indefinite particulars with singular existentials in (3*) and (4*) doesn't matter. Indeed, contemporary logicians don't even countenance distinct levels of generality in the subject or predicate—all first-order sentences deal with features of elements in the domain, where quantifiers range over those elements, and the features are all by nature general (at the very least not singular).

Such is the shape of the "problem" of existential import. Abelard questions each step of the reasoning on the medieval side, in particular the move from (3) to (4). To see why, we need to take a closer look at his understanding of how sentences work, which, at least in broad outlines, means taking a look at his views about the complex relationship between syntax and semantics.

2.2   Grammar and Logic

From the grammatical tradition stemming from Priscian, Abelard inherited an analysis of the sentence into *noun* and *verb*. From the logical tradition stemming from Aristotle, Abelard inherited an analysis of the statement into *subject* and *predicate*. The two kinds of analysis were not always in accord. William of Champeaux, one of Abelard's teachers, even held that the grammatical form of sentences was always distinct from their logical form in all cases, a view Abelard saw as going too far.[6]

The challenge, as Abelard saw it, was to show how the insights of each tradition complemented those of the other. His discussion of the categorical sentence in the *Dialectica* and the *Logica 'ingredientibus'* finds him doing exactly that, and the results are directly applicable to existential inference.

Abelard begins with the most basic sentence-type imaginable: the assertoric present-tense affirmative categorical sentence consisting in a single simple noun (as opposed to a noun phrase) and an incomplex intransitive personal[7] finite verb-phrase: "Socrates runs" or "Socrates is reading," for instance. Once Abelard has an account of these basic sentences, he extends his account to cover cases of negative sentences, complex verb phrases, different moods and tenses, impersonal verbs, and the like. The first order of business, though, is to figure out what's going on in the simple case—that is, to identify and describe the logical roles of subject and predicate in such logically basic sentences.

Aristotle, and some mediaeval grammarians, drew a distinction between 'two-piece' predication in which the verb is *secundum adiacens*, as in "Socrates runs" (*Socrates currit*) or "Socrates is/exists" (*Socrates est*), and three-piece predication in which the verb-phrase consists in the copula with a participle which is *tertium adiacens*, as in "Socrates is running" (*Socrates est currens*). There is no real difficulty in identifying the subject and predicate in two-piece predication: the noun is the subject, the verb the predicate.

---

[6] See Abelard, *in Top.* 271.32–273.3 for a description of the view of William of Champeaux (*noster praeceptor*), and for his characterization: "According to his theory, individual sentences have two senses: (*i*) dialectical, which is broader and in a certain way better, according to simple inherence; (*ii*) grammatical, which is more determinate, according to the connection of things."

[7] As opposed to 'impersonal' verbs, as in sentences such as "It is raining."

The key to understanding sentences, Abelard holds, is understanding that verbs are the ingredient that make a well-formed utterance (*congrua oratio*) into a statement. He describes the logical role of verbs, at least of verbs in two-piece predication, as follows (*dial.* 134.28–34):[8]

> We shouldn't pass over the fact that the verbs that are put into statements are said to be predicated properly on some occasions and incidentally on others. They are predicated properly like this: "Peter is/exists" and "Peter runs." Here they are employed with a twofold force, for not only do they retain their function of linking [themselves to the subject], they also signify the feature that is predicated. However, [a verb] is said to be predicated incidentally rather than properly when it is adjoined to the predicate only to link it [to the subject], as in "Peter is a man."

Abelard makes the same point in his *in Per.* 3.88 (120.652–121.658):[9]

> Note that personal verbs which can be predicated, no matter what their signification might be, are all able to link themselves [to their subjects]. For example, if one says "Socrates is/ exists" or Socrates reads," *being* and *reading* are themselves predicated *per se*, and are employed with a twofold force, because they have the force of the predicate and of linking, so that they simultaneously are predicated and link themselves [to their subjects]. Thus when one says 'runs' it is as though one were to say 'is running'.

A personal verb in two-piece predication properly has not one but two semantic functions, according to Abelard: (*a*) to express whatever feature may be embodied in the verb, so that 'runs' expresses running; (*b*) to link that feature to the subject in a way that produces a unified statement—in short, to say that something is such-and-so, in keeping with Aristotle's general characterization of a simple categorical sentence as one "saying something of something" (*De int.* 5 17ª21–22).[10]

Abelard is following tradition: the twofold function of verbs is put forward in the eleventh-century compendium of grammatical theory, the *Glossulae super Priscianum*,[11] and the equivalence of two-piece and three-piece predication is endorsed by Aristotle in the *De interpretatione*. Yet Abelard makes these views of his predecessors uniquely his own. On the one hand, he clearly thinks that two-piece predication is the proper and strict form of predication, though he retains its

---

[8] Non est autem illud praetermittendum quod uerba in enuntiationibus posita modo proprie, modo per accidens praedicari dicuntur; proprie autem praedicantur hoc modo: *Petrus est, Petrus currit*; hic enim gemina ui funguntur, cum non solum copulandi officium tenent, sed etiam rei praedicatae significationem habent. Per accidens autem et non proprie praedicari dicitur, cum ipsum praedicato ad eius tantum copulationem apponitur, ita: *Petrus est homo*.

[9] Et sciendum, quod personalia uerba quae praedicari possunt, cuiuscumque significationis sint, omnia sese copulare possunt, ut, si dicatur: *Socrates est, Socrates legit, esse* et *legere* per se ipsa praedicantur, et gemina ui funguntur, quia et uim praedicati habent et copulantis, ut simul et praedicentur et se ipsa copulent. Sic enim dicitur currit quasi diceretur est currens.

[10] See also *De int.* 6 17ª25–26. Note the problem with 'quantifying in' here: to say that something is such-and-so is to say of something that it is such-and-so (a notational variant), which is not the same as saying of some thing that it is such-and-so; the latter is an explicit ontological commitment not entailed by the former, at least not in Abelard's eyes, as we shall see shortly.

[11] For the *Glossulae* see Grondeux & Rosier-Catach [2017]. Tweedale [1988] 212–218 discusses Abelard's use of the *Glossulae* on the substantive verb.

equivalence to three-piece predication in order to be able to state rules of conversion in a symmetric fashion; it is far easier to give formal rules for "*S* is *P*" than for "*S* φs." On the other hand, he takes the semantics of three-piece predication to be explained by the complexities of two-piece predication. We can see how this works if we focus on the substantive verb "to be" (*a.k.a.* the copula).

Abelard holds that when the substantive verb is employed in two-piece predication, it exhibits the same semantic behaviour as any other verb; "Peter is/exists" is on a par with "Peter runs," as remarked above. He continues (*dial.* 135.6–8):[12]

> When [the substantive verb] is said properly, it contains the predicated feature and indeterminately attributes something being among existing things, so that "Peter is/exists" is as if to say "Peter is among the existing things."

The same point is made in his *in Per.* 3.106 (125.769–771):[13]

> But the verb 'is/exists', which contains everything in its nature, conjoins '(a) being' predicated in its primary sense; when we say "I am/exist" it is as though to say "I am among the existents."

Just as in "Socrates runs" the verb 'runs' expresses the feature running and links it to the subject of its sentence, so too "Socrates is/exists" expresses the feature existing and links it to the subject of its sentence.

We'll come back to this type of sentence shortly, since it is the vehicle for existential commitment, but first we need to look at how the substantive verb functions when it is not predicated properly but rather incidentally, in three-piece predication.[14] This broadens the scope of Abelard's discussion considerably, of course, since when the substantive verb appears in three-piece predication, the third 'piece' need not be a participle—that is to say, it need not be a verbal adjective; it could just as well be an ordinary adjective ("Socrates is white") or a noun ("Socrates is an animal"). Since the linking function is provided by the substantive verb, the third piece need only express some feature, as the predicate adjective 'white' expresses

---

[12] Cum autem proprie dicitur, rem etiam praedicatam continet atque aliquam rerum existentium indeterminate attribuit, ueluti eum dicitur: *Petrus est*, hoc est *Petrus est aliqua de existentibus rebus*.

[13] At uero est uerbum, quod omnia in essentia continet, primo loco praedicatum ens coniungit, cum dicitur: *Ego sum* ac si dicerem: *Ego sum aliquid de exsistentibus*.

[14] Two points. First, the substantive verb has some company; Abelard thinks that the nuncupative verb [*nuncupor*] has many of the same unusual features. Second, note that only the substantive verb is predicated incidentally, since it is the only verb that can be used as an auxiliary; we can say "Socrates is reading" but we cannot say "Socrates runs reading" and even have a well-formed sentence, much less a sensible one. Abelard holds that modal verbs and other periphrastic forms require the substantive verb, forming complex verbal compounds, so they are not counterexamples: see Jacobi [1980] and Martin [2001].

whiteness. In short, the substantive verb in three-piece predication welds itself to whatever it is combined with to create a single verb (*dial*. 138.11–17):[15]

> Accordingly, if I may venture to say so, it seems more reasonable to me that we should defer to reason—so that just as we took adjectival opposition according to composition rather than [mere] adjunction, so too let us construe incidental predication, and when we say 'is a man' or 'is conceivable' or 'is white' we should understand being a man or being conceivable or being white as a single verb.

He reiterates the point, referring to his earlier discussion (*dial*. 170.21–25):[16]

> But if here too we want to maintain the view we proposed earlier, namely when we declared that the [substantive] verb adjoined to a predicate-term makes up a single verb, we also have to take the conjunction involved in incidental predication according to composition [rather than mere adjunction]...

Abelard had argued that apparently conflicting juxtapositions of terms, such as 'dead man' (a case of "adjectival opposition"), should not be given a sense that is merely the addition of the sense of their constituents. Instead, they should be treated as a single unit "according to composition" with a single sense of its own.

The same, Abelard maintains, applies to three-piece predication: "Socrates is white" should properly be understood as the two-piece predication "Socrates is-white" with the newly coined verb 'to-be-white'.[17] The predicate noun or adjective lends the new verb the feature that it expresses, and the substantive verb endows the new compound with its linking force. Intuitively, the "force of the predicate" normally belonging to the substantive verb is cancelled and replaced by the predicative force of the predicate noun or adjective (*dial*. 134.34–135.1):[18]

> The interposed [copula 'is' in "Peter is a man"] does not also contain here the predicated feature. Indeed, it would be superfluous to supply '(a) man' then. Rather, it only links the predicated feature that is joined on to it—and if something other than 'man' were then attributed in it, it would not link the 'man' that is joined on to it in the same place.

The substantive verb cannot also link the predicated feature it has in two-piece predication because that would make the addition of anything further in the sentence superfluous, and in fact gibberish: "Socrates is white" would be properly read as "Socrates exists white," ill-formed since 'exists' is intransitive, not taking an

---

[15] Unde mihi, si profiteri audeam, illud rationabilius uidetur ut rationi sufficere ualeamus, ut scilicet, quemadmodum oppositionem in adiecto secundum compositionem* magis quam secundum appositionem sumimus, ita accidentalem praedicationem accipiamus, ac cum dicitur *est homo* uel *est opinabile* uel *est album* pro uno uerbo esse hominem uel esse album uel esse opinabile intelligamus. [* = Reading *compositionem* for *oppositionem*, as suggested in Wilks [1993] 90 n.16.]

[16] Si uero eam sententiam et hic quoque uelimus tenere quam in Tertio Postpraedicamentorum posuimus, quando scilicet uerbum cum adiuncto praedicato unum componere uerbum diximus, oportet accidentalis quoque praedicationis coniunctionem secundum compositionem accipere...

[17] See Kretzmann [1988], Tweedale [1988], Wilks [1993]. The example is natural in Latin: *Socrates est albus* is to be read as *Socrates albescit*.

[18] Neque enim hic interpositum quoque rem praedicatam continet, quippe iam *homo* superflue supponeretur, sed tantum quod subiungitur praedicatum copulat; nec si iam aliquid praeter hominem in ipso esset attributum, in eodem loco hominem copularet subiunctum.

object. Instead, the predicated feature belonging to what is joined on to the 'new' composite verb takes its place, and the result is that in three-piece predication, the verb phrase really—logically—becomes a single verb.

2.3 Existential Commitment

Abelard's view of simple categorical sentences has many virtues. But it has vices as well,[19] one of which is that it effectively blocks the reasoning from (3) to (4) given in §1, that is, the existential inference from "Socrates is P" to "Socrates is/exists." The reasoning is straightforward. If the substantive verb loses its predicated feature *existence* when it appears in three-piece predication—this feature being replaced by whatever feature is expressed by the predicate noun or adjective, as Abelard has argued—then it isn't available for its two-piece existential use. In short, we cannot infer 'is' predicated properly from a case of its incidental predication. Hence from (say) "Socrates is ugly" we cannot infer "Socrates exists." And since the argument is purely general, we are never entitled to an existential inference on the basis of anything other than an existential categorical sentence.

Surprisingly, Abelard endorses the conclusion that simple categorical sentences do *not* have existential commitment. More precisely, Abelard holds that simple categorical sentences do not have existential commitment in virtue of their logical form, their formal features. Rather, whether a sentence permits existential inference depends on its semantics, and in particular the semantics of the terms it involves (a 'material' rather than a 'formal' feature), as he remarks (*dial.* 136.37–137.6):[20]

> But every incidental predication of the verb seems to be improper when, as described, it is inserted as a third piece, since it does not then contain any feature that is predicated, as stated, but has the sole function of linking, as it does for instance in "Peter is a man" or "Peter is white." The fact that "Peter is/exists" can be inferred from "Peter is a man" pertains not to the interpretation of [the interposed substantive verb] but perhaps instead to the predication of 'man', which is the name of an existing thing only.

In three-piece predication, the substantive verb does not permit existential inference. Rather, Abelard suggests, the fact that we do draw the existential inference

---

[19] As noted earlier, one apparent vice is that if the substantive verb is combined with a predicate-term to form a single semantic unit, it seems that neither rules of conversion nor of the syllogism, which are usually taken to refer to the subject-term and the predicate-term independent of the copula, will work any longer. Abelard has to hold that the welding of the component pieces of three-piece predication into a single verb always permits certain kinds of logical decomposition, so that from "Every S is P" we can infer "Some P is S" (for instance).

[20] At uero mihi omnis illa uerbi praedicatio per accidens atque impropria uidetur, quando ipsum, ut dictum est, tertium adiacens interponitur, cum non rem, ut dictum est, praedicatam contineat, sed solius copulae officium habeat, ut in ea quoque qua dicitur: *Petrus est homo* uel *albus*. Nec quidem quantum ad eius interpretationem pertinet, ex eo quod dicitur: *Petrus est homo*, inferri potest *Petrus est*, sed fortasse quantum ad praedicationem hominis, quod existentis rei tantum nomen est.

might have more to do with the semantic value of the predicate: the term 'man' applies to all and only existing things.

This view might seem hopeless. It appears to have the counterintuitive consequence that we can only speak of living human beings, whereas in truth we speak of non-living humans all the time—people like Aristotle or Abelard. Whatever its virtues, this seems too high a price to pay.

Yet Abelard's suggestion that existential inference depends on the meaning of the terms rather than the formal features of a simple categorical sentence is, in fact, his considered view. He reasons his way to it by lengthy dissection of two problem sentences: "Homer is a poet" and "A chimaera is conceivable."

The difficulty with "Homer is a poet" is that Homer is now dead, and dead men aren't poets. (They tell no tales.) If one were still wedded to the idea that the interposed 'is' always carries existential commitment, then we could conjure Homer into existence just by saying something about him. As Abelard puts it (*dial*. 135.32–36):[21]

> When we say "Homer is a poet" once Homer is dead, if we consider the signification of what is signified by the words and take 'poet' in such a way that it's a name for the man Homer, then it's simply true that Homer exists in that he has the characteristic poet and the locution is proper.

Abelard tells us that his teacher 'Master W.' (presumably William of Champeaux) held, perhaps on these grounds, that the sentence "Homer is a poet" is *not* a proper locution; instead, it is merely figurative (135.28–31), and it has something like the meaning "Homer's fame lives on through the poem he wrote" (135.24–25).

A similar treatment was available to William for the other problem sentence, "A chimaera is conceivable" (136.32–36):[22]

> Likewise, "A chimaera is conceivable" is said [by William] to be a figurative and improper locution on the grounds that it proposes in its sense something other than the words in its utterance seem to. For no property is given to the chimaera (which doesn't exist) by 'conceivable'; instead, a conception of it is attributed to someone's mind, as though to say: "Someone's mind has a conception of a chimaera."

Although it looks as though "A chimaera is conceivable" ascribes a property to a something nonexistent, which would be a problem, William holds that such a claim is really a disguised way of talking about thoughts people have. Thus William of Champeaux proposes to rid himself of the apparent existential commitments to a living Homer and a real chimaera by recourse to reductive paraphrases, in the style later made popular by William of Ockham.

Yet Abelard rejects William of Champeaux's way out. There is no reason, in Abelard's eyes, to think that either of these sentences is figurative, that is, requires

---

[21] Cum enim dicimus Homero defuncto *Homerus est poeta*, si significatarum significationem dictionum pensemus atque Homeri nomen hominis ut *poeta* sumamus, uerum est et simpliciter Homerum esse, ex eo scilicet quod poetae proprietatem habere dicitur, atque propria fuit locutio.

[22] Sic quoque et *Chimaera est opinabilis* in eo figuratiua atque impropria locutio dicitur, quod aliud uerba quam uideatur in uoce, proponant in sensu; non enim chimaerae, quae non est, aliqua proprietas per opinabile datur sed magis animae alicuius opinio de ipsa attribuitur, ac si ita diceremus: Anima alicuius opinionem habet de chimaera.

paraphrase of the sort William proposed.[23] Unlike a sentence like "The meadow is cheerful" (*Prata rident*), which wears its figurative character on its face for the simple reason that meadows don't have moods, the claims that Homer is a poet and that chimaeras are conceivable do seem to be literal—the former is taken literally up to the point of Homer's death, after all, and the latter (much like "Sherlock Holmes is fictional") is straightforwardly true. The only rationale for taking them as figurative is that they are thought to land us with unwelcome existential commitments, which is a rationalization rather than a reason for thinking they are figurative: being inconvenient isn't grounds for rejecting their literal sense. But the problem, Abelard points out, is a problem only on the assumption that three-piece predication licenses existential inference. As we have seen, Abelard does not think that it does, and these sentences are further grounds to support his view.

William might protest that if "A chimaera is conceivable" is literally true, as Abelard seems to think it is, then it must have existential import. After all, it says that a chimaera is something. Doesn't 'something' require an existent subject?

Abelard holds that it does not. In considering Aristotle's discussion of the related sentence "Homer is something, namely, a poet" in *De int.* 11 21ᵃ25–26, Abelard points out that 'something' does not involve any existential commitment (*dial.* 137.14–16):[24]

> When [Aristotle] put 'something' in, he took it as the name of nonexistents as well as of existents in his claim that 'goat-stag' signifies something [*De int.* 1 16ᵃ16–17].

Abelard endorses the point generally (*in Per.* 6.32 (194.305–309):[25]

> Accordingly, we should grant something's being something that it is is taken as the meaning of an expression: wherever 'something' appears, it is a name of everything, existents as well as non-existents, just it is when we say that something is what it is not, for instance "A chimaera is a man" or "A chimaera is a chimaera."

'Something' is not equivalent to 'some thing', that is, some existing thing; Abelard follows Aristotle's lead in taking it to be a general term that applies to existents and nonexistents alike, as well as making the general point that existential commitment does not follow on the predicate-term: 'poet', like 'something', picks out existents and nonexistents equally.[26]

---

[23] Kretzmann [1980] 506: "Abelard's fundamental objection to this maneuver seems to be that it is only a maneuver."

[24] Cum *aliquid* posuit, ipsum tam existentium nomen quam non-existentium accepit secundum quod dictum est hircoceruus aliquid significare.

[25] Unde potius concedendum est Aliquid esse aliquid quod ipsum est in ui orationis accipi; et *aliquid*, ubicumque ponitur, nomen est omnium tam exsistentium quam non-exsistentium, sicut et quando dicitur aliquid esse id quod non est, ut *Chimaera est homo* uel *Chimaera est chimaera*.

[26] Abelard uses 'something' like a schematic letter. In the sentence "Homer is something (namely a poet)," the term 'something' stands in for whatever Homer is—in this case a poet, but it might as well have been any other word. Likewise, 'saying that something is something' is Aristotle's general characterization of what it is to make a statement, which of course might be true (when we say of something that it is something it is) or false (when we say of something that it is what it is not), no matter what word we put in for the various occurrences of 'something'.

There is a way, however, in which a sentence like "Homer is a poet" requires the existence of its subject to be true. Abelard insists that the present tense of the substantive verb has to be taken seriously; the new 'composite' verb forged from the copula and the predicate-term ('is-a-poet' or perhaps 'poetizes') will inherit its tense unless there is a reason for it not to do so. The sentence "Homer is a poet" is therefore a claim that Homer is presently a poet, and hence is simply false. It was true, though it is no longer; it is false because Homer is no longer. But the closely-related sentence "Homer was a poet" is true, taking its past tense seriously. A proper name does not fail to be a name because its subject does not exist (*dial.* 181.5–8):[27]

> The name 'Socrates' must be taken in the same signification in an affirmation and in a negation, namely in the designation of him who perished as much as of an existent...

The name 'Socrates' refers to Socrates whether he exists or not, which is how a present-tense negative existential statement like "Socrates does not exist" can be true; so too (with complications) for "Socrates is dead."[28] Likewise for 'Homer', and proper names generally. Now since Abelard is a strict presentist—he holds that only present things exist—many sentences will have empty subject-terms.[29] But a shift in tense will often produce the correct statement: Homer was a poet, Socrates was ugly, there will be a sea-battle tomorrow.

Sentences about the past or the future can therefore be true or false without involving existential commitment. The same is true for sentences about the present, depending on what they say, because the present tense of the verb-phrase itself doesn't always make an existential commitment. Take the second problem sentence under consideration, namely "A chimaera is conceivable." According to Abelard, there is a clear reason to override the import of 'present existence' in the tense of the verb-phrase, namely that the correct use of the predicate adjective 'conceivable' doesn't require the existence of that to which it applies. Anyone who thinks it does is making a serious error about what it is to be conceivable. As Abelard points out, that isn't why or how the term was devised (*dial.* 137.28–34):[30]

> Just as a chimaera is properly called a non-man, *i.e.* one of those which are not men, why should it not also be called conceivable, *i.e.* one of those of which a conception is held? Indeed, the imposition of their names is the same as regards existents and nonexistents. For just as in the imposition of 'man' we say "Let this thing be called 'man'!" so too we say in the case of a nonexistent thing "Let this thing be called 'conceivable'!"

---

[27] Oportet itaque *Socratis* nomen tam in affirmatione quam in negatione in eadem significatione accipi, in designatione scilicet eius qui periit tamquam existentis...

[28] Ebbesen [1979] discusses how later medieval philosophers dealt with this problem sentence.

[29] For Abelard's presentism see King [2004] IV.2.2 100–103.

[30] Sicut enim chimaera proprie non-homo dicitur, hoc est unum ex his quae non sunt homines, cur non etiam opinabilis diceretur, idest unum ex his de quibus opinio habetur, quippe eadem exstitit ad non-existentia nominum suorum impositio quae ad existentia suorum. Sicut enim dictum est in impositione hominis *Dicatur ista res homo*, sic etiam dictum est in huiusmodi re non existente: *Dicatur ista res opinabilis.*

Words have as part of their meaning the nature of the things to which they apply. A term like 'actual' picks out only what exists, whereas a term like 'conceivable' picks out something that may or may not exist. Roughly, Abelard holds that the sense of a predicate can determine the sense of the statement as a whole. Predicates such as 'dead', 'artificial', 'conceivable', or the like effectively prevent the present existence implicit in the present-tense verb from carrying existential commitment. Presumably the sentence "A chimaera is conceivable" is true partly because its subject-term was imposed on nonexistents and its predicate adjective is indifferent to existence, whereas "A chimaera is hungry" is false because being hungry at present requires a presently existing subject. Nor are these considerations limited to predicate nouns and adjectives; they apply to ordinary verbs and to subjects as well. Abelard can therefore admit the literal truth of "Mythical beings do not exist" or "Caesar crossed the Rubicon" without a blink. There is no special problem about negative existentials, sentences about times other than the present, and so on.

All these advantages come at a price. Since the sense of a sentence determines its truth-conditions, there is no way to read off the existential commitments of a sentence from its purely formal features: to know whether "S is P" is true depends on the sense of S and P in the sentence, and, being part of the semantics, this is not a purely syntactical affair. (To the extent that such features are formal they can be captured by logic, and if not, then not.) Hence there is no immediate inference from "Socrates is P" to "Socrates is/exists," and the burden of existential commitment is carried by the sense of the constituent sentences. Put another way: inferring the existence of the subject-term is not formally valid, though the inference may hold materially, that is, in virtue of the meanings of the terms involved.

2.4 Quantifiers

Recall the four sentences that play a role in the "problem" of existential import, laid out in §1 in their medieval and modern versions:

(1) Every S is P	(1*) $(\forall x)(Sx \rightarrow Px)$
(2) Some S is P	(2*) $(\exists x)(Sx \,\&\, Px)$
(3) Socrates is P	(3*) $Sa \,\&\, Pa$
(4) Socrates is [OR: Socrates exists]	(4*) Sa

Even if we grant Abelard his cautious approach to existential commitment and reject the entailment from (3) to (4), questions remain about relations among (1)–(3). Does (1) entail (2)? Does (2) entail (3)? If not, why not? When no S exists, contemporary logic takes (1*) to be true, (2*) to be false, and (2*) to entail (3*) and thence (4*). Yet as we have already seen, Abelard rejects the move from (3) to (4) as part of his view that existential commitment is not a formal feature of sentences. His view of the relation of (2) to (1) and in turn to (3) is not a simple matter. To understand it, we have to look at a feature conveniently ignored up to this point, namely the semantics of quantifiers.

Abelard recognizes the traditional four types of sentence, only the first two of which have explicit quantifiers: universal, particular, indefinite, and singular. It turns out that both universal and particular sentences have features which make them an ill match for their contemporary correspondents. Consider the universal sentences "Every S is P" or "All S is P" for some general term S. The terms 'every' and 'all' are traditionally said to appear here as a "sign of quantity," that is, to signal how much of the subject-term is covered by the ensuing assertion. How does the signal work? Aristotle tells us right from the beginning that "by the universal [sentence] I mean belonging to all or to none of something" (λέγω δὲ καθόλου μὲν τὸ παντὶ ἢ μηδενὶ ὑπάρχειν, *Prior Analytics* 1.1 24ᵃ18), which uses ὑπάρχειν combined with a dative expression, suggesting a mereological part/whole relation as the best explanation or analysis.[31] How universal sentences manage to say these things Aristotle leaves obscure.

Abelard takes a different tack. He distinguishes 'every' (*omnis*) from 'all' or 'the whole of' (*totum*) as follows (*dial.* 185.19–24 and 186.13–17):[32]

> Now 'the whole of' and 'every' differ in that 'every' applies to kinds (*i.e.* to what falls under it), whereas 'the whole of' applies to parts (*i.e.* to constituents). Each is able to be a quantifier: 'every' a sign of the universal quantity of a thing as it comprehends each of its kind, 'the whole of' a sign of an individual composite as its component constituents... 'Every' is comprehensive of many things taken singly, and when adjoined to a word collects the same things singly and is called a 'sign of universality' according to the comprehension of each and every thing that falls under it. For the quantity of a universal thing consists in its diffusion through what falls under it.

A quantifier-term such as 'every' is neither an operator nor any kind of name. It is instead a sign which works in tandem with the expression to which it is adjoined, to determine its kind of reference. When 'every' is adjoined to a term like 'weasel' (say), then 'every weasel' as the subject of a categorical sentence is used to talk

---

[31] How to interpret this suggestion, and which mereological relation it might involve, have long been matters of dispute. Modern logicians ever since Russell have faulted Aristotle for conflating class-membership (∈) with class-inclusion (⊆); Leśniewski takes the part/whole relationship literally and builds a logic around it, an approach that continues to command adherents today (see for instance Vlasits [2019]); the literature on the subject is extensive. Contemporary logic ignores Aristotle altogether, instead representing quantifier-terms as sentential operators binding variables that occur within expressions determined by translation-rules.

[32] In hoc enim *totum* et *omne* discrepant quod *omne* ad species, id est ad inferiora, *totum* uero ad partes, scilicet constituentes, ponitur. Et utrumque quidem quantitatis signum esse potest, illud quidem quantitatis uniuersalis rei secundum comprehensionem singularum specierum, hoc uero indiuidui compositi secundum constitutionem componentium partium... *Omnis* autem multorum est singillatim comprehensiuum et eadem singillatim colligit quae uox ipsa cui apponitur, signumque uniuersalitatis secundum comprehensionem omnium singulorum inferiorum dicitur. Nam uniuersalis rei quantitas in diffusione sua per inferiora consistit. —There are parallels in the use of plural general terms, 'every horse' and 'horses' for example; see *dial.* 64.31–65.7 and *in Cat.* 170.34–171.10.

about each and every (existing) weasel: it collects distributively everything that falls under the term to which it is adjoined, unlike 'the whole of' or 'all', which collect collectively all of what the term to which it is adjoined refers to—'the whole of (the) weasel' picks out the weasel as a whole, that is, to all existing weasels taken together, the way 'all of Socrates' picks out his feet, hands, shoulder, and so on.

Abelard's proposal is that the quantifier-term and the common term with which it is combined in a sentence form a single semantic unit. He makes this explicit when wrestling with the question what kind of word a quantifier-term is (*dial.* 188.26–31):[33]

> Perhaps we could resolve the matter more easily if we were to take the sign 'every' along with the name to which it is adjoined as a composite word, following not so much authority as reason. For example, when we say 'every man', we are dealing with individual men through 'every man' as though by a composite name in what is called a universal sentence, namely that something is proposed about every one with none excluded (whereas a particular or singular sentence would propose something indeterminately or determinately [respectively]).

Thus 'every weasel' is an expression that, when it appears in subject-position in a sentence, makes the sentence propose something about each weasel (getting the weasels from 'weasel' and the collective distribution from 'every'), much the way an adjectival combination like 'red wagon' can be used to say something about only wagons that are red.[34]

The novelty of Abelard's proposal, which follows "not so much authority as reason," lies in his insistence that the 'quantity' of a sentence is a semantic feature of what it says—when a quantifier-term appears with a general expression in subject-position, the combination spells out how the sentence says something about whatever satisfies that general expression. It isn't a matter of intentions or pragmatics; it's built into the logic of the subject-position itself.[35]

Furthermore, it's clear that Abelard's novel approach applies to all quantifier-terms. His parenthetical throwaway remark makes the generality of his approach

---

[33] Fortasse autem facilius nos absolueremus, si *omnis* signum cum adiuncto nomine tamquam compositam dictionem acciperemus—non tam quidem auctoritatem quam rationem sectantes. Veluti cum dicitur *omnis homo*, per *omnis homo* tamquam per compositum nomen de singulis hominibus ageremus in ea quae uniuersalis propositio diceretur, quod de omnibus nullo excluso proponeretur aliquid, particularis uero uel singularis, quod de aliquo indeterminate uel determinate proponeret.

[34] As before with his proposal that in three-piece predication the substantive verb is welded together with the predicate-phrase to form a single semantic unit, Abelard will have to explain how the rules of conversion can decompose such semantic units, as in the case of (say) "Every S is P" and "Some P is S." His answer is that conversion is designed to 'decompose' the semantic composition of a sentence and transform it into an equivalent, which is very different from the function the sentence was designed to accomplish in the first place, namely saying of something that it is something.

[35] And not just the subject-position! There is no reason to think that such a composite term could not appear as a predicate noun-phrase, in three-piece predication. Abelard recognizes and endorses this consequence, and permits both subject and predicate to be quantified. "Socrates is every animal" is false if there is some animal other than Socrates; "Every man is some animal" is straightforwardly true, since each man is the animal he is. Abelard offers a sketch of double-quantificational logic, with its own Square of Opposition and the like.

clear: particular sentences, that is, sentences with the quantifier-term 'some' as part of their subject, "propose something indeterminately" in contrast with singular sentences. In other words, particular sentences like (2), unlike sentences such as (1) or (3), neither say nor entail anything about a given object. For the combination 'some S' doesn't refer to any individual thing or things; it is used to talk about something or other that may be S, whatever that something may be, rather than about some thing that is S.

Abelard's distinction here between proposing something determinately and proposing something indeterminately is very similar to the distinction between referential and attributive uses introduced in Donnellan [1966] in regard to definite descriptions, but applicable more widely. Consider the sentence "The murderer is left-handed": sometimes the speaker may have a determinate person in mind (and might equally have used a proper name instead), using the description referentially; sometimes the speaker may have no determinate person in mind but rather be describing a feature that the murderer must possess, whoever the murderer might be, using the description attributively. Abelard's claim that sentences which have the quantifier-term 'some' combined with a general expression in subject-position propose something indeterminately is to hold that such particular sentences are attributive rather than referential as a matter of their semantics, regardless of the speaker's intentions. For Abelard, 'some S' is always to be taken as 'some S or other'; that is what the sentence means. If the speaker has someone determinate in mind, then a singular sentence is appropriate, not a quantified particular sentence.

We're now in a position to look more closely at (1) and (2). Abelard holds that when a universally quantified expression appears in subject-position in a categorical sentence, as it does in (1), the sentence is about each and every thing that the expression adjoined to the quantifier-term signifies. Consequently, Abelard would reject the modern formalization (1*) of (1) as mistaken, and this because (a) the quantifier is an operator with scope over not only the subject-term but also the predicate-term, and (b) the conditional form of a sentence does not actually say anything about the subject-term (or the items that fall under the subject-term), but instead asserts that a certain relationship holds between the antecedent and the consequent, whereas a universal sentence for Abelard proposes something about each and every item that falls under the general expression. While (a) points up the different underlying logical analyses, (b) is the more important, for it is what licenses the inference from (1) to (2). Making a statement about each and every S is to say something about any of the items that are S, no matter which; in brief, to speak of every one is to speak of any one, so (1) entails (2). Note that this isn't simply a reduction in the extent of the domain in question, that is, it isn't a mere matter of quantity; in moving to (2), the type of reference has shifted, from determinate to indeterminate, or as we might say from referential to attributive. Yet if (1) entails (2), it can't be the case that (1) can be true and (2) false, that is, that a universal claim is true while its corresponding subalternate particular is false, subject to the strictures of the preceding discussion. Hence the situation that led to the modern "problem" of existential import cannot arise.

As described, the move from (2) to (3) also holds, though here the character of the sentences shifts back from indeterminate to determinate. Since (3) is singular, with a proper name appearing in subject-position, there is no issue about how to take the reference of the subject-term (it has to be used 'referentially'). If (2) is true for some *S* or other, then a sentence with the composite expression 'some *S*' replaced by the name of one of the *S* that is *P* must also be true. This is something like a version of existential instantiation, though it need not involve 'existence', as we have noted in the preceding sections. But at this point we have left quantifiers behind.

2.5   Conclusion

To summarize: Abelard admits that (1) entails (2), and that (2) depends on (3), subject to the analyses he offers; but he rejects the move from (3) to (4) in general, as not being a matter of the logical form of the sentences but rather of their meaning. So let's return to the question with which we began. Should Abelard be credited with recognizing the "problem" of existential import? Yes, if we think that his recognition of the possibility that subject-terms might be empty in their intended domain is enough. Otherwise the answer should be a clear and resounding *no*: He did not think that there was a special problem in existential inference; he permits the inference from (1) to (2) in such a way that no problem arises; he does not think that existential commitments can be read off sentences solely as a matter of their logical form; there is no general inference from (3) to (4). On the whole, I think we can say that Abelard leaves the "problem" of existential import a shambles. But matters are much more interesting for it, since Abelard's unique approach to the semantics of simple categorical sentences, with the wealth of difficulties they involve, show the virtues of a non-traditional 'traditional' logic in the twelfth century.[36]

Bibliography

Abelard, *Dialectica* [abbreviated *dial*.]. 1969. *Logica 'ingredientibus'*, Book 7 (Commentary on Boethius's *De topicis differentiis*) [abbreviated *in Top*.]. Edited by Mario Dal Pra in *Pietro Abelardo: Scritti di logica*, Firenze (second edition). References are to the page and line numbers of this edition.
———. 1970. Edited by L. M. De Rijk in *Petrus Abaelardus: Dialectica*, Assen: Van Gorcum (second edition). References to the page and line numbers of this edition.
———. 1921. *Logica 'ingredientibus'*, Book 2 (Commentary on Aristotle's *Categories* [abbreviated *in Cat*.]. Edited by Bernhard Geyer in *Beiträge zur Geschichte der Philosophie des Mittelalters* XXI.2, Münster: Aschendorf, 111–305. References to the page and line numbers of this edition.

---

[36] See Yi [2021] §3.3.3 for a detailed discussion of Abelard's account of how the Square of Opposition works in relation to other medieval philosophers as a matter of formal logic.

———. 2010. *Logica 'ingredientibus'*, Book 3 (Commentary on Aristotle's *De interpretatione*) [abbreviated *in Per.*]. Edited by Klaus Jacobi and Christian Strub in *Petri Abaelardi Glossae super Peri Hermeneias. Corpus christianorum continuatio mediaeualis* tom. 206. Turnhout: Brepols. References to the chapter and section numbers, with page and line numbers in parentheses, of this edition.

Binini, Irene. 2018. 'My future son is possibly alive': Existential presupposition and empty terms in Abelard's modal logic. *History and Philosophy of Logic* 39: 341–356.

Donnellan, Keith. 1966. Reference and definite descriptions. *Philosophical Review* 75: 281–304.

Ebbesen, Sten. 1979. The dead man is alive. *Synthese* 40: 43–70.

Grondeux, Anne, and Irène Rosier-Catach. 2017. William of Champeaux (c.1070–1121), the *Glosule* on Priscian and the *Notae Dunelmenses. Historiographica Linguistica* 44: 107–179.

Jacobi, Klaus. 1980. Diskussionen über Prädikationstheorie in den logische Schriften des Petrus Abailardus. In *Petrus Abaelardus (1079–1142): Person, Werk und Wirkung*, ed. R. Thomas, 165–179. Trier.

King, Peter. 2004. Metaphysics. In *The Cambridge companion to Abelard*, ed. J. Brower and K. Guilfoy, 65–125. Cambridge University Press.

Kretzmann, Norman. 1982. The culmination of the old logic in Peter Abelard. In *Renaissance and renewal in the twelfth century*, ed. R. Benson and G. Constable, 488–511. Harvard University Press.

Martin, Christopher J. 2001. Abaelard on modality: Some possibilities and some puzzles. In *Potentialität und Possibilität: Modalaussagen in der Geschichte der Metaphysik*, ed. T. Buchheim, C.H. Kneepkens, and K. Lorenz, 97–124. Stuttgart/Bad Cannstatt: Frommann-Holzboog.

Parsons, Terry. 1997. "The Traditional Square of Opposition" in *The Stanford encylopedia of philosophy* (Fall 1997 Edition and thereafter): https://plato.stanford.edu/archives/fall1997/entries/square/. As of this writing (2021) the claim still stands.

Seuren, Pieter A.M. 2010. *The Logic of language: Language from within.* Vol. 2. Oxford University Press.

Tweedale, Martin M. 1982. Abelard and the Culmination of the Old Logic. In *The Cambridge history of later medieval philosophy*, ed. N. Kretzmann, A. Kenney, and J. Pinborg, 143–157. Cambridge University Press.

———. 1988. Logic from the late Eleventh Century to the time of Abelard. In *A History of twelfth-century Western philosophy*, ed. P. Dronke, 196–226. Cambridge University Press.

Uckelman, Sara L. 2008. Course on core logic given in AY 2008–2009 at the Institute for Logic, Language, and Computation, at the Universitaet van Amsterdam.: http://staff.science.uva.nl/~suck\-el\-ma/teaching/CL2008/2008-CL-L6.pdf. Slight modifications have been made in the Core Logic course in AY 2009–2010 and the course "Formal Logic before Frege" in AY 2010–2011.

Vlasits, Justin. 2019. Mereology in Aristotle's Assertoric Syllogistic. *History and Philosophy of Logic* 40: 1–11.

Wilks, Ian. 1993. *The logic of Abelard's Dialectica.* Doctoral dissertation, University of Toronto.

Yi, Byeong-Uk. 2021. "Categorical Propositions and Existential Import: A Post-Modern Perspective" in *History and Philosophy of Logic* 42 (forthcoming 2021).

Chapter 3
Rereading "Saint Anselm's Proof"

Daniel Patrick Moloney

Keywords Anselm · Aquinas · Ontological argument · Proslogion · God proofs

I first met Gyula Klima as a junior at Yale in the spring of 1993, and I think I read a version of his paper "Saint Anselm's Proof" (Klima 2000) soon after.[1] The article immediately impressed me as being obviously right, both as an interpretation and defense of Anselm's argument in *Proslogion* 2 (after all, he provided a formal reconstruction that proved its validity!), and as an explanation of why St. Thomas would demur from accepting Anselm's argument as a *demonstration*, and why a more traditional proof of the existence of God was necessary. Along the way, Klima introduced some of his favorite causes: that modern theories of semantic reference are different from medieval theories; that the medieval theory of ampliation deals with what modern theories call modality, with some important differences; that *entia rationis* (beings of reason) can be objects of reference in medieval, but not in modern semantic theories; and that medieval and modern conceptual frameworks can be brought into fruitful conversation…with the medievals more than holding their own. Within the cottage industry of those writing on the "ontological argument," the paper seems to have become a standard point of reference; it is cited both by Wikipedia and the Stanford Encyclopedia of Philosophy.[2]

---

[1] In addition to citing the hard-to-find official text, I will try to make my references clear to readers using the substantively identical text on Klima's website, since it is likely that many readers will access it there: https://faculty.fordham.edu/klima/anselm.htm

[2] Wikipedia 2021, fn. 186; Williams 2020.

D. P. Moloney (✉)
St. John Vianney Theological Seminary, Denver, CO, USA

Archdiocese of Boston, Braintree, MA, USA
e-mail: father.moloney@archden.org

© The Author(s), under exclusive license to Springer Nature Switzerland AG 2023
J. P. Hochschild et al. (eds.), *Metaphysics Through Semantics: The Philosophical Recovery of the Medieval Mind*, International Archives of the History of Ideas Archives internationales d'histoire des idées 242, https://doi.org/10.1007/978-3-031-15026-5_3

I believed Klima to be right about Anselm's argument for most of my adult life. But as I have spent more and more time studying and thinking about the rest of St. Anselm's works outside of *Proslogion* 2, I have developed some reservations about Klima's view *qua* an interpretation of Anselm. I would like to take the opportunity of this volume to suggest that Klima's interpretation of "Saint Anselm's proof" in the paper of that name and in others[3] is best thought of, not as an interpretation of Anselm, but as an interpretation of *Aquinas's reading of Anselm*, especially Aquinas's distinction between what is known *per se* in itself and what is known *per se* to us (*per se notum in se* vs. *quoad nos*). I want to conclude by suggesting that, as a reading of Aquinas, Klima's interpretation should be given significant attention in Thomistic circles, since it would help clarify a lot of confusion in the literature about how to read, for example, Aquinas's comments about the knowability of the first principles of natural law.

First, it will be helpful to review Klima's classic paper. The paper has two major parts. The first part is a defense of Anselm's argument against contemporary objections (#1–3 below), and the second is a critique of Anselm's argument following Aquinas's critiques in *Summa Theologiae* (henceforth *STh*) I.2 and *Summa Contra Gentiles* (henceforth *SCG*) I.10–11. The argument of the paper is as follows (the sections of Klima's paper are given in brackets):

1. Klima begins by addressing, not specialists in medieval philosophy, but contemporary philosophers who dismiss Anselm's argument in chapter 2 of the *Proslogion*[4] for technical reasons related to Russell's theory of descriptions, the Kantian-Fregean idea of existence as a second-order predicate, and Quine's concept of existence as "to be the value of a bound variable."

2. He then introduces what he calls *the medieval conception of reference*, which allows reference to range over beings that are thought of (or desired, or imagined) but that don't exist outside the mind (or desire, or imagination)—namely, "beings of reason" (*entia rationis*). Anselm's argument will be shown to depend on this conception of reference. [Section 1]

3. Klima presents a simple reconstruction of Anselm's argument arranged into numbered propositions, and then a formal restatement of the same. The conclusion of both is that Anselm's argument is valid, given the assumption that "that than which nothing greater can be thought" can be thought (a condition that the theist clearly satisfies). [Section 2]

4. He then considers the conditions for the possibility of dialogue between the theist and atheist in light of Anselm's further conclusion in *Proslogion* 3 that God cannot be thought not to exist—a claim that the atheist's atheism seemingly disproves. [Section 3]

---

[3] Klima returned to the argument in Klima 2017. He replies to Tony Roark's criticism of the original paper in Klima 2003.

[4] Klima simply refers to "Anselm's famous argument," but in section 3 of his paper he refers to "the next argument" (after the one he modeled) in a way that makes it clear he means *Proslogion* 3.

5. Klima then introduces the idea of *parasitic reference*, in which one person can refer successfully to another person's thought object (concept) without forming that concept in his own mind (as in the game "20 Questions," where I can refer to and ask questions about the properties of your thought object, without yet being able to think that same thought myself). *Constitutive reference*, by contrast, requires that the person hold the thought object as his own. Klima proposes that in the dialogue between the theist and atheist, the atheist refers to God parasitically while the theist refers to God constitutively, and that Anselm's proof will only go through if one uses constitutive reference. Thus, Anselm's proof doesn't prove anything *to the atheist*. [Sections 3 and 4]
6. But since the atheist is able to remain consistent only by placing the theist's conception of God in its own "sandbox" through parasitic reference, the way to convert the atheist (or at least convict him of rational inconsistency) is to lead him to realize that the thought objects to which he is already committed further commit him to making constitutive reference to something that can be identified as God. [Section 4]
7. This is what Aquinas does through his natural theology developed in *STh* I.3–11. His example provides a model for how those inhabiting different conceptual schemes can start to develop mutual understanding, while Anselm's does not. [Section 5]

The key idea to section 4 might be explained by the allusion to the practice of what computer programmers call *sandboxing*. If a programmer wants to execute a program or some lines of code (perhaps to study how it works) but is afraid that doing so might release a virus or crash his computer, he creates a separate, self-contained partition of the computer that is capable of executing the code or program in isolation from the rest of the computer—as if it is playing in its own sandbox.[5] Klima's idea is effectively that if the atheist can keep Anselm's argument in its own sandbox, he can study it and refer to it without releasing the theist "virus" into his own mind. Aquinas' more apologetic approach is meant to break down this sort of partition, and so to release the theistic virus.

3.1   Some Reservations About "Saint Anselm's Proof"

1. *For a work ostensibly about Anselm, the paper rarely refers to his texts*

I want to argue that Klima's papers about "Saint Anselm's Proof" are not primarily about St. Anselm's own work but are rather about St. Thomas Aquinas's

---

[5] See Sylvain 2008: "In a nutshell, a sandbox is a security mechanism used to run an application in a restricted environment. If an attacker is able to exploit the browser in a way that lets him run arbitrary code on the machine, the sandbox would help prevent this code from causing damage to the system. The sandbox would also help prevent this exploit from modifying and even reading your files or any information on the system."

characterizations of an argument that is a lot like Anselm's (we could call it Anselm*ian*) in *STh* I.2.1 and *SCG* I.10–11. There are several reasons I have come to think this, but the most straightforward is that Klima's paper has more references to later thinkers than to Anselm's own works.

Simply reviewing the footnotes and bibliography suggests that the focus of these papers is not primarily Anselm scholarship. In his original paper, Klima has only two footnotes to Anselm's works, one to *Response to Gaunilo*, and one to *Monlogion* 10. In the text of the paper, he mentions "Saint Anselm's proof for God's existence in his *Proslogion*," but does not clarify what he means by this until section 3, when he makes reference to *Proslogion* 3 as "the next argument," implying that the proof he formalized was from *Proslogion* 2. In his later restatement of the argument (Klima 2001), he adds two citations to Anselm's works (*Monologion* 2, *De Causu Diaboli* 1), as well as the claim that Anselm's description of God is derived from Augustine's *De Doctrina Christiana*. But these citations do not do much philosophical work (which is, presumably, why he did not include them in the earlier paper). By contrast, the references in the original paper (Klima 2000) to later medieval philosophers—not just to Aquinas, but to John Buridan, Albert of Saxony, Lambert of Auxerre, and to several twelfth-century theories of ampliation—are relatively abundant and do real work in the paper.

When I propose that Klima's paper is not primarily "Anselm scholarship," I mean that it is not the sort of paper that looks at the historical context of Anselm's semantics and the context of his *Proslogion* argument in particular.[6] Those who do such scholarship pay attention to probable sources for Anselm's thought, such as Boethius, Augustine, and Seneca; they study other works of Anselm, especially the *Monologion*, to understand Anselm's mindset when writing the *Proslogion*; and they also call attention to the context of *Proslogion* 2 within the rest of the *Proslogion* itself (which Klima does not but should have—more on that later). Klima does not consider the question urged by Holopainen (2020), whether Anselm's "*unum argumentum*" is found only in *Proslogion* 2 or is a reference to the whole *Proslogion*, a consideration that is relevant to Klima's critique of Anselm's position. Others (Sweeney 2012, 116–118; Walz 2010, 136–139) argue that Anselm's suggestion that he is writing not as himself but under a literary persona is relevant to the proper interpretation of his argument.[7]

John Marenbon describes Klima's article as combining "historical accuracy with logical acuity" (Marenbon 2005, 28), and Klima's speculation about Anselm's semantic framework *is* historically accurate. But outside of a few suggestions in the footnotes noted above, Klima never shows that the general medieval semantic framework he describes in section 1 is Anselm's own. In another article, Marenbon is able to sketch the semantic framework of the *Monologion* in just a couple of pages

---

[6] Major examples of this can be found in Marenbon 2002, 2005; Holopainen 1996, 2007, 2009, 2020; Logan 2009; and Sweeney 2012, esp. 147–169.

[7] *Proslogion*, Proemium (S I.93.21). Cf. *Monologion*, Prologus (S I.8.18–20). References to Anselm's works are to the edition in Schmitt 1968. Volume number, page number(s), and line number(s) of Schmitt 1968 are given thus: S Volume.Page.Line. Translations are my own.

(Marenbon 2002, 74–76); Klima could probably have done the same, had he been interested in doing Anselm scholarship.

Klima is obviously technically competent to have presented Anselm's argument in its own historical context, rather than as just an early example of later semantic frameworks. That he didn't choose to do so suggests that his purpose was not that of these other authors. His audience was also clearly not the same. Rather than writing primarily for other scholars of the Middle Ages, his audience (at least in section 1) is presumed to be more worried about the critiques of "the ontological argument" from Frege, Kant, Meinong, and Quine, and to be comfortable with symbolic formalization.[8] Especially in the first part of the paper, he is trying to make his case to contemporary analytic philosophers and those trained in contemporary logic, who might be familiar with Anselm's argument from, say, teaching it in an undergraduate class rather than as a professional concentration.[9]

My point in this section is not to claim that Klima's reconstruction of Anselm's proof is wrong, or that his claims about Anselm's semantic principles are historically inaccurate. Rather, I am arguing that Klima did not give the close attention to the nuances of Anselm's text that he might have, and that others have done. Further, I want to propose that this is because he was not primarily interested in defending Anselm from Aquinas's criticism.

2. *Anselm uses parasitic reference frequently and discusses its conditions*

In *STh* I.13.10 ad 1, Aquinas points out that one can refer to the "gods" of the pagans without holding that their idols are really divine. In section 5 of "Saint Anselm's Proof," Klima cites this passage as evidence that Aquinas was aware of parasitic reference:

> Aquinas is evidently aware of the possibility of the type of reference I called parasitic… Given the awareness of this possibility on Aquinas' part and the possibility to evade by its help the force of Anselm's argument, we may risk the assumption that this awareness played some role in Aquinas' rejection of Anselm's argument.[10]

I read this as Klima implying that Anselm was not aware of the phenomenon of parasitic reference, or else Anselm would not have argued as he did. But Anselm certainly understands the phenomenon of parasitic reference, since he frequently uses it when he writes. In fact, as other authors have noted (Sweeney 2012, 116–118; Walz 2010, 136–139), Anselm writes the entire *Monologion* and *Proslogion* using parasitic reference: he's referring to what someone *would* say *were* he meditating on the topics of the *Monologion* (Prologus; S I.8.18–20) or *were* he raising his mind to God using the method of the *Proslogion* (Prooemium; S 1.93.21). Later, Anselm would write philosophical dialogues in which he made parasitic reference to the thoughts of the characters. In the *Cur Deus Homo*, the characters make parasitic

---

[8] This difference in audience might account for Eileen Sweeney's surprising omission of Klima's article from her lengthy survey of the literature on Anselm's argument (Sweeney 2012, 147–169).

[9] Tony Roark seems to be just this sort of reader. See Roark 2003.

[10] Klima 2000, 80. The citation to *STh* I.13.10 ad 1 is in fn. 23.

reference to the views of non-Christians when *for the sake of argument* they agree to reason *remoto Cristo*, assuming Christ did not exist (Praefatio; S II.42.12). Anselm even uses parasitic reference in the argument of *Proslogion* 2 itself, when he refers to the thought processes of the Fool.

Anselm shows his alertness to the importance of constitutive reference for his *Proslogion* 2 argument in the opening salvo in his *Response to Gaunilo*. There he points out that the monk Gaunilo is not an atheist, even though he is (parasitically) making reference to the atheist's thoughts, and so rather than having a fight about parasitic reference, Anselm will respond directly to the monk (Preface and 1; S I.130.3–5). Since Gaunilo is a Christian, Gaunilo clearly makes constitutive reference to God; thus, Gaunilo's own Christianity has proved that God exists, since (as Klima's argument implies) if *anyone* makes constitutive reference to that-than-which-nothing-greater-can-be-thought-of, it follows that God exists.[11] Anselm calls this his "strongest argument" (*firmissimo argumento*), albeit against Gaunilo rather than against the Fool.[12] Whatever else, this text seems to indicate that Anselm is aware of the need to make constitutive reference in order for his argument to work.

3. *Anselm's argument was not meant to be* per se notum *or a* priori *or "ontological"*

Anselm never claims the view frequently attributed to him, that his argument is not supposed to depend on any reference to our experiences of the world. Quite the contrary. In *Response* 8, he explains that since all of us have *a posteriori* experiences of goodness and greatness in varying degrees, by using the word "greater," he is appealing to our ordinary human capacity to judge that something is better than something else, a capacity "evident to every rational mind."[13] Therefore, his argument continues, Gaunilo's atheist is denying something evident to ordinary people, and so is irrational—a fool.

Anselm seems to think that "greater than" is an intuitive enough notion that ordinary people can work out its implications. As Klima observes (Klima 2001, 76, fn. 3), Anselm means by "greater" and "greatest" something that is *better* than something else (or in the case of "greatest," better than *everything* else) in at least some respect. Since "better" and "best" are the comparative and superlative forms of "good," greatness is clearly related to goodness: "What is supremely good is also supremely great" (*Monologion* 2; S I.15.21–23). In *Monologion* 1, Anselm says:

---

[11] Klima doesn't make a big deal out of this in "Saint Anselm's Proof," but in Klima 2001, 78–79 he explores this implication. His argument clearly implies that if one person successfully makes constitutive reference to God, it follows that God exists outside the mind of that person. In which case, God *clearly* must exist outside the mind of those who *don't* have him in *their* minds (whether because they don't think of God or because they make parasitic reference to him). So, the question of how to convince the atheist is more one of apologetics—how to change another person's mind—rather than to determine whether God exists.

[12] *Response* 1 (S I.130.15–16): "fide et conscientia tua pro firmissimo utor argumento."

[13] *Response* 8 (S I.137.14–19): "Quoniam namque omne minus bonum in tantum est simile maiori bono inquantum est bonum patet cuilibet rationabili menti, quia de bonis minoribus ad maiora conscendendo ex iis quibus aliquid maius cogitari potest, multum possumus conicere illud quo nihil potest maius cogitari."

> There are innumerable goods, the great diversity of which we both *experience through our bodily senses* and discern by reasoning of the mind [*ratione mentis*]… It is certain that all good things, if they are compared to one another, are either equally or unequally good…[14]

This observation is the first premise in Anselm's *a posteriori* or "cosmological" argument for God's existence in the *Monologion*, which has not generated much philosophical controversy over the centuries. As Jeffrey Brower notes in commenting on this passage, Anselm here "simply assumes that we will all know the sorts of [good] things he has in mind."[15] After all, we all have experience with good things, and experience of some things being better than others, which means we all have experience of something being *greater* than something else. To take a relevant example, the idea that it is better to exist than not to exist (or worse not to exist than to exist) is arguably basic to our natural fear of death; hence, our ordinary experience of the fear of death would "pack" the superiority of existence into the concept of "greater than," ready to be "unpacked" once "greater than" is well understood.[16] If this interpretation is correct, then the phrase "that-than-which-nothing-greater-can-be-thought-of" makes a much greater appeal to our ordinary experience than Klima suggests.

As the rest of Anselm's argument unfolds over the remaining chapters of the *Proslogion*, he makes explicit more and more implications of all that is packed into a clear understanding of what greatness is. But that unpacking depends on a prior "packing" of implications into the concept; and *that*, says Anselm, depends on our everyday experience of comparing one thing to another.

Klima praises Aquinas for doing something he calls a "conceptual buildup," which seems similar to what I am calling Anselm's "unpacking" of the concept of *greater than*:

> [T]his seems to be precisely Aquinas' program of natural theology in the *Summa Theologiae*. Given our normal everyday commitment to objects of the empirical, physical world, Aquinas' proofs for God's existence intend to show us that by this commitment we are also committed to make constitutive reference to a Prime Mover, a First Cause, a First Necessary Being, etc., which, he says, are all what a theist would identify as God ("*et hoc dicimus Deum*"). Then he goes on to show us that God, to whom we are thus committed to make constitutive reference by all these descriptions, is simple, perfect, good, infinite, ubiquitous, immutable, eternal and one. In this way the atheist is not allowed to keep God, as an object

---

[14] *Monologion* 1 (S I.14.5–6 & 15–16): "Cum tam innumerabilia bona sint, quorum tam multam diversitatem et sensibus corporeis experimur et ratione mentis discernimus… Ergo cum certum sit quod omnia bona, si ad is invicem conferantur, aut aequaliter aut inaequaliter sint bona…."

[15] Brower 2019, 7. See also Sweeney 2012, 157: "The [*Proslogion* 2] formula itself, more specifically, *understanding* the formula, which is crucial to Anselm's argument, already contains within it the notion which is laid out explicitly in the *Monologion* and the reply to Gaunilo: that we can order things from lesser to greater, less to better, as a condition for the possibility of understanding the formula… Figuring out what is greater or better occupies large parts of the *Monologion* and *Proslogion*… Anselm does seem to think that we can come to some basic agreements about what is better than what… [C]learly he takes real understanding of the [*Proslogion* 2] formula, attended to with understanding, to entail a grasp of at least some things that are better and some things worse."

[16] In *Monologion* 3, Anselm regards greatness as being "packed in" to our ordinary concept of goodness, and in *Monologion* 4, he says that existence or being is also packed in.

of sheer parasitic reference, in isolation from his own beliefs. Indeed, throughout Aquinas' argumentation no single description is given which would presumably give the full meaning of the term "God" for the atheist, in the possession of which he could claim to have a full grasp of the meaning of this term, and then use it parasitically to refer to what the theist believes satisfies this term. Instead, the term is given a gradually growing content with every conclusion concerning the thing to which we are already committed to make constitutive reference by five different descriptions, in virtue of the existence proofs... In fact, it is precisely this type of conceptual build-up that is missed from Anselm's proof by Gaunilo on behalf of the Fool.[17]

In both Anselm and Aquinas, the ability to refer to God is just the beginning of a process of adding to the concept (or unpacking the implications of the concept). And both Anselm and Aquinas make appeals to our ordinary experiences in order to help us gain enough of a concept of God to serve as the basis for further arguments that help build up the concept of God. Certainly, Aquinas in the Five Ways (*STh* I.2.3) is more technically precise in detailing the parts of our ordinary experience to which he is appealing (efficient causality, for example), but that greater precision does not make one argument *a priori* as opposed to *a posteriori*. So, perhaps the *Proslogion* argument is not *a priori* or "ontological" after all.

4. *Klima's critique follows Aquinas's arguments more closely than it does Anselm's*

Klima's paper considers the arguments of *Proslogion* 2–3, but curiously, not *Proslogion* 4. In chapter 2, Anselm concludes that that-than-which-nothing-greater-can-be-thought-of exists outside the mind, which leads him in chapter 3 to conclude that God cannot be thought not to exist. But immediately afterwards Anselm goes to head off the kind of criticism that Gaunilo and Klima make of him, namely that it is enough to have a vague or merely verbal thought of the phrase "that-than-which-nothing-greater-can-be-thought-of."

Proslogion 4 details the conceptual conditions for how the Fool can "say in his heart" what Anselm had just proven could not even be thought. His answer is that the Fool can think (*cogitare*) the word "God" or the phrase "that-than-which-nothing-greater-can-be-thought-of" without understanding (*intelligere*) it. But were the Fool (or anyone) *to acquire in his understanding the true concept* of "that-than-which-nothing-greater-can-be-thought-of," then he could not think that God does not exist. Anselm's distinction in chapter 4 between merely *thinking of* something and *understanding* it (S I.103.18–19), and *understanding it well* (*bene intelligit*; S I.104.3), indicates that he is sensitive to the conditions necessary for his argument to go through:

> For God is that-than-which-nothing-greater-can-be-thought-of. One who *understands* this *well*, understands *without fail* that this same being exists in such a way that not even in

---

[17] Klima 2000, 81–82. If the last sentence means that Gaunilo is critiquing Anselm for not having more of a conceptual build-up, it should be noted that Gaunilo not only limits his criticism to the initial argument for God's existence, but actually praises the conceptual build-up in the *Proslogion* after chapters 2–3. See *Pro Insipiente* 8.

thought is it able not to be. Therefore, whoever thinks of God *in such a way* cannot think of him as not existing.[18]

It would seem, then, at least *prima facie*, that Anselm's position is not vulnerable to the criticism that Klima levels against it in sections 4–5 of "Saint Anselm's Proof." Anselm does *not* think that his argument will work on an atheist who refers to God only parasitically, since that would not be to *understand* the phrase "that-than-which-nothing-greater-can-be-thought-of," but only to *think* it, when only understanding it would be sufficient to make the argument go through. Klima writes in section 4, "the atheist can claim that he perfectly *understands* Anselm's description, and still deny that he *has in mind* something of which he *thinks* satisfies Anselm's description." Yet Anselm explicitly denies this. Klima seems to be using "understand," "have in mind," and "think" interchangeably, when Anselm uses "understand" for a higher type of cognition than "think," one which at least includes making constitutive reference to the thought object.

As we saw above, *Proslogion* 4 shows Anselm making a distinction between merely thinking of something vaguely or verbally, and having true understanding of it such that one could unpack its implications. Anselm then claims that true understanding is necessary for his argument. In a different paper,[19] Klima argues that Aquinas makes a similar distinction in order to defend his own version of an "ontological argument." In "Aquinas' Real Distinction," Klima is responding to Anthony Kenny's criticism of the *"intellectus essentiae"* argument that Aquinas makes in chapter 5 of *De Ente et Essentia*. This argument is often thought to be (at least directly) about the real distinction between essence and existence in creatures; yet, as Klima argues, since that real distinction in creatures implies the real *identity* of essence and existence in God, it is (at least indirectly) also an argument for the *necessary existence* of God. Like Anselm's *Proslogion* argument, Aquinas' *intellectus essentiae* argument seems to depend on what individuals happen to know or happen to be able to conceive—taken by itself, it too seems like an "ontological" or *a priori* argument.[20] And it too, Klima believes, is subject to the kind of criticism to which he believes Anselm's argument is subject.

Klima reconstructs Aquinas' argument as follows (Klima 2017, 2:3; 2019, 12):

Let c be any arbitrarily chosen thing whose nature is known but whose existence is not known. Then

1. Since the *nature* of c is known
2. And the *existence* of c is not known
3. Therefore, the *nature* of c is not the *existence* of c.

---

[18] S I.104.2–4: "Deus enim est id quo maius cogitari non potest. Quod qui bene intelligit, utique intelligit id ipsum sic esse, ut nec cogitatione queat non esse. Qui ergo intelligit sic esse deum, nequit eum non esse cogitare."

[19] Klima 2017, a substantially similar version of which was published as Klima 2019. I will refer to the 2017 online version by section and page numbers (section 2 page 3 is 2:3), as well as to the 2019 *Roczniki Filozoficzne* version.

[20] In his opening sentence (2017; 2019, 7), Klima suggests that the overall argument in *De Ente* is causal or "cosmological," but this part of the overall argument (known in the literature as the *intellectus essentiae* argument when taken alone) has strong similarities to Anselm's argument.

We can see that this argument is similar to Anselm's argument in its dependence on an ampliative or intentional verb—"is known" works almost as the middle term of the argument. Like Anselm's argument, this argument has been criticized for "the logical particularities of the intentional verb it involves" (Klima 2017, 3:4; 2019, 12).

Assuming the role of Gaunilo to Aquinas's Anselm, John Buridan points out that premise 2 could be satisfied simply because someone is ignorant about c, and the happenstance of someone's ignorance does not imply anything about the world outside that person's mind—what Klima calls "the well-known phenomenon of the breakdown of the principle of the substitutivity of identicals in intentional contexts" (Klima 2017, 3:5; 2019, 13). One could know something as F and not know it as G, even though it is both. One can know that Venus is the morning star and not know it as the evening star, even though it is both. This general phenomenon Buridan brings to bear in his criticism of Aquinas's *intellectus essentiae* argument, a criticism which Klima summarizes:

> Thus it seems that as long as we can know the same item *qua* some essence but not *qua* some act of existence, it is quite possible for us to know the essence of a certain thing without knowing whether it exists or not, despite the fact that its essence and existence are the same (Klima 2017, 5; 2019, 13).

We could know God's essence but not his existence; for example, we could define God and know *what* he is, but that does not entail that we know *that* he is, even though his essence and his existence are identical. Thus, Aquinas's argument for the real distinction fails.

Or so it seems. Klima thinks that he can defend Aquinas's argument by making the following distinction: Buridan's critique of the argument above depends on the person who "knows" c knowing it *as a mere linguistic expression*, or with at most a partial or vague knowledge, whereas Aquinas's actual argument depends on the person who knows c knowing it with *scientific quidditative knowledge* (an idea he derives from Avicenna). As he explains:

> In this context, therefore, we need to distinguish between merely having some (no matter how vague and confused) concept of a thing, resulting from the mind's first, spontaneous abstractive act, and having its quidditative concept, which is a clear, distinct, articulate concept, resulting from scientific inquiry into the nature of the thing. Having this sort of quidditative concept, therefore, means clearly knowing its implications (Klima 2017, 3:5; 2019, 14).

> If there is a thing whose essence and existence are the same, then having a clear and distinct cognition of the thing's essence would immediately give us the knowledge that the thing actually exists (Klima 2017, 3:6; 2019, 15).

As we saw above, in *Proslogion* 4, Anselm insists that for that-than-which-nothing-greater-can-be-thought-of to be *in the understanding*, it is not enough to think of these words or this phrase as *mere words*; one must understand them *well*, including all they entail. Klima's response to Buridan on behalf of Aquinas is that in order to know something's nature, it is not enough to have a linguistic or merely vague knowledge of the thing; one must have a clear, distinct, *articulate* concept of the essence of the thing and all that is implied in it. There is more technical precision in

Klima's formulation than in *Proslogion* 4 (*quidditative definition* is more precise than *understand well*), but the point is substantially the same. Yet if the distinction works to defend Aquinas from Buridan's criticisms, it also works to defend Anselm from Klima's and Gaunilo's analogous criticisms.

Klima claims that the above distinction is implicit in Aquinas's original *De Ente* argument:

> If we take a closer look at Aquinas' actual formulation of the argument, we have to notice something that is entirely neglected in the version of it criticized by Buridan; namely Aquinas' talking about "parts of the essence" without which it [the essence] cannot be understood... By "parts of the essence" he means whatever is signified precisely by the parts of the quiddative definition of the thing (Klima 2017, 3:5; 2019, 13).

> If the existence of the thing were the same as the essence of the thing, or using Aquinas' phrase, if it were 'a part of' the essence of the thing, then... we could not have its quidditative knowledge without knowing it actually exists (Klima 2017, 3:6; 2019, 15).

Seeing this distinction in the proof requires a good bit of Thomistic scholarship, noticing that the phrase "part of the essence" is a reference to the quidditative definition, so that the argument avoids Buridan's critique. Other readers of *De Ente et Essentia* have not always caught this reference, as the examples of Kenny and Buridan show. Rather than follow Buridan's reading, Klima does the research necessary to save Aquinas's argument from their critique. As shown above, however, similar research into Anselm's texts suggests that the same distinction is also present in Anselm's argument, which would save it from Klima's critique.[21]

5. *Klima's criticisms of Anselm are really interpretations of Aquinas's criticisms*

All this suggests that Klima was not focused on *Proslogion* 4. Rather, his article closely follows Aquinas's arguments in the two Summas, which did not observe Anselm's distinction between "thinking" and "understanding." To see just how indifferent Aquinas is to the vocabulary of Anselm's argument, it helps to look at a fairly literal translation of his summary of the argument in the *Summa Theologiae*:

> Those things are said to be known through themselves [*per se nota*] which are known [*cognoscere*] immediately upon knowing the terms—which the Philosopher attributes to the demonstration of first principles in *Posterior Analytics* I. For when it is known [*scire*] what is a whole and what is a part, immediately it is known that every whole is greater than its part. But upon understanding [*intellectus*] what this name [*nomen*] 'God' signifies, immediately it is grasped [*habere*] what God is. For by this name is signified [*significare*] that-than-which-a-greater-cannot-be-signified. But that which exists both in reality [*in re*] and in the intellect is greater than that which exists only in the intellect. Therefore, when this name

---

[21] In his *Sentences Commentary* (1SN d.3, q.1, a.2, obj.4 and ad 4), Aquinas treats both arguments together and even suggests that they have similar strengths and weaknesses. Thanks to Turner Nevitt for calling this text to my attention. For a more elaborate discussion, see the next section.

'God' is understood [*intellectus*], immediately it is in the intellect, and it follows that it is in reality. Therefore 'God exists' is known through itself [*per se notum*].[22]

Aquinas uses several terms interchangeably: *notum, cognoscere, scire, intellectus, habere*, and *significare*. All of these terms can be translated as "know" or "understand." What is more, Aquinas uses a different synonym *in every sentence*. In the response to this objection, Aquinas again rephrases (without explanation) what it is that the name "God" signifies, replacing *significare* with *cogitare*: whereas in the objection "God" signifies that-than-which-a-greater-cannot-be-*signified*, in the reply "God" signifies that-than-which-a greater-cannot-be-*thought*.[23] Anselm, as we saw above, pays close attention to the difference between *cogitare* and *intelligere*, claiming that his argument hinges on that distinction. And, as we also saw above, Aquinas knows that these sorts of intentional arguments depend on a precise type of *quidditative* knowledge, and not just any sort of knowing. This suggests that perhaps Aquinas's loose language in the *Summa* is not naïve.

It should also be noted that Aquinas's summary of the argument makes the claim that Klima attributed to Anselm (and which Anselm denied), namely that one need merely know what the name "God" signifies—i.e., know the meaning of the words and hold them in one's mind—for it to be self-evident that God exists. Aquinas is even clearer on this point in his reply to the argument in the *Summa Contra Gentiles*:

> Nor is it necessary that, *immediately upon thinking* [cognita] *the signification of this name 'God'*, the existence of God be known, as the first argument above stated.[24]

This seems to be a reference to the criteria for something to be *known per se*, which does not interest Anselm in the *Proslogion*. In fact, Anselm denies that the existence of God is known immediately upon thinking "that-than-which-nothing-greater-can-be-thought-of" when he first introduces the formula.[25] This only makes sense—after all, the purpose of the argument of *Proslogion* 2 is to *draw out the implications* of this formula, not simply to state it and hope the atheist immediately assents to God's

---

[22] STh I.2.1 obj 2 (Aquinas 2000–2019): "Praeterea, illa dicuntur esse per se nota, quae statim, cognitis terminis, cognoscuntur, quod philosophus attribuit primis demonstrationis principiis, in I Poster., scito enim quid est totum et quid pars, statim scitur quod omne totum maius est sua parte. Sed intellecto quid significet hoc nomen Deus, statim habetur quod Deus est. Significatur enim hoc nomine id quo maius significari non potest, maius autem est quod est in re et intellectu, quam quod est in intellectu tantum, unde cum, intellecto hoc nomine Deus, statim sit in intellectu, sequitur etiam quod sit in re. Ergo Deum esse est per se notum."

[23] I.2.1 ad 2 (Aquinas 2000–2019): "Ad secundum dicendum quod forte ille qui audit hoc nomen Deus, non intelligit significari aliquid quo maius *cogitari* non possit…"

[24] SCG I.11.1 (Aquinas 2000–2019): "Nec oportet ut statim, cognita huius nominis Deus significatione, Deum esse sit notum, ut prima ratio intendebat."

[25] *Proslogion* 2 (S I.101.7–10): "Sed certe ipse idem insipiens, cum audit hoc ipsum quod dico: 'aliquid quo maius nihil cogitari potest', intelligit quod audit; et quod intelligit in intellectu eius est, etiam si non intelligat illud esse. Aliud enim est rem esse in intellectu, aliud intelligere rem esse. [But certainly this same fool, when he hears this very [phrase] that I say, "something than which nothing greater is able to be thought", understands what he hears; and what he understands is in his understanding, *even if he were not to understand it to exist*. It is one thing for a thing to be in the understanding, and another to understand the thing to exist.]"

existence. Anselm's actual text suggests that Aquinas's summary is not an exact statement of Anselm's own argument.

Aquinas rarely if ever criticizes a saint or sacred authority by name. When he does disagree with an authority, his usual practice is to summarize the position he wants to criticize without attributing it to the authority, and then to criticize the argument on its own. While this delicate practice allows him to correct the ideas of holy men without detracting from their reputations, it does create the possibility that he is not always arguing against the actual, contextualized, nuanced position of the authority, but rather, for example, the position as understood by a typical student. That is, there might be some dialectical purpose behind what could otherwise appear as sloppiness in his characterization of an authority's views. Thus, it might be possible that in *STh* I.2.1 and *SCG* I.10–11, Aquinas is criticizing an Anselm*ian* argument, one widely assumed to be Anselm's (even today), rather than the actual argument of the *Proslogion*.

This suggestion is supported by a text from Aquinas's *Sentences Commentary* (1SN d.3, q.1, a.2, obj.4), in which Aquinas also asks whether the existence of God is *per se notum*. Objection 4 mentions by name both Anselm and Avicenna (who developed the notion of a quiddative definition which Aquinas uses in the *intellectus essentiae* argument of *De Ente*). Two points about this passage jump out: first, that Aquinas uses the arguments of these two authorities interchangeably; and second, that Aquinas is clear that he is only using their arguments to prove a minor premise in an argument that is *his*, not theirs:

> Again, that is known per se which is *not able to be known not to be*. But God is *not able to be known not to be*. Therefore, being itself [*ipsum esse*] is known per se. The proof of the middle is through Anselm: God is that than whom a greater is not able to be thought. But that which is *not able to be thought not to be* is greater than what *is* able to be thought not to be. Therefore, God is not able to be thought not to be, since he is *that than which nothing greater can be thought*. Another proof: No thing is able to be thought without its quiddity, such as *man* without that by which he is *rational mortal animal*. But the quiddity of God is being itself [*ipsum suum esse*], as Avicenna says. Therefore God is not able to be thought not to be.[26]

Anselm's argument from Proslogion 2–3 is not engaged here on its own terms, but is simply used as proof of the minor premise of a syllogism on a different topic of interest to Aquinas. (As noted above, Anselm never asks whether the existence of God is *per se notum*). Interestingly, Aquinas also says that one could use a different argument to prove the middle term, namely: that nothing can be thought without its quiddity, and a quidditative definition of God includes that he exists, therefore God

---

[26](Aquinas 2000–2019): "Praeterea, illud est per se notum quod non potest cogitari non esse. Sed Deus non potest cogitari non esse. Ergo ipsum esse, per se est notum. Probatio mediae est per Anselmum: Deus est quo majus cogitari non potest. Sed illud quod non potest cogitari non esse, est majus eo quod potest cogitari non esse. Ergo Deus non potest cogitari non esse, cum sit illud quo nihil majus cogitari potest. Potest aliter probari. Nulla res potest cogitari sine sua quidditate, sicut homo sine eo quod est animal rationale mortale. Sed Dei quidditas est ipsum suum esse, ut dicit Avicenna. Ergo Deus non potest cogitari non esse." Thanks to Turner Nevitt for pointing this text out to me.

cannot be thought without also thinking his existence—a version of the argument Aquinas deploys in the *intellectus essentiae* argument discussed above. This seems to suggest that both the Anselmian definition and the quiddative definition can serve equally well to defend the middle premise in the syllogism that God's existence cannot not be thought.

In the reply to objection 4, Aquinas claims that it is possible to think merely vaguely that God does not exist, a claim familiar to us from the two Summas. But here he offers an interpretation of how to read Anselm's *Proslogion* argument and how to read Avicenna's argument about the quiddative definition of God:

> To the fourth, it should be said that the reasoning of Anselm *must* be understood thus [*ita intelligenda est*]: After we *understand* [*intelligimus*] God, it is not possible [both] that *what God is* be understood [*intelligi*] and [that] it be possible to think *that he is not*; but nevertheless it does not follow that someone isn't able to deny or think [*cogitare*] 'God is not'; for it is possible to think that nothing exists of this sort [i.e.] 'than which a greater cannot be thought'...And similarly must be said to the other proof [of Avicenna]. [That it proceeds from the supposition that one has the quiddative definition of God.][27]

The last sentence here agrees with Klima's point (Klima 2017) that the *intellectus essendi* argument is valid only if one has a quiddative definition of God, and not a merely verbal one. But it seems that Aquinas is here also agreeing with the reading of *Proslogion* 4 that I gave above, that Anselm's argument requires an *understanding* of his formula and not merely a verbal 'thinking' of it. In this passage, unlike in STh I.2.1, Aquinas is careful to observe Anselm's distinction between *intelligere* and *cogitare*; indeed he claims that Anselm's argument *must* be understood to depend on this distinction.

The text from the Sentences Commentary is different from the parallel texts in the Summas in that it mentions Anselm directly and purports to provide an interpretation of Anselm's own argument. The texts in the two Summas do not, leaving open the reading that they are not intended to be a direct criticism of Anselm. The virtue of this reading of STh I.2.1 and SCG I.11.1 is that if, in those texts Aquinas is *not* trying to interpret the *Proslogion* itself, it protects Aquinas's reputation as an interpreter of Anselm.[28] Since Aquinas is explicitly interested in the conditions for some-

---

[27] (Aquinas 2000–2019): "Ad quartum dicendum, quod ratio Anselmi ita intelligenda est. Postquam intelligimus Deum, non potest intelligi quod sit Deus, et possit cogitari non esse; sed tamen ex hoc non sequitur quod aliquis non possit negare vel cogitare, Deum non esse; potest enim cogitare nihil hujusmodi esse quo majus cogitari non possit; et ideo ratio sua procedit ex hac suppositione, quod supponatur aliquid esse quo majus cogitari non potest. Et similiter etiam dicendum ad aliam probationem."

[28] Klima clearly *does* think that Aquinas is criticizing Anselm, rather than a merely Anselmian position. See Klima 2007, 156: "Aquinas finds Anselm's *a priori* approach in his *Proslogion* unpersuasive, because he clearly sees, just as Gaunilo did, that the mere linguistic understanding of Anselm's description of God as that than which nothing greater can be conceived cannot provide a logical short-cut to the requisite conception of God without which Anselm's reasoning cannot work. Thus, Aquinas opted for his *a posteriori* approach, which, however, is intimately tied to his Aristotelian physical and metaphysical principles that can be open to attack from many different angles, especially from different conceptual frameworks."

thing to be known *per se*, a topic that Anselm does not address, it seems plausible that he is interested not so much in Anselm's actual text, but rather in the question of *whether Anselm's formula could serve as the predicate* in a proposition known *per se*. If this is so, then Klima went beyond Aquinas in equating the view he is criticizing with Anselm's own argument, rather than an argument that is Anselm*ian* or merely inspired by the *Proslogion* formula.

3.2 Despite the Reservations, "Saint Anselm's Proof" Is Outstanding

The primary goal of sections 3–4 of "Saint Anselm's Proof" was to explain Aquinas's critique of Anselm's argument. My reservations have been about the second half of the paper, where Klima explains Aquinas's partial defense of Anselm's argument (as he interprets it), and then explains Aquinas's critique of the argument thus understood. My reservations have been that Klima's criticisms of Anselm appear unfair to Anselm, since in the *Proslogion* and *Response* Anselm explicitly rejects the claims Klima attributes to him. But at every point where I have expressed my reservations, Klima is closely following Aquinas's views in *STh* I.2.1 and *SCG* I.10-11. Even his formal reconstruction of Anselm's argument, showing its validity, can be read as a defense of *Aquinas's* claim that the existence of God is *per se notum secundum se*. I think it is fair to say that Klima is either following Aquinas's misinterpretation of Anselm's argument or is himself misattributing Aquinas's remarks to Anselm, and that the apparent weaknesses of his treatment of Anselm are because his real purpose is to explain Aquinas's own subtle position. Most of the criticisms I have made here could be avoided if the paper (or at least its second half) were rebranded as Thomistic exegesis. Understood in this way, Klima's interpretation is brilliant and needed.

It is needed because it is rare to attempt an exegesis of either *STh* I.2.1 or *SCG* I.10–11. *The Cambridge Companion to Aquinas*, to take a prominent example, has four citations to these questions, and no serious exegesis.[29] To cite another example, Fr. John Jenkins's book *Knowledge and Faith in Thomas Aquinas*, which focuses on the opening questions of the *Summa Theologiae*, and which treats at length Aquinas's distinctions about what is known *per se*, never has any extended interpretation of *STh* I.2.1, despite its relevance (Jenkins 1997). Perhaps because *STh* I.2.1 is thought of primarily as a response to Anselm's argument, many Thomists have thought it not worth much attention. But Klima's exegesis in "Saint Anselm's Proof" shows how that would be a mistake.

Aquinas' purposes were not ours. We are interested in the question of whether or not God exists. Aquinas and his students were basically all priests or studying for the priesthood; their question was not *whether* God exists, but whether the existence

---

[29] Kretzmann and Stump 1993, 286 lists all the citations to STh. I.2.1.

of God *is known* in this way or that way. Klima's article is so special because it explores that subtlety.

Thus, an unexpected effect of "Saint Anselm's Proof" is that it places *Aquinas's* proofs in *their* context. Aquinas's project at the opening stage of the *Summa Theologiae* is to argue that, despite several difficulties, it is possible to organize *sacra doctrina* into an Aristotelian science (*STh* I.1).[30] Before he can conclude in *STh* I.2.2 that *sacra doctrina* requires a *demonstration quia* to arrive at the concept of the central term of the science ("God," in this case), he has to rule out the possibility that no demonstration is necessary to arrive at this concept because it is *per se notum*. Anselm had shown that his formula managed to refer to God uniquely. So perhaps, the objection proposes, Anselm's formula could serve as the predicate in a proposition known *per se*. Then there would be no need of a demonstration that begins with effects that we understand well in order to arrive at a concept of God as their cause, since God could be known as easily as we can understand the concepts of whole and part—just by knowing what the words signify. But, Aquinas responds, for the concept of God to serve its role in the science of *sacra doctrina*, the concept must be held in a particular way by the person who has the science: it must be held with what Klima calls constitutive reference. Since it is possible to hold the concept of God in other ways (or not to hold the concept at all), it is necessary to go through what Klima calls a process of conceptual buildup, the first part of which is the *demonstration quia* that God exists—the Five Ways of *STh* I.2.3.[31]

From one perspective, Klima's article simply explains that article 3 of question 2 depends on articles 1 and 2. That's not how Klima presents it, in part because "Saint Anselm's Proof" has as its audience those philosophically trained non-specialists who teach and/or are interested in proofs for the existence of God. Nevertheless, the order of *STh* I.2.1–3 provides the structure of Klima's paper. Section 2 of "Saint Anselm's Proof" defends Aquinas's claim in *STh* I.2.1 that the existence of "that-than-which-nothing-greater-can-be-thought-of" is *per se notum secundum se*. Section 4 defends Aquinas's critique in that same article that it is not also *per se notum quoad nos*. Section 5 then explains Aquinas's claim in *STh* I.2.2 that we need a *demonstratio quia*, one which moves from effects to causes, in order to arrive satisfactorily at the conclusion that God exists, a demonstration Aquinas provides in *STh* I.2.3 with the Five Ways. The implications of the Five Ways are further elaborated in the subsequent questions, building up the concept of God, first as logical implications of that initial concept (*STh* I.3–11) and then adding to the concept things that can be said by analogy to creatures (*STh* I.12–13). It might be surprising that an article that is apparently about Anselm provides an interpretive key to the structure of the beginning of the *Summa Theologiae*!

---

[30] Which was a part of his larger project to convince the University of Paris that Aristotle was relevant to the work of theology, and not just philosophy.

[31] This account also explains why in *STh* I.13 the question of analogous names of God arises: at that stage Aquinas is still trying to shore up the claim that God can be the central concept of an Aristotelian science, despite the difficulties of saying much about him. Analogy is thus an important tool in the "buildup" of the concept of God.

Klima's article also calls attention to the ways in which the science of sacred doctrine has to operate. On Klima's interpretation, Aquinas's program in natural theology strives to build up the store of concepts to which the student is committed, so that he will be able to understand (or even, will not be able *not* to understand) the principles upon which the science of sacred doctrine is founded. This "conceptual buildup" occurs over the course of multiple arguments, moving from the concepts to which the student makes constitutive reference to concepts that the student does not yet have or to which he is not yet committed. The goal here is not simply to build up an organized body of knowledge, but to transform the concepts of the individual reader of the *Summa*. It doesn't matter that something is *per se notum secundum se*, if it is not also *per se notum quoad nos*.

This is the basic idea behind what Aquinas (following Aristotle) calls a *demonstratio quia*—a demonstration "that" something *is* (either absolutely or in a certain way)—which is distinguished from a *demonstratio propter quid*. A demonstration "that" something is argues from effects known to us to the existence of their cause, with the ultimate goal of being able to develop a quiddative concept of that cause. A demonstration "on account of which" (*propter quid*) moves from an understanding of the quiddity of the cause to a knowledge of its effects, typically involving what Jenkins calls "an intellectual habituation" such that the person can no longer think of the effects except *qua* being caused by their cause.[32] As Jenkins insists, Aquinas's goal in the *Summa Theologiae* is to teach students *sacra doctrina* as a *scientia*, so that all the truths and doctrines are understood in relation to God, the principle of the science. Many interpreters of Aquinas and Aristotle do not understand that this is what is meant by a science; readers of Klima can understand this quite readily, because the idea of a demonstration *quia* is an instance of what Klima calls a "conceptual buildup."

Many authors today also do not understand what Aquinas means by *per se nota* propositions. This is perhaps most evident in the elaborate discussions about what Aquinas means when he describes the principles of the natural law as *per se nota* (*STh* I-II.94.2). Both Germain Grisez and his critics claim that propositions that are *per se nota* are "underivable" in Grisez's terminology, that is, that they cannot be the conclusion of a syllogism or demonstration:

---

[32] Jenkins 1997, 46–47: "In certain *scientiae*, such as mathematics, our belief in the effect flows naturally from our belief in the cause. But in other *scientiae*, such as all the natural *scientiae*, we naturally know the effects prior to the cause. In such *scientiae*, then, the second stage will involve not only the construction of syllogisms, but a kind of re-arrangement in our doxastic structure, so that the causes, which were formerly less familiar, become more familiar and better known; and the effects, formerly better known, come to be believed on the grounds of our belief in the cause. What is required at this second stage is what Burnyeat has called 'intellectual habituation.' We must undergo a process of familiarization with the principles so that they become the foundation of our thinking and reasoning within a certain area. Not only must we construct a *propter quid* syllogism within a particular field, but such syllogisms must come to express the way we think about the facts described. And this requires that what is better known by nature comes to be better known to us. It requires that, in some sense, our doxastic structure comes to mirror the causal structure of the world."

Self-evidence in fact has two aspects. On the one hand, a principle is not self-evident if it can be derived from some prior principle, which provides a foundation for it. On the other hand, a principle is not useful as a starting point of inquiry and as a limit of proof unless its underivability is known. The objective aspect of self-evidence, underivability, depends upon the lack of a middle term which might connect the subject and predicate of the principle and supply the cause of its truth. In other words, the reason for the truth of the self-evident principle is what is directly signified by it, not any extrinsic cause. The subjective aspect of self-evidence, recognition of underivability, requires that one have such an adequate understanding of what is signified by the principle that no mistaken effort will be made to provide a derivation for it (Grisez 1965, 173).

The important point to grasp from all this is that when Aquinas speaks of self-evident principles of natural law… he means the principles of practical inquiry which also are the limits of practical argument—a set of underivable principles for practical reason. To function as principles, their status as underivables must be recognized, and this recognition depends upon a sufficient understanding of their terms, i.e., of the intelligibilities signified by those terms (Grisez 1965, 174–5).

Grisez uses "the objective aspect of self-evidence" to translate *per se notum secundum se*, and "the subjective aspect" to translate *per se notum quoad nos*. He claims that something which is subjectively self-evident—self-evident to us—must be known to us *qua* underivable, known as not-able-to-be-demonstrated. A reader of Klima knows that this is not the purpose of Aquinas's distinction. Something is *per se notum secundum se et non quoad nos* when we do not have the concept of the subject and/or the concept of the predicate in the domain of thought objects to which we are committed, those to which we make constitutive reference; while something is *per se notum quoad nos* when we do possess (or perhaps better, when the typical person possesses) the concepts of the subject and predicate of the *per se* proposition.

Stephen Jensen, summarizing Grisez on this point, says that Grisez emphasizes "one single truth about Aquinas' natural law, namely that the first principles of the natural law are *per se nota*, that is, they are known immediately from an understanding of the terms, with no need for deductive reasoning" (Jensen 2015, 4). Jensen accepts Grisez's view of "per-seity," even arguing that "being the conclusion of a syllogism" entails that a proposition is not *per se notum*.[33] In his extensive treatments of what it means to be *per se notum*, Jensen is consistently puzzled by how statements that seem to be, or that Aquinas claims to be, *per se nota* are sometimes the conclusion of syllogisms, since on Jensen's understanding that could never happen. Michael Pakaluk also accepts Grisez's view that a *per se notum* proposition

---

[33] Jensen 2015, 30: "What of the second and fourth modes [of predicating *per se*]? Can they also involve *per se nota* propositions? Aquinas does not say. Indeed, Aquinas states that they are sometimes the conclusion of syllogisms, which would indicate that in these cases they are not *per se nota*."

cannot be the conclusion of a syllogism.[34] Yet any reader of Klima would be inoculated against the claim that *per se nota* propositions could never be the conclusion of a demonstration, since the very purpose of a cosmological argument is to arrive at the *per se notum secundum se* proposition that God exists! It seems that both advocates and critics of the New Natural Law theory could benefit from reading Klima's interpretation of Aquinas on this point.

3.3 The Effect of "Saint Anselm's Proof" on a Young Mind

The occasion of this volume gives me the opportunity to call attention to some aspects of Klima's paper that reveal something about his character, and highlight where Klima has had an influence on at least one of his students.

- *The footnote 4 manifesto*

In footnote 4 of "Saint Anselm's Proof" Klima writes:

> I provided this type of criticism in a paper I wrote ten years ago in Hungarian. See Klima, G. 1983. I think most of the more recent criticisms can be reduced to this type, *but showing this in detail would take another paper (or even a book that is not worth writing, for it would not be worth reading)*…

I think this tells us a few things about Klima's character. He is not going to spend his time correcting the mistakes of other scholars, or doing surveys of the literature and developing classifications, unless he thinks that the error or classification can help him to make some interesting point.[35] What is more, his primary genre is the paper or essay, not the detailed monograph where he surveys the literature on a topic and then weighs in.[36] I do not know if he thinks such books are worth reading, but he evidently does not think they are worth writing. Klima would rather just explain

---

[34] Pakaluk 2013, 165: "[W]hen St. Thomas claims that some proposition is not demonstrated from others, he means, precisely, that we do not affirm it in the manner of a conclusion of a syllogism, in which the terms of that proposition are linked to each other solely through their connection to a middle term. We do not affirm it as the conclusion of a syllogism, because we see the connection between the terms immediately and can assert the proposition on its own. For an expert, the proposition '*Angelus non est circumscriptive in loco*' is indeed derived from prior knowledge, according to the common way of speaking, as one cannot grasp the subject nor the predicate properly without expert knowledge. However, to that same expert, the proposition is *per se nota* and not 'derived', that is, not demonstrated on the basis of others, because the expert sees immediately the connection of the term, without needing to rely on a syllogism which connects them through a middle term."

[35] As in his reviews of Anthony Kenny's books on Aquinas, where he finds Kenny to be a useful foil for showing the limitations of the contemporary conceptual framework for correctly interpreting Aquinas.

[36] For example, I suspect that Klima would appreciate John Jenkins's book (op. cit), but he would not be interested in summarizing and correcting the wide array of authors and opinions that Jenkins does.

the right answer directly, rather than point out exactly why everyone else did not quite get there.

When I first read what I will call the footnote 4 manifesto, I laughed. But I later grew to interpret it as a call to magnanimity, to academic ambition. For a young scholar seeking tenure and looking for material for publications, it is often easier to criticize the mistakes of others than to come up with the right answer oneself. But I realized that I did not like reading those books any more than Klima did, and I still do not. I am not sure that Klima intended this footnote to have much of an impact, but the idea that academic writing should be worth reading, and academic research should be about topics worth understanding, has shaped my intellectual—and to a certain extent my spiritual—development.

- *Logical Pentecostalism, or overcoming conceptual divides*

Alasdair MacIntyre has promoted Aquinas as an example of how to solve the problem of how to communicate across different and even seemingly incommensurable conceptual frameworks (MacIntyre 1990, esp. 113–126). This is also a major interest of Klima's, and "Saint Anselm's Proof" both shows and tells the reader how it is done.

Klima's paper attempts to bridge two pairs of different conceptual frameworks. At the beginning of the paper is the first pairing: the modern framework of reference, in which Anselm's proof seems mere nonsense, and the medieval framework of reference, in which Anselm's proof is clearly formally valid. I think most readers of section 2 of the paper will instantly see the possibilities of Klima's project: once he suggests that medieval philosophers had a sophisticated theory that allowed them to refer to thought objects, he is able to explain to those operating from the contemporary framework why Anselm's argument works. And of course, in doing so, he provokes the question of why the contemporary framework doesn't allow semantic reference to *entia rationis* (beings of reason), and the further question of whether it could be expanded in order to do so. Klima does not try to give a theoretical account of Quinean conceptual schemes or Wittgensteinian grammars or Kuhnian paradigms or Macintyrean narrative traditions, of incommensurability or of relativism; he just shows, using the tools of formal semantics, how to explain what Anselm is doing in a way that those from the other framework can understand.

The second pair of conceptual frameworks is that of the atheist and the theist. Klima argues that Anselm's argument fails to convince the atheist because the atheist does not share the necessary concepts, thanks to his use of parasitic reference and conceptual sandboxing. Thus, the two have different conceptual frameworks that, at least on the question of God's existence, do not overlap. In this part of the paper, Klima presents Aquinas as a model of how to persuade someone who does not share one's own conceptual framework, and Anselm as a model of someone who stays within his own framework and calls those outside it Fools. The atheist and the theist, in Klima's hands if not in Anselm's, come to stand for all those who have fundamental disagreements but are willing to engage in dialectic "for the sake of what is true and good." This novel characterization leads Klima to return in the last paragraph of "Saint Anselm's Proof" to offer a theory of how to engage in work across different conceptual frameworks. Klima views this sort of engagement, with its attendant intellectual and moral virtues, as essential to the vocation to philosophy:

> Unless one is able to learn to think and live with the concepts of another person and the thought objects constituted by them, one will always fail to have a real grasp on the meaning of the other person... This, of course, requires openness, patience, and respect from both parties. Indeed, this requires that attitude which defines our profession, the Love of Wisdom (Klima 2000, 83).

The optimism and idealism of this passage, plus his own example in section 2, marks Klima as what we might call a *Logical Pentecostalist*. By this term, I mean someone who believes that (1) social divisions between people are in significant part due to misunderstandings, which are in turn the fault of our *natural* languages, and (2) *symbolic* formulations of our arguments can help people engage in dialectic without the misunderstandings characteristic of natural language discourse. Just as the miracle of Pentecost allowed the peoples who spoke different languages to understand each other, so formal logical systems can allow people to understand each other across conceptual paradigms without ambiguity. This vision places Klima, with Leibniz and the Vienna Circle, among those who believe that the level of clarity of thought and expression that can be achieved through formalization could end misunderstandings and lead to peace.

I do not know if Klima has ever expressed himself as enthusiastically in his later writing, and perhaps his enthusiasm has been tempered as he has gotten older and reckoned with the fallenness of the profession of philosophy. But "Saint Anselm's Proof" expresses a lively faith in the possibility of mutual understanding, and section 2 especially shows the potential for using the philosophical tools of formal languages to achieve it.

When I first read that section, I would have answered if Klima had made an altar call (if I as a cradle Catholic, or if Klima, who had only recently escaped from behind the Iron Curtain, had had any idea of what an altar call was). Philosophy can bring us together, and can help the post-Christian West see the error of its conceptual framework! (I talked that way in college.) "All" one had to do was study a lot of technical semantics, both medieval and modern, and then formalize the medieval arguments so that those with other conceptual frameworks could understand them— and we would be able to overcome the conceptual differences between theist and atheist, Catholic and secularist!

• *Boxing with shadows in the cave*

I became disillusioned with this idea sometime during the first months of graduate school at Notre Dame. In my naiveté, I was surprised that contemporary philosophers—by which I mean those assuming contemporary semantics and "metaphysics" in the tradition of Kant, Frege, Russell, Quine, and so on—did not seem willing to abandon their conceptual framework. Even after reading a couple of Klima's papers! At Notre Dame in the 1990s, there were a fair number of "philosophers of religion" or "Christian philosophers," some of whom would venture to interpret Aquinas and other medieval philosophers, but whose methodology involved working within the contemporary conceptual framework to arrive at and/or defend classic Christian conclusions.[37] There were obvious professional and apologetics advantages built into such a project. For example, their arguments seemed clever to contemporary philosophers, they seemed to be doing something that was to their colleagues recognizably philosophy, while to those same philosophers it seemed a little bizarre to advance medieval ideas as if they were true.

Yet Klima had shown me that we have to pay attention to the differences in conceptual frameworks in order to be able to understand the medievals correctly, and to learn from them. What's more, Klima showed—not just in "Saint Anselm's Proof," but already there—that on several issues the contemporary framework often lacked the conceptual resources that the medieval framework possessed. That spoiled for me the Christian philosophy project, which, as I said, requires one to agree to work within the contemporary framework, even when that framework is inadequate. Why fight with one hand tied behind your back? Why stay in Plato's cave and shadow-box? A Kuhnian paradigm shift is supposed to leave one with a broader conceptual framework, from which one can answer the puzzles that the narrower paradigm answered, as well as puzzles that it could not answer. So why agree only to use conceptual tools that, for example, lacked a subtle enough mereology to explain how two natures could be in one person in Christ, or a rich enough notion of being to be able to see that being and goodness could be convertible, or strapped one with a view of "properties" that rendered the notion of Divine Simplicity unintelligible rather than reasonable? Having seen the broader conceptual framework that could handle both the questions of the contemporary framework and the questions (including important ones of doctrine and dogma) that the contemporary framework could not, it was hard to want to do Christian philosophy, at least with any conviction. This was even more true when I met real professional philosophers who were not much like the Lovers of Wisdom that Klima describes at the end of "Saint Anselm's Proof," but were earning a living doing a job that did not always reward them for changing their minds in a medieval direction.

"Saint Anselm's Proof" encouraged at least this (formerly) young intellectual to be ambitious despite all that, or better to be magnanimous, in the sense of working on the more important problems rather than wasting time pedantically correcting everyone else's mistakes. This is great advice in general in the age of social media, and has been on balance probably a net good for my intellectual and spiritual life. There are a lot of wonderful things I can say about my former teacher, but the importance of intellectual magnanimity might be the single most important conclusion I drew from "Saint Anselm's Proof."

---

[37] I am thinking of professors such as Alvin Plantinga and others associated with *Faith and Philosophy*, the "Cornell school" of medieval philosophy including some of Norman Kretzmann's students and their students, some of those who work on "analytic theology," and on the New Natural Law.

References

Aquinas, Thomas. 2000–2019. *Opera omnia.* Fundación Tomás de Aquino. Ab Enrique Alarcón collecta et edita. Pompaelone ad Universitatis Studiorum Navarrensis aedes ab AD MM. www. corpusthomisticum.org.

Brower, Jeffrey E. 2019. Platonism about goodness—Anselm's proof in the Monologion. *TheoLogica* 3 (2): 3–30.

Grisez, Germain. 1965. The first principle of practical reason: A commentary on the Summa theologiae, 1-2, question 94, article 2. *Natural Law Forum* 10 (1): 168–201.

Holopainen, Toivo. 1996. *Dialectic and theology in the eleventh century*, Studien und Texte zur Geistesgeschichte des Mittelalters, vol. 54. Leiden: Brill.

———. 2007. Anselm's argumentum and the early medieval theory of argument. *Vivarium* 45 (1): 1–29.

———. 2009. The Proslogion in relation to the Monologion. *The Heythrop Journal* 50 (4): 590–602.

———. 2020. *A historical study of Anselm's Proslogion: Argument, devotion and rhetoric.* Leiden: Brill.

Jenkins, John I. 1997. *Knowledge and faith in Thomas Aquinas.* Cambridge: Cambridge University Press.

Jensen, Steven J. 2015. *Knowing the natural law: From precepts and inclinations to deriving oughts.* Washington, DC: Catholic University of America Press.

Klima, Gyula. 2000. St. Anselm's proof: A problem of reference, intentional identity and mutual understanding. In Medieval philosophy and modern times, ed. Ghita Holmström-Hintikka, 69–87. Dordrecht: Kluwer. Also available online at https://faculty.fordham.edu/klima/anselm.htm.

———. 2001. On whether *id quo maius cogitari potest* is in the understanding. *Proceedings of the Society for Medieval Logic and Metaphysics* 1: 70–80. https://faculty.fordham.edu/klima/SMLM/PSMLM1/PSMLM1.pdf. Reprinted in *The immateriality of the human mind, the semantics of analogy, and the conceivability of God*, edited by Gyula Klima and Alexander W. Hall, 93–106. Newcastle Upon Tyne: Cambridge Scholars Publishing, 2011.

———. 2003. Conceptual closure in Anselm's proof: Reply to Professor Roark. *History and Philosophy of Logic* 24: 131–134.

———. 2007. *Medieval philosophy: Essential readings with commentary.* Edited by Gyula Klima with Fritz Allhoff and Anand Jayprakash Vaidya. Malden, MA: Blackwell.

———. 2017 Aquinas' real distinction and its role in a causal proof of God's existence. In *Symposium Thomisticum*, Porto, Portugal, 22–24 June 2017. https://www.academia.edu/34812683/Aquinas_Real_Distinction_and_Its_Role_in_a_Causal_Proof_of_Gods_Existence.

———. 2019. Aquinas's real distinction and its role in a causal proof of God's existence. *Roczniki Filozoficzne* 67 (4): 7–26.

Kretzmann, Norman, and Eleonore Stump, eds. 1993. *The Cambridge companion to Aquinas.* Cambridge: Cambridge University Press.

Logan, Ian. 2009. *Reading Anselm's Proslogion: The history of Anselm's argument and its significance today.* Farnham: Ashgate.

MacIntyre, Alasdair C. 1990. *Three rival versions of moral enquiry: Encyclopedia, genealogy, and tradition.* Notre Dame, IN: University of Notre Dame Press.

Marenbon, John. 2002. Some semantic problems in Anselm's De Grammatico. In *Latin culture in the eleventh century*, ed. M.W. Herren, C.J. McDonough, and R.G. Arthur, vol. 2, 73–86. Turnhout: Brepols.

———. 2005. Anselm's Proslogion. In *Central works of philosophy I: Ancient and medieval*, ed. John Shand, 169–193. Chesham: Acumen.

Pakaluk, Michael. 2013. Some observations on natural law. *Diametros* 38: 153–175.

Roark, Tony. 2003. Conceptual closure in Anselm's proof. *History and Philosophy of Logic* 24 (1): 1–14.

Schmitt, Franciscus Salesius. 1968. In *S. Anselmi Cantuarensis archiepiscopi Opera omnia*, ed. F.S. Schmitt, 5 vols ed. Stuttgart: Friedrich Frommann Verlag.

Sweeney, Eileen. 2012. *Anselm of Canterbury and the desire for the word*. Washington, DC: Catholic University of America Press.

Sylvain, Nicolas. 2008. *A new approach to browser security: The Google Chrome sandbox*. https://blog.chromium.org/2008/10/new-approach-to-browser-security-google.html. Accessed 26 July 2021.

Walz, Matthew D. 2010. The 'logic' of faith seeking understanding: A propaedeutic for Anselm's Proslogion. *Dionysius* 28: 131–166.

Wikipedia. 2021. *Anselm of Canterbury*. Last modified 25 October 2021. https://en.wikipedia.org/wiki/Anselm_of_Canterbury.

Williams, Thomas. 2020. Saint Anselm. In *The Stanford encyclopedia of philosophy (Winter 2020 Edition)*, ed. Edward N. Zalta. https://plato.stanford.edu/archives/win2020/entries/anselm/.

Chapter 4
Albert the Great Among the Pygmies: Explaining Animal Intelligence in the Thirteenth Century

Peter G. Sobol

Keywords Albert the Great · Animal intelligence · Aristotle · Avicenna · *Estimativa*, internal senses · Comparative psychology – history · Pygmies · Universals

Open a book on the history of psychology and you are likely to find Charles Darwin named as the founder of comparative psychology and ethology (Hearnshaw 1987, 122; Hothersall 1984, 280; Watson 1978, 322). But to trace the history of human concern with animal intelligence back no further than Darwin is to miss most of the story. Our modern fascination with how animals think and what animals know is only the latest manifestation of more than two thousand years of uneasy conjecture—uneasy because the behavior of animals, to anyone who studied it in depth, raised a difficult question: can we explain that behavior while preserving a firm boundary between animals and humans?

Aristotle seems to have believed in that firm boundary. In Aristotle's world, all living things possessed a soul with abilities that determined their place in a hierarchy. The soul granted all living things the ability to absorb nourishment, to grow, and to reproduce. The souls of animals granted them additional powers that allowed them to become aware of and, in most cases, to move about in their environment. Additional powers of the sensitive soul allowed some animals to assemble the information from their external senses into images of external objects (the common sense), to use and manipulate such images (the imagination) and to save and recall them (memory). The souls of humans alone granted them the powers of intellect.[1]

---

[1] At *On the soul* II.3, 414b18, *dianoetikon* and *nous* belong to "man, and any other being similar or superior to him." Aristotle 1975, 83.

P. G. Sobol (✉)
University of Wisconsin, Madison, WI, USA
e-mail: pgsobol@wisc.edu

J. P. Hochschild et al. (eds.), *Metaphysics Through Semantics: The Philosophical Recovery of the Medieval Mind*, International Archives of the History of Ideas Archives internationales d'histoire des idées 242, https://doi.org/10.1007/978-3-031-15026-5_4

But Aristotle also studied animals in depth. His zoological works fill more pages than his works on all other subjects. In among his descriptions of animal anatomy and physiology, movement and reproduction, he referred to animals as clever (*phronemos* – Aristotle 1991, 8.1.608a14), teachable (*mathematikos* – Aristotle 1991, 8.1.608a27), possessed of mind (*nous* – Aristotle 1991, 8.3.610b20), and thought or intellect (*dianoia* – Aristotle 1991, 8.7.612b20). Coming across this passage in his *On the Movement of Animals* (DMA),

> Now we see that the things which move the animal are intellect [*dianoian*], imagination, purpose, wish, and appetite (Aristotle 1983, 6.700b16),

a reader new to Aristotle might be forgiven for coming away with the belief that Aristotle attributed intellect to animals. How different, then, are animals and humans?

Judging by their literary output, medieval scholars did not view this question as a critical problem. These were, after all, Christian scholars for whom the exclusive possession of reason by humans was a theological as well as a philosophical truth. They more readily pondered the immortality of the human soul than its unique rationality. But although the apparently rational behavior of animals was not a popular problem, it was nevertheless a persistent one. From the thirteenth to the seventeenth century, a few scholars searched for an explanation of animal intelligence which would preserve humans' unique possession of intellect.

This was never going to be easy. On the one hand, Aristotle's psychology remains even today fertile ground for commentators who follow in the footsteps of their medieval forebears in their efforts to demonstrate the consistency that they know must lie hidden beneath the "dark and sparse statements"—to quote Franz Brentano in 1867—of Aristotle's extant writings.[2] The task is confounded by what Deborah Modrak has called Aristotle's "usual aversion to technical terms" (Modrak 1987, 69) and what William Fortenbaugh has called Aristotle's willingness to use "the metaphors of everyday language" (Fortenbaugh 1971, 143).

On the other hand, there are the complex phenomena of animal behavior, examples of which have always been readily available to even the casual observer. Birds' nests, bee hives, and spider webs all reveal in their makers an ability to successfully manipulate their environment. Aristotle's own *History of Animals* provided many examples of animal intelligence,[3] and, later, the Roman encyclopedist Pliny the Elder, in his *Natural History*, preserved for posterity even more enchanting tales. Pliny tells of good animals such as the lion that is merciful to those of its victims who beg to be spared (Pliny 1983, 8.19.48), of sagacious animals such as the fox that puts its ear to the frozen surface of a river to detect whether the ice will bear its

---

[2] Brentano 1977, 25. "den dunkelen und spärlichen Ausgaben des Aristoteles." Brentano 1867, 37. Brentano was confident that a coherent theory would emerge. "Es muss aber, wenn anders mein Vertrauen auf Aristoteles mich nicht täuscht, ein Ausweg bleiben, und dieser wird es dann sein, der uns das richtige Verständniss der Lehre vermittelt." *Ibid*, 38. Urs Dierauer, in his valuable *Tier und Mensch in der Denken der Antike*, has remarked of Aristotle's ideas of animal intelligence, "Und doch bleibt vieles in dunkeln." Dierauer 1977, 108.

[3] See esp. Aristotle 1991, VIII, *passim*.

weight (Pliny 1983, 8.42.103), and of the team of horses in a chariot race in which the charioteer

> was thrown at the start, and his team took the lead and kept it by getting in the way of their rivals and jostling them aside and doing everything against them that they would have had to do with a most skillful charioteer in control (Pliny 1983, 8.65.160).

Most remarkable are the stories about elephants. Pliny described one tame elephant found in the middle of the night practicing a task that it had earlier been beaten for failing to master (Pliny 1983, 8.3.6). Elephants mate in secret because of their modesty and "adultery is unknown among them" (Pliny 1983, 8.5.13). They even perform religious rituals for the new moon (Pliny 1983, 8.1.1–2).

Some of these tales suggest that animals have a moral sense, and in fact teachers of morals, following the precedent set in the book of Proverbs,[4] adopted many such stories.[5] In the fourth century, St. Basil and St. Ambrose both drew attention to the temperance and the prudence of animals to shame their hearers into behaving as well. In the seventh homily of his *Hexameron*, St. Basil wrote,

> If a fish knows what it ought to seek and what to shun, what shall we say, who are honored with reason, instructed by law, encouraged by the promises, made wise by the Spirit, and are nevertheless less reasonable about our own affairs than the fish?[6]

Didactic tales of animal behavior were also preserved in secular literature, most notably in the bestiary known as *Physiologus*, which may have been compiled during the second century CE (*Physiologus* 1979).[7]

There are thus two strands in the history of animal behavior that begin in antiquity and continue into the seventeenth century. One strand consists of encyclopedic and hortatory literature and includes many works in addition to those already mentioned.[8] These works contain anecdotes of intelligent animal behavior but make no attempt to explain them. The other strand consists of philosophical and academic works, mainly commentaries on Aristotle's *De anima*, which occasionally do attempt to explain intelligent animal behavior. The first strand posed no problem for later scholars, who could devote their efforts to correcting errors and adding new information. It was the second strand that challenged them, as they tried to delineate the internal faculties of the sensitive soul about which Aristotle had been so vague, and from which animal behavior must arise. The remainder of this paper will focus on a specific problem at the animal-human divide: are animals able to acquire and

---

[4] Proverbs 6:6 and 30:24–28.

[5] E.g., Aristotle (*Historia animalium* 9.47.631a1–7) included a report, also mentioned by Pliny (8.64.156.), of a stallion that threw itself off a cliff when it discovered that it had been bred with its mother.

[6] St Basil, *Hexameron* VII.5.

[7] See also White 1954. The bestiary remained a tool of Christian moral instruction into the nineteenth century. See Fisher 1834.

[8] See esp. Aelian 1958–1959, for a veritable circus of strange tales, purposefully offered in no discernable order and occasionally accompanied by exhortations to behave as well as animals do.

use universal concepts to guide their behavior, and, if so, how, lacking intellect, do they do it?

This question appears in the following way in the works of the Islamic scholars whose efforts would eventually accompany Aristotle's works into the Latin west: How do animals know to pursue or avoid things that are not immediately pleasant or painful? The pursuit of what is immediately pleasant and avoidance of what is immediately painful need not rely on intelligence; an animal need not possess an intellect to be able to stay out of the fire or to eat what tastes good. Yet much animal behavior involves reactions that cannot be based directly on sensory qualities. To use the familiar example, why does a sheep run away from a wolf even when it has never seen one before? Not because the color of the wolf irritates the sheep's eyes or because the odor of the wolf irritates the sheep's nose. Arab authors, particularly al-Farabi and Avicenna, believed that, beyond the five senses, animals possessed an internal sensitive power—not proposed by Aristotle—that allowed them to assess objects based on something other than sense data. That "something" had to arrive at the perceiving creature in much the same way as sensory information arrived. Avicenna's word for it was *ma'na*, which became in Latin *intentio*, or intention. The power that perceived intentions was called *wahm*, which became in Latin *æstimativa*. "Sometimes," Avicenna wrote,

> we judge of sensible things by means of intentions which we do not sense, either because they are not sensible in their nature in any way, or because they are sensible but we do not sense them when we judge. But those things that are not sensible in their nature are such things as enmity and malice and whence animals flee, which the sheep apprehends in the form of a wolf; it is the intention which make the sheep flee from the wolf; and the rapport that the sheep apprehends from its fellow sheep is by means of an intention. These are things which the sensible soul apprehends in such a way that sense teaches the soul nothing about them; therefore the virtue by which such things are apprehended is another virtue and is called *æstimativa*.[9]

Intentions thus revealed the relationship of the object to the perceiving animal and conveyed either positive values such as benevolence or utility, or negative values such as danger.

Avicenna employed the *æstimativa* to explain two groups of phenomena. The first group consisted of instinctive or unlearned behaviors. The instinct that makes an infant seek its mother's breast or seek support when it feels itself falling has its

---

[9] "Deinde aliquando diiudicamus de sensibilibus per intentiones quas non sentimus, aut ideo quod in natura sua non sunt sensibiles ullo modo, aut quia sunt sensibiles sed nos non sentimus in hora iudicii. Sed quae non sunt sensibiles ex natura sua, sunt sicut inimicitiae et malitia et quae a se diffugiunt quam apprehendit ovis de forma lupi et omnino intentio quae facit eam fugere ab illo, et concordia quam apprehendit de sua socia et omnino intentio qua gratulatur cum illa: sunt res quas apprehendit anima sensibilis ita quod sensus no doceat eam aliquid de his; ergo virtus qua haec apprehenduntur est alia virtus et vocatur æstimativa." Avicenna 1968, 6:79–7:88.

origin in God's concern for the infant's well-being.[10] Animals' unlearned responses, on the other hand, are natural rather than divine in origin and allow the animal to react to the value of a perceived body. According to Avicenna, a sheep runs away from the first wolf it has ever seen because the celestial spheres have prepared the *æstimativa* of each sheep to recognize that wolves are harmful.[11]

In learned behavior, however, intentions were created in the animal soul by the linking of two sensory images. A dog that has been beaten with a stick learns to recognize that all sticks are dangerous, because the image of a stick and the image of pain are linked in the dog's memory, creating an intention, a judgment that sticks are bad. The next time the dog sees a stick, the dog's *æstimativa* recognizes the link between that image and the image of pain, and the dog runs away.[12]

But while a sheep flees from a wolf not because it is recognized as a wolf but because it is the source of the intention of harm, a dog that has learned to fear a wielded stick now fears all sticks, not just the one that was raised against it. Hence, the dog seems able to recognize that sticks are members of a class to which the intention of danger applies. It would seem then that animals can, through experience, acquire universal concepts, an ability supposed to be a prerogative of intellect.

---

[10] "Dicimus igitur quod ipsa æstimatio fit multis modis. Unus ex illis est cautela proveniens in omne quod est a divina clementia, sicut dispositio infantis qui cum nascitur mox pendat ab uberibus, et sicut dispositio infantis qui, cum elevatur ad standum et vult cadere, statim currit ad adhaerendum alicui vel ad custodiendum se per aliquid." Avicenna 1968, 37:19–38:27.

[11] "et per istas cautelas apprehendit æstimatio intentiones quae sunt commixtae cum sensibilibus de quod obest vel prodest." IV.3 van Riet, 38.33–34. The precise origin of the natural instincts is not clear in the Latin of Avicenna's text. "Praeter hoc etiam animalia habent cautelas naturales. Cuius rei causa sunt comparationes quae habent esse inter has animas et earum principia quae sunt duces [a note here states "duces: confusion probable entre *qa'ida* (duces) et *da'ima* (semper)."] incessantes, praeter comparationes quas contingit aliquando esse et aliquando non esse, sicut considerare cum intellectu et quod subito in mentem venit: omnia etenim illinc [a note here states "illinc: *ar*. «de la-bas», du monde des *principia* ou substance célèstes."] veniunt. Et per istas cautelas apprehendit æstimatio intentiones quae sunt commixtae cum sensibilibus de eo quod obest vel prodest; unde omnis ovis pavet lupum, etsi numquam videri illum nec aliquid mali pertulerit ab illo." Avicenna 1968, 38:29–39:36.

It is less clear in the French translation of the Arabic text: "De même, les animaux possèdent des instincts naturels. La cause en est aux rapports existant entre ces âmes, et que les principes des rapports sont constants, non interrompus, autres que les rapports auxquels il arrive une fois d'être ou ne pas être, exemple la perfection de l'intelligence, et exemple l'idée du juste. Car toutes les choses viennent d'ici-bas..." Avicenna 1950, II:130.

Albert states that only man is imprinted from the heavens. Albertus Magnus 1920, 1325:15–16.

[12] "Alius autem modus est sicut hoc quod fit per experientiam. Animal etenim cum habuerit dolorem aut delicias, aut pervenerit ad illud utilitas sensibilis aut nocumentum sensibile adiunctum cum forma sensibili, et descripta fuerit in formali forma huius rei et forma eius quod adiunctum est illi, et descripta fuerit in memoria intentio comparationis quae est inter illas et iudicium de illa, scilicet quod memoria per seipsam naturaliter apprehendit hoc, et deinde apparuerit extra imaginativam forma ipsa, tunc movebitur per formam et movebitur cum illa id quod adiunctum fuerat illi de intentionibus utilibus aut nocivis, et omnino procedet memoria ad modum motus et perquestitionis quae est natura virtutis imaginativae; sed æstimatio hoc totum sentiet simul et videbit intentionem per formam illam, et hic est modus qui accidit per experientiam; unde canes terrentur lapidibus et fustibus et similia." Avicenna 1968, 39:39–582.

If Latin scholars were daunted by this consequence of Avicenna's theory, most of them nevertheless adopted the concept that humans and animals possessed an internal sensitive power that informed them of the value of sensed objects by means of intentions, not by means of sense images. Dominicus Gundissalinus, the twelfth-century translator of Avicenna's *De anima*, also wrote a *De anima* of his own, which borrows not only ideas from Avicenna but large chunks of text as well. Frequent borrowing occurs in the section on the internal senses, and it is tempting to conclude that, faced with this difficult text, Dominicus here threw up his hands and bequeathed the task of explicating Avicenna to posterity, thereby sparing himself the task of addressing the implication in Avicenna's theory that animals make use of universal concepts.[13]

That implication was addressed by John Blund in a *Treatise on the Soul* written around the year 1210. Blund admitted that, at first glance, it seemed as if Avicenna allowed the *æstimativa* of animals to recognize universals and also to recognize the truth or falsity of propositions. A sheep that flees from a wolf seems able to recognize the individual wolf as a member of a class of objects that should be avoided. By its flight, it seems to assent to the proposition "Wolves are harmful."[14] In order to debunk this conclusion and restrict to humans the recognition of universals and the truth or falsity of propositions, Blund explained that when a sheep sees a wolf and, by means of its *æstimativa*, recognizes its harmful intent, it does not reach the conclusion in a universal sense, of all wolves, but only of the present one.

> Whence it is not perceived by the *æstimativa* [of the sheep] that it should flee from a wolf, but it is perceived that it should flee from this wolf, which is sensed, or was sensed; and because the term "this wolf" connotes a singular, that which the term "to be fled" connotes is brought to the singular "from this wolf" via this designation.[15]

Instead of attributing the sheep's reaction to its detecting the intention of harm, Blund here suggests that the sheep perceives that this thing is to be fled because this thing is a wolf. But to accomplish that recognition, the sheep must have the universal concept of "wolf." Blund's explanation for why the sheep is unaware of the truth of its perceptions of the wolf consists of no more than stating that perception of truth or falsity is by definition only possible by means of intellect.[16]

---

[13] Dominicus Gundissalinus 1940. For the borrowed sections cf. Avicenna 1968 IV.3 *passim*, which refers to the pages in Muckle's text of Gundissalinus's *De anima*.

[14] Aristotle had anticipated this idea. "Sensation, then, is like mere assertion and thinking [*noein*]; when an object is pleasant or unpleasant, the soul pursues or avoids it, thereby making a sort of assertion or negation." Aristotle 1975, 3.7.431a9–12. The sheep's flight would then be the conclusion of a practical syllogism.

[15] "Unde secundum vim estimativam non apprehenditur quod a lupo sit fugiendum, sed apprehenditur quod ab hoc lupo sit fugiendum, qui est in sensu, vel prius fuit in sensu; et cum per hunc terminum, 'hoc lupo,' significetur singulare, illud quod significatur ulterius per hunc terminum 'fugiendum' trahitur ad singulare per hanc determinationem 'ab hoc lupo.'" Blund 1970, 70.

[16] "Non enim apprehendunt veritatem vel falsitatem, cum intellectu careant et ratione." Blund 1970, 71. But do animals lack practical intellect?

By the mid-thirteenth century, scholars had adopted the Aristotelian division of soul powers expanded by Avicenna's claim that animals and humans react to the value of a perceived object because the *æstimativa* detects intentions of which the exterior senses are unaware. But little effort was made to actually apply Avicennan psychology to animal behavior. In his *On the Properties of Things*, Bartholomeus Anglicus placed Avicennan psychology in Book 3 and natural history in Book 18, where, likely drawing on Pliny the Elder, he reported that sick elephants gather herbs to cure themselves, but before using them, "they raise their upturned heads to heaven, and ask for the aid of divine powers in a certain religion."[17] One can imagine Bartholomew, at the end of the day, thanking God that it was not the task of an encyclopedist to apply what he had written in Book 3 to explain the phenomena he reported in Book 18. But the problem awaited anyone with the interest and the knowledge to attempt a solution.

Albert the Great had both the interest and the knowledge. The Universal Doctor touched on animal intelligence in his *On the Soul* and in his *On Man*, but it was in his *On Animals*—the most comprehensive work on zoology since Avicenna's book of the same title—that he directly confronted the intelligence and trainability of animals. A survey of these three sources reveals a scholar who, true to his sobriquet, strove to unify psychology and what would someday be called ethology. But faced with the intricacies of animals' behavior—and of one "animal" in particular—he found himself treading warily at the animal-human boundary. In the end that boundary held, but it was now a thinner border wall than ever before.

Albert's understanding of human and animal behavior involves a complex interplay of sensation, intention, appetite, imagination, will, reason, and intellect. What follows is not a thorough presentation of that understanding but an attempt to discern just where Albert located the boundary between humans and animals. A thorough presentation of Albert's understanding must wait.

In Book II of his *De anima*, Albert wrote that, in addition to the reception of primary sensory qualities, animals and humans learned about the world in

> another way, which concerned intentions that were never in sense, but yet are not distinct from the trappings of matter, such as being beneficial or harmful, a friend or a foe, an offspring or not, a mother or not, just as a sheep recognizes its progeny.[18]

Intentions differed from mere images in that intentions could serve as initiators of action. When Aristotle had broached the topic of animal action toward the end of Book III of *On the Soul*, he had written that

---

[17] "...supino capite eas ad celum levant, et quadam religione a numinibus sibi adjutorium postulant." Bartholomeus Anglicus 1505, Lib. 18, c. 41.

[18] "alia autem quae est circa intentiones quae numquam in sensum fuerunt, sed tamen sensibilium conditionibus non sunt separatae, sicut esse conveniens vel inconveniens, et amicum vel inimicum, et esse filium et non filium, matrem et non matrem, sicut ovis noscit filium..." Albertus Magnus 1890, II:4.7.5:303a; "nec unquam lupus miseretur nato suo, nisi habet cognitionem et huius individui, et quod individuum est natus eius." III:1.2, *ibid.* V:317a. Also mentioned in the dubious *De apprehensione, ibid.* V:581.

the speculative mind thinks of nothing practical, and tells us nothing about what is to be avoided or pursued; but movement is characteristic of one who is pursuing or avoiding something (Aristotle 1975, 3.9.432b28–29).

If intellect is to have a role in action, then, it cannot be purely speculative. In the ninth chapter of Book III, Aristotle proposed that "practical mind" [*praktikos nous*] and "practical thought" [*praktike dianoia*] fill that role (Aristotle 1975, 3.10.433a10–20).

If the practical intellect and the *æstimativa* are both involved in animal action, then they are likely related in some way. In Book III of his *On the Soul*, Albert proposed that the *æstimativa* related to imagination in the same way that practical intellect related to speculative intellect. Just as the speculative intellect and imagination handled images entirely separate from any particular instance, so the practical intellect and the *æstimativa* handled images that remained connected to particular things in the world. While the speculative intellect dealt with universal concepts, it was the practical intellect in humans that allowed them to comprehend individual things and circumstances. It was the way intellect could play a role in human action.

Albert devoted the 39th question of his *De homine* to the *æstimativa*. He concluded that the object of the *æstimativa* could not be universal because, if animals were able to perceive universals, they would be able to acquire fields of knowledge "through discovery, doctrine, and study,"[19] which, clearly, they do not. He further concluded that intentions are perceived either "by reason of the universal [*per rationem universalis*]"[20] or "as they remain associated with the senses [*per intentiones numquam separatas a sensibus*]."[21] This second class of perceptions he further divided into those that bore upon truth or falsity, and those that bore upon the value of sensed objects.[22] Animals possessed of *æstimativa*, he allowed, were capable of this latter class of perceptions.

As if he had seen Blund's brief discussion, Albert stated that a sheep detects hostility (*inimicum*) in each wolf, but not by investigation or deliberation, the way humans detect the class of an individual thing. Instead of acting to discover the class of a thing, animals are acted upon by what their *æstimativa* presents to them.[23] Yet even if it be granted that a sheep neither investigates nor deliberates, it still seems able to react in the appropriate manner to any wolf presented to it.

---

[19] "Si ergo bruta animalia perceptiva essent universalium, perceptiva etiam essent scientiarum per inventum et doctrinam et studium, quod falsum est." Albertus Magnus 1896, I.39.2.35:338a.

[20] *Ibid.*

[21] *Ibid.*

[22] "Dicendum cum Avicenna, quod intentiones acceptae a sensibus non apprehensae per sensum, apprehenduntur per duos modos, scilicet per rationem universalis: et sic elicere eas a sensibus est experientiae et virtutis intellectivae. Alio modo accipiuntur per intentiones numquam separatas a sensibus, quae sunt hic et nunc: et sic accipiuntur duobus modis, scilicet prout sunt principium veri et falso in partibus, et sic sunt phantasiae: vel prout determinant nocivum vel conveniens in appetibilibus, et sic sunt æstimativae." *Ibid.*

[23] "Bruta potius aguntur quam agant," he wrote, citing John Damascene. *De homine*, q. 39, a. 2. Albertus Magnus 1896, 35:338b.

The 63rd question of *De homine* addresses the practical intellect, and explains that, while the universal forms that reach the speculative intellect have been entirely abstracted from matter, the forms that reach the practical intellect, because it deals with individual actions, are composite forms that are "individualized through a relationship to matter."[24] At this point, the *æstimativa* and the practical intellect begin to sound very much alike. Both deal with images or intentions that have not been completely divorced from the particulars that distinguished them out in the world.

The 63rd question also presents an important distinction between practical intellect, which deals with principles, and practical reason (*ratio*), which relates one thing to another (*ordinat unum ad alterum*).[25] On occasion, however, the practical intellect is part of reason.[26] It was this admission, perhaps, that led Albert to propose a still further distinction regarding reason when he came to discuss animals themselves.

In Book XXI of the *De animalibus*, Albert upheld the rigid distinction between humans and animals on the basis of intellect. Following Avicenna, Albert claimed that their reason made humans the most perfect animals, not because of their reason itself but because the presence of reason in humans improved and ennobled their sensitive and even their vegetative powers.[27] Only humans are moved by intellect. But "certain animals," he wrote, "seem to have few or none of the interior virtues, and others have them to such an extent that they even seem to be rational."[28] One way that an animal might evince a semblance of rationality is in its ability to acquire something like a universal concept.

> Certain animals seem to have a little of the ability to learn from experience. Learning from experience arises out of many memories [of the same thing] because many memories of the same thing create (*faciunt*) the power and faculty of learning; and we see that many animals besides man have some experiential cognition in singular things.[29]

---

[24] "particularizantur tamen per comparationem ad materiam." Albertus Magnus 1986, 35:541a.

[25] "ratio enim ordinat unum ad alterum, sed intellectus proprie est principiorum secundum quae est ordinatio illa." *Ibid.*, 542a.

[26] "Quando ratio dividitur contra concupiscibilem et irascibilem, tunc intellectus practicus includitur in ratione." *Ibid.*

[27] "et ideo vegetabilis in sensibilibus elargatam habet potentiam, et sensibilis et vegetabilis in rationali largissimae quae secundum naturam esse possunt, sunt potentiae." Albertus Magnus 1916, 21.1.1, § 3. 1323:2–4. "...virtutibus hominis propter consortium rationis accidit aliquid propter quod virtutes eius interiores differunt a virtutibus animalium." Avicenna 1968, IV:3.36:4–8.

[28] "Quaedam enim animalium videntur de interioribus potentiis paucas aut nullas habere, et quaedam in tantum in hiis vigent quod etiam aliquid simile rationi habere videntur." Albertus Magnus 1916, 21.1.2.1326:11–14. Albert made a similar admission regarding the ability to acquire an art: "Quaedam autem in tantum elevantur in hiis potentiis ut artis quamdam habeant imitationem, licet artem non attingant." *Ibid.*, 1328:39–40.

[29] "Quaedam autem animalia videntur aliquid licet parum experimenti participare. Experimentum namque ex multis nascitur memoriis quia eiusdem rei multae memoriae faciunt potentiam et facultatem aliquid experimenti; et nos videmus quod multa animalia praeter hominem aliquid experimentalis habent cognitionis in singularibus." Albertus Magnus 1920, 21.1.2, §11.1327:28–32.

But, of course, Albert went on to say, animals cannot use experience to arrive at a universal and hence they cannot have knowledge in the same sense that humans do.[30]

Among the animals capable of experiential cognition, the highest place belongs to the pygmies. These creatures seem to have something like reason, although they do not in fact possess it.[31] To make his point, Albert first reminded his reader what "reason" means.[32] But, as he then went on to point out, there are two kinds of reason. One kind entails reflection on the content of sense and memory, leading to a perception of experience. The other takes that experience further to create the principles of art and science.[33] The whole light of reason, Albert wrote, is present only in the second kind. The first kind he called the shadow of reason (*umbra rationis*). "By 'shadow' I mean a vague reverberation from the matter of sensibles, not separated from the trappings of matter."[34] He drew no explicit identity here between the shadow of reason and the *æstimativa*, but they both seem to deal with images that, while abstracted from matter, nevertheless retain some association with matter. The shadow of reason allows a creature to acquire these "individualized" universal concepts—the kind that can be used to initiate animal behavior. The light of reason—a human prerogative—allows universals to become the bases of arts and sciences.

Although they possess only the shadow of reason, pygmies resemble humans in many ways. Their upright stance confers upon them, as it does upon humans, a certain amount of spiritual clarity.[35] Pygmies have rounded heads, brains with three ventricles, and immobile ears. Their hands closely resemble human hands. They have a language in which they can discuss particular things.[36] But they lack the ability to elicit universals; their society has no laws. They are clearly higher on the scale of perfection than other animals although the power which so elevates them, which

---

[30] "Sufficienter autem non participant experimento quia non veniunt per experimentum ad universale et artem et rationem, sed tamen secundum aliquid participant experimento, ut iam diximus." *Ibid.*, 1327:35–38.

[31] "…ita quod videtur aliquid habere imitans rationem, sed ratione caret." *Ibid.*, 1328:7–8.

[32] "Ratio enim est vis animae discurrendo per experta ex memoriis accepta, per habitudinem localem aut syllogisticam, universale eliciens et ex illo principia artium et scientiarum per similes habeitudines conferens." *Ibid.*, 1328:8–11.

[33] "Ratio enim duo habet quorum unum est ex reflexione sua ad sensum et memoriam, et ibi est perceptio experimenti. Secundum autem est quod habet secundum quod exaltatur versus intellectum simplicem: et sic est elicitiva universalis quod est principium artis et scientiae." *Ibid.*, 1328:15–22.

[34] "Dico autem umbram idem quod resultationem obscuram a sensibilium materia et appendiciis materia non separatam." *Ibid.*, 1328:24–26.

[35] "Quod autem erigitur semper, facit in eo spiritualium maiorem claritatem." *Ibid.*, 1328:42–43.

[36] "Causatur enim loquela sua ex umbra resultante in occasu rationis." *Ibid.*, 1328:14–17.

he has called the shadow of reason, "is not named by philosophers" and is something added to the *æstimativa*.[37]

And then Albert may have made his greatest concession to the animal mind.

> We must not forget here that what has been received by the *æstimativa* [*æstimatum*] and by sense [*expertum*] refers to the universal in two ways. 1) in a contemplative way, so that, from sensed and remembered things that were received via the senses, the quiddity of things—which is the truth of things—is acquired per se or by means of a common sign, and the pygmy does not have things received or remembered in this way. 2) What is received by sense and remembered exists in another way, so that it bears upon what to seek and what to avoid, and in this way received and remembered things are acquired by the pygmy, and so we said above that the pygmy participates just a bit in experience [*experimento*].[38]

Here Albert admitted that an animal can possess a universal, even if not the kind that is of use to the speculative intellect.

Pygmies thus occupy a place on the scale of perfection between humans and the rest of the animal kingdom. Other apes are incapable of bringing memory to bear on experience, yet apes have what might be called a trans-specific *æstimativa*. Seeing one small ape show to another its mother's breasts, an ape will then, if possible, show to a boy a woman's breasts.[39] No other animal can recognize homologous values in another species. Apes are also the only animal that can be taught by vision and in fact will immediately imitate any human action. Other trainable animals must be trained by sounds.[40]

Proceeding in his treatment of animals lower on the scale of perfection—quadrupeds, birds, aquatic animals, reptiles, insects, worms—Albert traced intelligent behavior to the animals' organs of *æstimativa*. Even lowly snakes are credited with foresight (*prudentia*), shrewdness (*sagacitas*) and cunning (*astutia*), which Albert traced to their "quite clear *æstimativa*."[41] There is no mention of universals or reason here. Perhaps, having traversed the "uncanny valley" of so human-like an animal as

---

[37] "Virtus autem illa animae quam umbram rationis quamdam vocavimus superius, innominata quidem est a philosophis, sed circumloquendo cognoscimus quod haec vis aliquid potentie addit super æstimativam." *Ibid.*, 1329:5–7.

[38] "Est autem hic non praemittendum quod æstimatum et expertum dupliciter referuntur ad universale, uno quidem modo contemplative prout ex expertis et memoratis in sensu acceptis, quidditas rerum quod est rerum veritas accipitur per se vel in signo communi: et hoc modo memoratum et expertum non est in pigmeo. Alio modo inest memoratum et expertum prout in ipso est conferans ad appetitum vel fugam: et hoc modo expertum et memoratum accipiuntur a pigmeo et ideo diximus superius quod experimento parum participat pigmeus." *Ibid*, §14, 12–20.

[39] "et ideo videns parvulum exhibet parvulo ubera, non propria, sed matris quae peperit eum si permittatur: puero enim exhibet ubera feminarum si permittatur: et hoc alia non faciunt animalia." *Ibid.*, §17, 1331:26–29.

[40] "Alia autem bruta-- in visu quidem nichil disciplinale accipiendo, solum auditu aliquid disciplinae percipiunt." *De animalibus*, XXI.1.3. *Ibid.*, 16:1331, §16.

[41] "æstimativam valde lucidam, hoc est lucidi spiritus." *Ibid.*, §42, 1343:1–2. No mention here of Matthew 10:16: "Estote ergo prudentes sicut serpentes, et simplices sicut columbae."

the pygmy, and thus having moved away from the border between human and animal, he may have felt that the border no longer needed defending.

The irony of course is that if Albert had recognized that pygmies were humans, the threat to that border would have been much reduced. But given the history of the centuries to follow, and given the debates of the present day, Albert cannot be faulted for striving to keep that border intact.

Bibliography

Primary Sources

Aelian. 1958–1959. *On the characteristics of animals.* Ed. and trans. A.F. Scholfield, 3 vols. Cambridge, MA: Harvard University Press.

Albertus Magnus. 1890. *De anima.* In *Opera omnia,* ed. Augustus Borgnet, vol. 5. Paris: Vivès.

———. 1896. *Summa de creaturis.* In *Opera omnia,* ed. Augustus Borgnet, vol. 35. Paris: Vivès.

———. 1916. *De animalibus libri XXVI: Books I–XII,* ed. Hermann Stadler. Münster: Aschendorf.

———. 1920. *De animalibus libri XXVI: Books XIII–XXVI,* ed. Hermann Stadler. Münster: Aschendorf.

Aristotle. 1991. *History of animals (books VII – X).* Ed. and trans. D.M. Balme. Cambridge, MA: Harvard University Press.

———. 1975. *On the soul; Parva naturalia; On breath.* Ed. and trans. W.S. Hett. Cambridge, MA: Harvard University Press.

———. 1983. *Parts of animals; Movement of animals; Progression of animals.* Ed. and trans. E.S. Forster. Cambridge, MA: Harvard University Press.

Avicenna. 1950. *Psychologie d'Ibn Sina (Avicenna) d'après son oeuvre As-Sifa'. Éditée et traduite en français par Ján Bakos.* Prague: Éditions de l'Academie Tchécoslovaque des Sciences.

———. 1968. *Avicenna Latinus: Liber de anima seu sextus de naturalibus.* Brill: Ed. and trans. S. van Riet. Leiden.

Bartholomeus Anglicus. 1505. *De proprietatibus rerum.* Strasbourg: G. Husner.

Basil, St.. *Hexaemeron.* https://www.fisheaters.com/hexaemeron7.html.

Blund, John. 1970. Tractatus de anima. Eds. D.A. Callus and R.W. Hunt. London: Oxford University Press.

Gundissalinus, Dominicus. 1940. The treatise *De anima* of Dominicus Gundissalinus, ed. J.T. Muckle. *Mediaeval Studies* 2: 23–103.

Fisher, Jonathan. 1834. *Scripture animals.* Portland: William Hyde.

Physiologus. 1979. Trans. Michael J. Curley. Austin: University of Texas Press.

Pliny. 1983. *Natural history.* Ed. and trans. H. Rackham. Cambridge, MA: Harvard University Press.

White, T.H. 1954. *The bestiary: A book of beasts.* New York: G.P. Putnam's Sons.

Secondary Sources

Brentano, Franz. 1867. *Die Psychologie des Aristoteles, insbesondere seine Lehre vom ΝΟΥΣ ΠΟΙΗΤΙΚΟΣ.* Mainz: Franz Kirchheim.

———. 1977. The psychology of Aristotle: In particular his doctrine of the active intellect. Ed. and trans. Rolf George. Berkeley: University of California Press.

Dierauer, Urs. 1977. *Tier und Mensch in der Denken der Antike*. Amsterdam: B.R. Grüner.

Fortenbaugh, William. 1971. Aristotle: Animals, emotion, and moral virtue. *Arethusa* 4: 137–165.

Hearnshaw, L.S. 1987. *The shaping of modern psychology*. New York: Routledge and Keegan Paul.

Hothersall, David. 1984. *History of psychology*. Philadelphia: Temple University Press.

Modrak, Deborah K.W. 1987. *Aristotle: The power of perception*. Chicago: University of Chicago Press.

Watson, Robert I., Sr. 1978. *The great psychologists*. 4th ed. Philadelphia: Lippincott.

Part II
Aquinas

Chapter 5
"The Essential Differentiae of Things are Unknown to Us": Thomas Aquinas on the Limits of the Knowability of Natural Substances

Fabrizio Amerini

Keywords Thomas Aquinas · Theory of knowledge · Definition · Sense perception · Essentialism · Semantics

Preface Thomas Aquinas is often presented in the literature as a philosopher with a realist and optimistic attitude toward human knowledge. This is not unsurprising. On many occasions, Aquinas confesses to believe that our process of natural knowledge does not falsify reality and that we can arrive at knowing the 'what it is' of external things. In fact, Aquinas is mitigated in his optimism and realism, since, for him, it is not a mystery that both God, at the top, and the essences of natural things, at the bottom, remain hidden from us. We do not have any direct cognitive access to them. God is beyond our possibility of experiencing Him. We can have only an indirect and analogical knowledge of God, moving from His effects in the created world. This means that although we can prove that God exists, we can never know what God is. We discover Him as the uncaused first cause or the necessary being, but we can have a positive knowledge of God through Revelation alone. In the case of the knowledge of natural things, the limit is of a different kind. We can ascertain whether a thing exists and arrive even at defining what a thing is, but we cannot be sure that, through defining that thing, we really have known its essence as it is in itself. This limit is summarized by the dictum that the essential principles or differentiae of things are unknown to us.

These two cognitive limits—one at the top, the other at the bottom—require us to be cautious about Aquinas's epistemic realism, if not about his optimism. These

F. Amerini (✉)
University of Parma, Parma, Italy
e-mail: fabrizio.amerini@unipr.it

© The Author(s), under exclusive license to Springer Nature
Switzerland AG 2023
J. P. Hochschild et al. (eds.), *Metaphysics Through Semantics: The Philosophical Recovery of the Medieval Mind*, International Archives of the History of Ideas Archives internationales d'histoire des idées 242,
https://doi.org/10.1007/978-3-031-15026-5_5

limits are above all a consequence of the fact that Aquinas convincingly endorses Aristotle's theory of knowledge, which means, most importantly, that, for Aquinas, our natural knowledge always starts from the sensory acquaintance with a thing's accidents and only later do we arrive at knowing its essence. Accidents play a role in the knowledge of what a thing is, but, at the same time, they are also an obstacle for any direct intellection of what a thing is. A sensory-rooted account of intellective knowledge such as Aristotle's has indeed two relevant implications for Aquinas. First, Aquinas denies that we can have acts of intellective intuition of external things. Both the singularity and materiality of a thing impedes our intellect from direct contact. As is known, for Aquinas we can have intellective knowledge of an extramental singular *qua* singular only secondarily, by reflecting on the sensory process. Second, Aquinas holds that there is a gap between the senses and the intellect; the senses deal with singulars, while the intellect deals with universals. Accordingly, the process of natural knowledge cannot be described as a case of local motion of one and the same thing that transits from sensation to intellection. In the intellect, a thing is replaced by an intelligible species that has only a relation of representation to the thing.[1] With respect to this bottom limit, one could ask what, for Aquinas, does it mean exactly for the essential principles or differentiae of things to be unknown to us. In this paper, I want to respond to this question by reconsidering the places where Aquinas subscribes to this Aristotelian dictum.

5.1 Accidents Give a Great Contribution to the Knowledge of What a Thing Is

Let me begin with a preliminary point however, viz., the role that, according to Aquinas, accidents play in the knowledge of what a thing is. The celebrated dictum of Aristotle's *De anima* that "accidents give a great contribution to the knowledge of what a thing is"[2] (in Latin: *accidentia magnam partem conferunt ad cognoscendum quod quid est*) recurs at least five times in Aquinas's works. In the *Summa contra Gentiles* one can find a clear formulation of the sense Aquinas gives to such a dictum. Aquinas assumes that our intellect is naturally predisposed to know what a thing is. The knowledge of what a thing is significant especially when we attempt to demonstrate the inherence of proper accidents (*propria*) in a substantial subject: in that case, in fact, we take the knowledge of what a thing is as the middle term of a syllogism concluding to the inherence of such accidents in the subject. But in the

---

[1] The representationalist interpretation of Aquinas's theory of intellective knowledge is a highly debated issue. For arguments in favour, see, e.g., Panaccio 2001; for arguments against, see Perler 2000; Baltuta 2013. On Aquinas's representationalism, see also Brower and Brower-Toland 2008, and Klima 2011. Discussions have especially concerned the nature of intelligible species and the evolution of Aquinas's position on it. For a discussion of this notion and further bibliographical references, see Spruit 1994–1995; D'Onofrio 2008; Scarpelli Cory 2020.

[2] See *De anima*, I, 1, 402b16–403a2.

case of the process of natural knowledge acquisition, the direction of fit is reversed and we arrive at knowing the substance of a thing through knowing its accidents. This happens because our natural knowledge always starts from the senses and these acquaint us with a thing's accidents. Aquinas, however, expresses his confidence that in the end we can reach the knowledge of the substance of the thing. For everything that cannot be known through the knowledge of its substance simply remains unknown (*ignotum*) to our intellect.[3] In this process, Aquinas features accidents as signs that facilitate the knowledge of the thing in which they inhere insofar as they are supposed to depend on the essence of that thing. In his early *Commentary on the Sentences*, Aquinas clarified this point with an example. The mixture of a different flour with that of wheat in the host does not change the substance of the host, if the accidents one perceives are still those of the wheat host.[4] The idea that accidents are reliable signs of a thing's substance one is experiencing seems unproblematic. It entails that in an ordinary process of natural knowledge, an inquiry into a thing's accidents may help us to discover the properties that are essential to that thing.

The passage from a thing's accidents to its substance is far from being obvious, however. In the *Quaestiones de veritate*, Aquinas himself recognizes that an external thing produces the knowledge of it in us through the features of it that appear externally (*per ea quae de ipsa exterius apparent*). Again, Aquinas says that this happens because our natural knowledge starts from the senses and these acquaint us with a thing's accidents. But when the accidents refer us to a thing that is not what naturally lies under those accidents, the thing may be called 'false'.[5] Here Aquinas realizes that the Aristotelian dictum needs a qualification. Consider the example given by Aquinas. If there is a thing that has all the accidents of gold but it is not gold, I may say that it is a false gold. But one could ask: how can I know that it is not gold but, for example, orichalcum, if it has all the accidents of gold? At first, one could answer that the false gold directly produces in me the knowledge of the false gold. Aquinas, however, excludes that this is the case. He does not distinguish indeed between the appearances of the gold and those of the orichalcum. They manifest themselves in the same way. Quoting Aristotle's *Metaphysics*, in the *Quaestiones de veritate* Aquinas only notes that false things are either those things that are seen as they are not (*qualia non sunt*) or those things that simply are not (*quae non sunt*). But a thing is false not because it produces a false apprehension, he says, but because it induces false inferences from the features of it that appear externally. In other words, I realize that the thing in front of me is false gold not because it exhibits some features that conflict with the features typical of gold, but because it exhibits the very same features of gold although the thing behind such features is not gold. The reason that I can say that I am not seeing true gold is that I can make

---

[3] See Aquinas 1926, 155 (*Summa contra gentiles*, III, c. 56) [Hereafter referred to as *SCG*.]

[4] See *Scriptum super libros Sententiarum*, I, d. 44, q. 11, a. 2, a. 2, q.la 2. [Hereafter referred to as *Sent*.] For a chronology of Aquinas's life and works, see Porro 2016.

[5] See Aquinas 1970a, 31, 102–111 (*Quaestiones de veritate*, q. 1, a. 10) [Hereafter referred to as *Q. de ver.*]

a judgment concerning the thing I am seeing and this judgment leads me to the conclusion that it is not gold. Arguably, my act of judgment is the result of an act of comparison of my perceptions with the external thing.[6]

One could feel unsatisfied yet with Aquinas's answer. Since my intellective knowledge is based on the sense perception of a thing's accidents, as Aquinas established in the *Sentences* commentary, there is no way of knowing that what I am seeing is not gold if I am perceiving it as gold. Aquinas's answer presupposes in fact two things: first, that I am able to know what a thing is without transiting through the knowledge of its accidents and second, that I am able to perform some collative act through which I can compare my perceptions with the thing. If this were the sense of Aquinas's answer, I would be in such a situation that I always know if the thing I am seeing is or is not a true gold; no perceptual deception could ever occur.

I do not think, though, that this is what Aquinas meant. Probably, Aquinas was only conjecturing that when I am in doubt about the thing I am seeing, viz., if it is or is not gold, in order to dissolve the doubt I can search for other empirical proofs besides visual perceptions. Aquinas does not say much about this, but according to what he says in a couple of texts from the *Sentences* commentary and the *Summa theologiae*, he could agree that I can verify the nature of the thing I am seeing by considering other conditions. For example, I could wet the apparent gold and verify if it produces rust or I could check if it induces nausea, like orichalcum but not gold does.[7] So, even if there is no apparent falsity in what I am seeing, nonetheless I can manage things in a way that I can discover the potential falsity of what I am seeing.

Some years later, in the *Commentary on the De anima*, I, c. 1, Aquinas seems to be less optimistic about our capacity of knowing the essences of natural things. He acknowledges that if we did know and define correctly the essential principles of a thing, our definition would do without referring to accidents. But since the essential principles are unknown to us, we need to use accidental differentiae in the place of the essential ones. It is only through the accidental differentiae that we can obtain the knowledge of the essential principles of a thing.[8] Two things may be noted here. First, according to Aquinas's commentary, in that place of the *De anima* Aristotle is underscoring a difficulty: it is not easy to appreciate the contribution given by the accidents to the knowledge of a thing's essence, since the definitional practice involves a certain circularity. In fact, we cannot know what the accidents of a thing are if not by knowing what a thing is; but on the other hand, when the accidents are somehow pre-known, they can give a contribution to knowing what a thing is.

---

[6] See Aquinas 1970a, 31, 111–127. In the *Commentary on the Sentences* Aquinas notes that I can have a true or a false apprehension of a thing, and that both depend on what externally appears of that thing. In both cases, I make inferences about the thing moving from those appearances. See *Sent.*, I, d. 19, q. 5, a. 1. On this, see also *Expositio libri Peryermenias*, I, c. 3.

[7] On orichalcum's properties of producing rust and inducing nausea, and hence on the prohibition of making the Eucharistic chalice out of orichalcum, see *Sent.*, IV, d. 13, q. 1, a. 2, q.la 5, ad 4, and *Summa theologiae*, III, q. 83, a. 3, ad 6. [Hereafter referred to as *ST*]

[8] See Aquinas 1984, 7, 247–273 (*Sentencia libri De anima*, I. c. 1). [Hereafter referred to as *Sent. De an.*]

Aquinas's reconstruction of the difficulty that Aristotle seems to underscore at the end of *De anima*, I, c. 1, reveals that knowing a thing's substance is necessary for knowing 'more easily' (*facilius*) the thing's accidents, but the knowledge of a thing's accidents, in turn, facilitates the knowledge of a thing's substance.

Aquinas tries to avoid such an apparent circularity by distinguishing two perspectives. The knowledge of a thing's substance precedes the knowledge of a thing's accidents in the order of definitions. As Aquinas will explain in the *Commentary on the Metaphysics*, VII, c. 1, we can define the substance of a thing without mentioning the accidents, but we cannot define the accidents of a thing without mentioning the substance.[9] But according to the temporal order of natural knowledge acquisition, the knowledge of a thing's accidents precedes the knowledge of a thing's substance. This means that when we form a complete definition of a thing, we also obtain the knowledge of the accidents of that thing, but we arrive at defining a thing always by transiting through the knowledge of its accidents. A result of this apparent circularity is that, since I know a thing's substance only through its accidents, there seems to be no way of escaping the conclusion that when I am seeing the accidents of the gold, I know that the thing in front of me is a piece of gold. Aquinas, however, does not explain how the inference from the perception of the accidents of gold to the knowledge that it is not gold obtains. Referring to other empirical proofs beyond visual perceptions may thus be necessary.

The second thing to be noted about the text from the *Commentary on the De anima* is that Aquinas links the Aristotelian dictum to a second Aristotelian dictum, which we shall discuss in the next section: the essential principles or differentiae of a thing are unknown to us (*essentiales differentiae sunt incognitae*).[10] This linking permits us to put Aquinas's position in the right perspective. In our definitions of things, we make use of accidental differentiae and as accurate as our definitional practice may be, we never go beyond the plane of the accidentality of things, so to speak. This has repercussions on the process of intellective knowledge. How can we be sure that through the accidental differentiae we arrive at picking out those essential to the thing?

5.2 The Essential Differentiae are Unknown to Us

Aquinas does not give an explicit answer to the above question. Nonetheless, he gives us some indications for responding. Clearly, when Aquinas quotes this dictum, he has in mind something more complex than the case of the simple apprehension of a false thing, such as false gold or orichalcum. It is not simply a question of seeing a thing that seems to be gold but is not gold, but of selecting opportunely the

---

[9] See Aquinas 1964, 317, n. 1257–1259 (*Expositio in XII libros Metaphysicorum Aristotelis*, VII, lec. 1) [Hereafter referred to as *Exp. Met.*]

[10] On this principle, see Reynolds 2001; Klima 2002; Pasnau 2007. On the issue of the knowability of substances in the age of Aquinas, see also Noone 2011.

properties that permit a definition of gold and hence verifying whether the thing in front of me is or is not gold. As has been said, for deciding whether the thing I am seeing is or is not gold, I need to consider not only visual perceptions but also other empirical proofs. In order to reconstruct Aquinas's response to the above question, I shall examine, first, Aquinas's formulations of the dictum that the essential principles or differentiae of things are unknown to us; then, I shall try to extrapolate from these formulations Aquinas's answer.

As René-Antoine Gauthier noted, Aquinas refers the dictum that the essential principles or differentiae of things are unknown to us sometimes to Book VII, and other times to Book VIII of Aristotle's *Metaphysics*. In fact, he probably borrowed it from Averroes's *Commentary on the Metaphysics*.[11] The dictum includes two claims.

(i) First, Aquinas says that the essential principles or differentiae of things are unknown to us (*non notae, incognitae, ignotae*) since they are occulted (*propter occultationem*) or hidden (*propter latentiam*).[12]

(ii) Second, he also says that although the essential principles or differentiae cannot be known in themselves (*per se*),[13] they can be known by means of some accidental differentiae (*per aliqua accidentia*) which are as their signs (*per signa*).[14]

These claims are understandable when they are set in the context in which this dictum occurs, which is that of the real definition of a thing.[15] Nonetheless, they seem to introduce a certain conflict: on the one hand, Aquinas says that the essential principles or differentiae of things are unknown to us since we never know them as they are in themselves; but on the other hand, Aquinas says that we can know them in some way, i.e., by means of the accidents that make them manifest.

---

[11] See Averroes 1562, 212vbM–213raA (*Commentarium in XIIII libros Metaphysicorum Aristotelis*, VIII, t.c. 5). On this, see Aquinas 1989, 222, ad lin. 122 (*Expositio libri Posteriorum*, II, c. 13). [Hereafter cited as *Exp. Post.*] See there for a complete list of the texts where this dictum recurs.

[12] See, e.g., Aquinas 1976, 379, 72–84 (*De ente et essentia*, c. 5). See also *Sent.*, II, d. 3, q. 1, a. 6; II, d. 35, q. 1, a. 2, ad 3; IV, d. 14, q. 1, a. 1, a.la 6, ad 1; IV, d. 44, q. 2, a. 1, q.la 1, ad 1; *Q. de ver.*, q. 4, a. 1, ad 8; *Quaestiones de potentia*, q. 9, a. 2, ad 5. [Hereafter referred to as *Q. de pot.*] In *ST*, I, q. 29, a. 1, ad 3, Aquinas appears to distinguish two cases. He says that the essential principles are unknown to us or even are unnamed ("substantiales differentiae non sunt nobis notae, vel etiam nominatae non sunt"). It is not clear if the text of the *Summa* witnesses a supplementary note introducing a disjunction of cases or simply, as is more probable, an overlap between not knowing and not naming the essential differentiae (in this respect, note that one ms., the Vatic. Ottob. 206, only has "vel etiam nominatae"). In the *Q. de pot.*, q. 9, a. 2, ad 5, the two cases are posed in coordination ("ignotae [...] et innominatae").

[13] See, e.g., *ST*, I, q. 77, a. 1, ad 7; *Quaestio de spiritualibus creaturis*, a. 11, ad 3. [Hereafter referred to as *Q. de spir. Creat.*]

[14] See, e.g., Aquinas 1989, 222, 118–122 (*Exp. Post.*, II, c. 13). See also *Exp. Met.*, VII, lec. 12.

[15] In the wake of Aristotle, Aquinas distinguishes between nominal and real definitions (approximately, between definitions expressing what nouns signify and definitions expressing what things are). I do not linger on such a distinction here. For my argument, the only important thing is that in the case of the Aristotelian dictum only real definitions are concerned. For more on such a distinction, see Aquinas's *Commentary on the Posterior Analytics*. See Aquinas 1970b.

In some texts, Aquinas gives some clues for a possible way out, by adding two further details.

(iii) In the *Commentary on the Posterior Analytics*, he explains that it is not necessary to select the accidental differentiae among the accidents that are proper
(*propria*) to the thing. As has been said, the reason is that through the definition
of a thing, one can prove the inherence of such accidents in a substantial subject. So the species, which is the object of our definition, must be made known
through accidents that have an extension larger than that of the species. This
claim in part rectifies what Aquinas said in the *De ente et essentia*.[16] In chapter
5 of his early treatise, Aquinas made no distinction between different kinds of
accidents. There, he only noted that natural substances and supernatural substances have in common that the essential principles or differentiae are
unknown and are knowable only by means of a thing's accidents. There is
however a difference: in the case of natural substances, we can identify the
proper accidents, while in the case of supernatural substances, not even these
latter are knowable. Regardless of how one is disposed to explain these oscil-
lations in Aquinas's texts, it is certain that in the case of natural substances we
know the essential differentiae by means of the accidental differentiae. These
must not be the proper accidents if we are going to demonstrate the inherence
of these accidents in a substantial subject. By contrast, if we search for the
accidents that better manifest the essential differentiae of a thing, then the
proper accidents are the most suitable candidates.

(iv) A second point is stated in the *De ente et essentia* (c. 5) and clarified in the
Commentary on the Sentences (I, d. 44, q. 2, a. 1, a.la 1, ad 1). Aquinas explains
that the accidental differentiae are linked to the essential differentiae as an
effect to its cause. The *causality relation* holding between the accidental differentiae that enter into the definition of natural substances and the essential
differentiae sheds further light on point (ii) above: the causal relationship that
is supposed to hold between a thing's accidents and a thing's essence allows
inferring the latter from the former.[17] Earlier in the *Sentences* commentary, i.e.,
commenting on Book II, d. 3, q. 1, a. 6, Aquinas stated that different accidental
properties can be associated with the essential principles of a natural thing, but
that it is better to choose the properties that are *closer* to the essential principles.[18] This is an important claim, although Aquinas does not dwell on explaining how to establish if a property P is closer than a property Q to the essence
of a thing. Presumably, the degree of closeness is given by the position a property has in the Porphyrian tree: a generic property is farther from the essence

---

[16] See *De ente et essentia*, c. 5 (see above, note 12). See also *Q. de spir. creat.*, a. 11, ad 3.

[17] See *Sent.*, IV, d. 44, q. 2, a. 1, q.la 1, ad 1.

[18] See Aquinas 1929, 104 (*Sent.*, II, d. 3, q. 1, a. 6): "Unde possunt plures differentiae pro specificis
assignari, secundum plures proprietates rerum differentium specie, ex essentialibus differentiis
causatas; quarum tamen istae melius assignantur quae priores sunt, quasi essentialibus differentiis
propinquiores."

than a specific property. But one cannot exclude that also considerations concerning the explanatory power of properties are in play in Aquinas's statement. Property P could be closer to the essence than property Q because the fact that P explains the fact that Q and not vice versa. If this is what Aquinas had in mind, he could accept that our selection of the accidental differentiae that, in a definition, play the role of essential differentiae can be revised over time. This implication may be only conjectured, however, since Aquinas does not elaborate on it.

Aquinas highlights this causal aspect on many occasions, but especially when he explains Anselm's claim that philosophers mention 'being mortal' in the definition of man since they did not believe that a man could be immortal. Aquinas proposes this reading of Anselm, but he notes that Anselm's claim could also be explained in the light of the Aristotelian dictum that the essential principles or differentiae are unknown to us. Being mortal is an accidental differentia that is taken in the place of the essential differentia that causes it. Specifically, the accidental differentia of being mortal is caused by the composition of contrary properties of human beings, which is the cause of mortality according to the natural course of events, and it is this composition that belongs to human beings' essence.[19] The discussion of Anselm's claim gives the occasion to Aquinas to add a further detail to the picture we are reconstructing:

(v) The use of accidental differentiae instead of essential differentiae obtains *sometimes* (*aliquando*, *interdum*) or *frequently* (*frequenter*, *multoties*).[20]

It is not clear why Aquinas says this. There are two possible interpretations of this claim.

(1) The first is that not all the essential differentiae of natural things are unfamiliar to us. In the *De ente et essentia* (c. 5) and in the *Commentary on the De anima* (I, c. 1) Aquinas says that all the essential differentiae are unknown,[21] but in other texts, more usually, he says that since the essential differentiae are unknown, we sometimes use accidental differentiae in the place of the essential ones. If one follows what Aquinas says in the *De ente et essentia* and in the *Commentary on the De anima*, one would expect that we *always* use accidental differentiae in the place of the essential ones. But this does not seem to be what Aquinas had in mind, since there are texts such as the *Quaestiones de potentia* (q. 9, a. 2, ad 5) in which he says that the essential differentiae are unfamiliar frequently but not always, so that only frequently we use accidental differentiae in the place of the essential ones. In any case, whether we generalize over all the essential differentiae or limit to some of them, this first interpretation suggests

---

[19] See, e.g., *Sent.*, IV, d. 44, q. 2, a. 1, q.la 1, ad 1.
[20] See, e.g., *Sent.*, I, d. 25, q. 1, a. 1, ad 8; III, d. 26, q. 1, a. 1, ad 3; IV, d. 27, q. 1, a. 1, q.la 2, ad 2; *ST*, I-II, q. 49, a. 2, ad 3; *Q. de pot.*, q. 9, a. 2, ad 5; *Expositio in librum De generatione*, I, lec. 8.
[21] See *De ente et essentia*, c. 5 (see above, note 13); *Sent. De an.*, I, c. 1 (see above, note 9).

that in some cases we use accidental differentiae in the place of the essential ones, while in other cases we do not. Aquinas's example of the stone, which we shall consider in the next section, could teach that in the case of unanimated things we do not know which their essential principles are, while in the case of animated things we do know. However, this does not seem the right understanding because Aquinas discusses the replacement of essential differentiae with the accidental ones in the case of man too.

Nevertheless, if one did understand Aquinas's claim according to the criterion Aquinas indicates for replacing, in a real definition, the essential differentiae with the accidental ones (i.e., the closeness of the accidents to the essence), one could continue to distinguish the case of stone from that of man. One could think that while we arrive at knowing the accidental differentiae of a human being that are closer to the essence, we cannot determine this in the case of a stone.[22] Aquinas's discussion of the example associated with the name of Anselm could support this interpretation. Philosophers, for example, believe that 'being mortal' must be included in the definition of human beings, since all human beings and they alone have the property of being mortal. This property looks therefore essential, while in other cases we may be in doubt if a given property is essential or not. It is not certain, though, that this is the right understanding of the first interpretation, because Aquinas at times states the unknowability of all the essential differentiae. Thus, it is doubtful that Aquinas wanted to differentiate the case of unanimated things from that of animated things.

(2) We can therefore turn to the second interpretation of the point (v) above, namely that the use of accidental differentiae in the place of the essential ones obtains *sometimes* or *frequently*. Here the partition of cases does not concern substances, but the opposition between substances and accidents. Aquinas could think that while in the case of accidents, we can grasp directly their essences and define them in themselves, this does not happen in the case of substances. The reason is that accidents veil the substance, while accidents are not veiled by anything else, so they can be known in what they are.[23] This interpretation is in general plausible, but I am not sure that it is the right interpretation of the claim that the essential principles or differentiae of things are unknown to us sometimes or frequently. Aquinas draws the conclusion that we sometimes or frequently use accidental differentiae in the place of the essential ones from the premise that *all* essential differentiae are unknown to us. This leads me to think that Aquinas, rather, wanted to distinguish the case of natural substances, in which we can however make inferences from the apparent accidents to the hid-

---

[22] Aquinas seems to suggest this when he explains that Aristotle indicated 'cold' and 'warm', which are accidental differentiae, as the differentiae in the definition of earth and fire, respectively, because we do not know their essential differentiae. See, e.g., *Expositio in librum primum De generatione et corruptione Aristotelis*, lec. 8. Also *ST*, I, q. 29, a. 1, ad 3.

[23] See, e.g., *ST*, I, q. 13, a. 8. For this interpretation, see Pasnau 2002, 143ff.; also Pasnau 2007.

den essences, from that of supernatural substances, in which no such inferences are possible, as Aquinas already clarified in *De ente et essentia*, c. 5.[24]

By the way, we may leave undecided the question of which interpretation of point (v) is the right one. My point is that our choice does not change the fact that, for Aquinas, the differentiae that are taken as essential and are mentioned in the real definition of a thing are in fact nothing other than accidental differentiae. In the *Quaestio de spiritualibus creaturis*, Aquinas offers some evidence for this point. There, he recalls the dictum that the essential principles are unknown to us, so that we are compelled to use accidental differentiae in the place of those essential. He proposes two readings of this dictum when applied to the case of human beings. The first is that we are accustomed to use differentiae such as 'being bipedal' (*bipes*) or 'able to walk' (*gressibile*) instead of the essential differentiae such as 'being sensible' or 'being rational'. But also a second reading is possible. Even 'being sensible' or 'being rational' are accidental differentiae, which we take in the place of those essential, which are unknown. In fact, they are not derived from the senses and the reason understood as the powers of the human soul, but from the sensible soul and rational soul themselves.[25] As Aquinas clarified in the *Quaestiones de veritate*, the powers of the soul flow from the essence of the soul, but we can come to the latter only from the former.[26] If what Aquinas had in mind was precisely to create a rift between what externally appears of a thing and what is internally hidden, one may conclude that for him our knowledge of natural things is always and only *phenomenal*. We generalize from accidental features but the causal principle of such features as it is in itself remains inaccessible. We reproduce this cognitive mechanism in our real definitions of things: 'being sensible' and 'being rational' are assumed as essential differentiae, but in fact they are derived from sensibility and rationality, which are the principles of the accidental differentiae with which we are acquainted, and such principles remain unknown to us.[27]

5.3   We Impose Names on Things Moving
   from Their Accidents

The procedure for selecting accidental differentiae envisaged by Aquinas is also associated with the process of naming natural things and this further aspect confirms the interpretation of the second claim we have given in the previous section. On occasion Aquinas explains the procedure for naming things by referring to the fancy etymologies of Isidore of Seville. The case is well-known. His preferred example is that of 'stone' (*lapis*). This word has been imposed on the basis of the

---

[24] On this, see Wippel 2000, 511, n. 39; 542.

[25] See *Q. de spir. creat.*, a. 11, ad 3.

[26] See *Q. de ver.*, q. 10, a. 1, ad 6; also *ST*, I, q. 77, a. 1, ad 7; *Quaestiones de anima*, q. 12, ad 8.

[27] See Aquinas 1976, 374, 10–13 (*De ente et essentia*, c. 3).

property of hurting the foot. This etymology becomes evident in Latin where the word '*lapis*' is associated with the expression '*laedere pedem*'. Clearly, not all stones hurt the foot and not only stones do that. But this is unimportant. What should be retained is that the property of 'hurting the foot' plays the role of a placeholder for a specific class of things, viz., that of stones. We impose the name 'stone' from the property of hurting the foot, but we impose it with the purpose of naming a specific class of things. Aquinas expresses this point by stating that that from which a name has been imposed to signify does not coincide with that which a name signifies. In the case of 'stone', the property of hurting the foot is not what the name signifies, but only the occasion that led us to impose a name to signify a thing that has, among others, that property.[28] Thus, the reference of the name 'stone' is fixed with the help of some definite description, something like 'this thing and all the similar things that can hurt the foot'. The name 'stone' signifies a thing of a certain nature which happens to have the property of hurting the foot, but we do not know yet which are the similarity-properties that permit grouping those things together and naming them stones. The process of naming mirrors the process of understanding, so since we cognize things through accidents, we have to name them through accidents.[29]

What results from such a conception? What has been at times considered in the literature as a 'negative' side of Thomas Aquinas's philosophy, viz., the unknowability of things' essences,[30] reveals instead the positive empiricism that characterizes Aquinas's philosophy of knowledge. The accusation of promoting a 'magical' or 'naïve' realism is groundless in his case, it would seem.[31] True, Aquinas often says that our real definitions express the essences of things, that they are the formulas of essence, and this is a way of speaking that could be criticized as imprecise, as will be done by John Duns Scotus.[32] One should more correctly say that our real definitions express the concepts of things' essences and not the essences on their own. But this criticism looks ungenerous given that Aquinas denies that we can have any direct access to the essences of things in themselves. Our knowledge is phenomenal, as was said, although our intellect is made in such a way that it can make true inferences about the essences of things. In accord with its etymology, our intellect is naturally predisposed to 'read into' the things,[33] to go beyond the phenomenal appearances and to grasp the principle that is causally responsible for all the accidental features of the thing with which we are acquainted, from the closer to the farther.

---

[28] See, e.g., *Q. de ver.*, q. 4, a. 1, ad 8.

[29] For an introduction to Aquinas's theory of signification, see Buersmeyer 1987; Ashworth 1991; also Pini 1999. For an assessment of the role played by semantics in Aquinas's metaphysics, see Klima 1996.

[30] See, e.g., Pieper 1953.

[31] On this, see also Haldane 1988.

[32] On Scotus's criticism of Aquinas's doctrine of essence, see Pini 2003.

[33] For the etymology of the word 'intellect' (*intellectus*), see, e.g., *Q. de ver.*, q. 1, a. 12; *ST*, II–II, q. 8, a. 1.

This distinction between the thing as it is supposed to be in itself and the thing as we know and name it gives us an argument for understanding why the alternative between representationalism and direct realism concerning Aquinas's theory of intellective knowledge is incapable of reaching the core of his doctrine. Essences in themselves are unknown to us. We can say how they are only through defining them, moving from their accidents; this entails that, in a way, essences can exist with respect to us only at the end of our definitional practice. Thus, if, on the one hand, it is understandable that Aquinas says that real definitions express the essences of things since we propose to define things and not concepts, on the other hand, it is also clear that we can define things only to the extent to which they are known. When, in his *Commentary on the Metaphysics*, Book V, Aquinas finds Aristotle exclaiming about the word 'limit' that "it also means the reason for which something is done; and the substance or essence of each. For this is the limit or terminus of knowledge; and if of knowledge, also of the thing" ("*et substantia cuiuslibet, et quod quid erat esse cuique. Cognitionis enim hic terminus: sed si cognitionis, et rei*"),[34] he glosses that the substance of a thing, which is both the essence of a thing and the definition expressing the 'what it is' of the thing, is the limit of knowledge. Our knowledge starts from certain external signs of the thing, from which we move to the knowledge of the definition of the thing. When we obtain this, we obtain the perfect knowledge of the thing. This is one possible understanding of Aristotle's claim that the definition is the limit of knowledge. Aquinas also proposes a second understanding. The definition can be called the limit of knowledge because under it is contained all that which is needed to know the thing. In fact, if one differentia were changed, added or subtracted, the definition would not remain the same and consequently neither would our knowledge of the thing. In any case, if the definition is the limit of the knowledge of the thing, it is necessary that it is also the limit of the thing itself, because knowledge is the outcome of the assimilation of the knower to the thing that is known.[35]

Aquinas's gloss is significant. It reveals how important is the definitional practice for him and consequently the active role the intellect plays in bringing to light, through definitions, the essences of things. The two limits mentioned by Aristotle – viz., that of the knowledge and that of the thing – entail that we cannot know a thing except by the procedure of defining what a thing is. This implies that we could not even say that the essence of a thing is unknown to us, since we would need to know the essence in order to say that we do not know it. This paradoxical implication is not underscored by Aquinas but it may be inferred by the assumption that our natural knowledge obtains only when there is complete assimilation of the knower to the thing known. By contrast, this paradoxical implication could be what led Aquinas to equate the essence of a thing and the definition of the essence. A thing's essence may be known only as a defined essence and there is no way of knowing that what

---

[34] See Aquinas 1964, 273, n. 504 (*Exp. Met.*, V, lec. 19), for the Latin texts. English translation is from Aquinas 1961, 338.

[35] See Aquinas 1964, 274, n. 1048 (*Exp. Met.*, V, lec. 19); Aquinas 1961, 339.

we are defining is not the essence of the thing defined. In the end, definitions play, so to speak, a sort of constructional role with respect to things' essences.[36]

5.4 Conclusion: About the Skepticism of Aquinas

Should Aquinas's affirmation that the essential principles or differentiae of things are unknown to us be understood as a skeptical claim? In one respect, yes.[37] It is known that the distinction between things in themselves and things *qua* known traces back to at least Sextus Empiricus and it is one of the principal devices to make skepticism viable. The affirmation that things in themselves are unknown to us might be read as raising the white flag on the possibility for us to know things in what they are. But it might be read also in a more nuanced manner, i.e., as an exhortation to avoid any paradoxical inquiry. Aquinas seems to believe that we can arrive at the things' essences through our sensory and intellective process. Knowledge does not falsify reality, and it is so because the things with which our mind enters into contact are, at the end of the process, internal to our acts of knowledge. This makes understandable Aquinas's conviction that our mental representation of a thing's essence is the essence itself to a certain degree.[38] Clearly, it is not the essence that the thing has on its own; but we may only suppose that it is so since we cannot know what the essence is in itself; the defined essence is the only essence we can know. For this reason, *pace* Scotus, it could be not imprecise to say that when we define what a thing is, we are expressing its essence.

Bibliography

Amerini, Fabrizio. 2004. Thomas Aquinas, Alexander of Alexandria, and Paul of Venice on the nature of essence. *Documenti e studi sulla tradizione filosofica medievale* 15: 541–589.
Aquinas, Thomas. 1926. *Summa contra Gentiles*. In Sancti Thomae Aquinatis *Opera omnia*, t. XIV. Rome: Typis Riccardi Garroni.
———. 1929. In *Scriptum super libros Sententiarum*, ed. Pierre Mandonnet, 2 vols ed. Paris: Lethielleux.
———. 1961. *Commentary on the metaphysics*. Trans. J.P. Rowan. Chicago: Henry Regnery Company.
———. 1964. In *Expositio in XII libros Metaphysicorum Aristotelis*, ed. Raymundus Spiazzi. Turin/Rome, Marietti.
———. 1970a. Quaestiones de veritate, ed. Antoine Dondaine. In Sancti Thomae de Aquino *Opera omnia*, t. XXII/I-2. Rome: Ad Sanctae Sabinae.

---

[36] For further details on Aquinas's account of definition, see Galluzzo 2001.

[37] For a recent assessment of Aquinas's skepticism, see Klima 2009.

[38] Aquinas equates intelligible species and essence in *Quodlibet* VIII, q. 2, a. 2. This equation has been greatly discussed in the literature. It is not possible to dwell on this aspect here. For details, see Pini 2004. On the topic, see also Galluzzo 2004; Amerini 2004.

————. 1970b. *Commentary on the posterior analytics of* Aristotle. Trans. F.R. Larcher. Albany: Magi Books, Inc.

————. 1976. De ente et essentia, ed. Hyacinthe-François Dondaine. In Sancti Thomae de Aquino *Opera omnia*, t. XLIII. Rome: Editori di San Tommaso.

————. 1984. Sentencia libri De anima, ed. René-Antoine Gauthier. In Sancti Thomae de Aquino *Opera omnia*, t. XLV/1. Rome/Paris: Commissio Leonina/J. Vrin.

————. 1989. Expositio libri Posteriorum, ed. René-Antoine Gauthier. In Sancti Thomae de Aquino *Opera omnia*, t. I 2. Rome/Paris: Commissio Leonina/J. Vrin.

Ashworth, E. Jennifer. 1991. Signification and modes of signifying in thirteenth-century logic: A preface to Aquinas on analogy. *Medieval Philosophy and Theology* 1: 39–67.

Averroes. 1562. Commentarium in Libros Metaphysicorum. Venice: apud Iunctas, t. VIII.

Baltuta, Elena. 2013. Aquinas on intellectual cognition: The case of intelligible species. *Philosophia* 41 (3): 589–602.

Brower, Jeffrey E., and Susan Brower–Toland. 2008. Aquinas on mental representation: Concepts and intentionality. *Philosophical Review* 117 (2): 193–243.

Buersmeyer, Keith. 1987. Aquinas on the 'modi significandi'. *The Modern Schoolman* 64 (2): 73–95.

D'Onofrio, Sandro R. 2008. *Aquinas as representationalist: The ontology of the species intelligibilis*. Ph.D. Dissertation, State University of New York at Buffalo.

Galluzzo, Gabriele. 2001. Il problema dell'oggetto della definizione nel commento di Tommaso d'Aquino a 'Metafisica' Z 10–11. *Documenti e studi sulla tradizione filosofica medievale* 12: 417–465.

————. 2004. Aquinas on common nature and universals. *Recherches de théologie et philosophie médiévales* 71 (3): 131–171.

Haldane, John. 1988. San Tommaso e Putnam: realismo ontologico e realismo epistemologico. *Intersezioni* 8: 171–188.

Kenny, Anthony. 1993. *Aquinas on mind*. London/New York: Routledge.

Klima, Gyula. 1996. The semantic principles underlying saint Thomas Aquinas's metaphysics of being. *Medieval Philosophy and Theology* 5: 87–141.

————. 2002. Contemporary 'essentialism' vs. Aristotelian essentialism. In *Mind, metaphysics, and value in the Thomistic and analytical traditions*, ed. John Haldane, 175–194. Notre Dame: University of Notre Dame Press.

————. 2009. The anti-skepticism of John Buridan and Thomas Aquinas: Putting skeptics in their place versus stopping them in their tracks. In *Rethinking the history of skepticism: The missing medieval background*, ed. Henrik Lagerlund, 145–170. Leiden/Boston: Brill.

————. 2011. Intentional transfer in Averroes, indifference of nature in Avicenna, and the representationalism of Aquinas. In *Universal representation, and the ontology of individuation*, Proceedings of the Society for Medieval Logic and Metaphysics Volume 5, ed. Alexander W. Hall and Gyula Klima, 45–52. Newcastle upon Tyne: Cambridge Scholars Publishing.

Kretzmann, Norman J. 1993. Aquinas's philosophy of mind. *Philosophical Topics* 20 (2): 85–90.

MacDonald, Scott. 1993. Theory of knowledge. In *The Cambridge companion to Aquinas*, ed. Norman J. Kretzmann and Eleonore Stump, 160–195. Cambridge: Cambridge University Press.

Noone, Timothy B. 2011. The problem of the knowability of substance: The discussion from Eustachius of Arras to Vital du Four. In *Philosophy and theology in the middle ages: A tribute to Stephen F. Brown*, ed. Kent Emery, Russell L. Friedman, and Andreas Speer, 63–90. Leiden/Boston: Brill.

Panaccio, Claude. 2001. Aquinas on intellectual representation. In *Ancient and medieval theories of intentionality*, ed. Dominik Perler, 185–201. Leiden: Brill.

Pasnau, Robert. 1997. *Theories of cognition in the later middle ages*. Cambridge: Cambridge University Press.

————. 2002. *Thomas Aquinas on human nature. A philosophical study of Summa theologiae 1a 75–89*. Cambridge: Cambridge University Press.

———. 2007. Abstract truth in Thomas Aquinas. In *Representation and objects of thought in medieval philosophy*, ed. Henrik Lagerlund, 33–63. Aldershot: Ashgate.

Perler, Dominik. 2000. Essentialism and direct realism: Some late medieval perspectives. *Topoi* 19: 111–122.

Pickavé, Martin. 2012. Human knowledge. In *The Oxford handbook of Aquinas*, ed. Brian Davies and Eleonore Stump, 311–325. Oxford: Oxford University Press.

Pieper, Josef. 1953. On the 'negative' element in the philosophy of Thomas Aquinas. Trans. Fred Weick. *CrossCurrents* 4 (1): 46–56.

Pini, Giorgio. 1999. Species, concept, and thing: Theories of signification in the second half of the thirteenth century. *Medieval Philosophy and Theology* 8: 21–52.

———. 2003. Scotus's essentialism: A critique of Thomas Aquinas's doctrine of essence in the 'Questions on the metaphysics'. *Documenti e studi sulla tradizione filosofica medievale* 14: 227–262.

———. 2004. Absoluta consideratio naturae: Tommaso d'Aquino e la dottrina avicenniana dell'essenza. *Documenti e studi sulla tradizione filosofica medievale* 15: 387–438.

Porro, Pasquale. 2016. Thomas Aquinas: A historical and philosophical profile. Trans. J.G. Trabbic and R.W. Nutt. Washington, DC: The Catholic University of America Press.

Reynolds, Philip L. 2001. Properties, causality and epistemological optimism in Thomas Aquinas. *Recherches de théologie et philosophie médiévales* 68 (2): 270–309.

Cory, Scarpelli, and Therese. 2020. Aquinas's intelligible species as formal constituents. *Documenti e studi sulla tradizione filosofica medievale* 31: 261–309.

Spruit, Leen. 1994–1995. *Species intelligibilis: From perception to knowledge*. Vol. 2. Leiden/New York/Köln: Brill.

Wippel, John F. 2000. *The metaphysical thought of Thomas Aquinas: From finite being to uncreated being*. Washington, DC: The Catholic University of America Press.

Chapter 6
Aquinas, *perversor philosophiae suae*

Gábor Borbély

Keywords Thomas Aquinas · De unitate intellectus · Intellective soul · Siger of Brabant · Anonymous of Giele · Religious commitment · Faith · Belief · Double truth

As is well known, Aquinas makes some indignant remarks about one of his unnamed opponents' use of language and philosophical views in the closing passages of the *De unitate intellectus*.[1] This man, notes Aquinas, speaks of the Christian religion as

---

[1] See Thomas Aquinas 1976, 314, 397–430; Keeler 1936, 78–80, no. 122–123. The *De unitate intellectus* was written during Aquinas's second teaching period in Paris, most probably in 1270 (see Keeler 1936, XX–XXI. Thomas Aquinas 1976, 248–249; Torrell 1996, 348). I will abbreviate the title of Thomas Aquinas's *De unitate intellectus* throughout this paper as DUI, and the thesis of the unity of the possible intellect as TUI. For the sake of simplicity, and since the distinction is not relevant to the argument that follows, I am going to refer to the ensemble of the possible and active intellect as "intellect". I will quote the Latin text of DUI according to the Leonina edition (Thomas Aquinas 1976). In addition to the page number, I will also give the line numbers of the Leonina edition as can be seen above. Since the paragraph numbers of Leo W. Keeler's earlier edition are still in use for reference, I will also indicate these numbers as it is usual in the literature (e.g. no. 122–123; this latter will be the standard reference to the closing passages of the DUI discussed in this paper). As a rule of thumb, I am going to use Beatrice H. Zedler's fairly literal English translation (Zedler 1968), and if needed, I will also indicate the page number of Ralph McInerny's later rendering (see McInerny 1993). I am going to refer to Aquinas's unnamed opponent's individual claims presented by Aquinas as AC1, AC2 and so forth. In Aquinas's account his opponent makes the following claims. **AC1:** "Latini pro principiis hoc non recipiunt, (…) quia forte lex eorum est in contrarium." ("the Latins do not hold this as a principle, (…) because perhaps their law is against it"); **AC2:** "Hec est ratio per quam Catholici uidentur habere suam positionem." ("this is the reasoning by which Catholics seem to hold their supposition"); **AC3:** "Deus non potest facere quod sint multi intellectus, quia implicat contradictionem." ("God cannot make many intellects, because

---

G. Borbély (✉)
Eötvös Loránd University (ELTE), Budapest, Hungary
e-mail: borbely.gabor@btk.elte.hu

© The Author(s), under exclusive license to Springer Nature Switzerland AG 2023
J. P. Hochschild et al. (eds.), *Metaphysics Through Semantics: The Philosophical Recovery of the Medieval Mind*, International Archives of the History of Ideas Archives internationales d'histoire des idées 242, https://doi.org/10.1007/978-3-031-15026-5_6

irreverently as if he were an outsider to it, he calls the propositional content of Catholic faith a "position", and—presumptuously—forms a judgement about the limits of divine omnipotence concerning the multiplication of the intellect. Aquinas adds that one of his utterances is downright intolerable "for the believer's ears" as it implies that the object of faith is something false and impossible. Finally, the man's unscrupulous audacity is indicated by the fact that he presumes to discuss problems that do not belong to philosophy, such as the soul's suffering from hell's fire, and dares to say that the teaching of the theologians should be rejected in this matter (Thomas Aquinas 1976, 314; Zedler 1968, 74).[2]

By making these remarks, Aquinas goes beyond the philosophical issues discussed in the previous parts of his treatise and seeks to expose his opponent's hidden frame of mind: his presumption of knowledge and his hostility toward religious faith.

Let us call this allegedly arrogant opponent of Aquinas "Athaq" (Anonymus Thomae Aquinatis). We cannot be certain whether Athaq is identical to any philosopher known to us from the 1260s.[3] We have no idea whether Aquinas was directly

---

this would involve a contradiction."); **AC4**: "Per rationem concludo de necessitate quod intellectus est unus numero, firmiter tamen teneo oppositum per fidem." ("I necessarily conclude through reason that the intellect is one in number; but I firmly hold the opposite through faith."); **AC5**: "sententiae doctorum de hoc sunt reprobandae" ("the teachings of the doctors on this point should be rejected"). This unspecified claim happens to be in connection with the problem whether "the soul may suffer hell fire" ("anima patiatur ab igne inferni"). See Thomas Aquinas 1976, 314, 400–427; Keeler 1936, 78–79, no. 122–123. Zedler 1968, 74; McInerny 1993, 143. AC3 and AC5 have slightly been modified due to the different syntactic configuration. Aquinas's comments are going to be discussed later in this paper.

[2] Aquinas's text clearly implies that his remarks in no. 122–123 refer to the utterances of one and the same person, in all probability one of the contemporary arts masters at Paris. One of his claims (AC3) is mentioned earlier by Aquinas in no. 100 and no. 105 as a corollary of one of the central arguments of his opponents. It seems therefore likely that his adversary mentioned in no. 122–123 can be identified with at least one of those philosophers who are referred to in the earlier paragraphs. What is more, since plural references in medieval Latin often indicate individuals, it seems possible that the same person is implied by at least some of Aquinas's plural references to his contemporary adversaries. For these references see Van Steenberghen 1977, 58–59; De Libera 2004, 250 and 503–504. Nevertheless, it is unlikely that the person mentioned in no. 122–123 was the only master Aquinas bore in mind when writing his polemical tract. Famously, Aquinas coined the term "averroista" for his opponents (Thomas Aquinas 1976, 294, 308; Keeler 1936, 12, no. 17), considering them the followers of Averroes with respect to the problem of the unity of the intellect. On this latter point, see Van Steenberghen 1966, 369; 1974, 542–546; 1977, 394–395. The word "averroistae" became widely used to designate those philosophers who are thought to have been targeted by Aquinas's polemical tract. For the titles, incipits and explicits of the work in the manuscript tradition that used the term "averroista" see Thomas Aquinas 1976, 251–255. On the early use of the term in a different sense see, however, Bianchi 2015, esp. 73–76.

[3] The common opinion supported by a robust tradition is that Aquinas's main contemporary adversary throughout the DUI as well as his unnamed opponent cited and referred to in no. 122–123 was Siger of Brabant. For the extant manuscripts indicating that Siger was Thomas's target, see Thomas Aquinas 1976, 247–248. For the interchange between Siger and Thomas on the nature of the intellect see, among many others, Mandonnet 1911, esp. 103–112; Nardi 1938, 67–89; Zedler 1968, 5–11; Van Steenberghen 1977, esp. 57–70 and 338–383. Bazán 1972; Bazán 1974; Imbach and Putallaz 1997, esp. 27–55 and 154–168; Mahoney 1974, 532–551. De Libera 1994, 33–65; De Libera 2004,

or indirectly informed of Athaq's claims.[4] It seems likely, however, that Aquinas refers to Athaq's written utterances, even though Aquinas's quotations, as they appear in the closing passages of DUI, are not attested by any extant manuscript.[5]

---

passim. For those who happen to read in Hungarian see my *De unitate intellectus* volume (studies, commentaries, translation) from 1993 and the dialectical dispute between Gyula Klima and myself. See Thomas Aquinas 1993, and Borbély–Klima 2000. See further Klima 1998. For Siger as Aquinas's unnamed opponent in no. 122–123 see Mandonnet 1911, 151–153. Nardi 1938, 187–189; Van Steenberghen 1977, 60 and 1980, 53 where he says it is "morally certain" that the master targeted by Aquinas in the epilogue of the DUI is Siger of Brabant; see further De Libera 1994, 49–58, Imbach and Putallaz 1997, 46–47, and De Libera 2004, 503–504. For an overview of Siger's works that also indicates important chronological issues with reference to further literature see Calma 2006, 190–193. It seems prudent to keep in mind that Siger of Brabant's *Quaestiones in tertium de anima* that has often been regarded as an occasion for Aquinas to write the DUI was probably composed around 1265 and not 1269/70 as it had previously been thought. See Gauthier 1983, 209–212. (Bazán eventually accepted 1265 as the date of the work despite his and Van Steenberghen's earlier objections, see Bazán 2005, 603). Furthermore, aside from some rather general issues that had been discussed in Siger's *Quaestiones* and were also debated a few years later by Aquinas, it is hard to find direct and clear connections between the two texts. For these issues see Van Steenberghen 1977, 60. Although Siger's *Quaestiones* might have been one of the texts Aquinas used when writing the DUI, it was certainly not the text he referred to in the epilogue. Furthermore, it seems highly unlikely that the "great master", "one of the most eminent philosophers" at Paris who Giles of Rome famously refers to in his *Sentences* commentary could be identified with either Siger of Brabant or Boethius of Dacia. See Luna 1999, 656–658; De Libera 2004, 271–272. For his identification with Siger see Nardi 1938, 88, 143; Giele 1971, 20; Van Stenberghen 1977, 70, although hesitantly. For his identification with Boethius of Dacia, see Dales 1995, 154–155, who also suggests that the unnamed opponent of the epilogue of the DUI could have been Boethius (ibidem, 149). This "great master" is certainly identical to the author of the anonymous *De anima* commentary edited by Maurice Giele. The commentary of the "Anonymous of Giele" dates from 1270 (most probably from before 10 December when Stephen Tempier's condemnation was issued, see Luna 1999, 656–657) and it contains an immediate and straightforward response to the DUI. For this latter, see Giele 1971, 70–77. Because of the alleged prominence of this master and due to the obvious connection of his work with the DUI, it is not unreasonable to suppose that the Anonymous of Giele could have been at least one of those arts masters whose Aristotle-interpretation had been salient enough in the second part of the 1260s in Paris to provoke Aquinas's reaction to start writing the DUI. See Piron 2006, 304, and Calma 2006, 211. Be that as it may, I am no longer pursuing the issue of Athaq's identity in this paper. I will confine myself as strictly as possible to the examination of the problem indicated below in the main text.

[4] It could be a *reportatio* that Aquinas had before his eyes.

[5] Aquinas uses the phrase "et quod postmodum dicit" ("and what he somewhat later says") twice, and, in addition, the slightly different phrase "postmodum asserere audet" ("what he dares to assert later") within a few lines in no. 122–123. See Thomas Aquinas 1976, 314, 405–406; 314, 409–410; and 314, 412–413. Keeler 1936, 78–79. Zedler 1968, 74; McInerny 1993, 143. We can certainly assume, in accordance with Aquinas's usage, that these expressions just like "deinde cum dicit", "postmodum ostendit" etc. refer to a written text he has at his disposal. Cf. e.g. "Set Aristotiles postmodum ostendit quod anima cognoscit omnia in quantum est similis omnibus in potentia, non in actu." with reference to *De anima* III, 4, 429a18–24 and 429b29–430a2. See *Quaestiones disputatae de anima*, q. 8, Thomas Aquinas 1996, 73, 453–456. Similarly, "de hiis enim que pertinent ad unumquemque sensum specialiter, postmodum dicet." See *Sententia libri De anima*, Lib. II., Cap. X., Thomas Aquinas 1984a 107, 18–19. "Deinde cum dicit: *Set si quidem tale* etc., argumentatur ad questionem prius propositam." See *Sentencia libri De sensu et sensato*, Tr. II., Cap. 3; Thomas Aquinas 1984b, 114, 119–120.

Yet one thing seems clear from the last passages of the DUI: Aquinas does not intend to accommodate Athaq's claims in his own system of beliefs by maximizing the truth or rationality of Athaq's utterances. On the contrary, Aquinas tries to render these claims as outlandish as possible in an effort to expose what he supposes to be Athaq's true intention. Aquinas's theoretical unkindness, however, comes at a price, as it makes himself less rational and coherent, at least with regard to the issues concerned. Borrowing the expression that Aquinas himself coined and applied to Averroes, we can even say that he perverts his own philosophy in an attempt to transform Athaq into the person Aquinas believes he really is: a philosophical stranger who is recklessly committed to the Catholic faith.[6]

Athaq's first claim (AC1) is that, regarding the claim that there is only one intellect, the Latins do not accept this as a principle, because perhaps their law is contrary to it.[7] Aquinas makes two indignant remarks on this sentence and then—as a corroboration of these reproaches—makes a third one on Athaq's subsequent claim (which will be discussed below). Aquinas's first comment is that Athaq doubts whether the thesis of the unity of the intellect is "against the faith" (Thomas Aquinas 1976, 314,403–404; Zedler 1968, 74).[8]

But is this actually the case? Just a few lines later, Aquinas cites a more important claim (AC4) by Athaq, which clearly contradicts Aquinas's above reproach. Aquinas notes here with utmost indignation that Athaq—when contending that he "firmly holds the opposite" of TUI "through faith"—"thinks that faith is of things whose contrary can be necessarily concluded" (Thomas Aquinas 1976, 314, 412–415; Zedler 1968, 74).[9] Evidently, Aquinas's comment makes sense only if we suppose that Athaq is convinced of TUI being contrary to faith. But Athaq cannot doubt whether TUI is contrary to the faith and claim at the same time that he firmly holds through faith the opposite of TUI.

---

[6] See Thomas Aquinas 1976, 293, 139–140: "ut Commentator peruerse exponit et sectatores ipsius"; 293, 150–151: "sicut Commentator et sectatores eius peruerse exponunt"; 293, 163–164: "ut Commentator peruerse exponit"; 294, 251–252: "sicut Auerroys peruerse exponit"; 302, 93–96: "Quod autem Alexander intellectum possibilem posuerit esse formam corporis, etiam ipse Auerroys confitetur; quamuis, ut arbitror, peruerse uerba Alexandri acceperit"; 314,389–393: "Patet etiam quod Auerroys peruerse refert sententiam Themistii et Theophrasti de intellectu possibili et agente; unde merito supra diximus eum philosophie peripatetice peruersorem." He also calls Averroes the "philosophie peripatetice deprauator." See Thomas Aquinas 1976, 302, 156.

[7] "«Latini pro principiis hoc non recipiunt », scilicet quod sit unus intellectus tantum, «quia forte lex eorum est in contrarium»." "the Latins do not hold this as a principle, that is, that there is only one intellect, because perhaps their law is against it." See Thomas Aquinas 1976, 314, 400–403; Zedler 1968, 74; Keeler 1936, 78, no. 122.

[8] "Vbi duo sunt mala: primo, quia dubitat an hoc sit contra fidem (…)" "Here there are two evils: first, because he doubts whether this be against the faith (…)." See also Keeler 1936, 78, no. 122. If Athaq is identical to Siger of Brabant, then Aquinas's reproach would appear to miss the mark. Based on Siger's extant writings he seems to have been clearly aware of TUI being contrary to faith.

[9] "Adhuc autem grauius est quod postmodum dicit «Per rationem concludo de necessitate quod intellectus est unus numero, firmiter tamen teneo oppositum per fidem»." "But what he says later is still more serious: I necessarily conclude through reason that the intellect is one in number; but I firmly hold the opposite through faith." See Zedler 1968, 74; Keeler 1936, 79, no. 123.

Provided that Aquinas accurately quotes Athaq's text, a different reading would be simply "perhaps because" instead of "because perhaps".[10] In this case we should not assume that Athaq doubts what he asserts. Athaq would simply imply that perhaps the reason the Latins do not accept TUI is that their "law" (i.e. religion) is contrary to it. What would be the point of making such a claim? It may sound somewhat sarcastic to some. Still, even if Athaq's intention is to make use of verbal irony here, Aquinas does not seem to notice it.[11] On the contrary, he seems to be committed to a reading that clearly makes Athaq less intelligible. As a third option, "because perhaps" (*quia forte*) could perhaps be substituted simply by "quia" without causing much collateral damage to the meaning of the sentence. In this case, Athaq would simply say: "the Latins do not accept this as a principle, because their law is contrary to it." This reading would make Athaq more rational and coherent, although less sarcastic, and much less odd.[12]

Be that as it may, Athaq's same sentence serves as the basis for Aquinas's second comment on AC1. Athaq is signaling here, notes Aquinas, that he is outside of the "law" of "the Latins", i.e. he is signaling he is an outsider to the Catholic religion and its immense edifice, the Latin Church.[13] It seems obvious that it is not the use of the word "lex" ("religion") that makes Aquinas think Athaq behaves as an outsider. This usage of "lex" as a synonym for "secta" and "fides" was common in the thirteenth century and Aquinas clearly adopts this usage when he says that Athaq would like to signal he is "outside of this law", that is the Catholic religion.[14] Rather, Aquinas disapproves of Athaq's reference to *the Latins* and *their* law, because—in Aquinas's view—with this kind of speech, Athaq clearly indicates that he considers himself as an outsider to the religious community of the Western Christians. However, the general usage of these terms ("the Latins", "their law", i.e. "their religion") does not seem to justify Aquinas's interpretation. A reference to "the Latins"

---

[10] Zedler's and McInerny's translations reflect this difference: "the Latins do not hold this as a principle, that is, that there is only one intellect, because perhaps their law is against it. See Zedler 1968, 74. "the Latins do not accept this as a principle, namely, that there is only one intellect, perhaps because their law is contrary to it." See McInerny 1993, 143.

[11] Whereas Aquinas himself is certainly trying to use irony at the beginning of DUI to indicate that his adversaries' high ambitions pair with ignorance: "Et quia quibusdam, ut dicunt, in hac materia uerba Latinorum non sapiunt, sed Peripateticorum uerba sectari se dicunt, quorum libros numquam in hac materia uiderunt nisi Aristotilis, qui fuit secte peripatetice institutor (…)" "Latin writers on this matter not being to the taste of some, who tell us that they prefer to follow the words of the Peripatetics, though of them they have seen only the works of Aristotle, the founder of the school (…)" R. McInerny's translation: see McInerny 1993, 19. See Thomas Aquinas 1976, 291, 32–36.

[12] An example of a "quia forte" sufficiently close to "quia" can be found e.g. in Albert the Great's *Liber de sensu et sensato*: "et ideo ex albo et acuto in sonis non fit unum permixtione, sed fit unum ex eis per accidens in hoc subjecto: quia forte utrumque accidentium illorum sensibilium est cum altero in eodem subjecto, sed non fit ex eis unum formaliter permixtione, sicut ex acuto in voce, et gravi in voce mixtura proportionis fit symphonia." See Albertus Magnus 1890–98, Vol. 9, 84.

[13] "secundo, quia alienum se innuit esse ab hac lege." "secondly, because he implies that he is outside this law." Thomas Aquinas 1976, 314, 404–405; Zedler 1968, 74; Keeler 1936, 78, no. 122.

[14] For the use of "lex", "fides" and "secta" in the thirteenth century see, Biller 1985, 360–369, esp. 366.

by someone who was evidently one of them, or a reference to the religion of the Western Christians by someone who was a committed member of the Latin Church, was not uncommon in the 1260s.

A well-known example of the former is Albert the Great's reference to "all the Latins of our age" (*omnes moderni Latinorum*) who are—almost without exception—committed to a position not shared by Albert with regard to the cognition of the separate substances (Albertus Magnus 1968, 220).[15] Albert adds that the problem he discusses in this part of his commentary is extremely difficult and "the Latins" had neglected it so far (Albertus Magnus 1968, 220–221).[16] A further example is when Albert in his *De unitate intellectus* writes about the three souls in Plato's *Timaeus*. "Some people say that these three souls" (i.e. the souls in Plato's *Timaeus*) "are three different substances in man. I do not regard this as an opinion, but as something that is worthy of ridicule. And the source of this confabulation is not to be found among Peripatetic philosophers, but among those Latins who were ignorant of the nature of the soul. I refuted it many times, because saying that many substances belong to the same subject is the worst error of all, for these 'substances' can only be forms" (Albertus Magnus 1975, 16).[17] And a last example: "and, because we aim to investigate here the most difficult things, we would like to explain first Aristotle's doctrine of the soul (...) then bring in the opinion of other Peripatetic philosophers and Plato, and, finally, bring in my own opinion, for I do not agree with the Latin doctors at all" (literally: "I completely abhor the words of the Latin doctors") "concerning the solution of these problems", since their words "do not calm the soul, because they do not expose the truth and they do not reach it with their own words" (Albertus Magnus 1968, 177).[18]

As for "the law of the Latins", i. e. the religion of Western Christianity, it is also not unprecedented in thirteenth century literature to decouple one's own religious self-designation from the references to different religious groups in a philosophical discourse. A well-known example is Roger Bacon's classification and comparison

---

[15] "Et haec est via, quam fere sequuntur omnes moderni Latinorum, sed isti in principiis non conveniunt cum Peripateticis." See *De anima* L. 3, Tr. 3, Cap. 10. For Albert's position see, Nardi 1947, 200; Nardi 1960, 105; Fioravanti 1970, 580–581.

[16] "Et ex omnibus his patet, quod difficillima quaestio est, quae supra est inducta, et Latini quidem huc usque neglexerunt illam quaestionem; et huius causa est, quia non convenerunt in positionibus suis cum dictis Peripateticorum, sed diverterunt in quandam alteram viam et secundum illam finxerunt alia principia et alias positiones."

[17] "Quod autem dicunt quidam, has tres esse tres substantias in homine, non reputo opinionem, sed ridiculum, et hoc non dixerunt aliqui Peripateticorum, sed quidam Latini naturam animae nescientes hoc confinxerunt, et est expresse a nobis in multis locis improbatum, quia error pessimus est dicere unius subiecti plures esse substantias, cum illae substantiae non possint esse nisi formae."

[18] "Et quia res difficillimas hic perscrutari intendimus, ideo volumus primo totam Aristotelis sententiam pro viribus nostris explanare et tunc inducere aliorum Peripateticorum opiniones et post hoc videre de opinionibus Platonis et tunc demum nostram ponere opinionem, quoniam in istarum quaestionum determinatione omnino abhorremus verba doctorum Latinorum (...) in verbis eorum nullo modo quiescit anima, propterea quod sententiam veritatis nec ostendunt nec verbis propriis attingunt."; *De anima*, L. 3, Tr. 2, Cap. 1.

of (past, present and future) religions (in his terminology: *sectae* vel *leges*) based on cultural, habitual, moral and astrological considerations.[19] In Roger Bacon's view, the religion of the Christians (which he refers to variously as "lex Christiana", "secta Christianorum", "secta Christi") is one of the six major religions of the world.[20] Roger Bacon emphasizes that different religions can only be compared through philosophy, seeing as philosophy is common to believers and unbelievers, whereas considerations based solely "on our own religion" ("lex nostra") are inappropriate.[21]

Is Albert the Great signaling that he is not one of the Latin doctors when he says that he "completely abhors the words of the Latin doctors"? Is Roger Bacon signaling that he is not a member of the religious community of the Christians when he intends to compare—without prejudice—the "secta Christianorum" and the other religions? I do not think so. We should rather say that Albert takes a different perspective when saying he "completely abhors the words of the Latin doctors" because they "do not expose the truth" and "do not reach it with their own words". Similarly, Roger Bacon—regardless of his own religious affiliation—takes a different perspective, i.e. the perspective of philosophy that he finds appropriate for investigating the characteristics of the religions of the world, among them the "lex" or "secta" of "the Christians".

Obviously, both Albert and Roger make it clear that they belong to the Latin Church. But so does Athaq: Aquinas himself says that Athaq professes to be a Christian.[22] It would certainly be rather odd if Athaq intended to indicate that he is an outsider to the Latin Church, while considering himself a committed member of the Latin Church—as Aquinas suggests. Based on the contemporary usage of "Latini" and "lex eorum", we can easily read Athaq's words in a way that would make him sound more rational and coherent. Signaling a fully functional shift of perspective by using "Latini" and "lex eorum", seems to be just as compatible with

---

[19] "secta vel lex": Moralis philosophia, Pars quarta, Distincio prima (Roger Bacon 2010, 188–189); "fines principales legum et sectarum": *Compendium studii philosophiae*, Cap. IV; (Roger Bacon 1859, 421).

[20] In his *Opus maius* Roger Bacon gives two, partially different lists of the six "sectae principales". Cf. Roger Bacon 1897, I, 254. and Roger Bacon 1897, II, 367. "secta Christianorum": Roger Bacon 1897, II, 389; "secta Christi": Roger Bacon 1897, II. 392; "lex Christiana": Roger Bacon 1897, II, 252; 389; 396. Similarly, Bonaventure also seems to include the Christian religion among the "leges et sectae" when saying that "anima rationalis, secundum philosophos et secundum etiam omnes leges et sectas, est incorruptibilis ergo non est per naturam propagabilis ergo non est ex traduce." In Sent 2, Dist. XVIII. Art. II. Q. III; see Bonaventura 1885, 452. The term "secta" as it stands for "religion" was frequently used after the thirteenth century, mainly among English Franciscans, and had no negative connotations whatsoever. See Kaluza 1996, 340–341.

[21] "(...) qualiter oporteat persuadere de sectae veritate (...)"; "Sed non possumus hic arguere per legem nostram, nec per auctoritates Sanctorum, quia infideles negant Christum Dominum et legem suam et sanctos. Quapropter oportet quaerere rationes per alteram viam, et haec est communis nobis et infidelibus, scilicet philosophia." See Roger Bacon 1897, II, 372–373. For a similar approach see Aquinas, *Summa contra Gentiles* 1.2 (abbreviated as SCG below).

[22] "(...) aliquis Christianum se profitens (...)" "someone who professes that he is a Christian". See Thomas Aquinas 1976, 314, 398–399; Zedler 1968, 74.

Athaq's religious affiliation as it is with Albert the Great's or Roger Bacon's. All things considered, a charitable interpretation of Athaq's aforementioned words seems to be a difficulty only for those who presuppose that Athaq wishes to indicate his exclusion by talking about "the Latins" and "their law".[23]

Should anyone still be unsure of accepting that Aquinas's reading makes Athaq's utterance unnecessarily inconsistent with the contemporary usage of the respective words, Aquinas's subsequent—but still related—remark will probably leave no further room for doubt. Aquinas denounces what Athaq "somewhat later says" (AC2) on the ground that Athaq calls "the doctrine of the faith" ("sententia fidei") a "position" (Thomas Aquinas 1976, 314, 405–408; Zedler 1968, 74).[24] With this remark, Aquinas clearly intends to reinforce what he has previously said about Athaq's socio-cultural status (he is an outsider).[25] Athaq's reference to "the Catholics" runs parallel with his reference to "the Latins", and calling the doctrine of the faith a "position" seems to be at least as presumptuous as Athaq's transgressions cited previously by Aquinas.[26] As modern commentators of this passage emphasize, calling a teaching of the Catholic faith a "position" puts it on the same level with the often doubtful views of philosophers or philosophical schools, thus degrading it to mere opinion.[27]

This is, however, an astonishing reproach for any reader of the works of Aquinas from his second *magisterium* at the university of Paris, given that the first sentence of Aquinas's De aeternitate mundi (from about the same time as DUI)[28] starts with the following words: "Supposito secundum fidem catholicam quod mundus duratio-

---

[23] For a similar reasoning, see Aquinas's SCG 1.11: "Et sic nihil inconveniens accidit ponentibus Deum non esse: non enim inconveniens est quolibet dato vel in re vel in intellectu aliquid maius cogitari posse, nisi ei qui concedit esse aliquid quo maius cogitari non possit in rerum natura." See Thomas Aquinas 1918, 24b.

[24] For the usage of the term "sententia" as it is applied – from the thirteenth century on – to certain and authoritative propositions: Paré-Brunet-Tremblay 1933, 267–274, esp. 272. The phrase "sententia fidei" was used by both Siger of Brabant and Boethius of Dacia. See e.g. Boethius of Dacia's De aeternitate mundi (Boethius de Dacia 1976, 335; 340; 346) and Siger of Brabant's De anima intellectiva (Siger de Brabant 1972, 88).

[25] According to Alain de Libera, Aquinas's remarks in no. 122–123 display a rhetorical progression towards the worst (De Libera 2004, 501). As Aquinas seems to strictly follow Athaq's claims up until AC4 this would imply that Athaq's text displays a similar rhetorical progression.

[26] Aquinas refers twice to "the Catholics" in DUI. (1) "Quicquid autem circa hoc dicatur, manifestum est quod ex hoc nullam angustiam Catholici patiuntur, qui ponunt mundum incepisse." "But whatever may be said on this point, it is clear that Catholics, who hold that the world has had a beginning, have no reason for concern." See Thomas Aquinas 1976, 313, 340–343; Keeler 1936, 76, no. 118; Zedler 1968, 72; McInerny 1993, 139. (2) "uel Deus secundum Catholicos, uel intelligentia ultima secundum Auicennam"; "either God, according to Catholics, or the last intelligence, according to Avicenna." See Thomas Aquinas 1976, 314, 368–370; Keeler 1936, 77, no. 120; Zedler 1968, 73; McInerny 1993, 141. Taken out of context, these references could also be regarded as an indication that they were written by someone who did not consider himself a Catholic.

[27] See e.g. Nardi 1938, 187 and De Libera 2004, 503.

[28] The date of composition is most probably 1271. See Torrell 1996, 348.

nis initium habuit (…)", i.e. "If we suppose, in accordance with Catholic faith, that the world has not existed from eternity but had a beginning of its duration (…)" (Thomas Aquinas 1976, 85, 1–2; Thomas Aquinas 1964, 19). Aquinas's choice of words here seems to imply that he considers a doctrine of the Catholic faith (i.e. that "the world has not existed from eternity but had a beginning of its duration") as something that is supposed to be true, i.e. as a supposition. Someone might object that what is being supposed by Aquinas in this passage is not exactly the doctrine of the Catholic faith. On the contrary, a claim is being used here as a supposition in an argument and it happens to be in complete accordance with a propositional content of Catholic faith, even if the latter is not a supposition by itself. Aquinas's peculiar formulation of his introductory sentence serves the sole purpose of introducing his examination of the central problem of the work: whether or not being created and being eternal in a temporal sense involves a contradiction. We can find similar *ablativus absolutus mancus* constructions in Aquinas's works.[29] In most of these cases it can also be argued that although the doctrine of faith is being supposed as a premise by Aquinas, this fact does not entail that the doctrine of faith itself could properly be called a supposition.

Fortunately or not, we do not need to get entangled in the web of syntactic and semantic issues raised by quotation. For elsewhere Aquinas himself calls the doctrine of faith ("sententia fidei") a "position" and this corresponds to the usage of his contemporaries. What is more, this usage can be considered as a result of proper philosophical-theological considerations. An ample example which is also highly relevant with regard to our subsequent discussion comes from Aquinas's *Sentences* commentary (Thomas Aquinas 1929, 482–483).[30] Aquinas clearly asserts here that one of the positions concerning the problem of the corruptibility of the human soul is "that which our faith holds". Since, however, what the Catholic faith holds is a doctrine of the faith, a doctrine of the faith is called a position here by Aquinas. A further example would be when Aquinas refers to the proposition "that things have been brought into being by God, at the beginning" as "the position" of the faith and

---

[29] See e. g. SCG 2. 29: "(…) supposito quod Deus hominem facere vellet, debitum ex hac suppositione fuit ut animam et corpus in eo coniungeret, et sensus, et alia huiusmodi adiumenta, tam intrinseca quam extrinseca, ei praeberet." Thomas Aquinas 1918, 335b; and SCG 3.97: "Supposito autem quod Deus creaturis suam bonitatem communicare, secundum quod est possibile, velit per similitudinis modum: ex hoc rationem accipit quod sint creaturae diversae." Thomas Aquinas 1926, 301a.

[30] In Sent II.19.1.1 co.: "Quarta positio est quam fides nostra tenet, quod anima intellectiva sit substantia non dependens ex corpore, et quod sint plures intellectivae substantiae secundum corporum multitudinem, et quod, destructis corporibus, remanent separatae, non in alia corpora transeuntes; sed in resurrectione idem corpus numero quod deposuerat unaquaeque assumat." "The fourth position is that which our faith holds that the intellective soul is a substance that does not depend on the body, that there is more than one intellective substance corresponding to the multitude of bodies, and that they remain separate when bodies are destroyed, not passing into other bodies. Rather, in the resurrection each soul assumes the same body numerically that it had laid aside." (English translation is from https://aquinas.cc/la/en/~Sent.II.D19.Q1.A1.C.4)

contrasts it with the position of certain philosophers (Thomas Aquinas 1926, 184b; Thomas Aquinas 1956, 217).[31]

It is not unreasonable for Aquinas to call the teaching of faith a position, or even a supposition. In his view, the propositions that represent what he calls the second aspect of the "twofold truth with regard to divine things" cannot be known by natural reason, i.e. they cannot be either self-evident principles of human cognition or conclusions in demonstrative syllogisms.[32] The reason that these incomprehensible claims can still be used as principles in *sacra doctrina* is that theology receives them from a higher science which is the science of God and the blessed.[33] Now, the idea that a subalternated science can receive its principles from a higher science comes from Aristotle's *Posterior Analytics*. In his commentary, Aquinas—following Aristotle—makes a distinction between two types of immediate principles of syllogism: positions ("positiones") and axioms ("dignitates", "maximae propositiones"). "Positions" are immediate principles, whose terms are not known for everyone even if they are self-evident in themselves (Thomas Aquinas 1989, 25a).[34] These principles are therefore "received by a certain position" (Thomas Aquinas 1989, 25b).[35] Again, positions can be subdivided into two groups, suppositions and definitions. In Aquinas's view, we call the members of the first group suppositions, because we are positing them under the assumption that they are true propositions (Thomas Aquinas 1989, 25b).[36] Suppositions as immediate principles cannot be proved in the science in which we deploy them; they can only be proved by the principles of a higher science. This clearly seems to be the case with the principles of theology, as the doctrines of faith that can be regarded as positions or suppositions are "established by the light of a higher science" (Thomas Aquinas 1911, 4).[37] Therefore, calling a doctrine of faith a "position" or a "supposition" is in complete

---

[31] SCG 3.65: "Circa rerum originem duplex est positio: una fidei, quod res de novo fuerint a Deo productae in esse; et positio quorundam philosophorum, quod res a Deo ab aeterno effluxerint. Secundum autem utramque positionem oportet dicere quod res conserventur in esse a Deo."

[32] See the first nine chapters of the *Summa contra Gentiles*. Thomas Aquinas 1918, 3–22; Thomas Aquinas 1955, 59–78.

[33] See STh 1a.1.2 co: "Respondeo dicendum sacram doctrinam esse scientiam. Sed sciendum est quod duplex est scientiarum genus. Quaedam enim sunt, quae procedunt ex principiis notis lumine naturali intellectus, sicut arithmetica, geometria, et huiusmodi. Quaedam vero sunt, quae procedunt ex principiis notis lumine superioris scientiae, sicut perspectiva procedit ex principiis notificatis per geometriam, et musica ex principiis per arithmeticam notis. Et hoc modo sacra doctrina est scientia, quia procedit ex principiis notis lumine superioris scientiae, quae scilicet est scientia Dei et beatorum. Unde sicut musica credit principia tradita sibi ab arithmetico, ita doctrina sacra credit principia revelata sibi a Deo."

[34] *Expositio libri Posteriorum* I, 5.: "Quaedam uero propositiones sunt inmediate quarum termini non sunt apud omnes noti."

[35] "Et ideo cum quadam positione recipiuntur huiusmodi principia."

[36] "(…) et hec positio suppositio dicitur, quia tanquam ueritatem habens supponitur."

[37] STh 1a.1.2. See also *Expositio libri Posteriorum* I, 5.: "Sunt enim quedam propositiones que non possunt probari nisi per principia alterius sciencie, et ideo oportet quod in illa sciencia supponantur, licet probentur per principia alterius sciencie (…)". Thomas Aquinas 1989, 25b.

accordance both with Aquinas's theoretical considerations and with his practice. If it is a serious transgression, as Aquinas suggests with regard to Athaq, then either Athaq is a serious transgressor and Aquinas is much less consistent than he is supposed to be (provided he is not a serious transgressor himself), or Aquinas intends to render Athaq's claim much more odd than it is in reality.

This latter option can be corroborated by the contemporaries' use of the terms "position" and "supposition" with regard to the doctrines of faith. Albert the Great's reference to "the positions of faith" in his *De coelesti hierarchia* seems to be based on similar considerations as Aquinas's in the *Summa theologiae*. Investigating the problem whether there is essential composition in intelligences, Albert contends that although they are immune from matter, their existence is nevertheless distinct from their essence. However, we do not need to find a way to prove this kind of composition of the angels, adds Albert, since it is based on faith that is not demonstrated, but suffices only to be sustained. Therefore, we accept the composite nature of the intelligences "through the positions of faith" (Albertus Magnus 1892, 308b).[38]

As a matter of fact, quite a few contemporary theologians call the teaching of faith a "supposition" or a "position". Bonaventure enumerates doctrines of theology that "we have to suppose" in his *Collationes in Hexaemeron* (Bonaventura 1934, 141),[39] Giles of Rome denies that "the position of faith" would be irrational or impossible (Aegidius Romanus 1554),[40] John Peckham contends that between two extreme and erroneous positions there is a third one that "the Catholic faith confesses" (Johannes Peckham 1918, 32)[41] and Robert Kilwardby says that the natural generation of the human soul is "against the position of the Catholics and the faith" as it entails that also the intellect as one of the powers of the soul comes into being through natural processes (Ehrle 1889, 626).[42]

According to Aquinas, Athaq's next claim (AC3) is "not less presumptuous" than the earlier one: "God cannot make many intellects, because this would involve a

---

[38] "Sic ergo concedimus, quod est in eis compositio essentialis, et concedimus rationes ad hoc. Nec oportet a nobis quaerere aliquam demonstrativam viam deveniendi in Angelos hoc modo compositos: quia fides non demonstratur, sed sufficit quod sustineatur. Haec autem accipimus per positiones fidei." *De coelesti hierarchia*, Cap XI, Q. unica.

[39] "Supponendum est ergo quod Deus est rerum conditor, gubernator actuum, doctor intellectuum, iudex meritorum." *Collationes in Hexaëmeron*, Visio II. Collatio V.

[40] See *Theoremata de corpore Christi*, propositio XXXIX, fo. 27va: "positio fidei de existentia accidentis absque subiecto, non est irrationabilis, si diligenter videatur modus ponendi."; 27rb:,,(...) non est impossibilis positio fidei, cum solam quantitatem in sacramento altaris sine subiecto ponat: quae sine implicatione contradictionis, ut patet per habita, sine subiecto esse potest (...)."

[41] "Dicendum circa corruptionem et rebellionem in appetitu rationis et sensualitatis duae sunt positiones extremae erroneae, et tertia iuxta quam fides catholica confitetur." See further: "Placuit autem Augustino communis positio, dum communis teneatur fides redemptionis." Johannes Peckham 1918, 6.

[42] See Robert Kilwardby's letter to Peter of Conflans: "Si autem ubique per generationem, tunc intellectiva potentia in nomine est ex traduce, quod est contra catholicorum positionem et fidem."

contradiction"[43] (Thomas Aquinas 1976, 314, 408–411; Zedler 1968, 74). Aquinas's reproach is nothing new to the DUI reader, as the argument on which Athaq's claim is based has previously been discussed by Aquinas.[44] What is more, Aquinas has already expressed his strong resentment over Athaq's reasoning, saying that his opponent had argued "in a highly uneducated manner" so as to produce the desired conclusion from the aforementioned argument (Thomas Aquinas 1976, 311, 96–99).[45]

In fact, Aquinas's indignation is perfectly understandable as one of the most famous proponents of the theory that provides the background for Athaq's argument is Aquinas himself, as is well known. In Aquinas's view, within a species, at a given time, the principle of individuation for the specifically same form is what he calls designated matter ("materia signata").[46] Since he completely rejected that separate substances have matter of any kind if we use the word "matter" in the proper sense,[47] he held the view throughout his career that there could not be multiple individuals within the distinct species of intelligences.[48] Had Aquinas agreed with the view that

---

[43] "Nec minoris presumptionis est quod postmodum asserere audet, Deum non posse facere quod sint multi intellectus, quia implicat contradictionem." "What he dares to assert later is no less presumptuous that God cannot make many intellects, because this would involve a contradiction."

[44] See Chap. 5. no. 99–105. Thomas Aquinas 1976, 310, 1–311, 117; Keeler 1936, 63–68; Zedler 1968, 65–67.

[45] "Valde autem ruditer argumentantur ad ostendendum quod hoc Deus facere non possit quod sint multi intellectus, credentes hoc includere contradictionem." See also Keeler 1936, 67; Zedler 1968, 67; McInerny 1993, 127. I deviate here from the English translation of both Zedler and McInerny. For Aquinas's plural references see footnote 2 above.

[46] As Gyula Klima emphasizes, in Aquinas's view "all matter in reality is designated matter, i.e., concrete chunks of matter existing under the determinate dimensions of the individual bodies they constitute." The distinction between "designated" and "non-designated" matter therefore is not a real distinction, but a distinction of two different conceptual approaches to the same thing. See Klima 2007, 231, footnote 18. For more on the principle of individuation see Roland-Gosselin 1926, 51–134. For the various interpretations of Aquinas's theory and the spatial and temporal dimensions of individuation see further Wood 2015, esp. 114–116.

[47] Matter would prevent them from exercising their proper act of thinking. Aquinas says that "matter" can only be used homonimously for the separate substances. They are being composed of what makes them actual (*esse*) and of what is made actual (*quidditas*). See In Sent II.3.1.1: "intelligentia non est esse tantum, sicut causa prima; sed est in ea. esse, et forma, quae est quidditas sua et quia omne quod non habet aliquid ex se, sed recipit illud ab alio, est possibile vel in potentia respectu ejus, ideo ipsa quidditas est sicut potentia, et suum esse acquisitum est sicut actus; et ita per consequens est ibi compositio ex actu et potentia et si ista potentia vocetur materia, erit compositus ex materia et forma quamvis hoc sit omnino aequivocum dictum; sapientis enim est non curare de nominibus." Thomas Aquinas 1929, 88.

[48] See e.g. in the *De ente et essentia*: "(…) the essences of composite things, since they are received in designated matter, are multiplied by the division of designated matter, whence in their case it happens that there are numerically distinct things in the same species. However, since the essence of a simple thing is not received in matter, in their case there cannot be this kind of multiplication; therefore, in the case of these substances, there cannot be several individuals in the same species, but there are as many species as there are individuals, as Avicenna expressly claims." See Klima 2007, 239. See further as especially relevant for our investigation a well-known passage from SCG 2.93: "Quaecumque sunt idem specie differentia autem numero, habent materiam differentia enim

the intellective soul, or a part of it, was a *substantia separata* (or, as he puts it in DUI no. 99, a "separate form"), the philosophical refutation of the TUI would obviously have caused just as much difficulty for him as it actually did for his opponent(s).[49] However, even in this case we can safely assume that Aquinas would certainly have found a way out of the conundrum, as we are provided with a counterfactual reasoning in no. 105 that clearly meant to be a sophisticated alternative to Athaq's argument carried out "in a highly uneducated manner".

Aquinas concedes—*per impossibile*, for the sake of argument—that it is "not of the nature of the intellect to be multiplied", i.e. it is a separate substance. He continues with making a distinction between two states of affairs. The first is when "it contradicts a certain thing's nature to be such and such", and the second is when "it does not belong to a certain thing's nature to be such-and-such". In the first instance it is impossible for the thing in question to be such-and-such, whereas in the second it is only impossible if the property in question is regarded as an effect of a cause which is a part of its nature. If such is the case, argues Aquinas, nothing prevents that another cause would bring about the desired effect, for instance when a heavy thing is high up, not from its own nature—as that would involve a contradiction— but from an extraneous cause. On the basis of these considerations, Aquinas denies the consequence that the multiplication of the intellect as a separate substance would involve a contradiction, since even "if the intellect were naturally one for all men because it would not have a natural cause of the multiplication, it could nevertheless receive multiplication from a supernatural cause, and this would not imply a contradiction" (Thomas Aquinas 1976, 311, 108–113; Zedler 1968, 67).[50]

Somewhat surprisingly, Aquinas adds that he does not say this "because of the case in question, but rather lest this form of arguing be applied to other topics", where it is not a contradiction to suppose a supernatural intervention (Thomas Aquinas 1976, 311, 113–117; Zedler 1968, 67).[51] This disclaimer is confounding,

---

quae ex forma procedit, inducit diversitatem speciei; quae autem ex materia, inducit diversitatem secundum numerum. Substantiae autem separatae non habent omnino materiam, neque quae sit pars earum, neque cui uniantur ut formae. Impossibile est igitur quod sint plures unius speciei." See Thomas Aquinas 1918, 563a. For further references to Aquinas's account of the multiplication of intelligences see Hissette 1977, 83, footnote 2.

[49] Johannes Peckham was certainly right when he remarked that the immateriality of the possible intellect is the "fundamentum" of the TUI. See Johannes Pecham 1918, 49.

[50] "Sic ergo si intellectus naturaliter esset unus omnium quia non haberet naturalem causam multiplicationis, posset tamen sortiri multiplicationem ex supernaturali causa, nec esset implicatio contradictionis." See also Keeler 1936, 68, no. 105.

[51] Aquinas applies his recurring examples for miracles here ("the dead rise again", "the blind's sight is restored"). It is important to mention that in no. 105 Aquinas uses essentially the same reasoning as he had set forth in his *Quaestiones disputatae de potentia* (QDP) VI. 1 ad 5 (most probably from 1265–1266; see Torrell 1996, 335), just relying on the somewhat more obscure concept of "a cause in a thing's own nature" in place of "an intrinsic principle": "Just as God cannot make yes and no to be true at the same time, so neither can he do what is impossible in nature in so far as it includes the former impossibility. Thus for a dead man to return to life clearly involves a contradiction if we suppose that his return to life is the natural effect of an intrinsic principle, since a dead man is essentially one who lacks the principle of life. Wherefore God does

because what Aquinas says about supernatural causation is highly relevant in regard to the case in question for at least two reasons. First and foremost, it is relevant with respect to Athaq's position who thinks, in opposition to Aquinas, that the intellect is a separate substance,[52] and also thinks, in accordance with Aquinas, that in the case of separate substances there cannot be several individuals in the same species.[53] Secondly, the supernatural cause of the multiplication of the intellect is certainly relevant with regard to Athaq's next—and probably most famous and most frequently cited—claim (AC4): "I necessarily conclude through reason that the intellect is one in number; but I firmly hold the opposite through faith (Thomas Aquinas 1976, 314, 413–415; Zedler 1968, 74)."[54]

Athaq's claims (AC3 and AC4) taken together prove hopelessly inconsistent again. Athaq maintains, in Aquinas's account, that God cannot possibly make many intellects since it is not of the nature of the intellect (being a separate substance) to be multiplied. According to Aquinas, however, Athaq also maintains that he firmly holds through faith the opposite of the unity of the intellect thesis. The opposite of the unity of the intellect thesis says that there are several intellects within the same species. Athaq therefore firmly holds through faith that there are several intellects within the same species. However, firmly holding through faith that there are several intellects within the same species while claiming that it is not of the nature of the intellect to be multiplied: this does not seem possible without assuming that God as a supernatural cause can make several intellects within the same species beyond the

---

not do this but he makes a dead man to regain life from an extrinsic principle: and this involves no contradiction. The same applies to other things that are impossible to nature, and which God is able to do." See Thomas Aquinas, *On the Power of God*. Translated by the English Dominican Fathers Westminster, Maryland the Newman Press, 1952, Reprint of 1932. HTML Edition by Joseph Kenny, O.P., as retrieved in https://isidore.co/aquinas/QDdePotentia6.htm

[52] See e.g. "Hoc autem ultimum uerbum maxime assumunt ad sui erroris fulcimentum, uolentes per hoc habere quod intellectus neque sit anima neque pars anime, sed quedam substantia separata.": "Now it is especially this last word that they take over to support their error, intending by this to hold that the intellect is neither the soul nor a part of the soul, but some separate substance." See Thomas Aquinas 1976, 296, 450–453; Zedler 1968, 33; Keeler 1936, 17. no. 25.

[53] As it is clear from no. 99: "Si ergo est separatus et non est forma materialis, nullo modo multiplicatur secundum multiplicationem corporum." "If, therefore, it is separate and is not a material form, it is in no way multiplied according to the multiplication of bodies." Thomas Aquinas 1976, 310, 12–14; Keeler 1936, 64; Zedler 1968, 65.

[54] "Per rationem concludo de necessitate quod intellectus est unus numero, firmiter tamen teneo oppositum per fidem." See also Keeler 1936, 79, no. 123; McInerny 1993, 143. "Firmiter teneo": there is nothing peculiar in this expression. It had been in use since the Patristic era and was still widely used in the thirteenth century. In its various forms, this phrase tipically refers to a mental attitude regarding the doctrines of faith and expresses an obligation of the faithful. See e. g. the phrasal idiom "firmissime tene, et nullatenus dubites" in Ivo of Chartres's *Decretum* (PL 161, passim). However, it is important to emphasize that it does not have anything to do with epistemology or logic, as it is related only to the rule-following behaviour of the believer in a religious context. For the occurrence of the phrase in the contemporary arts magisters' works, see e.g. Siger of Brabant's *Quaestiones super Librum de causis*, q. 27: "firmiter tenendum quod hominum multiplicatione multiplicatur" or Boethius of Dacia's *De aeternitate mundi*: "ut sententia fidei firmiter teneatur." See Marlasca 1972, 115; Boethius de Dacia 1976, 335.

ordinary course of nature. Athaq, therefore, thinks and firmly holds through faith that God can make several intellects within the same species and, at the same time, he also thinks that God cannot make several intellects within the same species. In addition to this, Athaq says that he necessarily concludes through reason that the intellect is one in number.

It is obvious that Athaq's claims as they are presented by Aquinas do not make any sense. It is not an option for us, however, to attempt to modify Athaq's sentences in an effort to amend them. Our only source for Athaq's text is Aquinas's report and we have no other choice but to assume that his report represents correctly what Athaq said or—most probably—wrote, or what someone else said or—most probably—wrote about what Athaq had said or had written.

Let us see Aquinas's famous comment on AC4 that has formed the starting point for a considerable number of speculations later: "Therefore he thinks that faith is concerned with some propositions whose contraries can be necessarily concluded. But since only a necessary truth can be concluded necessarily, and the opposite of this is something false and impossible, it follows, according to his remark, that faith would be concerned with something false and impossible, that not even God could effect. This the faithful cannot bear to hear" (Thomas Aquinas 1976, 314,415–422; Zedler 1968, 74).[55] Aquinas's comment is astonishing because AC4 states exactly what Aquinas himself concluded in no. 105, save the counterfactual phrasing: the intellect is naturally one for all men because it does not have a natural cause of the multiplication; it can nevertheless receive multiplication from a supernatural cause. In addition, Aquinas strongly emphasizes in no. 105 that the intellect's multiplication from a supernatural cause would not imply a contradiction.[56]

Indeed, Athaq asserts with regard to the intellect in AC4 that it does not have a natural cause of multiplication. This is precisely what Aquinas maintains with respect to the separate substances throughout his career and, more importantly, this is what he concedes *per impossibile* with regard to the intellect at the beginning of no. 105. Furthermore, we are safe to assume that Athaq also thinks, in accordance with Aquinas, that the philosopher, by means of the investigation of natural reason, considers those things that belong to creatures by their proper nature.[57] Consequently,

---

[55] "Ergo sentit quod fides sit de aliquibus quorum contraria de necessitate concludi possunt; cum autem de necessitate concludi non possit nisi uerum necessarium, cuius oppositum est falsum impossibile, sequitur secundum eius dictum quod fides sit de falso impossibili, quod etiam Deus facere non potest: quod fidelium aures ferre non possunt." See also Keeler 1936, 79, no. 123.

[56] See footnote 50 above.

[57] See e.g. SCG 2.4: "Philosophus (…) considerat illa quae eis secundum naturam propriam conveniunt (…)"; Similarly, Siger of Brabant with regard to the multiplication of the intellect: "As to the seventh point raised above, viz. whether the intellective soul is multiplied in accord with the multiplication of human bodies, it must be carefully considered insofar as such pertains to the philosopher and can be grasped by human reason and experience, by seeking the mind of the philosophers in this matter rather than the truth since we are proceeding philosophically." (*On the Intellective Soul*, Chap. VII; Klima 2007, 203). See further Boethius de Dacia, *Super Libros Physicorum* I Quaestio 1–2 (Boethius de Dacia 1974, 139–142) and Roland Hissette's remarks in Hissette 1977, 23–26.

Athaq claims that "I necessarily conclude through reason that the intellect is one in number". He is certainly convinced that this sentence properly expresses the fact that the intellect cannot be multiplied as a result of natural processes, for this would involve a contradiction. Nevertheless, since at this stage of the reasoning he might already be aware that although it does not belong to the intellect's nature to be multiplied, and therefore we cannot say through natural reason that it can be multiplied, it does not contradict its nature to be multiplied by a higher, extraneous cause.[58] As a result, Athaq—as someone who professes that he is a Christian—is pleased to recognize the God of the Catholic faith as this higher, external cause. So, he adds: "but I firmly hold the opposite through faith."

I think this reading of Athaq can seamlessly be accommodated within the conceptual framework developed by Aquinas earlier in Chap. 5 of the DUI. What is more, it seems to be in complete accordance with Aquinas's general views on the use of modal terms in philosophy and theology with regard to intellective substances. As a case in point, when investigating the use of the concept of "impossible" in logic and mathematics, Aquinas does not hesitate to declare that the natural philosopher applies the concept "impossible" to what is impossible with regard to "determined matter". Nonetheless, it does not follow, notes Aquinas, that anything could prevent God from being able to do what is impossible for agents inferior to him, as the only limitation of divine power is what is *per se* impossible.[59]

Aquinas caused serious headaches to his commentators by claiming several times that intelligences are impossible to multiply within a species, while arguing in the DUI that the multiplication of the intelligences within a species is possible from a supernatural cause.[60] If it is correct to say that Aquinas's apparent inconsistency in this matter can easily be solved by a simple extension of the distinction he makes in QDP VI. 1., by introducing e.g. the concept pair "impossibile quantum ad modos multiplicationis nobis notos" and "impossibile simpliciter", then it would seem just

---

[58] Perhaps because he has grown out of his *ruditas* by now. If Athaq is identical to Siger of Brabant, this would miraculously shorten the period of his development into a Thomist. For what has been called Siger's "evolution" see, among many others, Van Steenberghen 1942, 551–560; Zimmerman 1967–68, 206–217; Fioravanti 1972, 407–464; Marlasca 1972, 18–22; Mahoney 1974; Bazán 1980, esp. 236–243; Van Steenberghen 1977, passim; Imbach and Putallaz 1997, 154–168, Bazán 2005, 613–625. For the historiography of Siger's "evolution", see Imbach 1991, 202–205. For the opposite case see Calma and Coccia 2006, 284–317.

[59] See QDP VI. 1: "(…) logicus et mathematicus considerant tantum res secundum principia formalia; unde nihil est impossibile in logicis vel mathematicis, nisi quod est contra rei formalem rationem. Et huiusmodi impossibile in se contradictionem claudit, et sic est per se impossibile. Talia autem impossibilia Deus facere non potest. Naturalis autem applicat ad determinatam materiam unde reputat impossibile etiam id quod est huic impossibile. Nihil autem prohibet Deum posse facere quae sunt inferioribus agentibus impossibilia." See also footnote 51 above.

[60] See e.g. the commentary by Francis Sylvester of Ferrara on SCG 2.93 with reference to DUI no. 105. See Thomas Aquinas 1918, 565a, VI. 3. See further Descoqs 1922; Balthasar 1922; Keeler 1936, 67–68, notes to no. 105; Hissette 1977, 82–87; Hissette 1977, 5–7; Wippel 1995, 243–248; De Libera 2004, 395–402.

as correct to introduce a similar distinction in the case of Athaq.[61] This could even solve the inconsistency between AC3 and AC4 and this solution, as thirteenth century sources show, would not be outlandish at all.[62] Conversely, if we are not generous enough to charitably interpret Athaq's words, and furthermore, if we would like to be fair in distributing malevolence, we must apply the same unkindness to Aquinas himself who seems to be at least as inconsistent with regard to the impossibility of multiplication of separate substances within a species as is Athaq—on Aquinas's account—in his treatment of the intellect as a separate substance. This would undoubtedly inflict considerable harm on Aquinas's thought, and we could say—yet again—that an uncharitable interpretation of Athaq's claims has a destructive effect on Aquinas's philosophy and theology.

In spite of all that, in order to eliminate the inconsistency of AC3 and AC4, Aquinas chooses to simply ignore the propositional content of what is firmly held by Athaq through faith: that there are several intellects within the same species. He provides us with an elementary logic lesson instead that he presents as an interpretation of AC4, while, as we have just seen, he could also have interpreted this passage as being fully in line with his own previous argument no. 105 and his own distinction between two different senses of the relevant modal terms. In the light of his earlier remarks, we can simply regard his choice as a further consequence of his overall interpretative malice towards Athaq. It is possible, however, that there is more to it than that.

It is widely held that Aquinas's comment on AC4 has always been seen as a kind of testimony for something that has usually been referred to as "veritas duplex".[63] In accordance with the "veritas duplex" type of approaches, a fairly obvious reading of Aquinas's comment would be that Aquinas would like to point out in this passage that we cannot possibly have two contradictory beliefs, a belief-that-p and a belief-that-non-p simultaneously.[64] This reading would provide us with a further contribution to the already familiar image of Athaq *ruditer argumentans* (as a matter of fact, he is quite close to being represented as cognitively disabled here), but, first and

---

[61] For this concept pair which is just an example borrowed from an author writing centuries later, see Francis Sylvester of Ferrara's commentary referred to in the previous footnote.

[62] For the strong emphasis of the arts masters on the inscrutability of divine will and the distinction of true or false *simpliciter* and true or false *secundum quid/secundum naturam* in contexts where doctrines of faith and propositions of philosophy are compared and evaluated see, again, among many others, Fioravanti 1970, esp. 530–531, 557; Pinborg 1974, esp. 169–181; Hissette 1977, esp. 45–49., 275–276; Knuuttila 1993, 99–137, esp. 136; Bianchi 1999, esp. 175–187; De Libera 2004, 25. It is also important to note that, in Aquinas's view, the second aspect of truth with regard to divine things "totally exceeds the ability of human reason", even though certain "intelligibilia divinorum" can be expressed in propositional form as articles of faith. See SCG 1.3, Thomas Aquinas 1918, 7–8.

[63] For the historiography of the "notion" or "theory" of "double truth" see, Van Steenberghen 1974; Bianchi 2008. For Aquinas's *De unitate intellectus* no. 123 as a precursor of the "interpretive schema" found in the introductory letter to Stephen Tempier's 1277 syllabus, see De Libera 1998, 82–83.

[64] See e.g. De Libera 2004, 506–511.

foremost, would provide us with a further contribution to the image of Athaq who intends to hide his true intention behind a blatant inconsistency. In Aquinas's interpretation, Athaq wraps his most important message in meaningless expressions. And his most important message is that faith is concerned with impossible things, things that even God cannot do.

A significant aspect of AC4, however, vanishes here. If we call what is necessarily concluded by Athaq a "belief", then we cannot say that AC4 expresses that Athaq has two contradictory beliefs. Most importantly, we cannot say Athaq has two contradictory beliefs even by Aquinas's standards. Let us take as a basis for what follows a standard description of some of the most important features of belief. (1) Beliefs are involuntary: we cannot decide whether or not we have a particular belief. (2) Beliefs "aim at truth", i.e. they are shaped by evidence and are adjusted to the state of affairs and not the other way around, as in the case of desires. (3) Beliefs do not have to be conscious for the one who possesses them. Our beliefs are usually not conscious. An important feature of them, however, is that even if they are not conscious, they can be made conscious. (4) In order to attribute beliefs to others, we must assume that their beliefs form a network that is subject to the requirements of consistency and coherence.[65]

It is obvious that faith, on Aquinas's account, has different properties.[66] Most importantly, what Aquinas calls faith is a result of a free and dramatic choice of the will and this choice is directed at something that we do not have evidence for, as in the case of science.[67] Furthermore, it cannot be seen how it would be possible for a religious "belief" not to be conscious if its acceptance, as Aquinas emphasizes, is a result of a dramatic choice and this choice has considerable moral weight. Finally, Aquinas stresses that since the entire consistent and coherent set of *fides* (the set of propositions identified and analyzed by theology) is not generally known explicitly by the ordinary believer, it is sufficient for most of them to learn the most important articles of faith and to be prepared to have faith in others.[68]

We cannot say, therefore, even by Aquinas's standards, that AC4 reveals that Athaq has two contradictory beliefs. Athaq has a belief "that the intellect is one in

---

[65] On these characteristics of belief, see Williams 1973; Bratman 1999; Engel 2000; Crane 2014.

[66] It is not relevant from the perspective of the "duplex veritas" approaches that keep revolving around the idea of having two contradictory beliefs simultaneously that Aquinas contrasts faith with science and opinion.

[67] For Aquinas's emphasis on the fact that the commitment to the incomprehensible and indemonstrable articles of the Catholic faith is a result of a purely voluntary act and not a termination of natural cognitive processes, see Borbély 2020, 75–77.

[68] ST 2a2ae.2.5. co.: "Quantum ergo ad prima credibilia, quae sunt articuli fidei, tenetur homo explicite credere, sicut et tenetur habere fidem. Quantum autem ad alia credibilia, non tenetur homo explicite credere, sed solum implicite vel in praeparatione animi, inquantum paratus est credere quidquid in divina Scriptura continetur." "As regards the first believable things, which are the articles of faith, man is held to believe them explicitly, just as he is also held to have faith. As regards the rest of the believable things, man is not held explicitly to believe, but only implicitly or by preparation of soul, so far as he is prepared to believe whatever is contained in divine Scripture." See Thomas Aquinas 1990, 78.

number" and—as a result of a free and dramatic choice of the will—he has a different attitude, i.e. the attitude of faith that "there are several intellects within the same species".[69] As a matter of fact, probably the philosopher himself, who I decided to call Athaq in this paper, also thought that faith and justified true belief (*scientia*) are essentially different attitudes.[70] But all of this is of little significance, since Aquinas himself is clearly convinced that the mental attitude of faith is significantly different from the attitude of knowledge, even if they have some common features.[71] Therefore, and again, Aquinas could have given a consistent and coherent interpretation of Athaq's words based on what he himself held of the features of the attitude of "faith", sparing thereby himself from the inconsistencies he is self-inflicting with his own interpretation of Athaq's words.

Why would not Aquinas attempt to do that? Why would he insist on Athaq's serious oddity, even if he thereby makes himself less rational and more incoherent? Athaq, as is represented by Aquinas in DUI, seems to be Aquinas's worst nightmare: someone who is recklessly committed to the articles of the Catholic faith "as though following artificial fables" (Thomas Aquinas 1918, 17; Thomas Aquinas 1955, 71).[72] Aquinas is convinced that, in the case of Athaq, "firmly holding" something "through faith" is tantamount to a pure act of social commitment regardless of the propositional content of what is believed by faith. As far as Aquinas is concerned, it is impossible to demonstrate the truth of such contents, as the articles of faith represent the incomprehensible aspect of truth with regard to the highest good and ultimate end, God. Yet it is not possible either that these contents be "apart from reason", because Aquinas believes that what is apart from reason is evil.[73] In con-

---

[69] Even though I will not discuss this issue in this paper, it deserves to be mentioned that the multiplicity of the intellect within the same species is a doctrine of faith for Aquinas, too. See footnote 30 above. On Aquinas's admirable attempt to provide us with a semantic solution for the problem of the *duplex entitas* of the human soul, i.e. for the problem that the human soul alone seems to be both an inherent and a subsistent being, see Klima 2018.

[70] On this point see footnote 54, and the literature in footnote 62 above.

[71] See e.g. ST 2a2ae.2.1. co: "(...) actus iste qui est credere habet firmam adhaesionem ad unam partem, in quo convenit credens cum sciente et intelligente, et tamen eius cognitio non est perfecta per manifestam visionem, in quo convenit cum dubitante, suspicante et opinante." "But the act of believing has firm adherence to one alternative, in which the believer agrees with the knower and the one who understands. Yet its apprehension is not completed by manifest vision, in which the believer agrees with the doubter, the suspecter, and the opiner." See Thomas Aquinas 1990, 67–68.

[72] See SCG 1.6 with reference to 2 Peter 2:16. In Aquinas's view, "imagination" (*phantasia*) can metaphorically refer to the erroneous choice of the intellect (see e. g. QDP VI.6 ad 3: "utitur autem metaphorice" (i.e., Dionysius) "nomine phantasiae pro intellectu errante in eligendo.") In contrast to human reason which "is always correct either in that it is disposed toward first principles about which it does not err, or in that error results from defective reasoning rather than the properties of reason", it is an essential property of imagination that it apprehends the images or likenesses of absent (including non-existent) things. Its operation therefore leads to error. See *Quaestiones disputatae de malo* 7.5 ad 6; for the English translation, see Thomas Aquinas 2003, 291.

[73] As for whether the assent to the articles of faith can rationally be justified according to Aquinas, see Borbély 2020. In Aquinas's view, although the will "takes a leading role" "in the knowledge of faith", still "the good of the will" consists in the fact that "it follows the understanding". Therefore,

trast, for Athaq—as Aquinas seeks to point out—the propositional content firmly held by faith could even be what is impossible, i.e. something that is, at least from Aquinas's perspective, obviously "apart from reason". It is needless to say that this interpretation does not make Athaq an atheist. This interpretation makes Athaq a stranger who—at least in Aquinas's eyes—simply does not care about the propositional content of faith when doing philosophy, or if he does, he regards this content as something that can be subject to rational inquiry and philosophical analysis like everything else.

This latter point is reflected in Aquinas's last comments on the behavior of Athaq, who "dares to dispute about those things that do not pertain to philosophy but are matters of pure faith."[74] Far beyond the issue of the unity of the intellect, this is a clear and unequivocal declaration that, in Aquinas's view, there is no reciprocity between the philosopher and the theologian when it comes to the domination of the territories of human cognition.[75] It is hardly surprising that there seems to be a link between Aquinas's words and the statute of the Parisian Arts Faculty of 1 April 1272. This statute decrees that "no master or bachelor" of the arts faculty "should presume to determine or even to dispute any purely theological question, as concerning the Trinity and incarnation and similar matters, since this would be transgressing the limits assigned him (Thorndijk 1944, 85)."[76] The forced restraint or self-restraint of the arts masters including Athaq is perfectly understandable, as they can lose everything by firmly adhering to their universalistic approach. A dedicated spiritual warrior, however, such as Aquinas can lose nothing in this fight, except for the consistency and coherence he had always been striving for.

"what is apart from reason is evil." See SCG 3.40 and SCG 3.107. Cf. Thomas Aquinas 1926, 99a and 336b; Thomas Aquinas 1956 (Part I), 131 and Thomas Aquinas 1956 (Part II), 102.

[74] "With equal reasoning he could argue about the Trinity, the Incarnation, and other teachings of this kind" that "he could only discuss as someone who is blind to these matters," adds Aquinas. Again, I deviated from the English translation of both Zedler and McInerny. See Zedler 1968, 74, and McInerny 1993, 143. Keeler 1936, 79–80, no. 123. Thomas Aquinas 1976, 314, 422–430: "Non caret etiam magna temeritate, quod de hiis que ad philosophiam non pertinent, sed sunt pure fidei, disputare presumit, sicut quod anima patiatur ab igne inferni, et dicere sententias doctorum de hoc esse reprobandas; pari enim ratione posset disputare de Trinitate, de Incarnatione et aliis huiusmodi, de quibus nonnisi cecutiens loqueretur." For Aquinas's famous reference to the issue of whether the soul can suffer from fire see De Libera 1994, 281 and De Libera 2004, 511–521.

[75] In Aquinas's view, "human philosophy" "serves" theology as the highest wisdom: "et propter hoc sibi, quasi principali, philosophia humana deservit." See SCG 2.4 (Thomas Aquinas 1918, 279b).

[76] For the text of the statute, see Denifle and Chatelain 1889, 499–500; Weijers 1995, 140–142. For the interpretation of the statute, see Gauthier 1984, 20–25; Imbach and Putallaz 1997, 123–142; Bianchi 1999, 165–201; Pluta 2002; Bianchi 2008, 98–115. For the apparent link between the DUI and the statute, see Van Steenberghen 1977, 84; Imbach and Putallaz 1997, 47; De Libera 1998, 86; Bianchi 1999, 171–172.

Bibliography

Aegidius Romanus. 1554. *Theoremata de Corpore Christi*. Roma: Antonius Bladus.

Albertus Magnus. 1890–98. Liber De sensu et sensato. In *Opera Omnia*, Vol. 9, ed. August Borgnet, 1–93. Paris: Vivès.

———. 1892. De Coelesti Hierarchia. In *Opera Omnia*, ed. August Borgnet, vol. 14, 1–451. Paris: Vivès.

———. 1968. De anima, ed. Clemens Stroick. In *Opera Omnia*, Tomus VII Pars I, ed. Albertus-Magnus-Institut, 1–250. Münster: Aschendorff.

———. 1975. De unitate intellectus, ed. Alfons Hufnagel. In *Opera Omnia*, Tomus XVII Pars I, ed. Albertus-Magnus-Institut 1–30. Münster: Aschendorff.

Balthasar, Nicolas. 1922. À propos d'un passage controversé du "De Unitate Intellectus" de saint Thomas d'Aquin. *Revue néoscolastique de philosophie* 24: 465–478.

Bazán, Bernardo Carlos. 1972. Introduction. In *Siger de Brabant: Quaestiones in tertium de anima, De anima intellectiva, De aeternitate mundi*, 7*–80*. Louvain: Publications Universitaires—Paris: Béatrice-Nauwelaerts.

———. 1974. La dialogue philosophique entre Siger de Brabant et Thomas d'Aquin. *Revue philosophique de Louvain* 72: 53–155.

———. 1980. La réconciliation de la foi et de la raison était-elle possible pour les aristotéliciens radicaux? *Dialogue* 19: 235–254.

———. 2005. Radical Aristotelianism in the Faculties of Arts, The Case of Siger of Brabant. In *Albertus Magnus und die Anfänge der Aristoteles-Rezeption im lateinischen Mittelalter*, ed. Ludger Honnefelder, Rega Wood, Mechthild Dreyer, and Marc-Aeilko Aris, 585–629. Münster: Aschendorff.

Biller, Peter. 1985. Words and the medieval notion of religion. *The Journal of Ecclesiastical History* 36: 351–369.

Bianchi, Luca. 1999. *Censure et liberté intellectuelle à l'Université de Paris (XIIIe–XIVe siècles)*. Paris: Les Belles Lettres.

———. 2008. *Pour une historie de la "double vérité"*. Paris: Vrin.

———. 2015. L'averroismo di Dante. *Le Tre Corone* 2: 71–109.

Boethius de Dacia. 1974. Quaestiones Super Libros Physicorum. In *Boethii Daci Opera* V, Pars II, ed. Géza Sajó, 139–322. Hauniae: Det Danske Sprog- og Litteraturselskab.

———. 1976. De aeternitate mundi. In *Boethii Daci Opera* VI, Pars II, Opuscula. ed. Nicolaus Georgius Green-Pedersen, 335–366. Hauniae: Det Danske Sprog- og Litteraturselskab.

Bonaventura. 1885. Commentaria In Quatuor Libros Sententiarum Magistri Petri Lombardi: In Secundum Librum Sententiarum. In *Opera Omnia*, Tomus II. Ad Claras Aquas (Quaracchi): Ex Typographia Collegii S. Bonaventurae.

———. 1934. *Collationes in Hexaëmeron*, ed. F. Delorme. Ad Claras Aquas (Quaracchi): Ex Typographia Collegii S. Bonaventurae.

Borbély, Gábor, and Gyula Klima. 2000. Dialektikus disputa az értelem egységének skolasztikus kérdéséről. *Magyar Filozófiai Szemle* 44: 361–404.

Borbély, Gábor. 2020. The triumph of renouncement: Religious signals, the secrets of the heart, error, deception and happiness in Thomas Aquinas's Summa contra Gentiles. *Hungarian Philosophical Quarterly* 64: 63–132.

Bratman, Michael E. 1999. Practical reasoning and acceptance in a context. In *Faces of intention: Selected essays on intention and agency*, 15–34. Cambridge: Cambridge University Press.

Calma, Dragos, and Emanuele Coccia. 2006. Un commentaire inédit de Siger de Brabant sur la "Physique" d'Aristote (Ms. Paris, BnF, lat. 16297). *Archives d'histoire doctrinale et littéraire du Moyen Âge*. 73: 283–349.

Calma, Dragos. 2006. Le corps des images: Siger de Brabant entre le *Liber de causis* et Averroès. *Freiburger Zeitschrift für Philosophie und Theologie* 53: 188–235.

Crane, Tim. 2014. Unconscious belief and conscious thought. In *Aspects of psychologism*, 261–280. Cambridge, MA: Harvard University Press.

Dales, Richard C. 1995. *The problem of the rational soul in the thirteenth century*. Leiden-New York-Köln: Brill.

De Libera, Alain. 1994. *Thomas d'Aquin contre Averroès: L'unité de l'intellect contre les averroïstes suivi des Textes contre Averroès antérieurs à 1270. Texte latin. Traduction, introduction, bibliographie, chronologie, notes et index*. Paris: GF-Flammarion.

———. 1998. Philosophie et censure. Remarques sur la crise universitaire parisienne de 1270–1277. *Was ist Philosophie im Mittelalter?* ed. Jan A. Aertsen and Andreas Speer, 71–89. Berlin-New York: de Gruyter.

———. 2004. *L'Unité de l'intellect: Commentaire du De unitate intellectus contra averroistas de Thomas d'Aquin*. Paris: Vrin.

Denifle, Heinrich and Emile Chatelain. 1889. *Chartularium Universitatis Parisiensis*, Tomus I. Paris: Delalain.

Descoqs, Pedro. 1922. La théorie de la matière et de la forme et ses fondements. *Troisième article. Revue de Philosophie* 29: 181–207.

Ehrle, Franz. 1889. Beiträge zur Geschichte der mittelalterlichen Scholastik II: Der Augustinismus und der Aristotelismus in der Scholastik gegen Ende des 13. Jahrhunderts. *Archiv für Literatur- und Kirchengeschichte des Mittelalters* V: 603–635.

Engel, Pascal. 2000. Introduction: The varieties of belief and acceptance. In *Believing and Accepting*, ed. Pascal Engel, 1–30. Dordrecht: Kluwer Academic Publishers.

Fioravanti, Gianfranco. 1970. "Scientia", "fides", "theologia" in Boezio di Dacia. *Atti dell'Accademia delle Scienze di Torino* 104: 525–632.

———. 1972. Sull'evoluzione del monopsichismo in Sigieri di Brabante. *Atti dell'Accademia delle Scienze di Torino* 106: 407–474.

Gauthier, René Antoine. 1983. Notes sur Siger de Brabant: I. Siger en 1265. *Revue des sciences philosophiques et théologiques* 67: 201–232.

———. 1984. Notes sur Siger de Brabant: II. Siger en 1272–1275. Aubry de Reims et la scission des Normands. *Revue des sciences philosophiques et théologiques* 68: 3–49.

Giele, Maurice. 1971. Un commentaire averroïste sur les livres I et II du traité de l'âme (Oxford, Merton College 275, f. 108–121). In *Trois commentaires anonymes sur le Traité de de l'âme d'Aristote*, ed. Maurice Giele, Fernand Van Steenberghen and Bernardo Bazán, 13–120. Louvain: Pulications Universitaires-Paris: Béatrice-Nauwelaerts.

Hissette, Roland. 1977. *Enquête sur les 219 articles condamnés à Paris le 7 mars 1277*. Louvain: Publications Universitaries – Paris: Vander-Oyez.

Imbach, Ruedi. 1991. L'Averroïsme latin du XIIIe siècle. In *Gli studi di filosofia medievale fra Otto e Novocento. Contributo a un bilancio storiografico*, ed. Ruedi Imbach and Alfonso Maierù, 191–208. Roma: Edizioni di storia e letteratura.

Imbach, Ruedi, and François-Xavier Putallaz. 1997. *Profession: Philosophe. Siger de Brabant*. Paris: Cerf.

Johannes Pecham. 1918. Quaestiones de anima, ed. H. Spettmann. *Beiträge zur Geschichte der Philosophie des Mittelalters: Texte und Untersuchungen* 19: 1–104.

Kaluza, Zénon. 1996. Bulletin d'histoire des doctrines médiévales: les XIVe et XVe siècles (I). *Revue des Sciences philosophiques et théologiques* 80: 317–349.

Keeler, Leo W. 1936. *Sancti Thomae Aquinatis Tractatus de unitate intellectus contra averroistas*. Editio critica. Roma: Apud Aedes Pont. Universitatis Gregorianae.

Klima, Gyula. 1998. Ancilla theologiae vs. domina philosophorum: Thomas Aquinas, Latin Averroism and the autonomy of philosophy. In *Was ist Philosophie im Mittelalter?* ed. Jan A. Aertsen and Andreas Speer, 393–402. Berlin-New York: de Gruyter.

———. 2007. *Medieval philosophy: Essential readings with commentary*, ed. Gyula Klima with Fritz Allhoff and Anand Jayprakash Vaidya. Oxford: Blackwell.

———. 2018. Aquinas' balancing act: balancing the soul between the realms of matter and pure spirit. *Bochumer Philosophisches Jahrbuch für Antike und Mittelalter* 21: 29–48.

Knuuttila, Simo. 1993. *Modalities in medieval philosophy*. London-New York: Routledge.

Luna, Concetta. 1999. Quelques précisions chronologiques à propos de la controverse sur l'unité de l'intellect. *Revue des Sciences philosophiques et théologiques* 83: 649–684.

Mahoney, Edward P. 1974. Saint Thomas and Siger of Brabant revisited. *The Review of Metaphysics* 27: 531–553.

Mandonnet, Pierre. 1911. *Siger de Brabant et l'averroisme latin au XIIIe siecle*. Ire partie, Etude critique. Deuxième édition revue et augmentée. Louvain: Institut Supérieur de Philosophie de l'Université.

Marlasca, Antonio. 1972. *Les Quaestiones super Librum de causis de Siger de Brabant*. Louvain: Pulications Universitaires-Paris: Béatrice-Nauwelaerts.

McInerny, Ralph M. 1993. *Aquinas against the Averroists: On there being only one intellect*. West Lafayette, IN: Purdue University Press.

Nardi, Bruno. 1947. Note per una storia dell'averroismo latino II: La posizione di Alberto Magno di fronte all' averroismo. *Rivista di Storia della Filosofia* 2: 197–220.

———. 1960. Alberto Magno e San Tommaso. In *Studi di filosofia medievale*, 103–117. Roma: Edizioni di Storia e Letteratura.

———. 1938. *S. Tommaso d'Aquino, Trattato sull'unita dell'intelletto contro gli averroisti*. Traduzione, commento e introduzione di Bruno Nardi. Firenze: Sansoni.

Paré, Gérard Marie, Adrien Marie Brunet, and Pierre Tremblay. 1933. *La renaissance du XIIe siècle: les écoles et l'enseignement*. Paris: Vrin-Ottawa: Institut d'études médiévale.

Pinborg, Jan. 1974. Zur Philosophie des Boethius de Dacia: Ein Überblick. *Studia Mediewistyczne* 15: 165–185.

Piron, Sylvain. 2006. Olivi et les averroïstes. *Freiburger Zeitschrift für Philosophie und Theologie* 53: 251–309.

Pluta, Olaf. 2002. Persecution and the art of writing: The Parisian statute of April 1, 1272, and its philosophical consequences. In *Chemins de la pensée médiévale: Études offertes à Zénon Kaluza*, ed. Paul J. J. M. Bakker avec la collaboration de Emmanuel Faye et Christophe Grellard, 563–585. Turnhout: Brepols.

Roger Bacon. 2010. *Operis maioris pars VII (Moralis philosophia)*. Turnhout: Brepols.

———. 1859. Compendium studii philosophiae. In *Opera quaedam hactenus inedita*, ed. J. S. Brewer, 393–519. London: Longman, Green, Longman, and Roberts.

———. 1897. *The Opus Majus of Roger Bacon*. Edited, with Introduction and Analytical Table, by John Henry Bridges, 2 vols. Oxford: Clarendon Press.

Roland Gosselin, Marie-Dominique. 1926. *Le "De ente et essentia" de S. Thomas d'Aquin*. Le Saulchoir, Kain: Revue des Sciences philosophiques et théologiques.

Siger de Brabant. 1972. *Quaestiones in tertium De anima, De anima intellectiva, De aeternitate mundi*. Edited Bernardo Bazán. Louvain: Pulications Universitaires-Paris: Béatrice-Nauwelaerts.

Thomas Aquinas. 1911. *The "Summa theologica" of St. Thomas Aquinas*. Part I. Literally translated by the Fathers of the English Dominican Province. London: Washbourne-New York: Benziger Bros.

———. 1918. *Summa contra Gentiles*. Sancti Thomae Aquinatis Doctoris Angelici Opera Omnia iussu Leonis XIII P. M. edita. Tom. XIII. Roma: Typis Riccardi Garroni.

———. 1926. *Summa contra Gentiles*. Liber tertius. Sancti Thomae Aquinatis Doctoris Angelici Opera Omnia iussu Leonis XIII P. M. edita. Tom. XIV. Roma: Typis Riccardi Garroni.

———. 1929. *Scriptum super libros Sententiarum Magistri Petri Lombardi Episcopi Parisiensis*. Editio nova, cura R. P. Mandonnet, O. P. Tomus I–IV. Paris: Lethielleux.

———. 1955. *On the truth of the Catholic faith: Summa contra Gentiles book one: God*. Translated, with an Introduction and Notes, by Anton C. Pegis. Garden City, NY: Image Books.

———. 1956. *On the truth of the Catholic faith: Summa contra Gentiles book three: Providence*. Part I-II. Translated, with an Introduction and Notes, by Vernon J. Bourke. Garden City, NY: Image Books.

———. 1964. *St. Thomas Aquinas on the eternity of the world*. Translated from the Latin with an Introduction by Cyril Vollert. In *St. Thomas Aquinas-Siger of Brabant-St. Bonaventure: On the eternity of the world.* Translated from the Latin with an Introduction by Cyril Vollert, Lottie H. Kendzierski, and Paul M. Byrne, 19–25. Milwaukee: Marquette University Press.

———. 1976. *Opera omnia.* Tomus XLIII. Cura et studio Fratrum Praedicatorum. Roma: Editori di San Tommaso.

———. 1984a. *Sentencia libri De anima.* Opera omnia, Tomus XLV, 1. Cura et studio Fratrum Praedicatorum. Roma: Commissio Leonina-Paris: Vrin.

———. 1984b. *Sentencia libri De sensu et sensato.* Opera omnia, Tomus XLV, 2. Cura et studio Fratrum Praedicatorum. Roma: Commissio Leonina-Paris: Vrin.

———. 1989. *Expositio libri Posteriorum.* Opera omnia, Tomus I*, 2. Editio altera retractata. Cura et studio Fratrum Praedicatorum. Roma: Commissio Leonina- Paris: Vrin.

———. 1990. *On Faith: Summa theologiae 2-2, qq. 1–16 of St. Thomas Aquinas.* Translated by Mark D. Jordan. Notre Dame: University of Notre Dame Press.

———. 1993. *Az értelem egysége.* Fordította, a kötetet szerkesztette és a kommentárokat írta Borbély Gábor. Budapest: Ikon.

———. 1996. *Quaestiones disputatae de anima.* Opera omnia, Tomus XXIV, 1. Ed. B. C. Bazán Roma: Commissio Leonina-Paris: CERF.

———. 2003. *On Evil.* Translated by Richard Regan. Edited with an introduction and notes by Brian Davies. Oxford: Oxford University Press.

Thorndike, Lynn. 1944. *University records and life in the middle ages.* New York: Columbia University Press.

Torrell, Jean-Pierre. 1996. *Saint Thomas Aquinas: Volume 1: The person and his work.* Translated by Robert Royal. Washington, D.C.: The Catholic University of America Press.

Van Steenberghen, Fernand. 1942. *Siger de Brabant d'après ses oeuvres inédites.* Second volume. Siger dans l'histoire de l'aristotélisme. Louvain: Éditions de l'Institut Supérieur de Philosophie.

———. 1966. *La philosophie au XIIIe siècle.* Louvain: Pulications Universitaires-Paris: Béatrice-Nauwelaerts.

———. 1974. Une légende tenace: la théorie de la double vérité. In *Introduction a l'étude de la philosophie médiévale,* 555–570. Louvain: Pulications Universitaires-Paris: Béatrice-Nauwelaerts.

———. 1977. *Maître Siger de Brabant.* Louvain: Publications Universitaires de Louvain-Paris: Vander-Oyez.

———. 1980. *Thomas Aquinas and radical Aristotelianism.* Washington, D.C.: The Catholic University of America Press.

Weijers, Olga. 1995. *La 'disputatio' à la Faculté des arts de Paris (1200–1350 environ). Esquisse d'une typologie.* Turnhout: Brepols.

Williams, Bernard. 1973. Deciding to believe. In *Problems of the self: Philosophical papers 1956–1972.* Cambridge: Cambridge University Press.

Wippel, John F. 1995. Thomas Aquinas and the condemnation of 1277. *Modern Schoolman* 72: 233–272.

Wood, Adam. 2015. Mind the gap? The principle of non-repeatability and Aquinas's account of the resurrection. *Oxford Studies in Medieval Philosophy* 3: 99–127.

Zedler, Beatrice H. 1968. *Saint Thomas Aquinas: On the unity of the intellect against the Averroists (De unitate intellectus contra Averroistas).* Translated from the Latin with an Introduction by Beatrice H. Zedler. Milwaukee, Wisconsin: Marquette University Press.

Zimmerman, Albert. 1967–68. Dante hatte doch Recht. *Philosophisches Jahrbuch* 75: 206–217.

Chapter 7
Knowing Non-existent Natures: A Problem for Aquinas's Semantics of Essence

Turner C. Nevitt

Keywords Aquinas · Essence · Existence · Definition · Logic

The question, "What is it?" is one of four questions that Aquinas considers basic to every science in Aristotle's sense, i.e. a body of knowledge unified by a common subject and established by sound reasoning.[1] Aquinas thinks every such body of knowledge will consist of the answers to four questions, which he considers basic because they cannot be reduced to any other questions of a different form; in fact, he thinks all other questions can be reduced to them.[2] These four basic questions are of the following form: (1) if an *F* exists (*si est*); (2) what is an *F* (*quid est*); (3) whether an *F* is *G* (*quia*); and (4) why an *F* is *G* (*propter quid*).[3] The first of these questions asks about a thing's existence; the second asks about its nature or essence; the third asks about its accidents or attributes; and the fourth asks for their cause. Aquinas follows Aristotle in calling a thing's nature or essence *what the thing was to be*, which he explains as the fitting answer to the question, "What is it?"[4] He says that this question is fittingly answered by terms predicated of a thing *per se* rather than *per accidens*; such terms comprise a thing's definition, through which we comprehend its essence. To understand essence this way—viz. as what we are thinking

---

[1] On Aquinas's view of science, see the introduction to Aquinas 1986 and Martin 1997, cc. 1–6.

[2] *Expositio Libri Posteriorum Analyticorum* (henceforth *In Post. An.*) II, l. 1, n. 2. References to the works of Aquinas are to Aquino 2000-. Translations are my own.

[3] Ibid. Cf. *Sententia Libri Metaphysicae* (henceforth *In Met.*) VII, l. 17, n. 4; *Summa Contra Gentiles* (henceforth *SCG*) III, c. 50, n. 4. On Aquinas's view of these questions, see Lonergan 1997, 24–29; Aertsen 1988, 12–33; and Martin 1997, c. 3.

[4] *In Met.* VII, l. 3, n. 4. Cf. *In Met.* VII, l. 3, n. 2ff; *In Met.* VII, l. 17, n. 11.

T. C. Nevitt (✉)
University of San Diego, San Diego, CA, USA
e-mail: tnevitt@sandiego.edu

© The Author(s), under exclusive license to Springer Nature
Switzerland AG 2023
J. P. Hochschild et al. (eds.), *Metaphysics Through Semantics: The Philosophical Recovery of the Medieval Mind*, International Archives of the History of Ideas Archives internationales d'histoire des idées 242,
https://doi.org/10.1007/978-3-031-15026-5_7

about when we use a thing's *per se* predicates to answer the question, "What is it?"—is to approach essence "logically," Aquinas says; he considers such an approach proper to the science of metaphysics and the way it ought to begin.[5]

In Aquinas's later commentaries on Aristotle he says that the first question about a thing's existence is logically prior to the second question about its essence. Non-existent things are not anything, and hence there is no asking what they are.[6] We must first know that a thing exists before we can ask what it is. As Aquinas says: "In this question which asks, 'What is a human being?' it is necessary to know the truth that this very *what it is to be a human being* exists, otherwise nothing would be asked."[7] Yet in his earlier works Aquinas claims just the opposite, namely that we can know what something is without knowing whether it exists. This claim is part of his famous "*intellectus essentiae* argument" for the real distinction between a creature's essence and existence in the *De ente et essentia*.[8] As he says there: "Every essence or whatness can be understood without knowing anything about its existence. For I can know what a human being or a phoenix is, and yet not know whether it has existence in reality. Thus, it is clear that existence is other than essence or whatness…"[9] Here and in other early works Aquinas claims that it is possible to do what he later insists "is impossible, namely that we know what something is, not knowing if it exists."[10]

What should we make of this apparent contradiction between Aquinas's works? Of course, it is possible that he simply changed his mind about this over the course of his career. Perhaps that is why the "*intellectus essentiae* argument" does not appear in Aquinas's later works. Another possibility is that in his later commentaries Aquinas is not expressing his own view, but merely explaining Aristotle's view, with which he disagrees; that was the solution favored by Joseph Owens.[11] Yet a third solution is possible, one that does not require a change in Aquinas's mind or a dis-agreement on his part with Aristotle. For in fact Aquinas distinguishes between two ways of knowing what something is—one way "by means of a definition" and another "by means of a proposition"—and he says that in the one way a thing's essence can be known without its existence and in the other way it cannot. Thus, the problem may be solved by making just such a distinction. Yet understanding this third solution requires an examination of the semantics of definitions and proposi-tions informing Aquinas's logical approach to essence. Such an examination will not only allow us to resolve the apparent contradiction between his earlier and later

---

[5] *In Met.* VII, l. 3, n. 3. Cf. *In Met.* VII, l. 2, n. 18; *In Met.* III, l. 1, n. 8; *In Met.* IV, l. 4, nn. 3–8. On Aquinas's view of logic, see Schmidt 1966. On Aquinas's view of the use of logic as a method in metaphysics, see Reichman 1965 and Doig 1972, c. 6.

[6] *In Post. An.* II, l. 6, n. 2.

[7] *In Met.* VII, l. 17, n. 19.

[8] On this argument, see Wippel 2000, 137–150.

[9] *De Ente et Essentia* (henceforth *DEE*) c. 4. Cf. *Scriptum Super Sententiis* (henceforth *In Sent.*) II, d. 1, q. 1, a. 1. Cf. *In Sent.* I, d. 8, q. 3, a. 3, exp.; *In Sent.* I, d. 8, q. 4, a. 2; *In Sent.* II, d. 3, q. 1, a. 1.

[10] *In Post. An.* II, l. 7, n. 5. Cf. *In Post. An.* II, l. 8, n. 6.

[11] Cf. Owens 1958, 6–7.

works; it should also give us a better understanding of Aquinas's logical approach to essence.

Aristotle begins his treatment of essence in the *Metaphysics* by speaking "logically," Aquinas says, "insofar as he investigates what essence is from the way of predicating, for this pertains properly to logic."[12] He immediately elaborates, explaining the logical approach to essence: "So, concerning *what a thing was to be*, it should first of all be known that it is predicated *per se*. For those things which are predicated of a thing *per accidens* do not pertain to its *what it was to be*."[13] Aquinas goes on to recognize that "not everything predicated of a thing *per se* pertains to its *what it was to be*," and thus excludes from essence "what is predicated *per se* as passions are predicated of their subjects."[14] The term "passions" is one of Aquinas's technical terms for a thing's necessary or proper accidents, which flow from a thing's essence, but are not part of that essence. So, according to the "logical" approach to essence, a thing's essence is what we are thinking about when we use its *per se* predicates, except for the *per se* predicates that signify a thing's necessary accidents.

Yet what are *per se* predicates? Aquinas often explains the distinction between *per se* and *per accidens* predication by appeal to the notion of definition. He makes such an appeal in his commentary on the *Posterior Analytics*, where he explains two different ways of saying something *per se*.[15] Concerning the first way he says:

> The first way of saying something *per se* is when that which is attributed to something pertains to its form. Since the definition signifies the form and essence of a thing, the first way of saying something *per se* is when the definition itself or something placed in the definition is predicated of a thing.[16]

The proposition "A human being is an animal" is one of Aquinas's stock examples of such a *per se* predication, since he thinks "animal" is part of the definition of a human being.[17] Concerning the second way of saying something *per se* he says: "The second way of saying something *per se* is when the subject is placed in the definition of the predicate, which is a proper accident of it."[18] As we just saw, Aquinas excludes this second way of predicating something *per se* from the logical approach to essence. Thus, for the purposes of the logical approach to essence, a *per se* predication is one whose predicate is contained in the definition of its subject. A *per accidens* predication, on the other hand, is one that is not *per se*, i.e. one whose predicate is not contained in the definition of its subject.[19] The proposition "A human

---

[12] *In Met.* VII, l. 3, n. 3.

[13] *In Met.* VII, l. 3, n. 4.

[14] Ibid, n. 6.

[15] *In Post. An.* I, l. 10, nn. 3–4. Cf. *In Met.* V, l. 19, nn. 11.–12.

[16] *In Post. An.* I, l. 10, n. 3.

[17] *Sentencia Libri De Anima* (henceforth *In De An.*) II, l. 14, n. 3.

[18] *In Post. An.* I, l. 10, n. 4.

[19] Cf. *In Met.* V, l. 9, nn. 1–4.

being is white" is one of Aquinas's stock examples of such a *per accidens* predication.[20]

So, *per se* predicates are those terms that comprise a thing's definition. Yet what is a definition? Aquinas often explains a definition as the phrase that signifies a thing's essence, as he does in the account of *per se* predication just quoted. But now the logical approach to essence appears to risk vacuous circularity: essence is explained logically by appeal to *per se* predication, *per se* predication is explained by appeal to definition, and definition is explained by appeal to essence.[21] It is perhaps significant, then, that Aquinas does *not* appeal to definition when presenting Aristotle's logical approach to essence through *per se* predication in the *Metaphysics*. Instead, he appeals to our practice of asking certain questions. As he says:

> About *what it was to be* it should first be known that it is predicated *per se*. For those things that are predicated of a thing *per accidens* do not pertain to its *what it was to be*. For by something's *what it was to be* we understand what can fittingly be replied to the question asked about it, "What is it?" But when we ask about something, "What is it?" we cannot fittingly reply with those things that apply to it *per accidens*; as when it is asked, "What is a human being?" one cannot reply that it is white or sitting or a musician. So, none of those things that are predicated of something *per accidens* pertain to that thing's *what it was to be*.[22]

According to Aquinas, a thing's *per se* predicates, which comprise the definition signifying its essence, are those terms that can fittingly answer the question, "What is it?" Thus, an essence can be understood logically as what we are thinking about when we raise and answer this type of question. Of course, Aquinas often goes back and forth, sometimes explaining *per se* predication by appeal to our sense of the question, "What is it?" and sometimes explaining the question itself by appeal to *per se* predication. Nevertheless, I think the logical approach to essence, and the explanation of the related notions of definition and *per se* predication, must ultimately bottom out at our intuitive sense of the question, "What is it?" Our intuitive sense of this question is supposed to make it clear that, for example, "What is a human being?" cannot fittingly be answered by reference to things like being white, or seated, or a musician: "For being a musician is not being *you*... since you are not a musician *according to your very self*."[23]

As I said, the question, "What is it?" is one of Aquinas's four basic scientific questions, which have the following form: (1) if an *F* exists (*si est*); (2) what is an *F* (*quid est*); (3) whether an *F* is *G* (*quia*); and (4) why an *F* is *G* (*propter quid*).[24] In his commentary on the *Posterior Analytics* Aquinas gives a number of examples of each type of question.[25] His examples of question (1) include: "Does a centaur exist or not?" "Does a human being exist?" "Does the moon exist?" "Is it night?" "Does a triangle

---

[20] Ibid.

[21] Cf. Galluzzo 2013, 67; Galluzzo and Mariani 2006, 68.

[22] *In Met.* VII, l. 3, n. 4. Cf. *In Met.* VII, l. 3, n. 2ff; *In Met.* VII, l. 17, n. 11.

[23] *In Met.* VII, l. 3, nn. 4–5

[24] Cf. supra n. 3.

[25] *In Post. An.* II, l. 1, n. 2ff.

exist?" His examples of question (2) include: "What is God?" "What is a human being?" "What is harmony?" "What is an eclipse?" His examples of question (3) include: "Is the sun eclipsed?" "Is the moon waxing or waning?" "Is the earth moved in an earthquake?" "Is the earth at the center of the universe?" "Does a triangle have three angles equal to two right angles?" His examples of question (4) include: "Why is the sun eclipsed?" "Why does the earth quake?" "Why is the moon waning?"

The difference between the second question, "What is an *F*?" and the third question, "Is an *F* a *G*?" is the same as the difference between the questions, "What is it?" and, "What is it like?" The question, "What is it?" asks for a *definition* that signifies a thing's nature or essence. The question, "What is it like?" asks for a *description* that signifies a thing's accidents, both necessary and contingent. But Aquinas says that we cannot ask either question until we have affirmatively answered the first question, "Does an *F* exist?" Moreover, he says that we cannot ask that question until we have answered the question, "What does the word '*F*' mean?" As Aquinas explains:

> Before we know about something *if it exists* (*an sit*), we cannot know properly about it *what it is* (*quid est*): for there are no definitions of non-existents. So, the question, "If it exists" precedes the question, "What is it?" But *if it exists* cannot be shown about something unless one first knows what is signified by the word.[26]

Thus, Aquinas recognizes a certain ambiguity in the question, "What is an *F*?" The question can mean either, "What *thing* is an *F*?" or merely, "What does *the word* '*F*' mean?" Usually when we ask, "What is an *F*?" we are looking for an answer to both questions, since the word "*F*" usually means what thing an *F* is, and we are usually ignorant of both or neither. But the questions clearly differ, and it is on that basis that Aquinas distinguishes between what are traditionally called real definitions and nominal definitions. A *real* definition answers the question, "What is *the thing* (*res*)?" Whereas a *nominal* definition answers the question, "What does *the word* (*nomen*) mean?" The difference between the two questions comes out most clearly in their different uses. For sometimes it is possible to ask the latter question about the meaning of words when it is not possible to ask the former question about what things are.

In his later commentaries on Aristotle, Aquinas says that in the case of non-existent things, we can only ask and answer the question, "What does the word mean?" We cannot ask and answer the question, "What is the thing?" As Aquinas explains:

> For since there is no whatness or essence of a non-existent, no one can know *what it is* (*quid est*) about that which is not; but one can know the signification of the word, or the formula (*ratio*) composed of many words; as one can know what is signified by the word "tragelaphus" or "goat-stag," which is the same thing, since it signifies a certain animal composed of a goat and a stag; but it is impossible to know the *what it is* of a goat-stag, since nothing is such in reality.[27]

---

[26] *In Post. An.* I, l. 2, n. 5. Cf. *Commentaria in Octo Libros Physicorum* (henceforth *In Phys.*) IV, l. 10, n. 2; *Summa Theologiae* (henceforth *ST*) I, q. 2, a. 2, ad 2.

[27] *In Post. An.* II, l. 6, n. 2.

Aquinas never offers more support than he does here for the claim that non-existent things lack essences. Apparently, he considers it sufficient to point out that non-existents like goat-stags are not anything; nothing in reality is a goat-stag. The only reply to the question, "What is it?" when asked properly about such non-existent things is, "Nothing." We can say what *something* is, but we cannot say what *nothing* is, since *there isn't anything* that nothing is. Since goat-stags don't exist, there is nothing that it is to be a goat-stag, and so there is no asking what it is to be one. In the case of non-existent things like goat-stags, Aquinas thinks the best we can do is say what the word "goat-stag" means.

Thus, according to Aquinas in his later commentaries, the question, "Does an *F* exist?" is logically prior to the question, "What is an *F*?" Of course, Aquinas recognizes that we might discover that something exists and what it is at the same time.[28] If we were above the moon during a lunar eclipse, for example, he says that we would know at once that an eclipse exists, what it is, and why it exists, since we would see that the moon is eclipsed by passing through the shadow cast by the earth's interposition between the moon and the sun.[29] But what we cannot do, Aquinas thinks, is discover what something is *without* also knowing that it exists. Doing that, he says, "is impossible."[30] The same thing goes for the logical priority of the question, "What does the word '*F*' mean?" We could not even ask the question, "Does an *F* exist?" if we did not already know what the word "*F*" means. Thus, nominal definitions are logically prior to real definitions, and knowledge of a thing's existence is logically prior to knowledge of its essence.

Yet in the "*intellectus essentiae* argument" of his early works Aquinas claims that it is possible to know what something is without knowing whether it exists. His examples of such knowledge include knowing what a human being is, what a phoenix is, and what an eclipse is, without knowing whether any of them exist.[31] The example of a human being is puzzling, since it is hard to see how we could fail to know whether a human being exists, given that we are human beings. The example of the phoenix is complicated by the fact that it is not clear whether Aquinas took the bird to be mythical or not. The example of the eclipse is the most helpful, since it seems obvious that we can know what an eclipse is without knowing whether one is happening right now. But, of course, we know that eclipses have happened in the past, and at least in that sense we know that eclipses exist. Is there an example of something whose nature we can know without knowing whether it exists at all? Consider elements on the periodic table that have not yet been discovered in nature or synthesized in a lab. Ununennium, for example, is the metal with atomic number 119. We know exactly what ununnenium is, and we know many of its proper

---

[28] *In Post. An.* II, l. 7, n. 5.

[29] *In Post. An.* II, l. 1, n. 10.

[30] *In Post. An.* II, l. 7, n. 5. Cf. *In Post. An.* II, l. 8, n. 6.

[31] *In Sent.* II, d. 1, q. 1, a. 1. Cf. *In Sent.* I, d. 8, q. 3, a. 3, exp.; *In Sent.* I, d. 8, q. 4, a. 2; *In Sent.* II, d. 3, q. 1, a. 1; *DEE* c. 4.

accidents, such as its mass, its melting point, its boiling point, its density, and so on. But we still do not know whether ununnenium exists at all.

In his earlier works Aquinas recognizes just this possibility, that we might know what something is without knowing whether it exists. So why does he deny that possibility in his later commentaries on Aristotle? Of course, it is possible that Aquinas simply changed his mind about this over the course of his career. It is also possible that in his later commentaries Aquinas was merely explaining Aristotle's view rather than his own. Of these two possibilities, the second seems to me the less likely. For Aquinas usually goes out of his way to interpret Aristotle in line with his own views; indeed, he even goes so far as to attribute his doctrine of creation *ex nihilo* to Aristotle.[32] Aquinas is also usually explicit in his commentaries when he thinks Aristotle needs correcting, yet he never hints at correcting Aristotle's view that we cannot know what something is without knowing whether it exists. Moreover, Aquinas follows Aristotle's logical ordering of the four basic scientific questions in his own later works: "Once that it exists (*an sit*) is known about something, it remains to inquire how it exists, in order to know about it what it is (*quid est*)."[33] So, it seems to me more likely that Aquinas changed his mind than that he disagreed with Aristotle about whether we could know a thing's essence without its existence.

Nevertheless, there is a third possibility. For in his disputed questions *De veritate* Aquinas makes a distinction between two ways of knowing what something is—one by means of a definition and another by means of a proposition—and says that in the one way we can know what something is without also knowing whether it exists, but in the other way we cannot.[34] If this distinction applies to Aquinas's earlier and later claims about our knowledge of essence without existence, then we can resolve the apparent contradiction between those claims without attributing to him a change of mind or a disagreement on his part with Aristotle.

Aquinas distinguishes these two ways of knowing what something is in a discussion of Adam's knowledge before the fall.[35] Aquinas wants to maintain that Adam knew all creatures in their proper natures from the time of his creation. But doing so causes trouble for Aquinas since, at least according to one creation account, Adam was created before all other plants and animals.[36] So, the objection goes, Adam could not have known all creatures in their proper natures from the time of his creation, since not all creatures existed in their proper natures at that time. In reply to this objection Aquinas says:

---

[32] For a list of all the texts in which he does so, see Aquinas 1997, 128, n. 20. On Aquinas's attribution of the doctrine of creation to Aristotle, see Johnson 1989, Dewan 1991a, Carroll 1994, Knasas 1996, and Carroll 2010.

[33] *ST* I, q. 3, pr. Cf. *SCG* III, c. 50, n. 4.

[34] Thanks to Gaston LeNotre for first bringing this text to my attention, and for so many helpful conversations over the years.

[35] *Quaestiones Disputatae de Veritate* (henceforth *QDV*) q. 18, a. 4. Cf. *In Sent.* II, d. 23, q. 2, a. 2; *ST* I, q. 94, a. 3.

[36] Genesis 2:4–25.

"Knowing a thing in its proper nature" is said in two ways. In one way [a thing is known in its proper nature] by means of a proposition: when, namely, a thing is known to exist in its proper nature: which cannot be [done] except when it exists in its proper nature. Adam did not know all creatures in their proper nature in this way, since not all creatures existed in their proper nature yet... In another way someone is said to know a thing in its proper nature by means of a definition: when, namely, someone knows what the proper nature of a thing is. In this way even a non-existent thing can be known in its proper nature. If all lions died, for instance, I could still know what a lion is. Thus, in this way Adam was able to know in their proper nature even things that did not exist at that time.[37]

Here Aquinas says that the nature of a thing can be known by means of a definition even when the thing does not exist, but its nature cannot be known by means of a proposition when the thing does not exist. This is just what one might expect, given Aquinas's semantics of propositions.[38]

Historians of medieval philosophy often call Aquinas's semantics of propositions the inherence theory of predication. The inherence theory can be understood by comparing it with its medieval rival, the identity theory of predication.[39] Both theories agree in supposing that every proposition is made up of three basic parts: a subject, a predicate, and a copula. But the two theories disagree about the semantic roles played by these parts. According to the identity theory, the semantic roles of both the subject and the predicate are the same: they are both used to name or refer to things. The copula, on the other hand, is used to express the identity of the thing named by the subject and the thing named by the predicate. According to the identity theory, for example, the proposition "Socrates is white" is true if and only if the subject "Socrates" and the predicate "white" actually name or refer to one and the same thing. In other words, the sentence is true if and only if Socrates and a white thing are identical.

Aquinas does recognize what he calls "predications by identity," which he says are true because their subjects and predicates name or refer to the same thing.[40] Yet he contrasts such predications with what he calls "predications by information" or "by inherence," which he says are "more properly predications" because their subjects and predicates play different semantic roles.[41] Aquinas even insists on the difference between these semantic roles in cases where the subject and predicate are the same, such as the proposition "A human being is a human being."[42]

In the inherence theory of predication, the subject of a proposition is used to name or refer to something, whereas the predicate is used to say something about it. Most often Aquinas expresses this difference by an analogy to Aristotelian hylomorphism, saying that the subject of a sentence is taken *materially* whereas the

---

[37] *QDV* q. 18, a. 4, ad 10.

[38] My understanding of Aquinas's semantics is greatly indebted to Klima 1996 and 2002. See also McInerny 1986, Ashworth 1991, Schoot 1993, and Sweeney 1995.

[39] For brief overviews of the two theories, see Moody 1953, 32–38; Abelard 1956, xxxvii–xl. For a critique of the standard dichotomy between the two theories, see Malcolm 1979.

[40] *In Sent.* III, d. 5, q. 3, a. 3, exp.

[41] Ibid. Cf. *In Sent.* III, d. 7, q. 1, a. 1.

[42] *ST* I, q. 13, a. 12.

predicate is taken *formally*.[43] Less often he expresses the same difference between subject and predicate by an analogy to Aristotle's ten categories, contrasting the *substance* of a word with the *quality* of a word.[44] (Sometimes he expresses the same difference again by a distinction between *that on which* a word is imposed and *that from which* a word is imposed.[45]) Aquinas uses these analogies to mark the difference between the *supposition* of a word and the *signification* of a word, which are similar to (though importantly different from) what contemporary philosophers call a word's *reference* and its *sense*.

So, according to the inherence theory, the subject of a proposition supposits or stands for a thing represented as matter and a substance—existing in itself and *potentially* such and such.[46] The predicate of a sentence signifies a thing represented as a form and accident—existing in something else and making it *actually* such and such.[47] And the copula is used to signify the actual existence of the form or quality signified by the predicate in the matter or substance supposited for by the subject at the time connoted by the copula's tense. As Aquinas explains:

> This verb "is" ...signifies first that which falls in the intellect by way of actuality absolutely. For "is," said by itself, signifies existence in actuality, and thus it signifies as a verb. But since actuality, which this verb "is" principally signifies, is commonly the actuality of every form, whether a substantial or accidental act, hence when we want to signify that a certain form or act actually exists in some subject, we signify that through this verb "is," either absolutely or with qualification—absolutely according to the present time; with qualification, however, according to other times.[48]

Thus, according to the inherence theory, a proposition is true if and only if the form or quality signified by its predicate actually exists in the matter or substance supposited for by its subject at the time connoted by its copula's tense.[49] For example, a proposition like "Socrates is white" is true if and only if the quality signified by "white" actually exists in the substance supposited for by "Socrates" at the time connoted by "is."[50] In other words, the sentence "Socrates is white" is true if and only if the whiteness of Socrates actually is or exists at the present time.

Thus, in Aquinas's semantics, these two propositions are equivalent:

(A) Socrates is white.
(B) The whiteness of Socrates is, i.e. exists.

---

[43] *ST* I, q. 13, a. 12. Cf. *ST* III, q. 16, a. 7, ad 4; *In Meta.* IX, l. 11, n. 4.

[44] *In Sent.* I, d. 22, q. 1, a. 1, ad 3; *ST* I, q. 13, a. 1, ad 3.

[45] *In Sent.* III, d. 6, q. 1, a. 3.

[46] *In Sent.* I, d. 22, q. 1, a. 1, ad 3. Cf. *In Sent.* I, d. 4, q. 1, a. 2; *In Sent.* I, d. 33, q. 1, a. 2; *SCG* I, c. 30, n. 3; *ST* I, q. 13, a. 1, ad 2; *ST* I, q. 45, a. 4.

[47] *In Met.* IX, l. 11, n. 4. Cf. *In Sent.* I, d. 4, q. 1, a. 2; *In Sent.* I, d. 33, q. 1, a. 2; *SCG* I, c. 30, n. 3; *ST* I, q. 13, a. 1, ad 2; *ST* I, q. 45, a. 4.

[48] *Expositio Libri Peryermeneias* (henceforth *In Pery.*) I, l. 5, n. 22. Cf. *ST* I, q. 16, a. 2.

[49] On Aquinas's theory of truth, especially as it relates to his theory of existence, see Wippel 2007, 65–112 and Maurer 1990, 43–58.

[50] Cf. *In Pery.* I, l. 9, n. 4.

It is precisely this equivalence that allows Aquinas to maintain that existence is signified, explicitly or implicitly, in every predication whatsoever. "In as many ways as something is predicated," he says, "in just so many ways is something signified to exist (*esse*)."[51] Of course, Aquinas is aware that not every predication contains the verb "is," whether as a copula or as a predicate. But he insists that "every [other] verb is resolved into this verb 'is' and a participle."[52] In this connection he points out that "it makes no difference whether one says 'A human being convalesces' or 'A human being is convalescing,' and the same goes for other [finite verbs]."[53] So, in Aquinas's semantics, every predication without a copula can be reduced to a predication with a copula, and every predication with a copula can be reduced to a predication with an existence predicate. That is why Aquinas thinks that every affirmative proposition has existential import. As he says, "in as many ways as a predication is made, in so many ways is 'existent' said."[54]

Since Aquinas thinks that the copula of an affirmative proposition signifies the existence of what the proposition is about at the time connoted by its tense, such a proposition is true if the things the proposition is about actually exist at that time; otherwise the proposition is false. Thus, according to Aquinas's semantics, the proposition "A lion is an animal" is false when a lion does not exist.[55] That is why Aquinas says in the *De veritate* that we cannot know the nature of a lion by means of a proposition when lions do not exist: no affirmative propositions about non-existent lions are true, and thus no such propositions can be a means of knowledge. Nevertheless, Aquinas recognizes that we can still ask and answer the question, "What is a lion?" even when lions do not exist. This is what he calls knowing what a lion is by means of a definition.

Of course, we often express definitions by means of propositions. We might define what a human being is, for example, by means of the proposition, "A human being is a rational animal." But Aquinas thinks that the latter proposition is *not* a definition; only *part* of it is a definition, namely the *per se* predicate "rational animal." As Aquinas himself says: "*In a definition nothing is predicated of anything.*"[56] In other words, definitions are *not* propositions. The distinction between definitions and propositions is what allows Aquinas to maintain that we can know the definition of a thing even when there are no true affirmative propositions about the thing, i.e. even when the thing does not exist. For propositions have existential import, he

---

[51] *In Met.* V, l. 9, n. 6.

[52] *In Meta.* V, l. 9, n. 9. Cf. *In Pery.* I, l. 5, n. 18.

[53] Ibid.

[54] Ibid.

[55] Cf. Ross 1990, esp. 180–181. For critical responses to Ross, though not touching on the present point, see Maurer 1991 and Dewan 1991b. For Ross's response to both Maurer and Dewan, see Ross 1991. For a "Thomistic" attempt to save the truth of essential propositions after the things they are about have all perished, see Frost 2010.

[56] *In Post. An.* II, l. 2, n. 11 (emphasis mine).

thinks, but definitions do not. As he says, "a definition is not a proposition signify-ing existence or non-existence."[57]

It may seem paradoxical to suppose that a thing's real definition can be known even when the definition is not truly predicable of the thing defined. After all, as Aquinas himself says, "once a definition is known, it is clear that the definition can be truly predicated of the subject [so defined]."[58] Perhaps the air of paradox can be dispelled by considering false tautologies such as, "The present king of France is the present King of France." That proposition is only true when there is a king of France; it does not matter that the subject and predicate are the same. The same goes for propositions whose predicates are contained in the definitions of their subjects. "The present King of France is a monarch," for example, is only true when there is a king of France; it does not matter that a king is a monarch by definition. In the same way, Aquinas thinks that the proposition "A human being is a rational animal" is only true when a human being exists; it does not matter that the definition of a human being is a rational animal. Aquinas has to say this about the truth conditions of such propositions, otherwise the entailments of his Aristotelian logic would break down—a point that, unfortunately, I cannot pursue further here.[59]

Aquinas's distinction between knowing a thing's essence without its existence by means of a definition and by means of a proposition can be applied to the apparently contradictory claims he makes about this in his earlier and later works. When Aquinas claims in his later works that it is impossible to know what something is without knowing whether it exists, he can be read as only denying that possibility by means of a proposition. I think it is unsurprising that Aquinas would deny this possibility in the context of his later commentaries on Aristotle. For those commen-taries are concerned with the development of science in Aristotle's sense, i.e. a body of knowledge unified by a common subject and established by sound reasoning. And reasoning, of course, proceeds by means of propositions. In the context of Aristotelian science, asking for a thing's definition amounts to asking for the middle term in the demonstration of its necessary accidents.[60] As Aquinas often says, "the definition is the middle term in a demonstration in which proper accidents are dem-onstrated of their subjects."[61] But, according to Aquinas's semantics, a definition cannot be used as a middle term in a demonstration unless the thing whose defini-tion it is exists; otherwise the propositions of the demonstration would be false. Thus, in the context of Aristotelian science, which proceeds by means of demon-stration through propositions, Aquinas says that the question, "Does it exist?" is logically prior to the question, "What is it?"

---

[57] *In Post. An.* I, l. 5, n. 9.

[58] Ibid.

[59] For a full explanation of the point, see Klima 2001.

[60] *In Post. An.* II, l. 1, n. 8. Cf. *In Post. An.* II, l. 7, n. 2.

[61] *In Phys.* IV, l. 5, n. 3. Cf. *In Post. An.* I, l. 2, nn. 2–3; *In Post. An.* II, l. 1, n. 9; *In De An.* I, l. 1, n. 15; *SCG* I, c. 25, n. 8; *ST* I, q. 3, a. 5.

When Aquinas claims in his earlier works that it is possible to know what something is without knowing whether it exists, he can be read as only granting that possibility by means of a definition. I think it is also unsurprising that Aquinas would grant that possibility in the context of the *"intellectus essentiae* argument" of his earlier works. For, given Aquinas's logical approach to essence, the *intellectus essentiae* argument is concerned with the content of real definitions. The argument claims that existence is not part of any creature's essence, since a created thing's essence can be known without knowing whether it exists. But Aquinas thinks that a thing's essence is comprehended by means of its real definition. So, determining whether a thing's essence includes existence requires examining the parts of its real definition in order to see whether existence is among them. Thus, in contexts in which Aquinas is concerned with the parts of a creature's real definition, he says that what something is can be known without knowing whether it exists, since we can examine the parts of a thing's definition without having to predicate the definition of the thing in a proposition. That is how we can know what the thing is without knowing whether it exists.

As long as propositions and definitions are kept distinct, as Aquinas's semantics requires, there is no inconsistency involved in granting the possibility of knowing a thing's essence without its existence by means of a definition, while also denying the possibility of knowing a thing's essence without its existence by means of a proposition. For propositions have existential import, while definitions do not. Hence, one can know a thing's real definition without knowing any true propositions about the thing; in that sense one can know what something is without knowing whether it exists. Of course, there is the further question of how one could ever discover and properly formulate a thing's real definition if the thing did not in fact exist. Answering that question would require a fuller examination of Aquinas's semantics of real definitions and of the methods by which he thinks we can discover such definitions and thus answer the basic scientific question, "What is it?" Nevertheless, the semantics informing Aquinas's logical approach to essence at least show that he need not have changed his mind or disagreed with Aristotle about whether it is possible to answer the question, "What is it?" without first answering the question, "Does it exist?" Rather than simply affirming or denying that possibility, Aquinas seems to have wanted to make a distinction.

Bibliography

Abelard, Peter. 1956. Petrus Abaelardus Dialectica. Edited by L.M. De Rijk. Assen: Van Gorcum and Company.
Aertsen, Jan. 1988. *Nature and creature: Thomas Aquinas's way of thought*. Leiden: E.J. Brill.
Aquinas, St. Thomas. 1986. *The division and methods of the sciences: Questions V and VI of his Commentary on the De trinitate of Boethius*, 4th rev. ed. Trans. Armand Maurer. Toronto: The Pontifical Institute of Mediaeval Studies.
Aquinas, St. Thomas. 1997. *Aquinas on creation*. Trans. Steven Baldner and William Carroll. Toronto: The Pontifical Institute of Mediaeval Studies.

Aquino, S. Thomae de. 2000-present. *Opera omnia.* Ab Enrique Alarcón collecta, edita, recognita et instructa automato electronico. Pompaelonae ad Universitatis Studiorum Navarrensis. Online. URL = <www.corpusthomisticum.org>.

Ashworth, E.J. 1991. Signification and modes of signifying in thirteenth-century logic: A preface to Aquinas on analogy. *Medieval Philosophy and Theology* 1: 39–67.

Carroll, William. 1994. San Tommaso, Aristotele, e la creazione. *Annales Theologici* 8: 365–376.

———. 2010. Thomas Aquinas on Aristotle, the eternity of the world, and the doctrine of creation. In *Tomás de Aquino: Comentador de Aristóteles*, ed. Héctor Velázquez Fernández, 13–42. Mexico: Universidad Panamericana.

Dewan, Lawrence. 1991a. St. Thomas, Aristotle, and creation. *Dionysius* 15: 81–90.

———. 1991b. St. Thomas, James Ross, and exemplarism. *American Catholic Philosophical Quarterly* 65: 221–234.

Doig, James. 1972. *Aquinas on metaphysics: A historico-doctrinal study of the commentary on the metaphysics.* The Hague: Martinus Nijhoff.

Frost, Gloria. 2010. Thomas Aquinas on the perpetual truth of essential propositions. *History of Philosophy Quarterly* 27: 197–213.

Galluzzo, Gabriele. 2013. *The medieval reception of book zeta of Aristotle's metaphysics, Vol. 1: Aristotle's ontology and the middle ages: The tradition of metaphysics book zeta.* Leiden: E.J. Brill.

Galluzzo, Gabriele, and Mauro Mariani. 2006. *Aristotle's metaphysics book Z: The contemporary debate.* Pisa: Edizione della Normale.

Johnson, Mark. 1989. Did St. Thomas attribute a doctrine of creation to Aristotle? *The New Scholasticism* 63: 129–155.

Klima, Gyula. 1996. The semantic principles underlying Saint Thomas Aquinas's metaphysics of being. *Medieval Philosophy and Theology* 5: 87–141.

———. 2001. Existence and reference in medieval logic. In *New essays in free logic: In honour of Karel Lambert*, ed. Alexander Hieke and Edgar Morscher, 197–226. Dordrecht: Kluwer Academic Publishers.

———. 2002. Aquinas's theory of the copula and the analogy of being. *Logical Analysis and History of Philosophy* 5: 159–176.

Knasas, John. 1996. Aquinas' ascription of creation to Aristotle. *Angelicum* 73: 487–506.

Lonergan, Bernard. 1997. *Verbum: Word and idea in Aquinas.* Toronto: University of Toronto Press.

Malcolm, John. 1979. A reconsideration of the inherence and identity theories of the copula. *Journal of the History of Philosophy* 17: 383–400.

Martin, Christopher F.J. 1997. *Thomas Aquinas: God and explanations.* Edinburgh: Edinburgh University Press.

Maurer, Armand. 1990. *Being and knowing: Studies in Thomas Aquinas and later medieval philosophers.* Toronto: The Pontifical Institute of Mediaeval Studies.

———. 1991. James Ross on the divine ideas. *American Catholic Philosophical Quarterly* 65: 213–220.

McInerny, Ralph. 1986. Being and predication. In *Being and predication: Thomistic interpretations*, 173–228. Washington, D.C.: The Catholic University of America Press.

Moody, Ernest. 1953. *Truth and consequence in medieval logic.* Amsterdam: North-Holland Publishing Company.

Owens, Joseph. 1958. The accidental and essential character of being in St. Thomas Aquinas. *Mediaeval Studies* 20: 1–40.

Reichman, James B. 1965. Logic and the method of metaphysics. *The Thomist* 29: 341–395.

Ross, James. 1990. Aquinas's exemplarism; Aquinas's voluntarism. *American Catholic Philosophical Quarterly* 64: 171–198.

———. 1991. Response to Maurer and Dewan. *American Catholic Philosophical Quarterly* 65: 235–243.

Schmidt, Robert J. 1966. *The domain of logic according to St. Thomas Aquinas.* The Hague: Martinus Nijhoff.

Schoot, H.J.M. 1993. Aquinas and supposition: The possibilities and limitations of logic in divinis. *Vivarium* 31: 193–225.

Sweeney, Eileen. 1995. Supposition, signification, and universals: Metaphysical and linguistic complexity in Aquinas. *Freiburger Zeitschrift für Philosophie und Theologie* 42: 267–290.

Wippel, John F. 2000. *The metaphysical thought of Thomas Aquinas: From finite being to uncreated being*. Washington, D.C.: The Catholic University of America Press.

———. 2007. *Metaphysical themes in Thomas Aquinas II*. Washington, D.C.: The Catholic University of America Press.

Chapter 8
Metaphors, Dead and Alive

Martin Klein

Keywords Aquinas · Ockham · Burley · Abelard · Boethius · Metaphor · Equivocation · Signification · Imposition · Transference

8.1 Introduction

Medieval philosophers were well aware of the fact that language permits many kinds of figurative speech and metaphors. At the same time, they were concerned about the use of figurative speech and metaphors in philosophy. As logicians, they worried about the ambiguities which result from metaphorical expressions, which they took to be a use of words in a non-literal sense. A common medieval example of a metaphor was the expression 'The meadows laugh': properly, the verb 'to laugh' applies to human beings, whereas a meadow (or the flowers in a meadow) are said to bloom (Rosier-Catach 1997). From this metaphorical use of the verb 'to laugh', a paralogism such as the following can result: Whatever laughs has a mouth; but the meadow laughs; therefore, the meadow has a mouth. We arrive at this wrong conclusion because we have confused a metaphorical sense of a word with its literal sense (Peter of Spain 2014, 276–78: *SL* 7.32). But metaphors were not seen only as a potential source of misleading talk and fallacies. For one, they were also considered to be important for preparing prospective students of theology for careful interpretations of the Bible, which is full of metaphors, and according to Thomas Aquinas, ambiguous expressions even have a value in themselves when it comes to religious instruction (Aquinas 1888, 23–24: *ST* I.1.9; Dahan 2009, 249–282).

Metaphors were explained as a deviant use of language which would be wrong if the words were understood in the literal sense. Laughing is properly attributed to

M. Klein (✉)
University of Würzburg, Würzburg, Germany
e-mail: martin.klein@uni-wuerzburg.de

© The Author(s), under exclusive license to Springer Nature
Switzerland AG 2023
J. P. Hochschild et al. (eds.), *Metaphysics Through Semantics: The Philosophical Recovery of the Medieval Mind*, International Archives of the History of Ideas Archives internationales d'histoire des idées 242, https://doi.org/10.1007/978-3-031-15026-5_8

creatures that have a mouth, but wrongly attributed to meadows. Hence medieval philosophers discussed metaphors within the broader context of how to distinguish the literal sense from a non-literal one. In line with Aristotle's remark in the *Poetics* (Aristotle 1968, 1457b6–9), *metaphora*, translated as *translatio* or *transumptio*, was conceived of as a transfer of sense. Medieval philosophers accounted for the distinction between a word's literal sense and any metaphorical sense by reference to what we would call foundational theories of meaning.[1] Words are considered to have their 'proper' signification when used in accordance with how they were originally instituted. When usage deviates from the sense given to a word by its original institution the signification is considered 'improper'.[2]

However, what once might have involved a transference of sense can become well established over time. Even if 'foot' in English is supposed to have been instituted for "the terminal portion of a limb which bears weight and allows locomotion" (as the English entry in Wikipedia defines the term), we also use it to refer to a unit of length. This is clearly a case where a word originally used for one thing gets applied to another. But although this new application creates an ambiguity, we would not say that 'foot' has a metaphorical sense when used to mean a unit of length. Similarly, the expression 'foot of a mountain' might originate from the feet of vertebrates, given that it is the lowest part of an elevated landform; as an established technical term, however, it should rather be called a conventional expression and distinguished from those figurative expressions that actually go against the literal sense of words.

Even though our languages have many established figurative expressions (some of which we might not even be aware when speaking), they should be distinguished from actual metaphorical uses of a term, that is, when we use a word in such a way that it deviates even from established ambiguous expressions. To put it differently, the metaphorical use of a word should be distinguished from those expressions which are so common and deeply seated in our language that it seems odd to call them metaphors.

The question I want to explore in this paper is how a distinction between proper and improper signification can give a plausible explanation of both metaphorical use and the usual transformations a language can undergo. In Sect. 8.2, I will show how Thomas Aquinas distinguishes between ordinary ambiguous terms and metaphors, whereas William of Ockham and Walter Burley do not leave room for this distinction. In Sect. 8.3, I will argue that Ockham's conception of transfer of sense through subsequent institution of words is best thought of as an explanation of how ordinary usage can contain ambiguities, whereas Burley's conception of transfer of sense without new imposition is more plausible when it comes to explaining metaphors, as I will argue in Sect. 8.4. In the end, if metaphorical use is lumped together with equivocation, the account of how they work cannot do full justice to either.

---

[1] On medieval views on the origin of language(s), see, e.g., Eco 1993; Ashworth 2013b.

[2] Jennifer Ashworth has provided excellent surveys on this matter. See Ashworth 1991, 2007, 2013a. See also Purcell 1987 for the increasing use of *transumptio* for metaphor instead of metalepsis in the thirteenth century.

8.2   *Translatio* and **Proper Usage**

Aquinas gives various examples of terms that have different interpretations without being improper. As he makes clear with regard to the term 'light', which we use for corporeal and incorporeal things, the proper way to use the term is surely to refer to corporeal things; however, Augustine claims that 'light' is properly predicated of spiritual things, and not, or at least only metaphorically, of corporeal things. As a solution, Aquinas proposes that there are two ways in which we can apply a name: in accordance with its original institution or "first imposition," or in accordance with how the name is used by our contemporaries (Aquinas 1889, 163: *ST* I.68.1). Accordingly, 'light' can be said properly of both corporeal and spiritual things, in a way similar to the verb 'to see', which was originally instituted for the act of seeing, though people later started using it for other kinds of cognitions in relation to other sense modalities ("See how it tastes!") and even in relation to the understanding ("Now I see what you mean!").

In the same way, Aquinas concludes, the name 'light' can be properly used for both corporeal and spiritual things:

> Any word may be used in two ways—that is to say, either according to its first imposition or according to the usage of a word. [...] And thus it is with the word 'light'. For it is first instituted to signify that which makes manifest to the sense of sight; afterwards it was extended to that which makes manifest to cognition of any kind. Therefore, if the name 'light' is taken according to its first imposition, then it is said metaphorically in the case of spiritual things. [...] But if it is taken according to the way it is extended in the usage of speakers to any kind of manifestation, then it is properly said in the case of spiritual things (ibid.).[3]

As this passage makes clear, if someone uses the word 'light' for spiritual things but in accordance with its original institution, it is used metaphorically, since 'light' was instituted for corporeal and not spiritual things. By custom, however, the term has obtained a broader application and is also used for spiritual things. Hence, if we use it in accordance with this established usage we do not speak metaphorically, nor do we when we extend the verb 'to see' to other kinds of cognition.

From this we can extract the following threefold distinction between proper and improper signification:

1. When a term is applied to a thing for which it was originally instituted, then it is used *properly*. (For instance, when we use 'light' for corporeal things.)
2. When a term is applied to a thing for which it was not originally instituted but for which it has acquired an established use, then it is likewise used *properly*. (This is the case when we use 'light' for spiritual things.)

---

[3] "[...] de aliquo nomine dupliciter convenit loqui: uno modo, secundum primam eius impositionem; alio modo, secundum usum nominis. [...] Et similiter dicendum est de nomine 'lucis'. Nam primo quidem est institutum ad significandum id quod facit manifestationem in senu visu: postmodum autem extensum est ad significandum omne illud quod facit manifestationem secundum quamucumque cognitionem.—Si ergo accipitur nomen 'luminis' secundum suam primam impositionem, metaphorice in spiritualibus dicitur [...] Si autem accipiatur secundum quod est in usu loquentium ad omnem manifestationem extensum, sic proprie in spiritualibus dicitur."

3. When a term is applied to a thing for which it was not instituted and for which it has *not* acquired an established use, then it is used *improperly* or *metaphorically*. (This is the case of light, when it is used "according to its first imposition" but said of spiritual things.)

How is the third case different from the second? If the original institution of a word provides its literal signification, it seems that only derivative usage could explain how we come to metaphorical expressions, precisely because they deviate from the original meaning. However, as Aquinas makes clear, usage too provides ways of speaking properly even if the use of a word differs from its original signification. As he puts it, "it is usual for words to be "twisted away (*detorqueantur*) from their original signification," from which they "are derived" (*derivatum*) to signify something else (Aquinas 1897, 4: *ST* II-II.57.1ad1). For this derivation of a new sense of a word from its original meaning as an instance of proper signification, Aquinas also uses the technical term *translatio* (Aquinas 1903, 22–23: *ST* III.2.1; Ashworth 2013a, 227). He also uses this term frequently as equivalent to the Greek-derived *metaphora* (though he more often uses *transumptio*); it turns out, however, that he recognizes two kinds of transfer of sense, only one of which is improper.[4] Thus, what distinguishes cases (2) and (3) above is not their deviation from the original institution of a word, since both cases deviate from the original signification, but rather the different ways in which we use a word.

The difference lies not just in whether we use a word either according to its original institution or according to usage, but in how this comes about. First of all, it has to do with the frequency with which we use a word. When a word is used frequently by speakers differently from its original meaning—for example, the more often they use the word "light" for spiritual things—the more common, and thus more proper, it is for them to use the word in this new sense. But frequency alone seems not to explain how proper use according to common usage is different from metaphorical expressions, since the latter can also have a quite long history of usage. Take the typical medieval example of a metaphor already mentioned: the laughing meadows, which appears to be of biblical origin in the Book of Isaiah and is explained by Aquinas in his commentary on this book.[5] We can assume that this metaphor was well known to the medieval congregant and theologian; and the more they heard and used it, the more it would be commented on and used as an example in other contexts. It seems it could equally count as a regular use like 'light' for spiritual things.

It is generally recognized that what allows the transfer of sense in both (2) and (3) is a similarity between two different things. As Aquinas explains with regard to the example of a real human being and a painted human being (used by Aristotle to

---

[4] For *metaphora* connected to *translatio/translative*, see Aquinas 1970, 202a: *De veritate* 7.2. For the pair *metaphora–transumptio/transumptive* see Dahan 2009, 261–262.

[5] See Is 35:1 in Aquinas 1974, 153: *Exp. Iasia* 35: "letabitur deserta et inuia, et exultabit solitudo et florebit quasi lilium." Aquinas comments (ibid., 153): "Primo (*ed. add.* ponit) hominum iocunditatem, quam comparat prato florenti, quod etiam ridens dicitur, quod quidem habet pulcritudinem in flore." Also Aquinas 1892, 132: *ST* I-II.88.1 seems to allude to the Isaiah passage.

introduce equivocals in the opening passage of the *Categories*), the real human and the painted one share a certain similarity (Aquinas 1884, 354: *In Phys.*7.8.8). The same might be said about seeing (the example used by Aquinas to make clear how 'light' can be used properly in a transferred sense): seeing is used not only for sight but also for the intellect, since both "make manifest to cognition." But it is also similarity of things which allows us to use a word metaphorically. A meadow full of flowers in bloom can be said to smile because its blooming is somehow similar to a smiling human being (Aquinas 1888, 150: *ST* I.13.6co).

The distinctive feature in this metaphorical use is that we linguistically relate two different things, on account of the similarity we attribute to them, from the one for which the word has proper signification to the other for which it has not. In saying that flowers smile, one does not just apply words to things as they usually apply, but one intends to apply them against custom and in deviation from the common use. In this sense, a metaphorical expression is not the result of *translatio*, but consists in *translatio* itself, which comes about when one produces a metaphor by transferring a word from one thing to another and when one notices a metaphorical expression and tries to fathom its meaning (Dahan 2009, 261–264).[6]

Plausibly, a metaphorical expression can come to seem natural as it is used more and more frequently in ordinary language. It might then be the case that a word acquires an established use which is proper even though it was originally transferred. However, Aquinas does not give *translatio* in terms of accustomed usage a conceptual clarification. *Ex negativo*, we can determine that in Aquinas the transference of sense is not something we have to actively bring about; rather, we use the word in a different sense because that is just the way we are accustomed to speak. Quite naturally, we call different things by the same name in this case. To be sure, what grounds both metaphor and usage is similarity, but in usage we do not intend to allude to certain characteristics of things that would not be accentuated by the normal expressions we use for them but only to signify one thing rather than the other, even though originally it was also some similarity which motivated the transference of sense. But when using an ordinary ambiguous word, we can be totally ignorant of this.

Shouldn't we then say that such regular and yet deviant use is characterized as proper for similar reasons as it is when it is used in accordance with the original institution, namely, precisely because there has been an imposition to which a speech community conforms? In fact, since Aquinas speaks of a "first imposition" of a word in the passage quoted above, one might think that he has in mind something like a second imposition which would explain a derivative and yet proper use

---

[6] Cf. Reginaldo of Piperno's *reportatio* of Aquinas' *Super I Cor.* 11.2 (Aquinas 2019, n. 87584): "Dicendum quod in omni figurata locutione, commune est quod sensus non est ille quem primo aspectu verba praetendunt, sed ille quod ille qui loquitur significare intendit, sicut si dicam: pratum ridet, non est sensus huius locutionis quod illud pratum rideat, sed illud quod ego significare intendo, scilicet quod pratum similiter se habet in decore cum floret sicut homo cum ridet. Hoc etiam modo se habet in locutionibus ironicis: cum enim non intendo hoc quod verba praetendunt significare, sed contrarium, ille est verus sensus quem ego intendo, et ideo nihil falsitatis est ibi."

of a word. However, he nowhere speaks of a second imposition being the reason for a term becoming proper by transference (Ashworth 2013a, 227).[7]

Unlike Aquinas, Burley and Ockham treat any *translatio* as belonging to a certain type of equivocal words called "deliberate equivocals". Consequently, every use of a word not according to its original signification counts as improper in their view. Generally, a word is equivocal when it is applied to two essentially different things because it is related to two concepts (Ockham 1974, 45: *SL* 1.13; Burley 1967, 16ra: *In Praed.*). This can occur in two different ways. Ockham and Burley resort to the distinction between *chance equivocals* (*aequivocum a casu*) and *deliberate equivocals* (*aequivocum a consilio*) made by Boethius when he comments on the opening passage of Aristotle's *Categories* (Boethius 1891, 166; cf. Aristotle 1961, 1a1–12). In equivocation *by chance*, the occurrences of equivocal expressions are totally unconnected; as Ockham characterizes it, "a name is imposed on one thing so that it will not be imposed on another thing, and it is not imposed on both." (Ockham 1978b, 124: *In Praed.* 1). In order to show how two expressions can be totally unconnected in this sense, both Ockham and Burley refer to the institution of proper names. To use an example from Ockham, the name 'Socrates' can be imposed on a person in Rome, and it can be imposed on a different person in England. The name given to a person in Rome has been imposed on that person only and no one else, especially not the person in England baptized with the same name, which has been instituted exclusively for the person in England. On the other hand, an equivocal is *deliberate* if there is a connection between the different concepts that are expressed by the same word. This applies to Aristotle's example of 'man', which is used equivocally for real human beings and painted ones. According to Ockham and Burley, the same term refers to both because 'man' was imposed for real human beings and then was deliberately applied to pictures of human beings on account of some similarity between the two. Hence, unlike in chance equivocals the word is intended to be linked to two different concepts. Given that real and painted human beings look similar, our mental representations also share some resemblance on account of which the term is applied to two different kinds of thing (Ockham 1974, 45: *SL* 1.13; 1978b, 142: *In Praed.* 1; 1980, 353: *Quodl.* 4.12; Burley 1967, 16ra: *In Praed.*; 2003a, 62: *EVP* 1.1.1).

In the *Sophistical Refutations*, Aristotle distinguishes three cases of how an equivocation can come about: first, when a name principally signifies more than one thing; second, "when we are accustomed to speak in that way"; and third, when in a propositional context words have ambiguous signification (Aristotle 1975, 166a15–20). Ockham and Burley, however, adopt Boethius's distinction from the context of the *Categories*, and link equivocation by chance to a word's proper signification of more than one thing. Deliberate equivocation, on the other hand, applies to language use as a case in which one word has a proper signification and an

---

[7] Of course, Aquinas uses the distinction between first and second imposition but in a different sense and in line with the common medieval distinction between first and second intentions. A second imposition is a case when words are imposed for words (Aquinas 1929, 624: *Super Sent.* I.26.1.1ad3).

improper signification in virtue of being instituted first for one thing and then later being transferred to signify something else. Hence, in the case of deliberate equivocals, the use of an already established term comes into play. As Ockham and Burley insist, *every* usage by transference is a case of improper signification. Thus, on their account Aquinas's distinction between (2) and (3) is a misconception.

Burley and Ockham disagree, however, on how to understand transference of signification. Ockham claims that a word is transferred to signify a new thing because of another imposition of the term. Burley objects that terms can be imposed only once, which is why usage cannot be a case of imposition. Jennifer Ashworth has pointed out this difference on several occasions (Ashworth 1991, 31–32; 2007, 325–327; 2013a, 226). But in what sense does it make a difference whether a term acquires a new meaning by imposition or by transference without imposition? In what follows I want to show that *translatio* as *impositio* gives a plausible explanation of how a word can get used as an ordinary equivocal term, whereas metaphorical use of a term is better conceived of as *translatio* without *impositio*. Unlike Aquinas, Ockham and Burley fail to acknowledge that these are two quite different modes of how transference works.

8.3   *Translatio* and Imposition

In the *Summa logicae*, Ockham describes the process by which a term becomes equivocal by deliberation and not by chance as follows:

> Another kind is equivocal by deliberation, when an utterance is first imposed on some thing or things and is subordinated to one concept, and later on, on account of some likeness of the first significate to something else or on account of some other reason, it is imposed on that other [thing], in such a way that it would not be imposed on that other [thing] except because it was first imposed on the former. This is the case with the name 'human being' (*homo*). For it was first imposed to signify all rational animals in such a way that it was imposed to signify all that is contained under the concept 'rational animal'. But later on, the users, seeing a likeness between such a human being and the image of a human being, at some time used the name 'human being' for such an image, so that if the name 'human being' had not first been imposed on human beings, the name 'human being' would not be used or imposed to signify or to stand for such an image (Ockham 1974, 45: *SL* 1.13).[8]

---

[8] "Aliud est aequivocum a consilio, quando vox primo imponitur alicui vel aliquibus et subordinaretur uni conceptui et postea propter aliquam similitudinem primi significati ad aliquid aliud vel propter aliquam aliam rationem imponitur illi alteri, ita quod non imponeretur illi alteri nisi quia primo imponebatur alii, sicut est de hoc nomine 'homo'. Primo enim imponebatur ad significandum omnia animalia rationalia, ita quod imponebatur ad significandum omne illud quod continetur sub hoc conceptu 'animal rationale', postea autem utentes, videntes similitudinem inter talem hominem et imaginem hominis, utebantur quandoque hoc nomine 'homo' pro tali imagine, ita quod nisi hoc nomen 'homo' fuisset primo impositum hominibus, non uterentur nec imponeret hoc nomen 'homo' ad significandum vel standum pro tali imagine" (trans. Spade 1995, 34, slightly modified).

How does a term, such as *homo*, become equivocal? First, it had to be already established as a sign for real human beings by being originally instituted. According to Ockham, words and concepts both directly signify things (ibid., 7–8: *SL* 1.1). While concepts are said to signify naturally, words do so conventionally. What makes a word a sign is its being related to a concept, although the term does not signify the concept. The conception might be very vague—indeed, sometimes it is merely a description of what the speaker intends to name[9]—but there must be some mental sign in order for a term to be imposed as a linguistic sign for something.

Instead of signifying the concept, a word is *subordinated* to a concept. Thus, a word has signification if and only if it is subordinated to a concept having signification, and once a word is subordinated to a concept, it signifies the same thing as the concept. Moreover, subordination is not something that has to be brought about actively by someone; rather, it first and foremost describes the relation between word and concept, of which the person can be entirely unconscious. For instance, the impositor does not need to know that her word is subordinated to a concept. What she wants do is to name things. What she *does* is to impose a sound on a thing of which she has a concept, and by this imposition a mere sound, in being subordinated to a concept in virtue of being imposed on a thing, is turned into a word.[10]

The original institution of a term fixes the relation between the word and the concept to which it is subordinated. No further reimposition is needed when the word is used subsequently, not even if the concept to which it is subordinated were to change its significates.[11] Of course, the word needs to be accepted by other language users, since it is possible to imagine original institutions of terms which are simply ignored and so do not get established in a language community. In fact, Ockham is well aware that someone wanting to establish a term must communicate this linguistic sign to others. Without shared understanding between speakers and listeners the sign is unlikely to become established; this is how they become conventional signs (Ockham 1979b, 471: *Ord.* 35.4).

A word can take on an additional meaning and become equivocal. The term is then related to a different concept by being reimposed, as Ockham makes clear for the case of transference of signification in the passage quoted above. People using a word according to its original institution can become aware that the things signified by a term bear striking similarities to other things, to which they start applying the

---

[9] "[…] potest aliquis imponere hoc nomen 'a' ad significandum quodcumque animal quod occurret sibi cras. Hoc facto, distincte significat illud animal, et significabit apud omnes volentes uti voce sicut imposita est, quantumcumque illud imponens non distincte intelligat, nec forte distincte intelliget quando sibi occurret." Ockham 1979b, 47: *Ord.* 22.

[10] I am following Schierbaum 2014, 82–87 here, but with one qualification. According to her, subordination should in no sense be thought of as a mental activity. If it were, the only way to subordinate a word to a concept would be by imposition, but this does not seem to be entirely Ockham's view; see below.

[11] It is open to discussion what exactly Ockham means by a change of the concept's natural signification. See Schierbaum's discussion in Schierbaum 2014, 87–92. Ockham himself gives the example that a concept (and thus the subordinated word) loses its signification when all of its individual significates cease to exist; see Ockham 1978a, 347: *In De int.*, prooem. 2.

same word; in our example, they start to use *homo* not just for human beings but also for images of human beings such that the word becomes related to an additional concept, that of images of human beings. As we have seen, in order for a word to conventionally signify something it needs to be subordinated to a concept. Hence, the relation between a term and a new concept needs to be one of subordination as well. But why does it also need to be imposed in this case? The reason seems to be that subordination in this sense is a semantic relation, not an activity. One does not subordinate a term to a concept; rather, subordination results from instituting a term for a thing. Ockham thus seems to hold that, generally, subordination can be established only by imposition.

If this is indeed his view, he has to explain deliberate equivocals, which come into existence by subordination to a new concept, in terms of reimposition. But does Ockham really mean that we need to reimpose a term every time we want to use it in a sense different from how it was originally instituted? In the passage quoted above, Ockham seems at first sight to be focusing on what is the case every time an individual speaker uses a word in its derivative meaning. In order to use *homo* not according to its original institution for real human beings, but subordinated to the concept for paintings of human beings, a speaker would need to impose the term anew every time she wants to talk about, say, portraits.

Ockham seems to be alluding to a view similar to the one defended by Roger Bacon (Schierbaum 2014, 97). According to Bacon, after the original institution, the imposition of words needs to be constantly renewed by speakers, often silently in their minds, when they use them. Bacon illustrates his position with the example of the utterance of 'John is dead' in reference to poor John who has just died. The problem is that John's corpse is strictly speaking no longer John, since it is no longer an animated being. How then can we say that it is *John* who is dead? Of course, while pointing to the corpse, the bearer of the news of John's death does not first say: "Let this name 'John' be imposed for the corpse." Instead, the utterer of 'John is dead' and the hearer silently renew the word's signification. According to Bacon, this process is to be regarded as imposition (Bacon 1988, 16–17: *CST* 125).[12]

It is a position like this which Walter Burley seems to have in mind when he argues that the transference of sense does not come about through subsequent acts of imposition and that only usage explains a word's transfer of sense. Burley claims:

> By virtue of the fact that there is a similitude between two things, the utterance that is imposed on the one is transferred to the other. Thus, because the beam of a bridge supports the bridge just as the foot of an animal supports the animal, and because the word 'foot' is imposed to signify the foot of an animal, the word 'foot' is transferred to signify the beam of the bridge. But this is not by imposition, since imposition is totally *ad placitum*, and the intellect is led by some reasoning to make 'foot' signify such a beam or to be taken for it,

---

[12] The example of a dead man goes back to Aristotle and inspired the popular sophism of the dead man alive; see Ebbesen 1979. Ockham mentions the dead man as an example of metaphorical speech but without referring to imposition; see Ockham 1974, 758: *SL* 3-4.3.

and so it is not [a case of] imposition but [of] transference (Burley 2003b, 201–202: *In Fallac.*, dub. 1.2).[13]

The example that Burley gives, though apparently not very common, is brought up by his contemporary Thomas de Wyk to arrive at the same conclusion, namely, that the transfer of sense is not by imposition (Thomas de Wyk 1997, 143: *Fallaciae*). It appears to be an adaptation of Boethius's example for the *translatio* from *pes hominis* to *pes navis* and *pes montis* as instances of the case in which a word is transferred from one thing to something else for which no separate word exists (Boethius 1891, 166: *In Cat.* 1). However, Burley and Thomas seems to treat the other thing for which the word is newly used as if someone wants to linguistically point it out for the first time and it lacks the proper word (because there is none). Burley insists that the intellect is led here by some reason when transferring a word; therefore, he claims, this cannot be an arbitrary choice, unlike when a word is originally instituted. He seems to be saying that if we were to think of imposition as what goes on in the mind of an individual speaker when applying a term to a different thing, we would be introducing an unfortunate ambiguity in the term 'imposition', since unlike when we transfer a word, in imposition we are not led by reason, but rather we relate a term to a thing arbitrarily.[14]

Ockham can readily agree with Burley that in originally instituting a name an impositor is free to name whatever she wants to name, and that it is entirely up to her which sound she imposes on a given thing. However, he is careful to distinguish between two cases of how deliberate equivocals can come about by subsequent imposition. On the one hand, a term can be subsequently imposed when it is not considered under the same concept, precisely because of some similitude or relation between the things to which the term now applies. On the other hand, a name can be deliberately imposed on different things without any consideration on the part of the impositor but simply because the impositor wants to. Ockham gives the example of a baptizer imposing the same name on the same occasion on three different persons (Ockham 1979b, 277: *Ord.* 29). One might argue that this is precisely what happens in chance equivocals. The difference seems to be that it is the same person on the same occasion who baptizes different people, while a chance equivocal is at work when there is no relation whatsoever between the instances of baptismal ceremonies. Now, the case is obviously different when different things share features which

---

[13] "Ex hoc enim quod est aliqua similitudo inter duas res, vox quae imponitur uni transfertur ad aliud, ut quia sicut pes animalis substat animali, sic lignum substat ponti, et hoc nomen 'pes' imponitur ad significandum pedem animalis, transumitur tamen hoc nomen 'pes' ad significandum lignum substans ponti. Sed hoc non est ex impositione, quia imponitur totaliter ad placitum; modo quod 'pes' significet tale lignum vel pro tali accipiatur, ad hoc intellectus quodammodo ratione ducitur, et ideo non est impositio sed transumptio" (trans. Ashworth 2013c, 146, slightly modified).

[14] Like Ockham, Burley claims that our words directly signify things, not our concepts of things. However, they disagree about whether the things directly signified by words are particular objects or their common natures. Ockham holds the former, Burley the latter. Burley on signification, see Cesalli 2013, 93–99. For a comparison of their views on signification see Dutilh-Novaes 2013, 74–79.

lead us to refer to them with the same word, such as the similarity of shape in humans and their portraits, or the similarity of function between the foot of an animal and the beam of a bridge.[15] Moreover, we might object against Burley that there are already cases of original imposition which are not totally *ad placitum* but are led by reason as well, as in onomatopoeic words for example.

Burley's objection does not actually apply to a conception like Ockham's, since it would take Ockham to be talking about transference as something happening in the mind of an individual speaker when the comparison of some objects is being made and a word is attributed to a new object. But this is not what Ockham is talking about in the passage quoted above. What he actually claims to be giving an account of when explaining the existence of deliberate equivocals in our language is how equivocal terms become commonly accepted within a language community. As Ockham says, a term could not be subsequently imposed on a second thing if it had not been originally imposed on some first thing; that is, the term not only has to have been originally instituted, but also has to be established within a language community. The same acceptance condition for imposition also applies to reimposition, since Ockham claims that reimposition requires that a plurality of speakers start to use the term for a different thing. According to him, not all the words we use gain their signification by an arbitrary original institution; for instance, in the case of the use of the word *homo* for pictures of human beings, a different story has to be told, since the new usage is established communally.

Admittedly, there is one difference between imposition and reimposition. There could be an original institution without subsequent use, since a language community might just not be willing to adopt the term. A subsequent imposition, however, not only is in need of a first imposition and accepted usage, but itself occurs *in the course of the speakers' frequent use of the word in the new sense*. As Ockham's passage indicates, it does not suffice that some person relates a term to a new thing occasionally; rather, the term has to be used in this way frequently or repeatedly, since otherwise no subsequent imposition will take place. It is established use itself that amounts to a further imposition and explains why we can use words in a sense different from their original meaning (see also Ockham 1974, 756: *SL* 3-4.3).

Of course, those speakers who are the first to use a word in a derivative sense have to somehow relate the term to a concept which differs from the one to which the word was subordinated by its original institution. After all, before the word *homo* can be regularly used for pictures of human beings as well as for actual human beings, some similarities between the two things have to be discovered so that people can begin to apply the word to pictures of human beings. Even if subordination is usually not something which the impositor brings about actively in her mind, our relating a word to a different concept is not ruled out—not to signify the concept but

---

[15] From an exegetical point of view, one finds both aspects in Boethius, that is, the user's reason and will; however, Boethius does not mention imposition, see Boethius 1891, 166: *In Cat.* 1. The larger background, of course, is the dispute between linguistic naturalism and conventionalism, which we already encounter in Plato's *Cratylus*.

to subordinate the word to it in order to apply the word to something other than its original significates. But once the word is regularly used in an equivocal sense—that is, once it is reimposed—its additional signification is an established fact for subsequent speakers. Unless we invent a new word that might make its way into common usage, we use words whose institution and fixed signification is just given for us.

This even enables us to use words of which we do not have a clear understanding because we lack proper concepts. We use words whose signification has already been established and which were subordinated to a concept at the moment of their original imposition. As Claude Panaccio and Sonja Schierbaum have shown, in Ockham the subordination of a word to a proper concept does not need to take place in our mind at the moment of utterance (Panaccio 2015; Schierbaum 2010). As Ockham claims we can use words for things we have never seen and yet those words have a signification on account of their original institution (Ockham 1974, 558: *SL* 3-2.29). This can be applied not only to our use of chance equivocals but also of deliberate equivocal terms. The proper sense of an equivocal term, once it is established, can be external to subsequent speakers, and they do not need to relate their words to the proper concept at the moment of utterance; instead, they rely on an established signification by imposition, regardless of whether this imposition was dependent on the original institution or on subsequent reimposition. In this sense, speakers take meanings that were derivatively imposed as if they had been originally instituted; it is quite natural for us to use the same word for real human beings and for pictures of them, for example. When using words, speakers do not necessarily have to know their origins and meanings, when meaning is taken to be the signification that is fixed by original institution. In fact, we are often surprised when we finally learn the etymology and original meaning of a word after we have already been using the word correctly for a long time.

Usage taking on the role of original institution has a significant consequence which Ockham himself does not address. When a word gets used so naturally for different things—in the case of *homo*, human beings and depictions of humans—we might ask whether the difference between deliberate and chance equivocals still applies, no matter how differently they came about originally. Recall that the different meanings of a chance equivocal are totally unconnected, and their signification is thus considered proper, unlike a deliberate equivocal, which is considered an improper use. In his discussion of Aristotle's three modes of equivocation, Peter of Spain pointed out that the same thing can happen to deliberate equivocals through frequent use:

> Or else we must reply (and this is better) that the signification said to belong properly to a word is the one that usage commonly accepts. Hence, what some word signifies now by transference will be signified properly when usage has increased, and then the word will be equivocal as to the first mode. And therefore it happens in this way that a signification that

is not proper now, but transferred, becomes proper later through frequent use (Peter of Spain 2014, 296: *SL* 7.54).[16]

It might be asked why a transferred signification should be treated as an improper use of a word if, as Peter puts it, the same word signifies a variety of things equally. Ockham does not venture this step, and still less does Burley's account consider this consequence of communal language use. His view of the signification of our words strictly fixed only by original institution conceives of every further development of their application within a language community as deviant. But this does not seem to give us a plausible account of how words can be so frequently used that they take on a secondary meaning that is nonetheless proper.

8.4 Metaphor and Equivocals

Does Ockham's conception of transference through imposition give us a suitable account for the signification of words used metaphorically? I think it does not, and that Burley's conception of *translatio* without imposition gives a better account.

Ockham claims that metaphorical meanings too should be thought of as deliberate equivocals that come about by reimposition, usually calling them *metaphorice*, *transumptive*, *improprie*, *equivoce*, *large*, or even *false* (Ockham 1974, 236–237, 264 and 757: *SL* 1.77, 2.4 and 3-4.3; 1967, 164: *Ord.* prol.5; 1970, 34, 41 and 467: *Ord.* 2.1 and 3.5; 1979b, 252 and 544: *Ord.* 27.3 and 36; 1984, 26: *Quaest. var.* 1). According to him, "there is hardly a word in the books of the authorities which is not used sometimes properly and according to its primary signification, and sometimes improperly and metaphorically and according to its improper signification" (Ockham 1979a, 312: *Exp. SE* 2.18.3).[17] Although the improper usage is clearly a matter of how the words supposit in a propositional context, Ockham traces improper supposition back to improper signification of words in the second and third modes of Aristotle's equivocals in the *Sophistical Refutations* (ibid.).[18] He gives a long list of how a word can be transferred from its proper signification to an improper one, which would introduce the risk of fallacies of equivocation, among them

---

[16] "Vel dicendum (et melius) quod propria significatio dicitur dictionis quam recipit usus communiter. Unde quod modo per aliquam dictionem significatur transsumptive, cum usus inoleverit, significabitur proprie, et tunc erit dictio equivoca quoad primum modum. Et ideo [...] contingit sic significationem que non est modo propria, sed transsumptiva, fieri postea propriam per frequentem usum" (trans. Copenhaver et al., slightly modified).

[17] "Vix etiam est aliquod vocabulum, quin in libris auctorum aliquando sumatur proprie et secundum suam primam significationem, et aliquando improprie et metaphorice et secundum significationem impropriam."

[18] Recall that Ockham relates Aristotle's second mode of equivocation with Boethius' deliberate equivocals. See also ibid., 22–23: *In SE* 2.2.8. For improper supposition, see Ockham 1974, 236–237: *SL* 1.77.

"metaphora, senecdoche, metonymia", all of which "are called by Boethius equivocal by consideration" (Ockham 1974, 759: *SL* 3-4.3).[19]

However, when treating this type of equivocation, Ockham does not discuss these cases—and nowhere does he mention Boethius' example of 'charioteer' for helmsman, and at best he alludes to the famous example of the laughing meadows (Ockham 1979a, 23: *Exp. SE* 2.8)—but always resorts to Aristotle's example of real and painted human beings. However, this is not an apt example for cases in which someone, for ornamental reasons and perhaps only to "show off with rhetorical brilliance or erudition", comes up with "different words" although she could easily use the words that are common in usage (Ockham 1974, 758: *SL* 3-4.3),[20] since it is quite ordinary to refer to a sculpture of a person as a human being. Ockham seems to have a profound lack of interest in poetic language, which leads him to simply subsume metaphors under equivocation. This leads him to overlook the fact that metaphors do not (or at least do not necessarily) amount to an established ambiguous use of language. If this were the case, then they would no longer be metaphors.

Boethius himself, however, whom Ockham claims to follow closely, saw metaphorical use as a special case of equivocation. For after introducing the distinction between chance and deliberate equivocals, Boethius adds a little later that there seems to be another type of equivocals which Aristotle does not take into consideration (in the *Categories*). He claims that if there does not exist a term for the thing to which a word is transferred, *translatio* amounts to equivocation. His example is the one we have already encountered in the previous section, namely, the application of 'foot' to a part of mountains and ships, to which Boethius also adds the example of *homo* for real and painted human beings. There is neither a special name for painted human beings nor for the bottom of a mountain; by transference, they are named for the first time. Metaphorical use differs from those examples where a term is transferred from its original sense in order to signify something which does not yet have a name. Suppose a word is said of something for which a proper linguistic expression already exists. If it is for ornamental reasons that we use a word for a thing which already has its own proper word, Boethius thinks that this should not be considered an equivocation. His example is the transference of the name for

---

[19] "Istis modis et multis aliis possunt dictiones a proripa significatione tranferri ad impropriam, cuiusmodi translationis grammatici diversas docent species. Inter quas continentur istae: metaphora, synecdoche, metonymia, antonomasia, emphasis, catachresis, metalempsis, anthropopathos, onomatopoeia, phantasia, paralange et multae aliae [...]. Et nota quod aequivocum tale, iuxta istum secundum modum, vacatur a Boethio aequivocum a consilio."

[20] "[...] scriptores veteres, quia tam profunditate scientae quam splendore eloquentiae praepollebant, necesse fuit eos propter ornatum eloquii per diversa vocabula et varias dictionem orationum formas suam intentionem exprimere [...]."

the "navigator" of a chariot, the charioteer (*auriga*), to the navigator of a ship, whom we usually call a helmsman (*gubernator*) (Boethius 1891, 167: *In Cat.* 1).[21]

Transference is different when it comes to things that are already significates of terms, since here a term which is usually used for one thing is transferred to refer to another thing for which we already have a proper expression. And for this it is Burley who seems to have the more plausible explanation, when he thinks that transference happens without imposition:

> An utterance is made a sign of a thing [...] by transference when the utterance, taken as having the *ratio* of a sign, is imposed on a thing primarily and by means of a proper *ratio*, and then, because of a similitude to the thing on which it was primarily imposed, or because of a proportion of relation which it has to some other thing, this utterance is transferred to represent some other thing, as is clear. In fact, 'to laugh' is properly attributed to, and by means of imposition it signifies the laugh of a human being, and, because of a certain similitude of this act with flourishing, this sound 'to laugh' is transferred to represent or signify flourishing (Burley 2005, 280: *QSE* 12).[22]

As Burley goes on to say, 'laughing' signifies flourishing only by usage and not by imposition; if it were by imposition, then the difference between proper and improper signification would vanish. Hence, the word by transference signifies a thing that it does not signify in its proper use. We cannot account for this by appealing to reimposition, since this would explain only how the signification of a word gets fixed and established for new things. But we need to explain how words can be applied occasionally to different things although they have a proper meaning. Hence, the question is what it means for the word being transferred to signify improperly in such cases.

For a speaker to transfer a word it is crucial that she have some intention to use the word differently. Burley mentions that there need to be discovered some similarities which tempt a speaker to transfer a word. Note that Burley prefers to say that the word is transferred to represent something else. In a sense, of course, Burley also says that the word signifies the thing to which it is metaphorically applied, but he seems to take this kind of signification as something different from the signification which words inherit from their original institution. Burley is not explicit on this

---

[21] "Videtur autem alius esse modus aequiuocationis quem Aristoteles omnino non recipit. Nam sicut dicitur pes hominis, ita quoque dicitur pes nauis, et pes montis, quae huiusmodi omnia secundum translationem dicuntur. Neque enim omnis translatio ab aequiuocatione seiungitur sed ea tantum cum ad res habentes positum uocabulum, ab alia iam nominata re nomen ornatus causa transfertur, ut quia iam dicitur quidam auriga, dicitur etiam gubernator, si quis ornatus gratia cum qui gubernator est dicat aurigam, non erit auriga nomen aequiuocum, licet diuersa, id est, moderatorem currus nauisque significet. Sed quoties res quidem uocabulo eget, ab alia uero re quae uocabulum sumit, tunc ista translatio aequiuocationis retinet proprietatem, ut ex homine uiuo ad picturam nomen hominis dictum est."

[22] "Sed vox fit nota rei [...] ex transumptione autem ut quando vox imponitur rei primo in ratione signi et sub propria ratione, deinde, propter similitudinem rei illius cui primo imponebatur vel propter proportionem vel relationem quam habet ad aliquam aliam rem transumitur ista vox ad aliquid aliud repraesentandum, ut patet: 'ridere' enim proprie attribuitur et ex impositione significat risum hominis, propter quandam similitudinem huius actus ad florere transumitur haec vox 'ridere' ad repraesentandum vel significandum florere."

point, but the opposition between proper signification by imposition and improper signification by transference can be interpreted in terms of modern pragmatist accounts as a distinction between what words mean and what a speaker means (see, e.g., Grice 1969). Someone who says "the meadows laugh" usually does not intend to act as an impositor and to give the word a new sense or to extend the literal sense. We use a metaphor in order to convey certain aspects about things that are not captured by the literal sense of the word, but we do not establish a new meaning for the word.

What Ockham and Burley confounded, we find neatly distinguished in Peter Abelard. He noticed clearly that Boethius is making a distinction between two types of *translatio*. First, it can occur "due to the necessity of signification", when there is not yet a word for a thing to name and one uses an already existing word for the thing; second, it can be done for rhetorical reasons, when one transfers a word to a thing which already has an established term. Following Boethius in conceiving of only the first case as equivocation, Abelard emphasizes that in the second case, the transference of a name does not come about through an act of imposition, because the things signified have already been subjected to a name. He distinguishes this latter case from equivocation, claiming that transference leading to equivocation comes about through a new imposition (Abelard 1921, 121: *LI* 2).[23] This is plausible, given that Abelard thinks that imposition endows a word with what he calls natural signification, in that it fixes the reference of the word for subsequent speakers. This is precisely *not* what happens with metaphorical expressions.[24]

8.5   Conclusion

Medieval authors agreed that the proper signification of a word is given according to its original institution, but they disagreed about when a signification of a word should be considered improper. A clear-cut distinction would be to consider every signification of a word improper when it deviates from the word's original signification. However, this would make it difficult to do justice to deviant but commonly accepted usages, as well as to metaphors. The term *translatio* itself turns out to be an ambiguous expression and can mean either the institution of equivocal words in the course of language development or the production of metaphors; but the two phenomena should get distinct explanations.

Aquinas wants to do justice to cases in which a certain usage of a word has become so prevalent that it would be misleading to consider the signification improper. His distinction between original imposition and usage can be fleshed out

---

[23] "[…] quando sermonem exornamus […] non novam impositionem vocis facimus […] Quod itaque in 'auriga' vel in 'ridere' quandoque aliud intelligimus ex adiunctis sibi, quam habeat eorum propria impositio, non est hoc aequivocationis multiplicitati deputandum."

[24] However, Abelard also saw that metaphorical expressions can also make their way into ordinary usage and thus get a "quasi-imposition" (Rosier-Catach 1991, 164). See also Martin 2011.

with Ockham's approach of subsequent imposition. A usage that deviates from the original sense and yet is well established has pretty much the same effect as the original institution of a word. However, Ockham should have drawn the consequences of this: such a usage should not be counted as improper merely because it deviates from the word's original signification. Moreover, Ockham was certainly misled in thinking that metaphors should be explained in the same way. For if they were, they would already be so well established as equivocals that they are no longer metaphors.

Here Burley has a point against Ockham in claiming that a metaphor does not establish a new signification as a result of imposition. Rather, what happens in the case of metaphor is that a word with a proper signification is applied to another thing. However, Burley makes a parallel mistake on the other extreme, for he fails to acknowledge that words can take on a quite ordinary equivocal sense which is not metaphorical. Words taken metaphorically are properly used neither in the sense of their original institution nor in a common usage which can deviate from the original meaning.

In treating both metaphors and quite ordinary equivocal expressions as cases of Boethius's deliberate equivocals, Ockham fails to give a plausible explanation of metaphors, while Burley similarly fails to account for ordinary equivocal expressions. The transfer of sense in a metaphor is best explained by usage rather than imposition, but a transferred sense becoming proper in itself seems to be best conceived of as a case of imposition. Aquinas, who acknowledges cases in which words which already name something can acquire another proper signification through frequent figurative usage, distinguishes metaphors from the original sense and the ordinary ambiguities of language. What seems to allow him to do so is to keep metaphors out of the box of deliberate equivocals where already Boethius did not want to put them in the first place.

Abelard draws this consequence when he explicitly keeps metaphors entirely separate from equivocation. Perhaps we can say that Abelard comes close to what Donald Davidson wanted to show about the semantics of metaphorical expressions: that words used metaphorically do not have an additional meaning. Words have an ordinary meaning (whether univocal or equivocal), and they can also be used in an unusual way but without taking on a new meaning. Metaphors belong exclusively to the realm of usage, but not in the sense of bringing about new significations, as happens when a term is transferred to name something which does not yet have its own name. If a word used metaphorically thus acquired a transferred sense — that is, a sense additional to the sense (or senses) it already has — then a metaphor would function like the other transferred senses that language already has anyway. Abelard was aware that on such an account, in Davidson's words, "to make a metaphor is to murder it" (Davidson 1978, 249).

Bibliography

Abelard, Peter. 1921. *Die Logica 'Ingredientibus'. Glossen zu den Kategorien*, ed. Bernhard Geyer. Aschendorff: Münster.

Aquinas, Thomas. 1884. *Commentaria in octo Libros Physicorum Aristotelis*. In *Opera omnia*, vol. 2, ed. Commissio Leonina. Rome: Ex Typographia Polyglotta S. C. de Propaganda Fide.

———. 1888. *Pars prima Summae theologiae, q. 1–49*. In *Opera omnia*, vol. 4, ed. Commissio Leonina. Rome: Ex Typographia Polyglotta S. C. de Propaganda Fide.

———. 1889. *Pars prima Summae theologiae, q. 50–119*. In *Opera omnia*, vol. 5, ed. Commissio Leonina. Rome: Ex Typographia Polyglotta S. C. de Propaganda Fide.

———. 1892. *Prima secundae Summae theologiae, q. 71–114*. In *Opera omnia*, vol. 7, ed. Commissio Leonina. Rome: Ex Typographia Polyglotta S. C. de Propaganda Fide.

———. 1897. *Secunda secundae Summae theologiae, q. 57–122*. In *Opera omnia*, vol. 9, ed. Commissio Leonina. Rome: Ex Typographia Polyglotta S. C. de Propaganda Fide.

———. 1903. *Tertia pars Summae theologiae, q. 1–59*. In *Opera omnia*, vol. 11, ed. Commissio Leonina. Rome: Ex Typographia Polyglotta S. C. de Propaganda Fide.

———. 1929. *Scriptum super libros Sententiarum. Commentum in primum librum*, ed. Pierre Mandonnet. Paris: Lethielleux.

———. 1970. *Quaestiones disputatae de veritate, q. 1–7*. In *Opera omnia*, vol. 22 1/2, ed. Commissio Leonina. Rome: Ad Sanctae Sabinae.

———. 1974. *Expositio super Isaiam ad litteram*. In *Opera omnia*, vol. 28, ed. Commissio Leonina. Rome: Editori di San Tommaso.

———. 1976. *De fallaciis*. In *Opera omnia*, vol. 43, ed. Commissio Leonina, 383–418. Rome: Editori di San Tommaso.

———. 1989. *Expositio libri Peryermenias. Editio altera retractata*. In *Opera omnia*, vol. 1/1, ed. Commissio Leonina. Rome: Commissio Leonina.

———. 2019. *Super I Epistolam B. Pauli ad Corinthios lectura, cap. XI–XIII.9. Reportatio Reginaldi de Piperno*. In *Corpus Thomisticum*, ed. Enrique Alarcón. corpusthomisticum.org/c1r.html.

Aristotle. 1961. *Categoriae vel Praedicamenta. Translatio Boethii, Editio Composite, Translatio Guillelmi de Moerbeka, Lemmata e Simplicii commentario decerpta, Pseudo-Augustini Paraphrasis Themistiana*. In *Aristoteles Latinus*, vol. I, 1–5, ed. Lorenzo Minio-Paluello. Bruges: Desclée De Brouwer.

———. 1968. *De arte poetica. Translatio Guillelmi de Moerbeka*. In *Aristoteles Latinus*, vol. XXXIII, ed. Lorenzo Minio-Paluello. Bruxelles: Desclée De Brouwer.

———. 1975. *De sophisticis elenchis. Translatio Boethii, Fragmenta Translationis Iacobi et Recensio Guillelmi de Moerbeke*. In *Aristoteles Latinus*, vol. VI, 1–3, ed. Bernard G. Dod. Leiden: Brill.

Ashworth, Jennifer E. 1980. Can I speak more clearly than I understand? A problem of religious language in Henry of Ghent, Duns Scotus and Ockham. *Historia linguistica* 7: 29–38.

———. 1991. Equivocation and analogy in fourteenth-century logic. Ockham, Burley and Buridan. In *Historia Philosophiae Medii Aevi. Studien zur Geschichte der Philosophie des Mittelalters. Festschrift für Kurt Flasch zu seinem 60. Geburtstag*, ed. Burkhard Mojsisch and Olaf Pluta, 23–43. Amsterdam: Grüner.

———. 2007. Metaphor and the logicians from Aristotle to Cajetan. *Vivarium* 45: 311–327.

———. 2013a. Analogy and metaphor from Thomas Aquinas to Duns Scotus and Walter Burley. In *Later mediaeval metaphysics. Ontology, language, and logic*, ed. Charles Boylard and Rondo Keele, 223–248 and 291–299. New York: Fordham University Press.

———. 2013b. Aquinas, Scotus and others on naming, knowing, and the origin of language. In *Logic and language in the middle ages: A volume in honour of Sten Ebbesen*, ed. Jakob L. Fink, Heine Hansen, and Ana Mariá Mora-Márquez, 257–272. Leiden: Brill.

———. 2013c. Being and analogy. In *A companion to Walter Burley, late medieval logician and metaphysician*, ed. Alessandro D. Conti, 135–165. Leiden: Brill.

Bacon, Roger. 1988. *Compendium studii theologiae*, ed. Thomas S. Maloney. Leiden: Brill.
Boethius. 1891. *In Categorias Aristotelis libri quatuor*. In *Migne Patrologia Latina*, vol. 64, 159–294. Paris: Garnier.
Burley, Walter. 1967. *Super artem veterem Porphyrii et Aristotelis*. Venice, 1497. Repr. Frankfurt a.M.: Minerva.
———. 2003a. *Expositio vetus super librum Praedicamentorum*, ed. Mischa von Perger. *Franciscan Studies* 61: 55–95.
———. 2003b. *Super tractatum fallaciarum*, ed. Sten Ebbesen. *Cahiers de l'institut du moyen-âge grec et latin* 74: 197–207.
———. 2005. *Quaestiones super Sophisticos Elenchos 4-12*, ed. Sten Ebbesen. *Cahiers de l'institut du moyen-âge grec et latin* 76: 239–281.
Cesalli, Laurent. 2013. Meaning and truth. In *A companion to Walter Burley, late medieval logician and metaphysician*, ed. Alessandro D. Conti, 87–133. Leiden: Brill.
Dahan, Gilbert. 2009. Saint Thomas d'Aquin et la métaphore. Rhétorique et herméneutique. *Medioevo. Rivista di Storia della Filosofia Medievale* 18(2008): 85–118. Repr. Dahan, Gilbert. *Lire la bible au Moyen Âge: essais d'herméneutique médiévale*, Geneva: Droz, 249–282.
Davidson, Donald. 1978. What metaphors mean. *Critical Inquiry* 5 (1): 31–47.
Dutilh-Novaes, Catarina. 2013. The Ockham-Burley dispute. In *A companion to Walter Burley, late medieval logician and metaphysician*, ed. Alessandro D. Conti, 49–84. Leiden: Brill.
Ebbesen, Sten. 1979. The dead man is alive. *Synthese* 40: 43–70.
Eco, Umberto. 1993. *La ricerca della lingua perfetta nella cultura europea*. Rome: Laterza.
Grice, Herbert Paul. 1969. Utterer's meaning and intentions. *The Philosophical Review* 68: 147–177.
Martin, Christopher G. 2011. "What an ugly child". Abaelard on translation, figurative language, and logic. *Vivarium* 49: 26–49.
Ockham, William. 1967. *Scriptum in librum primum Sententiarum. Ordinatio, prol., d. 1*. In *Opera theologica*, vol. 1., ed. Gedeon Gál and Stephen Brown, St. Bonaventure, N.Y: The Franciscan Institute.
———. 1970. *Scriptum in librum primum Sententiarum. Ordinatio, d. 2–3*. In *Opera theologica*, vol. 2, ed. Stephen Brown and Gedeon Gál. St. Bonaventure, N.Y: The Franciscan Institute.
———. 1974. *Summa logicae*. In *Opera philosophica*, vol. 1, ed. Philotheus Boehner, Gedeon Gál, and Stephen Brown. St. Bonaventure, N.Y: The Franciscan Institute.
———. 1978a. *Expositio in librum Perihermenias Aristotelis*. In *Opera philosophica*, vol. 2, ed. Angelo Gambatese and Stephen Brown, 345–504. St. Bonaventure, N.Y: The Franciscan Institute.
———. 1978b. *Expositio in librum praedicamentorum Aristotelis*. In *Opera philosophica*, vol. 2, ed. Gedeon Gál, 135–339. St. Bonaventure, N.Y: The Franciscan Institute.
———. 1979a. *Expositio super libros elenchorum*. In *Opera philosophica*, vol. 3, ed. Francesco del Punta. St. Bonaventure, N.Y: The Franciscan Institute.
———. 1979b. *Scriptum in librum primum Sententiarum. Ordinatio, d. 19–48*. In *Opera theologica*, vol. 4, ed. Gerald Etzkorn and Francis E. Kelley. St. Bonaventure, N.Y: The Franciscan Institute.
———. 1980. *Quodlibeta septem*. In *Opera theologica*, vol. 9, ed. Joseph C. Wey. St. Bonaventure, N.Y: The Franciscan Institute.
———. 1984. *Quaestiones variae*. In *Opera theologica*, vol. 8, ed. Gerald Etzkorn, Francis E. Kelley, and Joseph C. Wey. St. Bonaventure, N.Y: The Franciscan Institute.
Panaccio, Claude. 2015. Ockham's externalism. In *Intentionality, cognition, and mental representation in medieval philosophy*, ed. Gyula Klima, 166–185. New York: Fordham University Press.
Peter of Spain. 2014. *Summulae logicales. Summaries of logic. Text, translation, introduction, and notes*, ed. Brian P. Copenhaver, Calvin Normore, and Terence Parsons. Oxford: Oxford University Press.
Purcell, William. 1987. *Transsumptio*. A rhetorical doctrine of the thirteenth century. *Rhetorica: A Journal of the History of Rhetoric* 5: 369–410.

Rosier-Catach, Irène. 1991. La notion de translatio, le principe de compositionalité et l'analyse de la prédication accidentelle chez Abélard. In *Langage, sciences, philosophie au XIIe siècle*, ed. Joël Biard, 125–164. Paris: Vrin.

———. 1997. Prata rident. In *Langages et philosophie. Hommage à Jean Jolivet*, ed. Alain de Libera, Abdelali Elamrani-Jamal, and Alain Galonnier, 155–176. Paris: Vrin.

Schierbaum, Sonja. 2010. Knowing lions and understanding 'lion': Two jobs for concepts in Ockham? *Vivarium* 48: 327–348.

———. 2014. *Ockham's assumption of mental speech. Thinking in a world of particulars*. Leiden: Brill.

Spade, Paul Vincent. 1995. *William of Ockham. From his* Summa of logic, *part I*, pvspade.com/Logic/docs/ockham.pdf.

de Wyk, Thomas. 1997. *Fallaciae*, ed. Sten Ebbesen, "Texts on equivocation. Part II. Ca. 1250–1310". *Cahiers de l'Institut du Moyen-âge Grec et Latin* 67: 139–143.

Chapter 9
Truth and Person in Aquinas's *De veritate*

Robert J. Dobie

Keywords Aquinas · Truth · Person · Goodness · Transcendentals · Faith

In a series of articles, Gyula Klima (2002, 2009, 2016, 2018) has expounded Thomas Aquinas's philosophical anthropology and defended it with great skill from modern misunderstandings. In particular, he has shown how Aquinas's doctrine of the human mind or intellect and its relation to the body is not only philosophically defensible, but is in many ways superior to contemporary philosophical accounts. What I want to do in this essay is situate Klima's defense of Aquinas's account of the human mind and its relation to the human person in Aquinas's wider account of the transcendentals: i.e., that being as being is also intrinsically intelligible (true) and desirable (good). For Aquinas it should be remarkable to us that the world is knowable: that things existing quite apart from and independent of our intellect, can nevertheless cause true judgments in our intellect. What then, Aquinas asks, is the ground of this essential conformity between intellect and material thing? Why should the forms of material things be intelligible in the first place? Just as Klima argues that Aquinas's understanding of the soul and intellect in relation to the body goes beyond a simple and indefensible dualism of mind and body by showing how the substantial form of the human being can inform and yet transcend matter, so, I argue, Aquinas argues that the *ground* of the world's intelligibility is that it is rooted in a creative intellect that is also *personal*, i.e., that being is, as the Czech phenomenologist Erazim Kohak puts it, fundamentally *meaningful being*: "*Meaningful being*, not pure meaning or sheer being, is reality." Thus, Kohak continues: "Philosophy can claim to be the *scientia generalis* because it seeks to see and articulate the sense of being as it presents itself primordially, prior to the imposition of any special perspective or purpose" (Kohak 1984, 49). In this sense, Aquinas's

R. J. Dobie (✉)
Department of Philosophy, La Salle University, Philadelphia, PA, USA
e-mail: dobie@lasalle.edu

J. P. Hochschild et al. (eds.), *Metaphysics Through Semantics: The Philosophical Recovery of the Medieval Mind*, International Archives of the History of Ideas Archives internationales d'histoire des idées 242, https://doi.org/10.1007/978-3-031-15026-5_9

exploration of the nature of truth in his *Disputed Questions on Truth* reveals the phenomenon of being in a far more fundamental and comprehensive way than most modern philosophers since Descartes.

Precisely because Aquinas's examination of the truth of being is so fundamental, the complete sense of being eludes any full understanding by our finite intellect. But, as Aquinas notes, we desire more than we can understand:[1] the truth of being points to a cause of that truth that eludes cognition but awakens desire, for the good of the intellect is truth and the supreme Good of the intellect is the supreme Truth, that which is essentially true and the cause of all truth. Hence, Aquinas argues, the virtue that perfects our knowledge of this personal ground of all existence, truth, and goodness *in this present life* is the virtue of *faith*: for faith is that virtue by which our intellect is oriented to a truth and good that transcend the natural ability of our intellect to understand. More particularly, it is by faith that the intellect enters into the mystery of the Person of Christ, in whom the fallen human being encounters the *ground* of being. For the person of Christ reveals the truth of the human person, who, as incarnate intellect, both reveals and conceals intelligibility, and thus can evoke love and desire in a pre-eminent fashion. But since Christ, as the Gospel of John asserts, is the *Logos* or *Ratio* of all creation, what scripture reveals and what faith knows is Christ as the personal ground of the truth of being.

9.1   Truth and the Human Soul

Aquinas starts his *Disputed Questions on Truth* by arguing that the convertibility of truth and being makes sense only insofar as being as such is inherently and essentially related to a being that can at least potentially assimilate itself intellectually to all beings as beings.[2] In other words, we can predicate "true" of being as being only to the extent that it is "relatable" to the human soul, for the human soul, according to Aristotle, *is* all things insofar as it takes in by cognition the intelligible forms of all things. This assertion was not self-evident to most of Aquinas's contemporaries,

---

[1] It is interesting to note here that Descartes observes more or less the same thing in the fourth meditation of his *Meditations on First Philosophy*. But he draws a very different conclusion from this phenomenon: that the will outstrips the intellect or understanding is a defect to be remedied by the rigorous application of method so that the mind only contemplates "clear and distinct ideas," i.e., only ideas proportionate to our intellect. For Aquinas, it is this phenomenon that should draw the mind upward to a contemplation of the ground of being, truth, and goodness and, moreover, to finding some sort of understanding of this ground in our understanding of the mystery of the human person.

[2] "Thomas's important innovation in the doctrine of the transcendentals is the correlation he introduces between *anima* and being. He understands the transcendentals 'true' and 'good' in relation to the faculties of a spiritual substance, man" (Aertsen 1996, 257). In an earlier article, Aertsen goes so far as to say that Thomas begins a "Copernican Revolution" in philosophy by making the soul essential to understanding the transcendental properties of being (Aertsen 1992, 165). See also Seidle 1973, 171.

as most clung to the argument found in Aristotle that being as truth is in some way merely "accidental" to being qua being, for the relation of any entity to a particular human intellect is clearly something fortuitous or accidental and not essential to any being. Thus, many thirteenth-century theologians attempted to explain what is meant by truth by giving a purely "ontological" account of truth, i.e., an account that does not make any reference to the human intellect—or any intellect at all.[3] Aquinas thought these attempts futile, for reasons I will explain presently.

In the first article of the first question of the *De veritate*, Aquinas begins by observing that we can predicate certain properties of being said to be "transcenden-tal"—that is, properties that "cut across" all the ten categories of being—without adding anything real to being (for this is impossible). The way we can do this is by adding the notion of relation to being, for relation in itself adds nothing to being. But even more fundamentally, "being" cannot be even understood as such without a relation to a being that is intellectually "in some way all beings" This being is the human soul. And this relation is twofold: insofar as every being is related to an intel-lect which can know being as such and insofar as every being is related to a rational appetite or will, which can desire being as such. Thus,

> Every cognition is perfected through the assimilation of the knower to the thing known, such that the said assimilation is the cause of cognition: just as vision knows color by being disposed through the species of that color. This is said to be the adequation of thing and intellect; and in this the conception of truth is formally perfected.... But cognition [itself] is a certain effect of truth (*De ver.*, 1, 1).[4]

Notice here that for Thomas, the act of knowing does not cause truth nor is it a pre-condition for truth; rather, it is the other way around: knowing is caused by the intelligible forms of the things known. The intelligibility of being is prior to human knowing. And yet, being is intrinsically open to human knowing insofar as the proper effect to which it is essentially oriented is human knowing. In short, being

---

[3] Philip the Chancellor, who is the first author in the medieval tradition to write explicitly and sys-tematically on the transcendentals, tried to assimilate the transcendental truth to the definition of the one as indivision, i.e., as a property "added" to being in a purely negative fashion (i.e., as posit-ing nothing positive in addition to being, which is logically impossible). But Thomas breaks deci-sively with this tradition of trying to give a negative or purely ontological definition of truth. See Van de Wiele 1954, 550. For the development of Aquinas's thought on the nature of truth, espe-cially between his *Disputed Questions on Truth* and the *Summa Theologiae*, see Wippel 1989–1990.

[4] "Si autem modus entis accipiatur secundo modo, scilicet secumdum ordinem unius ad alterum, hoc potest esse *dupliciter*: Alio modo secundum convenientiam unius entis ad aliud: et hoc quidem non potest esse nisi accipiatur aliquid quod natum sit convenire cum omni ente. Hoc autem est anima, quae quodammodo est omnia, sicut dicitur in III *de Anima*. In anima autem est vis cognitiva et appetivia. Convenientiam ergo entis ad appetitum exprimit hoc nomen *bonum*.... Convenientiam vero entis ad intellectum exprimit hoc nomen *verum*. Omnis autem cognitio perficitur per assimi-lationem cognoscentis ad rem cognitam, ita quod assimilatio dicta est causa cognitionis: sicut visus per hoc quod disponitur per speciem coloris, cognoscit colorem. Adaequatio rei et intellectus dici-tur; et in hoc formaliter ratio veri perficitur.... Sed cognitio est quidem veritatis effectus." All translations from Aquinas are the author's.

defines itself as true (and good) in relation to the human intellect.[5] And the intellect can reveal being as such because the intellect itself is not determined, as intellect, to any one form, but open to all forms as such (*In De Anima*, III, lect. 7, n. 681).[6] Beings, in other words, are intrinsically ordered to the soul, although the existence of any particular being does not obviously depend on the soul knowing it.

Thus, as Mark Jordan puts it: "*Ens* as such is intrinsically ordinable. This ordinability is not one of the categories of relation which accrue to being *per accidens*. It is, rather, the fundamental source for the supra-categorical features of *ens*" (Jordan 1980, 15).[7] That beings are actually related to a particular human intellect is something that is purely accidental—they exist and thus remain knowable whether human beings exist or not (*Metaphysics* E, 3; 1027b30—end of book). But since intelligibility is an intrinsic feature of beings as beings, they must always and everywhere be related in actuality to *some* intellect; and this intellect can only be an eternal and creative intellect. Indeed, Thomas asserts in the second article of question one of the *De veritate* that "natural things are," as it were, "constituted between two intellects": things are said to be true insofar as they are adequated to an intellect. But, while a being is said to be true accidentally when related to the human intellect, it is said to be true essentially and fundamentally when related to the divine intellect, such that if on the impossible supposition that there is no divine intellect, nothing, not even that assertion, *could be* true, even potentially. Indeed, nothing would be at all, since being is convertible with intelligibility (and there certainly could be no meaningful statements either). Or as Jan Aertsen puts it: "Essential for the truth of things is the relation to the divine Logos. Ontological truth has a divine ground" (Aertsen 1992, 169).[8] This, then, confirms for Aquinas the Neoplatonic principle that the intrinsic "ordinability" of things, which is merely potential in created beings, cannot belong to being without it being somehow ordered in actuality to these properties in their maximum perfection (Jordan 1980, 19).[9]

In order to understand this, we must look at the distinction Aquinas makes between the speculative and practical intellect. In the latter, the maker is the measure of the truth of what he or she makes: the thing is true to the degree that it

---

[5] Indeed, the otherness of the intellect appears so stark that some philosophers from Meister Eckhart to Jean-Paul Sartre have called the intellect a "nothing." That is because the intellect does not have a definite nature; it is "empty of all form" so that it may be capable of receiving all form. But the relation is also reversible: intellect is only such in relation to being. See Breton 1963, 53.

[6] "Non contigit naturam intellectus esse 'neque unam', id est nullam determinatam, sed hanc solam naturam habet, quod est possibilis omnium."

[7] Or, as he writes a bit later in the same article, "*Ens* itself is intelligibly ordinable" (Jordan 1980, 16). In the same vein, Aertsen remarks: "It is noteworthy that Thomas consistently speaks of ontological truth in terms of 'aptitude'. Being is knowable through itself, on the basis of its act of being. Knowability is the possibility for truth, but it is not yet truth in the formal sense, which is a conformity" (Aertsen 1996, 271).

[8] This is, of course, a wholly different issue from that of to what extent the transcendental perfections of being are "appropriated" to the divine Persons of the Trinity. See Kretzmann 1989.

[9] "If the transcendentals constitute the minimum view of order, the perfections are the maximum."

conforms to the idea or intention in the mind of its maker. But in the former, the intellect is true to the extent that it conforms to what is intelligible in the thing itself (its form). Since, however, human beings do not make the natural world, they can only relate to it *speculatively*, i.e., by their minds being conformed to the intelligible form or species in things. The implication of this is that, if truth is properly (that is to say, actually) in the intellect (for truth properly resides in the judgment of the intellect), then truth in its most proper sense cannot be in the human intellect but in a divine creative intellect, i.e., one that creates the natural world itself. For, as Aristotle demonstrated, the actual is absolutely speaking prior to the potential. Natural things, if they are to be intelligible, must always and already be actually conformed to at least one intellect, the divine intellect: "Thus the divine intellect is measuring and not measured; natural things, however, are measuring and measured; but our intellect is measured, not measuring any natural things but artificial things only. A natural thing, therefore, as constituted between two intellects is said to be true according to its adequation to one or the other." Or, as Thomas puts it, whatever we experience is true to the extent anything we experience "is born (*nata est*) to form from itself a true judgment..." Thus, within the very notion of a "nature" is for it to be "being born" in an intellect. This implies for Aquinas, that natural things must then also be by their very nature "born" to be con-formed in a non-contingent manner, to the divine intellect (*De ver.*, 1, 2).[10] Or, to put it another way, the world as we experience it is, as it were, "constituted between the activities of two intellects." In other words, the sensible world, as it is known to the human intellect, is a sort of "screen" between two intellects, one, the human intellect, the other, the divine intellect.

By the same token, the human intellect knows, and actualizes itself as intellect, only to the extent that it becomes the beings it knows, that is, only insofar as it assimilates formally into itself *qua* intellect the intelligible species of other beings. And the more the human intellect knows the created world, to that degree it is assimilated to the cause of their intelligibility in the divine intellect and thus the

---

[10] "Sed sciendum, quod res aliter comparatur ad intellectum practicum, aliter ad speculativum. Intellectus enim practicus causat res, unde est mensuratio rerum quae per ipsum fiunt: sed intellectus speculativus, quia accepit a rebus, est quodammodo motus ab ipsis rebus, et ita res mensurant ipsum.... Sic ergo intellectus divinus est mensurans non mensuratus; res autem naturalis, mensurans et mensurata; sed intellectus noster est mensuratus, non mensurans quidem res naturales, sed artificiales tantum. Res ergo naturalis inter duos intellectus constituta, secundum adaequationem ad utrumque vera dicitur: secundum adaequationem ad intellectum divinum dicitur vera, in quantum implet hoc ad quod est ordinata per intellectum divinum,... Secundum autem adaequationem ad intellectum humanum dicitur res vera, in quantum nata est de se formare veram aestimationem.... Prima autem ratio veritatis per prius inest rei quam secunda, quia prior est comparatio ad intellectum divinum quam humanum; unde, etiam si intellectus humanus non esset, adhuc res: diceretur verae in ordine ad intellectum divinum. Sed si uterque intellectus, quod est impossibile, intelligeretur auferri, nullo modo veritatis ratio remaneret." "Being knowable, even being known, by a *human* mind is not constitutive of an object's essence; being known or not being known by *God*, however, means to be or not to be" (Pieper 1989, 55).

more intimately it becomes related to God. This assimilation and even intimacy between knower and known is something to which Josef Pieper draws our attention:

> For a thing to have knowledge, then, means to carry in itself the identity (*quidditas*) of some other being or thing, and not only its "image" but indeed its "form." A being's ability to know, therefore, is its ability to transcend its own delimitations, the ability to step out of its own identity and to have "also the form of the other being," which means: to *be* the other being. "Knowing" constitutes and establishes the most intimate relationship conceivable between two beings (a fact that is expressed and confirmed through the age-old usage of "knowing" to indicate sexual intercourse) (Pieper 1989, 37).

The two aspects of the transcendentals—the ontological and the cognitive—cannot for Thomas be isolated from each other. There is an inner and intimate relationship between being and thinking (Aertsen 1988, 315). But we should note something interesting here: this intimate union between intellect and the thing known has behind it or as its basis an intimate union of the thing with the divine mind. Indeed, to the degree that we know the truth of a creature, to that degree that creature communicates the truth it has in the divine mind (however limited this communication might be). As Thomas puts it, "the thing existing outside the soul through its form imitates the art of the divine intellect and thereby it has an inborn capability of forming a true apprehension on the human intellect" (*De ver.*, 1, 8).[11] For, as he goes on to argue, just as it is the essence of the divine goodness to communicate itself to creatures, so it is of the essence of creatures to radiate their own being, goodness, and intelligibility, as the sun not only illuminates the bodies it shines upon but also makes them luminous in turn (*De ver.*, 5, 8).[12] In this sense, then, creatures in general and (for the human intellect), material creatures in particular are essential to the communication of divine truth. They are not, as a certain Platonism would have it, a hindrance or obstacle to knowing the truth of things. Hence, the notion that we saw above that material creatures are a sort of "screen" between the human intellect

---

[11] "Res autem existens extra animam, per formam suam imitatur artem divini intellectus, et per eandem nata est facere de se veram apprehensionem in intellectu humano, per quam etiam formam unaquaeque res esse habet; unde veritas rerum existentium includit in sui ratione entitatem earum, et superaddit habitudinem adaequationis ad intellectum humanum vel divinum."

[12] "Voluit enim Deus perfectionem suae bonitatis, secundum quod possibile est creaturae, alteri communicare. Divina autem bonitas *duplicem* habet perfectionem: *unam* secundum se; prout, scilicet, omnem perfectionem supereminenter in se continent; *aliam* prout influit in res, secundum scilicet, quod est causa rerum, unde et divinae bonitati congruebat ut utraque creaturae communicaretur; ut, scilicet, res creata non solum a divina bonitate haberet quod esset et bona esset, sed etiam quod alii esse et bonitatem largiretur; sicut etiam sol per diffusionem radiorum suorum non solum facit corpora illuminata, sed etiam illuminantia; hoc tamen ordine servato, ut illa quae magis sunt soli conformiora, plus de lumine recipient, ac per hoc non solum sufficienter sibi, sed etiam ad influendum alii."

and divine intellect is not a defect of creation, but rather essential to the communication of truth and a fundamental feature of its goodness (*De ver.*, 10, 7).[13]

In other words, there cannot be for Thomas, as least for the *homo viator*, a "mind to mind" relation between God and the human being that is not mediated by material creation. Now, the human intellect is measured by the things it knows; but as we have seen, the intelligibility of things is more than what the human intellect can know or measure, for no finite creature can instantiate perfectly what it is in the divine mind. As such, this "super-intelligibility" of things not only underlines the limits of human reason;[14] it also awakens a desire for what is beyond or above human reason. In other words, this super-intelligibility awakens a desire for the good beyond created beings, which is itself a truth beyond the finite truths we can comprehend. It is therefore no accident that Thomas finds it necessary to discuss the nature of the good in his *Disputed Questions on Truth*. Again, like the true, the good adds nothing to being except conceptually; the good is added to being neither as an accident is added to a substance nor as a genus is contracted to a specific type of being. Rather, the term "good" adds to the notion of "being" that of "desirability," the intrinsic relation of being to a universal appetite that desires beings insofar as they exist. In other words, being as good (i.e., "good" as understood transcendentally) is revealed, at least among sensible, material creatures, only to the being that desires being as such universally, and this is, again, the human soul.

But there is a slight yet significant difference in how the terms "true" and "good" add to being. According to Thomas, perfection in creatures can be understood in two ways. In one way, being is perfected according to its rational species. But this

---

[13] "In cognitione ipsa qua mens ipsum Deum cognoscit mens ipsa Deo conformatur, sicut omne cognoscens, inquantum huiusmodi, assimilatur cognitio. Maior autem est similitudo quae est per conformitatem, ut visas ad colorem, quam quae est per analogiam, ut visus ad intellectum, qui similiter ad sua obiecta comparatur. Unde expressior similitudo Trinitatis est in mente secundum quod cognoscit Deum, quam secundum quod cognoscit seipsam. Et ideo proprie imago Trinitatis in mente est secundum quod cognoscit Deum *primo* et *principaliter*; sed *quodam modo secundario* est secundum quod cognoscit seipsam et praecipue prout seipsam considerat ut est imago Dei." It follows from this that for Aquinas, knowledge of God can be gotten only partially either from knowledge of creatures outside of us or from knowledge of ourselves. Created beings in their intelligibility point, of course, to God; but as we have seen, they do not manifest the full intelligibility that they have in God. For that matter, the mind, insofar as it knows created beings, sees a reflection of the divine Trinity in itself insofar as it remembers, knows, and desires; but this knowledge is only by a certain analogy with the divine Trinity. It is not a direct knowledge or intuition. In short, knowledge of God comes naturally from an intellect assimilating itself to created being first and primarily; but by doing so the embodied human intellect actualizes its own intellectual nature to the degree that it sees the divine nature reflected in itself. But again, this reflection is only an analogy of the divine nature; as not only created beings but as *material* created beings, human beings cannot know the divine mind directly—not in other creatures nor in itself.

[14] In fact, Rudi te Velde remarks perceptively how the manifestation of the limits of reason in the face of the very intelligibility of the world is the objective of Aquinas's *Summa contra Gentiles*: "So the issue is not a defense of the 'reasonableness' of Christian faith before reason. Aquinas's objective is to confront natural reason with its own condition, to make reason aware of its limitations in order to prevent reason from unreflectively imposing its own limits on the search for truth. We need more truth than our reason can grasp" (Te Velde 2002, 58).

happens only insofar as it is known in some intellect. Thus, the perfection predicated of the true is found only in the intellect and can be said really only of the intellect. By contrast, we can talk of a thing being perfected in its real existence apart from or "outside" the intellect. And we can only say something approaches its "perfection" or is "perfected" to the degree that it approaches an ideal standard (i.e., the standard according to which it was *created*). To the degree that things are perfected in their created, existent nature, to that degree they are good. And to the degree that its ultimate perfection in God lies "outside" or "beyond" the thing's created nature, to that degree is the good a goal or end that lies beyond the thing itself and, by extension, a goal or end that lies beyond the soul insofar as it is a created being and coincides with its exemplar in the divine mind: "It follows therefore that the true and good add over the understanding of being a relation to perfection." The true adds the notion of being perfected in its intelligible species by being known by and existing in an immaterial intellect. But: "In another way being is perfective of another not only according to the concept of its species, but also according to the existence (*esse*) it has in the natural world (*in rerum natura*). And through this mode the good is perfective." And with this understanding comes the understanding that natural things have an end or final cause—that for the sake of which they act and thus their good (*De ver.*, 21, 1).[15]

That truth and goodness are convertible with being indicates that there is a dual and parallel "movement" within beings: while the true is an assimilation of things to the intellect, the good is a movement of the soul towards things.[16] There is a tight

---

[15] "Oportet igitur quod verum et bonum super intellectum entis addant respectum perfectivi. *Uno modo* secundum rationem speciei tantum. Et sic ab ente perficitur intellectus, qui perficitur per rationem entis. Nec tamen ens est in eo secundum esse naturale; et ideo hunc modum perficiendi addit *verum* super ens. Verum enim est in mente, ut Philosophus dicit in VI *Metaphys.*; et unumquodque ens in tantum dicitur verum, in quantum conformatum est vel confomabile intellectui; et ideo omnes recte definientes verum, ponunt in eius definitione intellectum. *Alio modo* ens est perfectivum alterius non solum secundum rationem speciei, sed etiam secundum esse quod habet in rerum natura. Et per hunc modum est perfectivum *bonum*. Bonum enim in rebus est, ut Philosophus dicit in VI *Metaphys.* In quantum autem unum ens est secundum esse suum perfectivum alterius et conservativum, habet rationem finis respectu illius quod ab eo perficitur; et inde est quod omnes recte definientes bonum ponunt in ratione eius aliquid quod pertineat ad habitudinem finis; unde Philosophus dicit in I *Ethicorum*, quod *bonum optime definiunt dicentes, quod bonum est quod omnia appetunt.* Sic ergo *primo* et *principaliter* dicitur bonum ens perfectivum alterius per modum finis; sed *secundario* dicitur aliquid bonum, quod est ductivum in finem: prout *utile* dicitur bonum; vel natum est consequi finem: sicut et sanum dicitur non solum habens sanitatem, sed perficiens et conservans et significans."

[16] Jan Aertsen characterizes the differences in the two accounts of the transcendentals in the *De veritate* in this way: "The differences between *De veritate* 1.1 and 21.1 are primarily determined by the fact that their subjects are different: the first text deals with the true, the last with the good. Both are relational transcendentals, but there are two dissimilarities between the true and the good which make the perspective of the true the reverse of the perspective of the good. The true is the end-term of a movement of things toward the soul; knowledge is a process of assimilation. The good is the end-term of a movement of the soul toward things; appetite is an inclination. The second dissimilarity is that while everything desires the good, one cannot say that 'everything knows the true'. Truth is a perfection that can only be found in a spiritual substance" (Aertsen 1996, 262).

correlation between intellection and desire in things that can only make sense if they are constituted between two intellects. Of course, this correlation is never completely fulfilled in created things, including the human soul; truth is in the intellect, goodness is in things. But this parallelism does point, on the one hand, to their union or coincidence in God, who, as the creator of all things, is the source of the truth and goodness of all things, but, on the other hand, to the necessity of this truth being mediated through material creatures: "Because God is himself the purpose for the sake of which beings are created, he directs them to return to him. He not only creates beings, but invests them with an intrinsic and dynamic order by which they return to their source" (O'Rourke 1992, 234). Put differently, the transcendent Good, which is by nature self-diffusive and sharing of itself, is also intrinsically communicative and thus the essence of Truth itself. The existential act of the transcendent first cause, God, is in itself generous and communicative; "its nature is to communicate itself as far as possible."[17] It follows that every creature, insofar as it is the product of that self-communication, communicates something of God's goodness and is therefore said to be good by participation in that goodness; but insofar as every creature communicates something of God's being and goodness, that creature is also intelligible and true (*De ver.,* 21, 1, ad 1).[18] As Milbank and Pickstock note, truth as adequation is not a simple mirroring of the world or a passive registering of things in the mind, but rather an act that "fulfils the being of things known, just as much as it fulfils the truth in the knower's mind" and thus completes them at least partially in their goodness.[19] Hence, to quote Milbank and Pickstock again: "Aquinas shows us that he does not intend to *refer* truth to being, as if were at a kind of static speculative epistemological remove from being. Rather, he is asking about truth as a *mode of existence*."[20] Truth in its primary or transcendent (as opposed to *transcendental*) sense is not a form or idea—these are vehicles of truth. Rather truth in its first and primary sense is identical with the intellect who constitutes creatures in their being and communicates itself in and through them.

The world, then, as creation, is "constituted between two intellects." That is to say, being as being is not only true, but it is constituted by intellects (even if accidentally in relation to the human intellect). The created world as created is always already in relation to an intellect and thus also already and always potentially a part

---

[17] "God acts, not through desire for an end to be attained, but through love for an end which he wishes to communicate" (O'Rourke 1992, 246). "Of itself, act tends to realise itself according to its fullness; it is limited only by potency. Act is, therefore, of itself essentially generous: its nature is to communicate itself in so far as possible. This is signified in the very notion of act: *communcatio enim sequitur rationem actus*" (O'Rourke 1992, 247).

[18] "Et inde est quod essentia Dei, quae est ultimus finis rerum, sufficit ad hoc quod per eam dicatur Deus bonus; sed essentia creaturae posita non dicitur res bona nisi ex habitudine ad Deum, ex qua habet rationem causae finalis. Et pro tanto dicitur quod creatura non est bona per essentiam, sed per participationem."

[19] "Correspondence here is a kind of real relation or occult sympathy—a proportion or harmony or *convenientia*—between being and knowledge, which can be assumed or even intuited, but not surveyed by a measuring gaze" (Milbank and Pickstock 2001, 5).

[20] Milbank and Pickstock (2001, 6).

of a world of intellects. In short, the world as creation is shot through with intellectual relations and is thus eminently an inter-personal world and the various finite intellects in that world reflect in their judgments, as so many faces of a mirror, the transcendent Truth of things (*De ver.*, 1, 4).[21] Thus, relations between persons is not an accidental or contingent feature of being as such; rather it is an essential and constitutive property of being in its most fundamental sense.

9.2 Personhood and the Ground of Truth

To see where Aquinas is going with this exposition of the nature of truth in the *De veritate*, I think it helpful to look at what he says about truth in his scriptural commentaries, for after all, the principal aim of the disputed questions was to understand the words of scripture more deeply. And perhaps the place in his writings where Aquinas engages the question of truth in relation to scripture most deeply and directly is in his commentary on the Gospel of John. In his exposition of verse four of the first chapter of the Gospel, *In ipso vita erat* or "in him was life," Thomas expansively develops the nature of God as the transcendent ground of truth.[22] This first Truth (*prima Veritas*) is not only living, but all that He creates, insofar as it exists in the first cause, is also living within Him (*Expositio in Ioh.*, I, lect. II, n. 90).[23]

Now, of course, most creatures are not living beings: some, like the earth and metals, are completely inanimate; others, like animals and the human being, are living but are not identical to life itself (*Expositio in Ioh.*, I, lect. II, n. 91).[24] When we observe the scale of perfection in creatures, we notice that they run from the most primitive elements like earth through to plants, animals, and human beings. As sub-

---

[21] "Veritas ergo intellectus divini est una tantum, a qua in intellectu humano derivantur plures veritates, sicut ab una facie hominis resultant plures similitudines in speculo…. Veritates autem quae sunt in rebus, sunt plures, sicut et rerum entitates. Veritas autem quae dicitur de rebus in comparatione ad intellectum humanum, est rebus quodammodo accidentalis, quia posito quod intellectus humanus non esset nec esse posset, adhuc res in sua essentia permanerent."

[22] See the first question of the *Summa Theologiae*. Also, the first four questions of Aquinas's *Expositio super librum Boethii De Trinitate*.

[23] "Quod factum est in ipso, idest per ipsum, hoc vita erat non in seipso sed in sua causa. In omnibus enim causatis hoc commune est, quod effectus, sive per naturam sive per voluntatem producti, sunt in suis causis non secundum proprium esse, sed secundum virtutem propriae suae causae; sicut effectus inferiores sunt in sole ut in causa, non secundum eorum esse, sed secundum virtutem solis. Quia ergo causa omnium efectuum productorum a Deo, est vita quaedam et ars plena rationum viventium, ideo omne, quod factum est in ipso, idest per ipsum, vita erat in sua causa, scilicet in ipso Deo."

[24] "Res enim dupliciter considerari possunt, secundum scilicet quod sunt in seipsis et secundum quod sunt in Verbo. Si considerentur secundum quod sunt in seipsis, sic non omnes res sunt vita nec etiam viventes, sed aliquae carent vita, aliquae vivunt. Sicut facta est terra, facta sunt etiam et metalla, quae nec vita sunt, nec vivunt; facta sunt animalia, facti sunt homines, quae secundum quod sunt in seipsis, non sunt vita, sed vivunt solum."

stances gain in fullness and complexity, they also become living substances. So, Aquinas refers to the common example of the chest in the mind of the artisan: *in rerum natura*, the chest is nonliving, but insofar as it pre-exists as a chest in the mind of the artisan it is living or, more precisely, it is part of the life of the artisan, subsisting in him and in relation to all that makes up his life (*Expositio in Ioh.*, I, lect. II, n. 91).[25] Analogously, non-living creatures are, in a certain sense, living when in the divine mind and living creatures, while indeed alive, only have the fullness of life insofar as they exist as intentions in the divine mind.

Aquinas, therefore, in his commentary on John is saying more than that being and truth in their primary instance and first cause are living. Aristotle's god is also living; but Aristotle's god is not creative, it does not "pre-contain" everything within itself, and least of all does it communicate itself to substances "lower" than it, intellectual or otherwise. Showing his debt to the Neoplatonic understanding of the First Principle, Aquinas rather argues that a full understanding of divine life is of a life that communicates itself in and to creatures by creating beings that reflect in a limited or finite way the divine being, truth, and goodness. Now, this communication of divine truths through creatures is not automatic or necessary. This is partly due to the fact that human beings are contingent beings, dependent for their existence entirely on their Creator; but it is also partly due to the fact that the human being, due to his or her intellectual nature, possesses free will and thus an activity that is not completely determined by his or her finite nature. The perfection of the human being lies in his or her "intellectual or rational nature" (*Expositio in Ioh.*, I, lect. III, n. 99),[26] but divine truth can only be communicated fully to such a nature by moving it by free assent, because only such a being can "move [itself] perfectly" and thus be freely open to the full perfection of its being in God:

> Since those things are said to be living, which move themselves in some way, those are said to have perfect life who move themselves perfectly. But to move oneself perfectly and properly in inferior creatures belongs to man alone. Now even if other things move themselves by some intrinsic principle, this principle is still not indifferent to opposites; and therefore they are moved by necessity and not freely. Things moved, therefore, by such a principle are acted upon rather than act. Man, by contrast, since he is the lord of his own action, moves himself freely to all that he wishes; and thus, man has perfect life, and simi-

---

[25] "Si vero considerentur secundum quod sunt in Verbo, non solum sunt viventes, sed etiam vita. Nam rationes in sapientia Dei spiritualiter existentes, quibus res factae sunt ab ipso Verbo, sunt vita; sicut arca facta per artificiem in se quidem nec vivit nec vita est, ratio vero arcae, quae praecessit in mente artificis, vivit quodammodo, inquantum habet esse intelligibile in mente artificis, non tamen est vita, quia per ipsum intelligere artificis non est in sua essentia, neque suum esse. In Deo autem suum intelligere est sua vita et sua essentia: et ideo quicquid est in Deo, non solum vivit sed est ipsa vita, quia quicquid est in Deo, est in sua essentia. Unde creatura in Deo est creatrix essentia."

[26] "In hoc etiam ostenditur perfectio et dignitas huius vitae, quia est intellectualis seu rationalis."

larly [it is the case with] whatever is by nature intellect. (*Expositio in Ioh.*, I, lect. III, n. 99).[27]

In this way, the human intellect is moved to an assent of divine truth in such a way that it strengthens not only the human intellect as intellect, but the human being as a free being who is *dominus sui actus* and thus freely desires the highest good, who is God.

The human intellect, therefore, is not just a passive receptor of truth, but to the degree it knows, to that degree it becomes a real, actualized intellect; and the more it becomes a real actualized intellect, the more it grasps that the intelligibility of the world points to a cause beyond the world that is like it in its living and intellectual nature, even if infinitely more perfect, for it comes to grasp all the more that the cause of truth must be a subsistent intellect analogous to itself (for the human intellect is only self-subsistent *secundum quid*). Even more, it comes to grasp that this subsistent intellect is also free, a will that freely, perfectly and all at once desires itself as the supreme Good. Thus, any revelation of divine truth that is other than in the personal mode, i.e., as a free and subsistent (whether *per se* or *secundum quid*) intellect—such as an abstract emanation from a higher intellect, for example— would in fact be false. This is because, as Josef Pieper comments: "The concept of transcendental truth affirms the relatedness of every being to the *inner core* of another being, the knowing mind."[28] Truth in its deepest sense is always a dialectical interplay of the inner and outer, the hidden and manifest. Truth, then, in its primary instance is personal and since being is convertible with truth, being can only be understood as "being" insofar as it is situated in a world that is personal, viz., a world of things or natures whose intrinsic intelligibility manifests and conceals an eminently creative intellect that is also in essence self-communicative (Zimmerman 2005, 277).[29] As Mark Jordan observes: "Thomas understands by 'person' nothing but a subsisting thing within the genus of an intellectual nature. The transcendental features of *esse* are the characteristics of persons. The transcendentals are shadows of the entity which is eminently personal" (Jordan 1980, 25–26). Thus, the person is always a mysterious manifestation of intelligibility that is both manifested and hidden by the body, which reflects the nature of our knowledge of the truth of things

---

[27] "Cum enim illa dicuntur viventia, quae se aliquo modo movent, illa dicuntur vitam habere perfectam, quae perfecte seipsa movent; movere autem seipsum perfecte et proprie, in inferioribus creaturis soli homini convenit. Nam etsi alia ex seipsis ab aliquo principio intrinseco moveantur, non tamen illud principium se habet ad opposite; et ideo ex necessitate moventur, et non libere. Mota igitur a tali principio magis aguuntur quam agunt. Homo vero, cum sit dominus sui actus, libere se movet ad omnia quae vult; et ideo homo habet vitam perfectam, et similiter quaelibet intellectus natura. Vita ergo Verbi, quae est lux hominum, est vita perfecta."

[28] Pieper (1989, 77).

[29] "Sicut autem esse creatum, quantum est de se, vanum est et defectibile, nisi contineatur ab ente increato; ita omnis creata veritas defectibilis est, nisi quatenus per veritatem increatum rectificatur. Unde neque hominis neque angeli testimonio assentire infallibiliter in veritatem duceret, nisi quantum in eis loquentis Dei testimonium consideratur" (*De ver.*, 14, 8).

itself and the nature of material creation as a sort of "bodily screen" between the divine and human intellects.[30]

9.3 Faith and Personal Knowledge

Faith is a *habitus*—a disposition or, more accurately, virtue—by which we judge the truth of things in light of the First Truth of things revealed to us by God. Aquinas reduces these first principles to two: (1) that God exists and (2) that he loves us (Torrell 2003, 14). Having faith in the first point is a necessary, but not sufficient condition—even Satan and the damned believe that God exits (indeed, with far more certainty than any human intellect in this life). The second principle, that God loves us, therefore, is just as crucial for a living and efficacious faith (and therefore, a principle inaccessible to the demons). Faith, Aquinas argues, is a *habitus* or virtue that is both cognitive and volitional: to be sure, its object is the First Truth and thus faith strains to *know* what it believes; and yet, it cannot know with the clarity that usually comes with our knowledge of natural things. What is required is an act of will that adheres to what is revealed to the intellect with firmness and certainty despite the intellect not having a clear and complete grasp of what is revealed (*De ver.*, 14, 1).[31] This follows necessarily from the fact that the objects of faith—the *Summum Verum* and *Summum Bonum* and all the other objects of faith that bear relation to these—exceed our natural powers to know; we cannot know them naturally even in principle (*De ver.*, 14, 2).[32] Thus, in faith, the intellect assents to what

---

[30] "We can of course know things; we cannot formally know their truth. We know the copy, but not the relation of the copy to the archetype, the correspondence between what has been designed and its first design. To repeat, we have no power of perceiving this correspondence by which the formal truth of things is constituted. Here we can notice how truth and unknowability belong together" (Pieper 1957, 59). And Fr. Clarke asserts: "To be a person is to be intrinsically expansive, ordered toward self-manifestation and self-communication. This is the decisive advance over the Aristotelian substance, which was indeed, as nature, ordered toward action and reception, but, as form, was oriented primarily toward self-realization, the fulfillment of its own perfection as form, rather than sharing with others. The Neoplatonic dynamism of the self-diffusiveness of the good as taken over by St. Thomas is needed to expand this orientation toward action beyond the self-centered viewpoint of form towards the wider horizon of other persons and the universe as a whole" (Clarke 2004, 71–72).

[31] "Sed in fide est assensus et cogitatio quasi ex aequo. Non enim assensus ex cogitatione causatur, sed ex voluntate, ut dictum est. Sed quia intellectus non hoc modo terminatur ad unum ut ad proprium terminum perducatur, qui est visio alicuius intelligibilis; inde est quod eius motus nondum est quietatus, sed adhuc habet cogitationem et inquisitionum de his quae credit, quamvis firmissime eis assentiat."

[32] "Unde oportet huiusmodi cognitionis supernaturalis aliquam inchoationem in nobis fieri; et haec est per fidem, quae ea. tenet ex infuse lumine, quae naturaliter cognitionem excedunt."

is proposed to it by revelation by means of the will, which assents to it as something to which it is good to assent (*De ver.*, 14, 2).[33]

In other words, faith is a virtue that governs and moves both the intellect and will and, indeed, must do so. What causes someone to have faith and another not to? Faith is first a divine gift, but it has its basis in an attraction or love for what it proposes (Davies 1992, 280). We assent to faith because we have "suffered" the things of which it speaks. "For this reason, faith's assent to what God teaches amounts to a 'certain participation in... and assimilation to God's own knowledge, in that by faith infused in us we cling to the first truth for its own sake' (*De Trin.*, q.2, a2c). And so '*sacra doctrina* is like an impression of God's own *scientia*' (*S.Th.*, I, 1, 3 ad 2) in us" (Marshal 2005, 14). The question becomes, then, how can God most effectively make an "impression" of his own *scientia* on us? The answer is through the Incarnation.

As we saw above, faith is a virtue that involves both the intellect and will in equal measure. Now, while faith, properly speaking, is an intellectual virtue that has the intellect as its subject, it can only be moved to assent by the will, which loves the good (eternal life) that is proposed to it by revelation.[34] Thus, the perfection of faith demands the perfection of both the intellect and the will: the intellect must be perfected insofar as it is prepared to assent to the truths of revelation (by understanding properly first principles, by having objections and other intellectual obstacles to the faith removed, etc.) (*S.Th.*, II-II, 4, 2).[35] But the will must also be "prompt at obeying" what is revealed to it by God. "And thus, not only is it necessary that the

---

[33] "Voluntas autem mota a bono praedicto proponit aliquod intellectui non apparens, ut dignum cui assentiatur; et sic determinat ipsum ad illud non apparens, ut scilicet ei assentiat."

[34] "Unde facile est secundum dicta, definitionem artificialiter formare: ut dicamus quod *fides est habitus mentis, qua inchoatur vita aeterna in nobis, faciens intellectum non apparentibus assentire*" (*De ver.*, 14, 2). "Already present in the *De veritate*, the same definition was explained at length there: faith realizes in a believing subject that anticipation of eternal life through a certain similarity to the desired end" (Torrell 2003, 325).

[35] "Dicendum quod, cum fides sit quaedam virtus, oportet quod actus eius sit perfectus. Ad perfectionem autem actus qui ex duobus activis principiis procedit requiritur quod utrumque activorum principiorum sit perfectum: non enim potest bene secari nisi et secans habeat Artem et serra sit bene disposita ad secandum. Dispositio autem ad bene agendum in illis potentiis animae quae se habent ad opposita est habita, ut supra dictum est. Et ideo oportet quod actus procedens ex duabus talibus potentiis sit perfectus habitu aliquo praeexistante in utraque potentiarum. Dictum est autem supra quod credere est actus intellectus secundum quod movetur a voluntate ad assentiendum: procedit enim huiusmodi actus et a voluntate et ab intellectu. Quorum uterque natus est per habitum perfici, secundum praedicta. Et ideo oportet quod tam in voluntate sit aliquis habitus quam in intellectu, si debeat actus fidei esse perfectus.... Credere autem est immediate actus intellectus: quia obiectum huius actus est verum, quod proprie pertinent ad intellectum. Et ideo necesse est quod fides, quae est proprium principium huius actus, sit in intellectu sicut in subiecto."

habitus of the virtue be in the will as it commands, but also in the intellect as it assents" (*S.Th.*, II-II, 4, 2, ad 2).[36]

The upshot of this is that the only correlate to faith can be a person. This is because only the mystery of the person can move both the intellect and will into an act of faith, which, in turn, is the only way we can know what is beyond our natural powers to know in this life. For the person is both an object and subject of intellection and for that reason is both luminous to our intellect and beyond its grasp. Or, as we saw in the passage from Josef Pieper, only the human person as we experience it has an "inner" and "outer" dimension. The person is also a principle of desire and love: again, as both an object and subject of love, the person is able to elicit a love and desire that is of "mind to mind." It is to this personal mode of knowing that, I would argue, Aquinas refers when he distinguishes the "natural" mode of knowing of the philosopher from the "supernatural" mode of knowing of the theologian or believer. Concerning the philosopher, Aquinas remarks:

> The ultimate good that the philosopher and theologian consider is different. The philosopher considers as the ultimate good what is proportionate to human powers, and consists in the act of the man himself; hence happiness is said to be a certain operation. And thus according to the philosopher, an act, whose principle is said to be virtue, is said to be good absolutely insofar as it is fitting to a potency and perfecting it. Thence, whatsoever *habitus* the philosopher finds eliciting such an act, he calls a virtue, whether it be in the intellective part, as knowledge (*scientia*) and other such intellectual virtues, whose act is the good of its own potency, such as to consider the truth, or whether it be in the affective part, such as temperance, courage, and other moral virtues (*De ver.*, 14, 3).[37]

For the philosopher, then, faith is superfluous and even incomprehensible: what is perfective of the human being is only that which is proportionate to the powers, intellectual or otherwise, of human nature to know and desire. But this involves a paradox, because the First Truth, from which all other truths derive, cannot be proportionate to the human intellect or to human nature in general. The philosopher seeks truth; and yet, the Truth itself, the First Truth which is the cause of truth in creatures, cannot be known in itself, even in principle, by the human intellect unaided by revelation. This is where, according to Aquinas, theology comes in:

> But the theologian considers as the ultimate good that which exceeds the powers of nature, which is to say, eternal life, as said previously. Hence, he does not consider the good in human acts absolutely, because they are endless, but in relation to that good which does

---

[36] "Dicendum quod non solum oportet voluntatem esse promptam ad obediendum, sed etiam intellectum esse bene dispositum ad sequendum imperium voluntatis: sicut oportet concupiscibilem esse bene dispositam ad sequendum imperium rationis. Et ideo non solum oportet esse habitum virtutis in voluntate imperante, sed etiam in intellectu assentiente."

[37] "Aliud est autem bonum ultimum quod considerat philosophus et theologus. Philosophus enim considerat quasi bonum ultimum quod est humanis viribus proportionatum, et consistit in actu ipsius hominis; unde felicitatem dicit esse operationem quamdam. Et ideo secundum philosophum actus bonus, cuius principium virtus dicitur, dicitur absolute in quantum est conveniens potentiae ut perficiens ipsam. Unde quemcumque habitum invenit philosophus talem actum elicientem, dicit eum esse virtutem; sive sit in parte intellectiva, ut scientia et huiusmodi virtutes intellectuales, quarum actus est bonum ipsius potentiae, scilicet considerare verum; sive in parte affectiva, ut temperantia, et fortitudo, et aliae virtutes morales."

posit an end: asserting that only that act is a complete good which is ordered proximately to the final good, i.e., that which is more meritorious of eternal life. And every such act he claims is an act of virtue; and whatever *habitus* that elicits such an act is said to be virtue in itself (*De ver.*, 14, 3).[38]

Faith is the virtue that orients the human intellect and will to that which transcends its natural powers to know or love. But also, faith is a *habitus* or virtue that transforms the entire human being from within. So, if the known is always known in the mode of the knower, knowledge of God is made possible by God taking on human nature Himself (*De ver.*, 14, 10).[39]

This points to one of the reasons Aquinas gives for why the Incarnation was most fitting for providing an object for faith: it was the most appropriate way for human nature to be restored so that the human person might know what is beyond his or her natural power to know. For without the Incarnation, Thomas finds it hard to see how, among the many reasons for the Incarnation, the highest end for human beings could be attained, namely a full participation in God's divinity, which is eminently a personal participation (*S.Th.*, III, 1, 2). And indeed, I think one can argue that the phrase, "personal participation," is somewhat redundant: participation in the divine truth for Aquinas by definition demands a personal relation of mind to mind, of an intellectual substance in relation to another intellectual substance. Thus, Thomas points out that Christ did not take on simply the intelligible species of humanity, but the being of an individual human being, flesh, blood and all. For the font of truth and intelligibility cannot be a separate Form on the Platonic model, since a thoroughgoing Platonism ultimately puts impersonal intelligibility before intelligence or intellect itself and what is known before the knower.[40] The divine Word cannot simply

---

[38] "Sed theologus considerat quasi bonum ultimum id quod est naturae facultatem excediens, scilicet vitam aeternam, ut praedictum est. Unde bonum in actibus humanis non considerat absolute, quia ibi non ponit finem, sed in ordine ad id bonum quod ponit finem: asserens illum actum tantummodo esse bonum complete qui de proximo ad bonum finale ordinatur, id est qui est meritorius vitae aeternae; et omnem talem actum dicit actum virtutis; et quicumque habitus elicit talem actum, ab ipso virtus appellatur."

[39] "Ultima autem perfectio ad quam homo ordinatur, consistit in perfecta Dei cognitione: ad quam quidem pervenire non potest nisi operatione et instructione Dei, qui est sui perfectus cognitor. Perfectae autem cognitionis statim homo in sui principio capax non est; unde oportet quod accipiat per viam credenda aliqua, per quae manuducatur ad pervenidendum in perfectam cognitionem."

[40] In arguing this, Thomas is responding to an objection citing St. John Damascene: "in Domino nostro Iesu Christo non est commune speciem accipere." Thomas answers: "Verbum Damasceni potest intelligi dupliciter. Uno modo, ut referatur ad humanam naturam. Quae quidem non habet rationem communis speciei secundum quod est in uno solo individuo; sed secundum quod est abstracta ab omni individuo, prout in nuda contemplatione consideratur; vel secundum quod est in omnibus individuis. Filius autem Dei non assumpsit humanam naturam prout est in sola consideratione intellectus; quia sic non assumpsit ipsam rem humanae naturae. Nisi forte diceretur quod humana natura esset quaedam idea separata; sicut Platonici posuerunt hominem sine materia. Sed tunc Filius Dei non assumpsisset carnem.... Similiter etiam non potest dici quod Filius Dei assumpsit humanam naturam prout est in omnibus individuis eiusdem speciei, quia sic omnes homines assumpsisset. Relinquitur ergo, ut Damascenus postea dicit... quod assumpserit naturam humanam *in atomo*, idest in individuo, *non quidem in alio individuo, quod sit suppositum vel hypostasis illius naturae, quam in persona Filii Deo*" (*S.Th.*, III, 2, 5, ad 2).

assume human nature insofar as it subsists in the human mind as an impersonal idea or intelligible species. As Thomas argues in Part III of the *Summa Theologiae*: "if [Christ] did not assume it [human nature] among really existent beings [*in rerum natura*], the intellect would be false. Nor would it be other than a certain figment of the incarnation, as the Damascene says" (*S.Th.*, III, 4, 4).[41] The mode of knowing by which we participate in God's existence and knowledge of Himself is, of course, faith, which, "In theology,… plays the role that the *habitus* of first principles plays in our natural knowledge" (Torrell 2003, 13). In this sense, then, Christ brings into focus the personal nature of the created world: material creatures are, indeed, as it were, a "screen" between the divine mind and the human intellect. But they are more than that: they prepare the human mind for God's manifestation in the flesh in the Person of Christ. So, in that sense, the very intelligibility and *materiality* of the world is a *praeparatio evangelii*. And through Christ, the human person, as the union of body and soul, can now be more clearly perceived, through its participation in the personhood of Christ, as the locus of truth and goodness in our world.

Hence, for Aquinas, God is known most fittingly in this life by faith (*S.Th.*, II-II, 1, 1).[42] A clear and inerrant knowledge of God in which our will plays no part is unavailable in this life because we cannot have in principle any standard independent of God to judge whether our knowledge of God, both of his existence and nature, is true or correct.[43] We can only know God with any certainty by participating in God's revelation of himself; and this happens primarily and concretely by God participating in our nature. For, Thomas repeats constantly, everything known must be known in the mode of the knower; hence, God makes himself known in the mode of human knowing not just in language but in the very mode of our existing.[44] We know God to the degree that we choose to participate in God's existence; but this is possible because God first participates in ours, presenting himself to us as an

---

[41] "Similiter etiam non potuit assumi natura humana a FIlio Dei secundum quod est in intellectu divino. Quia sic nihil aliud esset quam natura divina; et per hunc modum, ab aeterno esset in Filio Dei humana natura. Similiter non convenit dicere quod Filius Dei assumpserit humanam naturam prout est in intellectu humano. Quia hoc nihil aliud esset quam si intelligeretur assumere naturam humanam. Et sic, si non assumeret eam in rerum natura, esset intellectus falsus. Nec aliud esset quam *fictio quaedam incarnationis*, ut Damascenus dicit."

[42] "In fide, si consideremus formalem rationem obiecti, nihil est aliud quam veritas prima."

[43] As Rudi te Velde remarks, "One cannot step outside revelation in order to prove its truth from a logically independent standpoint" (Te Velde 2006, 3). Te Velde makes a similar point in this essay as well: Te Velde 2005, 112.

[44] Hence, in *S.Th.*, I, 1, 10, Aquinas argues that what is unique to Sacred Scripture is that it signifies divine reality not just with words (as written by the human authors of the various books of the Bible), but also with the *things* signified by the words.

embodied person.[45] This is why, as Gyula Klima argues in the articles referred to at the beginning of this essay, Aquinas defends so vociferously the essential unity of the intellect and body in the substantial form of men and women, for without that essential unity, the inherent goodness and intelligibility of matter and the created world would be denied and God would not be known personally, which is to say, not known at all.

Bibliography

Aertsen, Jan. 1988. Die Lehre der Transzendentalien und die Metaphysik: Der Kommentar von Thomas von Aquin zum IV Buch der Metaphysica. *Freiburger Zeitschrift für Philosophie und Theologie* 35: 293–316.

———. 1992. Truth as a transcendental in Thomas Aquinas. *Topoi* 11: 159–171.

———. 1996. *Medieval philosophy and the transcendentals: The case of Thomas Aquinas.* Leiden/New York: E.J. Brill.

Breton, Stanislas. 1963. L'idée de transcendental et la genèse des transcendentaux chez Saint Thomas d'Aquin. In *Saint Thomas d'Aquin aujourd'hui: Recherches de philosophie,* 45–74. Paris: Desclée de Brouwer.

Clarke, C. N., S. J. 2004. *Being and person: The Aquinas lecture, 1993.* Milwaukee: Marquette University Press.

Davies, Brian. 1992. *The thought of Thomas Aquinas.* Oxford: Oxford University Press.

Jordan, Mark. 1980. The grammar of *esse*: Re-reading Thomas on the transcendentals. *The Thomist* 44: 1–26.

Klima, Gyula. 2002. Man = body + soul: Aquinas's arithmetic of human nature. In *Thomas Aquinas: Philosophical perspectives,* ed. Brian Davies, 257–273. Oxford: Oxford University Press.

———. 2009. Aquinas on the materiality of the human soul and the immateriality of the human intellect. *Philosophical Investigations* 32: 163–182.

———. 2016. Mind vs. body and other false dilemmas of post-Cartesian philosophy of mind. In *Biology and subjectivity: Philosophical contributions to non-reductive neuroscience,* ed. Miguel Garcia-Valdecasas, Jose Ignacio Murillo, and Nathaniel F. Barrett, 25–39. Berlin: Springer.

———. 2018. Aquinas' balancing act: Balancing the soul between the realms of matter and pure spirit. *Bochumer Philosophisches Jahrbuch für Antike und Mittelalter* 21: 29–48.

Kohak, Erazim. 1984. *The embers and the stars: A philosophical inquiry into the moral sense of nature.* Chicago/London: University of Chicago Press.

---

[45] "Dicendum quod cognita sunt in cognoscente secundum modum congnoscentis.... Sic igitur obiectum fidei dupliciter considerari potest: Uno modo, ex parte ipsius rei creditae: et sic obiectum fidei est aliquid incomplexum, scilicet res ipsa qua fides habetur. Alio modo, ex parte credentis: et secundum hoc obiectum fidei est aliquid complexum per modum ennutiabiliis" (*S.Th.,* II-II, 1, 2). So, while the object of faith is simple and ineffable, it does not follow that this object cannot be expressed in propositions. Nevertheless, it has become fashionable in recent theology to assert that the essence of faith lies not in propositional truths but in an "experience" or "encounter" with Christ, risen or otherwise. But this is certainly not Aquinas's understanding of faith. To be sure, the object of faith is not propositional nor is the expression of faith exhausted by propositional state-ments. But faith certainly includes in a pre-eminent way intelligible content that can and, indeed, must be expressed in propositions. See Davies 1992, 276–277.

Kretzmann, Norman. 1989. Trinity and transcendentals. In *Trinity, incarnation, and atonement: Philosophical and theological essays*, ed. Ronald J. Feenstra and Cornelius Plantinga Jr., 79–109. Notre Dame: University of Notre Dame Press.

Marshal, Bruce D. 2005. *Quod scit una uetula*: Aquinas on the nature of theology. In *The theology of Thomas Aquinas*, ed. Rik Van Nieuwenhove and Joseph Wawrykow, 1–35. Notre Dame: University of Notre Dame Press.

Milbank, John, and Catherine Pickstock. 2001. *Truth in Aquinas*. London/New York: Routledge.

O'Rourke, Fran. 1992. *Pseudo-Dionysius and the metaphysics of Aquinas*. Notre Dame: University of Notre Dame Press.

Pieper, Josef. 1957. *The silence of saint Thomas*. Trans. S.J. John Murray, and D. O-Connor. South Bend: Saint Augustine Press.

———. 1989. *Living the truth: Reality and the good and the truth of all things*. Trans. L. Krauth. San Francisco: Ignatius Press.

Seidle, Horst. 1973. Die aristotelischen Quellen zur Transzendentalien-Aufstellung bei Thomas von Aquin. *Philosophisches Jahrbuch* 80: 166–171.

Te Velde, Rudi. 2002. Natural reason in the *summa contra gentiles*. In *Thomas Aquinas: Contemporary philosophical perspectives*, ed. B. Davies, 117–140. Oxford: Oxford University Press.

———. 2005. Schöpfung und Partizipation (S.th. I, qq. 44–47 und qq. 103–105). In *Thomas von Aquin: Die "Summa Theologiae," Werkinterpretationen*, 100–124. Berlin/New York: Walter de Gruyter.

———. 2006. *Aquinas on god: The "divine science" of the summa theologiae*. Farnham/Surrey/Burlington: Ashgate.

Torrell, Jean-Pierre O.P. 2003. *Saint Thomas Aquinas: Volume 2, spiritual master*. Trans. R. Royal. Washington, DC: Catholic University of America Press.

Van de Wiele, Jozef. 1954. Le problème de la vérité ontologique dans la philosophie de saint Thomas. *Revue Philosophique de Louvain* 52: 521–571.

Wippel, John F. 1989–1990. Truth in Aquinas, parts I & II. The Review of Metaphysics 43: 295–326.

Zimmerman, Albert. 2005. Glaube und Wissen (S.th. II-II, qq. 1–9). In *Thomas von Aquin: Die "Summa Theologiae," Werkinterpretationen*, 271–297. Berlin/New York: Walter de Gruyter.

Chapter 10
Transcendentals Explained Through Syncategoremata: Is Being as Truth a Transcendental According to Thomas Aquinas?

Giovanni Ventimiglia

Keywords Aquinas · Being as truth · Syncategoremata · Transcendentals · Affirmation and negation

Metaphysics "considers universal being in so far as it is being," while the other sciences have as their object "being in so far as it is a certain type of being."[1] Metaphysics also deals with the properties common to being as a being, the so-called *passiones entis* or transcendentals.[2] Thus a characteristic of the object of metaphysics, being, and of its properties, is their extension or universality. It is, in fact, the widest possible scope. Metaphysics is by its very nature the most all-inclusive science ever, because being is the predicate included in everything, or universally predicated of everything.

---

[1] "Nulla scientia particularis considerat ens universale inquantum huiusmodi, sed solum aliquam partem entis divisam ab aliis; circa quam speculatur per se accidens, sicut scientiae mathematicae aliquod ens speculantur, scilicet ens quantum. Scientia autem communis considerat universale ens secundum quod ens: ergo non est eadem alicui scientiarum particularium (Thomas de Aquino, *In IV Met.*, l. 1. Aquinas, *Commentary on the Metaphysics*, nr. 532).

[2] Et quod hoc pertineat ad philosophum et ad nullum alium, sic probat. Eius est considerare primas passiones entis, cuius est considerare ens secundum quod est ens. [...]. Similiter et ens inquantum ens, habet quaedam propria, quae sunt communia praedicta. Ergo consideratio eorum pertinet ad philosophum." (Thomas de Aquino, *In IV Met.*, l. 4. Aquinas, *Commentary on the Metaphysics*, n. 571.)

G. Ventimiglia (✉)
Faculty of Theology, University of Lucerne, Luzern, Switzerland
e-mail: giovanni.ventimiglia@unilu.ch

© The Author(s), under exclusive license to Springer Nature
Switzerland AG 2023
J. P. Hochschild et al. (eds.), *Metaphysics Through Semantics: The Philosophical Recovery of the Medieval Mind*, International Archives of the History of Ideas Archives internationales d'histoire des idées 242,
https://doi.org/10.1007/978-3-031-15026-5_10

However, being so considered is not a univocal predicate but, as Aristotle teaches, an analogous predicate. For being is said in many ways, but all in reference to substance. At this point Thomas, commenting almost literally on Aristotle, writes:

> And just as the above-mentioned terms have many senses, so also does the term being. Yet every being is called such in relation to one first thing, and this first thing is not an end or an efficient cause, as is the case in the foregoing examples, but a subject.
>
> For some things are called beings, or are said to be, because they have being of themselves, as substances, which are called beings in the primary and proper sense. Others are called beings because they are affections or properties of substances, as the proper accidents of any substance. Others are called beings because they are processes toward substance, as generation and motion. And others are called beings because they are corruptions of substances; for corruption is the process toward non-being just as generation is the process toward substance. And since corruption terminates in privation just as generation terminates in form, the very privations of substantial forms are fittingly called beings. Again, certain qualities or certain accidents are called beings because they are productive or generative principles of substances or of those things which are related to substance according to one of the foregoing relationships or any other relationship. *And similarly the negations of those things which are related to substances, or even substance itself, are also called beings. Hence we say that non-being is non-being (unde dicimus quod non ens est non ens). But this would not be possible unless a negation possessed being in some way.*[3]

The final three sentences of this text are not without difficulties. First of all, there seems to be an assertion of continuity between the being of substance and the being of negations: both types of being seem to belong to the same spectrum of being, albeit in a different scale of importance and degrees. From this point of view, negations would also seem to belong to the spectrum of metaphysics.

Nonetheless, there are statements to the contrary in both Aristotle and Thomas: negations and privations are beings of reason, and therefore would not fall within the realm of metaphysics, but in that of logic. This sounds strange, if it is true that metaphysics is the most all-inclusive science ever. Nevertheless, there are passages in which the investigation of negations and privations is declared to belong to the

---

[3] "Et sicut est de praedictis, ita etiam et ens multipliciter dicitur. Sed tamen omne ens dicitur per respectum ad unum primum. Sed hoc primum non est finis vel efficiens sicut in praemissis exemplis, sed subiectum. Alia enim dicuntur entia vel esse, quia per se habent esse sicut substantiae, quae principaliter et prius entia dicuntur. Alia vero quia sunt passiones sive proprietates substantiae, sicut per se accidentia uniuscuiusque substantiae. Quaedam autem dicuntur entia, quia sunt via ad substantiam, sicut generationes et motus. Alia autem entia dicuntur, quia sunt corruptiones substantiae. Corruptio enim est via ad non esse, sicut generatio via ad substantiam. Et quia corruptio terminatur ad privationem, sicut generatio ad formam, convenienter ipsae etiam privationes formarum substantialium esse dicuntur. Et iterum qualitates vel accidentia quaedam dicuntur entia, quia sunt activa vel generativa substantiae, vel eorum quae secundum aliquam habitudinem praedictarum ad substantiam dicuntur, vel secundum quamcumque aliam. Item negationes eorum quae ad substantiam habitudinem habent, vel etiam ipsius substantiae esse dicuntur. Unde dicimus quod non ens est non ens. Quod non diceretur nisi negationi aliquo modo esse competeret." (Thomas de Aquino, *In IV Met.*, l. 1. Aquinas, *Commentary on the Metaphysics*, n. 539. Italics mine.)

same science to which the investigation of the one and the many, namely metaphysics, belongs.[4] A text from *De ente et essentia* helps to take a step further:

> Notice therefore that, as the Philosopher says in Metaphysics 5, being as such is said in two ways: first as it is divided into the ten genera, and second as meaning the truth of propositions. These differ because anything can be called being in the second sense if an affirmative proposition can be formed of it, even if it posits nothing in reality: thus privations and negations are called beings, *as when we say that affirmation is opposed to negation,* and the blindness exists in the eye (*dicimus enim quod affirmatio est opposita negationi et quod caecitas est in oculo*). But in the first sense only that which posits something in reality can be called being; therefore, blindness and the like are not beings in this sense of the term.[5]

According to a tradition attributed to Aristotle, but which the medieval Latins actually read in Averroes, being has two senses: that of the act of being and that of being as truth (Menn 2012; Ventimiglia 2020). Negations and privations belong to being as truth.[6] The reason given is interesting: we say that affirmation is opposed to negation and that blindness exists in the eye (*dicimus enim quod affirmatio est opposita negationi et quod caecitas est in oculo*). This reason recalls the one already encountered above in the *Commentary on Metaphysics*: we say that non-being is non-being (*unde dicimus quod non ens est non ens*). What do all these examples given by Thomas have in common? The expression 'dicimus quod' ('we say that') followed by a true (whatever) proposition using the copula 'est,' concerning that which does not have an act of being, such as negations or privations. This points in a useful direction for further analysis.

Meanwhile, the question we asked earlier comes up again here in other terms: is being as truth a transcendental? It would seem not, since Aristotle, Thomas and other contemporary commentators on *Metaphysics* consider being as truth not only as existing in the soul as opposed to in the nature of things, but also as existing in an

---

[4] "Dicit ergo, quod, cum ad unam scientiam pertineat considerare opposita, sicut ad medicinam considerare sanum et aegrum, et ad grammaticam congruum et incongruum: uni autem opponitur multitudo: necesse est, quod illius scientiae sit speculari negationem et privationem, cuius est speculari unum et multitudinem. Propter quod utriusque est considerare unum; scilicet ex utroque dependet unius consideratio, de cuius ratione est negatio et privatio. Nam sicut dictum est, unum est ens non divisum: divisio autem ad multitudinem pertinet, quae uni opponitur. Unde cuius est considerare unum, eius est considerare negationem vel privationem" (Thomas de Aquino, *In IV Met.*, l. 3). Aquinas, *Commentary on the Metaphysics*, n. 564).

[5] "Sciendum est igitur quod, sicut in V metaphysicae philosophus dicit, ens per se dicitur dupliciter, uno modo quod dividitur per decem genera, alio modo quod significat propositionum veritatem. Horum autem differentia est quia secundo modo potest dici ens omne illud, de quo affirmativa propositio formari potest, etiam si illud in re nihil ponat. Per quem modum privationes et negationes entia dicuntur; dicimus enim quod affirmatio est opposita negationi et quod caecitas est in oculo. Sed primo modo non potest dici ens nisi quod aliquid in re ponit. Unde primo modo caecitas et huiusmodi non sunt entia." (Thomas de Aquino, *De ente*, cap. I. Aquinas, "On Being and Essence," 31. Italics mine.)

[6] Siger of Brabant's commentary on the passage in Metaphysics IV quoted above is also clear on this point: negations and privations refer to being as truth (Sigerus de Brabantia 1981: 301.)

accidental way.[7] Hence, it seems impossible for any accident to be a property that always follows being as being. Things are, however, richer and more complex than they seem at first sight.

At this point it is helpful to consider two decisive texts for understanding being as truth. The first is the following:

> Then he gives another sense in which the term being is used, inasmuch as the terms *being* and *is* signify the composition of a proposition, which the intellect makes when it combines and separates. He says that *being* signifies the truth of a thing, or *as another translation better expresses it, being* signifies that some statement is true (*Unde dicit, quod esse significat veritatem rei. Vel sicut alia translatio melius habet quod esse significat quia aliquod dictum est verum*). Thus, the truth of a thing can be said to determine the truth of a proposition after the manner of a cause; for by reason of the fact that a thing *is* or *is not*, a discourse *is true* or *false*. For when we say that something *is*, we signify that a proposition *is true*; and when we say that something is not, we signify that it is not true (*Cum enim dicimus aliquid esse, significamus propositionem esse veram. Et cum dicimus non esse, significamus non esse veram*). And this applies both to affirmation and to negation. It applies to affirmation, as when we say *that Socrates is white because this is true*; and to negation, as when we say that Socrates is not white, because *this is true, namely, that he is not white*. And in a similar way we say that the diagonal of a square *is not* incommensurable [read: commensurable]

---

[7] "Deinde cum dicit quoniam autem excludit ens verum et ens per accidens a principali consideratione huius doctrinae; dicens, quod compositio et divisio, in quibus est verum et falsum, est in mente, et non in rebus. Invenitur siquidem et in rebus aliqua compositio; sed talis compositio efficit unam rem, quam intellectus recipit ut unum simplici conceptione. Sed illa compositio vel divisio, qua intellectus coniungit vel dividit sua concepta, est tantum in intellectu, non in rebus. Consistit enim in quadam duorum comparatione conceptorum; sive illa duo sint idem secundum rem, sive diversa. Utitur enim intellectus quandoque uno ut duobus compositionem formans; sicut dicitur, homo est homo: ex quo patet quod talis compositio est solum in intellectu, non in rebus. Et ideo illud, quod est ita ens sicut verum in tali compositione consistens, est alterum ab his quae proprie sunt entia, quae sunt res extra animam, quarum unaquaeque est *aut quod quid est*, idest substantia, aut quale, aut quantum, aut aliquod incomplexum, quod mens copulat vel dividit. Et ideo utrumque est praetermittendum; scilicet et ens per accidens, et ens quod significat verum; quia huius, scilicet entis per accidens, causa est indeterminata, et ideo non cadit sub arte, ut ostensum est. Illius vero, scilicet entis veri, causa est *aliqua passio mentis*, idest operatio intellectus componentis et dividentis. Et ideo pertinet ad scientiam de intellectu. Et alia ratio est, quia *utrumque*, scilicet ens verum et ens per accidens, sunt circa aliquod genus entis, non circa ens simpliciter per se quod est in rebus; et non ostendunt aliquam aliam naturam entis existentem extra per se entia. Patet enim quod ens per accidens est ex concursu accidentaliter entium extra animam, quorum unumquodque est per se. Sicut grammaticum musicum licet sit per accidens, tamen et grammaticum et musicum est per se ens, quia utrumque per se acceptum, habet causam determinatam. Et similiter intellectus compositionem et divisionem facit circa res, quae sub praedicamentis continentur. Unde si determinetur sufficienter illud genus entis quod continetur sub praedicamento, manifestum erit et de ente per accidens, et de ente vero. Et propter hoc huiusmodi entia praetermittuntur. Sed perscrutandae sunt causae et principia ipsius entis per se dicti, inquantum est ens. De quo palam est ex his quae determinavimus in quinto libro; ubi dictum est, quoties unumquodque talium nominum dicitur, quod ens dicitur multipliciter, sicut infra in principio septimi sequetur" (Thomas de Aquino, *In VI Met.*, l. 4).

with a side, because this is false, i.e., its *not being* [non] incommensurable [read: commensurable].[8]

Being as truth does not mean the truth of things but means ("as another translation better expresses it" as we have just read) the truth of a *dictum*, of a statement. It is expressed with the formula: *it is true that p*. Thomas, following Aristotle, then juxtaposes the expression "it is true that" with the verb to be (*esse, est*): "when we say that something is, we signify that a proposition is true"; "we say that Socrates is white because this is true." The point is explained further on a page of the same commentary by Thomas:

> He says, then, that "in one sense being means what is true," (*Dicit ergo quod ens quoddam dicitur quasi verum*) i.e., it signifies nothing else than truth; *for when we ask if man is an animal, the answer is that it is [the case],* by which it is meant that this proposition *is true* (*Cum enim interrogamus si homo est animal, respondetur quod est; per quod significatur, propositionem praemissam esse veram*). And in the same way non-being signifies in a sense what is false; for when one answers that it is not *[the case]*, it is meant that the statement made is false. Now this being which means what is true, and non-being which means what is false, depend on combination and separation; for simple terms signify neither truth nor falsity, whereas complex terms have truth and falsity through affirmation or negation (*Voces enim incomplexae neque verum neque falsum significant; sed voces complexae, per affirmationem aut negationem veritatem aut falsitatem habent*). And here affirmation is called combination because it signifies that a predicate belongs to a subject, whereas negation is called separation because it signifies that a predicate does not belong to a subject.[9]

---

[8] "Deinde cum dicit amplius autem ponit alium modum entis, secundum quod esse et est, significant compositionem propositionis, quam facit intellectus componens et dividens. Unde dicit, quod esse significat veritatem rei. Vel sicut alia translatio melius habet *quod esse significat* quia aliquod dictum est verum. Unde veritas propositionis potest dici veritas rei per causam. Nam ex eo quod res est vel non est, oratio vera vel falsa est. Cum enim dicimus aliquid esse, significamus propositionem esse veram. Et cum dicimus non esse, significamus non esse veram; et hoc sive in affirmando, sive in negando. In affirmando quidem, sicut dicimus quod Socrates est albus, quia hoc verum est. In negando vero, ut Socrates non est albus, quia hoc est verum, scilicet ipsum esse non album. Et similiter dicimus, quod non est diameter incommensurabilis lateri quadrati, quia hoc est falsum, scilicet non esse ipsum non commensurabilem" (Thomas de Aquino, *In V Met.*, l. 9. Aquinas, *Commentary on the Metaphysics*, n. 895. Italics mine). It is evident that the term "incommensurable" does not make sense here, although it is reported in the Latin translations of Aristotle's text and even in the same text by Aristotle. The first to notice the incongruity was Alexander of Aphrodisias.

[9] "Dicit ergo *quod ens quoddam dicitur quasi verum*, idest quod nihil aliud significat nisi veritatem. Cum enim interrogamus si homo est animal, respondetur quod est; per quod significatur, propositionem praemissam esse veram. Et eodem modo non ens significat quasi falsum. Cum enim respondetur, non est, significatur quod proposita oratio sit falsa. Hoc autem ens, quod dicitur quasi verum, et non ens, quod dicitur quasi falsum, consistit circa compositionem et divisionem. Voces enim incomplexae neque verum neque falsum significant; sed voces complexae, per affirmationem aut negationem veritatem aut falsitatem habent. Dicitur autem hic affirmatio compositio, quia significat praedicatum inesse subiecto. Negatio vero dicitur hic divisio, quia significat praedicatum a subiecto removeri" (Thomas de Aquino, *In VI Met.*, l. 4. Aquinas, *Commentary on the Metaphysics*, nr 1223. Italics mine). I slightly modified the English translation in order to better expresses the propositional meaning of the phrase "respondetur quod est", which clearly refers to the whole proposition.

When we answer a question in the affirmative using the verb to be (as in the case of: "Yes, it is the case," answering "Is man an animal?"), that being (in Latin "est"), Thomas tells us, refers in fact to the whole proposition ("man is an animal") and not just to "man."

The same meaning is clear for example in German, that in such cases uses the neutral "das": *Ist der Mensch ein Tier? Ja, das ist so*; here "das" clearly does not refers only to the subject but to the whole state of affairs signified by the whole propositions.

As Charles Kahn has shown, in ancient Greek a simple "esti" (*is*) sometimes precedes a proposition, for example: "esti Sokrates mousikos." That means something along the lines of "It *is* that Socrates is musical" (Kahn 2003: 331–370). The same idea, expressed in Latin, comes out as "est" referred to a whole proposition in affirmative answers: "cum enim interrogamus si homo est animal, respondetur quod *est*, per quod significatur propositionem praemissam esse veram." Such an "est" corresponds to the modern expression "it *is* [the case] that" and to the answer to a sentence-question in terms of "Yes, it *is* the case," where to the "is" is given an emphatic position, as suggested by Sauer (2013; Antonelli and Sauer 2014; Ventimiglia 2020: 107, 118).[10]

In other words, the *est* at stake here is not the *est* of "Socrates est," nor is it the *est* of "Socrates est homo" or "Socrates est albus." Now, Klima has shown decisively that not only in the case of "Socrates is/exists" (*Socrates est*) but also in the case of the copula "Socrates is a man" or "Socrates is wise," the existential sense is not lost at all. In fact, for medieval authors at least, the sense was as follows: "Socrates exists humanly" and "Socrates exists wisely" (Klima 1996, 2002; Ventimiglia 2020: 52–55). Could the same be said of the *est* of "it *is* [the case] that"? It seems so. This *est* means, in fact, the existence of the relation between the propositional content and reality. The synonymous expression, at least for medieval authors, namely "it is true that," indicates that the relation between that content and reality exists.

Thus, even though it is true that the "est" is not a *passio entis* but a *passio mentis*, indeed precisely a *passio enuntiationis*, as Roger Bacon has written (Rogerus Baconus 1930: 190–191), still this "passio" expresses the existence of a relation between the *dictum* of that enunciation and reality.

To better understand all this, it is useful to consult some texts of logic that medieval authors, including Thomas, had at their disposal. An interesting logic text for our purpose is the *Sophistaria* attributed to an anonymous author "tentatively called Matthew of Orléans," written between 1220 and 1230. In it, a distinction is made between a "non" that refers to a term or "negatio termini" (e.g. "non homo"), and a "non" that refers to the whole proposition or "negatio orationis" (e.g. "non Socrates est sapiens"). The opposite of the *negatio orationis*, which denies the inherence of a predicate to the subject (e.g. "Socrates is not wise"), is the affirmation (e.g. "Socrates

---

[10] Incidentally, this seems to correspond to Frege's assertion sign (Sauer 2013; Antonelli and Sauer 2014; Ventimiglia 2020).

is wise") (Mattheus Aurelianensis 2001).[11] Now, a *negatio orationis* can be rephrased in terms of "non est verum quod dicitur per hanc propositionem," i.e. "it is not true that p" (Mattheus Aurelianensis 2001).[12]

This is a doctrine that was quite common among medieval masters of logic who were contemporaries of Thomas, although it is expressed with different nuances and expressions in each case. Important for our purpose are the treatises on *Syncategoremata*.[13]

In Robert Bacon's *Syncategoremata*, dated between 1200 and 1220, the author distinguishes between the content or "substance of the composition" and, on the other hand, "the act of composition" which makes a proposition affirmative. The *divisio*, expressed by the syncategorem "non" (e.g. "Socrates non est albus") does not deny the *est* of the copula (for without this *est* there would not even be a composition or proposition), but it does deny the act of composition. The substance of the composition remains identical (i.e. "Socrates est albus"), whereas the negation (i.e. "Socrates non est albus") actually negates the statement underlying the composition, that is, it says something like "it is not true that Socrates is white." As a result, affirmation is not the mere substance of the composition, "Socrates is white," but it is something more, something like: "it *is* [the case] that (Socrates is white)" or "it is true that (Socrates is white)" (Robertus Baconus 1979).[14]

Similarly, in Johannes Pagus's *Syncategoremata* (around 1230) and Petrus Hispanus's *Syncategoremata* (around 1230–1245), we find a distinction between a

---

[11] "Item. Omnis negatio aut est negatio termini infiniti aut est negatio orationis. Tunc igitur queratur de illa negatione que est in illis predictis orationibus: aut est negatio termini, aut orationis, que facit facit propositionem negativam. Et manifestum est quod non est negation termini, quia sic faceret terminum infinitum. Quod non est verum. Ergo est negatio orationis. Sed talis negation habet esse circa compositionem verbi. Ergo illa negation semper fertur ad verbum et non ad participium [...]. 22 Ad aliud dicendum quod huiusmodi negatio est negatio orationis, et non est negatio termini. Sed negatio orationis est duplex, sicut affirmatio; nam si unum oppositorum est multiplex, et reliquum. Est enim negatio orationis aut quia negatur inherentia predicati ad subiectum; et hec est negatio a qua est oratio negativa, sicut ab illa affrmatione dicitur affrmativa. Est iterum negatio orationis quando negatur aliquid in subiecto; et ab hac non dicitur oratio negativa, prout ab affrmatione sibi opposita non dicitur affrmativa" (Mattheus Aurelianensis 2001: 85, 91).

[12] "Et secundum hoc distinguitur hec multiplex NULLUS HOMO LEGIT PARISIUS, NISI IPSE SIT ASINUS. Et hec similiter NULLUS HOMO EST, SI ALIQUIS HOMO EST. Et hec similiter NON ANIMAL EST, SI HOMO EST. Si cadat negatio supra totam consequentiam, tunc est sensus 'nullus homo etc.' idest: *non est verum quod dicitur per hanc propositionem 'aliquis homo legit Parisius nisi ipse sit asinus'*; et sic est vera. Si vero cadat negatio supra partem, tunc est sensus sequitur quod si homo non est asinus quod nullus homo legit Parisius; et sic est falsa. Et per hoc manifesti sunt sensus in aliis" (Mattheus Aurelianensis 2001: 93).

[13] Gyula Klima wrote an excellent introduction to the topic of Syncategoremata (Klima 2006).

[14] "Nam substantiam compositionis facit orationem propositionem esse, actus vero compositionis facit propositionem esse affirmativam. Nam substantia compositionis et divisio non sunt opposita, sicut substantia puncti et ratio dividendi non sunt opposita; sic enim dicimus quod eadem est compositio in affirmativa et negativa, sicut dicimus quod idem punctus secundum substantiam et est continuans et dividens lineam tamen ex diversis rationibus [...]. Sic idem punctus numero est continuatio et divisio linearum, sic eadem compositio secundum substantiam potest esse in ratione compositionis et facere actum compositionis et sic propositionem affirmativam, vel in ratione divisionis et sic propositionem negativam" (Robertus Baconus 1979: 142).

"compositio generalis" and a "compositio specialis." The "not" of the negation "is not" only negates the "compositio specialis," namely the very affirmation (Johannes Pagus 1979: 229; Petrus Hispanus 1992: 90–92). Also in William of Sherwood's *Syncategoremata* (1230–1245) the author identifies a *negatio*, or "non," understood in an "extinctive" way, which concerns the whole proposition and is opposed to the affirmatio but not to the simple *composition* (Guillelmus de Shyreswood 2012: 42).

In other words, and to sum up the insights from the logicians: "Socrates is white" is a *compositio*, endowed with a copula like all propositions. This is the content both of an *affirmatio* or *actus compositionis*, expressed by an "est," such as "it *is* [the case] that (Socrates is white)" or "it is true that (Socrates is white)," and of a *negatio orationis* or "extinctive" *negatio*, expressed by a "non (est)," such as "it is not [the case] that (Socrates is white)" or "it is not true that (Socrates is white)."

It is as if the "is" of "Socrates is white" actually contained two "is's": the copula that links the predicate to the subject, which always has an existential meaning, and, moreover, the "is" of "it *is* [the case] that Socrates is white" or "it is true that Socrates is white." The latter "is" is implicit in the proposition in the indicative but is not identical with the copula. It is kept hidden, so to speak, only for practical linguistic reasons, because it would be time-consuming and redundant to always premise every proposition in the indicative also the expression "it *is* [the case] that...." However, in the affirmative answers to questions this second "is" emerges more clearly. And this 'is' also has an existential meaning, because it expresses the existence of the relationship between the *dictum propositionis* and reality.

Now, there are a number of texts on the genesis of transcendentals in which reference is made both to a first transcendental, *ens*, linked to a first *affirmatio* and a first *est*, and also to a first *negatio* or *divisio*, expressed by *non*.[15] The following is one such example:

> But the unity which is interchangeable with being implies the privation of formal division, which comes about through opposites, and whose primary root is the opposition between affirmation and negation. For those things are divided from each other which are of such a kind that one is not the other. Therefore being itself is understood first, and then non-being, and then division, and then the kind of unity which is the privation of division, and then plurality, whose concept includes the notion of division just as the concept of unity includes the notion of undividedness.[16]

---

[15] It is interesting that in the "Parisian" treatises on the syncategoremata, such as those by Peter of Spain and Nicholas of Paris, two syncategoremata are considered at the origin of all the others: "*est*" and "*non*", that is "*affirmatio*" and "*negatio*", precisely like in the case of the origin of the transcendentals.

[16] "Sed unum quod cum ente convertitur importat privationem divisionis formalis quae fit per opposita, cuius prima radix est oppositio affirmationis et negationis. Nam illa dividuntur adinvicem, quae ita se habent, quod hoc non est illud. Primo igitur intelligitur ipsum ens, et ex consequenti non ens, et per consequens divisio, et per consequens unum quod divisionem privat, et per consequens multitudo, in cuius ratione cadit divisio, sicut in ratione unius indivisio; quamvis aliqua divisa modo praedicto rationem multitudinis habere non possint nisi prius cuilibet divisorum ratio unius attribuatur." (Thomas de Aquino, *In VI Met.*, l. 3. Aquinas, *Commentary on the Metaphysics*, n 566. Italics mine.)

These texts and this doctrine, later taken up in the treatise *De natura contrariorum* by Theodoric of Freiberg, would indeed seem to refer to the *est* and the *non*, in the sense of affirmation and negation in the terms just clarified (Theodoricus Friburgensis 1983: 93–97).

The first transcendental, *ens*, seems to correspond to the *est* of the affirmation, not to the *est* of "Socrates est." Proof of this is the fact that the opposite of this *ens* is *negation* and *divisio*, which are expressed in a "non" in propositions such as "one is not the other."

However, the propositional feature of affirmation and negation does not emerge explicitly in these texts, since negation is sometimes interpreted as if it were a *negatio termini*, namely as a simple "non ens." For this reason it cannot be deduced with certainty from these texts that the being at stake is being as truth. And so our initial question remains: can being as truth, which is expressed in the *est* of an affirmation, and which is certainly referred to a whole proposition, be considered a transcendental of being?

There is no doubt that the *est* corresponding to being as truth is more extensive and universal than the *est* that expresses the act of being. For it can concern propositions that include negations or privations, such as "it *is* [the case] that (non-being is non-being)" or "it *is* [the case] that (affirmation is opposed to negation)." Although all or some of the *elements* making up these propositions *do not exist*, the *relations* of those propositions to reality *do exist*, because the propositions are true. Of course, there remains the problem of identifying the truth-makers of these true propositions on the side of reality, the states of affairs to which these true propositions correspond. In any case, the existence of the truth relation cannot be denied.

So problems remain on the side of the speaking and thinking subject. Certainly, in fact, affirmation and act of composition presuppose a subject who expresses his assent with "it *is* [the case] that p." In the case of man, this affirmation ("it *is* [the case] that p") is accidental, just as any habit or act of his intellect is accidental and contingent.[17] The divine intellect, however, is not contingent. For Thomas, truth is not a property of things, as it was for Roger Bacon and Albert the Great, but a property of the proposition, and is therefore on the side of the intellect.[18] But it is not human intellect which accounts for the truth. The existence and transcendence of

---

[17] "Accidit autem unicuique rei quod aliquid de ipsa vere affirmetur intellectu vel voce. Nam res non refertur ad scientiam, sed e converso" (Thomas de Aquino, *In V Met.*, l. 9). "Veritas autem quae dicitur de rebus in comparatione ad intellectum humanum, est rebus quodammodo accidentalis, quia posito quod intellectus humanus non esset nec esse posset, adhuc res in sua essentia permaneret" (Thomas de Aquino, *De ver.*, q. 1, a. 4).

[18] "Et ideo, cum verum dicatur per prius et posterius de pluribus, oportet quod de illo per prius dicatur in quo primo invenitur completa ratio veritatis […]. Et quia bonum, sicut dictum est, dicit ordinem entis ad appetitum, verum autem dicit ordinem ad intellectum; inde est quod philosophus dicit in VI Metaphys., quod bonum et malum sunt in rebus, verum autem et falsum sunt in mente. Res autem non dicitur vera nisi secundum quod est intellectui adaequata; unde per posterius invenitur verum in rebus, per prius autem in intellectu" (Thomas de Aquino, *De ver.*, q. 1, a. 2).

truth is guaranteed by the fact that all things have a relation to the divine intellect.[19] It is as if God himself, in the act of creating and preserving things in being, constantly pronounces his "it *is* [the case] that p."

Finally, we must not forget that God is the creator of everything that exists, including propositions, and that he knows both things and propositions, or *enuntiabilia*, including negations, and their relations to things. Here is a very interesting text from Thomas in this regard:

> God not only knows the things themselves, but also the *enuntiabilia* and the complexes; yet he does so with a simple cognition in his own way. Which is demonstrated as follows: Since there are two aspects in the thing, namely, its quiddity and its being, there is a twofold operation of the intellect corresponding to them. One, which is called by the philosophers formation, which apprehends the quiddity of things, which is also called the intelligence of the indivisibles. The other knows the being of the thing, composing the affirmation [...] which consists in combining the accident with the subject. Similarly, in God himself we must consider his nature and his being; and as his nature is the cause and exemplar of all nature, so his being is the cause and exemplar of all being. Wherefore, as by knowing his essence, he knows all things, so by knowing his being, he knows the existence of all things; and so he knows all *enuntiabilia*, to which being is ascribed; yet not by any other operation or composition, but simply; for his being is not other than his essence, nor is it consequently composed; and as by the same operation he knows good and evil, so by the same operation he knows affirmations and negations.[20]

In conclusion, being as truth is the property of any proposition—even those whose components are non-beings in the strict sense—and signifies the existence of a relation of the dictum of that proposition to reality. Thus, being as truth is more extensive than being as an act of being and would seem an excellent candidate for the status of an authentic transcendental. To be sure, there is no shortage of problems and obstacles along the path for being as truth to achieve recognition as a genuine

---

[19] "Est ergo veritas in intellectu divino quidem primo et proprie; in intellectu vero humano proprie quidem sed secundario; in rebus autem improprie et secundario, quia non nisi per respectum ad alteram duarum veritatum [...]. Veritas autem quae dicitur de rebus in comparatione ad intellectum humanum, est rebus quodammodo accidentalis, quia posito quod intellectus humanus non esset nec esse posset, adhuc res in sua essentia permaneret [...]. Sic ergo res aliqua principalius dicitur vera in ordine ad veritatem intellectus divini quam in ordine ad veritatem intellectus humani" (Thomas de Aquino, *De ver.*, q. 1, a. 4).

[20] "Deus non solum cognoscit ipsas res, sed etiam enuntiabilia et complexa; tamen simplici cognitione per modum suum; quod sic patet. Cum in re duo sint, quidditas rei, et esse ejus, his duobus respondet duplex operatio intellectus. Una quae dicitur a philosophis formatio, qua apprehendit quidditates rerum, quae etiam dicitur indivisibilium intelligentia. Alia autem comprehendit esse rei, componendo affirmationem, quia etiam esse rei ex materia et forma compositae, a qua cognitionem accipit, consistit in quadam compositione formae ad materiam, vel accidentis ad subjectum. Similiter etiam in ipso Deo est considerare naturam ipsius, et esse ejus; et sicut natura sua est causa et exemplar omnis naturae, ita etiam esse suum est causa et exemplar omnis esse. Unde sicut cognoscendo essentiam suam, cognoscit omnem rem; ita cognoscendo esse suum, cognoscit esse cujuslibet rei; et sic cognoscit omnia enuntiabilia, quibus esse significatur; non tamen diversa operatione nec compositione, sed simpliciter; quia esse suum non est aliud ab essentia, nec est compositum consequens; et sicut per idem cognoscit bonum et malum, ita per idem cognoscit affirmationes et negationes" (Thomas de Aquino, *In I Sent.*, d. 38, q. 1, a. 3).

transcendental. Yet its candidacy is strong, and in the centuries following the 13th, especially with modern attention to subjectivity, arguments will favor this path.

Bibliography

Primary Sources

Mattheus Aurelianensis (Matthew of Orléans). 2001. *Sophistaria sive Summa communis distinctionum circa sophismata accidentium*, edited with an Introduction, notes and indices by Joke Spruyt. Leiden/Boston/Köln: Brill.

Rogerus Baconus. 1930. *Quaestiones supra libros Primae Philosophiae Aristotelis* (Metaphysica, I–II, V–X), edited by Robert Steele, and Ferdinand M. Delorme (Opera hactenus inedita Rogeri Baconi X). Oxford: Clarendon Press.

Baconus, Robertus. 1979. Syncategoremata. In *In De 13de eeuwse tractaten over syncategorematische termen I: Inleidende Studie*, ed. Henricus Antonius Giovanni Braakhuis, 106–167. Leiden: Meppel, II.

Thomas de Aquino. 1882. *Opera omnia*, iussu impensaque Leonis XIII P.M. edita, Romae. *Quaestiones disputatae de veritate*, t. XXII, voll. I–III, 1972–1976. Translation: "De veritate," "Disputed Question on Truth." Translated by Ralph McInerny. In Thomas Aquinas: *Selected Writings*, edited by Ralph Mcinerny. London: Penguin, 1998c, 163–170. [De ver.]

———. 1929–1947. *Scriptum super Sententiis*, edited by R.P. Mandonnet, and M.F. Moos, 4 voll. Paris: Lethielleux. [In Sent.]

———. 1948. *Opera omnia*. Taurini/Romae: Marietti. *In XII libros Metaphysicorum Aristotelis expositio*, edited by M.R. Cathala, and R. Spiazzi, 1964. Translation: *Commentary on the Metaphysics of Aristotle*. Translated by Joseph P. Rowan. Chicago: Henry Regnery Co, 1961. [In Met.]

Sigerus de Brabantia. 1981. *Quaestiones in Metaphysicam*, éd. revue de la reportation de Munich, texte inédit de la reportation de Vienne, edited by William Dunphy. Louvain-La-Neuve: Éditions de l'Institut Supérieur de Philosophie.

De ente et essentia, t. XLIII (Opuscola IV). 1976. Translation: "On Being and Essence." Translated by Ralph McInerny. In Thomas Aquinas: *Selected Writings*, edited by Ralph McInerny. London: Penguin, 1998, 30–49. [De ente].

Theodoricus Friburgensis. 1983. *Tractatus de natura contrariorum*, edited by Ruedi Imbach. In Dietrich von Freiberg, *Opera omnia*, Tom II: *Schriften zur Metaphysik und Theologie*, mit einer Einl. Von K. Flash, edited by Ruedi Imbach, Maria Rita Pagnoni-Sturlese, Hartmutt Steffan und Loris Sturlese (Corpus Philosophorum Teutonicorum Mediii Aevi, II, 3). Hamburg: Felix Meiner Verlag.

Guillelmus de Shyreswood. 2012. *Syncategoremata*, edited by Cristoph Kann, and Raina Kirchhoff. Hamburg: Felix Meiner Verlag.

Pagus, Johannes. 1979. Syncategoremata. In *In De 13de eeuwse tractaten over syncategorematische termen I: Inleidende Studie*, ed. Henricus Antonius Giovanni Braakhuis, 168–246. Leiden: Meppel, II.

Petrus Hispanus Portugalensis. 1992. *Syncategoreumata*, edited by Lambertus Marie de Rijk. Leiden/New York/Köln: Brill.

Secondary Sources

Antonelli, Mauro, Werner Sauer. 2014. Einleitung. In *Von der mannigfachen Bedeutung des Seienden nach Aristoteles* (Franz Brentano-Sämtliche Veröffentlichte Schriften, Bd. IV), edited by Mauro Antonelli, and Werner Sauer, XI–XCI. Berlin: De Gruyter.

Kahn, Charles H. 2003. *The verb 'be' in ancient Greek.* Indianapolis: Hackett Publishing Company.

Klima, Gyula. 1996. The semantic principles underlying St. Thomas Aquinas's metaphysics of being. *Medieval Philosophy and Theology* 5 (1): 87–144.

———. 2002. Aquinas's theory of the copula and the analogy of being. In *Philosophiegeschichte und logische Analyse. Schwerpunkt: Philosophie des Mittelalters – Logical Analysis and History of Philosophy*. Focus: Medieval philosophy, edited by Uwe Meixner, and Albert Newen, 159–176. Paderbon: Mentis.

———. 2006. Syncategoremata. In *Elsevier's encyclopedia of language and linguistics*, 2nd ed., ed. Keith Brown, Vol. 12, 353–356. Oxford: Elsevier.

Menn, Stephen. 2008. Al-Fārābī's Kitāb al-Ḥurūf and his analysis of the senses of being. *Arabic Sciences and Philosophy* 18 (1): 59–97.

———. 2012. Fārābī in the reception of Avicenna's Metaphysics: Averroes against Avicenna on being and unity. In *The Arabic, Hebrew and Latin reception of Avicenna's Metaphysics*, ed. Dag Nikolaus Hasse, Amos Bertolacci, 51–96. Berlin/Boston: De Gruyter.

Sauer, Werner. 2013. Being as the true: From Aristotle to Brentano. In *Themes from Brentano*, ed. Denis Fisette, Guillaume Fréchette, 193–225. Amsterdam/New York: Rodopi.

Ventimiglia, Giovanni. 2020. *Aquinas after Frege.* London/New York: Palgrave Macmillan.

Chapter 11
Truth as a Transcendental

Edward Feser

Keywords Anti-realism · Conceptual relativism · Principle of sufficient reason · Realism · Transcendentals · Truth

I am not given to quoting Francis Bacon approvingly, but I must admit that one cannot improve upon the opening line of his own famous essay on our subject: "'What is Truth?' said jesting Pilate; and would not stay for an answer" (2002, 341). This is usually taken to reflect Pilate's cynicism. No doubt he also lacked a taste for metaphysics. Only slightly less cynical, but similarly devoid of an interest in metaphysics – remarkably, given some of his adventures – was that renowned archeologist Indiana Jones, who once assured his class that, as a science, his discipline was concerned with "the search for *fact*. Not *truth*. If it's truth you're interested in, Dr. Tyree's philosophy class is right down the hall."[1]

Yet most modern philosophy professors are in fact only somewhat more open-minded on the subject. To be sure, contemporary analytic philosophers are considerably more tolerant of metaphysics than were their logical positivist, pragmatist, and ordinary language philosophy forebears. But where the metaphysics of truth is concerned, that tolerance quickly reaches its limits. Their answer to Pilate would be that truth is a pretty mundane property. To be sure, they disagree about exactly what are the "truth-bearers" to which this property should be attributed. The candidates include: (a) *utterances*, understood as noises or marks generated at a particular time and place (as when you speak or write "Snow is white" at noon next Friday); (b) *sentences*, in the sense of the *type* of which particular utterances are *tokens* (for example, my utterance now of "Snow is white" and your utterance next Friday of

---

[1] In the movie *Indiana Jones and the Last Crusade* (1989).

E. Feser (✉)
Pasadena City College, Pasadena, CA, USA
e-mail: ecfeser@pasadena.edu

© The Author(s), under exclusive license to Springer Nature Switzerland AG 2023
J. P. Hochschild et al. (eds.), *Metaphysics Through Semantics: The Philosophical Recovery of the Medieval Mind*, International Archives of the History of Ideas Archives internationales d'histoire des idées 242, https://doi.org/10.1007/978-3-031-15026-5_11

"Snow is white" are tokens of the same sentence type); (c) *beliefs*, in the sense of the mental states of which sentences and utterances are expressions; and (d) the *propositions* that serve as the contents of beliefs and are conveyed through a sentence or utterance (as when you and a German speaker believe or convey the same proposition when you think or utter "Snow is white" and he thinks or utters "Schnee ist Weiss").[2]

Contemporary philosophers also disagree about the nature of the property they attribute to whichever of these candidate truth-bearers they favor. Some say that truth is the *correspondence* of the truth-bearer with reality; some say that it is *coherence* with other truth-bearers; others say that it has to do with the truth-bearer's having *pragmatic value*; yet others take the *deflationist* view that to say that "Snow is white" is true is really nothing more than simply to assert that snow is white, rather than to attribute some property whose nature needs to be captured by a correspondence, coherence, or pragmatist theory.[3]

But what these views have in common is a tendency to limit the application of the notion of truth to phenomena of a linguistic, psychological, or logical sort rather than anything having grand metaphysical significance. As William Alston notes, in recent philosophy the most popular of the candidate truth-bearers has been *sentences* – rather than the far more plausible candidate *propositions* – because the latter would seem to entail a commitment to the reality of "abstract entities" that is, for the tastes of most contemporary academic philosophers, too metaphysically extravagant (1996, 9).

Now, notwithstanding the generally greater anti-metaphysical animus of earlier generations of analytic philosophers, one will actually find somewhat more metaphysically adventurous attitudes at least on the question of truth if one looks at some earlier works in that tradition. For example, Alan White's 1970 book *Truth* allows that there are *two* sorts of things that can be said to be true (1970, 3–6). First, there is "what is said," which more or less corresponds to propositions.[4] But second, there are "things other than what is said," examples of which would be what we have in mind when we describe something as true courage or true mahogany, or characterize a person as a true patriot or a true Yorkshireman. However, White nevertheless takes the use of "true" to describe "what is said" to be the *primary* use.

Then there is Gottlob Frege's classic 1918 essay "Thoughts," the broadly Platonic tenor of which is certainly the opposite of anti-metaphysical (Frege 1988). By a "thought" Frege has in mind what he calls "the sense" of a sentence and what contemporary philosophers call a proposition, and he insists that it cannot be identified with anything linguistic or psychological. Our knowledge of propositions is in Frege's view knowledge of a "third realm" distinct from both the material world and the human mind (1988, 36 and 45). However, like White, he has little interest in how

---

[2] Cf. Horwich 1990, 17–18. For discussion of yet other possibilities, and of different senses in which philosophers have used the terms for the four just considered, see Kirkham 1992, 54–58.

[3] For a basic overview of the main theories, see Part I of Blackburn 2018.

[4] Though only more or less. White makes it clear at pages 13–15 that he objects to some of the ways philosophers have used the term "proposition."

"true" might be applied to things other than propositions, as when we use the term "in the sense of 'genuine,'" or when it "is prefixed to another word in order to show that the word is to be understood in its proper, unadulterated sense" (34). On the contrary, Frege claims that propositions are "the only thing that raises the question of truth at all" (36). Hence, he judges, truth is the subject matter of *logic*, just as beauty is the subject matter of aesthetics, goodness the subject matter of ethics, and weight and heat subject matters for physics (33).

It is likely that Frege is the immediate source of the modern analytic philosopher's reflexive tendency to suppose that linguistic, psychological, and logical phenomena exhaust the range of possible things to which truth might arguably be attributable. Certainly they rarely consider the views of earlier thinkers. For instance, in Michael Lynch's anthology *The Nature of Truth: Classic and Contemporary Perspectives* (2001), the "classic" readings go all the way back to… an 1878 essay by C. S. Peirce. The unwary reader might conclude that no philosopher had much to say about the topic prior to then – that Augustine was not in fact what one writer calls the "doctor par excellence of the philosophy of truth" (Gardeil 1967, 134), and that Aquinas had never written *De Veritate*.

And yet, occasionally a contemporary philosopher will evince a sense that there might be more to the story – indeed that, as even a philosopher as little given to piety as Simon Blackburn allows, "there is an air of divinity that hangs over the concept of truth" (2018, 13). In what follows, I will set out what the medievals, building on hints provided by the ancients, took to be the rest of the story about truth, and indeed the most important part of the story. As we will see, the Scholastics distinguish between *logical* truth and *ontological* truth. Modern analytic philosophers focus more or less exclusively on the former, but for Augustine, Aquinas, and other medieval philosophers, it is ontological truth that is more fundamental, and the proper understanding of it has dramatic metaphysical implications. Truth is one of the transcendental properties of all being, and in the final analysis is indeed literally divine.

Most contemporary analytic philosophers will no doubt find such claims mystifying, but that is precisely because they are fixated on truth in the logical sense. To see how there could be truth in some other philosophically interesting sense requires some stage-setting. I will begin, in the next section, with an exposition of the doctrine of the transcendentals in general. This will prepare the way for the subsequent section's explanation of what it means to say that truth is a transcendental property of being, which is central to the notion of ontological truth. In the final section, I will consider some of the philosophical and theological implications of the notion of ontological truth.

Of course, the contemporary philosopher will want to know, not only what the notion of truth as a transcendental amounts to and what its implications are, but also why we should believe there is such a thing in the first place. The short answer is that, as we shall see, the notion is a natural outgrowth of more fundamental metaphysical ideas which, as a result of the neo-Aristotelian revival currently underway, many contemporary philosophers are already willing to reconsider. I would submit that, if they are willing to push the envelope as far as reevaluating neo-Aristotelian essentialism and teleology, just a little further pushing is needed in order to regard the doctrine of the transcendentals too as a live option.

11.1   The Transcendentals in General

The concept of *being*, the Thomist holds, is the most fundamental and familiar of all concepts. "The first thing conceived by the intellect," says Aquinas, "is being" (*Summa Theologiae* I.5.2).[5] Precisely for that reason it is difficult to get one's mind around. Properly to grasp it, as Orwell said of what is in front of one's nose, needs a constant struggle. We might start by proposing "reality" as a synonym for "being." What has being is what is in some way real. But obviously, that only takes us so far.

Can we say more? Yes, much more, which is where the doctrine of the transcendentals comes in. But before turning to that, it is worthwhile considering further why the concept is so difficult to elucidate. For, ironically, this itself helps us begin to clarify its nature.[6] For one thing, the concept of being is *simple* or *primitive* in the sense that we cannot analyze it without remainder into more elementary notions. For any concepts we might appeal to in order to analyze the concept of being will themselves represent either a kind of being or the absence of being, and thus presuppose the concept of being. The concept of being is also the *first* of our concepts both logically and chronologically insofar as for us initially to grasp anything at all is to grasp it *as* a kind of being or reality, or at least a possible being or reality. Even when we judge a thing to be unreal, we do so precisely by contrast with what has being or is real. The concept of being is maximally *indeterminate* and *abstract* insofar as it covers all possible kinds of reality – actuality and potentiality, essence and existence, substances and attributes, form and matter, the corporeal and the incorporeal, and so on – but, without further specification, it refers to none of these in particular. Being cannot strictly be *defined*, as Thomists understand definition, because there is no genus that being falls under, let alone a specific difference to distinguish it from other species in a genus. For any species, genus, and specific difference are themselves kinds of being. At the same time, neither, for the Thomist, is being itself any kind of genus, not even the widest genus. For a genus is always divisible into species by way of specific differences that are outside the concept of the genus. For example, the specific difference *rationality* is outside the concept of the genus *animal*, which is why we can distinguish that genus into the species *rational animal* and the various kinds of non-rational animal. But since every specific difference has being, there is none that lies outside the concept of being, by which we might divide being into species.

---

[5] All quotations from the *Summa* are taken from the translation in Thomas Aquinas 1948.
[6] The points summarized in this paragraph are often made in manuals of Thomistic metaphysics. Particularly useful is the discussion in Coffey 1970, 32–36.

For this reason, being is a *transcendental* notion. That is to say, it transcends all genera, let alone all species, of thing, and applies to all of them. Now, the first thing the doctrine of the transcendentals says is that there are *several* concepts which in this way apply to all reality. There are six others in addition to being: *thing, one, other, true, good*, and (with qualifications to be noted presently) *beautiful*. The second thing the doctrine of the transcendentals says is that these are all *convertible* with being. That is to say, what all of them represent is really just being, considered from different points of view. To be sure, terms like "one," "true," and "good" are not *synonymous* with the word "being." But, to apply Frege's famous distinction, though they differ in *sense*, they are identical in *reference*. This is how they deepen our knowledge of the nature of being. They add to our understanding of being *itself* conceptual content that is not present in our *notion* of being.

To be more precise, proponents of the doctrine are in agreement that at least three of the transcendentals add conceptual content that is not contained in the concept of being, but that names features that follow immediately from a thing's having being: namely, *one, true*, and *good*. (The status of the other transcendentals is more controversial.) These three are, accordingly, often referred to as the *transcendental properties of being*. They are not properties in the strictest sense, since, again, they are not really distinct from being in the way that a substance and its proper accidents are really distinct. But they can in a loose sense be characterized as properties insofar as, again, the concept of being *one*, the concept of being *true*, and the concept of being *good* add content to our grasp of being that is clearly not contained in the concept of being itself. Moreover, they refer to features that follow immediately from a thing's having being in a way comparable to a property's following immediately from a substance's essence.

For being to be *one* is for it to be undivided. Aquinas argues that all being is one as follows (*Summa Theologiae* I.11.1). Any being is either simple or composite. If it is simple or non-composite, then it is undivided. If it is composite, then it has being only insofar as its parts are actually combined, in which case it is undivided. So, either way, any being is undivided.

For being to be *true* is for it to conform to the concept an intellect has of it, and thereby to be intelligible. For example, a dog has being qua dog insofar as it conforms to the concept of dog, which represents the essence of dogginess. In so conforming, it counts as a *true dog*. If it failed to conform to this concept, it would fail to have *being* qua dog, since it would lack the essence of a dog. Of course, it would in that case really be some other thing, such as a piece of wood that merely looked like a dog. But in that case it would have being *qua wood*, and thus conform to the concept of wood, and thus have the essence of wood. It would be *true wood*. In this way, any being is true, insofar as it is a *true something or other* and will fall under *some* concept or other. Now, this is the transcendental that we are primarily concerned with here, so I will have much more to say about it presently. But first let's round out our look at the other transcendentals.

For being to be *good* is for it to realize the ends toward which its nature directs it. For example, a dog has being qua dog insofar as it has actually developed the physiological and behavioral traits characteristic of dogs. To the extent it has done so, it is a *good dog* in the sense of a good specimen of its kind. To the extent it fails to do so, it would be an imperfect dog, and thus less good as a specimen. This might be because it is not yet fully mature, or because it has been damaged in some way. Either way, the absence of the traits in question, and thus the absence of what makes for a good specimen, will amount to a failure to realize some end toward which its nature directs it. Such failure entails less of the kinds of being that a dog qua dog is supposed to have. This yields an account of *badness* as a privation of being, the absence of some reality that a perfectly good specimen of a kind would exhibit.

Again, to say that something is *one*, *true*, or *good* clearly adds conceptual content that is not contained in the statement that something has *being*. This is why these can in a loose sense be characterized as transcendental *properties* of being. More controversial among proponents of the doctrine of the transcendentals is whether additional conceptual content is added by any of the other transcendentals. Hence, any *being* is also a *thing* of some sort. But the concept of *thing* arguably adds nothing that is not already implicit in the concept of *being*. The most that can be said is that the accent in the case of the concept of *thing* is on *essence*, whereas the accent in the case of the concept of *being* is on *existence*, but where both essence and existence are nevertheless implicit in both concepts. Any being is also *other than* a distinct being, but this is a consequence, not of it having *being*, but rather of its being *one*.

Then there is the concept of the *beautiful*, which Aquinas says applies to things insofar as they are pleasing when apprehended (*Summa Theologiae* I.5.4 and I-II.27.1). The claim that all being is beautiful is, when properly understood, true enough for proponents of the doctrine of the transcendentals. However, on analysis a thing's beauty will be a consequence of its being *true* or *good*. In particular, it will please when apprehended either because it is seen to conform to the concept that an intellect forms of its essence, or because it is seen to conform to the end to which it is directed. Hence, like the concept of *other*, the concept of *beautiful* names a feature that does not follow *immediately* from a thing's having being in the way that the features named by the concepts *one*, *true*, and *good* do.

So, though in addition to the concept of *being*, there are six further transcendental *concepts* (*one*, *true*, *good*, *thing*, *other*, *beauty*) only three of them are taken by all proponents of the doctrine of the transcendentals to name transcendental *properties* (*one*, *true*, *good*). Now, the order in which I have listed these three properties of being is by no means arbitrary, but is taken by writers like Aquinas to correspond to an order in reality (*De Veritate* 21.3).[7] Being is *one* in an absolute way, but it is *true* or *good* relative to something else – to the concept an intellect has of it in the one case, and to the end toward which an inclination or appetite is directed in the other. Moreover, the intellect understands a thing only insofar as it takes it to be one, and a thing is directed toward an end only by virtue of the essence of which the intellect forms a concept. Hence, Aquinas writes: "The order of these transcendent names,

---

[7] All quotations from *De Veritate* are taken from the translation in Thomas Aquinas 1994. For the passage referred to in the text, see Volume III, pages 13–16.

accordingly, if they are considered in themselves, is as follows: after being comes the one; after the one comes the true; and then after the true comes good" (1994, 14).

We might represent the transcendentals and their relationships to one another by way of the following diagram (other diagrams are possible) [8]:

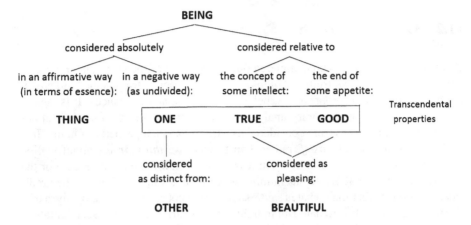

Now, much more could, of course, be said about the transcendentals in general. Not all proponents of the doctrine would spell it out exactly as I have and, needless to say, many philosophers would not accept it at all. My aim here has not been to provide a complete exposition and defense, but rather to provide context for the discussion of truth, specifically, as a transcendental property.

Suffice it for present purposes to say the following in defense of the general doctrine of the transcendentals. I would suggest that it is a natural view to adopt if one is already attracted to a broadly Aristotelian metaphysics, and that resistance to it tends to flow from metaphysical assumptions that no one attracted to Aristotelianism can sympathize with. In particular, I would submit that resistance to the idea that *good* is a transcendental property of being is a consequence of the reflexive tendency of modern philosophers to conceptualize nature in a broadly mechanistic or anti-teleological way. I would suggest that resistance to the idea that *truth* is a transcendental property of being is a byproduct of the sympathy many modern philosophers have for a broadly nominalist metaphysics on which the essences of things are created by the mind rather than discovered by it. I would suggest that resistance to the idea that *one* is a transcendental property of being is a result of the tendency to think of nature in reductionist terms. Even *being* might seem less than certainly objective to a philosopher influenced by idealism, relativism, or some form of anti-realism. The influence of such views has been so great in modern philosophy that even contemporary philosophers who do not accept them find it metaphysically adventurous to propose that concepts like *one*, *true*, and *good* represent features to be found in all of extra-mental reality. Hence if, with an increasing number of

---

[8] E.g. see the diagram proposed in Koren 1955, at page 52. My diagram was inspired by Koren's, but is significantly different.

contemporary philosophers, one is willing to question the assumptions of modern philosophy and to reconsider neo-Aristotelian ideas like essentialism and teleology, one ought also to be open to reconsidering the doctrine of the transcendentals.

11.2 Ontological Truth

The Scholastic thinkers who hammered out the doctrine of the transcendentals distinguish between *logical* truth and *ontological* truth. Logical truth is the kind which might be attributed to propositions, beliefs, sentences, and utterances. It is, again, the kind to which contemporary analytic philosophers tend to confine their attention. Ontological truth is truth considered as a transcendental property of being. It is truth attributed to reality *itself*, rather than to what we *think or say* about reality. Something is *true*, in this sense, when it is what we call the genuine article or the real McCoy. It is what White has in mind when he notes that truth might be predicated of "things other than what is said," such as true courage, true mahogany, a true patriot, or a true Yorkshireman. But in light of the doctrine of the transcendentals, it is a notion of greater metaphysical significance than White attributes to it.

Now, truth in either sense has to do with the relationship between being and intellect. But the direction of the relationship is different in each case. Logical truth has to do with the conformity of the intellect to being. Ontological truth has to do with the conformity of being to the intellect. To borrow some phrases from contemporary speech act theory, we might say that logical and ontological truth have different "directions of fit" (Searle 1983, 7 f.). Logical truth has a "mind-to-world" direction of fit, and ontological truth has a "world-to-mind" direction of fit.

It is clear enough what this means in the case of logical truth. To say that a belief, a proposition, a sentence, or an utterance is true when it corresponds to reality is a familiar thesis that goes back at least to Aristotle (*Metaphysics* 1011b25). And though concepts, not being complete thoughts, are not assigned truth values in logic in the way that propositions are, there is an obvious sense in which a concept can be true insofar as it can be said accurately to capture the essence of the thing it is a concept of – though, as Aquinas argues, what is true in the strictest sense is the intellect's *judgment* that its concept of some thing is accurate, rather than the concept itself, which is true only in a secondary sense (*De Veritate* I.3 and *Summa Theologiae* I.16.2). For an intellect to conform to being, then, is for its concepts accurately to convey the natures of their referents and for its beliefs to correspond to reality. But what is it for being to conform to intellect?

To a first approximation, and as I have already indicated, it has to do with something's conforming to the intellect's concept of its essence. For example, a true triangle is a triangle that conforms to the concept of *a closed plane figure with three straight sides*. Now, this might seem problematic, in two respects. First, it may seem to give the lie to my earlier remark that ontological truth is more fundamental than logical truth. Logical truth is a property of thought and language. Ontological truth is supposed to be something different, a property of reality *independent* of thought and language. But now, it might seem, it turns out that all that that amounts to is reality's reflecting the way that thought and language represent it. So, it might seem that logical truth is in the driver's seat after all, and that the notion of ontological truth is less interesting than I have suggested. Second, even if this problem can be resolved, it might seem that we are still left with a second and deeper one, which is that the account is viciously circular. Our concepts are true (in the logical sense) only insofar as they conform to being, but being is true (in the ontological sense) only insofar as it conforms to our concepts. How is this not a merry-go-round?

The first thing to say in response is that when it is claimed that ontological truth involves conformity of being to the intellect, what is meant is intellect in the abstract, not the human intellect in particular. What other intellects are there? I'll come back to that, but the point for the moment is that ontological truth is independent of *human* thought and language, and would exist even if they did not. Indeed, until the human mind makes contact with external reality by way of sensory experience, there are no concepts in it to which external reality might conform. The way this contact works according to Thomistic epistemology is that in forming a concept of a thing and thereby cognizing it, the intellect takes on the form of the thing it cognizes. As John Haldane suggests, we can begin to understand this by comparison with the way two physical objects of the same kind have the same form (1993, 33). For example, two triangles that you might draw on a marker board share the form of *a closed plane figure with three straight sides*. What happens in our cognition of a triangle is that the intellect too comes to share this form, but (by contrast with a physical object that has the form) in a way that is divorced from matter. Thought and the thing thought about are *formally* identical despite these relata not being materially identical or, in the case of the thought, not being material at all. In this sense cognition involves what Haldane calls a "mind-world identity" (1993, passim).

As John Wippel points out, for Aquinas, *truth* is like *universals* in that, though both are fully realized only when the intellect abstracts form from concrete particulars, neither is the free creation of the intellect, but has a foundation in mind-independent reality (2007, 66). Hence, when the intellect entertains the concept *triangularity* in abstraction from particular triangles, it is considering qua universal something that already really did exist in the particulars themselves before the mind abstracted it, but qua individualized. Similarly, when the intellect correctly makes a judgment to the effect that *this object before me is a closed plane figure with three straight sides*, what is present within it under the guise of *logical truth* is something that already existed in mind-independent reality under the guise of *ontological truth*.

Now, all of this illuminates logical truth, ontological truth, and the relationship between them in several ways. For one thing, it entails that the conformity of intellect to reality and reality to intellect has nothing to do with a relationship of *representation*, as that is typically understood in post-Cartesian philosophy of mind. It is much more intimate than that – again, it is a kind of *identity*, albeit only formal. For another thing, the account entails that ontological truth is prior to and independent of logical truth. To be sure, a thing's having a certain form gives it an inherent *aptness* or *potentiality* for being cognized. There is, in that sense, an implicit reference to the intellect in characterizing it as ontologically true. But until that potentiality is actualized by the presence of a human intellect, there are no concepts, beliefs, utterances or the like for the thing to conform to. Moreover, human intellects being what they are, they can of course sometimes *mis*conceive the objects of thought (as a result of misperception, confusion, or whatever). Ontological truth, then, is not fundamentally a matter of a thing's conforming to just any old concept that some human mind actually has in fact formed of it. Rather, it is a matter of a thing's conforming to the concept that an intellect *would* entertain *upon taking on that thing's form*, where that very same form is already actually to be found in the thing itself.[9] Whatever one thinks of this thesis, it is a substantive metaphysical claim about what things are like independently of any contingent facts about human thought and language. (Just how substantive, we will see in the next section when we look at the implications of the notion of ontological truth.)

It should also be clear why there is no circularity in the account, as there would be if we were simply defining the truth that exists in the intellect in terms of the truth that exists in being and the truth that exists in being in terms of the truth that exists in the intellect, and leaving it at that. Rather, the fundamental notion here is *form*, understood in the Aristotelian hylemorphist sense as the intrinsic organizing principle of a thing. The intellect is then defined in terms of the capacity to abstract form from matter altogether, thereby generating a concept. Truth is then in turn defined in terms of the way the intellect and the thing it knows conform to one another by virtue of their formal identity, where truth is characterized as logical if looked at from the point of view of the intellect and ontological if looked at from the point of view of the thing cognized.

There is still a puzzle to be resolved, however. I have explained how human thought and language presuppose a mind-independent reality from which the human intellect can abstract forms and thereby generate concepts, so that ontological truth is more fundamental than logical truth. Indeed, ontological truth would exist whether or not human beings had themselves ever existed. Yet I have also nevertheless defined ontological truth in terms of conformity to intellect, and I have said that it is a *transcendental* property of being – something attributable to *all* being as such, including what would exist even if human beings did not. How can these claims be reconciled? The answer is that they can be reconciled if there is an intellect to which all being would conform even in the absence of *human* intellects, specifically.

Keep in mind that the position I have been describing, since it is Aristotelian, is also *realist*. The human intellect *discovers* rather than creates the essences of natural objects, and thus it discovers rather than creates the truths it comes to know about these essences. Hence these truths do not depend on the existence of human minds. But they also do not depend on the existence of a material world. The proposition that the angles of a Euclidean triangle sum to 180 degrees remains true whether or not there are any actual triangles to be found in the material world; the proposition that *Tyrannosaurus Rex* is a bipedal carnivorous dinosaur remains true even though

---

[9] On the thesis that all being is true insofar as it has the *potential* to be cognized by a human intellect, whether or not it is *actually* so cognized, see Mercier et al. 1932, 462, and the discussion of Mercier's views in McCall 1938.

Tyrannosauruses no longer exist; and so on. Moreover, since these truths follow from the essences of things rather than from any contingent facts about them, they are necessary and eternal. There is also an infinite number of such truths, as can be seen just from the case of mathematics. So, realism entails the existence of a body of truths that is *immaterial*, *necessary*, *eternal*, and *infinite*. But for the Aristotelian (who rejects any Platonic "third realm"), if such truths are independent of matter, there is no other place to locate them than in an intellect. Hence there must be an intellect that is itself immaterial, necessary, eternal, and infinite – that is to say, a divine intellect.

What I am rehearsing here is, of course, what is sometimes called the "argument from eternal truths" for the existence of God, which has its roots in Neo-Platonism and is associated with the Augustinian tradition. Naturally, it raises all sorts of questions, but this is not the place for a defense, which I have in any case provided elsewhere (Feser 2017, chapter 3). Suffice it for present purposes to note that the Scholastics who hammered out the doctrine of the transcendentals, whether or not they endorse this particular argument for God's existence, do embrace the associated idea that the essences of things pre-exist their instantiation in the natural world as concepts in the divine mind, which function as the archetypes by reference to which God creates.

This is what grounds ontological truth as a transcendental property of being which would exist even in the absence of human minds, specifically. For all things exhibit ontological truth insofar as they conform to the concept the *divine* intellect has of them, which serves as the blueprint according to which they were made. Hence, though the truth that resides in human intellects presupposes ontological truth, and is therefore less fundamental than it, *ontological* truth in turn presupposes the truth that resides in the divine intellect, and is therefore itself less fundamental than *that*. Truth cannot get into our minds unless it is first in things, but it cannot get into things unless it is first in the mind of God. Hence truth is a property of human thoughts in only a secondary or derivative way, but of divine thoughts in a primary way.

But we can make a stronger claim even than that when we factor in other theological premises, such as the doctrine of divine simplicity. Since there are no parts in God, there is no distinction in him even between essence and existence. Accordingly, he does not merely *have* being in the sense of instantiating it. Rather, he just *is* subsistent being itself. But since truth is convertible with being – the same thing looked at from a different point of view – it follows that he just is *truth* itself. Moreover, talk about concepts and truths pre-existing in the divine intellect must be understood in analogical terms. We can say that there is in God something *analogous* to what we call concepts and thoughts, but whereas in our minds these are distinct entities, in God they are not. Given divine simplicity, God's knowledge, power, goodness, and other attributes are identical. We cannot grasp the divine nature except insofar as we bring it under these distinct concepts, but what they refer to in God is one and the same thing. In a similar way, in order to grasp the divine intellect to the extent that we are able to, we have to attribute to it distinct concepts and thoughts. But given divine simplicity, what these too refer to in God is one and the same thing.

Spelling all that out in greater detail would require delving into theological matters that would take us far beyond the metaphysics of truth. Suffice it for present purposes to note that the Augustinian thesis that concepts in the divine intellect are the archetypes according to which God creates is the *deepest* foundation for the claim that we need a notion of ontological or transcendental truth in addition to the notion of logical truth that is more familiar to modern philosophers. Hence we can add atheism to the list of "isms" (mechanism, nominalism, reductionism, etc.) whose influence on modern thought has, as I suggested earlier, made contemporary philosophers reluctant to credit the doctrine of the transcendentals.

I hasten to add that that is *not* to say that there are no non-theological considerations indicating that the ontological notion of truth as conformity of being to intellect cannot entirely be replaced by the logical notion of truth as conformity of intellect to being. John Peterson gives the example of Phidias working through several failed attempts to sculpt Athena before succeeding and declaring of the resulting statue: "That is the true *Athena*" (2015, 19). As Peterson points out, it will not do to suggest that what is expressed by this statement can be entirely captured by the thesis that Phidias' belief or utterance conforms to the final statue. Rather, it has to do, more fundamentally, with the final statue's conforming to Phidias's concept of it in a way that the failed attempts did not. In other words, we cannot make sense of Phidias's statement except as a remark about ontological truth rather than logical truth.

We ought also to factor in the familiar Scholastic thesis that whatever is in an effect must in some way first be in its cause. Logical truth resides in utterances, statements, and, more fundamentally, in the thoughts of which utterances and statements are expressions. But it gets into our thoughts only because of the contact the intellect makes with the reality outside it. Hence for truth to get into the intellect it must first in some way be in this external reality – that is to say, logical truth presupposes ontological truth.

So, there is much we can say in defense of ontological truth before making reference to distinctively theological considerations. But it is when we pursue things to the deepest level that we find that those considerations are unavoidable. For, again, truth of either the logical or the ontological kind essentially involves some relation to an intellect, and we therefore need to find some intellect to ground it in in real and imagined contexts where truth exists but no finite intellects are to be found.

If there is ontological truth, is there also ontological falsity? Obviously, a thing of one type might give the false appearance of being of another type. For example, pyrite can appear to be gold, and thus might be called false gold. But only in a loose sense, because the falsity in this case is really in our judgment that it is gold, not in the pyrite itself. Indeed, considered in itself it is *true* – that is to say, it is *true pyrite*. Aquinas's view is that, strictly speaking, and in relation to the *divine* intellect, nothing can be false (*De Veritate* I.10). Certainly the divine intellect is, unlike ours, incapable of making an erroneous judgment about what a thing is. Manualists generally seem to follow Aquinas in holding that, strictly speaking, nothing can be ontologically false.

It seems to me, though, that a thing itself might plausibly be said to be ontologically false in a stronger sense than that in which pyrite is false gold. After all, no line, circle, or triangle to be found in the physical world will have the perfection captured by our concepts of these geometrical entities – and by the concepts of them that pre-exist as archetypes in the divine intellect. In falling short of it, it seems that there is a sense in which they can be said to fail to be perfectly true, in a way that is analogous to how a thing can fail to be perfectly good. Indeed, since goodness and truth are both transcendental properties of being and thus convertible, it seems that there should be something like ontological falsity to parallel evil qua privation of goodness.

The nineteenth-century Neo-Scholastic philosopher Thomas Harper (1940, 438–44) considered and rejected such a view, but for reasons which do not seem to me to be strong. His opening move is to suggest that the notion of ontological falsity is a contradiction in terms (440). For if something has being, then, given the convertibility of being and truth, how can it be false? But this seems to me like saying that since being is convertible with goodness, no being can be bad. All that actually follows in the case of goodness is that no being can be bad *in every respect*. But it can be bad in some respects even if good in others. So why couldn't a being also be false in some respects even if true in others?

Harper also objects that if something counted as ontologically false by virtue of its defects, then it would follow that it is not conformable to intellect, which would contradict the thesis that all being is so conformable (440–1). But why couldn't a thing be conformable to intellect in *some* respects while not in others, just as it can be good in some respects while not in others? Harper says that the divine idea of every actual existing thing represents its defects along with its perfections, so that every thing will conform exactly to the divine idea and therefore not be ontologically false. But he goes on to admit that, since a defective thing will fail perfectly to correspond to what he calls the divine intellect's "generic or typal Idea" of the kind the thing falls under, the thing will exhibit "traces of something that bears a distant resemblance to Falsity" (441). Indeed, Aquinas too acknowledges that "a creature has some similarity to what is false in so far as it is deficient" (*De Veritate* I.4). This seems to me come pretty close to acknowledging that a thing can be ontologically false in a stronger sense than the sense in which pyrite is false gold. Perhaps the issue is ultimately semantic.

11.3   Some Implications

Having rashly given voice to this tentative disagreement with St. Thomas, let me hasten to change the subject and turn to the implications and applications of the account of ontological or transcendental truth that I have been setting out. I'll first address some philosophical implications and then briefly note some theological applications of the doctrine.

Perhaps the most fundamental philosophical consequence of truth's being a transcendental property of being is that it implies the Principle of Sufficient Reason (PSR). PSR has been formulated in various ways, not all of them equally plausible. But the basic idea is that anything that exists or occurs is intelligible. It can be explained or made sense of. Now, this thesis is not explicit in Aquinas or other medieval or ancient thinkers. It is commonly associated with Leibniz and other modern rationalists. For that reason, one occasionally comes across commentators who suggest that its presence in modern manuals of Thomist philosophy reflects a corruption of the tradition (e.g. Gurr 1959). The worry is related to Etienne Gilson's famous contrast of the "existentialism" he sees in Aquinas with the "essentialism" of the rationalists. The rationalists try to read reality off from our abstract concepts of the essences of things, whereas Aquinas insists that knowledge begins with awareness of concrete existents.

However, even Gilson himself accepted PSR (albeit its rationalist associations kept him from putting much emphasis on it), and the principle was more warmly embraced by prominent twentieth-century Thomists like Jacques Maritain precisely because of its connection to the thesis that truth is convertible with being.[10] Thomists certainly cannot accept rationalist epistemology or some of the dubious uses to which modern philosophers have put PSR. But the principle itself is sound, and follows from a claim that Thomists *do* accept, to the effect that all being is conformable to the intellect.[11]

A second implication of the idea of truth as a transcendental property of being is that we ought to be able to reason to God's existence by way of the notion of truth no less than by way of the notions of being, unity, and goodness. Or, to speak more cautiously, the notion of transcendental truth at least *suggests* this even if it does not strictly imply it. Arguments like St. Thomas's "existential proof" in *De Ente et Essentia* essentially reason to God's existence by way of the transcendental notion of being. Neo-Platonic arguments to the effect that composite things must derive from an absolutely simple or non-composite cause (an idea that is also clearly in Aquinas) essentially reason to God's existence by way of the transcendental notion of one or unity. Arguments that emphasize teleology, such as Aquinas's Fifth Way or Aristotle's argument that God moves the world as its final cause, essentially approach God by way of the transcendental notion of goodness. If being, one, goodness, *and truth* are convertible, then, it stands to reason that there should also be some way to arrive at God's existence by way of the transcendental notion of truth. The Augustinian argument from eternal truths is precisely such an argument.

Now, while some Thomists (myself included) have defended that argument, others are skeptical of it. Like PSR, it might seem to smack too much of rationalism to fit comfortably with Thomism. Yet as with PSR, it isn't really modern rationalism

---

[10] For discussion of the attitudes toward PSR of these and other Thomists, see Fitz Gerald 2002.

[11] I discuss and defend PSR at greater length in Feser 2014, 137–46, and Feser 2019, 74–85.

that is the inspiration behind the relevant ideas, but rather the notion of truth as a transcendental. Now, Augustine is commonly regarded as the seminal theorist of the notion of ontological or transcendental truth, just as Aristotle is seen as the fountainhead of theorizing about logical truth. But Aquinas was no less an Augustinian than he was an Aristotelian. Hence we ought to be wary of too quickly dismissing ideas like the ones in question as rationalist corruptions of authentic Thomism.

A third philosophical implication of the notion of ontological truth is that it suggests a critique of certain forms of skepticism and anti-realism about the world external to the mind. Haldane notes that epistemological realism, which holds both that a mind-independent world exists and that we can have knowledge of it, requires the following two claims:

1. The world is ontologically independent of thought, and
2. Concepts and what they represent are intrinsically related. (1993, 24)

For without (1), we wouldn't have realism, and without (2) we would be trapped behind a "veil of perceptions" which would be the same whether or not anything lay beyond it, making knowledge of the world impossible. The trouble, Haldane points out, is that (1) and (2) might seem to be incompatible. For if the world is ontologically independent of thought, how could concepts have an *intrinsic* relationship to it? Claim (1) might seem to lead to skepticism. But if concepts are intrinsically related to what they represent, how could the world be ontologically independent of thought? Claim (2) might therefore seem to lead to idealism, the collapse of the world into the mind.

The way out of this apparent impasse, as Haldane argues, is provided by the Thomist thesis that cognition involves the *formal* identity of the knower and the known without their *material* identity. Because the intellect and its objects are not materially identical, the world is ontologically independent of thought. Because they are formally identical, concepts and what they represent are intrinsically related and we are not trapped behind a veil of perceptions. In other words, (1) and (2) can be reconciled by conceiving of truth – the conformity of intellect and reality – as the doctrine of the transcendentals does, in terms of formal identity. Logical truth is a matter of the intellect having the same form as the thing known, and ontological truth is a matter of the thing known having the same form as the intellect.

As Haldane also points out, this account does not require commitment to the kind of semantic realism criticized by anti-realists like Michael Dummett, and expressed in the thesis that the meaning of a statement is given by truth-conditions that are recognition-transcendent. What this thesis entails is that the conditions that make a statement true may be such that we could never in principle known them. That kind of realism so exaggerates the independence of reality from thought that it threatens to make reality unknowable. Not only need realists not say this, in light of the doctrine that truth is a transcendental property of being, they should not say it. For if all reality is true in the sense of conforming to intellect, then there can be no such thing as an aspect of reality that is in principle unknowable.

Here is a fourth and related implication. Donald Davidson (1984) famously argued that conceptual relativism is incoherent. Fully to spell out his reasoning would require an exposition of his general philosophy of language. But the upshot is that we cannot intelligibly count something as a conceptual scheme in the first place unless we take it both to be commensurable with our own conceptual scheme and also accurately to capture reality at least in its broad outlines even if not in all its details. Hence we cannot make sense of the idea of *alternative* conceptual schemes for carving up reality. Indeed, strictly speaking, we cannot make sense of the very notion of a conceptual scheme *itself*, understood as a contingent way of carving up an otherwise unconceptualized reality. Davidson writes:

> In giving up dependence on the concept of an uninterpreted reality, something outside all schemes and science, we do not relinquish the notion of objective truth – quite the contrary. Given the dogma of a dualism of scheme and reality, we get conceptual relativity, and truth relative to a scheme. Without the dogma, this kind of relativity goes by the board... In giving up the dualism of scheme and world, we do not give up the world, but re-establish unmediated touch with the familiar objects whose antics make our sentences and opinions true or false. (1984, 198)

Davidson's position is sometimes read as a kind of pragmatism, but I would argue that it is better seen as an inchoate rediscovery of the Scholastic notion of truth as the conformity of intellect and reality, where this conformity has both "directions of fit," mind to world and world to mind. Reality in general must be as we conceptualize it, just as our concepts must conform to reality. Or in any event, whether or not Davidson himself would welcome such a Scholastic interpretation, the notion of transcendental truth affords us a way of making use of his insights without lapsing into pragmatism or the like.

The idea of truth as a transcendental property of being suggests lines of criticism of other philosophical "isms" as well. For example, if truth is a matter of conformity of being and intellect, then what do we make of views that either implicitly or explicitly deny the reality of the intellect? Modern empiricism implicitly does so insofar as it collapses the intellect into the imagination. Eliminative materialism explicitly does so insofar as it takes propositional attitudes and their intentional content to be illusions. Naturally, eliminativists would deny the reality of the divine intellect as well. Now as Aquinas notes in *De Veritate* I.2, if there were no such thing as intellect – not even, *per impossibile*, the divine intellect – then there would be no such thing as truth. That would entail that doctrines that deny the reality of intellect cannot, by their own lights, be true, and are therefore self-defeating. Of course, to suggest that eliminativism is self-defeating is not a novel idea, but my point is that the Scholastic notion of truth as conformity of intellect and being adds a new perspective on the matter.

Then there is the theme that the ultimate ground of truth must lie in the divine intellect, since it is the locus of the archetypes according to which all things are created. This, as I have said, is the standard Scholastic way of developing a realist account of the essences of things. What do we make, then, of views which hold that the essences of things have no foundation in reality outside human mind and language, such as nominalism and cognitive relativism? They essentially put human thought and language in the place of the divine intellect, thereby deifying them. Or, to be more precise, thereby making idols of them. Now, characterizing relativism as a kind of self-deification on the part of human beings is also not a novel idea. But what I am suggesting is that the idea of truth as a transcendental property of being also adds greater depth to that analysis.

This naturally leads us, finally, briefly to consider a theological application of the ideas we've been examining. Medieval theologians sometimes took the transcendental properties of being to illuminate the doctrine of the Trinity (Kretzmann 1989), and Aquinas at least implicitly agrees.[12] Here's how the idea works. Though the divine attributes are possessed by all the Persons of the Trinity equally, a given attribute can be "appropriated" to one Person in particular insofar as it reflects in a special way the manner in which we conceptualize that Person. Hence, though all the divine Persons possess power, wisdom, and love, power is associated in a special way with how we understand the Father, wisdom in a special way with how we understand the Son, and love in a special way with how we understand the Holy Spirit. Where the transcendentals are concerned, the idea is that *being* can be appropriated to the common divine essence, and each of the three properties of being to one of the divine Persons – *one* to the Father, *true* to the Son, and *good* to the Holy Spirit. For though these transcendental properties belong to each of the Persons, appropriating them to the Persons in this way reflects how we have to conceptualize each of the three Persons and their relations to one another.

The suitability of these appropriations is evident in light of Augustine's (2002) psychological model of the Trinity, in which the Father is compared to the mind, the Son to the mind's knowledge of itself, and the Holy Spirit to its love for what it knows (*On the Trinity* IX.3). Since to love is to will the good of another, the transcendental *good* is aptly appropriated to the Holy Spirit as Augustine conceives of him. Since knowledge entails truth, the transcendental *true* is aptly appropriated to the Son. Since unity is prior to multiplicity, the transcendental *one* is aptly appropriated to the Father as that from which the other Persons proceed just as knowledge and love proceed from the mind.

In *De Veritate* I.7, Aquinas does explicitly endorse the appropriation of truth to the Son, and also argues that there is a special metaphorical or figurative sense in which truth is to be predicated of the Son, specifically:

> For in [created things], truth is said to exist inasmuch as a created thing imitates its source, the divine intellect. Similarly, when truth is applied to God and is said to be the highest possible imitation of its principle, this is attributed to the Son. Taken in this way, truth properly belongs to the Son and is predicated personally.

Truth is specially attributed to the Son, then, insofar as he is a perfect imitation of the Father, as created things are imitations of the archetypes pre-existing in the divine mind. This particular predication is merely figurative or metaphorical, however, insofar as the Son is uncreated.

---

[12] As Kretzmann points out, though Aquinas does not put forward the thesis in his own voice, he does discuss the use others have put it to without seeming to disagree with the thesis itself even when he disagrees with that use (e.g. in *De Veritate* I.1).

The appropriation of truth to the Son is, of course, especially apt in light of scripture. John 1:1 tells us that Christ is the *logos* or Word, and of course the word of God must be true. Christ tells us in John 14:6 that he is the way, the *truth*, and the life. Had Pilate only stuck around after asking his famous question, perhaps it would have dawned on him that the answer was literally staring him in the face.[13]

Bibliography

Alston, William P. 1996. *A realist conception of truth*. Ithaca: Cornell University Press.

Aquinas, Thomas. 1948. Summa Theologica. In *Five volumes, translated by the fathers of the English Dominican Province*. New York: Benziger Bros.

———. 1994. Truth. In *Three volumes, translated by Robert W. Mulligan, James V. McGlynn, and Robert W. Schmidt*. Indianapolis: Hackett Publishing Company.

Augustine. 2002. *On the trinity, books 8–15, translated by Stephen McKenna*. Cambridge: Cambridge University Press.

Bacon, Francis. 2002. Of truth, from the essays or counsels civil and moral. In *The major works*. Oxford: Oxford University Press.

Blackburn, Simon. 2018. *On truth*. Oxford: Oxford University Press.

Coffey, P. 1970. *Ontology or the theory of being*. Gloucester, MA: Peter Smith.

Davidson, Donald. 1984. On the very idea of a conceptual scheme. In *Davidson, inquires into truth and interpretation*, 183–198. Oxford: Clarendon Press.

Feser, Edward. 2014. *Scholastic metaphysics: A contemporary introduction*. Heusenstamm: Editiones Scholasticae.

———. 2017. *Five proofs of the existence of god*. San Francisco: Ignatius Press.

———. 2019. *Aristotle's revenge: The metaphysical foundations of physical and biological science*. Neunkirchen: Editiones Scholasticae.

FitzGerald, Desmond. 2002. Gilson and Maritain on the principle of sufficient reason. In *Jacques Maritain and the many ways of knowing*, ed. Douglas A. Ollivant, 120–127. Washington, D.C: Catholic University of America Press.

Frege, Gottlob. 1988. Thoughts. In *Propositions and attitudes*, ed. Nathan Salmon and Scott Soames, 33–55. Oxford: Oxford University Press.

Gardeil, H.D. 1967. *Introduction to the philosophy of St. Thomas Aquinas, volume IV: Metaphysics*. St. Louis: B. Herder.

Gurr, John Edwin. 1959. *The principle of sufficient reason in some scholastic systems 1750–1900*. Milwaukee: Marquette University Press.

Haldane, John. 1993. Mind-world identity theory and the anti-realist challenge. In *Reality, representation, and projection*, ed. Haldane and Crispin Wright, 15–37. Oxford: Oxford University Press.

Harper, Thomas. 1940. *The metaphysics of the school, volume I*. New York: Peter Smith.

Horwich, Paul. 1990. *Truth*. Oxford: Basil Blackwell.

Kirkham, Richard L. 1992. *Theories of truth: A critical introduction*. Cambridge, MA: The MIT Press.

Koren, Henry J. 1955. *An introduction to the science of metaphysics*. St. Louis: B. Herder Book Co.

---

[13] For comments on an earlier version of this paper, I thank audience members at the Tenth Annual Aquinas Philosophy Workshop on the theme *Aquinas on Knowledge, Truth, and Wisdom* at St. Mary's Campus, Greenville, SC (June 23–27, 2021).

Kretzmann, Norman. 1989. Trinity and transcendentals. In *Trinity, incarnation, and atonement*, ed. Ronald J. Feenstra and Cornelius Plantinga Jr., 79–109. Notre Dame, IN: University of Notre Dame Press.

Lynch, Michael P. 2001. *The nature of truth: Classic and contemporary perspectives*. Cambridge, MA: The MIT Press.

McCall, Raymond J. 1938. St. Thomas on ontological truth. *The New Scholasticism* 12: 9–29.

Mercier, Cardinal, et al. 1932. *A manual of modern scholastic philosophy, volume I*. St. Louis: B. Herder.

Peterson, John. 2015. *Mind, truth and teleology: An introduction to scholastic philosophy*. Heusenstamm: Editiones Scholasticae.

Searle, John. 1983. *Intentionality: An essay in the philosophy of mind*. Cambridge: Cambridge University Press.

White, Alan R. 1970. *Truth*. New York: Anchor Books.

Wippel, John F. 2007. Truth in Thomas Aquinas. In *Wippel, metaphysical themes in Thomas Aquinas II*, 65–112. Washington, D.C.: Catholic University of America Press.

Part III
Ockham and Buridan

Chapter 12
Four Notes on the Grammar of Ockham's Mental Language

Claude Panaccio

Keywords William of Ockham · Mental language · Medieval grammar

Gyula Klima has long shown great interest in the idea of mental language in medieval philosophy. Not less than three chapters of his wonderful 2009 book on John Buridan, for example, are dedicated to Buridan's conception of mental language, totaling more than a hundred pages (Klima 2009, 27–142). Gyula was also the one who initially suggested that my own book in French on interior discourse from Plato to William of Ockham be translated into English and he eventually published the translation in his medieval philosophy series at Fordham University Press (Panaccio 2017)—for which I am extremely grateful to him.

One of the main points of this book of mine is that while the idea of mental discourse was present in Greek and medieval philosophy since Plato at least, William of Ockham accomplished a genuine revolution in the philosophy of mind by taking the linguistic model for human thought with utmost seriousness. Ockham purposefully transferred the categories of Latin grammar and medieval logic to the fine-grained analysis of intellectual thought and this move had a major impact for the next two centuries at least. In the recent literature about Ockham the accent has been on his use of the logical theory of the "properties of terms" in developing this linguistic conception of thought (see e.g. Panaccio 1999a, b; Schierbaum 2014). The approach clearly presupposes, however, that human thought be endowed with a syntax and for this, Ockham turns to grammar rather than logic. Which grammatical categories exactly, he asks, should be transferred to the analysis of thought?

Two parallel passages in his works are dedicated to this question: *Quodlibeta* V, 8 (Ockham 1980, 508–513) and *Summa logicae* I, 3 (Ockham 1974, 11–14). His answer is roughly the same in both: since mental language must have at least as

C. Panaccio (✉)
University of Quebec at Montreal, Montreal, Canada
e-mail: panaccio.claude@uqam.ca

© The Author(s), under exclusive license to Springer Nature
Switzerland AG 2023
J. P. Hochschild et al. (eds.), *Metaphysics Through Semantics: The
Philosophical Recovery of the Medieval Mind*, International Archives of the
History of Ideas Archives internationales d'histoire des idées 242,
https://doi.org/10.1007/978-3-031-15026-5_12

much expressive power as any conventional language, the grammatical distinctions that are liable to make a difference in the truth-value of spoken or written sentences must be reflected somehow in the syntax of human mental language. A distinction between singular and plural, for example, is to be postulated in mentalese since sentences such as "Some horse runs" and "Some horses run" can have different truth-values. The distinction between masculine and feminine, on the other hand, is not required: it affects the grammaticality of sentences, to be sure, but not their semantic import. The point is familiar in the Ockham-literature, but the two passages where it is developed raise a number of problems that have not yet been sufficiently clarified. In the present paper, I will address four such riddles.

12.1   The Structure of *Summa Logicae* I, 3

The first problem has to do with the structure of the *Summa logicae* chapter in the St. Bonaventure critical edition. The first paragraph states that the division of the "parts of speech" that is commonly accepted in grammar generally applies to mental terms as well as to spoken and written terms: there are mental names, verbs, adverbs, conjunctions, and prepositions just as there are spoken and written names, verbs, adverbs, conjunctions, and prepositions (Ockham 1974, 11, lines 1–12). After a discussion of whether there are participles as well as verbs in mentalese (lines 13–26), the text turns to the grammatical features of names and identifies those among these features that should be accepted as common to mental and conventional terms such as the distinction between singular and plural (lines 27–43), and those that are proper to spoken and written words such as the distinction between masculine and feminine (lines 44–68). Next comes the discussion of the grammatical features of verbs. As he did in the case of names, Ockham first lists the features that are common to mental and conventional verbs such as the distinction of moods, tenses, and persons (lines 69–83). At this point, however, the text surprisingly inserts a paragraph about why it is necessary to postulate mental names, verbs, adverbs, conjunctions, and prepositions in mental language (lines 84–94), thus returning to the distinction of the "parts of speech" that was discussed earlier in the chapter. And only then does it enumerate the grammatical features of verbs that are proper to spoken and written language such as the distinction of conjugations (lines 95–97). The chapter comes to a close with two short general remarks (lines 98–104).

The anomaly is that the development that occurs on lines 84 to 94 is not where it logically belongs. The justification of transferring the grammatical distinction of the parts of speech to the analysis of mentalese does not belong in the discussion about the grammatical features of mental verbs in particular. It is presupposed by this discussion and should have been provided before. My proposal is that the critical edition is to be amended here. The right place for the passage must be the one that is found in the manuscripts that the editors call A^1, D, and I, where it occurs at the end of the first part of the text, the one that has to do with the parts of speech rather than with the special features of names and verbs (Ockham 1974, 11, critical apparatus). This is confirmed by the parallel development in *Quodlibeta* V, 8 as the exact same argument (and partly with the same words) occurs in article 1 of the text, where Ockham argues that "mental concepts include names, verbs, adverbs, conjunctions, and prepositions" (Ockham 1980, 509; transl. Freddoso 1991, 425), rather than in article 2, where he discusses the grammatical features of mental names and verbs. My conclusion is that the edition of the *Summa* should be revised accordingly.

12.2   Ockham's Grammatical Source

The second question I want to raise is about Ockham's source for the grammatical categories he uses in *Quodlibeta* V, 8 and *Summa logicae* I, 3. Establishing what this source is sheds some light on the history of grammar in early fourteenth-century England and it also allows us to know what definitions exactly Ockham has in mind for the technical terms of grammar he employs there. That will help us understand what is at stake in his discussions of *qualitas* and *figura* in particular, about which there is some disagreement among recent commentators.

The sixth-century Latin grammarian Priscian was the most important authority during the Middle Ages for the development of grammar as a science (see e.g. Ebbesen and Rosier-Catach 1997, 107) and Priscian is the only grammarian indeed that Ockham mentions by name in the whole *Summa logicae*.[1] My conjecture, however, is that the list of grammatical categories Ockham uses in *Quodlibeta* V, 8 and *Summa logicae* I, 3 is borrowed not from Priscian but from the *Ars grammatica* of the fourth-century grammarian Donatus, and most probably from the part of the *Ars grammatica* known as the *Ars minor* that circulated during the Middle Ages as a separate elementary introduction to grammar (see e.g. Hayden 2017, section 4).[2]

In the two passages we are interested in, Ockham mentions the same grammatical categories:

1. the parts of speech, i.e. names, verbs, pronouns, participles, adverbs, conjunctions, and prepositions;
2. the "accidents" of names, i.e. case, number, gender, figure (*figura*), degree of comparison (*comparatio*), and quality (*qualitas*);
3. the "accidents" of verbs, i.e. mood, voice (*genus*), number, tense, person, conjugation, and figure (*figura*).

List number (1) provides no clue as to whether Ockham is using Donatus or Priscian since the parts of speech are the same in the two grammarians (Donatus 1981, 1, 585; Priscian 1855, II, 15–21, 53–56). Ockham's list differs from both of them only

---

[1] See *Summa logicae* I, 26 and I, 49 (Ockham 1974: 88 and 158). Nowhere in the *Quodlibeta*, on the other hand, is any grammarian explicitly mentioned.

[2] I have briefly proposed this conjecture in Panaccio 1995, 202, n.3. Here, I argue for it in more details.

by leaving out interjections; he simply ignores the possibility that there are interjections in mentalese. List number (2), on the other hand, is exactly the same as in
Donatus's *Ars minor* (Donatus 1981, 2, 585) and it significantly differs from what is
found in Priscian (Priscian 1855, II, 22, 57). While gender, number, figure, and case
are counted among accidents of names by Priscian as they are by Ockham and
Donatus, *qualitas* and *comparatio* are not. Priscian takes the "quality" of a name to
be an essential feature of it rather than an accident (Priscian 1855, II, 22, 56–57) and
he deals with *comparatio* in a separate chapter (Priscian 1855, III, 83–116). In addition, Priscian mentions what he calls *species* among the accidents of names, which
neither Donatus nor Ockham do. The *species* of a name for Priscian is its being
either "principal" or "derivative," his examples being "*Iulus*" and "*Iulius*" for proper
names and "*mons*" and "*montanus*" for common names (Priscian 1855, II, 22, 57).
This feature is utterly absent from Ockham's discussion in the *Quodlibeta* and the
Summa logicae.

As to the accidents of verbs—list number (3)—, Priscian has eight of those
instead of seven as in Donatus and Ockham. The additional one is *species* again,
which is whether the verb is "primitive" or "derivative" just as it is in the case of
names (Priscian 1855, VIII, 72, 427) and this is a feature that Ockham ignores in his
discussion of verbs just as he did in his discussion of names. It is true that one of
Donatus's seven accidents of verbs—the one he calls *qualitas*—does not appear as
such in Ockham's list, but this is easily explained. In the case of verbs, Donatus
identifies two kinds of "quality": mood (*modus*) and form (*forma*), among which
Ockham keeps only the former for reasons that can be safely guessed. The *forma* of
a verb for Donatus is whether this verb is "perfect," "meditative," "frequentative" or
"inchoative" (Donatus 1981, 4, 591). Those are notions that are altogether quite
technical and of no great importance in medieval grammar. Raising the question of
whether they correspond to a distinction in mental language or not would have significantly complicated the discussion without much benefit in the context of relatively short developments such as *Quodlibeta* V, 8 and *Summa logicae* I, 3 were
designed to be. Once the *forma* is left out, Donatus's *qualitas* reduces to mood in the
case of verbs and mood is what we find indeed in Ockham's list number (3) instead
of *qualitas*. Given that Ockham clearly follows Donatus rather than Priscian in his
enumeration of the accidents of names, it seems plausible that he does the same for
the accidents of verbs except by deliberately omitting the needlessly trouble-
some *forma*.

Donatus's *Ars minor*, indeed, was a most practical guide for Ockham to turn to
in the circumstances since it provided a relevant list of grammatical categories along
with their definitions in the form of very short questions and answers. It can be sur-
mised, in addition, that Ockham probably had direct access to the *Ars minor* while
writing the *Summa* since it came along with Alexander of Villedieu's grammar, the
Doctrinale, in a number of manuscripts (Holtz 1981, 505) and Ockham tacitly uses
the *Doctrinale* in the *Summa* (Gal and Brown 1974, 44*). It is true that the differences between Priscian and Donatus on these matters are not very important in the
end, but identifying Donatus's *Ars minor* as Ockham's direct grammatical source in
Quodlibeta V, 8 and *Summa logicae* I, 3 is interesting anyway. For one thing,

Ockham's use of Donatus and of Alexander of Villedieu's *Doctrinale* appears to be an early manifestation of a significant shift in the scholarly study of grammar. According to the historians of linguistics, Priscian was progressively supplanted by Alexander of Villedieu as the basic authority on grammar in most universities during the second half of the fourteenth century (Kneepkens 1995, 247–255; Ebbesen and Rosier-Catach 1997, 125; Kneepkens 2017, section 1; Hayden 2017, section 4). Supposing that Ockham's reliance on Donatus's *Ars minor* was in close relation with his use of the *Doctrinale* as documented by the editors of the *Summa logicae* (Gal and Brown 1974, 44*; Ockham 1974, 758, 776–777, 784), we can gather from our previous observations that the process was already on its way in the 1320s. Moreover, taking Donatus's definitions to be what Ockham had in mind while writing *Quodlibeta* V, 8 and *Summa logicae* I, 3 provides us with a good guide for understanding what he meant when using such technical grammatical notions as *qualitas* or *figura*, about which there are disagreements in the Ockham literature as we will presently see.

12.3   The "Quality" of Names

Ockham does not say much about the "quality" (*qualitas*) of names, but what little he says arouses curiosity. In the *Quodlibeta* version, he laconically remarks that "there is a problem (*dubium*) about whether the quality of a spoken name belongs to a mental name" (Ockham 1980, 510; transl. Freddoso 1991, 426), but he does not explain what the problem is. In the *Summa* Ockham briefly mentions the same difficulty and interestingly adds that he will deal with it "at its root" (*in sua radice*) in another context (Ockham 1974, 13). This remark suggests that a full discussion of this point might get complicated, but Ockham provides no additional clue as to what is at stake here. To understand it, we must first clarify of course what the quality of a name is supposed to be. Ockham presupposes that his readers would be familiar with the grammatical terminology he uses, but this is not the case with us anymore as is obvious from the disagreements that emerge among the few recent commentators who have proposed explanatory remarks on these passages. In a short footnote of the critical edition, the editors mention—without references—that the quality of a name here corresponds to its being proper or common (Ockham 1974, 13, n. 3) and so does Joël Biard, the French translator of the *Summa* (Biard 1993, 12, n.1). On the other hand, Alfred Freddoso, the English translator of the *Quodlibeta*, claims— also without references—that "*quality* includes affirmative and negative" and goes on to explain why Ockham would hesitate to countenance negative terms in mental language (Freddoso 1991, 426, n. 34).

This particular disagreement is easy to settle once Donatus is identified as Ockham's main grammatical source since the *qualitas* of a name is neatly defined in Donatus's *Ars minor* as its being either a proper name or a common name (Donatus 1981, 585). Joel Biard and the editors of the *Summa* are right about that.

The interesting question that arises at this point is to understand what the difficulty is for Ockham about whether there is a distinction between proper and common names in mental language. Since there undoubtedly are general concepts—and hence common names—in Ockham's mental language, the problem with deciding whether there is a distinction between proper and common names in mentalese must reduce to *whether or not there are mental proper names*. A proper name for Ockham is a simple linguistic unit that designates a single individual "such as this name 'Socrates' and this name 'Plato'," as he writes himself (Ockham 1974, I, 19, 66). The problem Ockham has in mind, then, is whether or not there are *simple singular concepts* in human thought. This is both a difficult and important question and Ockham seems to have oscillated about it. In his commentary on Aristotle's treatise *On Categories*, Ockham includes the distinction between proper and common names among those that "pertain only to conventional words" along with the distinction between concrete and abstract terms and the distinction between verbs and participles, but he provides no explanation as to why he does so (Ockham 1978a, 3, 145). In the original redaction of distinction 2, question 9 of the *Ordinatio*, he says that "with respect to any creature whatsoever, no proper concept can be naturally abstracted" (Ockham 1970, I, 2, 9, 308; my transl.). The reason he gives there is that "every concept that is abstracted from a thing equally relates to everything that is maximally similar (*simillimum*) to this thing" (Ockham 1970, I, 2, 9, 308; my transl.). In other words: a concept that is abstracted from a singular thing equally represents in the mind any other thing that is exactly similar to this thing. In a later addition to the text, however, Ockham specifies that this is so if a concept is taken to be a "certain *fictum*," i.e. a purely ideal mental representation produced by the act of the mind and distinct from this act (Ockham 1970, I, 2, 9, 307). If, on the other hand, the concept is identified with the act of intellection itself, as a rival theory of concepts claims, "a concept can be proper to a single thing," Ockham writes (*ibid.*, 308; my transl.).

Ockham's final stand on the matter is to be found in *Quodlibeta* I, 13 and V, 7. He is clear there that "a simple abstractive cognition is not proper (*propria*) to a singular thing" (Ockham 1980, I, 13, 77; transl. Freddoso and Kelley 1991, 67) and that "our intellect cannot have any such proper (*proprium*) and simple concept with respect to any creature" (Ockham 1980, V, 7, 506; transl. Freddoso 1991, 422). The reason he gives is the same as in the *Ordinatio*: "each such cognition or concept is equally a likeness of, and equally represents, all exactly similar individuals, and so it is no more a proper concept of the one than of the other" (*ibid.*; transl. Freddoso 1991, 422–423). Ockham's position in the *Quodlibeta* is nevertheless different from the one he held in the *Ordinatio*. In the latter, as we saw, the rejection of simple singular abstractive concepts is associated only with the *fictum*-theory of concepts, i.e. the idea that concepts are ideal objects produced by the acts of intellection. In the *Quodlibeta*, by contrast, Ockham endorses the *actus*-theory of concepts, according to which mental concepts are identified with the acts of intellection themselves.[3] In the meanwhile, therefore, he came to think that simple singular abstractive concepts are not acceptable in the *actus*-theory of concepts any more than they are in the *fictum*-theory. This must be because he realized that the similitude of an abstractive concept with external objects is as important in the *actus*-theory as it is in the *fictum*-theory for determining which objects the concept represents. Ockham is nowhere very clear—to put it mildly—about what this similitude between a concept and its objects amounts to, but it most probably has to do with the idea that a crucial role of a concept is to help us judge whether a certain thing falls under this concept or not. The concept of man, Ockham says, "equally refers to all men so that we can judge about anything whether it is a man or not" (Ockham 1970, I, 2, 8, 278). This is not to say that we can never be mistaken in such judgements, but there must be something about the concept that prompts us to judge with a good degree of reliability whether it applies or not in any given case. This feature of the concept is what Ockham calls the "likeness" (*similitudo*) of the concept with the objects that it represents. This is not the place to speculate further about how exactly to conceive this relation of likeness in the framework of Ockham's theory; I have done so in some details elsewhere (Panaccio 2004, 119–143; 2011; 2015, 176–177). What matters here is that insofar as mental names are identified with simple abstractive concepts, Ockham's considered view is that there is no distinction between proper and common names in human mental language because there are no mental proper names: no simple and proper concept can be naturally abstracted by the human mind.

This is not to say that there can be no singular terms at all in mental language. For one thing, Ockham does admit the possibility of *complex* singular cognitions. While "a simple abstractive cognition is not proper to a singular thing," he writes, "…a composite abstractive cognition can indeed be proper" (Ockham 1980, I, 13, 77; transl. Freddoso and Kelley 1991, 67). I can assemble a number of simple mental representations that taken together will ultimately represent Socrates and nothing else "because I have seen him as having such-and-such a shape, color, height, and girth, and as being in such-and-such a place" (*ibid.*). And secondly, a mental intuitive cognition is both simple and proper to a certain singular object according to Ockham: "an intuitive cognition is a proper cognition of a singular thing" (Ockham 1980, I, 13, 76; transl. Freddoso and Kelley 1991, 66). This is not, he explains, "because of its greater likeness to the one thing than to the other, but because it is naturally caused by the one thing and not by the other" (*ibid.*).[4] Yet neither

---

[3] See in particular *Quodlibeta* IV, 35, article 2 (Ockham 1980, 472–474). It is true that the original disputation of Ockham's Quodlibetal questions must have spread over a period of several years— presumably from 1322 to 1324 according to the editor (Wey 1980, 36*–38*)—but the text we now have is a revised version, and anyway the disputation and writing of *Quodlibeta* IV, 35, where Ockham unequivocally subscribes to the *actus*-theory of concepts, certainly antedated the disputation and writing of *Quodlibeta* V, 7, where he rejects the possibility of simple singular abstractive concepts.

[4] This thesis of Ockham about the object of an intuitive cognition being fixed by causality rather than similitude is the basis for the *externalist* understanding of his theory of intuitive cognition that I have proposed elsewhere (Panaccio 2010, 2015).

composite abstractive cognitions nor simple intuitive cognitions can plausibly be seen as mental proper names. In the case of complex abstractive cognitions, this is because they are semantically complex while names are supposed to be simple.[5] Intuitive cognitions, on the other hand, do not behave like names at all: since an intuitive cognition naturally exists in the mind only when its object is present, it cannot be used as a mental name for the object when the latter is away. In this respect, intuitive cognitions are more like a special kind of mental demonstrative pronouns than like mental proper names (Panaccio 2004, 11–14).

As to what Ockham had in mind in *Summa logicae* I, 3 when saying that he would discuss the point in another context, this remains unclear. He does not address the issue elsewhere in the *Summa* at least. It is true that he insistently mentions the distinction between common and proper names in *Summa logicae* I, 42 when discussing the Aristotelian category of substance, but his point there is only that the Aristotelian distinction between first and second substances must be understood as "a division among names": "proper names are said to be first substances and common names second substances" (Ockham 1974, 121; transl. Loux 1974, 133). There is no discussion in this context of whether this distinction occurs among concepts as well as among conventional words. And I see no other passage in the *Summa* where the latter question is raised. On the other hand, it would have been strange for Ockham to use the future tense in *Summa logicae* I, 3 ("*alias pertractabo*") if what he had in mind was his discussion in *Quodlibeta* I, 13 and V, 7 of whether there are simple abstractive concepts in the human mind since the disputation of the quodlibetal questions most certainly antedates the writing of the *Summa*. Even if we surmise that Ockham revised the text of the *Quodlibeta* after having completed at least the first chapters of the *Summa*, as has sometimes been suggested (e.g. by Baudry 1950, 80), it would still seem implausible that he would refer to any part of the *Quodlibeta* in the future tense when writing the *Summa* since what was left for him to do concerning the *Quodlibeta* was merely to finalize the text of previous public disputations. What seems more probable in my view is that Ockham is referring in *Summa* I, 3 to a commentary or set of questions on either the *De anima* or the *Metaphysics* that he intended to write but in the end never did because of the dramatic shift in his career that occurred after he fled Avignon for political reasons in 1324.[6] Whatever the case may be, it is certainly no wonder, given the complexity of the question, that Ockham did not consider it appropriate to discuss the matter of mental proper names in the context of *Quodlibeta* V, 8 or *Summa logicae* I, 3, where he simply wanted to establish that most grammatical categories are transferable to mental language.

---

[5] I will return to this point in the next section of this paper.

[6] In the Prologue to his Commentary on the *Physics*, Ockham expresses his intention to comment on the whole of Aristotle's natural philosophy, which would certainly include the *De anima* (Ockham 1985, 4). Later on in the same treatise, indeed, he does explicitly refer to a future work on the *De anima* (Ockham 1985, III, 2, 448–449, lines 276–277; see also footnote 10 of the editor in Ockham 1985, 14). With respect to the *Metaphysics*, Ockham often states that he will eventually comment on it, for example in his Commentary on the *Categories* (Ockham 1978b, 325, l. 22–24 and 326, l. 52–53) and in his Commentary on the *Physics* (Ockham 1985, 14, l. 118–119; 245, l. 55; and 282, l. 29–30).

12.4   The "Figure" of Names and Verbs

The last subject I want to deal with here is the "figure" (*figura*) of names and verbs. Ockham unambiguously counts this among the grammatical features that occur only in conventional language. Distinctions of figure, he says, are not introduced in language "because of any requirement of signification ... or because of any require- ment of expressiveness" (Ockham 1980, 510; transl. Freddoso 1991, 426). For both names and verbs, the argument is the same: certain synonymous words can differ in grammatical figure. Distinctions of figure, then, are not required in mental language for lack of semantic significance. Ockham, however, does not care to give examples of synonymous names or verbs that would differ in figure and the very idea of gram- matical figure turns out to be differently understood among Ockham translators and commentators.

In his translation of *Quodlibeta* V, Alfred Freddoso renders *figura* as "declen- sion" when it applies to names and he refers in a footnote to the distinction that exists in Latin between the "so-called" five declensions (Freddoso 1991, 426). In relation to verbs, Freddoso translates *figura* as "inflection" and prudently remarks in a footnote that "by differences of inflection (*figura*) Ockham might mean the dis- tinction between regular and deponent verbs" (Freddoso 1991, 428). Michael Loux also translates *figura* as "declension" when it applies to names (Loux 1974, 53), but simply keeps "figure" in the case of verbs without explanation (Loux 1974, 54). According to the French translator of the *Summa*, Joël Biard, on the other hand, what Ockham means by the technical term "*figura*" is the distinction between sim- ple and compound linguistic items (Biard 1993, 11).

As in the case of "*qualitas*," these divergences about "*figura*" are easily settled by looking at Donatus's *Ars minor*—and Joël Biard turns out to be right once more. Concerning names, Donatus states that they can have one of two "figures": they are either simple or compound (Donatus 1981, 586). And the same holds for verbs (Donatus 1981, 593).[7] Ockham's point about "*figura*," then, is that there is no dis- tinction in mentalese between simple and compound names or between simple and compound verbs. Since he certainly thinks that there are simple names and verbs (or at least participles) in mental language, his view is that there are no distinct com- pound mental names or mental verbs. This is not to say that different concepts can- not be assembled into a complex mental phrase capable of serving as subject or predicate of a mental proposition. In his Commentary on the treatise *On Interpretation*, Ockham mentions that there is a wide sense of the term "*oratio*" according to which it designates "any assemblage of words" such as "rational ani- mal," "animated sensible substance" or "white animal" (Ockham 1978b, I, 3, 390). And it is clear that the mind can form the corresponding mental complexes accord- ing to him. What he is denying in *Quodlibeta* V, 8 and *Summa logicae* I, 3 is that

---

[7] It should be noted that Priscian has exactly the same notion of what the grammatical "figure" is, both for names (Priscian 1855, V, 11, 177–183) and for verbs (Priscian 1855, VIII, 15, 434–442). Indeed, Biard refers to Priscian rather than to Donatus in this respect.

such conceptual assemblages are to be categorized as names or verbs. A mental name or a mental verb is always an "incomplex" sign in the strict sense that Ockham defines in his Commentary on the *Categories*, i.e. a sign that is not composed of several signs (Ockham 1978a, 4, 1, 148): "...no part of a name," he writes in his Commentary on the *On Interpretation*, "has a separate signification" (Ockham 1978b, I, 1, 379) and he is explicit that this holds for compound names as well. Strictly speaking, then, even the compound names of conventional languages are incomplex signs. Their complexity insofar as they have one is a matter of mere etymology, not of signification. But concepts do not have this kind of etymological complexity. No conceptual name or verb, therefore, is a compound term in the grammatical sense.

Take the English word "woodpecker." In Donatus's (or Priscian's) terminology it is a compound name since it is formed from two different words, "wood" and "pecker." But this is a particular feature of English (and of some other languages). The Italian name for woodpeckers is "*picchio*" and the German name is "*Specht.*" Grammatically speaking, those are simple terms, not compound ones. Taking "woodpecker" as a natural kind term, then, here is a case where a compound term is synonymous with simple ones in Ockham's preferred sense of what synonymy is.[8] In Ockham's mental language, the corresponding unit must be the same in all three cases: it is the absolute concept that a cognizer originally acquires by having intuitive cognitions of real woodpeckers. For Ockham, this concept is a simple mental unit (in the sense that no part of it has independent signification) and it can be grammatically counted as a mental common name. Certain speakers, of course, might lack this simple concept because they have never seen a real woodpecker. They could still use the word "woodpecker"—or "*picchio*" or "*Specht*" for that matter— but what they would have in mind in so doing, according to Ockham's view, is a complex description such as "a bird that pecks at wood."[9] And complex conceptual descriptions are not to be counted as mental names, as we saw.

---

[8] In Ockham's preferred sense of what synonymy is, "expressions are synonymous which simply signify the same thing (so that nothing is in any way signified by one of the terms which is not in the same way signified by the other)" (Ockham 1974, I, 6, 19; transl. Loux 1974, 58). This definition applies to terms of different languages such as "*picchio*," "*Specht*," and "woodpecker" (if the latter is taken as an "absolute" term rather than a connotative one).

[9] Ockham deals with a similar case in *Summa logicae* III-2, 29. He explains there that someone who has never seen a lion can nevertheless utter a sentence with the term "lion" as its subject, but what that person would have in mind in so doing is "a mental proposition the subject of which is composed of several incomplex cognitions" (Ockham 1974, 559; my translation).

12.5   Conclusion

I tried here to clarify four enigmas in Ockham's discussion of which grammatical categories are transferable to the analysis of human mental language. First, I suggested an amendment to the text of *Summa logicae* I, 3 as it appears in the critical edition and the corresponding translations, namely to move up ten lines of it from the third to the first part of the chapter. Second, I argued that Ockham was using Donatus's *Ars minor* as his main grammatical source when writing *Quodlibeta* V, 8 and *Summa logicae* I, 3. As to content, finally, I commented on two grammatical categories that were variously interpreted by Ockham's translators: *qualitas* and *figura*. In both cases there turns out to be more than meets the eye in Ockham's very short remarks about whether there are corresponding grammatical distinctions in mental language. What is at stake here are such far-reaching issues as the significance of intentional similitude, the possibility of singular cognition, the simplicity of basic concepts and the dependence of concepts on intuitive cognitions. As it happens, those are topics that played a prominent role in Gyula Klima's recent work on late medieval philosophy of mind.[10] "With Ockham and his followers," he writes, "there really is a big 'paradigmatic' shift in the conception of concepts" (Klima 2015a, 334). The two texts I have focused on here, *Quodlibeta* V, 8 and *Summa logicae* I, 3, were meant by Ockham to be brief and introductory discussions, but our discussion of *qualitas* and *figura* makes it clear that when combined with the Ockhamistic theory of concept formation, this grammaticalization of thought leads to precise and stimulating ideas about how exactly the human mind works. However allusive they are, Ockham's remarks on *qualitas* and *figura* in the *Quodlibeta* and the *Summa* show that he was well aware of this.[11]

Bibliography

Baudry, Léon. 1950. *Guillaume d'Occam: Sa vie, ses œuvres, ses idées sociales et politiques*. T. I: *L'homme et les œuvres*. Paris: Vrin.

Biard, Joël. 1993. *Guillaume d'Ockham: Somme de logique. Première partie*. 2nd ed. Mauvezin: Éditions Trans-Europ-Repress.

Donatus. 1981. *Ars Donati grammatici verbis Romae*. Critical Edition in Holtz 1981, 571–674.

Ebbesen, Sten, ed. 1995. *Sprachtheorien in Spätantike und Mittelalter*. Tubingen: Gunter Narr Verlag.

---

[10] See for example Klima 2009, 37–120, where Gyula proposes a profound and detailed discussion of conceptual complexity and singular conceptual cognition in John Buridan; or Klima 2011, 2013, and 2015a, b, where he addresses the topic of intentionality and representation in medieval philosophy at large.

[11] I am most grateful to Irène Rosier-Catach for having helped me find my way in the history of medieval grammar while writing this paper and for having provided me with several useful references.

Ebbesen, Sten and Irène Rosier-Catach. 1997. Le *trivium* à la faculté des arts. In Weijers and Holtz 1997, 97–128.

Freddoso, Alfred J. 1991. *William Ockham: Quodlibetal questions*. Volume 2: Quodlibets 5–7. New Haven: Yale University Press.

Freddoso, Alfred J. and Francis E. Kelley. 1991. *William Ockham: Quodlibetal questions*. Volume 1: Quodlibets 1–4. New Haven: Yale University Press.

Gal, Gedeon and Stephen Brown. 1974. Introductio. In *Ockham* 1974, 7*–73*.

Hayden, Deborah. 2017. Language and linguistics in medieval Europe. In *Oxford research encyclopedia of linguistics*. https://doi.org/10.1093/acrefore/9780199384655.013.380.

Holtz, Louis. 1981. *Donat et la tradition de l'enseignement grammatical*. Paris: Centre National de la Recherche Scientifique.

Klima, Gyula. 2009. *John Buridan*. Oxford: Oxford University Press.

———. 2011. Tradition and innovation in medieval theories of mental representation. In Klima and Hall 2011, 7–16.

———. 2013. Three myths of intentionality vs. some medieval philosophers. *International Journal of Philosophical Studies* 21: 359–376.

———. 2015a. Mental representations and concepts in medieval philosophy. In Klima 2015b, 323–337.

———, ed. 2015b. *Intentionality, cognition, and mental representation in medieval philosophy*. New York: Fordham University Press.

Klima, Gyula, and Alexander W. Hall, eds. 2011. *Mental representation*. Newcastle upon Tyne: Cambridge Scholars Publishing.

Kneepkens, C. H. 1995. The Priscianic tradition. In Ebbesen 1995, 239–264.

Kneepkens, C.H. 2017. The Donatus minor between via antiqua and via moderna: Grammar education and the Wegestreit. *Historiographia Linguistica* 44: 355–390.

Loux, Michael. 1974. *Ockham's theory of terms: Part I of the summa logicae*. Notre Dame: University of Notre Dame Press.

Ockham, William. 1970. Scriptum in librum primum Sententiarum. Ordinatio. Distinctiones II–III. In *Guillelmi de Ockham opera theologica*, ed. S. Brown, vol. II. St. Bonaventure: The Franciscan Institute.

———. 1974. Summa logicae. In *Guillelmi de Ockham opera philosophica*, ed. P. Boehner, G. Gal, and S. Brown, vol. I. St. Bonaventure: The Franciscan Institute.

———. 1978a. Expositio in librum Praedicamentorum Aristotelis. In *Guillelmi de Ockham opera philosophica*, ed. G. Gal, vol. II, 133–339. St. Bonaventure: The Franciscan Institute.

———. 1978b. Expositio in librum Perihermeneias Aristotelis. In *Guillelmi de Ockham opera philosophica*, ed. A. Gambatese and S. Brown, vol. II, 341–504. St. Bonaventure: The Franciscan Institute.

———. 1980. Quodlibeta septem. In *Guillelmi de Ockham opera theologica*, ed. J.C. Wey, vol. IX. St. Bonaventure: The Franciscan Institute.

———. 1985. Expositio in libros Physicorum Aristotelis. In *Guillelmi de Ockham opera philosophica*, vols. IV–V, ed. V. Richter et al. St. Bonaventure: The Franciscan Institute.

Panaccio, Claude. 1995. La philosophie du langage de Guillaume d'Occam. In Ebbesen 1995, 184–206.

———. 1999a. *Le discours intérieur: De Platon à Guillaume d'Ockham*. Paris: Éditions du Seuil.

———. 1999b. Semantics and mental language. In Spade 1999, 53–75.

———. 2004. *Ockham on concepts*. Aldershot: Ashgate.

———. 2010. Intuition and causality: Ockham's externalism revisited. *Quaestio* 10 (*Later medieval perspectives on intentionality*, ed. F. Amerini): 241–253.

———. 2011. Concepts as similitudes in William of Ockham's nominalism. In Klima and Hall 2011, 25–32.

———. 2015. Ockham's externalism. In *Klima* 2015b, 166–185.

———. 2017. *Mental language: From Plato to William of Ockham*. (Trans. J. P. Hochschild and M. K. Ziebart). New York: Fordham University Press (transl. of Panaccio 1999a).

Priscian. 1855. *Institutiones grammaticae*, ed. M. Hertz. Leipzig: Teubner.

Schierbaum, Sonja. 2014. *Ockham's assumption of mental speech: Thinking in a world of particulars*. Leiden: Brill.

Spade, Paul V., ed. 1999. *The Cambridge companion to Ockham*. Cambridge: Cambridge University Press.

Weijers, Olga, and Louis Holtz, eds. 1997. *L'enseignement des disciplines à la faculté des arts (Paris et Oxford, xiiie-xve siècles)*. Turnhout: Brepols.

Wey, Joseph. 1980. Introduction. In Ockham 1980, 7*–41*.

Chapter 13
Thoughts About Things: Aquinas, Buridan and Late Medieval Nominalism

Calvin G. Normore

Keywords Nominalism · Realism · Aquinas · Buridan · Universals

For more than a quarter century Gyula Klima has argued that the focus of the disagreements between those who were in the later Middle Ages termed Nominalists and those then called Realists has been, at least to some considerable extent, misunderstood. Whereas it has often been thought to lie in opposed semantic theories and in whether it is words or things that are classified by Aristotle's categories, Prof. Klima suggests it may lie instead in issues in epistemology and philosophy of mind. Taking John Buridan as his representative Nominalist and Thomas Aquinas as his representative Realist, he has argued that on the one hand, their semantic principles, though different, do not commit them to different ontologies, and on the other hand, there are issues in epistemology and philosophy of mind which separate them more decisively and lie nearer the root of the ongoing debates between their followers.

Whether or not the labels "Nominalism" and "Realism" are useful in contemporary philosophy, they were, throughout much of the Middle Ages, actors' categories, and it behooves historians of philosophy to attempt to discover what those actors meant by them. This project is a little different from that of attempting to discover what more recent scholars have thought they meant.[1] It is also a little different from that of attempting to discover what the *Wegestreit* was about or who were the *antiqui*, *moderni* or *termnistae*. It may turn out that medieval thinkers used some of these descriptors interchangeably or applied them to the same figures, but all of that is

---

[1] For a wonderfully helpful account of the latter see Courtenay 1991, reprinted as chapter 1 of Courtenay 2008.

C. G. Normore (✉)
University of California Los Angeles, Los Angeles, CA, USA
e-mail: normore@humnet.ucla.edu

© The Author(s), under exclusive license to Springer Nature
Switzerland AG 2023
J. P. Hochschild et al. (eds.), *Metaphysics Through Semantics: The Philosophical Recovery of the Medieval Mind*, International Archives of the History of Ideas Archives internationales d'histoire des idées 242,
https://doi.org/10.1007/978-3-031-15026-5_13

something we need to establish, not to assume. Of course, medieval thinkers may have simply used "*Nominales*" and "*Reales*" and their cognates as terms of identification or abuse, much as "conservative" and "liberal" are used in many contemporary political discussions but, like Prof. Klima, I think it a good working hypothesis that there was more to it than that.

13.1   History?

"*Nominales*" and "*Reales*" as labels for groups of thinkers are both twelfth-century terms. Though not entirely forgotten in the thirteenth century, they do not seem to be applied by thirteenth- and early fourteenth-century thinkers to themselves or their contemporaries, and it seems to be late in the fourteenth before they begin again to be widely used and retrofitted to thirteenth- and earlier fourteenth-century thinkers.[2]

The twelfth-century *Nominales* seem to have been a distinctive school, and various schools identified, for example, by their literal founders—the *Porretani*, students/followers of Gilbert of Poitiers; the *Robertini/Melidunensis*, students/followers of Robert of Melun; the *Parvipontani*, students/followers of Adam of Balsham; etc.—are identified as *Reales* by their differences from the *Nominales*. As far as I have been able to determine, this pattern continued throughout the Middle Ages.[3] By the sixteenth century there was a canonical family tree of Nominalist masters with whom contemporary masters identified. Again, there seem to have been several "schools" of Realists so grouped by their differences from the Nominalists, though this time identified not with particular teachers but with thirteenth- and early fourteenth-century authorities—Albertists, followers of Albertus Magnus; *Formalizantes*, presumably inspired by Duns Scotus, and *Thomistae*. By

---

[2] What are apparently the last references to the twelfth-century *Nominales* as an extant school are found in a text of Jacques de Vitry reprinted as text 53 in Iwakuma and Ebbesen 1992, 202. This text was originally brought to my attention by Professor Christopher J. Martin.

[3] I do not know who were the earliest post-twelfth-century medieval thinkers to be called "*Nominales*" or "*Nominalistae*" by themselves or their contemporaries. What is clear is that by even as early as 1340 there are references to *Ockhamistae*, by 1400 some were being called *Nominales*, and by 1474 some not yet precisely identified soi-disant Parisian *Nominales*, replying to an edict of the French king seizing their books and outlawing the teaching of the *renovatores* who inspired them, were claiming Ockham as a founding father. They did not exactly claim Buridan (who is mentioned by name in the king's edict but not in the reply), but they did not seek to distance themselves from him either, and in the first quarter of the fifteenth century we find references to the "*via Buridana*" and the "*seculum Buridanuum*."

sometime in the fifteenth century, John Buridan is indeed taken to be a Nominalist and Thomas Aquinas to be a Realist.[4]

Although it would be nigh impossible to overestimate the importance of Buridan to late medieval Nominalism, and although he may be in many ways typical, it is William Ockham who is the stormy petrel of the movement. Unlike Buridan, who seems to have avoided institutional trouble, the Venerable Inceptor was accused of heresy and later excommunicated (though for his political activity not for his larger philosophical and theological views), and his works were the subject of a number of censures both in his lifetime and after. Where he and Buridan disagree, it is almost always the case that those later called Realists would find Buridan's view more congenial than Ockham's. Near where he and Buridan agree we can plausibly assume lies the doctrinal center of the Nominalist movement.

To find the doctrinal center of late medieval Realism is more difficult. Even today Aquinas's Realism is often qualified as merely "moderate." To find someone who occupies a position among the Realists analogous to that of Ockham or Buridan among Nominalists may well be impossible. Ockham's contemporary Walter Burley was and is often thought to be an "extreme" Realist, and certainly does occupy positions extremely different from Ockham (and Buridan) on many issues. John Wyclif was a self-proclaimed Realist, a figure even more controversial than Ockham, and one who had significant followers. Neither of these, however, is claimed by fifteenth- or sixteenth-century *Reales* as a founder or a teacher. They instead look back to such earlier thinkers as Albertus the Great, Aquinas and Duns Scotus, and interpret their views in ways they find congenial. If, as seems the case, the *Reales* are unified in both medieval and later tradition more by their opposition to the *Nominales* than by any common doctrine, finding a truly representative Realist may be a mug's game. Still the *Thomistae* are early counted among the *Reales*, so Prof. Klima's choice of Aquinas is eminently reasonable.

If Aquinas is a Realist and Buridan a Nominalist, what then of the suggestion that it is less in semantics than in epistemology and philosophy of mind that the central disagreements between them lie?

13.2 Semantics

First then, how do their semantics differ? At the core of the conceptual vocabulary of medieval semantics is *significatio*, the term used to express the relation a sign has to its significates, that or those of which it is a sign. As Paul Spade in particular has stressed (Spade 1982), for most theorists the signification of a term was what was

---

[4] Here we are all indebted to the extensive work of Zenon Kaluza and in particular to Klauza 1988. Several scholars, including Prof. Klima, have pointed out that we can see battle lines drawn, for example, in the 1473 edict of Louis XI forbidding the teaching of the followers of these "*Nominales*" and contrasting the teaching of these *doctores reales*. See Normore 2017a, b and the references therein.

understood or brought to mind by that term. This has the consequence that for such theorists many terms do not signify the various things of which they might be predicated since typically most (and possibly even all) of those things would not be brought to mind by using them. For example, the term "human" (*homo*) applies to you and me but, unless we know each other (and likely not even then), it is not you and me as such who come to mind for either of us when we hear the term. The most common account was that what is brought to mind in that case was "humanity" or "human nature." When they are the subject (and later, among some, either the subject or predicate) in a declarative sentence, signs also have *suppositio*, and it is this property, not signification, that enters directly into the truth conditions of declarative sentences. Commonly there was thought to be various kinds of *supposition*, one of which was privileged in that a subject term (or among some theorists, both a subject and predicate term) which had it *supposited* or "stood for" what it signified, while in other kinds of supposition it might stand for itself or some other items. A third concept complexly related to these two is *appellatio*. Its history is complex and still not well understood. Its etymology suggests that a term *appellates* what can be "called" using it. Buridan often uses it and *connotatio* interchangeably for cases when a term "calls" or "suggests" or secondarily signifies items in the ontology that it does not properly signify and for which it cannot supposit. For example, "bipeds" connotes feet but does not supposit for feet, since it is animals and not feet that can be truly "called" bipeds.

Throughout the Middle Ages the basic items in any ontology were forms, matter(s) and substances. Thus, it was natural for terms to be taken to signify these. However, in *De interpretatione*, Aristotle, in Boethius's translation, had suggested that words signified *passiones animae*, which themselves signified items of the ontology. As far as I can tell, for proper names this difference was typically ignored, but for general terms it became a central issue. Ockham and some who followed him bypassed the issue, maintaining that, although which items a general term signified was determined by the *passio animae* to which it was (in his terminology) subordinated, it did not signify the *passio animae* but rather the same items that that signified. On the other hand, Buridan and others insisted that general terms (primarily) did signify such *passiones* though they also (ultimately) signified what those *passiones animae* signified. What such a theorist thought a *passio animae* to be might then have consequences for what a term signified.

Two other distinctions central to the discussion below are that between *absolute* and *connotative* terms and that between *abstract* and *concrete* terms. The distinction between abstract and concrete terms comes from the grammatical tradition. Exactly how it is to be drawn seems never to have been entirely clear. As Ockham has it, concrete terms such as "just" and "strong" typically can function as adjectives, as in "strong Socrates," and can be predicate adjectives, as in "Socrates is strong."

They cannot typically appear alone as subject terms in categorical sentences.[5] Abstract terms such as "justice" and "strength," on the other hand, are typically nouns, and not only can be subjects of categorical sentences, but typically cannot be predicated of individual substances like Socrates. Socrates may be just but not justice, and strong but not strength. The distinction between absolute and connotative or appellative terms, on the other hand, seems to have arisen among logicians and perhaps from efforts to interpret Aristotle's remarks about paronymy at the beginning of the *Categories*. A connotative term connotes (or appellates) items for which it does not supposit; an absolute term does not.

It would seem that an abstract term and the corresponding concrete term are typically not synonyms. How then are their significata related? Here Ockham takes a radical position. He notes that in an abstract concrete pair, sometimes one will signify a quality possessed by those things signified by the other, sometimes one will signify parts of each thing signified by the other, and sometimes one will signify things related to those signified by the other in one of a myriad of ways—as cause to effect, sign to signified, etc. He insists, however, that when none of these applies, the pair are synonyms in the sense that they signify the very same things in the same ways. He is thus able to conclude that no term, abstract or concrete, need signify anything other than one or more substances, qualities, or parts of substances or qualities.

Buridan's ontology is more inclusive than Ockham's but his picture of the relation between abstract and concrete terms is very similar. As he writes:

> on the part of the intention it is required that the concrete term should have appellation, that is, that it should appellate, or connote, some external disposition besides what it supposits for. Therefore, even if there were some derivation in the formation of the utterance, as [there is] in the case of 'man' [deriving] from 'manhood',[6] [or] of 'God' [deriving] from 'godhead', [or] of 'existent' [deriving] from 'existence', and so on in many other cases, still, nothing can be predicated denominatively here;[7] and this is what is noted by the above description when it says 'have appellation'. (Buridan 2001, 132–133)

Like Ockham, Buridan admits that there are some cases in which pairs of abstract and concrete terms co-predicate: He writes:

> Furthermore, we should note that in many cases an abstract connotative term is predicated of the subject just as truly as the concrete term; so that, for example, matter is not only deprived but is also a privation, and a magnitude is not only shaped [in some way], but is also a shape. Whence the question arises as to whether a predication such as 'Matter is privation' or 'A magnitude is a shape' is denominative.

---

[5] The situation with concrete terms is somewhat more complex than I here let on. The neuter form of at least some Latin adjectives, for example *album* (pale/white), is frequently used alone as a noun where in English it would now be customary to supply a "dummy" noun such as "one" or "thing." Thus "*currens est album*," which has the participle "*currens*" as subject and the neuter adjective as predicate, might well be translated as "Some runner (or running thing) is a pale thing."

[6] In the sense of "humanity" or "human nature," as this term would serve as the abstract counterpart of the term "man," differing from it only in *casus*, as is the case with *homo* and *humanitas* in Latin.

[7] Because, in Buridan's view, these terms are absolute terms, lacking any extrinsic connotation, whence they cannot have appellation, and thus cannot be predicated denominatively either.

> To this I reply that such a predication is denominative from the point of view of intention, but is not denominative properly speaking, for the requirement on the part of the utterance is not satisfied. Therefore it is not a proper locution, although it is a true predication, when it is said that matter is privation, or that a magnitude is a shape, or that an action is a passion, or that time is motion or that a blind [man] is a blindness. (Buridan 2001, 133)

Buridan insists that in typical sentences, a term supposits for what it ultimately signifies. Thus, for both when the pair of an abstract and concrete term are synonyms, either both are absolute or neither is, and Buridan makes clear what Ockham does not—that not all abstract terms are absolute and not all concrete terms are connotative.

None of this is news to Prof. Klima, who has done more than anyone else to make Buridan's semantic views clear. What, though, of Aquinas? Prof. Klima suggests that Aquinas's semantics can be characterized, at a certain level of abstraction, by four principles. In "Buridan's Logic and the Ontology of Modes," he puts these principles this way:

1. Concrete as well as abstract common terms signify ultimately whatever their concepts represent as their formal objects. I shall call what they ultimately signify their *significata*.
2. As the subject of a proposition, a common term supposits *personally* for (i.e., refers to) whatever is in actuality in respect of its *significata* (relative to the time and modality of the copula of the proposition, taking into account the possible ampliative force of the propositional context). What is thus supposited for by a term in the context of a proposition I shall briefly call here the term's *supposita*.
3. On account of their different mode of signifying (*modus significandi*), the *supposita* of abstract terms are the same as their *significata*, whereas the *supposita* of concrete terms may or may not be the same as their *significata*. In any case, the *supposita* (and hence also the *significata*) of abstract terms are always the same as the *significata* of their concrete counterparts. So, this semantic principle specifies only that the *significata* and *supposita* of abstract terms are the same, and that they are the same as the *significata* of their concrete counterpart, but it leaves open the question whether the *supposita* of a concrete term are the same as its *significata*...
4. An affirmative categorical proposition is true if and only if the *supposita* of its subject are actual in respect of the *significata* of its predicate (relative to the time and modality of the copula, taking into account the possible ampliative force of the propositional context) as determined by the quantity of the proposition. (This, of course, is just a general formulation of the familiar *inherence theory of predication*.) (Klima 1999, 476–478)

If we focus on personal supposition, as Prof. Klima does here, I see no reason why Buridan could not accept Principle 2. On his view, the personal supposita of a term are always among its ultimate significata and, since affirmative sentences have existential import, the personal supposita of a term are those of its significata that are actual. Principle 4 might give him pause, but if we understand supposita of the subject being "actual in respect of the significata of the predicate" as "the predicate suppositing for what the subject supposits for," then he could perhaps accept it. This is an issue to which I shall return below.

Principle 1 raises a particularly tricky issue. I have myself argued that Ockham thinks the concepts to which absolute terms are subordinated are produced by a process of abstraction from what he calls intuitive cognitions, and signify both what did produce them and whatever would have produced them if suitably situated (Normore 2011). I have gone on to suggest that there need be nothing intrinsic to the concept which would enable even an angel examining it to tell what it signified, and that it may well be that Ockham is committed to thinking that, although our thought is indeed about the world, we may be in no position to tell what descriptions best correspond to our absolute terms (Normore 2017a, b). On the other hand, Prof. Klima (e.g. Klima 2011a, b) agrees with Claude Panaccio (2004, 2011) that for Ockham and Buridan, the mental qualities (their interpretations of Aristotle's *passiones animae*) are intrinsically representational. From this Prof. Klima draws the conclusion that both Ockham and Buridan are committed to the signification of a general term being determined by what it intrinsically represents—and hence to Principle 1. This, however, is problematic, as Pannacio has argued.

Panaccio notes that both Ockham and Buridan have it that in the normal case a general mental term such as that picked out by "nuthatch" is indeed the causal product of an encounter with one or more objects in the world, and while he maintains that such a term is a *similitudo* of those objects which would ordinarily suffice to identify them, Panaccio admits that there could be a deviant causal chain which produced a mental term which would lead a thinker to, say, misidentify an arctic tern as a nuthatch. As he puts it with respect to Ockham:

> ...although intentional similitude is what opens the way for generality in representation, it does not adequately determine by itself the extension of our simple substance concepts. The extension of such concepts in Ockham's framework should contain only individuals which really belong to the same species as one another, individuals, that is, which have basically equivalent causal powers. (Panaccio 2004, 29)

I suggest Buridan has the same view. If Panaccio is right (and a fortiori if I am right), no intrinsic representational feature of a mental quality can, by itself, be sufficient necessarily to determine either the signification of that quality or the signification of a general term subordinated to (or, in Buridan's terminology, primarily signifying) it, and hence Ockham and Buridan cannot accept Principle 1. On the other hand, as Prof. Klima sees it, Ockham and Buridan are committed to the signification of a general term being fixed solely by its intrinsic features, and, since they also maintain that any created thing can exist without any other, are committed to the possibility that none of our general terms signify anything that exists.

As Prof. Klima has long urged (e.g. Klima 2013), it seems that Aquinas can maintain that the signification of a general term is fixed by its intrinsic features without this consequence. Aquinas can do so because, in some central cases at least, namely those where we have a quidditative concept, what is in the soul is, in some sense of "same" (*idem*), the very same as what it signifies. When this is the case there can be no mismatch between what is formally represented and what is signi-fied (since there can be no mismatch between an item and itself).

The restriction to central cases is needed. As Elizabeth Karger and E. J. Ashworth noted, Ockham maintains that one can subordinate a general term to a concept which one does not have but someone else does (as in, "by 'Fermium' I signify whichever substance the community of physicists has so named"). This is an extreme case of a familiar phenomenon: the incomplete possession of a concept. If, as Panaccio and I both would have it for Ockham, and as I at least suggest for Buridan, there are cases in which the causal chain leading from a thing to a general term trumps any intrinsic similarity the term might have, then Ockham and Buridan can account for mistaken identification easily enough. Aquinas may have a more difficult time. Whether he does depends in part upon how he understands the pro-cess which leads to the presence in the soul of the forms of what is in the world. That is a notoriously controversial issue in Aquinas interpretation, which I hope we need not settle here. What is crucial is that for Aquinas there are some cases at least in which the very same form found in a significatum of a term is also present in the soul as the content of the signifying *passio animae*, while for Ockham and Buridan the signifying concept and its significata are distinct things and either could exist without the other ever having existed.

If the foregoing is right, then Klima has put his finger on a crucial difference between our paradigmatic Nominalists and their opponents. Either, as Panaccio and I think, Ockham and Buridan deny that the intrinsic features of a concept necessar-ily suffice to fix its signification, in which case I claim we have no guarantee that we can describe what we are talking about; or, as Prof. Klima claims, they maintain that the intrinsic features of the concept do necessarily fix the signification, in which case, having granted that any creature can exist without any other, they cannot guar-antee that there is any case in which we can be certain that there is what we think there is. Aquinas, on the other hand, maintaining that what is in the soul is in some sense what it signifies, can both insist that we have access to what we are thinking about and that we can be certain, in central cases at least, that it existed.

Demon issues aside, Buridan's attitude to Principle 1 raises a central issue for his semantics. If the ultimate signification of a term is not determined by the intrinsic character of the concept to which it is subordinated, then why the emphasis on similitude, and what makes it also a concept anyway?

As Prof. Klima notes, Buridan describes concepts both as mental qualities and as similitudes. How are these related? One thought would be that they are related as vehicle and content. On this account, a concept is akin to a picture, which may have literally some of the properties shared by what it is a picture of but also lacks many. A picture may have the "same" color as a house but you can't walk inside it. In ordinary terms, it is less similar to a house than to another picture—but it is "of" the house and not the other picture. Why? The "content" account has it that there is a different sort of similarity at issue, one captured, perhaps metaphorically, by the thought that it "contains" the house "objectively" or "intentionally." On this view, the features of the significates are found in the concepts but in a different way from that in which they are found in the significates.

A second thought is Claude Panaccio's—that a concept has intrinsic features which, while not those of what it signifies, enable the recovery of them. Panaccio illustrates the view by pointing to the way in which the shape of a baseball glove or the cupping of a hand shows the shape of a ball caught. On this view, while the features of the significate are not found in the concept, there are found in the concept features which are not simply contingently related to those of the significate. It is not a contingent fact that to hold a convex ball a glove needs to have a concave shape.

Yet a third thought is that the features a concept has, it has because it is caused by what it signifies. On this picture, there may be no necessary connection between the features of the concept and those of the significate, but if causes of a given sort do in fact regularly produce effects of a certain sort, one can regularly though contingently infer to the cause from the effect: where there is smoke there is fire.

As far as I have been able to tell, Buridan's text underdetermines which picture of similitude he has. That he holds the first is implausible given that he does not speak as Auriol and Scotus do of objective being, or as Aquinas does of intentional or spiritual being, or even as the youthful Ockham did of fictive being. Perhaps he holds the second—though what features of a mental act could be intrinsically and necessarily connected with those of a horse or a house is a puzzle. The advantage of the third is that it does not require us to solve that puzzle. It is, moreover, explicitly endorsed by at least one theorist of Buridan's generation very frequently numbered in the fifteenth and sixteenth centuries among Nominalists: Robert Holkot. Holkot writes:

> I do not posit that the species is a natural similitude of the thing of which it brings about cognition, such that in an angel the similitude of a stone would be a stone. But I do posit a quality causative of a cognition of a stone when the stone is not present. For that reason it is called 'representative' [representativa] of the stone, or a likeness [similitudo] of the stone, or its species, and the same thing can be called a 'habit' because it facilitates or inclines the intellect toward the abstractive cognition of the stone.[8]

If Buridan agrees with Holkot here, then this would explain his use of *representativa* and of *similitudo* without saddling him with anything more in his ontology than that to which we have other reasons to think him committed.

So far we have seen how a difference in account of concept formation could, as Prof. Klima suggests, play a significant role in the disputes between Nominalists and Realists. What, though, of the claim centrally embodied in Principle 3 that Aquinas's semantics need not commit him to an ontology any more expansive than Buridan's? If we count Aquinas as a Realist and Buridan as a Nominalist, this would suggest that from the very beginning of the late medieval self-identification of these movements the terrain between them has been muddied.

As Prof. Klima and others have noted, among the early soi-disant fifteenth-century Nominalists who claimed fourteenth-century figures as ancestors were, apparently, the group at the University of Paris in the 1470s who authored a response

---

[8] Robert Holkot, II *Sent.*, q. 3 (Oriel fol. 159ra), quoted and translated in Tachau 1988, 249.

to an edict of the French king forbidding Nominalists from teaching. They characterize their teaching and their differences with certain "*Reales*" this way:

> [T]hose *doctores* were called *nominales* who do not multiply things designated in the first instance by terms as the terms are multiplied. But they are *reales* who, by contrast, contend that things are multiplied as terms are multiplied...

> Also: those were called *nominales* who zealously tried to understand all the properties of terms on which the truth and falsity of speech depend and without which one cannot make a complete judgment about the truth and falsity of propositions...

> *Reales* disregard all these, however, and disparage them, saying we go to things, and we don't care about terms. (Thorndike 1944, 355–356)

Some scholars see this as merely part of a polemic designed to denigrate the *Reales* and perhaps not even intended to capture truth, but these Nominalists trace their ancestry to Ockham, and as Prof. Klima noted long ago, their response echoes a criticism Ockham had made a century and a half century earlier (Ockham 1974, Pars I, c. 51, l. 240–247); prima facie, then, we should take it seriously as part of the self-conception of the Nominalists and of their views of their opponents. It appears that as they see it, issues of semantics and ontology do separate them. Since even issues about the extra-mental reality of universals can be seen as special cases of the more general debate about to what our semantics commits us, if, indeed, the differences between Aquinas's semantics and Buridan's need have no ontological significance, it is a striking result.

I suggested above that for Ockham and Buridan the distinction between abstract and concrete terms, though grammatically significant, is nearly orthogonal to the semantic distinction between absolute and connotative/appellative terms. A consequence of this is that for them, while a sentence like "Fido is a caninity" is grammatically deviant, it is true.[9] So, for that matter, is "A caninity barked at me yesterday." For Ockham and Buridan, these sentences, which involve only absolute terms, need commit only to individual dogs. If we turn to sentences involving connotative terms, things are different. There are two sorts of case. One is that in which the abstract term picks out real accidents. Both Ockham and Buridan take it that there are individual color qualities and that abstract terms like "*albedo*" (whiteness) are absolute terms signifying (and, when used personally, suppositing for) them. Thus, in a fusion of Latin and English that Terence Parsons (2014) might call "Linguish*," "An albedo is on my wall" might be true. The corresponding concrete terms, however, are connotative—they signify that of which they can be truly predicated and connote the quality instances in virtue of which that is so. Thus, "My wall is album" would be a true Linguish* sentence committing only to walls and individual color qualities. When we turn to cases in which Buridan or Ockham thinks there are no such real accidents, the abstract term is itself connotative. Thus, in Buridan's example "*Magnitudo est figura*," the term "*Magnitudo*" supposits for

---

[9] "Socrates is a humanity" would be a more intuitive example except for complications induced by the Incarnation.

magnitudes (to which Buridan is committed) and "*figura*" supposits also for magnitudes but connotes their parts (which are also magnitudes) and that they are arranged. In "*Magnitudo est figuratum*," the term "*figuratum*" signifies in exactly the same way. What is crucial here is that the abstract term commits to no more than does the concrete term.

If we turn to Aquinas as I take Prof. Klima to understand him, the situation is subtly different. Ockham and Buridan take the subject and predicate terms of a categorical sentence to be of the same semantic category, that of names (*nomina*), and adhere to what has become known as the "two-name" theory of predication. On their accounts, for example, a categorical universal sentence such as "All humans are bipeds" is true iff the items supposited or stood for by "humans" are all among those supposited or stood for by "bipeds." On the other hand, developing a line of thought pioneered by Peter Geach (1955), Klima sees Aquinas as recognizing a semantic difference between the behavior of subject and predicate terms, and (usually) subscribing to what has been termed the "inherence" theory of predication. As Prof. Klima notes:

> according to the inherence theory the function of the predicate is to signify particular forms, **inhering** in their subjects, and what makes a predication true is the actual inherence (inesse) of the form signified by the predicate in the thing supposited for by the subject. So, e.g., the proposition 'Socrates is white' is true, if and only if the whiteness of Socrates exists, or, the same expressed in the 'material mode of speech', Socrates is white by his whiteness. (Klima 1988, 24)

One might think that this picture builds in precisely the multiplication of entities of which the 1474 *Nominales* complain, but Prof. Klima argues that even if the forms this technique requires may be beings in some sense, they need not be beings over and above the substances they inhere in, so they do not *multiply* things after all.

To see why, consider the current Prime Minister of Canada, Justin Trudeau. Suppose Justin is just. On the inherence theory of predication, this is because a justice inheres in him. Which justice? Justin's justice. Thus, a necessary condition for Justin to be just is that Justin's justice exists. Is it a sufficient condition? Suppose it is; that what it is for Justin's justice to exist is precisely for him to be just, and in general whenever neither the faith nor physics requires otherwise, the existence of Y's x-ness is both necessary and sufficient for y to be x.[10] It would seem then that on the inherence theory, for an abstract term (Justin's justice) to signify, nothing more is required than for a sentence such as "Justin is just" to be true, and since the

---

[10] The proviso that neither the faith nor physics requires otherwise is necessary, of course. Neither Ockham nor Buridan would have thought that if Justin's justice were a being different from Justin, its existence would be sufficient for Justin's being just. Both thought that, for example God could bring it about that a whiteness existed without anything being white. Ockham thought that this is what would happen if a piece of bread made from bleached flour were transubstantiated as in the Eucharist. Aquinas's view in this case is more complicated, but he does seem to have thought that the bread's whiteness could exist without the bread—though perhaps not without the bread's quantity—which itself could exist without it.

truth of that sentence requires nothing more than that "Justin" and "just" supposit for Justin, then "Justin's justice" commits one to nothing more either.

So far, then, it would seem that Aquinas could be as ontologically parsimonious as Buridan. Since, for example, it seems very implausible that a relation could exist without its relata, we have as yet no pressure to conclude that a relation is a thing different from its relata taken together. Buridan so concludes and so far we have no reason why Aquinas could not agree.

But trouble looms. Prof. Klima attributes to Aquinas the general strategy of admitting that where Y is a substance and x-ness a property truly attributable to Y, Y's x-ness exists, while also claiming that if Y's x-ness exists iff Y is x (where x is the concrete term corresponding to x-ness), then Y's x-ness is not a thing distinct from Y. Abstracting still further, for x-ness as such to exist in such a case is for there to be something such that it is x, hence there is no thing, x-ness, apart from its instances. As Prof. Klima notes, this strategy invites the objection that if, say, Justin's justice is not distinct from Justin, then it is Justin, and since it cannot exist without Justin existing, Justin is necessarily just, but of course Justin could become unjust while continuing to exist, so if Justin's justice is anything, it must be something distinct from Justin.

Klima's response to this objection is to suggest that Justin's justice is Justin but is only contingently so. Thus, where Buridan would have it that a typical abstract term in one of the accidental categories is a name for one or more substances, qualities or quantities, and carries no further ontological commitment, Aquinas would have it that it names an accident that is contingently but not necessarily identical with the substance in which it inheres and that is incapable of existing apart from it.

At first glance these would seem equivalent strategies. Consider an analogy. As I write, Justin Trudeau is the Prime Minister of Canada. Are there here two things, Justin Trudeau and the Prime Minister, which are contingently identical, or is there one thing picked out on the one hand by a rigid designator ("Justin Trudeau"), and on the other by a definite description ("the Prime Minister of Canada")? If we choose the first alternative, are there more things than if we choose the second? If so, when are there more? Not right now: since Justin Trudeau is (contingently) the very same thing as the Prime Minister of Canada, we should not count two. Not before Justin Trudeau was the Prime Minister, or after he ceases to be the Prime minister, since then either there will not be a Prime Minister or someone else will be—and that person and the Prime Minister are not two.

I suggest, however, that this first glance is deceptive. Consider Justin's justice, JJ and Justin's current mass, JM. Grant that JJ exists iff Justin is just and that JM exists just in case Justin so masses. Suppose that each is contingently identical with Justin. Are they then currently identical with each other? What are we to make of the following argument?

$$JJ =_c Justin$$
$$Justin =_c JM$$
$$JJ =_c JM$$

If we accept the argument, it seems we should be able to substitute any one of these terms for any other in extensional contexts, as we can "Justin Trudeau" and "the Prime Minister of Canada." But this leads to some very odd results. That Andre the Giant's mass is greater than Justin's is true, but that Andre the Giant's mass is greater than Justin's justice may not even make sense. Justin's justice may weigh heavily upon him, but surely that is a metaphor!

Suppose, then, that we do not accept the argument. After all, there is some controversy about whether contingent identity is transitive. It would seem in that case that we have to admit that there may be perfectly ordinary extensional contexts in which a predicate applies to, say, JJ but not to JM—one of them is less than Andre the Giant's mass and the other is not. But in that case, it seems we are fully justified in counting JJ and JM as two, and so have multiplied entities after all. Of course, these entities may not be able to exist apart from others and, depending on to what one thinks counting commits one, they may not be beings in the same sense that substances are, but they are not just different ways of talking about those substances either!

Do Ockham and Buridan fare any better? On their pictures there are only substances, qualities, and for Buridan but not Ockham, quantities. The abstract terms in those categories are absolute terms, and they are willing to swallow hard and admit that their particularized forms can be substituted for each other (and indeed for the corresponding concrete terms *salva veritate*). If Justin is driving a Ford then Justin's humanity is driving a Ford and so is his animality. Abstract terms in the other categories, on the other hand, are connotative terms and, I suggest, Ockham and Buridan share the program of supplying nominal definitions for them, and so showing that what they connote is already accounted for by the absolute terms in the categories in which abstract terms are absolute. If this is right, then in the mental language that they both posit, there are no such abstract terms and the spoken and written sentences containing them should be expounded.

13.3   Conclusion

In "The Tradition of Medieval Nominalism," I suggested that a unifying thread running through the Nominalist tradition was that there were more truths than truthmakers. Put even more grandly, it would be that the structures of language and thought are not even approximately isomorphic with the structure of the world. If Prof. Klima is right, Aquinas too (and perhaps many others in the Realist tradition) could happily agree that the world may be rather different from our conceptions of it, but they would have to insist both that there are at least as many kinds of thing (or perhaps as many ways of being a thing) as we have fundamental ways of conceiving, and that our grip on our ways of conceiving could not be fundamentally mistaken.

If that is so, then Buridan and Aquinas may still be further apart in semantics and in epistemology than Prof. Klima has suggested, but closer together than I (and perhaps the Nominalists of 1474) have thought. I am deeply grateful to Prof. Klima for showing me that!

Bibliography

Boyard, C., and R. Keele, eds. 2013. *Later medieval metaphysics: Ontology, language and logic*. New York: Fordham University Press.

Buridan, John. 2001. *Summulae de Dialectica*. An annotated translation, with a philosophical introduction by Gyula Klima. New Haven: Yale University Press.

Courtenay, W.J. 1991. In search of nominalism: Two centuries of historical debate. In *Gli studi di filosofia medievale tra otto e Novecento: Contributo a un bilancio storiografico*, ed. A. Maierù and R. Imbach, 214–233. Rome: Edizioni di Storia e Letteratura.

———. 2008. *Ockham and Ockhamism*. Leiden: Brill.

Ebbesen, S., and R. Friedman, eds. 1999. *Medieval analyses in language and cognition*. Copenhagen: The Royal Danish Academy of Sciences and Letters.

Geach, P. 1955. Form and existence. *Proceedings of the Aristotelian Society* 55: 251–272.

Iwakuma, Y., and S. Ebbesen. 1992. Logico-theological schools from the second half of the 12th century, a list of sources. *Vivarium* 30: 173–210.

Kaluza, Z. 1988. *Les querelles doctrinales á Paris: Nominalistes et réalistes aux confins du XIVe et du XVe siècles*. Bergamo: P. Lubrima.

Klima, G. 1988. *Ars artium essays in philosophical semantics, mediaeval and modern*. Institute of Philosophy, Hungarian Academy of Sciences.

———. 1999. Buridan's logic and the ontology of modes. In Ebbesen and Friedman 1999, 473–495.

———. 2011a. Demon skepticism and concept identity in a nominalist vs. a realist framework. In Klima and Hall 2011a, 83–94.

———. 2011b. Demon skepticism and non-veridical concepts. In Klima and Hall 2011b, 117–126.

———. 2013. Aquinas vs. Buridan on essence and existence. In Bolyard and Keele 2013, 30–44.

Klima, G., and A. Hall, eds. 2011. *The demonic temptations of medieval nominalism*. Newcastle Upon Tyne: Cambridge Scholars Publishing.

Kretzmann, N., et al., eds. 1982. *The Cambridge history of later medieval philosophy*. Cambridge: Cambridge University Press.

Lagerlund, H., and B. Hill, eds. 2017. *The Routledge companion to sixteenth century philosophy*. Leiden: Brill.

Normore, C.G. 1987. The tradition of medieval nominalism. In Wippel 1987, 201–217.

———. 2011. Externalism, singular thought and nominalist ontology. In Klima and Hall 2011, 137–147.

———. 2017a. Nominalism in the sixteenth century. In Lagerlund and Hill 2017a, 121–136.

———. 2017b. Likeness stories. In Pelletier and Roques 2017b, 81–94.

Ockham, William. 1974. *Summa logicae, opera philosophica*, ed. P. Boehner, vol. 1. St. Bonaventure: The Franciscan Institute.

Panaccio, C. 2004. *Ockham on concepts*. Aldershot: Ashgate.

———. 2011. Late medieval nominalism and non-veridical concepts. In Klima and Hall 2011, 95–116.

Parsons, T. 2014. *Articulating medieval logic*. Oxford: Oxford University Press.

Pelletier, J., and M. Roques, eds. 2017. *The language of thought in later medieval philosophy*. Berlin: Springer.

Spade, P.V. 1982. The semantics of terms. In Kretzmann et al. 1982, 188–196.

Tachau, K. 1988. *Vision and certitude in the age of Ockham*. Leiden: Brill.

Thorndike, L. 1944. *University records and life in the middle ages*. New York: Columbia University Press.

Wippel, J., ed. 1987. *Studies in medieval philosophy*. Washington, D.C.: The Catholic University of America Press.

Chapter 14
Buridan's Reinterpretation of Natural Possibility and Necessity

Guido Alt

Keywords John Buridan · Natural necessity · Varieties of modality · Medieval modalities

John Buridan has provided different analyses of modal concepts in diverse contexts of his writings. As a logician, Buridan developed a theory of modal consequence and of modal syllogistics based on the semantics of ampliated sentences. It has been frequently argued that his framework approaches an understanding of modality as a form of generality tractable in the framework of possible worlds semantics (e.g., see Johnston 2021). As an interpreter of Aristotelian natural philosophy, Buridan used alternative descriptions of necessity and contingency the intended domain of which is the physical world. In the world around us, we observe some things coming about always, others for the most or for the minor part, and still others by chance, and philosophers traditionally tended to describe what comes about in those different ways by appeal to conceptions of necessity and contingency.

Buridan's picture of varieties of modality places Aristotelian conceptions of necessity in the restricted domain of natural necessity and possibility (Knuuttila 1989, 2001). In this paper, I shall revisit Buridan's picture of natural necessity on the background of his account of varieties of modality by addressing two contexts in the intersection of his logical and natural philosophical concerns. The first involves the Aristotelian doctrine of the necessity of natural cycles of alteration and generation at the beginning of his questions on *De Generatione et Corruptione,* in particular in a question about a consequence from possibilities of alteration to possibilities of generation debated both by Buridan and his near contemporaries. The second concerns a picture of causal necessity he discusses in connection with a

G. Alt (✉)
Stockholm University, Stockholm, Sweden

University of Cologne, Köln, Germany
e-mail: guido.alt@philosophy.su.se

J. P. Hochschild et al. (eds.), *Metaphysics Through Semantics: The Philosophical Recovery of the Medieval Mind*, International Archives of the History of Ideas Archives internationales d'histoire des idées 242, https://doi.org/10.1007/978-3-031-15026-5_14

received controversy between the views of Avicenna and Averroes about the appropriate description of causal necessity in commentaries to the second book of Aristotle's *Physics*. In that context, Buridan shows a tendency to approach causal necessity and contingency by making less appeal to essences than the Averroan model. By bringing both of these contexts to attention, I hope to shed further light on the relation between Buridan's logical analysis of modality and the interpretative uses of modal concepts in his natural philosophy and metaphysics.[1]

14.1   Degrees of Necessity

Contemporary Aristotelians often reject the category of natural necessity as distinct from the metaphysical necessities founded on substances just in virtue of what they are. Late medieval Aristotelians, on the other hand, customarily draw a midway distinction between what is logically and what is naturally necessary in terms of what God can bring about by his absolute power and what he can lawfully do by his ordained power, a distinction which is also reflected in Buridan's argumentative usage of supranatural and natural cases, applying obligational terminology from the arts faculty instead of theological language.[2]

Buridan's most elaborate account of varieties of modality is found in the treatment of demonstrative propositions at the eight book contained in the *Summaries of Logic,* where a doubt concerning the exhaustiveness of the classification of *per se* propositions motivates him to introduce a more refined distinction between absolute and a manifold of relative necessities in terms of degrees (*SD*, 8.6.3):

> The first grade of necessity occurs when it is not possible by any power to falsify the proposition while its signification remains the same, not is it possible for things to be otherwise than it signifies. Another grade occurs when it is impossible either to falsify it or for things to be otherwise by natural powers, although it is possible supernaturally or miraculously, as in 'The heavens are moving', 'The heavens are spherical', and 'Any place is filled'. The third grade occurs with the assumption of the constancy of the subject, as in 'A lunar eclipse takes place because of the interposition of the sun and the moon', 'Socrates is a man', and

---

[1] Hereafter, Buridan (2001a) refers to Gyula Klima's translation of the *Summulae de Dialectica* [*SD*], I also refer often to the Latin text of *De Demonstrationibus* edited by De Rijk in Buridan (2001b). Buridan (2015b) is Stephen Read's translation of *Treatise on Consequences* [*TC*]. The translations from passages of the modern editions and incunabula, where needed, are mine. The Latin sources will be referred to in the following texts: *Questiones super libros De Generatione et Corruptione* [*DGC*], edited by P. Bakker, J. Thijssen and M. Streijger in Buridan (2010), also the *Quaestiones super octo libros Physicorum Aristotelis* [*Phys.*] in Buridan (2015a), *Expositio et Quaestiones in Aristotelis de Caelo* [*DC*] edited by Benoît Patar in Buridan (1996), *Quaestiones longe super Perihermeneias* [*QSP*] in Van der Lecq's edition in Buridan (1983), and *In Metaphysicen Aristotelis Questiones* [*Met.*] in Buridan (1518).

[2] For representative treatments of some of these "supranatural cases" in Buridan's natural philosophy and metaphysics, Sylla (2001) presents some areas where natural philosophy and theology intersect in Buridan's writings, and Paul Bakker (2001, 256) examines the problem of separable accidents in particular.

'Socrates is risible'. These are said to be necessary in this way because it is necessary for Socrates, whenever he is, to be a risible man [....] There is yet a fourth mode, which involves restriction. For just as 'possible' is sometimes predicated broadly, in relation to the present, past, and future, and sometimes restrictively, in relation to the present or the future, in accordance with what is said at the end of *On the Heavens*—that no force or power can be brought to bear on the past [...]—the same goes for 'necessary' and 'impossible', which are also predicated either with restriction or broadly. (2001a, 733)[3]

Buridan's picture of degrees presents interesting refinements of the absolute and relative distinction; it was arguably also influential in later times, and a similar use of *gradus perseitatis* can be found as late as in Franco Burgersdijk's logical synopsis (1659, fol. 41). Whereas Buridan's maximal necessities involve the absence of any competing possibility, the manifold degrees of relative necessities are obtained by shifting what Pasnau described as modal spaces (2020). As we shall see in the next section, shifting modal contexts in relation to time provided Buridan with a logical tool for the mundane purpose of interpreting the Aristotelian doctrine of natural cycles of alteration and generation developed in his questions on *De Generatione et Corruptione*.

First, it is useful to note that Buridan's concept of absolute necessities is not a good match to the prevailing contemporary to us conception of metaphysical necessity, insofar as the latter is conceived of as based on the essences of the substances signified, or as Buridan puts it, on predications "indicating the quiddity of the thing" (Buridan 2001a, 127). Buridan's choice of examples rather seem to suggest he has in mind a category of logical necessity broadly construed, which covers less ground than the category of essential predications. Among the examples of first degree necessities he gives are predications involving correlatives—e.g., "A part is a part of some whole"—negative propositions with impossible subjects—e.g., "A chimera is not a chimera," and arguably necessarily vacuous conditionals such as "If a donkey flies, it has wings", which suggests he takes logical consequence to involve absolute

---

[3] Cf. Buridan (2001b, 141–2): "Est enim primus gradus necessitatis quia per nullam potentiam possibile est propositionem falsificari, stante significatione, vel aliter se habere quam significat. Alius gradus est quia impossibile est eam falsificari vel aliter se habere per potentias naturales, licet sit possibile supernaturaliter vel miraculose, ut 'caelum movetur', caelum est sphaericum, 'mundus est sphaericus', 'locus est plenus'. Tertius gradus ex suppositione constantiae subiecti, ut 'lunae eclipsis est propter interpositionem terrae inter solem et lunam', 'Socrates est homo', 'Socrates est risibilis'. Hae enim dicuntur necessariae sic quia necesse est quandocumque est Socrates, ipsum esse hominem risibilem [...]. Adhuc est quartus gradus, secundum restrictionem. Nam sicut 'possibile' aliquando ample dicitur, in ordine ad omne tempus praesens, praeteritum et futurum, et aliquando restrictive, in ordine ad praesens vel futurum, iuxta illud quod dicitur in fine primi *de Caelo* quod non est virtus sive potestas ad praeteritum [...]—ita etiam 'necesse' et 'impossibile' dicuntur secundum restrictionem vel ample." Normore (2013) presents an insightful discussion of these modal degrees in its broad philosophical context in the fourteenth century. Pasnau at (2020) discusses similar passages as evidence for Buridan's choices of modal spaces for different explanatory purposes. Note that a similar use of degrees of firmness of truth is made by Buridan in the epistemic sense of levels of evidentness, see in that respect Zupko (2001, 175–182) and Biard (2012, 38–39).

modality.[4] The feature these propositions share in common, in Buridan's words, is that they are bound to be true solely because of the concepts signified, provided a given conventional signification of the terms in the proposition is established (Buridan 2001a, 727).[5]

The second degree corresponds for Buridan to natural necessities. In fact, Buridan's conception of natural necessity is arguably closer to our contemporary concept of metaphysical necessity; after all, to that class belong the usual candidates for metaphysical necessity in the modern sense. Buridan lists essential definitions of absolute terms—e.g. "Every human being is an animal"—universal predications obtaining in virtue of thing's nature and natural operations—e.g. "Fire is hot"—and propositions expressing natural regularities. Even though all the latter have competing possibilities through a supranatural power, Buridan considers that they are nevertheless immune to natural powers and necessary on the assumption of the common course of nature (*ex suppositione communis cursus naturae*).[6] Buridan believes these competing negatives can be assumed actual without implying any contradiction. An illustrative case is Buridan's abovementioned example of a natural necessity, "Any place is filled"—the necessity of which is a famous tenet of Aristotelian physics—which he claims has a competing negative by supranatural possibility. Buridan appeals to the imagination of the supranatural case in which the contents of the sphere of the moon are annihilated by God, and claims that in such a scenario referring to the empty place inside that sphere by applying the concept of void would be logically possible (Sylla 2001).[7]

Which concept of possibility is associated with the second degree? Even though Buridan only speaks of necessities in the passage above, we can infer from the fact

---

[4]Buridan briefly mentions these examples, at *SD* 8.6.3 (2001a, 734–5). He justifies the first at *SD* 3.2.4, saying that a hand would not be someone's hand anymore if, by a supranatural possibility, it were cut off by God and preserved alive, but "still, it is not possible by any power that a part be a part without being the part of some whole" (2001a, 175). The second example is necessary assuming the logical convention that negative propositions with empty terms are true by default, since then propositions with impossible subjects will be necessary by default. Buridan also adds "God exists" as an example of absolute necessity, but there might be a line of argument for it being a logical necessity. For an argument that this is the case in in Scotus, see Cross (2015). For a treatment of the concept of absolute necessity as involved in the Buridanian approach to logical consequence, see Normore (2015).

[5]It is important to note that for Buridan even absolute necessities are relative to the conventional signification the terms have in a language and the formation of proposition, cf. *DGC* I.1 (2010, 39.3–29). See also the sophism on conventionality, "It is within our power that a man should be a donkey" (Buridan 2001a, 937). Buridan's solution to the latter sophism makes clear that the fact that linguistic conventions possibly change is the reason why he relativizes propositional necessity to the permanence of the linguistic conventions (*stante significatione*).

[6]The concept of a common course of nature has a wide use in Buridan's account of scientific knowledge, see in particular King (1987, 20–24).

[7]Cf. *SD* 8.6.3 (2001a, 735). Sylla (2001, 238ff.) presents a detailed discussion of Buridan's approach to the supranatural possibility of the void. For discussion of that problem in Buridan's immediate context and the use of *secundum imaginationem* methods in natural philosophy, see also Hugonnard-Roche (1989).

that whatever a secondary natural cause can bring about, a first supranatural cause can, that a possibility in the second degree entails a possibility in the first, but not the other way around; in other words, a logical possibility is a necessary but not a sufficient condition for natural possibility. What would be sufficient for the latter is the existence of natural powers acting as the concurring causes without which the diversity in the operations observed in the natural world cannot be accounted for.[8] Buridan understands natural powers as categorical qualities in respect of which the subject possessing them is said to be enabled or impeded to perform certain natural operations (Buridan 1983, 107; Klima 2018). Referring to the former acceptation of powers, he takes Averroes and Aristotle in the *Physics* to have understood the possible as that to which there correspond natural powers of generation, and possibility to be an attribute of those propositions which are made possible by the actual presence of such active or passive powers.[9]

The model of powers-based possibility Buridan attributes to Aristotle and Averroes substantially differs from his own logical interpretation of the modalities. At the core of Buridan's modal logic is a uniform treatment of divided modal propositions as ampliated to the possible; Buridan's famous example of an ampliated sentence in the *Treatise on Consequences*, "air can be made out of water, although that may not be true of any air that exists" (2015b, 97), is not based on the assumption of any actually existing powers. Insofar as Buridan claims that propositions in natural philosophy are said to be possible by the presence of active or passive powers, we seem to find a discrepancy. Buridan seems to be aware of that discrepancy; in his commentary to the *Physics* (2015a, 211), Buridan claims not intending to

---

[8] *Phys.* II.13 (2015a, 339.21–340.8), "Secundo dico quod necesse est post ipsum Deum ponere alias causas secudum quarum diversitates consequuntur diversitates transmutationum et effectuum in hoc mundo nobis apparentium, quia licet Deus per suam infinitam potentiam et voluntatem liberam posset sine aliis causis concurrentibus producere et creare diversos effectus contrarios sive in eodem tempore sive in diversis, et hoc modo supernaturali et miraculoso, tamen modo naturali non esset possibile quod ab eodem simplici et invariabili provenirent diversi effectus contrarii, ut nunc tales et cras alii, nisi essent aliae causae concurrentes diversae [...] Tertio etiam apparet mihi quod non potest sufficienter reddi causa talis diversitatis transmutationum et effectuum ex ipso Deo et prima materia [...]." Thus, Biard (2001, 84) notes that Buridan claims here that the diversity of observed causes can only be salvaged *naturaliter loquendo*.

[9] *Phys.* I.22 (2015a, 220.22–222.17): "Et videtur Commentatori et forte Aristoteli quod huiusmodi potentia vel possibile dicitur secundum attributionem ad potentiam activam vel passivam. Ex eo enim dicitur Antichristus est possibilis vel in potentia, quia iam est principium activum potens ipsum vel formam eius producere in esse et quod est subiectum vel materia potens ipsum vel formam eius suscipere; et illud principium activum est Deus et illud subiectum est prima materia. Sed nos diceremus quod ad huiusmodi esse in potentia sufficit potentia activa, quae est Deus. Vel etiam potest dici quod huiusmodi potentia vel possibile dicitur secundum attributionem ad possibilitatem propositionibus attributam. Ex eo enim dicimus Antichristum esse in potentia vel ens in potentia vel possibilem vel quod est in potentia ad esse Antichristum vel ad ipsum fieri etc., quia haec est possibilis 'Antichristus est', vel 'Antichristus fit, etc". Buridan here distinguished between three concepts of 'possibility or potentiality', cf. Knuuttila (2001). For the context of that question, see Friedman (2021). Because that question deals specifically with the powers of matter, Buridan does not mention the other *species* of qualities dealt with in Klima (2018). See further Buridan (1983, 107).

apply the same interpretation of modal sentences in logic and in natural philosophy.[10]

One strategy available to Buridan would seem to involve accommodating both interpretations of possibility by appealing to the conventionality of language uses and addressing this discrepancy as a foremost semantical issue. A similar strategy is used the fifth question of his commentary to the *Metaphysics,* book 9. There, Buridan discusses the principle that "everything that someone will be able to do, it is possible for them to do," which is a valid principle according to the ampliated reading. But Buridan draws on counterintuitive instances of that principle, such as "it is possible for a baby to lift heavy weight," to say that modal discourse (*modi loquendo ad posse*) should be adapted in accordance with conventions of communication in everyday life and in scientific disputation, and appeals to the need to contextually distinguish the senses of propositions, rejecting a modal proposition in accordance with one sense, and conceding it according to another (Buridan 1518, fol. 57rb).[11] However, that strategy seems to be quite isolated in Buridan's writings.[12] Van der Lecq and Braakhuis (1994, 30) argue that Buridan's appeal to ambiguity in that context should rather be understood in light of a late development in his career after a change of mind concerning the need for distinctions of the sense of propositions, probably motivated by the prohibitions in the Statute of 1340.

An alternative strategy, perhaps closer to Buridan's *ex professo* view, is to single out a fundamental concept of possibility and to provide principled semantical restrictions to get narrower concepts, rather than evoking an ambiguity of the corresponding concepts arising from language use. In fact, Buridan seems to hold the view that it is according to the logical concept of possibility and necessity that propositions are fundamentally (*primitus*) said to be possible or necessary.[13] Furthermore, as Calvin Normore (2013) pointed out, Buridan adopts such a strategy of *restrictiones* in his account of the relations of modality with time. We shall now see how that strategy is reflected in his interpretation of an Aristotelian doctrine in natural philosophy.

---

[10] *Phys.* I.22 (2015a, 211): "Et quia de huiusmodi potentia vel possibilitate non intendimus ad praesens, ideo non amplius hic discutio utrum universaliter sit bene dictum illud quod nunc est dictum." Buridan is referring to the logical concept of possibility in that context.

[11] Cf. *Met.* 9.5 (1518, fol.58va): "Et videtur mihi quod homines magis communiter utuntur illo sensu qui est secundum potentiam propinquam quam illo qui est secundum remotam: quia omnes communiter reputarent absurdum quod infans esset equipotens sicut vir robustus et perfectus, et quod tantum pondus posset levare sicut vir, quia sermones non habent virtutem nisi ex impositione et impositio non potest sciri nisi ex usu."

[12] *Pace* Knuuttila's (1989) opinion that Buridan's account of varieties of necessity represents "emergence of the view that the notion of necessity is equivocal and that conceptual necessities do not necessarily have anything in common with nomic natural necessities" (155), I think Buridan did not believe necessity to be an ambiguous concept.

[13] See *Phys.* I.22 (2015a, 221.7–10): "Primitus enim propositio dicitur necessaria, quia quandocumque proponitur, est vera et non potest esse falsa. Deinde propositio dicitur possibilis ex eo quod sua contradictoria non est necessaria."

14.2 The Necessity of Natural Cycles

In his main treatment of modal propositions, Buridan treats necessity as distributing universally over situations and possibility as distributing particularly (Buridan 2001a, 75). That conception interprets modality a form of generality, approaching the main intuition that possible worlds semantics imposes. In a Buridanian restricted sense, however, modality is intrinsically interwoven with time; possibility, he says, is taken "determinately for the present or the future", and necessity is taken "determinately for the past."[14] That restricted conception of modality corresponds for Buridan to the intuition that any agent is powerless with regard to the past (Pasnau 2020). As Normore (2013) explains it, a logical relation between Buridan's broad and restricted modalities obtains, such that:

> A claim is possible in the broad sense if it was, is or will be possible. A claim is possible in the restricted sense only if it is or will be possible. From the way Buridan distinguishes these two senses it is pretty clear that something is necessary *per accidens* (in the terminology of others) just in case it is possible in the broad sense, but not possible in the restricted sense (in his terminology). (2013, 397)

Normore sees Buridan's statement of the restricted sense as a concession to the Ockhamist conception of accidental necessity. Buridan seems to have thought a similar distinction between natural and accidental necessity to be useful in his interpretation of the Aristotelian doctrine of necessity in natural cycles of alteration and generation in his commentary to the first book of *De Generatione et Corruptione*.

At the beginning of Buridan's commentary, book I q. 4, Buridan and his contemporaries address the validity of the argument "if it is impossible for the elements to be generated, it is impossible for the elements to be altered" (*si impossibilia sit elementa generari, impossibile est ea alterari*).[15] He says that the locus from final causes warrants the inference, namely the maxim according to which if a given end is impossible, then the means ordered towards the end is impossible as well. In fact, a more general problem about the connection of alteration with generation motivates the discussion of the consequence at hand.

Buridan thought to be in keeping with Aristotle that, speaking naturally, it is impossible for the basic elements to be generated by natural powers, and also that

---

[14] Interestingly, the necessity of the present is absent in this discussion. In his *Quaestiones longe super Perihemeneias*, Buridan avoids the problem of the necessity of the present in an interesting interpretative move, saying that the only reason Aristotle suggested it was that the present continuously 'flows into the past' (1983, 55). Furthermore, Normore's (2013) characterization of Buridan's "pure divisibilist" position about moments would also imply that the problem of the necessity of the present could not arise for Buridan in the same way it did for Duns Scotus.

[15] Cf. Buridan *DGC* I.4 (2010, 56). Marek Gensler (2006) provides interesting texts of Walter Burley's corresponding question. According to Gensler (2006, 643), the background interest in the question was that qualitative alteration was thought to be a necessary condition for generation, whereas there can be generation without the other kinds of accidental change such as augmentation or change of place. For an approach to the problem of qualitative change more broadly, see Pasnau (2021).

each of the basic elements (water, earth, fire and air) are perpetually the same as they ever were throughout the natural cycles of generation and corruption by successive identity, just as the River Seine is the same river it was hundreds of years ago through a succession of its parts.[16] However, the Aristotelian theory of reciprocal changes claims that each of the basic elements change into another, in particular in alterations which involve contrariety; for example, when water is boiled it leads to the generation of new air, for which there must be passive and active powers to explain that change. There is a natural connection (*naturalis habitudo*) between alteration and generation in changes that involved the repugnance of contraries, which presupposes that the generation of new elements is possible after all. Buridan mentions two lemmas in addressing the goodness of the consequence. On the one hand, if substantial generation of air from water were impossible, then the natural end of such alterations cannot be achieved, making them only apparent and not real features of the world. On the other hand, there is a sense in which the elements cannot be regenerated by natural powers, since this water cannot recur as the same individual by natural powers.

As Buridan makes clear, no logical connection between the concepts of alteration and generation is involved in the consequence.[17] Therefore, the abovementioned consequence should be evaluated by a layer of validity according to natural necessity, and the candidate descriptions thereof lead us back to the interpretation of the broad and restricted (or accidental) modalities. At the *De Generatione et Corruptione* question at hand, Buridan further expands on these modal concepts, and it might be useful to quote him again at length:

> It should be noted that possibility and impossibility or necessity should be understood in two ways. In the first way insofar as they relate indifferently to every time, present, past and future. And in this way only what always was, is and will be and never could nor will fail to be is necessary. And then the impossible is what never was, is, will, nor could nor will be able to be. The possible, in that way, is what at some time is, was, or will be. Accordingly, we would say that Aristotle is possible, and not impossible, because we would concede that 'Aristotle exists' is a possible proposition and not an impossible proposition. In a second way possibility is taken determinately with regard to the present or the future, excluding the past. It is according to that way that Aristotle said in the first book of *De Caelo* that there is

---

[16] Cf. *DGC* II.13 (2010, 258.20–259.4) "Tertia conclusio ponitur ab aliquibus quod nulla generatio fuerit semper. Et ego credo quod oppositum potest sustineri. Nam numquam Sequana generabatur, quia si Sequana generatur, hoc non est quia tota simul, sed quia pars post partem. Et ita etiam de aere e de terra. Nam ille aer magnus in sphaera sua numquam generatus fuit totus simul, sed dicitur generatus, quia pars post partem generatus est totus. Ita fuit semper secundum Aristotelem et semper erit. Et est idem aer perpetue, sicut dicimus eandem sequanam nunc et in centum annis." Buridan comments that 'perpetuum' is meant here in the sense of specific identity.

[17] *DGC* I.4 (2010, 60.13–18): "Ad secundam, quando dicitur 'si unum potest esse sine altero, non oportet, si illud alterum est impossibile, quod primum sit impossibile', ego dico quod hoc est verum, nisi illa habeant ad invicem naturalem habitudinem. Sed si habeant habitudinem ad invicem, sicut finis et ordinatum in finem, dico quod si unum est impossibile, quod alterum est impossibile."

no power to the past. In that way we say that everything which was, could not fail to have been. And therefore, it is said that 'Aristotle exists' is naturally impossible. (2010, 57.5–29)[18]

As Buridan notes, the consequence from possibilities of alteration to generation is warranted taking the broad acceptation of natural possibility (2010, 58.6–15), for on the restricted acceptation there may well be present possibilities of alteration without their corresponding present possibilities of generation; for example, singular subjects which exist accidentally such as this horse and the moon can undergo alterations, but they are no longer generable by natural powers.[19]

The use of different descriptions of natural modality to assess the validity of the consequence is also made by some among Buridan's near contemporaries at the parallel passages of their commentaries on the first book of *De Generatione et Corruptione*. Nicole Oresme's reply, in the third question of book I of his commentary is representative of an alternative strategy adopted. Oresme's reply to the question is, in the end, very similar to Buridan's. He says that the consequence stated in the question is valid according to the concept of necessity the intended interpretation of which is the fact that nature exhibits intermittent regularities holding at the *species* level, since alterations involving contrariety are, in the common course of nature, essentially ordered towards generation.[20] However, the picture of modality which Oresme offers in that question seems to differ from Buridan's in some ways. Oresme uses a standard distinction between types of necessity in terms of temporal

---

[18] *DGC* I.4 (2010, 57.5–29). "Nota quod possibilitas et impossibilitas aut necessitas solent capi dupliciter. Uno modo prout respiciunt indifferenter omne tempus praesens, praeteritum et futurum. Et illo modo illud solum dicitur necessarium quod semper fuit, est et erit et numquam potuit vel poterit non esse. Et tunc dicitur illud impossibile quod numquam fuit, est vel erit nec umquam potuit aut poterit esse. Et illud dicitur possibile quod aliquando est, fuit vel erit. Et ita diceremus Aristotelem esse possibilem et non impossibilem, ita quod illo modo concederetur quod haec est possibilis 'Aristoteles est' et non impossibilis. Alio modo possibilitas, impossibilitas et necessitas accipiuntur prout determinate respiciunt praesens aut futurum, ita quod non praeteritum. Unde illo modo dicit Aristoteles primo *Caeli* quod potentia non est ad praeteritum. Illo modo etiam dicitur quod omne illud quod fuit, impossibile est non fuisse. Et sic diceretur quod illa est impossibilis naturaliter 'Aristoteles est'."

[19] Cf. Buridan's *DGC* I.4 (2010, 56.17–20), and also, referring to the restricted sense, see *DC* I q.26 (1996, 376): "Genitum non amplius potest generari; ergo genitum non est generabile, quia idem significat generabile quod possibile generari; et tamen genium est corruptibile; ergo aliquid corruptibile non est generabile." To be sure, Buridan ultimately rejects this restricted sense as a natural modality, saying that the latter pertain rather to 'narrative stories', but not to demonstrative sciences. Cf. Normore (2013).

[20] Oresme, *De Generatione et Corruptione* I.3 (1996, 21.118–128): "Tunc secunda conclusio est quod ista consequentia est bona: generatio est impossibilis, ergo alteratio est impossibilis. Probo et suppono primo quod ordinatio rerum naturalium est quod alteratio fiat propter generationem; secundo, quod talis ordo nature est necessarius secundum speciem, ita quod non potest impediri in toto, licet impediatur in parte, sicut intentum hominem non generare est possibile, sed non est possibile simul de quolibet. Tunc arguitur: alteratio est propter generationem, ergo istum ordinem in toto impedire est impossibile; sed si possibile esset alterationem esse et generatio esset impossibilis, iste ordo impedi(re)tur, ergo si alteratio est possibilis, generatio est possibilis; igitur a destructione consequentis: si generatio est impossibilis, alteratio est impossibilis, quod est propositum."

duration, perhaps taken in broad lines from Averroes.[21] He defines the necessary as what cannot eternally fail to be, understanding that necessity applies primarily to eternal beings in virtue of its meaning. Oresme offers a tentative explication of necessity as what has unceasing being (*sic dicitur necessarium quasi 'non cessans esse'*; Oresme 1996, 19.68–69), and develops that perpetuity model in a sixfold division of necessities based on the temporal duration of beings.[22]

Buridan has a simpler starting point in his account of varieties of necessity based only on the unrestricted (*ample*) and restricted (*restrictive*) distinction. That might be related to the fact that he criticizes the adequacy of standard temporal convertibilities which seem to underlie Oresme's model. His main line of criticism concerns Aristotle's claim in *De Caelo* that "generable" and "corruptible" are convertible, since both are convertible sometimes being, and sometimes not being, whereas "ungenerable" and "incorruptible" are convertible with being always (Buridan 1996, 377–9). Buridan claims that this convertibility is false as a matter of meaning (*de virtute sermonis*). Furthermore, since it presupposes that every generable will at some time be generated, a principle which he does not accept for logical possibility, and he considers Aristotle's argument for it logically faulty, although he says that the former principle should to some extent be conceded for natural possibility (Buridan 1996, 377).

14.3 Causal Necessity and Contingency

Besides locating natural necessities among categorical sentences in his picture of degrees of necessity, Buridan also refers to natural necessities as a conditional form. That concept makes an appearance in causal contexts. In the treatment of causal demonstrations about the past or the future, Buridan distinguishes between two kinds of conditional necessities; on the one hand, there are necessary

---

[21] Compare with Averroes' modal distinctions in his account of demonstrations discussed in Paul Thom (2019).

[22] Oresme, *De Generatione et Corruptione* I.3 (1996, 19.67–20.85): "Tunc est secunda distinctio quod sex modis dicitur 'necessarium'. Primo modo dicitur de eternitate continua ab utraque parte, et sic Deum esse est necessarium; et sic dicitur 'necessarium' quasi 'non cessans esse'. Secundo modo dicitur 'necessarium' de continua eternitate tantum ab una parte, ut a parte post, et sic Sortem fuisse dicitur necessarium; aut a parte ante, et sic solem eclypsari crastina die fuit necessarium. Et tale necessarium potest bene transire in impossibile. Tertio modo dicitur 'necessarium' eternaliter sed intercise, cuius quodlibet singulare inevitabiliter venit, sicut hoc quod est lunam eclypsari; et hoc etiam verum est secundum Aristotelem. Quarto modo dicitur sicut prius, scilicet intercise, sed quodlibet singulare evenit contingenter, et ita generationem esse est necessarium, quia non semper continue est generatio, et tamen ante infinitum tempus fuit necessarium generationem esse, et tamen nulla generatio fit necessario. Quinto modo est necessarium sicut aliquod singulare quod est solum una hora, et tamen inevitabiliter evenit, sicut est aliqua constellatio. Sexto modo dicitur 'necessarium' quod futurum erat contingenter, sed, quia ponitur in esse, ideo tunc, quando est, est necessarium, sicut Sortem esse, quando est, necessarium est esse."

concomitances, and on the other necessary consecution or precedence, and both are involved in different kinds of causal demonstration (*SD*, 8.10.6):

> For if the present being (*inesse*) of one requires the concomitance of the other, just as there is a demonstration from the present being of one to the present being of the other, so there is one from the future being of one to the future being of the other, and from the past being of one to the past being of the other and from the possible being of one to the possible being of the other, whether the demonstration be *quia* or *propter quid*. Also, if the concomitance is mutual, then there is likewise a demonstration from the coming to be to coming to be and from having come to be to having come to be. If, however, there is no mutual concomitance, but there is a necessary consecution or precedence of one with respect to the other, then there is no demonstration from being to being, but there is one from being to future or past being. (2001b, 206)[23]

That passage echoes a distinction Aristotle makes in the *Posterior Analytics* (II.12, 95b14–37), where he is concerned with the question of what makes causal inferences valid in the case where cause and effect are non-simultaneous particulars. This seemed problematic for Aristotle, since in the interval where a cause is present but its effect is not yet actualized, it seems that the conditional is not true.[24] Aristotle's thought seems to be that at the interval of time in which, for example, a match is struck but fire has not yet started, it is not necessarily true that if the match is struck then it will catch fire, since an impeding factor might intervene. For example, while the match is struck a drop of rain might fall on it preventing its ignition, such that the causal connection can be broken midway.[25]

Buridan's account of causal necessitation at the general level abstracts away from intervening factors in the common course of nature. In that respect, what seems to be required for causal necessitation in Buridan's picture is that under normal circumstances the same combination of active and passive powers produces a species similar effect, provided the circumstances are equal (*omnis rebus similiter se habentibus*), so that fire when applied to the log must, *ceteris paribus,* burn it and

---

[23] I have here modified Klima's translation (Buridan 2001a, 789) of the text, cf. Buridan (2001b, 206): "Nam si unum inesse requirit concomitantiam alterius, tunc sicut fit demonstratio de esse unius ad esse alterius, ita de fore ad fore, de fuisse ad fuisse et de posse esse ad posse esse, sive 'quia' sive 'propter quid'. Et etiam, si ista concomitantia sit mutua, fit similiter demonstratio de fieri ad fieri et de facto esse ad factum esse, si talia sint innata fieri. Sed si illa concomitantia non sit mutua, non oportet ita esse. Si autem non fuerit concomitantia, sed necessaria unius ad alterum consecutio vel precedentia, tunc non fit demonstratio de esse ad esse, sed de esse ad fore vel fuisse."

[24] Cf. *Analytica Posteriora* II 12, 95a27–34 (Aristotle 1993): "The deduction is possible if it starts from what has come to be later (but the principle in this case is something which has already come about), and similarly with what is coming about; but it is impossible if it starts from what is earlier (e.g. 'Since this has come about, this has come about later'). And similarly for what will be the case. For whether the time is indeterminate or determined it will not be the case that since it is true to say that this has come about it is true to say that this—the later item—has come about: in the interval, when the one item has already come about, the statement will be false."

[25] Kupreeva (2010) offers a detailed discussion of the Aristotle's approach of conditional necessity in *Analytica Posteriora* II.12. For a general discussion of Aristotle's account of hypothetical necessity across his writings, see Gaskin (1995).

it is impossible, *ceteris paribus,* that it fails to burn the log.[26] That is in effect a generalization of the standard Aristotelian account of deterministic propensities of the non-rational powers. However, the extent to which these deterministic propensities explain necessitation received alternative understandings in Buridan's time. In particular, a famous disagreement of Averroes' with Avicenna which Buridan rehearses in the eleventh question of his commentary to the second book of the *Physics* is revealing of alternative accounts of the role of natures in causal necessity (Buridan 2015a, 322–329).

The disagreement in that context concerns more directly the question of whether chance effects can be the outcome of causes which are contingent either way (*ad utrumlibet*), but it also includes also a long discussion about the proper definition of natural necessity and contingency with reference to causality.[27] One of Averroes' arguments which Buridan restates in that context involves a criticism of Avicenna's definition of causal necessity and contingency. Avicenna has understood the difference between causes which always bring about their effects and causes which only sometimes do in terms of the presence or absence of competing factors hindering their effects (Avicenna 1992, 111.85–91). According to Averroes, explaining necessity and contingency by reference to those competing impediments as Avicenna did eventually collapses necessity and contingency (Averroes 1562, fol. 66vb). Buridan explains Averroes argument in the following way:

> The second conclusion [i.e., Averroes'] is that Avicenna defines the necessary and the contingent ineptly and badly, when he operates by the presence or absence of an extrinsic impediment. Since if what is called contingent is so called because it has an extrinsic impediment, it would follow that every contingent thing is naturally necessary, which is false. The consequence is evident, since a thing should be said such as it naturally is from its intrinsic nature, abstracting away from the extrinsic factors which do not belong to that nature; but abstracting from the extrinsic factors there would be no such extrinsic impediment and therefore it would be necessary according to Avicenna; therefore, everything would be naturally necessary. (Buridan 2015a, 325)[28]

---

[26] *Met.* 9.3 (1518, fol. 58va): "[…] omnis potentia irrationalis est determinata ad alterum oppositorum, verbi gratia, si huic igni debite applicetur aliquod combustibile vel calefactibile necesse est, omnis rebus similiter se habentibus, ipsum comburere; et non est possibile, omnis rebus sic se habentibus, ipsum non comburere."

[27] That discussion emerges from Aristotle's tripartite division of the frequency of effects in into those that obtain always, for the most part, and those that only do so rarely, to which late ancient commentators added the class of those which are equally likely to occur or not (*ad utrumlibet*). For a helpful summary of Buridan's treatment, see Edith Sylla's introduction to Buridan's commentary on the *Physics* (Buridan 2015a). See further Knebel (2006) on Buridan's take on the disagreement between Avicenna and Averroes in that question, and also Maier (1949, 232).

[28] Buridan, *Phys.* II.11 (2015a, 325.6–12) "Secunda conclusio est quod Avicenna inepte et male definit necessarium et contingens, scilicet per non habere vel habere impedimentum extrinsecum. Nam si ex hoc diceretur contingens quod habet impedimentum extrinsecum, sequeretur quod omne contingens esset naturaliter necessarium, quod est falsum. Consequentia patet, quia tale debet dici unumquodque, quale esset naturaliter ex intrinseca natura sua circumscriptis extrinsecis quae non sunt de natura sua; sed circumscriptis extrinsecis non esset impedimentum extrinsecum et sic esset necessarium secundum naturam; igitur omnia essent naturaliter necessaria."

Averroes' argument seems to be based on a conception of modality according to which what is naturally necessary or contingent for some thing is entirely a matter of how that causal operation is compatible or not with the nature at hand, since being intrinsic to something is seen by Averroes as the very point to call a cause natural to start with. Accordingly, in the Averroan picture, it seems that necessity and contingency should not be explained on the basis of anything other than the causal powers of the essences involved, which might either contain the presence of or lack any possibility of deficiency.[29]

Avicenna's strategy exhibits a reversal of explanatory priorities. As mentioned above, he states the difference between causal necessity and contingency in terms of possibility of extrinsic competing alternatives; that is, the difference between causes that always bring about their effects and causes which only sometimes do is explained in terms of the presence or absence of contrary or prohibitive factors (see again Avicenna 1992, 111.85–91; and Belo 2007, 151). In the same passage, Avicenna embraces the corollary which Averroes criticized him for, namely that in some sense every contingent cause which is for the most part prevented from being actualized is possibly necessary, since we can easily isolate in imagination that causal nature from those competing factors hindering its actualization for the most part, which he claims we can evidently do concerning natural causes.[30] In fact, it seems that the idea that a contingent cause is conceivably necessary is precisely what seemed untenable for Averroes. One rationale Averroes appeals to is the common view that nature does nothing in vain. In accordance with that principle, as Averroes sees it, adding competing alternatives to the definition of causal necessity is theoretically superfluous, since if the necessary had an impediment, such an impediment would have to be eternally frustrated.[31]

Buridan says that although Averroes definitions are conceptually prior, since they make appeal to the nature of causes, he nonetheless prefers Avicenna's descriptions of causal necessity and contingency since, as he says, they should be described *a*

---

[29] Cf. Averroes, *De Physico Auditu* II (1562, fol. 66vb): "Et debes scire quod differentia inter contingens ut in pluribus et necessarium non est quod contingens ut in pluribus habet impedimentum ut in paucioribus, et necessarium non habet impedimentum, ut dicit Avicennam; secundum hoc sequitur, ut onia sint naturaliter necessario. Immo contingens ut in pluribus est illud, in cuius natura est possibilitas ut actio eius deficiat in minori parte, et immo invenitur illic impedimentum extrinsecum. Necessarium vero quia non habet hoc in sua natura, ideo non invenitur impedimentum illi extrinsecum."

[30] Avicenna, *De Causis et Principiis Naturalium* (1992, 111.85–91) "Et haec est differentia inter semper et saepe, eo quod ei quod est semper non adversatur aliquod contrarium <et ei quod est saepe adversatur aliquod contrarium>. Unde sequitur ut quod est saepe, condicione removendi contraria et prohibentia, fiat necessarium. Et hoc in <rebus> naturalibus manifestum est." See Belo (2007) for further discussion and comparison with Averroes.

[31] Averroes, *De Physico Auditu* II (1562, fol. 66vb-67ra): "Si ergo non invenitur impedimentum extrinsecum ei quod est contingens ut in pluribus, contingeret tunc ut possibilitas in illo esset ociosa; et si invenitur ei quod est necessarium, impedimentum, tunc esset impedimentum ociosum, et natura nihil agit ociose."

posteriori by the effects.[32] More generally, there are some features of causal necessity that Buridan takes Averroan definitions of natural necessity to have mistakenly ruled out. First, contrary to Averroes' position, Buridan sees nothing wrong in assuming that the same cause is described as necessary relative to some set of circumstances extrinsic to the nature of the cause, but contingent relative to another set of circumstances. Buridan's example is that while Socrates dying at a particular time is contingent and preventable relative to a king's decree, it is however necessary and unpreventable if that circumstance includes an omnipotent agent overpowering the king's will and bringing about Socrates' death at that time as a matter of necessity.[33] The second point which Buridan mentions in support of Avicenna's descriptions is that there is similarly nothing inconsistent in describing something as obtaining for the most part with respect to some circumstance, but only rarely with respect to another (Buridan 2015a, 327.27–328.4).

Buridan can thus be seen as modifying an originally essentialist view of causal necessity, and introducing modal constraints to explain causal necessitation in accordance with his own theory of natural necessity. In particular, he endorses a theory of causal necessitation that makes less appeal to essences than the Averroan model does. If that is the case, what Buridan says in this context coheres well with his picture of varieties of necessity. By defining causal necessity with reference to competing alternatives, rather than focusing on intrinsic causal natures, Buridan is able to maintain both that causal necessities are metaphysically contingent, and yet necessary on the common course of nature.

14.4   Concluding Remarks

In his account of varieties of necessity, Buridan modifies his logical analysis of modality to the target concepts of necessity and contingency in the domain of natural philosophy. I hope to have shown that he does so in a principled way, and that his picture of varieties of modality involves more than just stating a variety of contextual usages of modal concepts. Buridan's stance in applying his own modal concepts to interpret Aristotelian theories reflects also an awareness of alternative historical frameworks, and his introduction of philosophical innovations are often accompanied with a careful attitude towards the interpretation of the philosophical past. In one of his polemical works, Buridan neatly illustrates this stance by

---

[32] *Phys.* II.11 (2015a, 328): "Iterum quamvis descriptiones necessarii et contingentis quas ponit Commentator sint priores illis quas ponit Avicenna (contingit enim describere per posteriora), ideo non propter hoc debent reprobari illae quas ponit Avicenna. Et Commentator iam approbat eas, quia dicit eas sequi ex suis."

[33] *Phys.* II.11 (2015a, 328.4–10): "Iterum de necessitate consequentis posterioris ex priori necesse esset Socratem mori hodie respectu voluntatis Dei efficaciter hoc volentis, quia contra talem voluntatem non potest contingere impedimentum, sed hoc esset contingens et non necessarium respectu voluntatis regis, quia posset contra eum esse impedimentum."

proclaiming his attitude concerning authorities to be more often guided by the concern of explaining them rationally rather than by the intent to refute them.[34]

Acknowledgments I want to express my gratitude to Gyula Klima on this happy occasion for his friendly support and scholarly inspiration. I am also especially thankful to Henrik Lagerlund for his constant feedback, and to participants of the Stockholm History of Philosophy Seminar for lively discussions. I have also benefited from discussions of this text with Andreas Speer and Sven Bernecker, and with audiences at the Thomas-Institut in Cologne. Lastly, I am greatly indebted to Simo Knuuttila for many insightful remarks on earlier drafts of this paper.

Bibliography

Primary Sources

Aristotle. 1993. *Posterior analytics. Translated and with commentary by Jonathan Barnes*. Oxford: Clarendon Press.

Averroes. 1562. *Aristotelis de physico auditu libri octo cum Averrois Cordubensis variis in eosdem commentariis*. Venice: Venetiis apud Junctas.

Avicenna. 1992. *Avicenna Latinus. Liber primus naturalium* I. *De causis et principiis naturalium*, ed. S. van Riet. Leiden: E.J. Brill.

Burgersdijk, Franco. 1659. *Institutionum logicarum synopsis, sive rudimenta logica*. Amsterdam: Amstelodami apud Aegidium Valckenier.

Buridan, John. 1509. *Quaestiones super octo Physicorum libros Aristotelis*. Paris. Repr. Frankfurt am Main, 1968.

———. 1518. *In Metaphysicen Aristotelis questiones*. Paris. Repr. Frankfurt am Main, 1964.

———. 1983. *Questiones longe super librum Perihermeneias*. Edited by Ria van der Lecq. Nijmegen: Ingenium Publishers.

———. 1996. *Expositio et quaestiones in Aristotelis De caelo*. Edited by Benoît Patar. Louvain/Paris: Éditions Peeters.

———. 2001a. *Summulae de Dialectica*. Translated by Gyula Klima. New Haven: Yale University Press.

———. 2001b. *Summulae: De demonstrationibus*. Edited by L.M. De Rijk. Turnhout: Brepols.

———. 2010. *Quaestiones super libros De generatione et corruptione Aristotelis*. A critical edition with an introduction. Edited by Michiel Streijger, Paul J.J.M. Bakker, Johannes M.M.H. Thijssen. Leiden/Boston: Brill.

———. 2004. De dependentiis, diversitatibus et convenientiis, ed. Dirk-Jan Dekker. *Vivarium* 42: 109–149.

———. 2015a. *Quaestiones super octo libros Physicorum Aristotelis (secundum ultimam lecturam) Libri I-II*. Edited by Michiel Streijger and Paul J.M.M. Bakker. Leiden/Boston: Brill.

———. 2015b. *Treatise on consequences*. Translated by Stephen Read. New York: Fordham University Press.

Oresme, Nicole. 1996. *Quaestiones super De generatione et corruptione*. Edited by Stefano Caroti. Munich: Bayerische Akademie der Wissenschaften.

---

[34] Buridan (2004, 144.19–23) "Et huic responsioni sibi acquiesco, quia nolo me in hac opinione fundare super aliquam auctoritatem, sive Lincolniensis, sive Averrois, sive Aristotelis, quia auctoritates faciliter expononuntur, et etiam ipsi fuerunt homines. Tamen plus vellem probabiliter eos exponere quam negare."

Secondary Sources

Bakker, Paul J.M.M. 2001. Aristotelian metaphysics and eucharistic theology: John Buridan and Marsilius of Inghen on the ontological status of accidental being. In *The metaphysics and natural philosophy of John Buridan*, ed. J.M.M.H. Thijssen and Jack Zupko, 247–265. Leiden/Boston/Köln: Brill.

Belo, Catarina. 2007. *Chance and determinism in Avicenna and Averroes*, Islamic philosophy, theology and science. Texts and studies, 69. Leiden/Boston/Köln: Brill.

Biard, Joël. 2001. The natural order in John Buridan. In *The metaphysics and natural philosophy of John Buridan*, ed. J.M.M. Thijssen and Jack Zupko, 77–97. Leiden/Boston/Köln: Brill.

———. 2012. *Science et nature: La théorie buridanienne du savoir*. Paris: Libraire Philosophique J. Vrin.

Cross, Richard. 2015. Duns Scotus and divine necessity. *Oxford Studies in Medieval Philosophy* 3: 128–144.

Friedman, Russell L. 2021. Is matter the same as its potency? Some fourteenth century answers. *Vivarium* 59: 123–142.

Gaskin, Richard. 1995. *The sea battle and the master argument: Aristotle and Diodorus Cronus on the metaphysics of the future*. Berlin/New York: Walter de Gruyter.

Gensler, Marek. 2006. Averroes' influence in Walter Burley's commentary on 'De generatione et corruptione'. In *Wissen über Grenzen: Arabisches Wissen und lateinisches Mitterlalter*, Miscellanea Mediaevalia, 33, ed. Andreas Speer, 641–654. Berlin/New York: Walter de Gruyter.

Hugonnard-Roche, Henri. 1989. Analyse sémantique et analyse *secundum imaginationem* dans la physique parisienne au XIVe siècle. In *Studies in medieval natural philosophy*, ed. Stefano Caroti, 177–226. Florence: Leo S. Olschiki.

Johnston, Spencer C. 2021. Modal logic. In *The Routledge companion to medieval philosophy*, ed. Richard Cross and J.T. Paasch, 43–56. New York: Routledge.

King, Peter. 1987. Jean Buridan's philosophy of science. *Studies in History and Philosophy of Science* 18: 109–132.

Klima, Gyula. 2009. *John Buridan*. Oxford: Oxford University Press.

———. 2018. The metaphysics of habits in Buridan. In *The ontology, psychology, and axiology of habits (habitus) in medieval philosophy*, ed. Nicholas Faucher and Magali Roques, 321–331. Berlin: Springer.

Knebel, Sven. 2006. "Volo magis stare cum Avicenna": Der Zufall zwischen Averroisten und Avicennisten. In *Wissen über Grenzen: Arabisches Wissen und lateinisches Mitterlalter*, ed. Andreas Speer, 662–676. Berlin/New York: Walter de Gruyter.

Knuuttila, Simo. 1989. Natural necessity in John Buridan. In *Studies in medieval natural philosophy*, ed. Stefano Caroti, 155–176. Florence: L.S. Olschki.

———. 1993. *Modalities in medieval philosophy*. New York: Routledge.

———. 2001. Necessities in John Buridan's natural philosophy. In *The metaphysics and natural philosophy of John Buridan*, ed. J.M.M.H. Thijssen and Jack Zupko, 65–76. Leiden/Boston/Köln: Brill.

Kupreeva, Inna. 2010. In *Interpreting Aristotle's Posterior analytics in late antiquity and beyond*, ed. Frans A.J. de Haas, Mariska Leunissen, and Marije Martijn, 203–234. Leiden/Boston: Brill.

Lagerlund, Henrik. 2021. Aristotelian powers, mechanism, and final causes in the late middle ages. In *Reconsidering causal powers: Historical and conceptual perspectives*, ed. Benjamin Hill, Henrik Lagerlund, and Stathis Psillos, 82–93. Oxford: Oxford University Press.

Maier, Anneliese. 1949. Notwendigkeit, Kontingenz und Zufall. In *Die Vorläufer Galileis im 14. Jahrhundert: Studien zur Naturphilosophie der Spätscholastik*, 219–250. Rome: Edizioni di Storia e Letteratura.

Normore, Calvin. 2013. Buridanian possibilities. In *Logic and language in the middle ages. Essays in honor of Sten Ebbesen*, eds. Jakob L. Fink, Heine Hansen, and Ana María Mora-Marquez, 389–402. Leiden: Brill.

———. 2015. Ex impossibili quodlibet sequitur. *Vivarium* 53: 353–371.

————. 2016. Ockham and the foundations of modality in the fourteenth century. In *Logical modalities from Aristotle to Carnap: The story of necessity*, ed. Max Cresswell, Edwin Mares, and Adriane Rini, 133–153. Cambridge: Cambridge University Press.

Pasnau, Robert. 2020. Medieval modal spaces. *Aristotelian Society Supplementary Volume* 1: 225–254.

————. 2021. Qualitative change. In *The Routledge companion to medieval philosophy*, ed. Richard Cross and J.T. Paasch, 194–201. New York: Routledge.

Sylla, Edith. 2001. *Ideo quasi mendicare oportet intellectum humanum*: The role of theology in John Buridan's natural philosophy. In *The metaphysics and natural philosophy of John Buridan*, ed. J.M.M.H. Thijssen and Jack Zupko, 199–220. Leiden/Boston/Köln: Brill.

Thom, Paul. 2019. Averroes' logic. In *Interpreting Averroes: Critical essays*, ed. Peter Adamson and Matteo Di Giovanni, 81–95. Cambridge: Cambridge University Press.

Van der Lecq, Ria, and Henk A.G. Braakhuis. 1994. Introduction. In *Johannes Buridanus questiones elenchorum*, ed. Ria van der Lecq and Henk A.G. Braakhuis, ix–xxxvi. Nijmegen: Ingenium Publishers.

Zupko, Jack. 2001. On certitude. In *The metaphysics and natural philosophy of John Buridan*, ed. J.M.M.H. Thijssen and Jack Zupko, 165–182. Leiden/Boston/Köln: Brill.

————. 2003. *John Buridan: Portrait of a fourteenth-century arts master*. Notre Dame: University of Notre Dame Press.

Chapter 15
The Semantic Account of Formal Consequence, from Alfred Tarski Back to John Buridan

Jacob Archambault

Keywords Formal consequence · John Buridan · Alfred Tarski · Demarcation problem

15.1 Introduction

The resemblance between Buridan's and Tarski's theories of formal consequence has long been remarked upon, so much so that it accelerated the rediscovery of Buridan as a major medieval figure in the latter half of the twentieth century.[1] But while long noticed, it has not yet been subjected to sustained general analysis.

In this article, I provide just such an analysis. I begin by reviewing today's understanding of classical consequence, highlighting its differences from the account provided by Tarski (2002). Following this, I introduce Buridan's account of formal consequence, detailing its philosophical underpinnings, then its content. This prepares the ground for both a direct comparison between Buridan's and Tarski's respective accounts and a partial genealogy of the modern account.

---

[1] See Moody 1952; Kneale and Kneale 1962; Dumitriu 1974; Dutilh Novaes 2012, 2020; Parsons 2014. See also the editor introductions to Buridan 1976, Kretzmann et al. 1982, and King 1985.

J. Archambault (✉)
C# .NET developer, Louisville, KY, USA

15.2   From Classical Consequence Back to Tarski

15.2.1   Classical Consequence Today

15.2.1.1   Classical Syntax

Today, classical consequence is constructed as follows. One begins with an artificial language $L = (Paren, Trm, Pred, Con, F)$. $Paren = \{(,)\}$ are our parentheses, $Trm = N \cup Var$ is a collection of *terms*, itself the union of a set of *individual constants* $N = \{a, b, c, \dots\}$, and *variables* $Var = \{x, y, z, w, x' \dots\}$. *Pred* is an infinite set of n-ary relation symbols $\{P^1, Q^1, R^1, \dots, P^2, \dots, P^n\}$. $Con = \{\neg, \supset, \vee, \wedge, \equiv, \exists, \forall\}$ is a collection of logical constants. Occasionally, the two-place identity predicate = is also classified as a constant. The class of formulas F is then determined recursively as follows:

- If $t_1 \dots t_n$ are terms, and P^n is an n-ary relation symbol, then $P^n(t_1 \dots t_n)$ is a formula. These formulas are called *atomic formulas*. Any variables among the terms of $P^n(t_1 \dots t_n)$ are said to be *unbound*.
- If $A \in F$, then $\neg A \in F$. The unbound variables of $\neg A$ are the same as those of A.
- If A, B are formulae, then so are $(A \supset B)$, $(A \vee B)$, $(A \wedge B)$, and $(A \equiv B)$, their unbound variables being those of A, B.
- If $A \in F$, and $v \in Var$, then $\forall v A$, $\exists v A$ are formulae. Here, the quantifiers $\forall v$ and $\exists v$ are said to *bind* the free occurrences in A of v, which thereafter is called a *bound variable*. A formula all of whose variables are bound is called a *sentence*.
- Nothing else is a formula.

15.2.1.2   Classical Semantics

After giving conditions for what constitutes a formula, conditions are provided for determining when they are true or false. To do this, one defines a model $M = (D, I)$ as a pair of a *domain*, D, and an *interpretation I*. D is a non-empty collection of objects: cats and dogs, numbers, members of the Medici family, or whatever else one likes. The interpretation function I then assigns: each individual constant a to an element in the domain D; and each n-ary relation symbol R^n to a subset of D^n, the nth Cartesian product of the domain. In addition to interpretations, *variable assignments* $\{v, v', \dots\}$ on M each assign values in D to all the variables of L. A formula A is thus said to be true in I on a a variable assignment v.[2]

For notational convenience, we let $(v \star I)$ be the operation such that $(v \star I)$ agrees with v on the assignment of variables, and with I on the assignment of terms,

---

[2] The treatments of truth in a model and consequence given here are substantially those of Fitting and Mendelsohn 1998. Alternatively, one might let I assign a denotation for variables and introduce x-variants in the definition of quantifiers, or use a number of other approaches. See the various approaches discussed in Garson 2013.

and write $(v \star I)(t_1, \ldots t_n)$ for $((v \star I)(t_1), \ldots (v \star I)(t_n))$. Lastly, call a variable assignment v' an *x-variant* (*y-variant*, etc.) of v iff v' agrees with v on all assignments except perhaps x. The truth value of different formulae in a model M—i.e. *truth in a model*—is then recursively determined as follows:

1. For atomic formulae of arity n, $(v \star I)(Rt_1 \ldots t_n) = T$ iff $(v \star I)(t_1, \ldots t_n) \in I(R)$
2. $(v \star I)(\neg\phi) = T$ iff $(v \star I)(\phi) = F$
3. $(v \star I)(\phi \wedge \psi) = T$ iff $(v \star I)(\phi) = (v \star I)(\psi) = T$
4. $(v \star I)(\phi \vee \psi) = T$ iff $(v \star I)(\phi) = T$ or $(v \star I)(\psi) = T$
5. $(v \star I)(\phi \supset \psi) = T$ iff $(v \star I)(\phi) = F$ or $(v \star I)(\psi) = T$
6. $(v \star I)(\phi \equiv \psi) = T$ iff $(v \star I)(\phi) = (v \star I)(\psi)$
7. $(v \star I)(\forall x\phi) = T$ iff, for every x-variant v' of v, $(v' \star I)(\phi) = T$
8. $(v \star I)(\exists x\phi) = T$ iff, for some x-variant v' of v, $(v' \star I)(\phi) = T$

A sentence ϕ is *satisfiable* if it is made true on some model M. When this happens, M is said to be a *model* of ϕ. Next, let Γ denote a set of sentences $\{\phi, \psi, \ldots\}$. We say Γ is satisfiable iff there is some model M on which every sentence in Γ is satisfiable. Similarly, when this occurs, M is said to be a model of Γ. Lastly, a sentence ϕ is said to be a logical, i.e. formal, consequence of a set Γ, written $\Gamma \vDash \phi$, iff every model of Γ is a model of ϕ.

15.2.2   Tarskian Consequence

On Tarski's account of formal consequence, $\Gamma \vDash \phi$ precisely when there is no uniform substitution on non-logical constants in Γ, ϕ that models Γ but not ϕ. This agrees with the modern classical approach inasmuch as formality is determined by variation of models, though it differs with respect to what precisely is varied.

15.2.2.1   Tarskian Models

In model-theory today, the languages one works with are left uninterpreted until given an interpretation by the interpretation function. The languages Tarski worked with, by contrast, were fully interpreted artificial languages, like those for Riemannian geometry or Peano arithmetic. Thus, for Tarski, there is no question of assigning an interpretation to the non-logical constant '0', say, or varying its interpretation across models. Rather, where contemporary model theory varies the interpretation of non-logical constants across models to determine what follows logically from what, Tarski left these constants interpreted as they were, but replaced them uniformly with variables, whose assignments are then varied accordingly.[3] The same point also holds for predicate and relation symbols: where modern practice varies their interpretation, Tarski's replaces them with second-order variables, and then varies their assignments.[4] While there is a conceptual difference between the two approaches, both lead to the same material results.

For Tarski, in contrast with modern practice, a model does not include an interpretation, but is simply a sequence of objects. As Tarski puts it:

> One of the concepts which can be defined with the help of the concept of satisfaction is the concept of *model*. Let us assume that, in the language which we are considering, to each extra-logical constant correspond certain variable symbols, and this in such a way that, by replacing in an arbitrary sentence a constant by a corresponding variable, we transform this sentence into a sentential function. Let us further consider an arbitrary class of sentences L, and let us replace all extra-logical constants occurring in the sentences of class L by corresponding variables (equiform constants by equiform variables, non-equiform by non-equiform); we shall obtain a class of sentential functions L'. An arbitrary sequence of objects which satisfies each sentential function of the class L' we shall call a *model of the class L* (in just this sense one usually speaks about a model of the system of axioms of a deductive theory); if in particular the class L consists of only one sentence X, we will simply speak about a *model of the sentence X*. (Tarski 2002, 185–186)

Some examples may be helpful. The sentence "Andrew and Peter are brothers" may be formalized by $B(a, p)$. Since both the relation B and the individual constants a and p are non-logical constants, we replace them all to obtain a class of sentential functions $L' = \{X(x, y), X'(x, y')...\}$. On Tarski's definition, the models of $B(a, p)$ thus end up being those ordered pairs satisfying each sentential function of the form $X(x, y)$. This can be meant in two ways: in the first way, it can mean the models of $B(a, p)$ are those ordered pairs satisfying every binary function. If this were so, the resulting class would be empty, since, e.g. no ordered pair satisfies both the identity function and its converse. And following this line of reasoning, anything would follow from it: since the class of models would be empty, it would hold vacuously that every model of whatever else would be a model of $B(a, p)$. This isn't Tarski's intention. In the way Tarski did intend this, we consider $X(x, y)$ and $X(x', y')$ separately, as mere notational variants of each other, and take the class of models of $B(a, p)$ to be the class of ordered pairs satisfying some arbitrary binary relation which we let be designated by X. The class of models thus turns out to be just the class of ordered pairs.[5] This is counterintuitive to the degree one might expect the class of models of the *fully-interpreted* string $B(a, p)$ to simply be {<Andrew, Peter>}. But notice that Tarski's method gives the same result as the modern one, on which B, a, and p are treated as uninterpreted symbols whose interpretations are varied across models.

---

[3] According to Schiemer and Reck 2013, 433, the contemporary practice originates in the work of John Kemeny. See Kemeny 1956a, b.

[4] See e.g. Tarski 1941, 122–23. Cf. Etchemendy 1988, 69; Schiemer and Reck 2013, 448.

[5] The proof of this is simple: both the identity and non-identity functions are candidate values for the second-order variable X in $X(x, y)$. Since these partition the class of ordered pairs (i.e. every ordered pair satisfies one or the other of these), there is always some function the variable X may be mapped to to include an ordered pair as its arguments mapping to *Trm*.

15.2.2.2   Tarskian Domains

The most debated question concerning Tarski's work from both pre- and post-war periods is whether he allowed for domain variation across different classical models, as modern practice does; or whether in accordance with then-current logicist assumptions, he assumed a single fixed domain of quantification, viz. the actual universe. Unlike the above, this difference *does* affect the extension of the class of formal consequences. For instance, if the domain of quantification is not varied, $\exists x \exists y x \neq y$ is a logical truth, and hence follows formally from, e.g. $\exists x x = x$. But intuitively (and on the variant-domain approach followed today), "there are at least two objects" is not a truth *of logic*, nor does it follow from "there is at least one object."[6]

Today, all major parties to the debate agree that Tarski employs a fixed-domain framework in his 1936 "On the concept of following logically," this being his broadest and most philosophical discussion of formal consequence in the period. The main points of disagreement concern (1) whether Tarski made use of variable domains where the range of variables was restricted to some more specified domain of discourse—e.g. numbers, points, or segments; and (2) whether Tarski ever changed his mind about domain variation. Readings starting with Etchemendy 1988 and including those of Sagüillo, Corcoran, and Mancosu, suggest that Tarski changed from a fixed to variable domain approach in the late 40s or early 50s. Gómez-Torrente, however, holds Tarski's views did not change significantly throughout his life: rather, Tarski accepted a fixed-domain background theory for formal consequence, which permitted techniques for domain relativization when applied to more specified formal theories.

Gómez-Torrente (2009, 251–67) copiously details cases where Tarski's actual mathematical practice from the same period as his 1936 essay allowed for domain variation. Tarski 1953, often regarded as Tarski's first work to explicitly require domain variation in its approach to consequence (Corcoran and Sagüillo 2011, 367; Etchemendy 1988, 65), unproblematically refers his reader to his 1936 paper for formal definitions of its semantical notions, including logical consequence (Tarski 1953, 8, n. 7; Gómez-Torrente 2009, 259); and Tarski's *Introduction to Logic and to the Methodology of Deductive Sciences*, first published in 1941 with subsequent editions in 1946 and 1965, does not undergo any significant change in its treatment of formal consequence. Lastly, as Corcoran and Sagüillo (2011, 365–66) notes, the

---

[6] Alonzo Church had already read Tarski as varying the domain across models in 1956. The first paper to have suggested domain variation was *absent* in Tarski's original account appears to have been Corcoran 1972, 43. That Tarski assumed a fixed-domain in his account of formal consequence was then defended at length by Etchemendy 1988, 1990, 2008, and later taken up by Sagüillo 1997, 2009; Corcoran and Sagüillo 2011; Bays 2001; and Mancosu 2006, 2010b. A variable-domain reading of Tarski 2002 was accepted by Sher 1991, 1996; Ray 1996; and in Stroińska and Hitchcock's introduction to Tarski 2002, each broadly on grounds of interpretive charity. The most sophisticated proponent of a variable-domain interpretation in Tarski's pre-WWII work is Gómez-Torrente 1996, 2009. Mancosu has summarized the status of the current debate in Mancosu 2010a.

framework for Tarski's broadest later discussion of the issues involved in his 1936 work, his 1966 lecture "What are logical notions?" (Tarski 1986), is also domain-invariant.

In short, Tarski's pre-WWII mathematical work makes use of variable domains; where Tarski's use of domain variation is explicit in his post-WWII discussions of consequence, he refers his reader to his earlier work unproblematically; and his broadest later discussion of the issues of his 1936 paper also assumes an invariant domain. All of this suggests a high level of continuity between Tarski's earlier and later work on the subject.

To better understand the continuity as well as the differences between modern practice and Tarski's, it may be useful to reflect on the concerns and motivations behind Tarski's approach. Tarski's main concern was, positively, to secure the foundational unity of the deductive sciences; and negatively, to remove or overcome the main threats to that unity, found especially in Gödel's incompleteness results. Tarski's theory of formal consequence was not only meant to capture an intuitive notion of following from: it was also meant to provide a general theory for accommodating all then-known mathematical deductive practices.[7] To give a theory of formal consequence was thus to be engaged in philosophy of science at the most general level.[8] Though its details are different, Tarski's aim, to secure logic as a unified framework for all mathematics, remains one with Russell and Whitehead's *Principia*.

Tarski locates the problem with both Carnap's approach and the proof-theoretic approach of the Hilbert school in a certain relation to *language*. For Tarski, both these approaches are too dependent on language, albeit in different ways: Carnap's is linguistically impoverished, since, e.g. it is not sufficiently general to extend to languages lacking negation; it is the expressiveness embraced by the proof-theoretic approach to avoid ω-incompleteness, however, that allows Gödel's incompleteness results to go through.[9] The former failure justifies the shift to the model-theoretic approach; the latter, Tarski's limiting the concept of truth used in this approach so as to restrict self-reference.

---

[7] See Blok and Pigozzi 1988 and esp. Jané 2006.

[8] This same attitude persists in Tarski 1986, where logic is regarded as the most general of the sciences, and logical notions are accordingly identified as those remaining invariant for "all one-one transformations of the space, or universe of discourse, or 'world', onto itself" (49).

[9] Gödel's original proof only applied to languages strong enough to formulate Peano Arithmetic, and hence including rules for mathematical induction (or their equivalent). Later, Rosser 1936 and others extended Gödel's incompleteness results, showing they were replicable for all extensions of the weaker system Q, not including induction rules.

15.2.2.3   Summary

Though both Tarski's and the modern approach call a consequence $\Gamma \vDash \phi$ formal when every model of the set Γ is at the same time a model of ϕ, they differ to the degree that their underlying concepts of "model" differ. Tarski interprets "model of Γ" to mean a sequence of objects satisfying the sentential functions obtained from Γ—i.e. constant-free versions of the sentences of Γ, where like constants are replaced by like variables. The modern approach takes a model of Γ to be an interpretation of the (uninterpreted) strings in Γ, mapping them to a domain of objects arbitrary both in content and in number. Tarski's approach corresponds more fully to the intuitive *meaning* of "model," while the modern approach, if idiosyncratic in its choice of terms, corresponds more fully to the intuitive *extension* of following formally.

Let us then see how these compare to Buridan's account.

15.3   Buridan's Theory of Formal Consequence

15.3.1   Preliminaries

Buridan's *Treatise on Consequences* divides into four books: the first provides the theory of consequences, then discusses consequences holding between assertoric propositions; the second treats modal consequence; the third and fourth, respectively, provide detailed discussions of assertoric and modal syllogistic.

Buridan begins book 1 with a discussion of the truth and falsity of propositions (ch. 1), then the causes of the truth of propositions (ch. 2), before defining (ch. 3) then dividing consequence into its various kinds (ch. 4). After this, he treats the supposition (ch. 5) and ampliation of terms (ch. 6) and the matter and form of propositions (ch. 7) before providing a list of assertoric consequences (ch. 8).

Unlike Tarski, Buridan has no notion of a function, and unsurprisingly has even less the notion of a sentential function. However, the degree to which Buridan's remarks on propositions mimic the role played by the notion of sentential function in Tarski's is surprising. Earlier medieval logic treatises invariably discussed the signification of terms prior to propositions. In doing so, they followed the order charted by Aristotle in the Boethian translations of the "old logic."[10] Because terms signified things belonging to the different Aristotelian categories of being, and terms were the principal parts of the proposition, an adequate grasp of propositions was thought to presuppose a correct account of the categories. This was all the more so in the case of syllogistic and other consequences, which themselves presupposed

---

[10] I.e. those elements of the Aristotelian logical corpus that never disappeared from the Latin West: Porphyry's *Isagoge* and Aristotle's *Categories* and *On interpretation*. See Aquinas 1989 prologue, as well as the ordering of materials in Ockham 1974.

the theory of the proposition. In contrast with William of Ockham, whose approach was radical in proposing a different and more limited metaphysical basis for logical reasoning (Read 2007), Buridan's ordering of materials in both his *Tractatus de consequentiis* and his *Summulae* is radical in simply postponing the metaphysical question: what is important first and foremost for Buridan is the role terms play in a sentence.

Tarski both took the number of objects to be fixed and required constants referring to them to be stripped of any temporal or modal connotation.[11] For Buridan, by contrast, what exists changes from moment to moment; and with Prior and Kripke against Tarski and Quine, the propositional edifice upon which Buridan builds his account of consequence retains modality and tense.[12]

As a special case of the previous point, *propositions*, too, can come into and out of existence (Klima 2004; Dutilh Novaes 2005). Thus, unlike Tarski, Buridan didn't require the elements of language themselves to lie outside the range of semantic referents.

Buridan employs a version of truthmaker semantics, where the primary sense of "exists" ranges over presently existing entities. But his "presentism" leads to some modifications when compared to more common accounts of truthmakers, or what Buridan calls *causes of truth* (Buridan 2015 I. 1). Typically, presentist approaches to truthmaking require that one give *presently-existing* truthmakers for past- and future-tense statements. These may be existing concrete entities (Cameron 2008, 2011, 2013), abstracta (Crisp 2007), or even the entire universe (Bigelow 1996). Buridan, by contrast, employs a version of what Sam Baron has called *tensed-truthmaker theory* (Baron 2015). According to Buridan,

> If Colin's horse, which cantered well, is dead, 'Colin's horse cantered well'… is true because things were in reality as the proposition signifies they were. In the same way 'The Antichrist will preach' is true, not because things are in reality as the proposition signifies, but because things will be in reality as the proposition signifies they will be. Similarly, 'Something that never will be can be' is true, not because things are as the proposition signifies, but because things can be as it signifies them to be. And so it is clear that it is necessary to assign causes of truth to different types of propositions in different ways. (Buridan 2015 I. 1, 63)

Where Tarski prefaced his account of consequence by introducing the notion of a model, i.e. a sequence of objects satisfying a sentential function, Buridan uses the notion of the *causes of truth* or falsity of a proposition. A cause of truth of a present-tense assertoric proposition ϕ at time t is a state of affairs present at t making the proposition true, provided ϕ exists. If ϕ does not exist at t, it is neither true nor false. In tensed and modal cases the same basic idea is applied, making appropriate adjustments. But where Tarski stratifies the concept of truth, Buridan jettisons it: his account of consequence makes no use of truth apart from that required to arrive at the concept of a cause of truth (Klima 2008).

---

[11] In this, Tarski is following Russell, Ramsey, and Wittgenstein. See Ramsey 1931, 59ff.

[12] For the influence of Buridan on Prior's work, see Uckelman 2012.

As we can see from the above, where Tarski's notion of a model is general from the start, countenancing e.g. every object satisfying a unary function from objects to truth as a model of "Socrates runs," Buridan's remains particular at this point, countenancing only Socrates running as a cause of truth.

For Buridan, the relative number of causes of truth a typical quantified subject-predicate proposition can have is conditioned by the *supposition* of its terms. In his *Summulae*, Buridan divides the most common type of supposition, *common material supposition*, into determinate and confused, the latter being subdivided into distributed and merely confused. The subject and predicate of a particular affirmative proposition, as well as the subject of a particular negative, have determinate supposition: each implies the disjunction of all sentences where the determinately suppositing term is replaced by one of its instances, and is implied by any of these. The subject of a universal affirmative has confused distributed supposition, as do both terms of a universal negative proposition: each implies any sentence replacing the confused distributed term with any object falling under it, and is implied by the conjunction of all such sentences. Merely confused supposition is that kind had by the predicate of a universal affirmative proposition: here, one cannot descend from the original sentence to either the conjunction or disjunction of all sentences resulting from replacing the merely confusedly suppositing term with an object falling under it, though one *may* descend from the original sentence to one where the merely confusedly suppositing term is replaced by the term disjunction of all its instances. Buridan explains the relations between these as follows:

> I say that both terms being undistributed but suppositing determinately, then there are more causes of truth than if one were distributed and the other confused without distribution. This is clear because every cause of truth enough to make 'Every B is A' true is enough to make 'B is A' true, but not vice versa. Therefore a proposition [1] has most causes of truth with each term undistributed [2] and fewer with one term distributed and the other confused without distribution, [3] and fewer still with one distributed and the other used determinately without distribution, [4] and fewest of all with both distributed. (Buridan 2015 I. 2, 66)

What Buridan states here has a ready parallel in model theory, namely that every model of a sentence of the form $\forall x\phi$ is a model of "$\exists x\phi$." Buridan, however, extends the theory further, pointing out that whatever makes a proposition of the form "Every A is *this* B" true also makes "Every A is B" true (i.e. case 3), and that whatever makes "Every A is every B" true also makes "Every A is this B" true (case 4). Buridan is already operating on a highly abstract level in considering cases like 3 and 4, which hardly occur in natural language discussion. And by phrasing the point in terms of distribution rather than by mentioning specific determiners, he shows us that he knows this holds across a wide-variety of sentential forms, rather than merely those mentioned above.

What is perhaps surprising is that for Buridan, a cause of truth does not suffice for the truth of a proposition, but only does so on the condition that the proposition itself exist. Buridan introduces this caveat as a way of dealing with certain propositions whose existence falsifies them, that nevertheless describe possible states of affairs. For instance, the proposition "no proposition is negative" is self-falsifying whenever formed, but surely describes a possible state of affairs—indeed, it adequately captures each actual state of affairs before the advent of human speech (Buridan 2015 I. 3).

15.3.2 Formal and Material Consequence

After laying out the above preliminaries, Buridan provides us first with a definition and then a division of consequences.

Today, logicians distinguish consequence from hypothetical propositions, usually identifying the latter with conditionals. One then must provide a deduction theorem to establish that $A \vDash B$ iff $\vDash A \to B$. Buridan, by contrast, identifies these: "A consequence is a hypothetical proposition; for it is constituted from several propositions conjoined by the expression 'if' or the expression 'therefore' or something equivalent" (Buridan 2015 I. 3, 66, alt.).

Just as modern practice reserves the term "consequence" for formally valid consequence, Buridan reserves it for correct hypotheticals (Buridan 2015 I. 3, 66). But where the classical emphasis on formal validity arises already in removing nonlogical content from the models of a sentence, Buridanian consequences are not as such formal in this way.[13]

After considering definitions of consequence in terms of (1) the impossibility of the antecedent being true and the consequent not so, (2) the impossibility of the antecedent being true and the consequent false *when both are formed*, and (3) the impossibility of things being as the antecedent signifies without being as the consequent signifies, Buridan ultimately settles on the following definition of consequence:

> A consequence is a hypothetical proposition composed of an antecedent and consequent, indicating the antecedent to be antecedent and the consequent to be consequent; this designation occurs by the word 'if' or by the word 'therefore' or an equivalent. (Buridan 2015 I. 3, 67)

Unlike the model-theoretic definition, Buridan's is deflationary in spirit: Buridan takes "antecedent" and "consequent" to apply to the respective parts of a hypothetical proposition precisely when "consequence" applies to the whole. Thus, whether the definition is materially adequate or not,[14] it does nothing to further determine

---

[13] This difference in definition hints at a much deeper one. For Buridan, consequences are always individual sentence tokens, i.e. actually written or spoken hypothetical expressions, which are evaluated by determining whether the connections they express hold in all possible situations (including those where the expressions themselves do not exist, and hence are neither true nor false). For Tarski and the modern approach, by contrast, consequences are *never* actual sentences, both because of the aforementioned abstraction at the level of the models of a sentential function, and because the antecedent Γ of a classical consequence $\Gamma \vDash \phi$ is always at least countably infinite, since it is closed under entailment.

[14] It is not. See Archambault 2017, 55–60.

either the extension or the intension of "consequence" beyond what is already given in the name itself.

Buridan divides consequences into formal and material, dividing the latter into simple and as-of-now consequences. A simple consequence is one where things cannot be as the antecedent signifies and not as the consequent signifies; an as-of-now consequence, one where things cannot *now* be as the antecedent signifies, without also being as the consequent signifies. Thus, as-of-now consequence limits those cases considered in simple consequence to the present situation alone. Thus, every simple material consequence is an as-of-now material consequence, but not conversely.

Buridan explains the division between formal and material consequence as follows:

> A consequence is called 'formal' if it is valid in all terms retaining a similar form. Or, if you want to put it explicitly, a formal consequence is one where every proposition similar in form that might be formed would be a good consequence [...]. A material consequence, however, is one where not every proposition similar in form would be a good consequence, or, as it is commonly put, which does not hold in all terms retaining the same form. (Buridan 2015 I. 4, 68)

Buridan continues:

> It seems to me that no material consequence is evident in inferring except by its reduction to a formal one. Now it is reduced to a formal one by the addition of some necessary proposition or propositions whose addition to the given antecedent produces a formal consequence. (Buridan 2015 I. 4, 68)

Where the former passage shows formal and material consequence on equal footing with respect to their validity—both are true hypothetical propositions—the latter shows they are not so with respect to their evidential status: a material consequence is only evident in inference if it can be transformed into a formal one by appropriate additions to the antecedent. One might get the impression from this that for Buridan, material consequences are all enthymemes.[15] But Buridan lists enthymemes as only one kind of material consequence, alongside examples and inductions (Buridan 2015 III. 1, 113); and in Buridan's treatment of dialectical topics, inductions may be proven not "by virtue of being a formal consequence or by being reduced to a formal consequence, but by the natural inclination of the understanding towards truth" (Buridan 2013, 10-6:6.1.5). In this way, the peculiar importance of formal consequence lies not in its preserving *truth*, but *evidence*.

But to know which consequences exactly are formal, one must know what the form of a proposition is. And just as in both Tarski's earlier and later work, this is determined by a partition. Buridan writes:

> I say that when we speak of matter and form, by the matter of a proposition or consequence we mean the purely categorematic terms, namely the subject and predicate, setting aside the syncategoremes attached to them by which they are [1] conjoined [2] or denied [3] or

---

[15] Cf. Burleigh 1955, 66.

distributed [4] or given a certain kind of supposition; we say all the rest pertains to form.
(Buridan 2015 I. 7, 74)

There are two central differences between Buridan's division and its Tarskian counterpart. First, where Tarski's is a fixed division of terms in a *language* into two different *kinds*, Buridan's is one of terms in a *sentence* into two different *roles*. Thus,
for instance, in the sentence "if is a syncategoreme, therefore if is a word," Buridan's
analysis correctly characterizes "if" as a categorematic term, while Tarski's requires
it to be treated as a logical constant. Second, where Tarski's approach prioritizes
determining the set of logical constants of a language, Buridan's begins by defining
the *categorematic* terms of a sentence, i.e. the analogue of classical non-logical
constants, and then defines the syncategoremata of a sentence as those not belonging among the categorical terms of the sentence. The categorematic terms are simply those operating as the subject and predicate of the sentence.[16] Buridan then lists
four types of words as pertaining to form: (1) those conjoining the subject and
predicate (e.g. "is"); (2) those separating the subject and predicate (e.g. "not"); (3)
those giving the terms a certain distribution (e.g. quantifiers); (4) those giving terms
a certain kind of supposition (e.g. modal, tense, and other intensional operators).
These last two are the subjects to which Buridan's discussions of supposition and
ampliation in chapters five and six pertain. Notably absent from this list are propositional connectives, which Buridan doesn't consider in the *Treatise on Consequences*.

Though Buridanian formal consequences may be represented schematically,
these consequences are never themselves schematic,[17] but remain individual hypothetical propositions. As such, there is no problem on Buridan's account about
whether the *ordering* and choice of schematic variables in a schematic consequence
belongs to its matter or form.[18] For Buridan, while different good consequences may
be representable by the same schema (e.g. different instances of *modus ponens*);
while these same consequences may be representable by other schemata (i.e. by
uniformly replacing the schematic variables used in the first schema with others);
and while schemata for good and bad formal consequences may have the same
ordering of their syncategorematic parts (e.g. *modus ponens* and affirming the consequent): because schematic consequences are not properly consequences at all for
Buridan, these problems disappear. Buridan's formal consequences are hypothetical
propositions of a natural language; it is not because they belong to the same schema
that they are formal consequences; rather, these formal consequences evidently
belong to an equivalence class, and because of this can be represented schematically
under the same form.

---

[16] A note on the language of "syncategoremata": to my knowledge, the phrase "syncategorematic
terms" does not occur in Buridan. Terms are those words in which every sentence "bottoms out"
(hence the name "term," i.e. end or limit), and so are just those words against which syncategore-
mes are divided.

[17] This is also true on Tarski's account, though it is not so on the received classical analysis. The
basic reason for the latter is the decision to regard the constant symbols as uninterpreted.

[18] I thank Milo Crimi for bringing this problem to my attention.

15.4   Formal Consequence from Tarski Back to Buridan

Having set Buridan's, Tarski's, and the standard classical accounts of formal consequence in order, we can now contrast them summarily. Doing so provides us with a condition requisite for an adequate genealogy of the Tarskian concept, i.e. an account of the conditions that had to arise between Buridan and Tarski's account before Tarski's account became a real possibility. With this in mind, we first summarize the differences between the Buridanian and Tarskian accounts of formal consequence; then, we list historical conditions necessary for arriving at the Tarskian account from the Buridanian one.

Both modern and Tarskian approaches begin with a partition of all terms of a *language* into logical and non-logical terms; Buridan's partition of terms into categorical and syncategorematic occurs not at the level of a language, but at that of the sentence.

Tarski's project prioritizes determining the logical terms of a language, with the determination of the set of non-logical terms falling out of this. Buridan's partition begins by determining those terms pertaining to the matter of the sentence, fixing the set of formal terms in a sentence as the complement of those pertaining to the matter. For Buridan, the terms pertaining to the matter of a sentence are its subjects and predicates.

Tarskian consequence was designed for recursively defined artificial languages, particularly those being developed in mathematics. Buridanian consequence was designed to capture Buridan's stilted fourteenth-century scholastic Latin. *Pace* humanist objections, the latter remained a natural language, albeit one making use of mild regimentation when doing so aided discussion. Buridan counts the copula, negation, modalities, tenses, quantifiers, intentional operators, as well as disjunction, conjunction and negation for terms among the formal parts of a sentence. But because he explains the formal parts of a sentence as those affecting the supposition of *terms*, he does not mention sentential connectives as pertaining to form. While admitting sentential connectives, Tarski discounted modalities, tenses, and intensional operators. While initially silent on the status of identity, Tarski later explicitly admitted it as a logical notion. Since then, modalities and other intensional operators have become standard in extensions of classical logic.

For Tarski, consequences are distinguished from hypothetical propositions, not least because the set of premises from which a consequent is derived is closed under entailment, hence countably infinite. Buridan, by contrast, explicitly identifies consequences with hypothetical propositions.

Where Tarski provides an informative definition of consequence in terms of models, Buridan provides a deflationary one in terms of the correlative notions of antecedent and consequent. However, the work done by the notion of a model on Tarski's account is mimicked by that done by the notion of a cause of truth on Buridan's.

On the received classical account, a model of a sentence ϕ in a language L consists of a domain D and an interpretation I, i.e. a mapping of the sentences of L to truth or falsity, recursively determined by a mapping of terms to elements in D and n-ary predicates to sets of n-tuples in D^n.

On Tarski's account, a model of a set of sentences Γ is a sequence of objects in a fixed domain satisfying the sentential functions obtained by uniformly replacing each non-logical constant in the sentences of Γ with variables of the appropriate order and arity.

The differences between the received classical and Tarskian understandings of a model thus lead to differences in their understanding of both the intension and extension of the concept of formal consequence. Both the Tarskian and received classical accounts of the models of a sentence, however, are general from the beginning: for instance, the classical models of an atomic sentence will not be the objects making it true on the intended interpretation of its non-logical constants, but those making it true on *any* interpretation; and the Tarskian models will be sequences satisfying any sentential function of the same form as the initial sentence.

Buridan's account of causes of truth, by contrast, maps hypothetical propositions to states sufficient to make them true on their *intended* interpretation. The determination of the relative number of causes of truth a sentence has is given by the supposition of its terms, i.e. the manner in which one is permitted to descend from a general term modified by a determiner to a new sentence or sentences replacing the determined general term with a name (names) for an individual(s) falling under it. On Buridan's account, the causes of truth of a proposition are relative to a time of utterance; the models of a Tarskian sentence are not; and while not fixed, classical models are relativized in a way not based on external circumstances, but arbitrarily. On Buridan's account, formality is then achieved by the determination of the equivalence class of a hypothetical proposition: a Buridanian consequence is formal iff for every proposition equivalent in form to it that could be formed, it is impossible for things to be as the antecedent signifies without being as the consequent signifies (or to have been, or be able to be, etc., in accordance with the tense and modal requirements of the sentences from which the consequence is composed).

Those developments that *were* necessary historical conditions for the development of Tarski's account from the Buridanian one are comparatively few, but central. The first is the development of the concept of a model; the second, that of a function generally and of a sentential function in particular. Lastly, the decision to regard antecedents as premise sets closed under entailment, and hence infinite, presupposed the development of recursion and its application to logical entailment.

Other elements of Tarski's account, on the other hand, were straightforwardly available to Buridan, but not taken up by him. Tarski's rejection of modality is not historically dependent upon post-fourteenth-century developments. An understanding of the parts of consequence as non-linguistic was accepted in the fourteenth century by Walter Burley (Bulthuis 2016). And the assumption of a fixed, eternalist domain is present in Buridan's own discussion of natural supposition (Buridan 2001, 4.3.4). In assuming that the same terms may supposit differently (e.g. for themselves) in different sentences, Buridan implicitly rejects Tarski's construal of different parts of a language as belonging to different kinds.[19] Other differences, including Buridan's decisions to identify consequences and hypothetical propositions, to determine causes of truth relative to a time, and to distinguish formal consequence from logical consequence as such, represent further philosophical disagreements.

As for motivations, one of the main ones behind Tarski's approach to languages—the complete elimination of equivocation from scientific language—was present in a different form in Ockham's adoption of *mental*, rather than spoken or written, language as his point of departure (Trentman 1970; Spade 1980; Chalmers 1999), but not in Buridan. Buridan does not require the elimination of equivocation, hence neither does he have the concern one finds in Tarski with the consistency of languages.[20]

Tarski's worries about Carnap's account of semantic consequence don't arise for Buridan either: natural languages are sufficiently robust, and indefinitely extendable, thus sufficient to encounter most of Tarski's concerns with impoverished recursive languages.[21] The major exception to this is superdenumerable domains such as the real numbers, points of geometrical space, etc., which Buridan's theory was clearly not designed to handle. This discovery, while not a necessary historical condition for the development of the semantic approach to consequence, was and remains an important motivator for it.

15.5   Conclusion

The concept of formal consequence in classical logic today, in perfect verbal agreement with Tarski's 1930s definition, holds $\Gamma \vDash \phi$ iff every model of Γ is at the same time a model of ϕ. But behind this verbal agreement lies a substantive disagreement, grounded in different concepts of a model. Today's classical models interpret uninterpreted linguistic strings by mapping them to a domain of arbitrarily many objects. Tarskian models, by contrast, are sequences of objects, within the fixed domain of all objects in the world, satisfying sentential functions obtained from interpreted sentences.

Tarski's account represents a genuine development from the Buridanian account to the degree that it employs the concepts of model, sentential function, and recursion, which were unavailable to Buridan. Other differences, however, represent more substantive disagreements. Buridan's presentism; his acceptance of modality, tense, and variable domains; his prioritization of the determination of the material parts of the sentence over the formal; his adoption of a token-based semantics

---

[19] Even if Tarski's division exacerbates a tendency, already found in Buridan, to prescind from treating the meaning of terms prior to their propositional role.

[20] This is part of what allows Buridan to treat the liar paradox locally, rather than instituting a global ban on self-reference. See Buridan 2001, 9.2.6. Cf. Klima 2004, 2008; Dutilh Novaes 2011; Benétreau-Dupin 2015.

[21] Cf. Barcan Marcus 1978.

grounded in natural languages, all were taken up *against* analogues of the contrary positions, found in Tarski, in Buridan's own time. In other ways, the difference between Buridan and Tarski's approach to consequence is not so wide as their chronological distance from each other would suggest. In contrast with modern practice, neither construes the *relata* of formal consequence schematically; Buridanian causes of truth form analogues to the Tarskian concept of models of a sentential function; and both Buridanian and Tarskian accounts of following formally are given in terms of substitution—a Buridanian formal consequence is good if all sentences that could be formed by uniform substitutions on its categorematic terms are good, a Tarskian one if it is invariant under satisfaction of sentential functions obtained from it by substituting its non-logical constants with variables. Given this closeness, it is perhaps unsurprising that many of the genuine developments in formal logic over the past 60 years have involved a reappropriation of the Buridanian standpoint on just those topics where he disagrees with Tarski. In this reappropriation of the best elements of Buridan's account into the context brought about by genuine developments since it, one might hope to find progress toward—well, if not truth, at least how things are signified to be.

Bibliography

Aquinas, Thomas. 1989. *Expositio libri Peryermeneias.* Edited by R.A. Gauthier. Translated by Jean T. Oesterle. Leonine. Vols. I*-1. Opera Omnia. Paris: Cerf.

Archambault, Jacob. 2017. *The development of the medieval Parisian account of formal consequence.* PhD thesis, Fordham University.

Barcan Marcus, Ruth. 1978. Nominalism and the substitutional quantifier. *The Monist* 61: 351–362.

Baron, Sam. 2015. Tensed truthmaker theory. *Erkenntnis* 80: 923–944.

Bays, Timothy. 2001. On Tarski on models. *Journal of Symbolic Logic* 66: 1701–1726.

Bénétreau-Dupin, Yann. 2015. Buridan's solution to the liar paradox. *History and Philosophy of Logic* 36: 18–28.

Bigelow, John. 1996. Presentism and properties. *Philosophical Perspectives* 10: 35–52.

Blok, W.J., and Don Pigozzi. 1988. Alfred Tarski's work on general metamathematics. *Journal of Symbolic Logic* 53: 36–50.

Bulthuis, Nathaniel. 2016. The motivations for Walter Burley's theory of the proposition. *British Journal for the History of Philosophy* 24: 1057–1074.

Buridan, John. 1976. Tractatus de Consequentiis. In *Philosophes Médiévaux 16*, ed. Hubert Hubien. Louvain: Publications Universitaires.

———. 2001. *Summulae de Dialectica.* Translated by Gyula Klima. New Haven: Yale University Press.

———. 2013. *Summulae de Locis Dialecticis.* Edited by Niels Jørgen Green-Pedersen. Turnhout: Brepols.

———. 2015. *Treatise on consequences.* Translated by Stephen Read. Bronx: Fordham University Press.

Burleigh, Walter. 1955. *De puritate artis logicae.* Edited by Philotheus Boehner. St Bonaventure: Franciscan Institute.

Cameron, Ross. 2008. How to be a truthmaker maximalist. *Noûs* 42: 410–421.

———. 2011. Truthmaking for presentists. *Oxford Studies in Metaphysics* 6: 55–100.

———. 2013. Changing truthmakers: Reply to Tallant and Ingram. *Oxford Studies in Metaphysics* 8: 362–373.

Chalmers, David. 1999. Is there synonymy in Ockham's mental language? In *The Cambridge companion to Ockham*, ed. Paul Vincent Spade, 76–99. Cambridge: Cambridge University Press.

Corcoran, John. 1972. Conceptual structure of classical logic. *Philosophy and Phenomenological Research* 33: 25–47.

Corcoran, John, and José M. Sagüillo. 2011. The absence of multiple universes of discourse in the 1936 Tarski consequence-definition paper. *History and Philosophy of Logic* 32: 359–374.

Crisp, Thomas M. 2007. Presentism and the grounding objection. *Noûs* 41: 90–109.

Dumitriu, Anton. 1974. The logico-mathematical antinomies: Contemporary and scholastic solutions. *International Philosophical Quarterly* 14: 309–328.

Dutilh Novaes, Catarina. 2005. Buridan's *Consequentia*: Consequence and inference within a token-based semantics. *History and Philosophy of Logic* 26: 277–297.

———. 2011. Lessons on sentential meaning from mediaeval solutions to the liar paradox. *The Philosophical Quarterly* 61: 58–78.

———. 2012. Form and matter in later Latin medieval logic: The cases of *suppositio* and *consequentia*. *Journal of the History of Philosophy* 50: 339–354.

———. 2020. Medieval theories of consequence. In *The Stanford encyclopedia of philosophy*. https://plato.stanford.edu/archives/fall2020/entries/consequence-medieval

Etchemendy, John. 1988. Tarski on truth and logical consequence. *Journal of Symbolic Logic* 53: 51–79.

———. 1990. *The concept of logical consequence*. Cambridge: Harvard University Press.

———. 2008. Reflections on consequence. In *New essays on Tarski and philosophy*, ed. Douglas Patterson, 263–299. Oxford: Clarendon Press.

Fitting, Melvin, and Richard L. Mendelsohn. 1998. *First-order modal logic*. Dordrecht: Kluwer.

Garson, James W. 2013. *Modal logic for philosophers*. 2nd ed. Cambridge: Cambridge University Press.

Gómez-Torrente, Mario. 1996. Tarski on logical consequence. *Notre Dame Journal of Formal Logic* 37: 125–151.

———. 2009. Rereading Tarski on logical consequence. *Review of Symbolic Logic* 2: 249–297.

Jané, Ignacio. 2006. What is Tarski's common concept of consequence? *Bulletin of Symbolic Logic* 12: 1–42.

Kemeny, John G. 1956a. A new approach to semantics–part I. *Journal of Symbolic Logic* 21: 1–27.

———. 1956b. A new approach to semantics–part II. *Journal of Symbolic Logic* 22: 149–161.

King, Peter. 1985. *Jean Buridan's philosophy of logic: The treatise on supposition, the treatise on consequences*. Dordrecht: D. Reidel.

Klima, Gyula. 2004. Consequences of a closed, token-based semantics: The case of John Buridan. *History and Philosophy of Logic* 25: 95–110.

———. 2008. Logic without truth: Buridan on the liar. In *Unity, truth and the liar: The modern relevance of medieval solutions to the liar paradox*, ed. S. Rahman, T. Tulenheimo, and E. Genot, 87–112. Berlin: Springer.

Kneale, William, and Martha Kneale. 1962. *The development of logic*. Oxford: Oxford University Press.

Kretzmann, Norman, Anthony Kenny, and Jan Pinborg, eds. 1982. *The Cambridge history of later medieval philosophy*. Cambridge: Cambridge University Press.

Mancosu, Paolo. 2006. Tarski on models and logical consequence. In *The architecture of modern mathematics*, ed. José Ferreirós and Jeremy Gray, 318–470. Oxford: Oxford University Press.

———. 2010a. Fixed- versus variable-domain interpretations of Tarski's account of logical consequence. *Philosophy Compass* 5: 745–759.

———. 2010b. *The adventure of reason: Interplay between mathematical logic and philosophy of mathematics*. Oxford: Oxford University Press.

Moody, E.A. 1952. *Truth and consequence in medieval logic*. Amsterdam: North-Holland.

Ockham, William. 1974. Summa logicae. In *Opera philosophica*, ed. Philotheus Boehner, Gedeon Gàl, and Stephen Brown, vol. Vol. 1. St. Bonaventure: Franciscan Institute.

Parsons, Terence. 2014. *Articulating medieval logic*. Oxford: Oxford University Press.

Ramsey, Frank P. 1931. The foundations of mathematics. In *The foundations of mathematics and other essays*, ed. R.B. Braithwaite, 1–61. London: Kegan Paul.

Ray, Greg. 1996. Logical consequence: A defence of Tarski. *Journal of Philosophical Logic* 25: 617–677.

Read, Stephen. 2007. William of Ockham's *The sum of logic. Topoi* 26: 271–277.

Rosser, Barkley. 1936. Extensions of some theorems of Gödel and Church. *Journal of Symbolic Logic* 1: 87–91.

Sagüillo, José M. 1997. Logical consequence revisited. *Bulletin of Symbolic Logic* 3: 216–241.

———. 2009. Methodological practice and complementary concepts of logical consequence: Tarski's model-theoretic consequence and Corcoran's information-theoretic consequence. *History and Philosophy of Logic* 30: 21–48.

Schiemer, Georg, and Erich H. Reck. 2013. Logic in the 1930s: Type theory and model theory. *Bulletin of Symbolic Logic* 19: 433–472.

Sher, Gila. 1991. *The bounds of logic*. Cambridge: MIT Press.

———. 1996. Did Tarski commit Tarski's fallacy? *Journal of Symbolic Logic* 61: 653–686.

Spade, Paul Vincent. 1980. Synonymy and equivocation in Ockham's mental language. *Journal of the History of Philosophy* 18: 9–22.

Tarski, Alfred. 1941. *Introduction to logic and to the methodology of deductive sciences*. Oxford: Oxford University Press.

———. 1953. A general method in proofs of undecidability. In *Undecidable theories*, 1–35. Amsterdam: North-Holland.

———. 1986. What are logical notions? *History and Philosophy of Logic* 7: 143–154.

———. 2002. On the concept of following logically. Trans. Magda Stroińska and David Hitchcock. *History and Philosophy of Logic* 23: 155–196.

Trentman, John. 1970. Ockham on mental. *Mind* 79: 586–590.

Uckelman, Sara L. 2012. Arthur prior and medieval logic. *Synthese* 188: 349–366.

Chapter 16
Skeptical Motivators in Buridan's Philosophy of Science

Ariane Economos

Keywords Induction · *Nous* · *Intellectus* · John Buridan · Aristotle · First principles · Medieval skepticism

16.1 Introduction[1]

Jonathan Barnes has argued that, when it comes to interpreting the relation between induction and *nous* as presented in the *Posterior Analytics*, Aristotelian commentators typically take one of two routes: (1) Some argue that Aristotle recognizes that induction must always be incomplete, and so alone is insufficient to provide us with knowledge of principles, and that he introduces *nous* or "intuition" as a faculty which enables us to go beyond induction and "just see" principles, without any further rational process being required. Barnes calls this the "orthodox" view, and claims that the distinction between "intuitive" and "demonstrative" knowledge used by the rationalists and empiricists is ultimately based upon this interpretation of

---

[1] This paper is written with gratitude to Gyula Klima, who served as teacher, dissertation mentor, and friend while I was a PhD student at Fordham University, and who was never "skeptical" of my abilities (although he was occasionally skeptical of some of my ideas). Thank you for everything, Gyula!

A. Economos (✉)
The School of Humanities, Marymount University, Arlington, VA, USA
e-mail: aeconomo@marymount.edu

J. P. Hochschild et al. (eds.), *Metaphysics Through Semantics: The Philosophical Recovery of the Medieval Mind*, International Archives of the History of Ideas Archives internationales d'histoire des idées 242, https://doi.org/10.1007/978-3-031-15026-5_16

what Aristotle means by "intuition" (Barnes 1994, 267).[2] (2) The other interpretation is that *nous* is not a "faculty or method" of attaining knowledge of principles, rather it is simply the "state or disposition" of grasping the principles that have been acquired through induction. An "intuitive leap," on this view, plays no role whatsoever in the actual acquisition of the principles; *nous* is simply the state attained as a result of the inductive process. Barnes calls this the "unorthodox" view. Barnes and Modrak both suggest that the "orthodox" interpretation of Aristotle only gained popularity around the seventeenth century (Barnes 1994, 268).[3]

This paper examines John Buridan's account of induction and its relation to *intellectus*, the Latin equivalent of *nous*, and argues that Buridan's view of the relation between induction and *intellectus* is shaped largely by his sensitivity to skeptical concerns. Buridan includes induction in his account of our cognition of indemonstrable principles, but his recognition of these skeptical concerns leads him to the conclusion that induction itself is not productive of such principles. Rather, the primary role of induction is to train and cultivate the innate power of *intellectus* so as to ensure that its natural assent to universal principles does not go astray. Induction accomplishes this by providing counter-examples to generalizations, when available. In this way, Buridan is a fourteenth-century representative of Barnes's "orthodox" view.

16.2 The Purposes and Kinds of Indemonstrable Principles

Buridan holds that indemonstrable first principles are essential for the acquisition of scientific knowledge (*scientia*), and serve the function of providing a starting-point for scientific demonstration. He closely follows Aristotle in claiming that, strictly speaking, to have scientific knowledge of something means that one has demonstrated it. A demonstration, according to him, is a syllogism that produces

---

[2] Deborah Modrak describes this "traditional" view of *nous* in the following way: "… the traditional interpretation [is] championed by Le Blond (1939) among others. According to that interpretation of II, 19, the genetic account [of induction] describes a process of empirical generalization that yields general principles of some sort, but these principles fall short of the comprehensiveness and certainty required of first principles. First principles are apprehended through an immediate act of insight (nous), and this process is described in the final section." Modrak 1987, 172.

[3] Modrak describes the "non-traditional" view of *nous* in a similar way: "Kosman (1973) and Lesher (1973) both argue to the contrary that the connection between the two sections [of II, 19] is obvious and unproblematic: the first section describes the acquisition of first principles through *epagoge*; the second section talks about *nous*, which is the *hexis* (disposition) realized through *epagoge*." Modrak 1987, 171. Modrak herself argues for the non-traditional interpretation: "While a seventeenth-century philosopher might believe that *nous* is needed to confirm the apodictic certainty of principles reached through *epagoge*, Aristotle is not motivated by skeptical considerations; hence for him the interesting issues concern the apprehension of first principles, not the validation of our claim to know them. *Nous* is Aristotle's answer to the second question; it is the *hexis* of knowing the first principles." Modrak 1987, 173.

knowledge of the cause of a thing or event.[4] The premises of a demonstrative syllogism must be true, primary, immediate, prior to, and causative of the conclusion (Buridan 2009, 201–210). Most importantly for our purposes here, and again following Aristotle, he claims that the premises of such a demonstrative syllogism must not only be known, but must in fact be *better known* than the conclusion.

In order to establish the need for *indemonstrable* principles, Buridan produces versions of arguments similar to those we find in Aristotle's *Posterior Analytics*. Buridan claims that if there were no indemonstrable principles, then it would be necessary to "go to infinity" in our demonstrations and demonstrate every principle. This, he argues, is impossible, since it would either require that circular demonstration be valid, which he argues against, or it would lead to a regress, which "would be impossible, for it is impossible to go to infinity in the series of subjects and predicates; there has to be a halt... as is sufficiently proved by Aristotle in Book 1 of the *Posterior Analytics*" (Buridan 2001, 702). Thus, in order to avoid an account of knowledge that would fall prey to this kind of criticism, Buridan concludes that some premises must be immediate and indemonstrable.

In the *Summulae de dialectica* and the *Quaestiones in duos Aristotelis libros Posteriorum Analyticorum*, Buridan divides first principles into different kinds, namely, those which are self-evident and those which are not. According him, a principle is self-evident to us if it is "necessarily conceded on the basis of [its] nominal definition, provided the signification of the terms is known" (Buridan 2001, 719). He cites "every vacuum is a place," and "every pug is a nose," as examples. He also cites the Principle of Non-Contradiction, and other principles immediately derived from it, as another example of a self-evident principle:

> Some principles are at once evident to us when they are propounded to us. And this is the case with that most general and evident principle that Aristotle posits in Book 4 of the *Metaphysics* [i.e. the Principle of Non-Contradiction], and the principles that come under it, e.g., that it is impossible for a man to run and not to run, that it is impossible for the same line to be simultaneously equal to itself and not to be equal to itself, and it is impossible to dissent from such principles, or to assent to their opposites, because of the evident repugnance involved in contradiction (Buridan 2001, 719).

Such principles are evident in what Buridan calls "the most proper sense," that is, one immediately assents to them: "When it comes to evidence, you should note that 'evidence' may be taken in many ways. One sense is the most proper, and in this case the evidence of a proposition is that because of which the intellect, by its nature, is compelled to assent to the proposition and cannot dissent from it" (Buridan 2009, 163) Jack Zupko describes such principles as having "absolute evidentness"; that is, a proposition of this kind cannot be falsified and is absolutely certain, even in the worst of skeptical scenarios. Buridan distinguishes absolutely self-evident principles from those lacking this kind of evidentness at the end of his *Questions on the Posterior Analytics*:

---

[4] If we are talking about demonstration in the strict sense, that is, a demonstration *propter quid*.

It must also be noted that there are two kinds of indemonstrable principles. One kind is those of which the relations of the terms plainly include or exclude each other, once we know their meaning. The other <kind> is principles in which the meanings of their terms neither evidently include nor evidently exclude each other (Buridan 2009, 423).

The first of these two kinds refers to absolutely self-evident principles, and from what he says here and above, it seems clear that Buridan primarily has in mind definitions and axioms. As long as one knows the meaning of the terms involved in the proposition, one cannot help but concede a definition such as, "every pug is a nose," or an axiom such as, "it is impossible for a man to both run and not run."

The second kind of principles have a different sort of evidentness, where understanding the meanings of the terms of the proposition is not sufficient to make the intellect assent to their truth. When discussing this kind of principle, Buridan especially cites examples of moral principles: "Not every first principle is self-evident when it first occurs. And this is obviously true for moral principles, for it is possible to… deny them and assent to their opposites" (Buridan 2001, 718–719). Moral principles are not the only kind of principles that lack absolute evidentness, however; there are principles used in the speculative sciences which also lack this kind of evidentness: "even for speculative knowledge… a great number of first and indemonstrable principles in natural science are doubtful to us until we have had many experiences involving them, over a long period of time" (Buridan 2001, 719) The "doubtfulness" of these principles, for Buridan, is an indication that they cannot be classed with absolutely self-evident principles.

These principles, he claims, do have their own kind of evidentness: "natural evidentness." Something is "naturally evident" if "it is apparent to anyone and no human reasoning can make its opposite apparent" (Buridan 2009, 163). Natural evidentness, however, is not evident in the strictest sense, since "the intellect may be deceived about such evident propositions by a supernatural cause, since God could produce a fire without heat, and could produce and conserve in my senses a sensible species without an object" (Buridan 2009, 163). He refers to their evidentness as "natural" in the sense that such a proposition is evident assuming that the common course of nature holds, and no supernatural agent is intervening: "one cannot be deceived about it as long as he remains within the common course of nature, granted that he could be deceived by a supernatural cause; this evidentness is sufficient for natural science" (Buridan 2009, 164).

Into this category of principles that have "natural evidentness" we must place the principles that Buridan most frequently cites in his discussion of how we come to know first principles, that is, "every fire is hot," and "all rhubarb produces bile" (Buridan 2009, 423). Buridan is clear that this class of indemonstrable principles is entirely distinct from axioms and definitions; he explicitly claims that propositions such as axioms and definitions have absolute evidentness, since the relations of their terms "plainly include or exclude each other," while propositions such as, "all rhubarb produces bile," are not composed of terms which evidently include or exclude each other, and so can only ever be naturally evident.

16.3   Induction

In the *Questions on the Posterior Analytics*, Buridan claims that how we come to know a first principle differs depending upon the type of principle. As discussed above, he distinguishes between two kinds of principles, which he here calls first-mode and second-mode. First-mode principles include axioms and definitions, and second-mode include causal principles such as, "all rhubarb produces bile." He re-emphasizes he point that, when it comes to grasping a principle that belongs to the first-mode, it suffices that the intellect understands the meanings of the terms of the proposition for it to give assent to the proposition's truth (Buridan 2009, 423).

When it comes to understanding second-mode principles, however, understanding the meanings of the terms being used in these principles is not sufficient to produce assent to their truth. Rather, the intellect requires perception, memories, and past experience in order to grasp such principles:

> For example, the intellect does not immediately concede that all fire is hot and that all rhubarb makes bile; therefore, assuming that you had never seen fire, or that if you had seen it, you never touched it, it would not be known to your intellect whether all fire is hot. Therefore, for the intellect to firmly concede such principles, perception, memory, and experience are prerequisite (Buridan 2009, 423).

This process of what Buridan calls "induction," combined with "the intellect's natural disposition to assent" to the truth of such principles, produces our understanding of second-mode principles (Buridan 2009, 425). Thus, Buridan is clearly qualifying Aristotle's claim that we come to know indemonstrable principles through induction; according to Buridan, induction is involved only in coming to know certain kinds of principle, namely, those which are second-mode. According to Buridan, first-mode principles, such as the Principle of Non-Contradiction, or principles drawn from definitions, such as, "man is a rational animal," do not require induction in order for one to grant their truth.

Buridan discusses induction at length in only two of the questions of his *Questions on the Posterior Analytics*. The first mention of it is made in Question I.2, which examines whether it is possible for us to know anything and deals extensively with skeptical arguments. Many of the arguments found here are remarkably "modern," that is, they raise skeptical doubts that are nearly identical to ones found later in Descartes.[5] Most of the arguments begin from the assumption that scientific knowledge must be absolutely certain (Buridan 2009, 156–68). Each argument then proceeds to give various reasons why such certainty is impossible. For example, one argument presents a "deceiving God" scenario, with God making it appear that some object is present, when in fact it is not:

> A sensible species of the way things <presently> appear to you may be preserved by God entirely and perfectly in your senses <even when such> things are not present, in which case everything will appear to you exactly as it does right now. Believing <that such things are present>, you will form judgments as if <they were>, and your judgments will be incorrect, since this is false (Buridan 2009, 158).

---

[5] Many of the arguments can be found in Nicholas of Autrecourt. See Zupko 1993, 191–207.

The argument then proceeds to cut off what will be Descartes's means of escape from this doubt, by claiming that not only *could* God deceive us, but we have no way of knowing whether God *would wish* to do such a thing or not:

> Indeed, some argue that God can do this if he wishes, and you cannot know with certainty whether God wishes it; therefore, you cannot be certain whether this is the case, nor, as a consequence, <can you be certain> whether you are seeing any <actual> external thing (Buridan 2009, 158).

It is within the context of such skeptical concerns that induction is discussed. The point is raised that insofar as the assent to first principles relies upon sensation and experience, the knowledge of such principles can never be certain, since experience is fallible. Furthermore, no amount of experience can ever produce a "perfect induction," that is, one which takes into account every singular: "no <amount of> experience concludes in a universal proposition on account of its form, since no amount of experience can produce an induction <that includes> every singular. Therefore, it seems that principles are not certain" (Buridan 2009, 159).

In order to reply to this and to the "deceiving God" skeptical concern raised above, Buridan again draws on the distinction between kinds of principles and kinds of evidentness: first-mode principles possess absolute evidentness, and second-mode possess natural evidentness.[6] First-mode principles possessing this kind of evidentness are absolutely certain.[7] Principles that are acquired through inductive experience, according to Buridan, possess only natural evidentness. Nevertheless, while it is the case that a limited amount of experience will be productive of nothing but fallible principles, a wide range of well-examined experiences will produce second-mode principles that have very strong natural evidentness and, according to Buridan, that are not fallible (Buridan 2009, 166–167). Additionally, he argues, while a supernatural cause certainly could make principles appear evident to us that are in fact false, we do not need to exclude all possibility of supernatural interference in the natural sciences, and so natural evidentness suffices for the principles being used:

> Let us note that this <kind of> evidentness is not properly called "evident," because the intellect can be deceived about such evident principles by a supernatural cause… but, this natural evidentness is rightly called "natural," since a person cannot be deceived about it <as long as> he remains within the common course of nature, although he may be deceived by a supernatural cause. This <kind of> evidentness is sufficient for natural knowledge (Buridan 2009, 163–164).

In response to the deceiving-God skeptical scenario, Buridan appeals to the assumption of a "common course of nature" principle, that is, assuming that one remains

---

[6] I am borrowing the terminology of absolute and relative evidentness from Jack Zupko. See Zupko 2003.

[7] Buridan does suggest the possibility, however, that in a deceiving God scenario, we could be led astray even concerning absolutely evident principles. See Zupko 1993, 191–207.

within the common course of nature and is not being deceived by a supernatural agent, the truth of second-mode principles should not be doubted.[8]

In reply to the charge that experience can never produce a perfect induction, Buridan cites Averroes:

> The Commentator, in <his commentary on> the second book of the *Physics*, responds that although induction, or inductive experience, does not conclude on account of its form, nevertheless, the intellect, through its natural inclination toward the truth, grants that a universal principle <is> known and evident through natural and possible evidence, by repeatedly perceiving <something> to be the case for which there cannot or could not be a counterexample, <as long as> there does not seem to be a reason why this ought to be otherwise in other cases (Buridan 2009, 167).

This passage acknowledges that an induction that does not take into account every singular cannot validly conclude in a universal proposition, and Buridan makes no attempt to argue that any given number of particular experiences could ever validly conclude in a universal proposition. Additionally, it claims that what produces assent to a universal principle is not in fact induction, but rather the intellect's "natural inclination toward the truth," coupled with the absence of any counter-examples which would contradict such a universal proposition. It is significant that Buridan *could have* again appealed to something like his "common course of nature" principle, and then argued that a limited number of experiences is sufficient to produce knowledge of a universal proposition, assuming that nature continues to operate in future cases as it has in the observed ones. But Buridan *does not* appeal here to the common course of nature principle, and we shall later see that Buridan will in fact *deny* that adding such a principle to an induction is a useful approach when responding to the objection that induction cannot take into account every singular instance.

The other passage in which induction is discussed at length in the *Questions on the Posterior Analytics* is the last question of the second book, which roughly corresponds to bk. 2, ch. 19 of Aristotle's *Posterior Analytics*, and which examines whether the knowledge of first principles is innate. While in Question I.2 induction was discussed in the context of skeptical concerns, here the account of induction is at the center of an explanation of how we come to know first principles. Buridan again distinguishes between first and second-mode principles, and then claims that perception, memory, and experience are necessary prerequisites in coming to know second-mode principles:

> Therefore, for the firm acceptance of principles of this <second mode > by the intellect, perception, memory, and experience are prerequisite, in such a way that first you learn from perception that *this* fire is hot and immediately the intellect consequently judges that fire is hot, and yet it never judges that *every* < fire is hot> until you experience another fire to be hot, and thus many <instances> are possessed by the memory that these were hot, and then if you encounter another fire, which you do not perceive, because of the memory of the previous ones, you will judge this to be hot, and this is now a judgment of experience about something not perceived. Finally, it must be noted that the intellect, noticing that things were in the same way in many instances, and that no diverse circumstances prevented them

---

[8] For more on Buridan's use of the "common course of nature" principles, see King 1987, 109–132.

from being so… by its natural inclination toward the truth, forms a universal principle and assents to it as known, namely, that *every* fire is hot (Buridan 2009, 423–424).

Buridan then voices an objection to this description of how second-mode principles are acquired. If a principle is made evident through some prior cognition, then, even if that prior cognition does not constitute a demonstration, it is still the case that some cognitive process must precede the acquisition of the principle. If this is the case, then the "principle" acquired is not a principle in the sense that is needed, that is, it is not a starting-point for a demonstrative argument, but rather is the conclusion of an inductive argument. The objection runs as follows:

> No such judgment seems to be a principle, because it is made evident by preceding cognition, namely sensory cognition. Although it is not proved through demonstration, it seems to be proved by example or induction. For instance, saying, "this fire is hot, and so on for many others that have been sensed, and there is no reason why it should not be thus for the others; therefore, every fire is hot." But what is known and conceded through argumentation should not be taken to be a principle (Buridan 2009, 424).

This objection makes it clear that calling a second-mode principle "indemonstrable" is being taken to mean a good deal more than that it not being proven via a syllogism. Rather, if the appeal to first principles is to truly achieve its goal of avoiding an infinite regress, then one must deny that such principles are acquired through *any* reasoning process.[9] Being acquired through an inductive reasoning process would put the foundational status of such principles in just as much peril.

Buridan's reply to this objection clarifies his view of the role that induction plays in the acquisition of a principle. He argues that the sensory cognition which takes place prior to the intellect's assent to a principle is not what determines the intellect to assent to that principle: "perception is not primary in determining the intellect, but only shows an object to it; rather the intellect through its own nature is determined to concede the principle; that is why it is called an 'intelligible principle.'" (Buridan 2009, 424). Nor, then, is the intellect determined to assent to a principle on the basis of an inductive argument:

> Induction does not conclude on account of its form. First, no one is able to perform an induction over every single fire; indeed, no one touches every <fire>, nor is it possible that someone should touch every <fire>, and the conclusion does not follow on account of its form if the induction is not over every <instance>, and one knows that these are all <the instances that there are>. Second, it does not help to propose the addition of the clause, "and so on for the others," because this clause is neither known nor certain to the intellect… because you then are already positing a universal clause, namely that it is exactly this way for all the others (Buridan 2009, 424–25).

In other words, only a perfect induction could compel intellectual assent to the principle, and such an induction cannot be performed. Furthermore, Buridan here denies that the addition of something like a common course of nature principle—"and so

---

[9] That Buridan holds that the point of indemonstrable principles is to avoid an infinite regress in demonstrations is discussed above. See also Grellard 2007, 328–342.

on for the other cases"—to an induction is a viable solution, rather, he claims, this would do no more than beg the question.

Buridan concludes that although the intellect does in some way "need induction," its assent to the principles suggested by induction only occurs because the intellect itself is first and foremost inclined to this assent "through its own nature." What sensation and induction do is "show" or "present" to the intellect a series of appearances, at which point the intellect assents to a principle (Buridan 2009, 426). The inductive process itself is not what produces this assent, rather, Buridan argues, the power of *intellectus* is what determines this assent (Buridan 2009, 425).

The next step, then, is to investigate what exactly Buridan takes *intellectus* to be doing when it "determines us to assent to the truth of principles," but before we turn to this, we should note that almost the entirety of Buridan's discussion of induction is fueled by skeptical challenges. Buridan formulates his view of induction in response to the objections that experience is fallible, that particular experiences cannot validate the formulation of a universal principle, that foundational principles cannot be reliant on any prior reasoning process (whether inductive or deductive), and that the addition of a common course of nature principle only begs the question. Buridan's need to address such skeptical concerns, as we have already begun to see, shapes his interpretation of induction.

16.4 Intellectus

In the *Questions on the Nicomachean Ethics*, Buridan specifically discusses *intellectus* in the question, "Whether *intellectus* is a virtue?" (Buridan 1637, 515). His answer to this question occurs in three stages. First, he discusses how we come to know indemonstrable principles. Next, he examines whether or not the intellectual *habitus* which commands assent to such principles is a habit distinct from the intellective power itself. Finally, he ascertains whether this disposition to assent to principles is in fact a virtue.

Concerning the first point, that is, how we come to know indemonstrable principles, Buridan presents a truncated version of the division of principles that we find in the *Summulae*. Indemonstrable principles may be divided into the universal and singular. Singular principles, he claims, typically come to be known through perception, memory, or experience. For example, I perceive that *this* flame is hot, or I remember that *that* man ran, or I experience that *this* dose of rhubarb purges bile (Buridan 1637, 517). When a number of such perceptions, memories, and experiences have been compiled, *intellectus*, working along with this compilation, forms a universal concept of this multitude of singulars and assents to it as a universal principle, such as, "all fire is hot," or "all rhubarb purges bile." (Buridan 1637, 517).

At this point, Buridan raises "doubts" or objections to the view that first principles are acquired through induction, and these objections are variations of the skeptical concerns also found in the *Questions on the Posterior Analytics*. A principle, the first objection claims, is not truly a principle if it is known through some prior reasoning process. Simply claiming that the process through which we come to know principles is non-syllogistic, or non-demonstrative, is insufficient: the claim that such a principle is acquired through an inductive reasoning process still returns us to the problem of how the starting principles of *that* inductive process are acquired (Buridan 1637, 517). The objection then tacks on the additional complaint that an induction can never provide one with certitude of a universal principle, since it cannot take into account every singular (Buridan 1637, 517).

A second objection argues that a principle is not truly a first principle if it requires *any* prior knowledge for it to be cognized. In fact, it is just this lack of a need for any prior cognition that sets our cognition of principles apart from the knowledge of scientific, artistic, or prudential conclusions: "principles become cognized by us naturally, while conclusions become known to us through precognitions." (Buridan 1637, 517). To say that universal principles are cognized through perception, memory, experience, or induction is to say that they are not immediately cognized, but rather acquired through previous cognitions, like conclusions (Buridan 1637, 517). Thus, again, the point is that they can then hold no special epistemic status as foundational grounds for demonstrable knowledge if they must be known through some prior cognition.

A final objection proceeds along a different route and is brought against singular principles specifically. It begins with a very general question concerning whether singular principles are "in the senses or in the intellect," but then quickly turns to the more precise question of whether it is perception or intellection that establishes the certainty of such principles. If they acquire their certainty from perception, the objection runs, then we ought not call their cognition or cognitive habit *intellectus*, which seems to imply that they are established by the intellect. Furthermore, such principles ought not depend for their certainty upon something as prone to error as perception (Buridan 1637, 518).

Buridan's response to all three of these objections is the following:

> To these and also to all doubts of this kind, one ought to reply, in the manner of Eustratius, that neither the senses, nor induction proceeding from the senses, nor experience causally constitute intellectual cognition, nor its certitude, but only minister to the intellect by representing the sensible species of things (Buridan 1637, 518).

A few lines later, Buridan cites with approval Grosseteste's claim that the agent intellect "illuminates the interior of the mind, and reveals truth." (Buridan 1637, 518). He concludes with a summary of his own view:

> Anything we believe due to *intellectus*, <whether> through the senses, induction proceeding from the senses, or experience, without any other intellectual argument proceeding from other prior principles, ought to be called an intellectual and indemonstrable principle, the cognition or habit of which is called *intellectus*, because <such principles> are only cognized and believed due to the natural light of the intellect (Buridan 1637, 518).

Buridan concludes this description of induction's relation to *intellectus* by repeating the claim that although induction does "enter into demonstration," it only serves to "minister" to the intellect, and does not itself "certify" such principles (Buridan 1637, 518). In these passages, Buridan is arguing that not only is *intellectus* what inclines and determines us to *assent* to indemonstrable principles, but in fact *intellectus* is what enables us to *form* and *understand* such principles at all.

In particular, when the intellect first encounters second-mode principles, it does not immediately assent to their truth. The reason for this, Buridan argues, is that while it is not possible to err concerning the truth of first-mode principles once their terms are known, it is possible for the intellect to err in assenting to second-mode principles (Buridan 1637, 518). It is therefore clear, Buridan argues, that the normal intellective powers are insufficient to make the truth of these principles evident. Rather, the intellect requires some other power to be added to it:

> Therefore, when it comes to second-mode principles, there is no doubt that in order to state the truth promptly, easily, and firmly, we require an acquired disposition which goes beyond the intellective power. This is because a power, when it comes to those things which it naturally may guide or lead astray, is not itself sufficiently determined, without an added disposition, to guide firmly, promptly, and easily, and never lead astray (Buridan 1637, 518).

What then *is* this disposition which enables one to "quickly, easily, and firmly" grasp the truth of second-mode principles? As we have seen, induction alone does not result in the cognition of, or assent to, first principles. Rather, what is required is the innate virtue of *intellectus*:

> A certain virtue is innate to us that naturally inclines and determines us to assent to the truth of principles if they are appropriately presented to it, just as fire is naturally inclined toward burning when it is situated near a combustible thing, and this innate virtue is human *intellectus* (Buridan 2009, 425).

In other words, induction only concludes in a universal principle because *intellectus* is already at work.

Given the skeptical concerns that are motivating Burdian's interpretation of Aristotle, what role does induction really play in the acquisition of first principles? I would suggest two answers to this question. First, while the power of *intellectus* is innate, the *content* of such principles must be acquired. To use Buridan's own example, one would neither form nor give assent to a second-mode principle such as, "all rhubarb purges bile," unless she first had seen rhubarb and had some experience of its medical properties. However, to claim that it is *only* the *content* of our principles that is acquired through induction is insufficient. This is because, in the *Questions on the Ethics* at least, Buridan is making the stronger claim that the *habitus* of *intellectus* itself, and not just the content of principles, is acquired. While Buridan holds that *intellectus* is an innate intellectual power, its ability to "guide firmly, promptly, and easily," and most important of all, to "never lead astray" is perfected only though induction (Buridan 1637, 518). *Intellectus* is the natural tendency of the human intellect to produce and accept a universal principle based upon a limited amount of experience. Buridan claims that it is as natural for the intellect to assent to a universal proposition based upon a limited amount of experience as it is for a flammable thing to burst into flame when in the presence of a source of heat (Buridan 2009, 425). To continue his analogy, occasionally a flammable object may spontaneously combust, i.e., burst into flame even when heat has not been applied. Buridan needs an account of the operation of *intellectus* that rules out such "spontaneous combustion," that is, an account where *intellectus* does not simply assent to universal principles without sufficient evidence. This is precisely where induction comes into play in shaping the development of *intellectus*. It is only through sensation and repeated experiences that *intellectus* is trained not to leap to assumptions about what universal principles ought to be formulated and assented to. Buridan makes this point in the following passage:

> Although induction, or inductive experience, does not conclude on account of its form, nevertheless, when *intellectus* repeatedly perceives <something> to be the case and cannot discover a counterexample, nor does there seem to be a reason why it ought to be otherwise in other cases, <*intellectus* > through its natural inclination toward truth, grants that a universal principle is known (Buridan 2009, 167).

It is the function of induction to look for counter-examples and reasons why a principle should not be universalized. In the absence of any such limiting factors, the intellect follows its natural inclination to assent to the universal principle.

Thus, for Buridan, induction's function is twofold. First, it has the positive function of providing the content of our principles through perception and experience. Second, it has the negative function of stopping *intellectus* from pursuing its natural inclination to assent to a universal principle by providing counter-evidence for such universalization, again through perception and experience.[10] *Intellectus* in one sense, then, is innate: it is the innate inclination of the human intellect to assent to universal principles. In another sense, however, it is shaped through inductive experience and trained not to simply assume a universal in the face of insufficient evidence or counter-examples.[11]

16.5   Conclusion

As we have seen, with Buridan we find a medieval representative of what Barnes calls the "orthodox" interpretation of Aristotle (Barnes 1994, 267–68). While other Aristotelian commentators may hold that *intellectus* is simply the state of possessing principles that have been acquired through induction, Buridan cannot accept this interpretation of the *Posterior Analytics* precisely due to his skeptical concerns. He claims that induction alone can never confirm the universality of a principle, or, in fact, even *suggest* the universality of a principle. Thus, he argues that instead it is *intellectus*, Aristotle's *nous*, which forms and gives assent to such universal

---

[10] This discovery of counter-examples would be what prevents assenting to the universalization of accidental principles, for example.

[11] For a discussion of Buridan's understanding of evidence, see Zupko 2003, 194.

principles.[12] Induction's role, on Buridan's view, is not to provide us with universal principles, but rather to provide content for the universalizing power of *intellectus* to work with, and possible counter-instances that would falsify such universal principles.

Bibliography

Aristotle. 1960. *Posterior Analytics*, ed. and trans. Hugh Tredennick. Cambridge/London: Loeb Classical Library.

Barnes, Jonathan. 1994. *Aristotle: Posterior analytics*. Oxford: Clarendon Press.

Buridan, John. 1637. *Quaestiones in decem libros Ethicorum Aristotelis ad Nicomachum.* Excudebat L. L[ichfield] impensis Hen. Cripps, Ed. Forrest, Hen. Curtayne, & Ioh. Wilmot. English translations by Ariane Economos.

———. 2001. *Summulae de Dialectica: An annotated translation, with a philosophical introduction*, ed. and trans. Gyula Klima. New Haven: Yale University Press.

———. 2009. *Quaestiones in Duos Aristotlis Libros Posteriorum Analyticorum*, ed. Hubert Hubien, trans. Ariane Economos. In *Intellectus and induction: Three Aristotelian commentators on the cognition of first principles*, Ariane Economos, 145–426. Ann Arbor: ProQuest LLC.

Grellard, Christophe. 2007. Scepticism, demonstration, and the infinite regress argument (Nicholas of Autrecourt and John Buridan). *Vivarium: An International Journal for the Philosophy and Intellectual Life of the Middle Ages and Renaissance* 45 (2–3): 328–342.

King, Peter. 1987. Jean Buridan's philosophy of science. *Studies in History and Philosophy of Science* 18, no. 2: 109–132.

Klima, Gyula. 2004. John Buridan on the acquisition of simple substantial concepts. In *John Buridan and beyond: Topics in the language sciences 1300–1700*, ed. Friedman and Ebbesen. Kgl. Danske Videnskabernes Selskab.

Modrak, Deborah. 1987. *Aristotle: The power of perception*. Chicago: University of Chicago Press.

Zupko, Jack. 1993. Buridan and skepticism. *Journal of the History of Philosophy* 31 (2): 191–207.

———. 2003. *John Buridan: Portrait of a fourteenth-century arts master*. Notre Dame: University of Notre Dame Press.

---

[12] So, while a Humean might argue that assuming that other cases will resemble the few which we have experienced, and forming principles on this basis, is irrational, Buridan would perhaps reply that the human intellect is naturally determined to do this, and that this determination, being a very part of our intellectual structure, is thus quite "rational" after all. For a treatment of other ways in which Buridan may be read as providing a "medieval refutation" of British Empiricism, see Klima 2004.

Part IV
Other Scholastics

Chapter 17
Parody or Touch-Up? Duns Scotus's Engagement with Anselm's *Proslogion* Argument

Giorgio Pini

Keywords Anselm · John Duns Scotus · Proslogion · Ontological argument · God's existence · Evil · Possibility

Some arguments have a peculiar life. From the moment of their appearance, they start exerting an odd fascination on all those who come across them. Their resilience is exceptional: after each criticism and allegedly definitive refutation, they come back—sometimes in a new garb but still recognizable and with renewed energy. They seem to thrive on challenges.

The proof of God's existence Anselm presents in chapters 3 and 4 of his *Proslogion* is undeniably one of these arguments. (Anselm, *Prosl.*, 101–103). It attracted attention—and criticism—even before its official public appearance, when it came already accompanied by a set of objections and responses. That was just the first episode in a story that continued through a long and varied series of thinkers, including Descartes, Leibniz, and Kant, who finally called it "ontological" while celebrating its demise. Or so it was thought. For in the twentieth century, the *Proslogion* argument came back with a vengeance, so that even now, after more than ten centuries, it hasn't lost any of its vitality.[1]

What about the centuries between Anselm and Descartes? If we trust the standard histories of this argument, we might easily believe that nothing of note happened for almost 600 years, until Descartes gave the argument a second life in his *Fifth Meditation* (Oppy 1995, 4–46). In the long period in between, only Thomas Aquinas (and arguably not in one of his best moments) might occasionally receive

---

[1] No better demonstration of the *Proslogion* argument's good health can be given than a reference to the spectacular defense of its validity in Klima 2000.

G. Pini (✉)
Fordham University, New York, NY, USA
e-mail: pini@fordham.edu

J. P. Hochschild et al. (eds.), *Metaphysics Through Semantics: The Philosophical Recovery of the Medieval Mind*, International Archives of the History of Ideas Archives internationales d'histoire des idées 242, https://doi.org/10.1007/978-3-031-15026-5_17

a brief mention for his quick dismissal of Anselm's argument in the *Summa theolo-giae* (*ST* I, q. 2, a. 1, arg. 2 and ad 2).

As a matter of fact, however, the argument continued to be discussed all along the Middle Ages (Daniels 1909; Chatillon 1959; Cress 1976, 36, nt. 14). And some of these discussions were philosophically impressive. For example, it is in this period that the argument was parodied as a demonstration of the existence of the worst possible evil. Contrary to what has long been believed (Oppy 1995, 181–83), this perverse mirroring of Anselm's proof is not a recent invention: barring future discoveries, we can now say that it made its first appearance between the thirteenth and fourteenth century, courtesy of John Duns Scotus.

That Scotus formulated a parody of the *Proslogion* argument might be interest-ing, perhaps even amusing. But it also presents us with a problem. For Scotus is also known as the author of a "touch-up" (*coloratio*) of Anselm's proof.[2] Accordingly, Scotus seems to improve on the *Proslogion* argument with one hand while parody-ing it with the other.

What is the point of Scotus's parody? And what is the point of his "touch-up" of the *Proslogion* argument? And what is the relationship between his parody and his touch-up? In this paper, I try to answer these questions to shed some light on a remarkable episode in the surprising life of this unique argument. First, I give a short presentation of Scotus's parody. Second, I turn my attention to Scotus's own interpretation of Anselm's argument. Third, I reconstruct Scotus's "touch-up." Fourth and finally, I draw a few conclusions.

17.1 The Parody

In his *Remarks on Aristotle's Metaphysics,* when considering Aristotle's claim that, when evil things are concerned, act is worse than potency (*Met.* IX, 9, 1051a15–16), Scotus notes:

> This remark is a cause of trouble for those who posit and argue that God exists in this way: God is that than which a greater cannot be thought; but for the greatest good, to exist in act (and not only to be understood) is greater than to be only in the intellect and in potency to the external act. Against this: by the same argument, I demonstrate that the greatest evil exists, which is against what the Philosopher says here (*Met.* IX, 9, 1051a17–21). For the greatest evil is the evil than which a greater cannot be thought; therefore, if the greatest evil were in the intellect, it would be possible to think of one still greater, namely that which is

---

[2] Scotus, *Ord.* I, dist. 2, pars 1, qq. 1–2, nn. 137–138 (Vat. II, 208–209). In translating *coloratio* and *colorari* as "touch-up" and "touching up" I am following Wolter (Scotus, *A Treatise*, 122). Wolter's translation was also adopted by Craig 1980, 222.

both in the intellect and in act in reality; therefore, it will be both in the intellect and in reality.[3]

Scotus's point seems straightforward: Anselm's argument is criticized because it can be parodied to conclude something false, namely that the worst evil exists. Admittedly, Scotus does not say that it is *false* that there is a worst evil; rather, he states that positing that there is a worst evil is against Aristotle. But this does not seem to change things. Aristotle's claim is eminently plausible, and Scotus does not expect the people he is criticizing to be ready to reject it: there is indeed a greatest good, but no greatest evil exists.

Specifically, Scotus's parody is targeted at what has often been identified as a problematic point in the *Proslogion* argument, namely the claim that to exist in both the intellect and reality is greater than to exist only in the intellect.

Accordingly, Scotus seems to reject Anselm's argument.

Or does he? Appearances notwithstanding, I think it would be premature to draw this conclusion. One small detail might give us pause. Note that Scotus does not name Anselm as the author of the argument he is rejecting. True, it was common practice among medieval authors to refer to other thinkers as "some people" (*aliqui*), as Scotus does here. But that practice was usually reserved for authors who were not considered authoritative. Scotus and his contemporaries, by contrast, considered Anselm as an authority, just like Augustine and Aristotle. And we do not expect to find Augustine or Aristotle referred to as "some people" in scholastic works.

This textual detail is admittedly not decisive, but it does encourage us to look at the matter more closely. Isn't it possible that Scotus might not be criticizing Anselm's argument but the way some people interpret it? In the next section, I will argue that this is indeed the case.

17.2 Scotus's Formulation of the *Proslogion* Argument

In both his *Lectura* and his *Ordinatio*, Scotus presents Anselm's argument (in the version in which he parodies it in his *Remarks on Aristotle's Metaphysics*) as an argument in favor of the claim that God's existence is self-evident (*per se nota*).[4]

---

[3] Scotus, *Not. super Met.*, IX, 162, nn. 101–102: "Post dicit quod actus in malis est peior potentia. Hoc notabile contra aliquos qui ponunt et probant Deum esse sic: Deus est quo maius [ex]cogitari non potest; sed maius est quod non solum intelligatur summum bonum sed etiam quod est actu extra, quam quod est solum in intellectu et in potentia ad actum exteriorem. Contra: per idem argumentum probo summum malum, quod est contra Philosophum hic. Summum enim malum est quo maius [ex]cogitari non potest; ergo, si summum malum esset in intellectu tantum, maius adhuc [ex]cogitari potest, quia illud quod est in intellectu et[iam] extra in re actu; ergo erit in intellectu et in re extra, etc." I have slightly modified my own edition as indicated by the square brackets.

[4] Scotus, *Lect.* I, dist. 2, pars 1, qq. 1–2, n. 9 (Vat. XVI, 113); *Ord.* I, dist. 2, pars 1, qq. 1–2, n. 11 (Vat. II, 129). Scotus defines a self-evident proposition as a proposition whose truth and evidentness depends entirely on the meaning of its terms (*Ord.* I, dist. 2, pars 1, q. 1–2, n. 15 (Vat. II, 131).

Probably, here Scotus has in mind the reference Thomas Aquinas made to Anselm's argument in his *Summa theologiae* (*ST* I, q. 2, a. 1, arg. 2). Since Scotus, just like Aquinas, rejects the claim that God's existence is self-evident (at least if that claim is made in an unqualified way),[5] we might expect that he also rejects Anselm's argument, just as Aquinas did. This would explain Scotus's recourse to the parody I have considered in the previous section.

But things are not that simple. When addressing Aquinas's view that Anselm's argument can be taken as supporting the (false) claim that God's existence is self-evident, Scotus contends that Aquinas misread Anselm, because Anselm's intention was *not* to say that God's existence is self-evident. According to Scotus, this becomes clear once we consider that Anselm's proof is an *argument*, which includes two distinct syllogisms:

> ... when it is argued with regard to Anselm, "it is self-evident that that than which a greater cannot be thought exists," I say that this is not the case. Hence in that passage [Anselm] intends to show not that it is self-evident but that it is true that God exists. And he makes two syllogisms, of which the first is: "something is greater than anything that does not exist; but nothing is greater than the greatest; therefore, the greatest is not non-existent (*non ens*)". The other syllogism is: "what is not non-existent, exists; but the greatest is not non-existent; therefore, the greatest exists."[6]

What is going on here? Is Scotus just muddling the waters? As if there were any need for it! Before drawing any hasty conclusion, however, it is important to note that, when rejecting the claim that Anselm holds that God's existence is self-evident, Scotus does not repeat the "standard" formulation of the *Proslogion* argument—the one Aquinas had given and Scotus had quoted earlier. Rather, he now provides his own formulation of the argument. This is an indication, I believe, that Scotus does think the argument presented in the objection is subject to criticism, but that he also thinks that Anselm's own argument, if interpreted as *he*, Scotus, interprets it, does not fall prey to it.

So let us see what characterizes Scotus's formulation as opposed to the way Anselm's proof appears in the objection found in both Aquinas and Scotus himself. First (and obviously), Scotus reads the *Proslogion* argument as including two syllogisms; in that way, he makes it explicit that we are dealing with an *argument* and a *demonstration*. Second (and I believe more importantly), while the proof as presented in the objection is based on a comparison between being in the intellect and being in reality and on the assumption that being in reality is greater than being in the intellect, both this comparison and this assumption are—rather

---

[5] Scotus, *Ord.* I, dist. 2, pars 1, qq. 1–2, n. 26 (Vat. II, 138–139). See Wolter 1990, 255–257. For some more discussion, see Gilson 1952, 120–122.

[6] Scotus, *Lect.* I, dist. 2, pars 1, qq. 1–2, n. 35 (Vat. XVI, 123): "Ad aliud, quando arguitur de Anselmo 'illud quo maius cogitari non potest esse, est per se notum', dico quod non. Unde intentio Anselmi ibi non est ostendere quod Deum esse sit per se notum, sed quod hoc sit verum. Et facit duos syllogismos, quorum primus est: 'omni eo quod non est, aliquid est maius; sed summo nihil est maius; igitur summum non est non-ens'. Est alius syllogismus: 'quod non est non-ens, est; sed summum non est non-ens; igitur summum est'."

surprisingly—absent from Scotus's formulation. This will turn out to be essential to Scotus's interpretation of the *Proslogion* argument. Third, Scotus too thinks that the *Proslogion* argument includes a comparison, but that comparison is not between being in the intellect and being in reality but between a certain existent and any other object of the intellect that is only in the intellect.

Before moving on, I should note that some doubt might be raised about the last point. That the *Proslogion* argument includes a comparison between a certain existent and anything else that is only in the intellect is indeed what Scotus says in the *Lectura* passage I have translated above. But if we turn to the parallel passage in the *Ordinatio*, we find a different formulation: "something" (*aliquid*) is replaced by "being" (*ens*).[7] Accordingly, it seems that now we might interpret Scotus as stating that *any* existent (rather than "a certain existent," as in the *Lectura*) is greater than any non-existent. (To modify a famous example, this would mean that one cent in my pocket is greater than 100 dollars in my intellect.) Since Scotus's *Ordinatio* is a revision of his *Lectura*, we might think that the second interpretation of the key premise in Anselm's proof is the definitive one and that Scotus ended up discarding what he had said in the *Lectura*.

I believe, however, that this is not the case. Rather, I suggest that it is the *Lectura* formulation that should be taken as our guide to interpret the *Ordinatio* passage. Accordingly, my contention is that, even in the *Ordinatio*, Scotus's point is that *a certain existent is greater than any non-existent*. I find support for this interpretation in the very passage of the *Ordinatio* to which Scotus refers us if we want to find out how to make Anselm's argument safe from criticism.[8] It is in that passage that Scotus gives his "touch-up" (*coloratio*) of the *Proslogion* argument. So let us now turn to it.

17.3 Scotus's Touch

Scotus presents his touch-up of Anselm's proof when arguing that an infinite being is possible—specifically, *logically* possible: *being* and *infinite* are two concepts compatible with each other. He demonstrates this claim in several ways. The argument I am interested in makes appeal to the reliability of our cognitive powers. Scotus draws a parallelism between sensory and intellectual powers. It is an easily observable fact that we immediately perceive a dissonance: in other words, that a composite sound includes two simple sounds in disagreement with each other is

---

[7] *Ord.* I, dist. 2, pars 1, qq. 1–2, n. 35 (Vat. II, 145–146): "Ad secundum dico quod Anselmus non dicit istam propositionem esse per se notam, quod apparet, quia non potest inferri ex deductione eius quod ista propositio sit vera nisi ad minus per duos syllogismos, quorum alter erit iste: 'omni non-ente ens est maius, summo nihil est maius, ergo summum non est non-ens,' ex obliquis in secundo secundae; alius syllogismus est iste: 'quod non est non-ens est ens, summum non est non-ens, ergo etc.'"

[8] See next section. This passage has a literal parallel in *DPP*, 4, 104–106.

something that does not escape our attention. Thus, if we perceive no dissonance, we can infer that there is no dissonance in reality. Now Scotus remarks that we are capable of thinking about an infinite being. This indicates that we are not aware of any contradiction between the concept *infinite* and the concept *being*. Quite the contrary, Scotus holds that our intellect finds "rest" in the composite concept *infinite being*. This means that our intellect does not find contentment in the study of any finite object, rather, it moves onwards to another object until it finds an infinite object, in whose contemplation it can finally find peace. Now there is no reason to believe that our intellect is less reliable than our senses. So we can conclude that, if we are not aware of any contradiction in an object of thought, that object does not contain any contradiction, i.e., what that concept represents is logically possible. From this, Scotus further concludes that, if something includes a contradiction (for example, *round square*), it is not actually thinkable—not because of a limit of our intellect but because it is not *one* object of thought.[9]

It is at this point that Scotus introduces his touch-up of the *Proslogion* argument. His point, I believe, is that the *Proslogion* argument should be interpreted in light of the principle he has just established, namely that if we are aware of no contradiction in an object of thought, it is plausible to conclude that that object of thought does not contain any contradiction, and so it is one, logically possible object of thought.

Scotus's touch-up of the *Proslogion* argument can be divided into three main steps: (1) That than which a greater cannot be thought can be thought; (2) That than which a greater cannot be thought can exist in reality; (3) That than which a greater cannot be thought exists in reality. Let us consider each one of these three steps in turn.

1. *That than which a greater cannot be thought can be thought.* Scotus's first step is to posit that God is that than which a greater cannot be thought without a contradiction:

   ... Anselm's argument about the greatest good that can be thought can be interpreted in this way: God is that than which, when understood *without contradiction*, a greater cannot be thought *without contradiction*. And it is clear that we must add the expression "without contradiction," because something is not called an object of thought when there is a contradiction in its understanding, because in that case there are *two* objects of thought that in no way constitute *one* object of thought, because the one does not qualify the other.[10]

---

[9] *Ord.* I, dist. 2, pars 1, qq. 1–2, n. 136 (Vat. II, 208): "Item, quia intellectus, cuius obiectum est ens, nullam invenit repugnantiam intelligendo aliquod infinitum, immo videtur perfectissimum intelligibile. Mirum est autem si nulli intellectui talis contradictio patens fiat circa primum eius obiectum, cum discordia in sono ita faciliter offendat auditum: si enim disconveniens statim ut percipitur offendit, cur nullus intellectus ab intelligibili infinito naturaliter refugit sicut a non conveniente, suum ita primum obiectum destruente?"

[10] *Ord.* I, dist. 2, pars 1, qq. 1–2, n. 137 (Vat. II, 208–209): "Per illud potest colorari illa ratio Anselmi de summo bono cogitabili, *Proslogion*, et intelligenda est eius descriptio sic: Deus est quo cognito sine contradictione maius cogitari non potest sine contradictione. Et quod addendum sit 'sine contradictione' patet, nam in cuius cognitione vel cogitatione includitur contradictio, illud dicitur non cogitabile, quia sunt tunc duo cogitabilia opposita nullo modo faciendo unum cogitabile, quia neutrum determinat alterum."

By stressing the link between thinkability and lack of contradiction (what is usually called "logical possibility"), Scotus is indicating that the key point in this first step of the argument is that *that than which a greater cannot be thought* can be an object of thought (or rather, *one* object of thought rather than two distinct and incompatible objects of thought like *round square*) and consequently is something logically possible (i.e., it contains no contradiction). Although Scotus does not give an argument in support of this claim, he is clearly suggesting that this can be demonstrated the same way he has just argued that *infinite being* is a possible object of thought: just as in the case of *infinite being*, our intellect is not aware of any contradiction when it thinks about *that than which a greater cannot be thought* or *the greatest object of thought*, and it would be odd if there were a contradiction but it remained hidden to our intellect: this would amount to assuming, rather gratuitously, that our intellect is unreliable. Admittedly, this argument that *that than which a greater cannot be thought* is a logically possible object of thought is merely plausible (Copleston 1972, 526–527; Craig 1980, 222): it only shows that we have no reason to doubt that *that than which a greater cannot be thought* is a logically possible object of thought. In other words, the possibility of a hidden contradiction is not completely ruled out, it is only shown to be extremely implausible. But the burden of proof is now on those who deny that *that than which a greater cannot be thought* is an actual object of thought. If they want to do so, they must demonstrate that such a concept contains a contradiction of which we are not aware. And this does not look like an easy task.

2. *That than which a greater cannot be thought can exist in reality.* It is not only the case that that than which a greater cannot be thought exists as an object of thought (because it contains no contradiction); it can also exist in reality. Scotus demonstrates this further claim by introducing the concept of quidditative being (*esse quidditativum*):

> The aforementioned greatest object that can be thought without a contradiction can exist in reality. This is demonstrated concerning quidditative being, because the intellect finds complete rest in such an object of thought; it follows that that object includes the concept of the first object of the intellect, namely being, and this at the highest degree.[11]

The concept of quidditative being is akin to the concept of *esse essentiae*, originally introduced by Henry of Ghent. As Scotus explains elsewhere, he holds (whether correctly or not) that Henry of Ghent posited that God provides every object he thinks about with a special ontological status by the simple act of thinking about it. That special ontological status is called 'an essence's being' or 'essential existence'—*esse essentiae*. Scotus rejects Henry's position: according to Scotus, the objects of God's thought receive no special ontological status when God thinks about them. And what holds for the divine intellect holds for our intellect as well: we do not grant any special ontological status to our objects of thought by the

---

[11] *Ord.* I, dist. 2, pars 1, qq. 1–2, n. 138 (Vat. II, 209–210): "Summum cogitabile praedictum, sine contradictione, potest esse in re. Hoc probatur de esse quiditativo, quia in tali cogitabili summe quiescit intellectus; ergo in ipso est ratio primi obiecti intellectus, scilicet entis, et hoc in summo."

simple fact that we think about them.[12] From an ontological point of view, Scotus notices that, before any human being was created, there was no difference between the concept *human being* and the concept *chimera* (which is assumed to be a pseudo-concept, actually consisting of several incompatible concepts, whose combination is in turn incompatible with existence in reality).[13]

All this is true, but I believe that it would be wrong to conclude that Scotus denies any value to the concept of *esse essentiae* or quidditative being. Although there is no ontological difference between unactualized possibles and impossibles, there is nevertheless *some* difference between them, as Scotus explicitly admits: the former can exist in reality, the latter cannot. Now Scotus's point is that unactualized possibles (unlike impossibles) are objects of thought that are compatible with existence in reality and accordingly can be thought to exist in reality without any contradiction. For that reason, they are said to be capable of having quidditative being, the sort of being that characterizes real essences. So the concept *human being* is capable of having quidditative being (namely, it is capable of being the concept of a real essence) while the (pseudo-)concept *chimera* is not.[14]

So let us consider *that than which a greater cannot be thought*. Scotus has already claimed, in the first step of his argument, that this concept does not contain any contradiction and so can be an object of thought. Here I believe that Scotus is making a further step. He is saying that such a concept is the concept of something capable of having quidditative being, namely that we can think that that than which nothing greater can be thought can exist in reality.[15]

---

[12] *Ord.* I, dist. 36, q. unica, nn. 26–29 (Vat. VI, 281–282).

[13] *Ord.* I, dist. 36, q. unica, nn. 60–61 (Vat. VI, 296).

[14] *Ord.* I, dist. 36, q. unica, n. 50 (Vat. VI, 291). This second step adds something significant that was not established in the first step. Scotus thinks that there are some concepts that do not include any contradiction, and so can be objects of thought, which are nevertheless incompatible with existence in reality. Consequently, saying that an instance of such a concept can exist in reality would be a contradiction. Second intentions and more in general relations of reason are such: there is no contradiction in the concept *genus*, but that concept is incompatible with real existence (we never encounter *genera* in reality, we only encounter animals). As a consequence, we cannot think about an existing *genus*, strictly speaking (whereas of course we can think about an existing animal), because what contains a contradiction is unthinkable, in the sense that it cannot be *one* object of thought, as we have seen above. Scotus draws the distinction between the case of relations of reasons and second intentions, on the one hand, and objects of thought that are compatible with existence in reality in *Quodl.*, q. 3, n. 2 (Vivès XXV, 114): "Ens ergo vel res isto primo modo accipitur omnino communissime, et extendit se ad quocumque quod non includit contradictionem, sive sit ens rationis, hoc est praecise habens esse in intellectu considerante, sive sit ens reale habens aliquam entitatem extra considerationem intellectus. Et secundo, accipitur in isto membro minus communiter pro ente quod habet vel habere potest aliquam entitatem non ex consideratione intellectus."

[15] That this is a further step in the argument, distinct from the first step concerning logical possibility, is made explicit in the parallel treatment in Scotus, *Rep.* I-A, dist. 2, qq. 1–3, n. 73 (Wolter and Bychkov I, 137): "Redeo ergo ad propositum et arguo quod summum cogitabile est, quia summum cogitabile est cogitabile sine contradictione; sed tale possibile est in effectu, ergo potest cogitari in effectu esse."

How does Scotus demonstrate this further step? Remember that for Scotus think-ability and possibility are closely related. Specifically, if we can think of something and do not perceive any contradiction in it, we can conclude that that object of thought does not contain any contradiction and is (logically) possible. Now what Scotus is suggesting here is that we perceive no contradiction between the concept *that than which a greater cannot be thought* and real existence. (We would say that the concept *that than which a greater cannot be thought* is such that it can be instan-tiated.) Accordingly, we *can* think about an existent greatest being—this is actually a concept in which our intellect finds rest. Note that Scotus's argument is not that, because we can think of the greatest being and we experience no uneasiness when we do so, it follows that such a being can or even does exist: in other words, Scotus is not shifting from the claim that *that than which a greater cannot be thought* is logically possible to the claim that such an object is *really* possible. Rather, Scotus's argument is that we can think about the greatest being (a.k.a. that than which a greater cannot be thought) *as existing*, without perceiving any incompatibility between that than which a greater cannot be thought, on the one hand, and existence in reality, on the other hand. From this, we are entitled to conclude (making appeal to our intellect's reliability) that such an object can exist in reality.

3. *That than which a greater cannot be thought exists in reality.* In the third step of his argument, Scotus argues that, if the greatest object of thought (= that than which a greater cannot be thought) can be thought to exist in reality, then it does exist in reality:

> And then it is also argued that it exists, speaking of being of existence: the greatest object of thought does not exist only in the intellect of the one who thinks about it, because in that case, it would be both capable of existing—because it's an object of thought that is capable of existing (*possibile*)—and incapable of existing, because existing from a cause is incom-patible with its nature, as is evident from the second conclusion concerning efficient causal-ity given above.[16]

Scotus's argument here includes several sub-steps:

(3.1) Suppose that the greatest object of thought does not exist in reality;

(3.2) The greatest object of thought *can* exist in reality;

(3.3) Something that can but does not exist in reality can come to exist in reality only through the action of some cause (*ab aliqua causa*);

(3.4) The concept *greatest object of thought* is incompatible with *existing in reality through the action of some cause*;

(3.5) Therefore, the greatest object of thought *cannot* exist in reality (because of the conjunction of (3.3) and (3.4));

(3.6) Therefore, the greatest object of thought can exist in reality (3.2) and cannot exist in reality (3.5);

---

[16] *Ord.* I, dist. 2, pars 1, qq. 1–2, n. 138 (Vat. II, 210): "Et tunc arguitur ultra quod illud sit, loquendo de esse exsistentiae: summe cogitabile non est tantum intellectu cogitante, quia tunc posset esse, quia cogitabile possibile, et non posset esse, quia repugnat rationi eius esse ab aliqua causa, sicut patet prius in secunda conclusione de via efficientiae."

(3.7) In order to avoid the contradiction in (3.6), the premise (3.1) should be rejected;

(3.8) Therefore, the greatest object of thought exists in reality.

Steps (3.6) and (3.7) are implicit but can be easily figured out from what Scotus says, and it is clear that they must be provided to have the argument running. Even though the conclusion (3.8) is not stated at the end of the argument, it is presented at its beginning as what is going to be demonstrated. This leaves us with Scotus's three assumptions, which are (3.2), (3.3), and (3.4). Scotus has demonstrated premise (3.2) in the second step above. So let us first consider (3.3).

Premise (3.3) has also been demonstrated in a prior passage of the question of the *Ordinatio* devoted to demonstrating God's existence.[17] Scotus's point is that something exists either from itself (*a se*) or from a cause (*ab aliqua causa*) and it not the case either that what exists from itself can change into something that exists from a cause or that what exists from a cause can change into something that exists from itself: existence from itself and existence from a cause are mutually exclusive and each one of them pertains necessarily to what it pertains.

Let us now turn to premise (3.4). As Scotus has demonstrated in the very passage he has just referred to, the concept *first cause* is incompatible with the concept *being from a cause* (or *existing through the action of a cause*). Scotus's demonstration is based on the distinction between an essentially and an accidentally ordered causal series and is intended to prove that there cannot be an infinite regress in an essentially ordered causal series. Scotus's demonstration of this claim is sometimes identified as a weak point in his argument.[18] I think, however, that, if the first being is described as "the greatest object of thought" or "that than which a greater cannot be thought", as it is done here, Scotus has at his disposal a quick and hopefully less controversial argument to show that the greatest object of thought, if it exists, exists from itself and not from a cause. For suppose that the greatest object of thought exists from a cause; then, when you turn your attention to the cause of the greatest object of thought, you would be considering something on which the greatest object of thought depends, and that would be an object of thought greater than the greatest object of thought. This clearly cannot be. It might be objected that maybe we can always think of an object of thought greater than the one we are thinking about, and so there is no greatest object of thought. But this would amount to assuming that the concept *the greatest object of thought* (or equivalently, *that than which a greater cannot be thought*) cannot be thought, and the only reason for this could be that such a concept contains a contradiction of which we are not aware, contrary to what has been demonstrated in step (1) above.

Scotus concludes his touch-up of the *Proslogion* argument with what I take to be a corollary to the conclusion (3.8) or possibly an alternative formulation of that conclusion:

---

[17] *Ord.* I, dist. 2, pars 1, qq. 1–2, n. 57 (Vat. II, 162–164).
[18] O'Connor 1993, 24–26.

> Therefore, an object of thought that exists in reality is greater than what is only in the intellect. This last sentence, however, should not be taken to mean that one and the same thing, if it is thought, is a greater object of thought if it exists; rather, it means that some existing thing is greater than anything <else> that is in the intellect.[19]

In order to understand what Scotus is saying here, remember that what can be thought of as existing (and so can exist) but does not exist (and so is currently only in the intellect even though it can be brought to existence by a cause) has turned out *not* to be the greatest object of thought, because there is something greater, namely something that can be thought of as existing (and so can exist) and exists *by itself* (and so cannot be brought to existence by anything else). Now another way of making this point is to say that there is an object of thought (what exists by itself in reality) that is an object of thought greater than anything that is thought as being capable of existence but does not actually exist. Suppose, for example, that I think about a cat with seven tails but no cat with seven tails exists. Even if it does not exist, there seems to be no incompatibility between the concept of a cat with seven tails and real existence. (It would admittedly be a weird occurrence, but this doesn't seem to be impossible, either logically or naturally.) Now what could bring such a cat to existence? Only some cause, for example a mother cat and a father cat or a cruel scientist or an evil demon. Would a cat with seven tails that existed from itself be a greater being than a cat with seven tails brought to existence by a cause? Absolutely. The problem is that what can be thought of as existing but does not exist (like a cat with seven tails) can be brought to existence only by some cause, and this is incompatible with existing from itself. So a cat with seven tails that exists from itself is not an object of thought—it is unthinkable. By contrast, I *can* think of something that exists from itself, so that object is logically possible; and I can think of it as something existing, so that object is really possible—it can exist. But if it can exist, it does exist: otherwise, if it didn't exist, it could be brought to existence only by a cause, which is incompatible with existence from itself. So there exists in reality something that is an object of thought greater than any other object I can think about but does not exist in reality. In other words, there exists in reality something greater than anything that, although capable of existing, does not exist.

This formulation of the conclusion is Scotus's own reinterpretation (his final "touch-up," we might say) of the most famous and controversial step in Anselm's proof, often interpreted as stating that to exist in reality is greater than to exist in the intellect.[20] Note the extent of the transformation to which Scotus has subjected Anselm's claim: it is not an assumption anymore but the conclusion of (or, alternatively, a corollary to) the demonstration that that than which a greater cannot be

---

[19] *Ord.* I, dist. 2, pars 1, qq. 1–2, n. 138 (Vat. 210): "[M]aius ergo cogitabile est quod est in re quam quod est tantum in intellectu. Non est autem hoc sic intelligendum quod idem si cogitetur, per hoc sit maius cogitabile si exsistat, sed, omni quod est in intellectu tantum, est maius aliquod quod exsistit."

[20] Anselm, *Prosl.* 2, 101: "Et certe id quo maius cogitari nequit, non potest esse in solo intellectu. Si enim vel in solo intellectu est, potest cogitari esse et in re, *quod maius est.*" (Italics mine.)

thought exists. As such, it does not play any role in the *demonstration* of the actual existence of that than which a greater cannot be thought.

Scotus's warning about the correct way to interpret the conclusion phrased in this way is targeted, I believe, at a reading that, although possible, is nevertheless open to criticism. In Latin, the claim that I have translated as "an object of thought that exists in reality is greater than what is only in the intellect" can also be interpreted as meaning "the object of thought that exists in reality is greater than the one that exists only in the intellect."[21] And it is tempting to read this as meaning that the very same object of thought (say, a cat with seven tails) is greater if it exists in reality than if it is merely thought about, as if existence were a "great-making" property. My suggestion is that Scotus knows that, if the *Proslogion* argument is interpreted in this way, it is open to criticism—the sort of criticism that Peter of John Olivi moved against it (and with which it's possible that Scotus might have been familiar): from the claim that existence in reality is greater than existence in the intellect it can only be concluded that, if that than which a greater cannot be thought existed in reality, then it would be greater than if it existed only as an object of thought. But this does not mean that that than which a greater cannot be thought exists in reality; it only means that, if I think of it as existing in reality, I think of something greater than if I think of it as existing only in the intellect. In other words, I am comparing two objects of thought in my intellect, not something outside my intellect with something inside my intellect: there seems to be no way to jump from thought to reality.[22]

Indeed, if Anselm were establishing a comparison between the same thing as existing in reality and as merely thought about, his argument would be open to Scotus's own parody: I can think about the worst evil; but the worst evil existing in reality is worse than the worst evil existing merely as an object of thought; therefore, the worst evil exists. But that this reasoning is unsound causes no problem to

---

[21] See above n. 17.

[22] Olivi, *De Deo cognoscendo*, q. 3, n. 7 (Jansen, 523–524): "Ratio etiam eius [scil. Anselmi] quam facit in *Proslogion* non videtur necessaria. Arguit enim sic: Illud quo maius cogitari non potest, si est in solo intellectu et non in re, non est quo maius cogitari non potest; quia maius est illud quod in re est et in intellectu quam illud quod est in solo intellectu. Ergo illud quo maius cogitari non potest non potest esse in solo intellectu. Sed illud quo maius cogitari nequit potest esse in intellectu cuiucunque, etiam insipientis; potest enim ab omnibus intelligi et cogitari. Intellectum autem est in intellectu intelligentis seu cogitantis. Ergo illud quo maius cogitari nequit necessario est in re, alias enim non posset intelligi nec esse in intellectu cogitantem ipsum. Solum autem Deus est illud quo magis cogitari nequit et e contrario. Ergo Deus necessario est in re. Haec autem ratio videtur in hoc deficere, quia licet ab intellectu non possit intelligi vel cogitari illud quo magis cogitari nequit, nisi ab eodem intellectu supponatur et cogitetur esse in re, quia in ratione ipsius implicatur quod sit in re, alias non haberet rationem summi: tamen videtur posse cogitari absque hoc quod veraciter sit. Quamvis enim si ipsum est in solo intellectu, iam non sit summum: nihilominus tamen bene poterit cogitari quod, si tale esset in re, ipsum esset summum. Ex prima igitur propositione non videtur sequi quod ipsum non possit esse in solo intellectu ut obiectum, sed solum quod ipsum non possit esse actu, si est in solo intellectu, sed tamen esset ibi ut intellectum. Bene etiam sequitur quod non cogitari potest esse in solo intellectu, sed oportet conditionaliter ibi intelligi quod, si tale quid esset actu, necessario esset in re."

the *Proslogion* argument once we interpret it the way Scotus does. So I think we can now safely conclude that Scotus's parody is targeted not at the *Proslogion* argument, which can be rescued (if adequately "touched on"), but at the way some people (*aliqui*) read it—an interpretation that might look plausible and could even be taken as the standard one but should also be recognized as the most superficial and least charitable one.

17.4 Conclusion

By touching up the *Proslogion* argument, Scotus subjects it to a radical revision. The most spectacular aspect of Scotus's reinterpretation is that the key step in Anselm's proof—which Scotus idiosyncratically reads as a comparison between a specific existent and any object of thought that can but does not exist—plays no role in obtaining the conclusion that that than which a greater cannot be thought exists. Rather, Scotus presents that comparison as a rephasing of the *conclusion* of the argument. If we now turn back to Scotus's analysis of the Anselm's proof as an argument including two syllogisms,[23] we can see that step 3, as reconstructed above, can be interpreted as a demonstration of the first premise of the first of those two syllogisms: in that interpretation, the point of that step would be not be to demonstrate the existence of that than which a greater cannot be thought, strictly speaking, but that there is something greater than any object of thought that can but does not exist. Once this is established, we can then argue that nothing is greater than the greatest object of thought and conclude that the greatest object of thought is not something that can but does not exist. Then we can proceed to formulate a second syllogism and argue that what is not something that can but does not exist (i.e. a mere object of thought) is something that can and *does* exist, then notice that this applies to the greatest object of thought and conclude that the greatest object of thought can and does exist.

Scotus's own touch-up of the *Proslogion* argument has been criticized for what is taken to be an illicit shift from logical possibility to real possibility: Scotus would unwittingly shift from the claim that the concept *greatest object of thought* is non-contradictory—namely, that the greatest object of thought is a logically possible object—to the claim that the greatest object of thought can exist in reality—namely, that it is a really possible object (Scribano 2021, 26; Cross 2005, 36–37). As should be clear from my reconstruction above, I think that, if Scotus's argument is read correctly, it is not open to this criticism.[24] For we can think that there is a shift from logical to real possibility only if we draw no distinction between what I have identified as the first step and the second step in Scotus's argument. First, Scotus establishes that the greatest object of thought is something thinkable, because there

---

[23] See above, Sect. 17.2.

[24] Of course, this does not mean that it might not be open to other criticisms.

appears to be no internal contradiction in it; then, he moves on to establish, by a separate argument, that the greatest object of thought can be thought as something capable of existing, without any contradiction, and so can exist.[25] Also, I do not think that Scotus is shifting from a claim about what is logically possible to a claim whose truth depends on "the causal constitution of the world" (Cross 2005, 37).[26] That that than which a greater cannot be thought cannot exist from a cause is not something that depends on the causal constitution of the world (and so is nomologically, as opposed to logically, possible). Rather, that the first being—or the greatest object of thought or that than which a greater cannot be thought—is incompatible with existence from a cause is something that can be inferred from the very concept *first being*—or *greatest object of thought* or *that than which a greater cannot be thought* (Conti 2017, 421). Of course, when we draw that inference, we do not know yet if that concept is instantiated. That that concept is instantiated is the *conclusion* of Scotus's argument, and this is what he argues for in his *third* step. But before reaching that conclusion, Scotus demonstrates (purely *a priori*) that, *if* that concept is instantiated, necessarily its instantiation is not from a cause.

At the end of this analysis, we might wonder: is Scotus's reading of the *Proslogion* argument a faithful interpretation of Anselm's intentions? I seriously doubt that we can say so. But does it really matter? What Scotus wants to give is a "touch-up," a *coloratio* of Anselm's proof—and he thinks this is the most charitable interpretation that can be given of that argument. That interpretation incorporates several elements that are proper to Scotus's own argument for God's existence and for which we would look in vain in Anselm. And this is just what philosophers (as opposed to historians of philosophy) do: they want to keep arguments alive, not to preserve them intact. And sometimes, to keep them alive, they don't hesitate to subject them to radical transformations, starting up an exciting new episode in their long and, indeed, colorful existence.[27]

---

[25] Accordingly, I do not think that "[f]or something to exist in quidditative being is for there to be a coherent concept of it," as Cross says (Cross 2005, 36); rather, as I have argued above, for something to exist in quidditative being is for it to be capable of existing.

[26] I should clarify that if I take issue with Cross's interpretation of Scotus's touching up of Anselm's argument—and so of Scotus's own argument for God's existence—it is only because Cross provides one of the most compelling and precise treatments of Scotus's argument I am aware of.

[27] In this paper, I haven't considered Scotus's second "touch-up" of Anselm's argument, based on the concept of intuitive cognition, given immediately after the first one I have examined: *Ord.* I, dist. 2, pars 1, qq. 1–2, n. 139 (Vat. III, 210). Also, I haven't considered the version of his "touch-up" Scotus gives in his *Reportatio*, whose step 3 diverges at some point from what he says in the passage of the *Ordinatio* I have focused on here. See *Rep.* I-A, dist. 2, qq. 1–3, n. 73 (Wolter and Bychkov I, 137).

Bibliography

Primary Sources

Anselm. 1946. *Prosl.* = *Proslogion*, In S. Anselmi Cantuariensis Archiepiscopi *Opera Omnia*, ed. F.S. Schmitt, vol. 1, 89–139. Ebinburgh: Thomas Nelson and Sons.

Aristotle. 1957. *Met.* = Aristotelis *Metaphysica*, recognovit brevique adnotatione critica instruxit E. Jaeger. Oxford: Clarendon Press.

Olivi. 1926. *De Deo cognoscendo* = *Quaestiones de Deo cognoscendo*. In Petri Johannis Olivi *Quaestiones in II^{um} Sententiarum*. Edidit Bernard Jansen, 3, 517–554. Ad Claras Aquas: ex Typographia Collegii S. Bonaventurae.

Scotus. 1950. *Ord.* I, dist 2 = *Ordinatio. Liber primus: distinctio prima et secunda*. In Ioannis Duns Scoti *Opera Omnia studio et cura Commissionis Scotisticae ad fidem codicum edita*, II. Civitas Vaticana: Typis Polyglottis Vaticanis.

———. 1960. *Lect.* I, dist. 2 = *Lectura in primum librum Sententiarum. Prologus et distinctiones a prima ad septimam*. In Ioannis Duns Scoti *Opera Omnia studio et cura Commissionis Scotisticae ad fidem codicum edita*, XVI. Civitas Vaticana: Typis Polyglottis Vaticanis.

———. 1963. *Ord.* I, dist. 36 = *Ordinatio. Liber primus a distinctione vigesima sexta ad quadragesimam octavam*. In Ioannis Duns Scoti *Opera Omnia studio et cura Commissionis Scotisticae ad fidem codicum edita*, VI. Civitas Vaticana: Typis Polyglottis Vaticanis.

———. 1966. *A Treatise* = John Duns Scotus. In *A Treatise on God as First Principle*. Translated and Edited with Commentary by Allan B. Wolter O.F.M. Chicago: Franciscan Herald Press.

———. 1974. *DPP* = Johannes Duns Scotus. *Abhandlung über das erste Prinzip*. Heraugegeben und übersetz von Wolfgang Kluxen. Darmstadt: Wissenschaftliche Buchgesellschaft.

———. 2004. *Rep.* = John Duns Scotus. *The Examined Report of the Paris Lecture, Reportatio I-A*. Latin text and English translation by A.B. Wolter and O.V. Bychkov, 1, New York: Publications of the Franciscan Institute.

———. 2017. *Not. super Met.* = Ioannis Duns Scoti *Notabilia super Metaphysicam*. Cura et studio Giorgio Pini. *Corpus Christianorum Continuatio Mediaevalis*, 287. Turnhout: Brepols Publishers.

Thomas Aquinas. 1999. *ST* = Sancti Thomae de Aquino *Summa theologiae*. Cinisello Balsamo MI: Edizioni San Paolo.

Secondary Sources

Chatillon, Jean. 1959. De Guillaume d'Auxerre à Thomas d'Aquin: l'argument de saint Anselme chez les premiers scolastiques du XIIIe siècle. In Spicilegium Beccense I: *Congrès International du IXe Centenaire de l'arrivé d'Anselme au Bec*, 209–231, Paris: Vrin.

Conti, Alessandro D. 2017. L'argomento ontologico di Anselmo, la sua 'fortuna' presso Duns Scoto e le critiche di Ockham. Appunti per una storia della nozione di Dio nel Medioevo. In *La filosofia medievale tra antichità ed età moderna. Saggi in memoria di Francesco Del Punta*, a cura di Amos Bertolacci e Agostino Paravicini Bagliani, 411–429. Firenze: SISMEL – Edizioni del Galluzzo.

Copleston, Frederick. 1972. *A history of medieval philosophy*. London: Methuen & Co.

Craig, William Lane. 1980. *The cosmological argument from Plato to Leibniz*. London: The MacMillan Press.

Cress, Donald A. 1976. The "Coloratio" by Duns Scotus of the "Ratio Anselmi" and Vindobon. 1453. *The Modern Schoolman* 54: 33–43.

Cross, Richard. 2005. *Duns Scotus on God*. Aldershot: Ashgate.

Daniels, Augustinus. 1909. *Quellenbeiträge und Untersuchungen zur Geschichte der Gottesbeweise in dreizehnten Jahrhundert mit besonderer Berücksichtigung des Arguments in Proslogion des hl. Anselm*. Beiträge zur Geschichte der Philosophie des Mittelalters VIII, Hft. 1–2. Münster: Aschendorff.

Gilson, Étienne. 1952. *Jean Duns Scot. Introduction à ses positions fondamentales*. Paris: Vrin.

Klima, Gyula. 2000. Saint Anselm's proof: A problem of reference, intentional identity and mutual understanding. In *Medieval philosophy and modern times*, ed. Ghita Holmström-Hintikka, 69–87. Dordrecht: Springer.

O'Connor, Timothy. 1993. Scotus on the existence of a first efficient cause. *International Journal for Philosophy of Religion* 33: 17–32.

Oppy, Graham. 1995. *Ontological arguments and belief in God*. Cambridge: Cambridge University Press.

Scribano, Emanuela. 2021[2]. *L'esistenza di Dio: Storia della prova ontologica da Descartes a Kant*. Roma: Carocci Editore.

Wolter, Allan B. 1990. Duns Scotus and the existence and nature of God. In Allan B. Wolter. *The Philosophical theology of John Duns Scotus*, ed. Marilyn McCord Adams, 254–277. Ithaca/London: Cornell University Press.

Chapter 18
De se vs. *de facto* Ontology in Late-Medieval Realism

Laurent Cesalli

Keywords Medieval philosophy · Moderate realism · Ontology · Metaphysics · Universals

Medieval philosophy is often presented as dominated by an antagonism between realism and nominalism. While this view is something of a caricature, it is not entirely without justification. Indeed, the debate about universals—just to mention the most famous form taken up by the general issue—can be traced continuously from the eleventh through the fifteenth century[1]. That situation should not come as a surprise, given the nature of the issue—how is *generality* to be accounted for?—and its pervasiveness in (at least) the propaedeutic disciplines of grammar and logic. More surprising is the fact that in spite of the crucial significance of the historiographic categories of nominalism and realism, what they mean is not always clear. Thus, a formula like

1. whatever exists is particular

seems to capture pretty well medieval nominalism in all its different forms, for it is consistent with the fundamental claim that universality is always to be accounted for *in significando*, and never *in essendo* (common names and general concepts are singular entities). Realism, then, or so it seems, could be accurately captured by the contradictory of (1):

This paper was written in the frame of the SNF research project "Realisms. Universals, Relations and States of Affairs in the Austro-German and Medieval Traditions" (n° 100012_182858, Geneva, 2019–2023).

---

[1] Medieval accounts of universals are one among the many topics Guyla Klima deals with in his works. Exemplarily, and recently, in Gyula (2017), updated in 2022.

L. Cesalli (✉)
University of Geneva, Geneva, Switzerland
e-mail: laurent.cesalli@unige.ch

© The Author(s), under exclusive license to Springer Nature
Switzerland AG 2023
J. P. Hochschild et al. (eds.), *Metaphysics Through Semantics: The Philosophical Recovery of the Medieval Mind*, International Archives of the History of Ideas Archives internationales d'histoire des idées 242, https://doi.org/10.1007/978-3-031-15026-5_18

2. some entities exist that are not particular.

But that is not so. For (at least) some of medieval realists *accept* (1) and thus *reject* (2)—which, at first sight, might appear to be a severe form of philosophical confusion. One will of course immediately object that there is a patent equivocation on the term "realist" to the effect that, if it is to be used in that sense, the category loses its systematic relevance. However, things seem to be more complicated, for some thinkers who accept (1) also typically endorse

3. universals[2] exist,

a claim that is clearly incompatible with any form of nominalism. The question, thus, is this: if there are medieval philosophers who endorse (1) *and are not nominalists*, what exactly does "realism" mean in their case?

This paper aims at assessing and discussing a form of realism that accepts (1) and (3). My starting point are the views of two English fourteenth-century thinkers: Pseudo-Richard of Campsall (fl. 1330), author of a *Logica Campsale Anglicj ualde utilis et realis contra Ocham* (*LCO*) and Richard Brinkley (fl. 1350), who wrote an extensive *Summa logicae* (*SLB*).

I proceed in three main steps. I begin by assessing Pseudo-Campsall's and Brinkley's views on universals and the (necessary) qualifications they add to (1) and (3) in claiming that some entities are *de se* universals, although *de facto*, they are particulars (which amounts to developing an ontology that is partly counterfactual). I then briefly compare Pseudo-Campsall's and Brinkley's views with some other forms of medieval realism. Finally, I discuss their views with respect to the two following issues: (i) the systematic relevance of the distinction between *de se* and *de facto* ontology, and (ii) the meaning of the category of "moderate realism."

The general (and provisional) conclusion I am aiming at is that counterfactual ontology *à la* Pseudo-Campsall and Brinkley is systematically relevant (it is not fictional), and that it provides a better account of generality than its rival nominalist views.

18.1 Pseudo-Campsall and Brinkley on Universals

18.1.1 What Are Universals?

Pseudo-Campsall and Brinkley share a philosophical enemy: William of Ockham's nominalism. More than anywhere else, their critical stance comes to the fore in their views on universals. Both claim, against Ockham—who insists that whatever is universal can only be such *in significando*[3]—that there are universal things (*res*

---

[2] Universals *in essendo* (i.e. universals *besides* common names and general concepts).

[3] Ockham (1974) I, 14: "Quodlibet universale est una res singularis, et ideo non est universale nisi per significationem, quia est signum plurium."

universales, universale ex parte rei) that are neither concepts nor signs.[4] Pseudo-Campsall and Brinkley respectively define the universal as follows:

[1] "A universal is that whose formal nature does not prevent it to be common to many. And I prove that there are such universal things ...."[5]
[2] "... the term 'universal' is taken by the metaphysician to stand for the quiddity of a thing, in itself communicable to many inferiors."[6]

As made explicit by Brinkley, those answers are given from a metaphysical point of view. Both authors insist, however, that the universal is taken differently depending on *who* is defining it. Thus Pseudo-Campsall and Brinkley consider that for a *logician*, the universal is a *term*, that is: something predicable. As for the physicist, Pseudo-Campsall says she takes the universal as a compound of matter and form, whereas according to Brinkley, it is the indeterminacy of a cause able to produce many effects (*LCO* 24.07; *SLB* II, 2). Those differences, I take it, are mere variations that leave untouched the heart of the doctrine—metaphysical universals ground physical and logical ones:

[3] "... one should not concede that what is predicated of many is a universal; rather, one has to say that that for which what is predicated of many supposits, is a universal."[7]
[4] "... to a logical universal corresponds, as its primary counterpart, a real and metaphysical universal."[8]

As it should be, Brinkley and Pseudo-Campsall argue at length for the existence of metaphysical universals, providing positive arguments, and criticizing those of their opponents. My goal is not to go into those reasons, but rather to examine so to speak the consequences of the thesis endorsed by our two authors.

18.1.2   The **de se/de facto** *Distinction*

But how exactly are those metaphysical universals to be conceived of? What is their ontological status? And how are they related to particulars? The answers one can reconstruct from Brinkley and Pseudo-Campsall's works are based on the *de se/de facto* distinction, on which I shall focus in the rest of the paper.

---

[4] Pseudo-Richard of Campsall 1982, 13.12; *SLB* II, 4 and 22.

[5] Pseudo-Richard of Campsall 1982 13.12: "Universale est illud cui, ex sua ratione formali, pluribus convenire non repugnat. Et quod tales res universales sint ... probo."

[6] *SLB* II, 2: "... terminus 'universale' <accipitur> a metaphysico pro quidditate rei de se communicabili ad plura inferiora."

[7] Pseudo-Richard of Campsall 1982 13.11: "... non debet concedi quod illud quod praedicatur de pluribus sit universale, sed debet dici quod illud pro quo supponit illud quod praedicatur de pluribus est universale." In the same §, Pseudo-Campsall introduces the idea that predication is a metaphysical predicate, and that every true linguistic proposition (vocal, mental) is made true by a corresponding real proposition (*propositio in re*).

[8] *SLB* II, 10: "... universali logico tamquam eius primus terminus universale reale et metaphysicum correspondet."

The *de se/de facto* distinction, is, as I would like to call it, an *aspectual* distinction. It allows, for example, to say something like: "*de se*, item *x* is *F*" and/although "*de facto*, item *x* is not-*F*." Although *aspectual*, the *de se/de facto* distinction is not an *epistemic* distinction: it does not pertain to the ways a cognizing subject considers things, but to what can be truly predicated of things—depending on the perspective taken by a cognizing subject.

The items to which Pseudo-Campsall and Brinkley apply the *de se/de facto* distinction are natures, and the *prima facie* incompatible predicates it allows one to say about natures are "common," when natures are considered *de se*, and "not common," when the very same natures are considered *de facto*.

When talking about common natures, Pseudo-Campsall insists that they should not be understood as being some numerically *one* thing (*aliqua una res*) existing in several particulars, a view that would be absurd (*absurdum*). Rather:

> [5] "... the human nature that is in Socrates is one thing such that, in itself (*de se*), nothing prevents it from being in Plato, and Socrates, and to accord with Socrates, although in fact (*de facto*) it could not be such. And just as this holds for Socrates's humanity, it holds for Plato's. For the metaphysician, who considers the quiddity of the thing in itself (*de se*), does not consider the thing otherwise ... and considered in such a way, it is in itself (*de se*) indifferent and common with respect to any individual and thus, one such nature is in any individual, determined by a numerical difference."[9]

The reason for introducing the *de se/de facto* distinction seems to be this: generality is a fact (things come in kinds, our languages comprise general terms expressing general concepts); there are metaphysical universals; therefore, something general must exist in extra-mental (and extra-linguistic) reality, namely natures or quiddities; but "being general" in the extra-mental world cannot mean "being one and the same thing in many" (nor can it mean, for that matter, "being one and the same thing over many"[10]); therefore, one should distinguish, for a given quiddity or nature, between the way it is *de facto*, i.e. singularised in each particular, and the way it is *de se*, i.e., common and indifferent.

The same distinction is introduced by Brinkley in the context of his discussion of personal and simple supposition (*suppositio*). Roughly, the supposition of a term is its reference in a sentence. "Man" in "a man is running" has "personal" supposition (it stands for human beings), while in "man is a species" it has "simple" supposition (it stands for human nature). According to Brinkley, that division reflects a partition

---

[9] Pseudo-Richard of Campsall 1982 13.13: "... natura humana, quae est in Sorte, est una res cui, quantum est de se, non repugnat esse in Platone et Sorte et convenire Sorti, licet de facto sibi competere non possit. Et sicut est de humanitate Sortis, ita est de humanitate Platonis. Metaphysicus enim qui considerat quidditatem rei in se, non considerat rem nisi talem qualem ... sic, autem, considerata, de se est indifferens et communis ad quodlibet individuum et ita, una talis natura est in quolibet individuo, determinata per differentiam numeralem ..."

[10] Pseudo-Campsall decidedly rejects Platonic ideas: not even Plato himself believed in such monstrosities (*abusiones*) that were invented by Aristotle in his (unfair) critique of his master (see Pseudo-Richard of Campsall 1982 61.02).

among things: a term has simple supposition when it stands for a universal thing; it has personal supposition when it stands for a singular one.[11]

Given Brinkley's metaphysics—and in particular, given his acceptance of metaphysical universals—that seems relatively unproblematic. However, Brinkley also makes the following claim:

[6] "When it is said that there is a thing that is not singular, I deny that. For I say that every thing is singular..."[12]

But in what sense, then, can one say, as Brinkley wants, that a term taken in simple supposition supposits for a universal thing? Is a universal thing a singular one? Well... in a sense—that is, provided one makes a certain distinction—it is:

[7] "I say that what is expressed in the first place by a common term, as for example by this term 'man,' is in itself (*de se*) common or communicable with respect to every individual within the human species; yet, in fact (*de facto*), it is only one individual, such that it is not communicable, but really incommunicable..."[13]

[8] "Simple supposition occurs when a term supposits for a thing as non-contracted, that is: for a thing that, in extra-mental reality (*ex parte rei*), is communicable...".[14]

Brinkley also insists that a nature, say: humanity, as non-communicable (that is: non-common) thing exists *in* the individual whose nature it is:

[9] "Just as a line that is in Socrates can be understood without Socrates but cannot exist without Socrates, just the same, the humanity that is in Socrates can be understood without Socrates although it could not exist without Socrates."[15]

What turns a *de se* universal thing into a *de facto* particular one? In text [5], Pseudo-Campsall talks about a numerical difference determining a quiddity as to make it exist in an individual; and in text [8], Brinkley says that the universal thing for which a term in simple supposition supposits is a thing as non-contracted, thereby suggesting that the singular thing for which a term in personal supposition supposits

---

[11] *SLB* IV, 2.2: "Dividitur igitur suppositio propria secundum divisionem rerum; res enim primaria divisione dividitur in rem universalem et in rem singularem ... Ideo omnis terminus qui representat nobis in propositione res, vel representat nobis rem universalem vel rem singularem; si universalem tunc terminus pro illa supponens dicitur habere suppositionem simplicem; si singularem ab illo termino distinctam representat nobis terminus tunc debet dici in propositione ubi sic representat habere suppositionem personalem."

[12] *SLB* IV, 6.14: "Quando dicitur quod aliqua sit res que non sit res singularis, hoc nego. Dico enim quod omnis res est singularis ..."

[13] *SLB* IV, 6.14: "Quando dicitur quod aliqua sit res que non sit res singularis, hoc nego. Dico enim quod omnis res est singularis ... Dico quod illud quod primo exprimitur per terminum communem ut per illum terminum 'homo' est de se commune sive communicabile ad omne individuum in specie hominis; et tamen de facto est tantum unum individuum ita quod non communicabile, sed realiter ita incommunicabile ..."

[14] *SLB* IV, 2.3: "Suppositio simplex est quando terminus supponit pro re ut non contracta, sive pro re pluribus communicabili ex parte rei ..."

[15] *SLB* II, 10: "Sicut linea quae est in Socrate potest intelligi absque Socrate sed non potest esse absque Socrate, ita humanitas quae est in Socrate potest intelligi sine Socrate, quamvis non posset esse sine Socrate."

is precisely a contracted one. As a matter of fact, contraction is nothing but something like the metaphysical effect of a difference on a common nature, be that difference specific, or individual:

> [10] "…the physicist says that a genus is divided into species, because that thing that is a genus is contracted by the formal determination (*ratio formalis*) of the species."[16]

> [11] "In 'Socrates is sustaining human nature,' 'Socrates' signifies something by which human nature is contracted to a certain and determinate referent, and that is the individual difference."[17]

Summing up, one can express the gist of Pseudo-Campsall and Brinkley's views on universals as follows: (*i*) metaphysical universals (i.e. universals that are neither linguistic signs, nor concepts) exist; (*ii*) universals are common natures; (*iii*) natures are *de se* common, but *de facto* particular; (*iv*) particular natures are contracted common natures; (*v*) *de facto* natures exist in particulars. Alternatively, and in terms of the three theses formulated at the beginning of this paper, one can say that Pseudo-Campsall and Brinkley accept all three theses, but with some crucial qualifications: (1) only holds *de facto*, whereas (3) and (thus) (2) hold *de se*.

Provided such a reconstruction is correct, one may still legitimately be puzzled (to say the least) and wonder, since the *de se/de facto* distinction is not a merely epistemic distinction but pertains to real aspects *in things*, how one and the same item can truly be common *and* particular.

At this point, we are facing two antagonistic hermeneutical options: either the theory must be dismissed as being (at best) inconsistent; or, more charitably, one can believe that there is something philosophically worthwhile in the *de se/de facto* distinction as it is used by Pseudo-Campsall and Brinkley. But before issuing a verdict, and in order to make a fair decision, a bit of doctrinal sight-seeing is in order.

18.2　Comparison with Other Medieval Views

The thesis of the existence of metaphysical universals clearly locates Pseudo-Campsall's and Brinkley's views among realist theories of universals. Yet, exactly what kind of realism they advocate remains in need of clarification. In that respect, some comparative considerations might help.

---

[16] Pseudo-Richard of Campsall 1982 30.09: "… philosophus naturalis <dicit> genus in species dividi quia res illa quae est genus per rationem formalem speciei contrahitur."

[17] Pseudo-Richard of Campsall 1982 7.06: "Per 'Sortes' < in 'Sortes est sustentans naturam humanam' > importatur aliquid per quod natura humana contrahitur ad certum et determinatum suppositum, et illud est differentia individualis."

18.2.1 Negative Delimitations

The first view from which those advocated by our two authors have to be distinguished is sheer Platonism.

Another view against which those of Pseudo-Campsall and Brinkley have to be contrasted is Avicenna's essence neutralism—a position that is doctrinally located, so to speak, *beyond* the opposition between realism and nominalism. As is well known,[18] Avicennian essences are said to be indifferent with respect to existence (be it in the mind or *in re*), as well as to universality and particularity: existence, universality, and particularity are comparable to accidents occurring to essences. Thus, regarding universality, Avicenna claims that a genus like animal as such (*in se*) is neither universal nor particular.[19] As we saw above, however, Pseudo-Campsall and Brinkley insist that natures *de se* are common, that is: universal.

Turning to Latin medieval realist accounts of universals, Pseudo-Campsall's and Brinkley's views can be delimited *negatively* with respect to three theories, the first being a quite radical form of "immanentism," whereas the last two take universals either to "accompany," or to be identical with, individuals.

On the one hand, Pseudo-Campsall's and Brinkley's positions differ from the robust and famous realism originally endorsed by William of Champeaux in the early twelfth century, according to which universals exist *in* particulars in the strongest possible sense: a given genus and one of its species exist, as such, in each of the individuals of that species (Erismann 2011, 76–77). What accounts for the distinction between two individuals is nothing like an individual difference or any "contracting" metaphysical device, but the constellation of accidents uniquely possessed by each individual.

On the other hand, the kind of views described in the first section of this paper differs from other fourteenth-century forms of stronger realism, as found in the works of the *later* (that is: post-1324) Walter Burley and of John Wyclif.

According to the later Burley, universals exist as such in extra-mental reality, as items that essentially accompany individuals without being any of their parts or constituents (Conti 2008). Although that view has a distinctive Platonic flavour, it is not a genuine case of Platonism. True enough, Burley takes universals to exist *separately* from individuals and to be un-instantiated: humanity accompanying Socrates is just humanity accompanying Plato and any other member of the human species.

---

[18] Benevitch (2018), Bertolacci (2006), Di Vincenzo (2021), Germann (2010), Lizzini (2020), Libera (1996), Libera (1999), Porro (2002), Wisnovsky (2005).

[19] Avicenna (2018), 198: "Ponamus autem in hoc exemplum generis dicentes quod animal est in se quiddam et idem utrum sit sensibile aut sit intellectum in anima. In se autem neque est universale neque singulare. Si enim in se esset universale, ita quod animalitas, ex hoc quod est animalitas, esset universalis, oporteret nullum animal esse singulare, sed omne animal esse universale. Si autem animal ex hoc quod est animal esset singulare, impossibile esset esse nisi unum singulare tantum, scilicet ipsum singulare cui debetur animalitas, et esset impossibile aliud singulare esse animal."

But Burleyian universals do not exist in a *separate world*. Rather, they are concomitant or "adverbial" items existing *together with*, yet not in, individuals.

In his *De universalibus*, Wyclif goes one significant step further. He distinguishes three ways of conceiving (*considerationes*) universals in a vein reminiscent of the disciplinary variations pointed at by Pseudo-Campsall and Brinkley: grammarians see universals as mere (extra-mental) linguistic signs; logicians, for their part, reduce them to intellectual cognitive acts; metaphysicians, finally, agreeing with "the saint doctors," conceive of universals as common natures really identical with each singular: "every universal is a singular, and vice versa."[20]

It is clear, I take it, that Pseudo-Campsall's and Brinkley's views have to be distinguished from the realisms endorsed by William of Champeaux, Walter Burley and John Wyclif. Contra William and Burley, their universals exist in particulars and only as instantiated (or contracted) natures. Contra Wyclif, Pseudo-Campsall and Brinkley do not identify universals and particulars; although, as we saw, they are prepared to say that contracted common natures exist in individuals, they do not claim that every individual *is* its own *common* nature.

18.2.2   Positive Delimitations

So much for negative delimitations. Turning now to similarities, or even affinities, between other theories of universals and the kind of view advocated by Pseudo-Campsall and Brinkley, the first suspect on the list is Duns Scotus. The use of the notion of contraction, for example, seems to be a reliable indicator—strongly reminiscent of what Scotus himself has to say about universals.[21] Indeed, when, in his discussion of individuation in *Ordinatio* II, d. 3 Scotus explains how quiddity (or common nature) is to be conceived of, he writes:

> [12] "For although <quiddity> is never really (*realiter*) without some of these features <that is: unity, plurality, being universal, being particular>, yet it is not any of them of itself (*de se*), but is naturally prior to all of them"[22] (transl. Spade 1994, 63).

I take Scotus's *de se/realiter* distinction to be conceptually equivalent to Pseudo-Campsall's and Brinkley's *de se/de facto* distinction. However, and as the very same passage suggests, Scotus has an Avicennian conception of common nature—a point he explicitly makes clear in the immediate context of the passage just quoted. According to Scotus, then, and just as Avicenna wanted it, common natures, even

---

[20] Wyclif (1985), 4.57–58:"… omne universale est singular et econtra …"; see also *De universalibus* 3.213–240.

[21] Conti (2008), Hawthorne (2016), Libera (1996), McCord Adams (1982), Pini (2007), Spade (1994), Taieb (2017).

[22] Scotus, *Ordinatio* II, d. 3, prima pars, q. 1, n. 32: "Licet enim <quiditas> numquam sit realiter sine aliquo istorum <sc. unitas, pluralitas, esse universale, esse particulare (sive singulare)>, de se tamen est prius naturaliter omnibus istis."

considered *de se*, are not universals. Furthermore, Scotus rejects the existence of extra-mental universals:

> [13] "... I say that the universal in act is what has some indifferent unity according to which it itself, the very same, is in proximate potency to be said of each *suppositum* ... Nothing in reality, according to any unity at all, is such..."[23] (trans. Spade 1994, 65).

Thus, even though Pseudo-Campsall's and Brinkley's *de se/de facto* distinction might be derived more or less directly from Scotus's approach to common natures, the two accounts of universals diverge on two crucial points: contrary to Scotus, Pseudo-Campsall and Brinkley, first acknowledge the existence of extra-mental universals, and second insist that natures *de se* are universal and not indifferent with respect to universality.

The *Doctor subtilis* was the first name on my list of suspects—that is, of thinkers whose views about universals present some similarities with those of Pseudo-Campsall and Brinkley. Three further names are on the list: the *very* early Burley, Roger Bacon, and Albert the Great.

In question one of his so-called middle commentary on Aristotle's *Categories* (ca. 1302), Burley, in the course of an extended discussion regarding the proposition and its different kinds (*divisio enuntiationis*), says the following about universal propositions:

> [14] "There is another division of the proposition, for some proposition is singular, and some is universal; and that division is derived from a division among things: some among the things are universal, and some singular. Universal is what is apt to be predicated of many, and singular what is not apt to be predicated of many but only of one. One has to understand that *that* is called a universal, with respect to the nature of the form of which it is not impossible that it is in many, although on the side of matter, it is impossible that it is in many."[24]

Three points are salient in this passage: first, the idea that a linguistic distinction—here, the division of proposition—is ontologically grounded (*acciptur ex divisione rerum*); second, the thesis of the extra-mental existence of real universals among things, that is, universals *in essendo*, and not merely *in significando*; third, the distinction between what can be truly said of a universal with respect to its very nature (*ex natura formae*), and what is the case in the material world (*ex parte materiae*). The affinities with the views of Pseudo-Campsall and Brinkley are striking, but also the difference with respect to what we had in our first suspect, namely Scotus.

---

[23] Scotus, *Ordinatio* II, d. 3, prima pars, q. 1, n. 37: "... dico quod universale in actu est illud quod habet aliquam unitatem indifferentem, secundum quam ipsum idem est in potentia proxima ut dicatur de quolibet supposito ... Nihil enim est in re tale ..."

[24] Burley (1973), 84–85: "Alia divisio enunciationis accipitur, quia quaedam enunciatio est de subiecto singulari et quaedam de subiecto universali, et haec divisio accipitur ex divisione rerum: quaedam rerum sunt universalia et quaedam singularia. Universale est quod est aptum natum praedicari de pluribus et singulare quod non est natum praedicari de pluribus sed de uno solo. Intelligendum quod illud dicitur universale cui ex natura formae suae non repugnat reperiri in pluribus, etsi ex parte materiae impossibile sit ipsum in pluribus reperiri."

According to Burley, a nature or quiddity—say humanity[25]—is *ex natura formae suae* (that is, *de se*) universal, and not indifferent with respect to universality. Further, such a universal is found in the extra-mental world—it belongs to the realm of things as opposed to the one of concepts.

But what about the time *before* Scotus and Burley? Are there, before the last decade of the thirteenth century, say, accounts of universals that come close to those of Pseudo-Campsall and Richard Brinkley? Any attempt to answer such a (legiti-mate) question will necessarily be provisional and lacunar. Among the many pos-sible candidates, I picked out Roger Bacon and Albert the Great for a number of reasons (none of them being compelling, I am afraid): Albert, for his role of para-digmatic and tutelary figure in what has been called "13th-century moderate real-ism" (Conti 2008), and Bacon, for the highly sophisticated—and largely unstudied[26]—metaphysics on which his account of universals is based.

In his questions on the second book of Aristotle's *Physics*,[27] in the context of a discussion pertaining to the problem of abstraction, and more precisely to the pos-sibly mendacious character of abstraction, Bacon makes the following distinction:

> [15] "… one has to notice that the being of a thing is twofold: one is actual, natural, material being (*esse actuale, naturale, materiale*), and the physicist considers that being; thus, he considers a form in a matter, and with respect to the being it has in virtue of matter. Another being is of essence, formal, separate or abstract (*esse essentiae, formale, separatum, abstractum*), and that is the being possessed by something existing in matter, <but> not in virtue of the nature of matter; and the mathematician considers that being."[28]

Remarkably, according to Bacon, the two *esse*—namely material *and* essential being—belong to the *material* world, although only the former is possessed in vir-tue of matter, whereas the latter, though *in* matter, is not possessed *in virtue of* it. Only that, I take it, is meant by the two intriguing predicates "abstract" and "sepa-rate" that have thus to be taken in a deflationary sense (Bacon is not a Platonist).[29]

Thus, "abstract" and "separate" need not point to any third realm, but could just mean "in the mind." And indeed, what Bacon writes immediately after the passage just quoted seems to go into that direction:

---

[25] Although the notions of nature or quiddity do not appear in text [14], Burley frequently uses *natura* and *quidditas* in order to designate genera and species.

[26] With the notable exception of the anthology of translations (with a doctrinal introduction) pub-lished by Maloney back in the late 1980s (Maloney 1989).

[27] Note that Donati (2013) has questioned the attribution of those questions to Bacon with serious arguments. In order to take that possibility into account, I refer to the author of those questions as (Pseudo)-Roger Bacon.

[28] (Pseudo)-Roger Bacon (1928), 69–71: "… notandum quod duplex est esse rei: quoddam est actuale, naturale, materiale, et hoc esse considerat naturalis; unde considerat formam in materia et quantum ad illud esse quod habet per materiam. Aliud est esse essentiae, formale, separatum vel abstractum, et hoc est esse quod habet existens in materia, non per naturam materiae, et hoc esse considerat mathematicus." On that passage and its context, see Libera 2005, 245–64 (esp. 255).

[29] See Bacon (1905–1913) §47 [no one, nowadays, speaks like Plato], and below, text [19].

[16] "You can appreciate what has been said so far in considering the example of the universal: the universal, according to the actual and natural being it possesses in virtue of singular things, is one in many; however, in the being of essence and cognitive being it has from the soul, it is not like that <i.e. one in many>, but one over many."[30]

Applied to universals, the distinction between material and essential being amounts to distinguishing the being a universal has in virtue of matter (*per materiam*), namely material being, and the being it gets from the soul (*ab anima*), namely essential or cognitive (*cognoscitivum*) being. In text [15], however, being of essence had been introduced as a kind of being possessed by something existing in matter. Is Bacon incoherent on that point? I don't think so.

There is a slip, in text [16], from a metaphysical to a cognitive point of view, marked by the introduction of the predicate *cognoscitivum*. The fact that a universal has cognitive being in the mind and that, as such, it is something that is one *over* many, is not incompatible with the claim made in text [15], according to which essential being is possessed by what exists in matter, that is, outside the mind.

My reason for seeing a change of perspective, or a slip, in text [16] is that in other passages (to be quoted below) Bacon is quite explicit that the difference between material and essential being is a difference *within* extra-mental being, and not a difference *between* extra-mental and mental being. A universal in its cognitive being, then, is what one has in mind when cognizing an extra-mental universal in its essential being, that is: in the being it has *in* matter, but not *in virtue of* matter.

Let us now have a look at those other passages of Bacon's. They are all taken from his questions on book VII of Aristotle's *Metaphysics*, in his *Quaestiones supra libros Primae philosophiae Aristotelis*, written in Paris in the 1240s. There, one reads:

[17] "... I concede that universals have a common matter and a common form; thus, just as primary matter and this form make an individual, just the same, common matter and common form make the most general genus; and in that way, progressively, by means of assignation and contraction, they make species and individuals."[31]

[18] "... I say that something <exists> in matter in two ways: either immediately in designated and particular matter, and that is individuated; or it exists immediately in common matter ... and thus, there is no need for it to be individuated because it is immediately received in common matter" (trans. Maloney 1989, modified).[32]

---

[30] (Pseudo)-Roger Bacon (1928) p. 71: "Quae jam dicta per exemplum de universali potes perpendere: est enim universale quantum ad esse actuale et naturale quod habet per singularia unum in multis, tamen in esse essentiae et cognoscitivo ab anima non ut sic est, sed ut est unum praeter multa." On that passage and its context, see Libera 2005, 255.

[31] Bacon (1930), p. 237: "... concedo quod universalia habent materiam communem et formam communem; unde sicut materia prima et haec forma faciunt individuum, sic materia communis et forma communis faciunt generalissimum; et sic descendendo semper per assignationem et contractionem faciunt species et individua."

[32] Bacon (1930), p. 242: "... dico aliquid in materia dupliciter: aut immediate in materia signata et particulari, et tale individuatur; aliud est in materia communi immediate, et sic universale est in materia communi quia fit ex materia communi et forma communi ... et ideo non est necesse quod individuetur, quia immediate recipitur in materia communi."

As those two passages make clear, Bacon's ontology acknowledges something like two hylomorphic layers in extra-mental reality: there is particular matter and form on the one hand, and common matter and form on the other, the latter being the constituents of universals. Furthermore, a universal, since it is composed of common matter and common form, is an un-instantiated one. That sounds *very much* like Platonism. It would be mistaken, however, to draw such a conclusion:

[19] "Only three types of being are imaginable: either <being> in and of itself, <being> in the mind, or <being> in things; but a universal is not something that has being in and of itself and stands on its own, because then it would be a Platonic Idea; neither <does it have being> in the mind, as has been seen" (trans. Maloney 1989).[33]

It seems thus that Baconian universals are extra-mental, un-instantiated, and yet non-Platonic entities. But where do they exist, then? Do those two hylomorphic layers—that is, universals and particulars—exist *together* as constituents *within* every individual? As the following final passage suggests, the answer is affirmative:

[20] "... I say that a universal is in act, and likewise a particular, but they do not carry a numerical commitment (*non ponunt in numerum*), and thus, they are not two things. Because of this, it is necessary that they be one, which is precisely what they are, because a universal is in a particular ... a universal is received in the manner of the recipient, because the very essence of a universal is <to be> a one in many. Yet in being received in it, <the universal> has designated and participated being. Whence the essence of a universal is always one, though it is replicated (*replicatur*) in different things according to <its> being designated (*signata*), different and particularized"[34] (trans. Maloney 1989, modified).

Universals, then, exist *in* particulars. But not only that. They exist so to speak *twice* in particulars: once as universals in act (as the essence's being one in many), and a second time in so far as they have participated being (*esse participatum*). By something like "internal participation," the essence becomes replicated. The consequence is that the same item, namely the essence or common nature, is at the same time and within the same individual *universal* (as an un-instantiated universal) and *particular* (as a replicated universal).

Such a picture, however, can only be accepted under some strict ontological distinction. But as we saw above in text [15], Bacon employs precisely just such a distinction, namely that between material and essential being.

The picture, then, is this: both instantiated and un-instantiated universals coexist *in* individuals, *but not on the same mode of being.* Instantiated universals exist in individuals according to material being. Un-instantiated universals exist in

---

[33] Bacon (1930), p. 237: "Non contingit imaginari nisi triplex esse: aut in se, aut in anima, aut in rebus; sed universale non est in se per se stans, quia sic esset idea Platonica; nec in anima, ut visum est."

[34] Bacon (1930), p. 245–246: "... dico quod universale est actu, et similter particulare; sed non ponunt in numerum, ideo non sunt duo. Propter hoc oportet quod sint unum, immo sunt, quia universale est in particulari. ... universale recipitur per modum recipientis quia ipsa essentia universalis est unum in multis, tamen secundum quod recipitur in isto habet esse signatum et participatum. Unde ipsa essentia universalis est semper una, tamen illa replicatur in diversis, secundum esse signata et diversa et particulata ..."

individuals according to essential being—a being, as Bacon nicely puts it, they have *in* matter, but not it *in virtue of* matter.

A very short remark on Albert the Great, before turning to the evaluative (and last) part of my paper. Albert's definition of universals reads as follows:

[21] "The universal is that which, although being in one thing, is apt to be in several <things> ... And because it is in several <things> in virtue of aptitude, it is predicable of them. And thus, a universal is that which, by its aptitude, 'is in many, and of many.'"[35]

The key notion here is that of aptitude. Applied to the metaphysics of universals, it suggests a neat solution to several difficulties at once, difficulties that are familiar to the whole Aristotelian tradition: "to be in one thing while being apt to be in several things" (that's Albert's idea) is a smart ecumenical formula that somehow holds together the antagonistic aspects of "being *one*," "being *in* many," and "being *said of* many." That, I take it, explains the immense fortune of the definition. But beyond its undeniable irenic potential, Albert's definition also raises a lot of questions, the first of which is of course what exactly it means. The different doctrinal elements gathered in the first two sections of that paper might suggest a way to interpret it—something I shall now attempt to do.

18.3 Evaluation

18.3.1 A (Needed) Recap

Provided that I have understood them correctly, Pseudo-Campsall and Brinkley's accounts of universals are characterized by what appears at first sight to be a pair of incompatible claims stating, on the one hand, that metaphysical universals exist—thesis (3) in the introduction—but also, on the other hand, that the world is constituted of particular items only—thesis (1) in the introduction. As we saw in the first section of this paper, what allows them to maintain those two claims without being inconsistent is the *de se*/*de facto* distinction, to the effect that everything is *de facto* particular, whereas some things are (also) *de se* universal. In the terms of our two heroes: *de facto*, natures exist as not-common (contracted), whereas *de se*, the very same natures are common.

In Sect. 18.2, I have compared Pseudo-Campsall's and Brinkley's views to a selection of other accounts of universals. I distinguished three cases, under the labels of "negative delimitations" (Sect. 18.2.1), for the first two cases, and of "positive delimitations" (Sect. 18.2.2), for the third.

First there is the case of radical difference with Plato and Avicenna. Second there is the case of partial correspondence (but with crucial differences) with William of

---

[35] Albert the Great (1890), p. 17b: "Universale autem est quod, cum sit in uno, aptum est esse in pluribus ... Et per hoc quod in multis per aptitudinem est, praedicabile de illis est. Et sic universale est quod de sua aptitudine 'est in multis et de multis'".

Champeaux, the later Burley and Wyclif. Third there is the case of striking affinity with Scotus, the very early Burley, Roger Bacon, and Albert the Great.

That being said, let me turn (again) to Pseudo-Campsall's and Brinkley's *de se*/*de facto* distinction, and say a bit more about how, from a systematic point of view, it can, or perhaps should, be interpreted.

18.3.2   The **de se/de facto** *Distinction and Moderate Realism*

In Sect. 18.1.2. above, when introducing the *de se*/*de facto* distinction, I said that it was not an epistemic, but an aspectual distinction. What I mean by that—and I endorse now the point of view that I take to be the one of Pseudo-Campsall and Brinkley—is that natures, independently of our ways of thinking, are such that they possess a particular and a universal aspect—or better, they *are* particulars, possessing a universal aspect. Take humanity as it exists in Socrates, for example. In terms of what one can quantify over, there is only one thing, namely this particular nature: Socrates's humanity. Nonetheless, what Socrates's humanity is *de se*, namely common and universal, is a *real*, that is, non-fictional, aspect of it. Thus, an ontology making use of the *de se*/*de facto* distinction is partially *counterfactual* (*de se* natures do not exist as distinct entities besides *de facto* natures) without being fictional (*de se* natures are such independently of our way of thinking). To put it still differently: the *de se*/*de facto* distinction, as an aspectual distinction, does not have any *existential* import, although it does have a decisive *ontological* import. This means that although it does not increase the number of denizens in the world, it makes a metaphysical difference in the world.

But in what sense exactly? Take two particulars such that one, as such, has a universal aspect—for example, the particular humanity existing in Socrates—and the other does not—for example, the individual Socrates himself. One can say then, that the ontological difference captured by the *de se*/*de facto* distinction is that whereas the humanity existing in Socrates is the result of the "contraction" of something general (it is a "contracted" nature), the same does not hold for Socrates. Although Socrates might well be the final result of combined and multi-layered contraction processes, he himself does not instantiate anything general. His nature is a *particular*, i.e., something particularized, whereas he himself is just an *individual*.

Thus, one way to express the gist of the *de se*/*de facto* distinction in more familiar terms might simply be to say that it presents us with a medieval way of getting at (and articulating) the difference between what is particular (that is, particular*ized*, or "contracted") and what is individual: particulars and individuals share the property of being not-common, but only particulars have a universal aspect.

In contemporary terms, finally, one could perhaps suggest that the *de se* universal aspect of particular natures amounts to *repeatability*, to the effect that the *de se* clause could be appropriately rendered by "repeatable," and the *de facto* one, by "repeated." Such a reading of Pseudo-Campsall's and Brinkley's ontology leads to something that would probably be considered a sheer monstrosity by many contemporary metaphysicians, namely, an account of generality combining tropes and universals, *de facto* natures being comparable to tropes displaying a (*de se*) universal moment. This idea is possibly akin to what Jeffrey Brower suggests in a recent paper on Aquinas' account of universals in terms of "internal sameness" (Brower 2016), but also to some remarks made by John Hawthorne and Hamid Taieb in equally recent papers on Scotus on universals (Hawthorne 2016 and Taieb 2017).

This line of thought opens some perspectives with respect to the needed clarification of the notion of moderate realism, a notion wildly used in the historiography of medieval philosophy. Facing the massive *explanandum* of generality, and (i) endorsing strong epistemological realism (our concepts *do* tell us something about how the world is), and (ii) rejecting any form of Platonism (the *explanans* must be located within the realm of things), some late medieval philosophers go for the general strategy of "nature-immanentism." As its name indicates, nature-immanentism claims that natures exist *in* individuals. But once this much has been said—and it is not much—doctrinal ways depart from one another. Some philosophers hold that only *instantiated* natures exist in individuals, meaning that full universality is only achieved in (and by) the intellect (Avicenna, Scotus). Others, in contrast, insist that besides instantiated natures, *un-instantiated* natures also exist in individuals, either as entities possessing a distinct kind of being (Bacon's *esse essentiae*), or as mere (but non-fictional) aspects of instantiated natures (Pseudo-Campsall, Brinkley, and perhaps the very early Burley).

18.4   Conclusion

My conclusion is at the same time critical and programmatic. It is critical, because of the many authors, theories and arguments that I did not take into account. The programmatic aspect of my conclusion is the following. What we discovered in Pseudo-Campsall and Brinkley, but also in their fellow moderate realists, calls for a holistic approach of the notion of realism (medieval or not). I mean by this that it calls for an approach that goes beyond the relatively limited, though certainly crucial, problematic of universals, and addresses the more general and fundamental issue of ontological complexity in its different aspects: relational, predicative, propositional. In that respect, the seminal work of Donald Mertz, in his 1996 monograph *Moderate Realism and its Logic*, points exactly into the right direction.

Two last points. I owe a verdict regarding the consistency and philosophically interesting character of Pseudo-Campsall's and Brinkley's accounts of universals, together with a reason why these accounts are better than their nominalist rivals. Let me make *d'une pierre deux coups*. As I tried to show, Pseudo-Campsall's and Brinkley's moderate realism is complex, sophisticated, but not inconsistent: the *de se/de facto* distinction does a systematically relevant job. Furthermore, their realism offers a better account of generality in that it provides at least the beginning of a metaphysical analysis of what mainstream nominalism is compelled either to reduce to semantics, or to take as being primitive.[36]

---

[36] Many thanks to Clarisse Reynard for her careful reading of a first version of this paper.

Bibliography

Primary Sources

Albert the Great. 1890. *Super Porphyrium de V universalibus*, ed. I. Borgnet. Paris: Vivès.
Avicenna. 2018. Logica, ed. F. Hudry. Paris: Vrin.
Burley, Walter. 1973. *Commentarius in librum* Perihermeneias. In S.F. Brown, "Walter Burley's Middle Commentary on Aristotle's *perihermeneias.*" Franciscan Studies 33: 45–134.
Bacon, Roger. 1905–1913. *Communia naturalia*, 3 vols., ed. R. Steele, Oxford: Clarendon.
Bacon, (Pseudo)-Roger. 1928. Quaestiones supra Libros quatuor Physicorum Aristotelis (Physica I-IV), ed. F.M. Delorme, R. Steele. Oxford: Clarendon.
Bacon, Roger. 1930. In *Quaestiones supra libros Primae philosophiae Aristotelis*, ed. R. Steele and F. Delorme. Oxford: Clarendon.
Brinkley, Richard. 2008. *Summa logicae II* = *De universalibus*, ed. L. Cesalli, "Richard Brinkley *contra dialecticae haereticos*: une conception métaphysico-logique de l'universel" in *Documenti e Studi Sulla Tradizione Filosofica Medievale* XIX, 277–333.
———. 2013. *Summa logicae IV* = *De suppositionibus* (fragments), ed. L. Cesalli, "Richard Brinkley on supposition", *Vivarium* 51: 275–303. [also in E. P. Bos (ed.). 2013. *Medieval supposition theory revisited*, Leiden: Brill. 275–303].
Pseudo-Richard of Campsall. 1982. *Logica Campsale Anglicj, ualde utilis et realis contra Ocham* ed. E.A. Synan in *The Works of Richard Campsall*, vol. 2. Toronto: Pontifical Institute of Medieval Studies.
Scotus, John Duns. 1950. Ordinatio, dist. I-II in *Opera omnia* 2, ed. C. Balić, M. Bodewig, S. Bušelić, P. Čapkun-Delić, I. Jurić, I. Montalverne, S. Nanni, B. Pergamo, F. Prezioso, I. Reinhold, and O. Schäfer. Città del Vaticano: Typis Polyglottis Vaticanis
William of Ockham. 1974. Summa logicae, ed. G. Gál, R. Wood. St. Bonaventure: The Franciscan Institute.
Wyclif, John. 1985. *De universalibus*, ed. I. Müller. Oxford: Clarendon.

Secondary Sources

Adamson, Peter, Taylor, Richard C., ed., 2005. *The Cambridge companion to Avicenna*. Cambridge: Cambridge University Press.
Benevitch, Fedor. 2018. *The reality of the non-existent object of thought: The possible, the impossible and mental existence in Islamic philosophy* (eleventh-thirteenth centuries). In Oxford Studies in Medieval Philosophy 6. 31–61.
Bertolacci, Amos. 2006. *The reception of Aristotle's* Metaphysics *in Avicenna's* Kitab al-Sifa'. Leiden: Brill.
Bertolacci, Amos, Dimitri Gutas, John McGinnis, Tony Street, Johannes Thomann and Renate Würsch. 2021. "Ibn Sina" in Ulrich Rudolph, ed., *Die Philosophie in der Islamischen Welt*, II.1: *11. und 12. Jahrhundert. Zentrale und Östliche Gebiete*, Basel: Schwabe. 1–210.
Brower, Jeffrey. 2016. Aquinas on the problem of universals. *Philosophy and Phenomenological Research* 112 (3): 715–735.
Cesalli, Laurent. 2017. Pseudo-Richard of Campsall and Richard Brinkley on universals. In *Universals in the fourteenth century*, ed. F. Amerini and L. Cesalli, 225–240. Edizioni della Normale: Pisa.
Conti, Alessandro. 2008. Categories and universals in the later middle ages. In *Medieval commentaries on Aristotle's categories*, ed. L. Newton, 369–427. Brill: Leiden.

de Libera, Alain. 1996 [new edition: 2014]. *La querelle des universaux. De Platon à la fin du Moyen Âge*, Paris: Seuil.
———. 1999. *L'art des généralités. Théories de l'abstraction*. Paris: Aubier.
———. 2005. *Métaphysique et noétique*. Albert le Grand. Paris, Vin.
Di Vincenzo, Silvia. 2021. *Avicenna, The Healing, Logic: Isagoge*. A New Edition, English Translation and Commentary of the *Kitāb al-Madḫal* of Avicenna's *Kitāb al-Šifāʾ*. Berlin, De Gruyter.
Donati, Silvia. 2013. Pseudoepigrapha in the *Opera hactenus inedita Rogeri Baconi?* The Commentaries on the *Physics* and on the *Metaphysics*. In *Les débuts de l'enseignement universitaire à Paris (1200–1245 environ)*, 153–203. Turnhout: Brepols.
Erismann, Christophe. 2011. *L'homme commun. La genèse du réalisme ontologique durant le haut Moyen Âge*, Paris: Vrin.
Germann, Nadja. (2010). Ibn sina (Avicenna). In *Encyclopedia of medieval philosophy*, ed. H. Lagerlund, 515–522. Dordrecht: Springer.
Hawthorne, John. 2016. *Scotus on universals*. In Oxford Studies in Medieval Philosophy 4: 64–77.
Klima, Gyula. 2017. In *The medieval problem of universals*, ed. E. Zalta. Stanford encyclopedia of philosophy. https://plato.stanford.edu/entries/universals-medieval/.
Lizzini, Olga. 2020. In *Ibn Sina's Metaphyscis*, ed. E. Zalta. Stanford encyclopedia of philosophy. https://plato.stanford.edu/entries/ibn-sina-metaphysics/.
Maloney, Thomas. 1989. *Three treatments of universals by Roger Bacon*. Binghampton: Centre for Medieval and Early Renaissance Studies.
McCord Adams, Marilyn, 1982. Universals in the Early Fourteenth Century. In *The Cambridge history of later medieval philosophy*, ed. A. Kenny, N. Kretzmann, J. Pinborg, E. Stump, 413–439. Cambridge: Cambridge University Press.
Mertz, Donald. 1996. *Moderate realism and its logic*. New Haven: Yale University Press.
Piché, David. 2005. *Le problème des universaux à la Faculté des Arts de Paris entre 1230 et 1260*. Paris: Vrin.
Pini, Giorgio. 2007. Scotus on universals: A reconsideration. *Documenti e studi Sulla Tradizione Filosofica Medievale* 18: 395–409.
Porro, Pasquale. 2002. Universaux et *esse essentiae*: Avicenne, Henri de Gand et le 'troisième Reich'. In *Le réalisme des universaux*, Cahiers de Philosophie de l'Université de Caen 38–39, ed. V. Carraud and S. Chauvier, 9–51.
Spade, Paul-Vincent. 1994. *Five texts on the medieval problem of universals: Porphyry, Boethius, Abelard, duns Scotus, Ockham*. Indianapolis: Hackett.
Taieb, Hamid. 2017. Scotus' nature: From universal to trope. In *Universals in the fourteenth century*, ed. F. Amerini and L. Cesalli, 89–108. Pisa: Edizioni della Normale.
Wisnovsky, Robert. 2005. Avicenna and the Avicennian Tradition. In *The Cambridge companion to Avicenna*, ed. P. Adamson and R.C. Taylor, 92–136. Cambridge: Cambridge University Press.

Chapter 19
Connotation vs. Extrinsic Denomination: Peter Auriol on Intentions and Intellectual Cognition

Giacomo Fornasieri

Keywords Peter Auriol · Intellectual cognition · Intentions · Connotation · Extrinsic denomination · Radulphus Brito

19.1 Introduction

Intellectual cognition is surely one of the most favorite and thoroughly disputed topics among late medieval thinkers. As the subject matter of a number of exceptionally fierce debates, this issue engaged their minds at length, giving rise to an exceptional variety of theories, which surely make the fourteenth century one of the most vibrant periods in the Middle Ages. Among the questions that were most frequently addressed at that time, there were those concerning (i) the *categorization* of the intellectual act, (ii) the status of the concept and (iii) the relation between them. What is the nature of the cognitive act? Can it fit into one of the ten Aristotelian categories? If so, which one? What is a concept, specifically in relation to the object to which it refers? Is the concept somehow distinct from the intellectual act? Depending upon one's answers to these questions, different conceptions arise concerning the inner workings of intellectual cognition and the thought it produces.

In this paper, I will examine Peter Auriol's contribution on these issues, considering two major aspects of his theory of intellectual cognition, namely, his view on (i) what it is for a thing to be an intention or a concept and on (ii) what kind of relation connects the object cognized to the cognizing mind as soon as intellectual cognition is occurring. My analysis will comprise two steps. First, I will examine Auriol's criticism of Brito's thesis, according to which intentions are the same as cognitive acts, and "being cognized" is just an extrinsic denomination, which amounts to

G. Fornasieri (✉)
Lumsa University, Rome, Italy
e-mail: g.fornasieri@lumsa.it; giacomo.fornasieri@unicatt.it

© The Author(s), under exclusive license to Springer Nature Switzerland AG 2023
J. P. Hochschild et al. (eds.), *Metaphysics Through Semantics: The Philosophical Recovery of the Medieval Mind*, International Archives of the History of Ideas Archives internationales d'histoire des idées 242, https://doi.org/10.1007/978-3-031-15026-5_19

saying that for a thing to be objectively in the mind is just for there to be a cognitive act directed at that thing (Pini 2015, 340). Second, I will discuss Auriol's thesis, according to which each and every act of thinking must be thought of as a connotative notion, that is, as something implying or connoting (the production of) an intentional object appearing to the cognizer. In this regard, Auriol's view, as opposed to Brito's, allows him to think of "being cognized" as more than an extrinsic denomination of the object cognized, and thereby to incorporate into intellectual cognition a phenomenon that proves to be unique to our cognitive life, viz. the fact that we consciously experience what we cognize while we cognize it.

Since Auriol himself directly opposes Radulphus Brito to shape his own position on the matter, Auriol's thesis will be briefly read against Brito's view on intentions (*intentiones*). Once Brito's thesis on abstract/concrete first/second intentions and denomination is concisely discussed, and Auriol's criticisms presented, Auriol's understanding of intellectual cognition will be treated. Finally, I will offer some concluding remarks on Auriol's doctrine, as well as a brief evaluation of his theory.

19.2   Focusing the Target: Brito's View of Intentions and Cognitive Acts

In d. 23 of Book I of his Commentary on the *Sentences*, the late-medieval Franciscan theologian Peter Auriol questions whether the name "person" should be considered either a first or a second intention. Throughout his analysis, he delves at great length into what it means for a thing to be cognized, that is, what it means for it to be an intention. To that end, he lingers on the view of the modist master Radulphus Brito (ca.1320),[1] providing himself the opportunity both to reject that position and (what is most important for our purposes) shape his own. Thus, a survey of Brito's view proves a necessary prerequisite to getting the exact flavor of Auriol's position on intentions and the relation between a cognitive act and its object.

---

[1] The greater part of Radulphus's work exists only in manuscripts. While some of his philosophical texts have been edited, his theological oeuvre remains still basically unexplored. The backbone of the most recent research on Brito is surely represented by Pinborg's legacy, excellently filled out by Ebbesen's research. See, for example, Pinborg 1974, 1975, 1976, 1980; Ebbesen 1978, 1986, 2000. Alongside these works, essential are the studies done by Marmo, Mora-Márquez and Rosier-Catach. See, among others, Marmo 1995, 1999, 2013; Mora-Márquez 2013, 2015; Rosier-Catach 1995. On Radulphus's life and academic career, see Courteney 2005. To describe Brito's view on intentions and cognition in Sects. 19.2.1 and 19.2.2, I rely on their scholarship.

19.2.1   Brito on Intentions

Despite the fact that his philosophical work is still generally unexplored and further research needs to be done to get a more precise account of his thought, the modist master Radulphus Brito (ca. 1320) is well known among medieval scholars for developing a highly-sophisticated theory of intentions and intellectual cognition. His views on concepts and intentions played an active part in shaping the fourteenth-century philosophical debates on the matter, and this applies especially to Auriol's view.

According to Brito, an *intentio* is *that by which* (*illud quo*) one's own mind is made to aim at something other than itself (*in aliud tentio*),[2] a noetic tool (*cognitio*) with which the intellect equips itself to make something an object of cognition. This view comes out clearly in Brito's distinction between concrete and abstract intentions.[3] As he points out, abstract intentions (be they first or second) are intentions insofar as they are taken in *themselves*, which is to say, according to their nature. *Qua* abstract, an intention is just an informing of the intellect (i.e. its being informed), that by which the intellect itself is aimed at some extramental entity (De Rijk 2005, 219). Thus, an intention conceived abstractly is a form, a quality or, what is the same in Brito's account, the cognitive act (*cognitio*) by which the mind aims at the object cognized.

Concrete intentions, in contrast, are (abstract) intentions insofar as they are taken according to their content. They are abstract intentions concretely conceived and thereby counting as *what* is thought of by or contained within a concept or a cognitive act. It is no coincidence that Brito calls a concrete intention the *res sic cognita vel intellecta* (the thing thus cognized or understood) (De Rijk 2005, 220).[4]

According to Radulphus, what this means is that when we think of Socrates as a human being, we do so by having in mind the first abstract intention or cognitive act *humanity*. *Humanity* is a means of understanding (*ratio intelligendi*), as it is precisely *that by which* Socrates is cognized as a human being. By the same token, the relevant first concrete intention is *human being* (*homo*), as it is *what* is cognized (*res cognita*) by having in the mind the first abstract intention or cognitive act of

---

[2] Radulphus Brito, *Quaestiones in Aristotelis De Anima, I*, q. 6 (De Rijk 2005, 685): "Et primo ad hoc videndum est quid significetur nomine 'intentionis' in communi. Unde notandum est quod intentio est illud quo intellectus tendit ad aliud (et hec est cognitio in ipso intellectu existens). Et hoc est manifestum secundum interpretationem, quia *intentio* est *in aliud tentio*." See also Pinborg 1980, 124. For a discussion of these texts, see Dijs 2009, 216–217.

[3] Radulphus claims that the concrete/abstract distinction applies not only to simple apprehension, but even to what he calls composition or division (it stands for any kind of proposition, be it categorical, hypothetical or whatever) and complex reasoning, be it a syllogism, an enthymeme, an inference, or an induction. Since the aim of this paper is not to delve into Brito's theory of propositions and knowledge, these topics will not be treated. For an overall presentation of Brito's philosophy of mind, see, among others, De Rijk 2005, Ebbesen 2000, Mora-Márquez 2013, Van der Lecq 2008, and the literature referred to therein.

[4] See *infra*, n. 6.

humanity. *Human being* is the first concrete intention of *humanity*, as it is *humanity* concretely conceived.

Note that in this view nothing is involved in cognition (nor is required) beyond a cognitive act and the object that act is about. As concrete intentions are nothing other than abstract intentions concretely conceived, nothing but the cognitive act of humanity (insofar as it is concretely conceived) is referred to by "human being." No beings of reason are formed through cognition and thereby implied by concrete intentions. Conceiving of Socrates as a human being amounts to having in the mind the cognitive act or the first abstract intention of humanity as directed at Socrates.

For Brito, as abstract intentions are *that by which* something is conceived, while concrete intentions are abstract intentions insofar as they are concretely considered, and thereby count as *what* is conceived through those abstract intentions, first abstract intentions are to be expressed by abstract common terms like "humanity," "animality," and "rationality," while first concrete intentions are to be expressed by their concrete counterparts, that is, by concrete common terms like "man," "animal," and "rational." As mentioned, when we conceive of Socrates through the abstract intention of, say, *humanity*, we think of him precisely as a human being.[5]

As is well known, Brito argues that intentions (whether abstract or concrete) must be divided into first and second intentions. However, since this analysis is not of direct concern for our purposes here, it suffices to recall that, for him, a second intention is a cognitive act by which a particular entity (previously grasped through a first intention) is cognized in relation to other entities. So, when we cognize Socrates as a human being, the second abstract intention is the apprehension of the first concrete intention *human being* in view of its *aptitude* to be found in a variety of entities at once, i.e. in its universality, or, as we should more strictly say in this case, in its being

---

[5] Radulphus Brito, *Aliquis homo est species* (Pinborg 1975, §49, 141–142): "Intentio enim in abstracto nihil aliud est nisi quaedam informatio intellectus per quam intellectus intendit in aliud. Unde intentio est illud per quod intellectus tendit in rem, et istud est quaedam ratio intelligendi rem vel quaedam rei cognitio quam habet intellectus penes se. Modo duplex est rei cognitio; quaedam enim est prima rei cognitio qua res primo cognoscimus secundum modum essendi proprium rei, secundum quamcumque operationem intellectus. Hoc sit sicut per primam operationem intellectus: apprehendo hominem vel asinum secundum modum essendi proprium fantasiatum talis rei, sicut intelligendo hominem secundum istum modum essendi qui est ratiocinari, et animal secundum istum modum essendi fantasiatum qui est sentire, et sic de aliis. Et ista cognitio est prima intentio in abstracto, et res sic cognita dicitur prima intentio in concreto, unde omnis cognitio, quaecumque sit, habet denominare suum obiectum; dicimus enim 'scibile scitur': ibi scientia denominat scibile, et 'color est visus' et 'sonus auditus', et sic de aliis; ibi enim cognitio denominat suum obiectum... Et ideo cognitio hominis secundum se et absolute dicitur prima cognitio. Sed cognitio hominis ut est in pluribus dicitur secunda cognitio. Et ista cognitio rei in habitudine ad aliud dicitur secunda intentio in abstracto, et res sic cognita dicitur intentio secunda in concreto, sicut quantum ad primam operationem intellectus cognitio hominis ut est in pluribus est secunda intentio, quae est universalitas. Et homo sic cognitus est secunda intentio in concreto, quae est universale. Eodem modo genus, species, differentia etc. sunt quaedam intentiones secundae secundum primam operationem intellectus, secundum quod res habet intelligi ut est reperibilis in pluribus numero, praedicabilis de illis in quid. Et ita ista praedicatio denominativa 'homo est species', 'animal est genus' et sic de aliis, sicut esse intellectum est accidentale rei. Et ideo dicimus 'homo est universalis' et non 'universalitas'."

a species or its *specificity*. Likewise, the second concrete intention is the object being cognized through the second abstract intention, which is to say, the concrete counterpart of universality or specificity: *human being* as a universal, or as a species.[6]

Brito's map of intentions can therefore be summarized as follows[7]:

Intention	*Concrete*	*Abstract*
First	Man	Humanity
	Animal	Animality
	Rational	Rationality
Second	Species	Specificity
	Genus	Generality
	Difference	Differentiality

Now, what is important to keep in mind at the end of this quick treatment of Brito's theory of intentions is the answer Brito would give to the question what is an intention. If asked, in fact, he would firmly reply that an intention is a cognitive act. For him, abstract intentions (whether first or second) amount to what intentions are in themselves. In themselves, however, intentions are just absolute entities, intellectual acts, inhering in the soul as real accidents. They are some kind of mental dispositions or habits of the intellect; they are what make the mind able to refer to an object.[8] To put it differently, intentions or, what is the same, concepts *qua* concepts, are not what is signified *through* a concept. They are *that by which* the signification of what is signified *through* a concept takes place (i.e., the thing cognized, or what Brito calls a concrete intention). In this regard, it must also be noted (as it

---

[6] Dijs 2009, 216–217. See Radulphus Brito, *Quaestiones in Aristotelis De Anima, I*, q. 6 (De Rijk 2005, 685–686): "Sed prima intellectio rei qua intelligitur primo ex proprio suo fantasmate, est prima intentio in abstracto, et res sic intellecta dicitur prima intentio in concreto; sicut cognitio hominis vel asini que sumitur ex proprio suo fantasmate, dicitur prima intentio in abstracto, et res iste sic intellecte dicuntur intentio prima in concreto. Secunda autem intentio est secunda rei cognitio, que non sumitur a modo essendi proprio vel fantasmate proprio rei, sed est quedam secunda cognitio rei respectu alterius. Et sumitur ex aliquo modo essendi communi corespectivo, sicut esse universale vel universalitas est [secunda] cognitio [rei]. Unde universalitas [vel universale in abstracto] est cognitio vel ratio cognoscendi rem ut nata est esse in pluribus, et universale in concreto est esse cognitum rei ut est in pluribus." Radulphus Brito, *Quaestiones in I Sententiarum*, d. 23 (De Rijk 2005, 636): "Sed primo est intelligendum quod intentio nichil aliud est quam cognitio intellectus. Sed duplex est cognitio de re. Quedam est cognitio qua res cognoscitur in se; et ista vocatur prima rei cognitio vel intellectio. Alia est cognitio qua res cognoscitur in suis particularibus; et ista vocatur secunda rei cognitio, quia prius aliquis cognoscitur in se quam in suis particularibus. Et sicut est duplex cognitio, ita erit duplex intentio. Quedam enim [est] que vocatur prima rei cognitio. Alia est intentio que dicitur secunda rei cognitio; et ista dicitur secunda intentio. Et dicitur consecutive ad primam intentionem secundum quod aliquis primo cognoscitur in se quam in suis particularibus. Verbi gratia. Prima cognitio quam habeo de homine est quod sit animal et quod sit rationale; et istud est cognoscere hominem in se, et dicitur esse prima intentio quam habeo de homine. Sed secunda cognitio quam habeo de homine, est quod sit in pluribus et quod [de eis] predicetur in quid. Et ex hoc accipitur quod est species; et istud vocatur secunda intentio."

[7] My description here is drawn from Van der Lecq 2008, 379.

[8] Radulphus Brito, *Aliquis homo est species* (Pinborg 1975, §56–58, 146–147).

will be fundamental to Auriol's criticism) that Brito's theory of intentions sees no need to postulate the formation of entities other than the cognitive act: concrete intentions are nothing other than abstract intentions concretely conceived. *Qua* cognitive acts or qualities having real existence in the mind, then, (abstract) intentions are mainly meant as what makes a subject *cognizant*. As Mora-Márquez points out, (abstract) intentions are a kind of cognitive link to the object to which they refer, an epistemological condition for their being signified (Mora-Márquez 2013, 368).

19.2.2   The Relation Between Cognitive Acts and Their Objects

At this point, however, a question arises. Once this view of intentions is provided, one might ask, what is the relation between an object and its cognitive act? What does it mean for a thing to be objectively (i.e., as an object) in the mind, which is to say, what does it mean for it to be cognized and thereby to be a concrete intention? Radulphus's famous answer is that our intentions or concepts signify the objects of which they are concepts, in the same way as real accidents signify their subjects. They denominate them; they count as denominations of those subjects.[9]

Consider the term "white." Taken by itself, "white" signifies two things. On the one hand, it signifies the abstract form of whiteness. On the other, it denominates the subject wherein whiteness is received. An object is in fact called "white" only due to the whiteness informing it. It is *denominated*, that is, identified, by the abstract form of whiteness, which inheres in it. Likewise, "human being" signifies two things at once. On the one hand, it signifies the abstract intention of "humanity." On the other, it names the object which is cognized by virtue of the abstract intention, e.g. Socrates, a human being. Just as "white" denominates a white thing, "human being" denominates a human being, e.g. Socrates.[10]

Despite the similarities, however, Brito maintains that an important distinction differentiates how concrete intentions denominate their objects from how real concrete

---

[9] Radulphus Brito, *Aliquis homo est species* (Pinborg 1975, §49, 142): "et ita semper cognitio denominat suum obiectum, sicut accidentia abstracta denominant suum subiectum."

[10] De Rijk 2005, 231. See Radulphus Brito, *Quaestiones in Porph. Isag.*, q. 11a (De Rijk 2005, 680–681): "Sed propter solutionem rationum est intelligendum quod, sicut dicit Aristotiles septimo *Metaphisice*, in diffinitione accidentium habent poni sua subiecta. Sed hoc est differenter in accidentibus in abstracto et in concreto, sicut videtur esse de intentione Commentatoris in eodem septimo, quia (a) in diffinitione accidentium in abstracto ponitur suum subiectum loco differentie—sicut dicendo 'Simitas est nasi cavitas'; ibi enim ponitur subiectum loco differentie et aliquid sui generis loco generis—, sed (b) in diffinitione accidentium in concreto habet poni subiectum loco generis, sicut si diffiniatur *simus*, diceretur 'Simus est nasus cavus'; ibi 'nasus', quod est subiectum *simi*, ponitur in sua diffinitione loco generis. Modo sicut accidentia realia in concreto denominant sua subiecta et dicuntur in habitudine ad ipsa et propter hoc ponuntur in diffinitione sua, ita intentiones secunde denominant sua obiecta. (b1) Et ideo sicut in diffinitione propria ipsorum accidentium in concreto ponitur subiectum loco generis, ita in diffinitione secundarum intentionum concretarum debet poni obiectum suum loco generis." Radulphus Brito, *Aliquis homo est species* (Pinborg 1975, §49, 141–142).

accidents denominate their subjects. As he sees it, concrete intentions are not said of an object because they really inhere in their objects *qua* abstract inhering intentions. While a man cannot rightly be called (de-nominated) "white" unless whiteness fully inheres in him as a real quality, for an animal to be able to be called (de-nominated) a "human being" it is not required that humanity as such fully inhere in it as a real property. As concepts directly abstracted from extra-mental things, the subject wherein intentions occur is the cognizing mind (not the extra-mental particular they are drawn from). According to Brito, extra-mental particulars only serve as partial motive causes (together with the intellect) for bringing about intentions. For him, an entity can be called (de-nominated) a "human being" through the concrete intention "human being" inasmuch as "humanity" *qua* an abstract intention (or cognitive act) is found in the mind as in its subject, and in the really existent rational animal Socrates as in its object.[11]

To make this point, Brito relies on what he calls the difference between *formal* and *non-formal* denomination, that is, between *intrinsic* and *extrinsic* denomination, which also makes clear why a concrete intention (such as "human being") must be thought of as a denomination of the latter type.[12] As he sees it, formal or intrinsic denomination is a type of predication that occurs whenever what is meant by the predicate really inheres in its subject as a form informing it. Non-formal or extrinsic denomination, in contrast, is a type of predication according to which the predicate is attributed to its subject like an effect to its cause.[13] What this means can easily be seen by comparing "being white" and "being seen." When we say that x is white, besides whiteness, "white" denominates the white object, precisely because of the whiteness that inheres in that object. "Being white," in Brito's parlance, is thus a formal denomination or what we might call an *intrinsic* denomination. When we

---

[11] De Rijk 2005, 205 and De Libera 1999, 360–361. This is also why Brito claims that accidents can be denominatively predicated of certain things, insofar as they occur there as *in* a subject, whereas intentions can be denominatively predicated of certain things, insofar as they occur there as *in* an object. Radulphus Brito, *Quaestiones in Arist. I De anima*, q. 6 (De Rijk 2005, 691): "Sed adhuc circa dicta notandum est quod intentiones cum sint quedam intellectiones vel quedam intellecta in concreto sumpta, predicantur de re obiecta denominative, non quia sint in obiecto sicut in subiecto (sicut dicitur homo 'albus' ab albedine in ipso existente formaliter), sed quia sunt in eis sicut in obiecto, et hoc est esse in aliquo movente vel efficiente respectu earum. Et ideo, sicut dicitur 'Sor est percutiens' percussione que est in passo, et similiter 'Color videtur' visione que est in oculo, et similiter 'Scibile scitur' scientia que est in anima, sic intentiones concrete, que quantum ad suum esse formale quod per intellectio, sunt in anima, denominative predicantur de obiectis earum, quamvis non sint in eis sicut in subiecto. Unde sicut ista est vera 'Lapis intelligitur intellectione que est in anima', sic ista 'Homo est species' [vel 'Animal est genus'] (et sic de aliis), quia esse genus et species—et sic de aliis intentionibus secundis—sunt quedam intellectiones vel quedam esse intellecta. Et ideo predicantur denominative de obiectis suis."

[12] For a standard view on intrinsic and extrinsic denomination, see Thomas Aquinas, *Summa contra gentiles* II, c. 13 (Aquinas 1918, 293–294); *Scriptum super Sententiis* I, d. 32, q. 1, a. 1, co. (Aquinas 1929, vol. 2, 741–745).

[13] Radulphus Brito, *Quaestiones in Porph. Isag.*, q. 8A (Pinborg 1980, 116): "'Illud quod denominat alterum etc.' dico quod illud quod denominat alterum formaliter est in eo quod denominat sicut in subiecto. Sed illud quod praedicatur de alio denominative non formaliter, sed sicut effectus de sua causa, non oportet quod sit in eo sicut in subiecto, sictu est percutiens vel agens."

say that a wall is *seen*, in contrast, "being seen" does not denominate the wall because of a feature that inheres in it. The sight, in fact, is not within the wall; it is in the eyes. "Being seen" denominates the wall only because of a property that belongs to something else, i.e. the viewer (Taieb 2018b, 85). As a result, the wall is denominated, but only as the *object* that causes the vision in the eyes, which is precisely what makes "being seen" a non-formal or extrinsic denomination.[14]

By claiming that the concrete intention "human being" denominates Socrates simply because "humanity" *qua* abstract intention (or cognitive act) is found in the mind as in its subject, Brito is implying that "human being" denominates Socrates extrinsically. As mentioned in the previous section, Socrates owes his being thought of as, and thereby named "human being," to the presence of the abstract intention of humanity in the mind of whoever cognizes him. Nothing other than the abstract intention (or cognitive act) of *humanity* is supposited for by "human being." For Brito, then, a concrete intention is just a name that can be applied to things, not by virtue of something the particulars acquire as they are cognized, but only insofar as there is a cognitive act by which they are thought by the mind.

Of course, the same also holds for "being cognized" (*esse cognitum*), which can be treated along the same lines as "being seen" and "human being." Just like "human being" and "being seen," "being cognized" is not attributed to, say, Socrates because of a property that Socrates acquires by being cognized. The semantic value of "being cognized" is just the cognitive act really occurring in the mind cognizing Socrates. Nothing is produced beyond the cognitive act, which could eventually bear the property of being cognized. Beyond something's being cognized there is no cognized being for an object to acquire as the term of a cognitive act (Taieb 2018b, 85). "Being cognized," in other words, denominates Socrates (as soon as Socrates is being cognized) *extrinsically*. According to Brito's view, then, being cognized, which is to say, being objectively in the mind, is all about being named according to the relevant cognitive act occurring in the mind. It is taking on a name, so that nothing else is needed but the cognitive act and the thing grasped by the act in order to explain intellectual cognition. As Tachau points out, "[o]pposed… to distinguishing intellectual acts from concepts, Radulphus had insisted that for something to be known (*esse cognitum*) was merely a designation of the relation between an object and a cognitive act, not a name for a resulting mental entity" (Tachau 1988, 188).

19.3   Modelling the View: Auriol's Rebuttal of Brito's Thesis

In d. 23 of his Commentary on Book I of the *Sentences,* Auriol makes use of Brito's thesis as a target to model his own view of intentions and intellectual cognition. The core of Auriol's attack against Brito concerns two features, namely, (i) Brito's identification of intentions with cognitive acts and (ii) his view of the relation between

---

[14] *Ibid.,* 116–118.

the object cognized and its cognitive act, on account of (i), as an extrinsic denomination.

19.3.1 Intentions and Cognitive Acts

As to (i), Auriol's idea is that thinking of intentions as cognitive acts (i.e. as intentions abstractly considered), which only derivatively (*denominative*) signify the objects cognized, is a metaphysically grave misreading of our cognitive life.[15] Things, in fact, are precisely the other way around. In contrast to what Brito admits, cognitive acts (as well as any other kind of disposition of the mind, such as intelligible species) are called "intentions" only insofar as they are *that by which* someone's mind aims at *something* as the object of its own gaze (*tendit in alio obiective*). Cognitive acts, in other words, are thought of as intentions only by virtue of something else. Without that *something* being given, that is, without the object they make the mind cognize being present to it, cognitive acts cannot but aim at nothing, and are thus useless. Auriol's conclusion, then, is that rather than being an intention only in a derivative sense, that is by being denominated by (i.e. by being a denomination of) the cognitive act, the object cognized ought to be thought of as what an intention formally is. The object cognized is that in virtue of which any other noetic tool (be it an intelligible species or a cognitive act) can be meaningfully said to be (i.e. be denominated) an intention.

This view is rooted in Auriol's conviction that human cognitive powers (and thereby the intellect) are active. Cognition always involves the production of something over and above the mere cognitive act. More precisely, cognizing amounts to the placing of the object we aim at into cognized or (as Auriol famously names it) apparent being.[16] It entails the formation of an intentional object, which is put before the mind's eye, as the *appearing* content of each and every cognitive act.[17] This intentional object is what Auriol means by *intention*. Auriol also calls it the *objective concept*, as it occurs as the objectual content of each cognitive act, in contrast to the *formal concept* which stands for cognitive act.[18]

---

[15] Peter Auriol, *Scriptum I*, d. 23, a. 2 (De Rijk 2005, 710): "Primo quidem in hoc quod ait actum intellectus esse formaliter et in abstracto intentionem primam et secundam, et obiectum tantum denominative dici, et non formaliter, intentionem secundam vel primam." That Auriol here is attacking Brito is claimed also by Tachau. See Tachau 1988, 188. On this point see also De Libera 1999, 364.

[16] Petrus Aureoli, *Scriptum I*, d. 3, sect. 14, a. 1 (Auriol 1952–1956, vol. 2, 709): "De ratione autem actus intelligenti […] est habitudo prima, videlicet formare sive rem ponere in esse formato."

[17] Petrus Aureoli, *Scriptum I*, d. 27, 18, in The Electronic Scriptum (henceforth *ES*): "illa [apparitio] non est cogitatio formans sed formata … Haec autem non competent speciei intelligibili aut actui intellectus … nullum enim istorum est quod cogitamus, et quod vere scimus … sed solummodo res vera intentionaliter praesens aspectui cogitantis."

[18] Petrus Aureoli, *Scriptum I*, d. 2, sect. 9 (Auriol 1952–1956, vol. 1, 483): "considerandum est circa conceptum, quoniam potest concipi vel pro actu intellectus realiter inhaerente, vel pro con-

Auriol insists that experience shows it, as no cognition could ever occur without the cognizer's production of the appearing object and its experience of being appeared-to by what is conceived: if nothing is formed through the cognitive act, nothing is put before and thereby made to appear to the cognizing mind; as a result, we would be like sleeping. What follows, then, is that, rather than our *act of thinking* about something, what (intellectual) cognition formally consists of is our having something present through the mode of appearing. It requires the formal and the objective concepts to be distinct; it requires the formation and the appearing of an intentional object.

Granted, Auriol agrees that thinking of something is necessary for bringing about an intention. You would have no intention (at least, in Auriol's sense of the word) without a cognitive act or an intelligible species. Auriol's idea, however, is that, taken alone, the cognitive act or the intelligible species is insufficient to make someone acquainted with things. Despite its being a likeness of what is cognized, the cognitive act is only the tool *by which* the cognizer cognizes. According to this view, then, for a thing to be objectively in the mind involves much more than the cognizer having a cognitive act directed at that thing.[19] What is like for a thing to be cognized is much better accounted for by its appearing to and being seen by the cognizer that cognizes it. Likewise, concepts or intentions are much more suitably thought of as the *content* of our cognitive acts than as cognitive acts themselves. Equating intentions with cognitive acts, in other words, would mean, for Auriol, providing a description of what cognizing entails that is *formally* independent of *what* the mind intends or tends to—a price that seems to him too high to pay:

> Manifestum est enim quia: Illud dicitur formaliter in ordine ad quod omnia alia dicuntur—ut patet, quia sanitas animalis dicitur formalis quia in ordine ad ipsam medicina et dieta et omnia alia 'sana' dicuntur. Sed species vel actus ex hoc dicuntur intentiones quod per ea intellectus tendit in aliud obiective. Ergo obiectum cognitum sive conceptus obiectivus formaliter intentio dicetur[20]

At this point, however, one might ask: what is that *something* our cognitive acts tend to? What is the object our intentions or concepts are equated with? What is its status? Auriol's answer to these questions brings us to the core of his view, as it appeals to his theory of concept formation and the distinction between formal and objective concepts.

Now, Auriol endorses a view that may well seem paradoxical. On the one hand, he is firmly convinced that our words refer to the things they are meant to be about. On the other, he maintains that such a connection is provided through the mediation of the intentional object, which counts, in turn, as the *immediate* signification of our common and singular terms.

---

ceptu objectali." On the meaning of the term 'concept' in medieval philosophy and the distinction between formal and objective concepts, see Klima 2015.

[19] See below nn. 21–22. See also Friedman 2015, 155–156 and Auriol's texts referred to by there.

[20] Peter Auriol, *Scriptum I*, d. 23, a. 2 (De Rijk 2005, 710).

His way out is ever more creative. As Friedman nicely points out (Friedman 2013, 585), the inner conflict between representationalism and direct realism, which his view is apparently committed to, is solved by making the objective concept invisible, by identifying it with the thing it is a concept of.

This claim comes out clearly by considering Auriol's theory of concept formation. As to the subject-side of cognition, Auriol argues that whenever we think of, say, an apple, we thereby give birth to something above the mere cognitive act *by which* we think of the apple. We produce the intentional, appearing apple.

At the same time (and this holds for the object-side of cognition), Auriol is clear in stating that the production of the intentional object is a peculiar type of production. In the first place, producing an intentional object is not a real, but an intentional action: by our thinking about something, we do not give birth to something external to us. The intentional object is something devoid of autonomous existence; it is nothing in itself (*nihil in se*). It is an entity whose being entirely depends on the cognitive act.[21] Also, the production of the intentional object is a peculiar type of production, because, rather than yielding a reified, static intermediary between the mind and the extra-mental reality, it just amounts to occasioning a certain *situation*. It consists of making something apparent to the mind.[22] *Forming* an intentional object, then, means, for Auriol, just *putting* a thing *in the state* of being visible to whatever cognizes it.[23]

This analysis provides Auriol with the exact theoretical framework for proving his claim that our words stand for their referents, although they immediately signify the objective concept formed through the relevant cognitive act. By cognizing an apple, the mind produces the relevant intentional object. At the same time, Auriol argues that the intentional apple is not a third entity between the intellect and the real apple. It is the real apple as it acquires a new status, a new mode of being: that of being *apparent* to the cognizer. As a result (and this is the gist of Auriol's claim), whatever holds for the objective concept also holds for the external object that concept is a concept of, since the objective concept *just is* the external object, put into apparent or intentional being.[24] They are numerically the same thing.[25] For Auriol,

---

[21] Peter Auriol, *Scriptum I*, d. 9, pars. 1, a. 1 (*ES*, 8, ll. 364–369). See also Friedman 2015, 157 and Auriol's texts referred to there.

[22] Peter Auriol, *Scriptum I*, d. 35, pars. 1, a. 1 (*ES*, 9): "[n]on enim est aliud intellectio quam id quo alicui res apparent."

[23] Peter Auriol, *Scriptum I*, d. 9, a. 1 (*ES*, 10–12). On these passages about the production of the intentional object and its appearing to the cognizer, see Friedman 2015, esp. 154–157.

[24] Peter Auriol, *Scriptum I*, d. 27, q. 2, a. 2 (*ES*, 10). See also Friedman 2015, 143–144.

[25] Peter Auriol, *Scriptum I*, d. 9, a. 1 (*ES*, 8): "sunt unum et idem realiter, quamvis differant in modo essendi." Peter Auriol, *Scriptum I*, d. 23, a. 2 (De Rijk 2005, 718–719); Peter Auriol, *Scriptum I*, d. 27, pars 2, a. 2 (*ES*, 18): "res posita in esse formato non est aliquid aliud quam res extra sub alio modo essendi… vera res habet esse fictitium et apparens. Nec propter hoc fit bis, sed idem fit in duplici esse: realiter quidem exterius in natura, intentionaliter vero in mente." Peter Auriol, *Scriptum I*, d. 27, pars 2, a. 2 (*ES*, 16): "ubi considerandum est quod res in esse formato posita non claudit in se aliquid absolutum nisi ipsam realitatem. Unde non ponit in numerum res et sua intentio quantum ad aliquid absolutum, claudit tamen aliquid respectivum, videlicet apparere."

then, whenever we utter the word "apple," we indeed *signify* the intentional apple (i.e., the objective concept) we form through our cognitive act. However, since the intentional apple is literally the same as the real apple our mind is directed at, by uttering the word "apple," we nonetheless *refer* to (and thereby have acquaintance with) the really existent apple we think of.

Of course, that cognition entails a peculiar type of production just means, for Auriol, that cognition belongs to a special kind of action.[26] As he sees it, cognition partially eludes the classically assumed Aristotelian dichotomy between immanent and transitive actions,[27] as it can be genuinely envisioned both as a transitive *and* as an immanent action.

Consider the case of singing or playing music. As experience shows, music stops as soon as a musician stops playing or a singer stops singing. Nothing absolute is produced by moving the fingers on an instrument or vibrating the vocal cords. On this view, playing or singing is a fully immanent action. Still, no one could deny, on pain of contradiction, that by playing or singing, something is produced besides the act of playing and singing. The sound emerges *over* the physical movement that makes it; it exceeds the act, which makes it impossible to reduce the former to the latter. Accordingly, it seems that, besides the act of singing or playing, at least another feature needs to be included within our definition of "sound" or "music." This is the sound's being sensed or perceived, its bearing a *content* for whatever is said to sense it.

A similar situation, Auriol continues, obtains with intellectual cognition.[28] No matter how hard we try, experience shows that we cannot really give birth to the object of our thought by simply thinking about it (that is God's prerogative, at best). Then, like singing or playing, nothing absolute is produced through cognizing. Cognizing does not give birth to something external to the cognizer. It just results in something devoid of full, autonomous existence, and thus may count as an immanent action. At the same time (just as in the case of sounds and music), the fact that the intentional object vanishes as soon as the cognizer ceases to think about it does not prove that it can be entirely reduced to the cognitive act that produces it.[29] As

---

[26] See Lička 2017 and Fornasieri 2021.

[27] Aristotle, *Metaphysics* IX, 6, 1048b.

[28] Peter Auriol, *Scriptum I*, d. 27, pars. 2, a. 2 (*ES*, 15): "Prima siquidem non, non enim est omnino simile de vivere, intelligere, et videre. Vivere namque non est actus transiens realiter nec obiective, non est enim verum dicere 'vivo istum vel illum.' Videre autem, etsi non transit realiter (in quo assimilatur ipsi vivere), transit nihilominus obiective: unde proprie dicitur 'video te' vel 'illum.' Philosophus ergo et Commentator dicunt esse simile de vivere, intelligere, et videre, quantum ad hoc quod nullum reale agitur aut producitur per ipsa, sed non intelligunt quin videre et intelligere aliquid in esse intentionali producant... Ex quo patet quod tam videre quam intelligere est pati et agere: pati quidem realiter, sed agere intentionaliter et secundum iudicium, in quantum visio et intellectio, ultra hoc quod sunt reale aliquid, ponunt res in esse intentionali et iudicato, quod non facit vivere vel albere."

[29] *Ibid.* "Primo quidem quia non negat Philosophus nec Commentator nec Augustinus quin per actiones quae sunt fines possit aliquid produci, non tamen manens post operationem. Nullus enim dubitat quin per citharizare sonus producatur, et tamen secundum Commentatorem, I *Ethicorum*,

mentioned, besides the bare act of thinking, any cognitive act implies something that exceeds that act of thinking. The cognitive act always comes with the production of the intentional object, which appears to the cognizer and stands before the mind as its term.[30] Of course, such an intentional object is an *ens rationis*, that is, an entity whose *being* entirely equates to its *being thought by* and *appearing to* the mind.[31] Nonetheless, Auriol thinks that this is enough for claiming that the cognitive act and the intentional object cannot be reduced to one another, and thus for thinking of cognition as a transitive action.

According to Auriol's theory of concepts, cognizing involves the production of an intentional object, which just means making something apparent to the mind's gaze. In this sense, one may even say that, upon cognition, every object is somehow transformed. The apple cognized (i.e. the intentional apple) *is* the real apple, but in a different state or mode of being. It *is* the apple *plus* something more, i.e. the apple appearing.[32] As a result, the modification the (real) apple undergoes is just its becoming (through intellectual cognition) apparent to the mind; it consists of a change of its status. According to Auriol, then, it is impossible to conceive of intellectual cognition without also conceiving of the relevant intentional object appearing. What proves that a cognizer cognizes, i.e. that one has intentions, is one's having an intentional object given as present to one's mind. It is the object's appearing (rather than the bare cognizing or being cognized) that crucially characterizes intellectual cognition. Without it, no one can be rightly said to cognize. It is therefore the objective concept, i.e., the intentional object formed as opposed to the cognitive act, that most suitably deserves the name of *intention* or *concept*. Claiming otherwise, that is, reducing intentions to cognitive acts, Auriol concludes, would be the same as pretending to describe some painter's painting independently of *what* he actually paints.

---

cantare et citharizare sunt de operationibus quae sunt fines, ex quibus non sequuntur opera praeter eas. Unde verba commenti sunt quod Aristoteles 'opera' vocat quae operationibus quiescentibus manent; musico autem operante secundum musicam et cantante deinde quiescente, nullum opus relinquitur; fabro autem quiescente manet aliquod opus subsistens. Sic igitur intelligere et videre sunt operationes immanentes et fines ex quibus non relinquitur operatum, quoniam obiectum formatum quod praesens intellectualiter experimur non manet intellectione cessante."

[30] See *supra* n. 16. See also Peter Auriol, *Scriptum I*, d. 35, p. 1, a. 1 (*ES*, 7).

[31] Klima 1996a. On beings of reason (*entia rationis*) and their ontological status, see also Klima 1993.

[32] Peter Auriol, *II Sententiarum*, d. 3, q. 2, a. 4 (Fb, f. 27rb; Pg, f. 24rb): "Sic igitur est eadem res addita alia et alia apparentia, quae nihil est reale, sed tantum intentionale—non enim apparentia illa est in re, sed in intellectu tantum."

19.3.2   The Relation Between Cognitive Acts and their Objects

By defining intentions or concepts as formally the same as the object cognized, Auriol is now brought to the second criticism he makes against Brito's view. What is at stake here is how to think of the relation between the object cognized and its cognitive act, given a certain definition of what intentions are.

Auriol considers Brito's view to be philosophically untenable, insofar as it equates "being cognized" with "being denominated" and thereby implies that being extrinsically denominated by a cognitive act is enough for a thing to be an intention or, what is the same, to be objectively in the mind. The Franciscan master boils down the core of Brito's mistake to a few lines:

> Secundo vero deficit, quia ymaginatur quod res concepta denominetur tantummodo ab actu intellectus et non capiat aliquod esse intentionale plus quam *Cesar* qui pingitur capiat a pictura. Hoc enim est impossibile.[33]

Now, the rationale behind Auriol's claim that extrinsic denomination is not suited for describing intellectual cognition is that, for him, extrinsic denomination is an extrinsic relation:

> *x* is denominatively said of *y* or *x* is a denomination of *y* iff *x* names *y* not by virtue of a feature belonging to y, but exclusively of a respect *y* has toward something external or superadded to its very nature.[34]

To see what is entailed by his view, Auriol clarifies by comparing cognizing to the act of painting. As he points out, "being painted" is a genuine case of extrinsic denomination, because it does not name Caesar by virtue of a feature Caesar acquires as soon as he is being painted, but only due to the property of representing Caesar, which the portrait of Caesar has. 'Being painted' does not rely on some feature intrinsic to (painted) Caesar. It comes (as it were) from the 'outside': what 'painted Caesar' supposits for is just the picture representing Caesar. Thus, by being painted, Caesar does not undergo any relevant transformation; it is totally irrelevant for him.

By the same token, if "being cognized" were equated with an extrinsic denomination, then, Auriol concludes, "being cognized" (just like "being painted") would not be attributed to Caesar by virtue of an aspect Caesar takes on, as soon as he is cognized. It would be attributed to him only due to a property belonging to something else, viz. the property of cognizing Caesar had by a cognitive entity actually cognizing him.[35]

---

[33] Peter Auriol, *Scriptum I*, d. 23, a. 2 (De Rijk 2005, 713).

[34] For medieval treatments of extrinsic denomination as applied to intellectual cognition, see Walter Chatton, Prologus, q. 2, a. 2 (Chatton 1989, 88–89, ll. 73–86); William Ockham, *Ordinatio* I, d. 27, q. 2 (Ockham 1967, 252–253); d. 43, q. 2 (*ibid.*, 646). On extrinsic denomination in medieval philosophy, including a discussion of Brito and Auriol, see De Libera 1999.

[35] Taieb 2018b, 85–86. See also Lička 2016, 65.

Now, given Auriol's view of intentions, it is clear what he thinks is wrong with Brito's view here: conceiving of the intentional object (what Brito would call a concrete intention) as a denomination of the cognitive act is philosophically untenable, as extrinsic denomination entails neither the production nor the appearing of an intentional object.

As has been shown, Brito's idea is precisely that for a thing to be cognized or to be objectively in the mind is just to say that there is a cognitive act cognizing (i.e., naming) that thing. *Homo* is just a name drawn from the cognitive act occurring in the mind as an abstract intention (*humanitas*) and extrinsically applied to Socrates, whenever we think of him. *Denominating* a thing is thus just forming a name and thereby (extrinsically) applying to that thing, according to the relevant cognitive act. Likewise, cognizing implies the production of no intentional object beyond the very same cognitive act and thereby no cognized or intentional being is referred to by when we say that something is being cognized. No 'cognized being' lays behind 'being cognized'; no mode of being nor feature intrinsic to Caesar is referred to when one says 'Caesar is cognized' (Taieb 2018b, 85). What makes that predication correct is simply the fact that there is a cognitive act (a first abstract intention corresponding to Caesar, in Brito's parlance) by which the cognizer is thinking of Caesar. To put it more technically, the semantic value of 'cognized Caesar' is the cognitive act in the mind of the cognizer cognizing Caesar. According to this view, then, there is a strict identity between what Auriol calls a formal and an objective concepts: they are one and the same thing. (Tachau 1988, 188).[36]

Pace Brito, his account of is totally unacceptable to Auriol. As we have seen, he claims that a cognitive act is surely necessary for an object to become an intentional object, but it nonetheless can never be sufficient. Beside the mind's activity, an additional feature must be included to give a compelling account of intellectual cognition: the formation and the shining of the objective concept to the cognizer. For Auriol, this proves to be the case to the point that, if only the image of Caesar could ever appear to the wall actually depicting him (by implicitly being somehow distinct from it), even that wall could be paradoxically said to cognize.[37]

---

[36] See also Dijs 2009, 217.

[37] Petrus Aureoli, *Scriptum I*, d. 35, p. 1, a. 1 (*ES*, 7): "Illud enim videtur constituere formalem rationem intellectionis, quo dempto ab aliquo illud non dicitur intellectio, et quo posito dicitur intellectio [...] Sed manifestum est quod a quacumque re tollitur ne sit quoddam habere aliquid praesens per modum apparentis, ab illa tollitur ne sit formaliter intelligere; cuicumque vero hoc competit, illud dicitur quoddam comprehendere. Si enim menti nostrae nihil appareat obiective, nullus dicet se aliquid intelligere, immo erit in dispositione simili dormienti [...] Similiter etiam si per picturam in pariete existentem, Caesar pictus appareret parieti, paries diceretur cognoscere Caesarem pictum. Ergo manifeste apparet quod non est plus de formali ratione ipsius intelligere, aut cognoscere in universali, nisi habere aliquid praesens per modum apparentis." See also the following texts: Petrus Aureoli, *Scriptum I*, d. 9, pars 1, a. 1 (*ES*, 11): "Similiter etiam actus intellectus concipi non potest nisi ut faciens res obiective apparere."; Petrus Aureoli, *Scriptum I*, d. 3, sect. 14, a. 2 (Auriol 1952–1956, vol. 2, 708): "Nam intelligentia sive acies cogitantis dicitur dum est intellectio cum re intellecta *experimentaliter* posita in conspectu, sicut accidit illi qui loquitur attente de aliqua materia."

Recalling Auriol's example of Caesar's painting, his argument can therefore be boiled down to the following: (i) Caesar is not made to appear to the wall on which he is painted, (ii) by simply being painted on it; there is nothing in (ii) that might cause (i). Likewise, (iª) the object cognized is not made to appear to the mind's eye, (iiª) by simply being denominated by the cognitive act. Denominating does not entail appearing to the cognizer, because it does not entail the production (and thereby the appearing) of an intentional object; (iiª) is insufficient to bring about (iª):

> Denominari ab aliquo non est esse presens aut apparens denominanti, sed nec esse in conspectu aut prospectu ipsius, et nec illi obici aut offerri; sicut patet quod Cesar pictus non est presens aut apparens picture nec in conspectu aut prospectu illius nec sibi obicitur aut offertur. Sed experientia docet quod res cognita est apparens, presens, obiecta intelligenti necnon et in prospectu aut conspectu illius[38]

So, what Auriol thinks to be erroneous about conceiving of the intellectual cognition as an extrinsic denomination is that 'being cognized' is not attributed to Caesar (as soon as he is being cognized), by virtue of a feature *intrinsic* to him. His idea is that behind being cognized there indeed *is* a cognized being; behind Caesar cognized there indeed *is* a cognized Caesar. To put it differently, 'being cognized' denotes cognized Caesar, by virtue of a property which is *intrinsic* to him, as it is impossible to cognize Caesar without forming the relevant intentional object and thereby constituting some cognized being behind something's being cognized.

Nevertheless, a point I would like to stress here is that, besides denoting *cognized* Caesar, by implying a property *intrinsic* to him, Auriol seems also committed to the view that, in contrast to Brito, "being cognized" (precisely by being intrinsic to Caesar cognized) *intrinsically* denominates the real existent Caesar as well. "Being cognized" denotes cognized Caesar as it implicitly supposits for the cognized being Caesar acquires by being cognized, which is the same as the objective concept of Caesar we form through the relevant cognitive act. However, since, for Auriol, the cognized Caesar is nothing but the real Caesar insofar as he is being thought of by and thus made to appear to the mind, "being cognized" may indeed be thought of as attributed to the real Caesar through the mediation of Caesar as put into cognized or apparent being. It refers to something that is actually going on *in* Caesar (and thus is not completely irrelevant or extrinsic to him) as soon as he is cognized. Of course, this does not amount to saying that there is something necessary about Caesar (as an extra-mental particular) being cognized, nor that he undergoes a real modification. That would be absurd. Auriol's understanding aims only at saying that, in contrast to being depicted, being cognized (as he understands it) does not leave Caesar untouched.

As has already been shown,[39] his view is that every object is somehow transformed by being cognized. What follows, for him, is that, as the concept of Caesar is formed, it is (the real existent) *Caesar* that is being put into the state of being

---

[38] Peter Auriol, *Scriptum I*, d. 23, a. 2 (De Rijk 2005, 714).

[39] See *supra* n. 32.

apparent or *visible* to the cognizer. In a nutshell, the intentional object of Caesar (and thereby his appearing) *is of* (the real) Caesar.

On this view, then, Caesar cognized, which is the same as the real Caesar, becomes the subject of an appearance that is founded in Caesar cognized and terminates in whatever cognizes him.[40] Friedman makes this point, by stressing the idea that "for Auriol, it is *intrinsic* to each and every thing to have two different modes of being: real or extramental being, on the one hand, and intentional or objective being, on the other." What marks the difference between them is that "[u]nlike real being, the thing's intentional being needs a perceiver in order to actualize it" (Friedman 2013, 587).[41] The property of being apparent and thereby related to the intellect is a feature objects have in themselves (it is intrinsic to them), which just needs a cognizer to be brought into act. According to Auriol, then, by virtue of the strict identity between Caesar and his concept, "being cognized" is neither thought of as just a name extrinsically applied to Caesar, nor as one of his pictures or representations. "Being cognized," on the contrary, is somehow mediately, although not less truly, attributed to the real existent Caesar.[42]

These remarks compel us to make now explicit a detail of Auriol's arguments against the claim that intellectual cognition should be thought of as an extrinsic denomination, which has remained only partly expressed thus far. His idea is that, given that appearance is its distinctive feature, cognition is a unique event, which cannot therefore be described with any standard philosophical tool. As Auriol implies by contrasting them as he does, cognizing and representing through a painting (and thus extrinsic denomination) denote two crucially different experiences. Cognizing, as has been shown, always comes with the production of the intentional object. At the same time, for Auriol, the formation of an intentional object typically includes the appearing of such an object to the cognizing mind: forming an intentional object *is* being appeared-to by that intentional object. Representing an object through a painting, in contrast, lacks precisely this feature, as it does not involve the object's appearance to what it is painted on, say, the wall on which it is painted. The two experiences thus cannot be reduced to one another.

All in all, Auriol's idea is that appearing does not fall into any of the classes of the Aristotelian relations (i.e., the relations according to number, according to

---

[40] Note that "relation" is put into inverted commas; the reason for that will appear later. Friedman summarizes the *change* that an extra-mental object undergoes by being cognized in the following way (Friedman 2015, 144): "Upon intellectual acquaintance, Socrates as really existing is *converted* through the act of conception, that is, by being conceived, into Socrates as intentionally existing. Thus, for Auriol, Socrates and a concept grasping Socrates are the same thing with differing modes of existence" (italics mine).

[41] Italics mine. For a treatment of intentionality as a property of things rather than of mental states, see Klima 2013.

[42] Note that, as soon as it is compared with Brito's view, Auriol's view implies that being an intention or being cognized ends up being for cognized Caesar a property which is much closer to being white than to being seen for a seen thing. Just as "being white" is said of *x* because of the whiteness really inhering in it, "being cognized" is predicated of cognized Caesar because of the intentional being Caesar acquires by being cognized.

power, and according to measure and the measurable).[43] It denotes an experience that cannot be described in any standard manner and thus cannot be compared with a strict pictorial similitude: the intentional object, for Auriol, *is* nothing but a really existent object insofar as it appears to the cognizer.

The Franciscan master makes this point by claiming that cognitive acts relate to their objects in an intimate way, as something interior to them. By forming an intentional object and thereby making something appear to the cognizer, something is *present* to the cognizer. Cognitive acts, for Auriol, refer to their objects by implying the subject who performs them, as that *to which* the cognized object appears. They imply the cognizer's experience of being appeared-to by the object cognized.[44]

In fact, Auriol argues that cognizing requires by definition the object's appearing, what he calls (again) the object endowed with *esse apparens*: "[s]i enim menti nostrae nihil appareat obiective, nullus dicet se aliquid intelligere."[45] They are two symmetrical and indistinguishable features: nothing can appear to the mind without being cognized and nothing can be cognized without being made to appear to the mind that cognizes it. At the same time, Auriol continues, "omne quod apparet, alicui apparet, et omne quod lucet, alicui dicitur lucere,"[46] which is to say that cognizing involves appearing (or being cognized), but appearing (or being cognized) always connotes someone to whom that appearance appears. In a nutshell, intellectual cognition implies the cognizer's experience of seeing as present the object cognized.

The result is just that to give a compelling definition of the concept of Caesar, the cognizer to which Caesar appears must be necessarily included, as part of the definition itself. Cognizing implies the production of the intentional object and thereby entails the cognizer as *that which* cognizes, as well as *that to which* what is cognized appears. It is this dynamic, Auriol concludes, that is entirely lacking in Brito's understanding of cognition as an extrinsic denomination. By being depicted, Caesar does not appear, which is to say, is not present to the wall on which he is painted. Likewise, nothing is present to the cognizer by being merely denominated, because

---

[43] Peter Auriol, *Scriptum I*, d. 35, pars 1 (*ES*, 29): "Sic igitur intelligere connotat apparentiam obiectivam absque omni relatione media*, quia si poneretur relatio nec esset modo unius aut numeri*, nam apparere non est esse simile aut aequale; nec modo activi et passivi, nam apparere non est pati aut agere; nec modo mensurae et mensurati, nam apparere non est mensurare aut mensurari. Et ita non potest inter relationes collocari." See also Aristotle, *Metaphysics* V, 15, 1020b–1021b.

[44] See Friedman 2015 and Lička 2016.

[45] See *supra*, n. 37.

[46] Peter Auriol, *Scriptum I*, d. 9, q. 1, a. 1 (*ES*, 10): "Tertio autem, quia omne quod apparet, alicui apparet, et omne quod lucet, alicui dicitur lucere; talis autem conceptus dicitur apparitio et relucentia quaedam; habet ergo habitudinem ad intellectum in actu tamquam ad id cui lucet et cui apparet." Read this text against the one found in n. 19. Peter Auriol, *Scriptum I*, d. 9, pars 1, a. 1 (*ES*, 11). For the sake of brevity, this cannot be the place to dwell on all the complex details of Auriol's correlation between appearing and cognizing, and its incorporation into his theory of *esse apparens*. They are addressed separately in a paper entirely devoted to that topic, which I refer to as a preliminary study for this article. See Fornasieri 2021.

nothing is formed and made to appear by being denominated. There is only the cognitive act.[47]

In sum, according to Auriol, intellectual cognition involves the production of the intentional object. Something different from the cognitive act is formed. At the same time, Auriol claims that concepts and their referents are numerically the same: Caesar cognized is the same as Caesar. What a concept, a cognized thing, acquires for its being conceived, is just its becoming related and therefore *apparent* (*apparens*) to the cognizer. This is what the modification Caesar undergoes by being cognized (as opposed to being depicted) consist of, and the definitive reason why being cognized cannot be considered just as a denomination Caesar acquires from the fact that an act external to Caesar grasps him. The crucial point for the argument of this paper is that, falling outside the Aristotelian description of relations, appearing, in Auriol's sense, must be thought of as a connotation.

19.4   Auriol's View: Intellectual Cognition as Connotation

Having outlined the core of Auriol's position in light of his criticism of Brito's thesis, we can now turn directly to Auriol's thesis, according to which human cognition is a connotative concept, and the relation between an intentional object and the relevant cognitive act should be thought of as a connotation. In particular, my understanding is that Auriol considers connotation as an accountable model to describe intellectual cognition and the relation between the cognitive act and its object, insofar as it manages to include two features, which Brito's view leaves mostly untouched.

On the one hand, connotation provides Auriol with a semantic tool to explain how a cognitive act always entails the production of a cognized being or an intentional object. By stating that intellectual cognition is a connotative notion, his view is that each and every act of thinking must be thought of as something implying or connoting (the production of) an intentional object appearing to the cognizer. Connotation, then, provides Auriol with some semantical justification for his claim that 'being cognized' is not extrinsically attributed to the object cognized. Rather, he argues that "being cognized" is a connotation (as opposed to denomination) of the object cognized, in the sense that, behind something's being cognized there lies some cognized or (as he would call it) apparent being that an object acquires by being the term of a certain cognitive act.

---

[47] Peter Auriol, *Scriptum I*, d. 3, sect. 14 (Auriol 1952–1956, vol. 2, 713): "Praeterea, etiam a priori constat quod intellectio est simillima rei de qua est. Aut igitur per hanc similitudinem res capit aliquod esse, aut denominari tantum. Sed non potest dici quod denominari tantum, sic quod esse intellectum non sit nisi denominando quaedam, sicut Caesar pictus denominatur a pictura; per hanc enim denominationem Caesar non est praesens picturae, nec sibi obicitur nec apparet. Ergo necesse est dicere quod per intellectionem tamquam rei simillimam res capiat quoddam esse, ita ut esse intellectum non sit denominatio sola, sed quoddam esse intentionale diminutum et apparens."

On the other hand, by accounting for the production of the intentional object, through connotation Auriol manages to include the cognizer's awareness in the definition of cognition. Insofar as intellectual cognition is all about the appearance of the object cognized to the cognizer, the cognizer's experience of being appeared-to by what is conceived ends up being an irreplaceable feature of our cognitive life.

To address this view and get to the bottom of Auriol's words as much as we can, the best option is to start with what Auriol says once again in d. 35 of his *Scriptum*. There he provides the definition of what understanding (*intelligere*), or cognizing in act, essentially means. According to his view as presented there, an act of understanding is a connotative notion (*intelligere formaliter dicit determinatum connotatum*). To understand means to connote or co-signify something as apparent to the cognizer. The object cognized, in contrast, is what is connoted or co-signified by that cognitive act; it is what is produced and appears to the cognizer.

In line with what has been shown thus far, Auriol claims that thinking in act always implies something more than the sole cognitive act. Though secondarily or in a derivative manner, the intellectual act signifies something insofar as it appears to the cognizer:

> *intelligere formaliter dicit determinatum connotatum*, scilicet habere praesens aliquid ut apparens; non dicit autem determinate aliquid in recto… intelligere formaliter non includit determinate aliquid in recto, sed solum connotat aliquid ut apparens illi quod dicitur intelligere[48]

At this point, however, a question arises: what does it mean to conceive actual cognition as a connotation? Auriol's treatment of connotative terms might come in handy to answer this question.[49] Classically speaking (and Auriol agrees with this view), connotative terms are those that have a primary and a secondary meaning. What identifies connotative terms's primary meaning is that they linguistically refer to it by using Latin grammar's direct cases, such as nominative and accusative. For this reason, they are also said to refer to it directly or *in recto*. What identifies connotative terms's secondary meaning, in contrast, is that they linguistically refer to it by using Latin grammar's oblique cases, such as genitive, dative and ablative. For this reason, they are also said to refer to it implicitly, derivatively or *in obliquo* (Taieb 2018a, 116–117).

What is peculiar to Auriol's reading of connotative terms and particularly relevant to intellectual cognition, however, is his view on how primary and secondary signification comes to be related. In fact, Auriol claims that connotative terms are

---

[48] Peter Auriol, *Scriptum I*, d. 35, pars. 1, a. 1 (*ES*, 7). Italics mine. See also *supra* n. 34 and the texts that follow. See also Peter Auriol, *Scriptum I*, d. 9, pars 1, a. 1 (*ES*, 11): "Similiter etiam actus intellectus concipi non potest nisi ut faciens res obiective apparere."

[49] To address the issue of how connotation is applied to intellectual cognition, I refer to what I have already discussed in Fornasieri 2018 and 2021 and to the literature referred to therein. Note that Auriol takes connotative concepts to be the same as relative terms (instead of actual relations), which means, as Brower points out, that relative terms are things that are 'said of' in some way; they are terms whose correct predication essentially entails a relationship to something different from the subject of which they are spoken (Brower 2018).

mainly those terms that cannot even be conceived of without also conceiving (*quasi cointellecta*)[50] of what they signify *in obliquo*. While expressing their primary meaning, they simultaneously co-signify their secondary meaning. One of the examples Auriol most frequently provides to make this point is the term "flesh." As he puts it, "flesh" is a connotative term, since "flesh" cannot be said but to be the "flesh of someone." "Flesh," in other words, co-signifies "animal" just in virtue of what "flesh" mainly signifies.[51]

Now, in virtue of its being a connotative notion, Auriol holds that the concept of intellectual cognition has a primary and a secondary signification. In contrast with most other connotative concepts, however, Auriol claims that its primary meaning has a totally undetermined content. It does not formally (nor directly) refer to any definite entity. In fact, Auriol argues that cognition *in recto* is anything and everything (*id*) "by which" something is made to appear to the cognizer (Taieb 2018a, 117). As Auriol points out, what "*id*" actually means is the concept of being (*ens*),[52] a concept that means every possible and actual being in an utterly implicit manner, and therefore coincides with everything that exists.[53] The result is that cognition *in recto* is not something in itself. It can be anything which is able to instantiate it. As Auriol remarks, however, this is not the end of the story. In fact, undetermined entities cannot exist in extra-mental reality. It is impossible for a thing to make some-

---

[50] Peter Auriol, *Scriptum I*, d. 45, a. 1 (Auriol 1596; Fb, f. 1067D): "...et hoc est, quod appellat Simplicius super praedicamenta caracterizatam ab extrinseco, utpote a relatione cum ait, quod caput capitati dicitur, et manus manuati secundum dici, quia caracterizatur ipse ad aliquid... ex quo etiam patere potest, quo modo aliqua intelliguntur esse unum et idem in ratione intrinseca, quae tamen distinguuntur extrinsece et penes connotata, in quantum una et eadem ratio potest sibi plure habitudines appropiare, in tantum illa differet penes appropriata, quae includet extrinsece, quasi quaedam cointellecta, non tamen intrinsece distinguetur."

[51] Peter Auriol, *Scriptum I*, d. 8, q. 3, a. 2 (*ES*, no. 68, 14): "Est enim considerandum quod sunt aliqua quae nihil dicunt nisi in recto, utpote homo, leo, et ceterae substantiae; et sunt aliqua quae, cum hoc quod dicunt aliquid in recto, aliqua significant in obliquo, ut simitas dicit concavitatem in recto et nasum in obliquo, et similiter caro dicit substantiam propriam in recto et animal in obliquo, quia dicitur caro alicuius caro; similiter etiam os, manus et similia connotant aliquid in obliquo, principale autem significatum est illud quod dicunt in recto."

[52] Peter Auriol, *Scriptum I*, d. 35, pars. 1, a. 1 (*ES*, 9): "Sed formalis ratio intellectionis nullam rationem determinatam dicit in recto. Non enim est aliud intellectio quam id quo alicui res apparent, totum autem hoc est conceptus entis, quod importatur per 'id quo alicui'; conceptus vero entis indeterminatissimus est, et ita quod importatur per intellectionem in recto est indeterminatum." See also Peter Auriol, *Scriptum I*, d. 8, q. 3, a. 2, no. 60 (*ES*, 12): "'id' non dicit determinatum aliquid, nec rem nec rationem, immo totum conceptum entis qui caret omni re et omni ratione determinata."

[53] Peter Auriol, *Scriptum I*, d. 2, sect. 9, a. 2 (Auriol 1952–1956, v. 1, 487): "Communitas autem entis est confusus quidam et mixtus conceptus omnium rationum, non innixus alicui rationi determinatissime seu potentiali, sed denudatus ab omni distinctione et actuali ratione." See also Peter Auriol, *Scriptum I*, d. 2, sect. 9, a. 4 (Auriol 1952–1956, v. 1, 509): "conceptus denudatus sit ab omni ratione et omni conceptibili in actu." Auriol's view on the concept of being (*ens*) is quite complex and many studies have been devoted to it. For reason of space, this cannot be the place to dwell on this matter thoroughly. Here, we can only refer, among others, to the following: Aertsen 2012, 434–456; Brown 1995; Goris 2002.

thing appear without being something in itself. What follows is that, as soon as cognizing is incorporated into human minds, cognizing itself necessarily coincides (in its primary meaning) with something determined, real and able to make cognition occur.[54] Auriol's idea is that this is nothing but the mind's cognitive act. Cognitive acts, in fact, are endowed with categorial, non-relative existence (*aliquid absolutum*).[55] Also, they are that by which the intentional object is formed and made to appear to the mind.[56]

According to Auriol, then, intellectual cognition's primary meaning coincides with the cognitive act, which is a quality in the mind. Intellectual cognition's secondary meaning, in contrast, is what is co-signified by that cognitive act.[57] As Auriol puts it, this is the intentional object, that which is formed by and thereby appears to the cognizer. Intellectual cognition, in fact, is that (*id*, i.e., intellectual cognition's primary meaning) by which something (is formed and thus) appears to the cognizer (*quo alicui res apparent*, i.e. the intentional object).[58] The intentional, appearing object is what is obliquely referred to by intellectual cognition's primary meaning. Every cognitive act, in fact, is always *of* a certain intentional object: it is the act by which a certain intentional object is formed and made to appear.

By conceiving of cognition as a connotation, Auriol's idea is therefore that intellectual cognition's primary and secondary meaning relate to each other like any other connotative concept. Cognizing something in act involves the formation and appearing of the object cognized, because the cognitive act and the object cognized respectively count as the primary and secondary meaning of a connotative notion.[59]

---

[54] Peter Auriol, *Scriptum I*, d. 35, pars. 1, a. 1 (*ES*, 8–9): "Secunda vero propositio est quod ista formalis ratio, quae non dicit in recto, ut dictum est, determinatum aliquod absolutum, sed connotat determinatum aliquid, oportet quod fundetur, vel potius quod coincidat et determinatur per aliquod absolutum in creatura… Quod enim necessario coincidat in aliquid determinatum et absolutum apparet, quia nullum indeterminatum in recto potest poni in rerum existentia, quicquid sit de apprehensione… Ergo necesse est, dum intellectio ponitur existere in rerum natura, quod coincidat ille conceptus indeterminatus in aliquam realitatem determinatae rationis."

[55] Peter Auriol, *Scriptum I*, d. 35, pars. 1, a. 1 (*ES*, 14): "siquidem intellectio, formaliter et in recto loquendo in intellectu creato, non est aliud quam intellectus cum similitudine rei, in quantum id quod positum est in esse apparenti sibi apparet, unde connotat apparens ut sibi." See also Peter Auriol, *Scriptum I*, d. 9, pars 1, a. 1 (*ES*, 8): "Secunda vero propositio est quod res non potest habere tale esse apparens nisi ratione alicuius absoluti realis existentis in intellectu: omne namque deminutum reducitur ad aliquid reale, alioquin nihil esset et in se et in alio. Sed res in esse apparenti sive rei apparitio est omnino quid deminutum; unde nihil est in se. Ergo necesse est quod sit aliquod reale in intellectu, ratione cuius dicatur esse." See also *ibid.*, 10: "Omne enim absolutum potest concipi absque respectu. Sed actus intellectus, qui resultat ex potentia et ex reali similitudine obiecti, est aliquid absolutum." On these passages and Auriol's definition of the cognitive act as something composed by the intellect and a likeness of the object, see Friedman 2015.

[56] Peter Auriol, *Scriptum I*, d. 9, pars 1, a. 1 (*ES*, 10): "Primo quidem, quoniam res posita in esse apparenti dicitur concipi per actum intellectus, immo est conceptus intellectualis."

[57] See *supra*, n. 48.

[58] See *supra*, n. 52. See also *ibid.*: "intelligere est id quo res intellecta praesens est per modum apparentis."

[59] See *supra*, n. 52.

For Auriol, it is therefore impossible to even think of the former without also thinking of the latter.[60] As cognition's primary meanings, cognitive acts essentially co-signify their relevant intentional object. The production and the appearing of the intentional object are part and parcel of each cognitive act. Taieb makes this point when he says that "created cognition…is ontologically absolute, but can only be represented (that is, can only be thought about …) as having a relation to an object." (Taieb 2018a, 131–132).

This view fits very well with Auriol's claim that "being cognized" can no longer be conceived as an extrinsic denomination of the object cognized. In contrast to Brito's theory, "being cognized" here supposits for the cognized being an object inevitably acquires by being cognized. Its semantic value is no longer (nor can it be) the mere cognitive act, but is the mode of being an object comes to have as soon as it is cognized by that cognitive act. What connotation adds to this description, though, is that the object's being put in the intentional or appearing being occurs as the secondary meaning of a notion whose primary signification is the cognitive act. For Auriol, then, an intention is a real thing, insofar as it is related to the mind, but a real thing is being related to the mind, for Auriol, insofar as the relevant intentional object is formed and thereby that thing is made to appear to whatever is said to cognize.

Remarkably, conceiving of cognition as a connotation is also effective in making clear Auriol's claim that intellectual cognition is a special kind of action, as it can be thought of as both transitive and immanent.[61] Immanency and transitivity are compatible features as applied to cognition, inasmuch as, for Auriol, it is impossible to conceive of a cognitive act without the production of the relevant intentional object. In fact, considered as a co-signification of the relevant cognitive act, the intentional object is nothing other than the cognitive act while obliquely conceived. It is neither added, nor juxtaposed to the act. The intentional object simply "follows" or flows from the cognitive act. At the same time, by being thought of as a co-signification of the cognitive act, the object cognized cannot be equated with what instantiates the connotation's primary meaning. The intentional object is something which stands behind the cognitive act. The two must at least be *connotatively* distinct.

In contrast to Brito's identification of intention with cognitive acts, Auriol thus manages (through connotation) to give the object cognized a central place in the definition of intellectual cognition. As he sees it, the intentional object, given as present to the mind's gaze, cannot just be a name drawn from the cognitive act; it is essential for cognition to occur. As has been shown, for Auriol, there is no intellectual cognition without (the production of) an intentional object, because there is no intellectual cognition without a cognitive act. In this framework, connotation is precisely what provides him with the tool to think of the object cognized as something

[60] On the metaphysical background of Auriol's theory of concepts, see Friedman 2015, esp. 154–157.

[61] See *supra*, n. 26 and surrounding.

irreducible to the cognitive act (though intentionally distinct) and co-essential to intellectual cognition; it offers a view of intellectual cognition that involves the presence of the object cognized before the mind's gaze, a feature we might call "object-givenness" (Taieb 2018a, 132), i.e. the appearing of what we are thinking about while we are thinking about it (with everything that comes with it).

Now, these remarks introduce the second important feature of intellectual cognition that connotation serves to describe, i.e., the cognizer's awareness.

As has been shown elsewhere,[62] Auriol seems committed to the view that, as far as it is applied to intellectual cognition, connotation involves symmetry: (i) the concept of cognition, whose primary meaning as incorporated into human cognition is the cognitive act, connotes (ii) the concept of the intentional object, as much as (ii) the concept of appearing, which always coincides with the concept of the intentional object, connotes (i) the concept of the cognitive act. As we have just seen, (i) entails (ii). According to Auriol, (i) connotes or co-signifies (ii) as *that which* appears: (ii) is the cognitive act's secondary meaning (*intelligere connotat ipsum tamquam id quod apparet*). Nevertheless, he also seems convinced that (ii) obliquely entails (i), as (ii) is a connotative notion. As Auriol himself puts it, whatever appears (*apparens*) connotes or co-signifies the cognitive act and the cognizer who performs it as that *to which* it actually appears; the cognitive act counts as the secondary meaning of the concept of the intentional object (*apparens connotat intelligere, tamquam id cui apparet*).

What follows, then, is that both (i) the cognitive act (*isto* [*scil.*] *habere aliquid per modum apparentis*) cannot be thought of without also thinking of (ii) the intentional object (*apparens*), as a co-signification of the act itself, and (ii) the intentional object (*ipsa apparentia*) cannot be thought of without also thinking of (i) the cognitive act (*habere aliquid per modum apparentis*), as a co-signification of the intentional object itself. According to Auriol, (i) necessarily refers to (ii), as (ii) to (i):

> Et si dicatur quod ista habitio [*scil.* intellectio vel habitio alicuius per modum apparentis] erit quaedam relatio, dicendum quod apparens alicui apparet, nec est aliud habere aliquid per modum apparentis quam illud sibi apparere; propter quod [*scil.* habere aliquid per modum apparentis vel ista habitio vel intellectio] habitudinem non importat, sed potius [*scil.* habere aliquid per modum apparentis vel ista habitio vel intellectio] connotatur ab ipsa apparentia, et e converso apparens connotatur ab isto [*scil.* habere aliquid per modum apparentis vel ista habitio vel intellectio], sic quod apparens connotat intelligere, tamquam id cui apparet; sed e converso intelligere connotat ipsum [*scil.* apparens] tamquam id quod apparet.[63]

According to Auriol's account, cognizing something in act involves the production and the appearing of the intentional object.[64] Every time an appearance is going on,

[62] Fornasieri 2021.

[63] Peter Auriol, *Scriptum I*, d. 35, pars 1, a. 1 (*ES*, 8).

[64] See *supra*, n. 37. "[s]i enim menti nostrae nihil appareat obiective, nullus dicet se aliquid intelligere."

there indeed is an object formed and appearing.[65] At the same time, this passage from Auriol seems to imply that what is formed and thereby appears involves that which is receiving the appearance. Something appearing requires someone for and to whom it appears.[66]

Why is this claim so important for our purposes? Of course, as has already been touched upon,[67] symmetry here is not meant to prove that cognition should be thought of as a mutual relation. This is especially true for cognitive acts directed at extra-mental particulars. According to Auriol, the extra-mental object and the object endowed with apparent being are numerically the same. Notwithstanding, he firmly places cognition among what Aristotle calls the third-class relations, which in fact are non-mutual.[68] When a cognizer cognizes a thing, something happens to the cognizer, as a cognitive act directed at that thing comes to inhere in the cognizer's mind, as an accident in its subject; when that thing is cognized, in contrast, nothing of the sort happens to it. In contrast with the cognizer's mind, an object does not undergo any real change or modification by being cognized. Thus, no genuine object/act relation corresponds to the real, genuine act/object one.

Nonetheless, we cannot make Auriol claim something he does *not* claim. He cannot be meant to say here that being not a real mutual relation involves for cognition that the object cognized should be said to be objectively in or related to the mind by extrinsic denomination alone. This would amount to saying that Caesar is said to be objectively in the intellect or to be related to it, just because someone externally examining Caesar and the cognitive act about him thinks of Caesar as the foundation of a relation directed at the cognitive act, despite Cesar himself is not related to that cognitive act (Pini 2015, 356).[69] But we have seen that this is precisely how extrinsic denomination works and why Auriol claims it to be ineffective to describe intellectual cognition.

As far as I can see, Auriol's aim in this text is emphasizing that the cognitive act relates an object to the mind just by conceiving and thereby making it appear to itself. More precisely, I contend that it is connotation's symmetrical feature that provides the tool to describe the twofold nature of the intellectual cognition. By being a connotative notion, intellectual cognition cannot even be imagined without also thinking of the (production of) relevant intentional object. By being a connotative notion either, the object cognized cannot even be imagined without also thinking of the cognizer performing the act through which it is cognized. Cognition amounts to appearing and appearing involves something that appears. That the

---

[65] Peter Auriol, *Scriptum I*, d. 3, sect. 14, a. 2 (Auriol 1952–1956, vol. 2, 712): "impossibile est quin apparitioni formali aliquid appareat obiective. Sicut enim albedine aliquid albet et repraesentatione aliquid repraesentatur et pictura aliquid pingitur, sic apparitione aliquid apparet."

[66] See *supra*, n. 46.

[67] See *supra*, n. 32.

[68] On this point, see Taieb 2018a, 127–132. On Aristotle's third-class relation: Aristotle, *Categories*, 7, 6b1–6; *Metaphysics*, V, 15, 1021a26–b3.

[69] I owe this description of 'being cognized' as extrinsically attributed to the object of thought to his sharp treatment of Scotus' view on the matter.

cognized object appears to the cognizer is therefore a prerogative each thing acquires as soon as it is conceived of. We may put it by saying that by cognizing, the cognitive act forms the intentional object; by forming it, the cognitive act makes it appear to the mind; through its own appearing, the intentional object comes to be related to the intellectual act (Fornasieri 2021, 39).

In the particular case of cognitive acts directed at extra-mental particulars, this is especially remarkable as it means (if my interpretation is correct) that, since the extra-mental object is the same as the intentional one, the property of being cognized and thereby becoming apparent is something which is *connotatively* involved in each thing as it is grasped by the mind. The object's appearing is not added or superimposed to that object. It does not come from the outside: the intentional object is the real object appearing to the mind; it is therefore that real object that (by being cognized and thereby appearing) is connotatively related to the mind.[70]

This gist of Auriol's position is very well stressed by his claim that whenever we think of something, the very same thing is (said to be) cognized both *terminative* and *denominative*. What is grasped *terminative*, i.e., what terminates the mind's gaze, can be conceived as what is *immediately* cognized. This is the extra-mental thing, as it is put into intentional being and thereby being made to appear to the cognizer. What is grasped *denominative*, in contrast, is to be conceived as what is *ultimately* cognized, which is nothing but the very same extra-mental thing, insofar as it has real being. As Davenport rightly points out, «[h]aving made this distinction, he cautions however that the mind is not any less related [...] as a result to the extramental thing» (Davenport 2006, 64). Despite potential ambiguities, Auriol's idea is that the extra-mental thing and its relevant intentional object are the very same item, in precisely the same way as one's face appearing on a mirror as soon as he or she is self-mirroring is the same as the that viewer's real face. What appears to a self-mirroring viewer is not a representation of his or her face. It *is* just his or her face. According to Auriol, then, through the mediation of the intentional object, which terminates the mind's gaze being nothing but the real thing insofar as it is made to appear to the cognizer, what one ultimately gets acquainted with (and thereby what 'being cognized' is ultimately attributed to) is nothing other than the extra-mental thing, in precisely the same way as what is reached and touched by following the image on the mirror is, for the self-viewer, nothing other than the his or her own face itself.[71]

---

[70] Petrus Aureoli, *Scriptum I*, d. 27, q. 2, a. 2 (*ES*, 16): "considerandum est quod res in esse formato posita [...] claudit tamen aliquid respectivum, videlicet apparere. Quod non debet intelligi ut affixum aut superpositum illi rei, sicut ceterae relationes, sed omnino intrinsicum et indistinguibiliter adunatum."

[71] Petrus Aureoli, *Scriptum I*, d. 35, pars 2 (*ES*, 10): "Ubi considerandum est quod aliquid dicitur intelligi terminative, aliquid vero denominative:terminative quidem res extra quantum ad illud esse quod habet per modum nostri conspicui, quod est esse in anima et esse diminutum; denominative vero quantum ad illud esse quod habet in re extra, quod verum est et reale; et licet sit eadem res, non tamen esse reale et intentionale sunt idem esse. [...] Ut verbi gratia, si rosa quae lucet in mente haberet esse reale, sicut habet esse diminutum, ea. terminante intuitum intellectus, rosae omnes particulares exterius existentes denominative intelligi dicerentur, et non minus perfecte; et est exemplum ad hoc de imagine quae est intra speculum obiective, non quidem realiter sed intention-

In this regard, Auriol's terminology should not fear us: 'denominative' here does not mean that 'being cognized' is an extrinsic denomination of the extra-mental things. To the contrary, what is meant by 'denominative', according to Auriol, is just the fact that the real thing is cognized through the mediation of the intentional object, whose formation is co-signified in each and very cognitive act. Since, on Auriol's account, such a formation is nothing other than that thing's becoming apparent to the mind, 'being cognized' denotes and thereby is attributed to the extra-mental thing itself, precisely through the intentional object thus formed. By being cognized something happens to the object being cognized, as it is precisely that object that becomes apparent to the mind. 'Being cognized', in turn, connotes or intrinsically denominates a feature of the object cognized, which is the same as the extra-mental thing. To cut a long story short, by being cognized, the (extra-mental) object is connoted (instead of extrinsically denominated) by the cognitive act. Not by chance, Auriol himself claims that what is grasped *terminative* and *denominative* is the very same thing, although in two different modes of being.[72]

In Auriol's view, then, connotation seems perfectly equipped for taking up the task of making something related to the mind, by explaining how it is made to appear to the mind. It provides a description of how cognizing involves the production and causes the appearing of what is cognized. What follows is that for a thing

---

aliter, quae si haberet esse reale ibi, differret realiter a re extra speculum existente, quae diceretur visa denominative per hoc quod res alia, videlicet imago existens in speculo, terminaret intuitum videntis. Nec tamen minus propter hoc res exterior denominative videretur, immo aspiciens illam imaginem operari posset circa rem exteriorem, utpote circa propriam faciem maculam abstergendo vel componendo et ornando aut super ipsam secundum situs varios manus ducendo." On how we are acquainted with real things through the mediation of our concepts, this passage of Klima is illuminating: see Klima 1996b: "When you look into the mirror to fix your tie, you see your tie only *through* seeing its reflection. Still, of course, you do not fiddle with the reflection to fix your tie. Instead, you reach for your tie, because *what* you see by looking into the mirror is *your tie*, the *ultimate object* of your act of sight, which you see *through* its *immediate object*, the reflection. Indeed, for the reflection to be this immediate object is for it to function *only* as something that directs your act of sight to its ultimate object. That is to say, *to be* this immediate object is *to be recognized only* as something *through which* [*quo*] you see the object you want to see, and, at the same time, not to be recognized as *that which* [*quod*] you want to see, as the ultimate object, *to which* your intention, attention and action are directed *through* or *by* the former."

[72] On this point, it should be recalled what has already been said above. According to Auriol, 'being cognized' is to be thought of as a property which is much closer to being white, than to being seen for a thing. As a consequence, 'denominative' here is to be intended in terms of an intrinsic (as opposed to an extrinsic) denomination. Not by chance, Auriol himself uses 'connotation' and 'denomination' (in the sense of *intrinsic denomination*) as synonym. See, for example: Petrus Aureoli, *Scriptum I*, d. 35, pars 2, a. 2 (*ES*, 11): "Quamvis enim essentia quae terminat intuitum divinum simplex et una sit tam re quam ratione, nihilominus ea. cognita plura dicuntur cognita, non quidem terminative, sed denominative, ut patet ex praedictis. Et propter hoc rationes incommutabiles dicuntur plures, non quin sit una incommutabilis ratio in se, quae deitas est, sed quia ab ipsa unica existente, plura denominantur et connotantur, sicut apparebit inferius cum agetur de multitudine idearum"; Petrus Aureoli, *Scriptum I*, d. 36, pars 2, a. 3 (*ES*, 19): "Unde verum est quod intellectus aspicit omne verum, dum pervenit ad prima ideata; et quia ista pertinent ad ideas connotative et denominative, ut saepe dictum est, ideo omne verum dicitur in ideis videri, quia in aliquo quod extrinsece et oblique clauditur in ratione ideali."

to be objectively in the mind involves much more than the cognizer having a cognitive act directed at that thing. To recall Pini's formulation, we might say: that Caesar appears to the cognizer by being cognized is independent of any observer describing that event. It occurs without requiring any reflection on the cognitive act and its object.[73]

Notwithstanding, connotation requires no converse relation beside the act/object one to explain how something is related to the mind. To the truth, connotative notions do not imply (genuine) relations at all. According to Auriol, they co-signify their secondary meaning, implying no relation, but only in virtue of what they signify *in recto* (Fornasieri 2018, 263). Thus, the object's appearing involves no respect, as it is just what is co-signified by each and every cognitive act, and in turn connotes the cognizer, as its own secondary meaning. By being cognized, (the real) Caesar is being put in the state of being visible to the cognizer and thereby related to the mind cognizing him. Through cognizing, he becomes the subject of such appearing, which is founded in Caesar cognized (which is the same as the real one) and terminates in whatever cognizes him. Nothing more is required. This is explained by Auriol's claim that appearing (i.e., being cognized) is not a genuine relation. Since, for him (as mentioned), appearing or being cognized does not fall in any of the classes of the Aristotelian relations, connotation serves Auriol to explain *how* he may maintain that 'being cognized' (and thereby 'appearing') belongs to Caesar, so that he enters into a new relationship to the mind, without thereby denying that cognition is non-mutual.

Given this framework, one of the most remarkable consequences of Auriol's view (and this is the second important feature of intellectual cognition that connotation serves to describe) is that the cognizing mind comes to be deeply engaged with what it cognizes; it acquires an intimacy that denomination could never explain.[74] Due to connotation's symmetrical nature, in fact, the mind's *subjective* experience of intellectually seeing what is being thought is naturally involved in the concept of cognition. It is the very same cognizer (through the cognitive act) that both cognizes and is appeared-to by the object cognized: the property of becoming apparent to the cognizer is implied in each cognitive act as a co-signification of that act. At the same time, by becoming apparent to the mind, the object (as soon as it is cognized) connotes the cognizer as the viewer of the object's appearing. By appearing to the

---

[73] According to Auriol, it is denomination (rather than intellectual cognition) that requires (or is subsequent to) an external observer to make the attribution. Petrus Aureoli, *Scriptum I*, d. 23, a. 2 (De Rijk 2005, 714): "Preterea. Omne denominari presupponit intelligi; intellectus enim est qui facit denominationem unius rei ab alia, unde nec Cesar est in pictura intentionaliter nec denominatur ab ea. pictus, sed intellectus facit istam denominationem Cesaris a pictura, eoquod ducitur in notitiam eius per picturam; ex quo patet quod omnis denominatio pre- supponit apprehensionem. Sed constat quod hoc non esset nisi apprehendi esset aliquid plus quam ab apprehensione denominari; pari enim ratione hec denominatio presupponeret aliam apprehensionem, et illa aliam, et sic in infinitum. Ergo necessarium est rei intellecte attribui aliquid plus quam denominari."

[74] See *supra,* nn. 37–38. See also Friedman 2015 and Lička 2016. See *supra,* n. 37.

cognizer, the object's appearing makes something be a cognizant entity, it places that thing in a different state, i.e. the state of being a cognizer.

According to Auriol, then, for an object to appear or be cognized, it must always be through someone's cognizing and being appeared-to by that object. Furthermore, this occurs in an infinitely more intense sense than the sense in which the painting of Caesar *involves* Caesar by being a picture *of* him. On Auriol's view, cognizing involves the cognizer's subjective experience, insofar as it involves appearing, and appearing semantically involves (i.e. connotes) someone or something *to which* the appearance appears. The symmetrical semantic connection between cognition's first and secondary meanings incorporates into each cognitive act that act's capacity to receive something apparent, its ability to experience or see what is appearing. This makes intellectual cognition, of necessity, someone's mental activity, a completely non-transferrable experience[75].

To make this point clearer, by way of example Auriol compares the object cognized to the images in a mirror: without a viewer, the mirror still reflects certain images, but no appearing occurs, because nothing is there to receive that reflection.[76] In a similar way, cognizing involves appearing, insofar as it requires the cognizer's experience of seeing what the cognizer itself has made apparent; it requires the experience of being aware of some objective content.[77] Without an object's appearing going-on, that is, without the mind's seeing that ongoing appearing, no intellectual cognition could ever occur.

In this regard, something that neither Auriol's contemporaries, nor the majority of contemporary scholars have paid particular attention to, is that the *apparent* object (as the term itself suggests) is not something static; it describes an activity that lasts as long as the cognitive act does. In fact, the Latin word Auriol employs to describe the mode of being an object acquires by being cognized is *"esse apparens"* (*apparent* being), that is, a present participle. Now, a present participle expresses an action that does not have a determined beginning or end; it describes an ongoing process or an ongoing change brought about by a certain cause. As applied to intellectual cognition, this means that an object being cognized enters into a certain state, being literally made apparent (*apparens*) or visible to the intellect that conceives it. *Qua apparens*, then, the object cognized appears to the cognizer

---

[75] Searle 1992, 39.

[76] Peter Auriol, *Scriptum I*, d. 3, q. 14, a. 1 (Auriol 1952–1956, vol. 2, 697); Peter Auriol, *Scriptum I*, d. 27, a. 2 (*ES,* 16). On this point see Lička 2017. For a comment on Auriol's text, as well as on Lička's paper, see Fornasieri 2019, 343–345.

[77] Friedman 2015; Lička 2016. Friedman's study is at the moment the most relevant contribution on how Auriol claims consciousness and cognition intertwine. It deals with this matter by focusing on the description of the mechanics of intellectual cognition. For more detail on this topic, see this paper and its bibliography. The present paper may also serve as support for Friedman's reading, although moving from a different starting point. Rather than focusing on the mechanics of intellectual cognition, this paper mainly deals with its general definition, focusing on what it means to equate it with connotation.

(essentially co-implying the cognizer's experience of seeing and being appeared to by that object) as long as the mind keeps on conceiving of and focusing upon it.

What follows, for Auriol, is that, just as for mirror images, it is impossible even to think of intellectual cognition without also thinking of the cognizer's being appeared-to by or conscious of what appears. Each mental act is conscious in that it necessarily co-signifies the cognizer's awareness of what it thinks as its own activity's secondary meaning. Consciousness is as essential to intellectual cognition as H2O is to what we are used to calling water, and this precisely because the notion of "intellectual cognition" *essentially* is a connotative notion. In fact, intellectual cognition for Auriol includes what we might call a phenomenal feature: things are grasped as they *appear* (or are made to appear) to us. As Lička points out, "cognitive relations… include something we can call a 'phenomenal ingredient'. The cognized thing *appears* to the observer; it is experienced as present and introduced to him; it seizes his attention."[78] Intellectual cognition always involves the cognizer's point of view, because the object cognized is nothing but an extra-mental particular insofar as it appears to and is seen by the mind's eye:

> Nam intelligentia sive acies cogitantis dicitur dum est intellectio cum re intellecta *experimentaliter* posita in conspectu, sicut accidit illi qui loquitur attente de aliqua materia.[79]

19.5   Conclusion

The late-medieval Franciscan theologian Peter Auriol elaborates a complex theory of intellectual cognition. Its core content consists of conceiving of intellectual cognition as a connotative concept. What follows is that, like any other connotative notion, the concept of intellectual cognition has a primary and a secondary meaning, which are mutually correlated. According to Auriol, connotative concepts are those concepts that we cannot even think of without also thinking about what they obliquely refer to as their secondary meaning. The result, Auriol concludes, is that (i) the concept of intellectual cognition primarily refers to the cognitive act and obliquely refers to the object cognized, and that therefore (ii) cognitive acts cannot be thought of except as something implying (or connoting) an intentional object appearing to the cognizer. The intentional object is nothing other than the cognitive act, while obliquely conceived.

In sum, as applied to intellectual cognition, connotation provides Auriol with a device to account at once for both of the essential features involved in each and every cognitive act without making them merge into each other: the fact that we *think* about something and that *something* is always thought of, which can never be equated with the cognitive act. *Thinking* about something always implies *something* appearing to us; it always entails our receiving or being appeared-to by what we are thinking of.

---

[78] Lička 2016, 65.
[79] Peter Auriol, *Scriptum I*, d. 3, sect. 14, a. 2 (Auriol 1952–1956, vol. 2, 708).

Remarkably, this allows Auriol to take a step further. On the one hand, by employing connotation as the description of intellectual cognition, Auriol avoids reducing "being cognized" to an extrinsic denomination of the object cognized. As cognition necessarily implies the production of the intentional object as what is co-signified in each cognitive act, by the same token, "being cognized" cannot but imply a cognized being behind it. As has been shown, this does not mean that there is something necessary about a thing being cognized. Auriol's idea is only that being cognized does not leave a thing untouched. By being cognized, every object is somehow transformed, insofar as it is put into the state of being *apparent* or *visible* to the cognizer. However, insofar as the intentional object and the real object are one and the same thing, "being cognized" is attributed to the real thing through the mediation of the intentional object itself.

On the other hand, through connotation, Auriol also makes consciousness essential to intellectual cognition itself: the cognizer's experience of being appeared-to by the apparent object becomes inevitably, albeit obliquely, tied to our own cognitive activity.[80] Without it, that is, without our own being appeared-to by what we think of while we think of it (the fact that we are the ones who see what we are thinking of, while we are thinking of it), no intellectual cognition occurs. As mentioned, the cognitive act and the object cognized must be thought of as semantically correlated: the concept of the former obliquely co-signifies the concept of the latter as appearing to the mind's eye, as much as the concept of the latter obliquely co-signifies the concept of the former as that which conceives of it. The fact that we consciously experience what we cognize while we cognize it (a phenomenon that proves to be peculiar to our cognitive life) thus comes to be incorporated into intellectual cognition in an undoubtedly original manner. This peculiar feature of Auriol's account is precisely what lies behind his criticism of Brito's view, according to which intellectual cognition amounts to denominating an object. As the Franciscan theologian points out, denomination is insufficient to explain intellectual cognition since it does not entail the object's appearing to the cognizer; it is thus unable to account for the phenomenal quality of our cognitive life—something without which nothing can be a cognizant entity.

Bibliography

Manuscripts

Fb—Firenze, Biblioteca nazionale centrale, ms. conv. soppr. A.3.120.
Pg—Padova, Biblioteca Antoniana, ms. 161 scaff. ix.

---

[80] Grassi 2005, 56: "vivere comprendendo o coscientemente significa avere presente a sé qualcosa in forma del suo apparire."

Primary Sources

Aquinas, Thomas. 1918. *Summa Contra Gentiles II. Sancti Thomae Aquinatis Opera omnia iussu edita Leonis XIII P.M., v. XIII.* Romae: Typis Riccardi Garroni.
———. 1929. *Scriptum super Sententiis magistri Petri Lombardi.* Edited by P. Mandonnet, 2 vols. Paris.
Aristotle. 1928. *Metaphysics.* Edited by W. D. Ross. Oxford: Clarendon Press.
———. 1962. *Categories and De Interpretatione.* Edited by J. L. Ackrill. Oxford: Clarendon Press.
Auriol, Peter. 1952–1956. Scriptum Super Primum Sententiarum. In *Peter Aureoli Scriptum Super Primum Sententiarum*, ed. E. Buytaert, vol. I–II. New York: St. Bonaventure.
———. 1596. *Commentariorum in Primum Librum Sententiarum, Pars prima, Auctore Petro Aureolo Verberio Ordinis Minorum Archiespiscopi Aquensi S. R. E. Cardinali, Ad Clementem VIII Pont. Opt. Max.* Roma: Typographia Vaticana.
———. 1605. *Commentarii in Secundum Librum Sententiarum, Petri Aureoli Verberii Ordinis Minorum Archiepiscopi Aquensis S. R. E. Cardinalis Commentariorum in Secundum Librum Sententiarum, Tomus secundus.* Roma: Typographia Alojsii Zannetti.
———. 2020. *The electronic scriptum.* Edited by R. L. Friedman, L. O. Nielsen, and C. Schabel. http://www.peterauriol.net/editions/electronicscriptum/contents/.
Chatton, Walter. 1989. Reportatio et Lectura super Sententias: Collatio ad Librum Primum et Prologus. In , ed. J.C. Wey and CSB. Toronto: Pontifical Institute of Medieval Studies.
Ockham, William. 1967. *Scriptum in Librum Primum Sententiarum. Ordinatio (Dist. XIX–XLVIII). Opera theologica.* Vol. 4. Edited by G. Gál et al. St. Bonaventure: The Franciscan Institute.

Secondary Sources

Aertsen, J. 2012. *Medieval philosophy as transcendental thought: From Philip the Chancellor (ca. 1225) to Francisco Suárez.* Leiden: Brill.
Brower, J. 2018. Medieval theories of relations, the Stanford encyclopedia of philosophy (winter 2018 edition), Edward N. Zalta (ed.), https://plato.stanford.edu/archives/win2018/entries/relations-medieval/.
Brown, S.F. 1995. Petrus Aureoli: De unitate conceptus entis (Reportatio Parisiensis in I Sententiarum, dist. 2, p. 1, qq. 1–3 et p. 2, qq. 1–2). *Traditio* 50: 199–248.
Courteney, W.C. 2005. Radulphus Brito, master of arts and theology. *Cahiers de l'Institut du Moyen-Âge Grec et Latin* 76: 131–158.
Davenport, A. 2006. *Esse egressus* and *esse apparens* in Peter Auriol's theory of intentional being. *Mediaevalia Philosophica Polonorum* XXXV: 60–84.
De Libera, A. 1999. Dénomination et intentions: Sur quelques doctrines médiévales (XIIIe-XIVe siècle) de la paronymie et de la connotation. In *Medieval analyses in language and cognition*, ed. S. Ebbesen and R.L. Friedman, 355–376. Copenhagen: The Royal Danish Academy of Sciences and Letters.
De Rijk, L.M. 2005. *Giraldus Odonis O.F.M. Opera philosophica, Vol. II: De Intentionibus. Critical edition with a study of the medieval intentionality debate up to ca. 1350.* Leiden: Brill.
Denery, D.G. 1998. The appearance of reality: Peter Aureol and the experience of perceptual error. *Franciscan Studies* 55: 17–52.
Dijs, J. 2009. Intentions in the first quarter of the fourteenth century: Hervaeus Natalis versus Radulphus Brito. In *Philosophical debates at Paris in the early fourteenth century*, ed. S.F. Brown, T. Dewender, and T. Kobusch, 213–223. Leiden: Brill.
Ebbesen, S. 1978. The sophism 'Rationale est animal' by Radulphus Brito. *Cahiers de l'Institut du Moyen-Âge Grec et Latin* 24: 85–120.

———. 1986. *Termini accidentales concreti*: Texts from the late 13th century. *Cahiers de l'Institut du Moyen-Âge Grec et Latin* 53: 37–150.

———. 2000. Radulphus Brito: The last of the great arts masters; or: Philosophy and freedom. In *Geistesleben im 13. Jahrhundert*, ed. J.A. Aertsen and A. Speer, 231–251. Berlin/New York: De Gruyter.

Fauser, W. 1974. *Der Kommentar des Radulphus Brito zu Buch 3. De anima: Kritische Edition und Philosophisch-historische Einleitung*. Münster: Aschendorff.

Fornasieri, G. 2018. Peter Auriol on connotative distinction and his criticism of Scotus's formal distinction. *Documenti e studi sulla tradizione filosofica medievale* 29: 231–274.

———. 2019. Teoria degli universali e conoscenza della realtà in Pietro Aureoli. Unpublished doctoral dissertation, Università degli Studi di Salerno – KU, Leuven.

———. 2021. "Intelligere formaliter solum connotat aliquid ut apparens": Peter Auriol on the nature of the cognitive act. *Rivista di Storia della Filosofia* 1: 24–49.

———. Forthcoming-a. Teologia vestita di Poesia: Discorso retorico e discorso poetico nei Sermoni di Pietro Aureoli. Rivista di Filosofia Neo-Scolastica.

———. Forthcoming-b. Conception, connotation and essential predication: Peter Auriol's conceptualism to the test in II Sententiarum, d. 9, q. 2, art. 1. Analiza i Egzystencja.

Friedman, R.L. 1997. Conceiving and modifying reality: Some modist roots of Peter Auriol's theory of concept formation. In *Vestigia, imagines, verba: Semiotics and logic in medieval theological texts (XII–XIV century)*, ed. C. Marmo, 305–221. Turnhout: Brepols.

———. 1999. Peter Auriol on intentions and essential predication. In *Medieval analyses in language and cognition*, ed. S. Ebbesen and R.L. Friedman, 415–430. Copenhagen: The Royal Danish Academy of Sciences and Letters.

———. 2013. *Intellectual traditions at the medieval university: The use of philosophical psychology in Trinitarian theology among the Franciscans and Dominicans, 1250–1350*, 2 vols. Leiden: Brill.

———. 2015. Act, species, and appearance: Peter Auriol on intellectual cognition and consciousness. In *Intentionality, cognition, and mental representation in medieval philosophy*, ed. G. Klima, 141–165. New York: Fordham University Press.

Goris, W. 2002. Implicit knowledge – Being as first known in Peter of Oriol. *Recherches de Théologie et Philosophie Médiévales* 69: 33–65.

Grassi, O. 2005. *Intenzionalità: La dottrina dell'esse apparens nel XIV secolo*. Torino: Marietti.

Klima, G. 1993. The changing role of entia rationis in medieval philosophy: A comparative study with a reconstruction. *Synthese* 96: 25–59.

———. 1996a. The semantic principles underlying Saint Thomas Aquinas's metaphysics of being. *Medieval Philosophy and Theology* 5: 87–141.

———. 1996b. *Nulla virtus cognoscitiva circa proprium obiectum decipitur* – Critical comments on "Robert Pasnau: The identity of knower and known. http://faculty.fordham.edu/klima/APA.htm.

———. 2001. Aquinas' proofs of the immateriality of the intellect from the universality of thought. In *Proceedings of the Society for Medieval Logic and Metaphysics Volume 1*, ed. G. Klima, 19–28. http://faculty.fordham.edu/klima/SMLM/PSMLM1.pdf.

———. 2002. Contemporary 'essentialism' vs. Aristotelian essentialism. In *Mind, metaphysics, and value in the Thomistic and analytic traditions*, ed. J. Haldane, 175–194. Notre Dame: Notre Dame University Press.

———. 2004. The demonic temptations of medieval nominalism: Mental representation and 'demon skepticism'. In *Proceedings of the Society for Medieval Logic and Metaphysics Volume 4*, ed. G. Klima, 37–44. http://faculty.fordham.edu/klima/SMLM/PSMLM4/PSMLM4.pdf.

———. 2007. Thomistic 'monism' vs. Cartesian 'dualism'. *Logical Analysis and History of Philosophy* 10: 92–112.

———. 2010. The anti-skepticism of John Buridan and Thomas Aquinas: Putting skeptics in their place vs. stopping them in their tracks. In *Rethinking the history of skepticism*, ed. H. Lagerlund, 145–170. Leiden-Boston: Brill.

————. 2013. Three myths of intentionality vs. some medieval philosophers. *International Journal of Philosophical Studies* 21: 359–376.

————. 2015. Mental representations and concepts in medieval philosophy. In *Intentionality, cognition and mental representation in medieval philosophy*, ed. G. Klima, 323–337. New York: Fordham University Press.

————. 2017a. The medieval problem of universals. In *The Stanford Encyclopedia of Philosophy*, ed. E. N. Zalta. http://plato.stanford.edu/entries/universals-medieval/.

————. 2017b. Intentionality and mental content in Aquinas, Ockham, and Buridan. In *Universals in the fourteenth century*, ed. F. Amerini and L. Cesalli, 65–88. Pisa: Scuola Normale Superiore.

————. 2018. Aquinas' balancing act: Balancing the soul between the realms of matter and pure spirit. *Bochumer Philosophisches Jahrbuch für Antike und Mittelalter* 2: 29–48.

Lička, L. 2016. Perception and objective being: Peter Auriol on perceptual acts and their objects. *American Catholic Philosophical Quarterly* 90: 49–76.

————. 2017. Attention, perceptual content, and mirrors: Two medieval models of active perception in Peter Olivi and Peter Auriol. *Filosofický časopis, special issue 1: Perception in scholastics and their interlocutors*: 101–119.

————. 2019. What is in the mirror? The metaphysics of mirror images in Albert the Great and Peter Auriol. In *The senses and the history of philosophy*, ed. B. Glenney and J. Silva, 131–148. London: Routledge.

Marmo, C. 1995. A pragmatic approach to language in modism. In *Sprachteorien in Spätantiken un Mittelalter, Geschichte der Sprachteorie*, ed. S. Ebbesen and Peter Schmitter, vol. 3, 169–183. Tübingen: Gunter Narr Verlag.

————. 1999. The semantics of the Modistae. In *Medieval analyses in language and cognition*, ed. S. Ebbesen and R.L. Friedman, 83–104. Copenhagen: The Royal Danish Academy of Sciences and Letters.

————. 2013. Radulphus Brito on relations in his questions on the sentences. In *Logic and language in the middle ages: A volume in honour of Sten Ebbesen*, ed. J.L. Fink, H. Hansen, and A. Mora-Márquez, 373–388. Leiden: Brill.

Mora-Márquez, A.M. 2013. Radulphus Brito on common names, concepts and things. In *Logic and language in the middle ages: A volume in honour of Sten Ebbesen*, ed. J.L. Fink, H. Hansen, and A. Mora-Márquez, 357–372. Leiden: Brill.

————. 2015. Boethius of Dacia (1270s) and Radulphus Brito (1290s) on the universal sign 'every'. *Logica Universalis* 9: 193–211.

Pinborg, J. 1974. Zum Begriff der Intentio Secunda: Radulphus Brito, Hervaeus Natalis und Petrus Aureoli in Diskussion. *Cahiers de l'Institut du Moyen-Âge Grec et Latin* 13: 49–59.

————. 1975. Radulphus Brito's sophism on second intentions. *Vivarium* 13: 119–152.

————. 1976. Some problems of semantic representations in medieval logic. In *History of linguistic thought and contemporary linguistics*, ed. H. Parret, 254–278. Berlin: De Gruyter.

————. 1980. Radulphus Brito on universals. *Cahiers de l'Institut du Moyen-Âge Grec et Latin* 35: 56–142.

Pini, G. 2008. Scotus on the objects of cognitive acts. *Franciscan Studies* 66: 281–315.

————. 2015. Scotus on objective being. *Documenti e studi sulla tradizione filosofica medievale* 26: 81–103.

Rosier-Catach, I. 1995. *Res significata et modi significandi*: Les implications d'une distinction médiévale. In *Sprachteorien in Spätantiken un Mittelalter, Geschichte der Sprachteorie*, ed. S. Ebbesen and Peter Schmitter, vol. 3, 135–168. Tübingen: Gunter Narr Verlag.

Searle, J. 1992. *The Rediscovery of the Mind*. Cambridge-London: MIT Press.

Tachau, K.H. 1988. *Vision and certitude in the age of Ockham: Optics, epistemology and the foundation of semantics, 1250–1345*. Leiden: Brill.

Taieb, H. 2018a. What is cognition? Peter Auriol's account. *Recherches de théologie et philosophie médiévales* 85: 109–134.

————. 2018b. *Relational intentionality: Brentano and the Aristotelian tradition*. Cham: Springer.

Van der Lecq, R. 2008. Logic and theories of meaning in the late 13th and early 14th century including the Modistae. In *The handbook of the history of logic: Medieval and renaissance logica*, ed. D.M. Gabbay and J. Wood, vol. 2, 347–388. North-Holland: Elsevier.

Vanni Rovighi, S. 1958 [1960]. L'intenzionalità della conoscenza secondo P. Aureolo. In *L'Homme et son destin, 673–680*. Louvain/Bruxelles: Nauwelaerts.

———. 1960. Una fonte remota della teoria husserliana dell'intenzionalità. In *Omaggio a Husserl*, ed. E. Paci, 47–65. Milano: Il Saggiatore.

Chapter 20
Temporal Origins Essentialism and Gappy Existence in Marsilius of Inghen's *Quaestiones super libros De generatione et corruptione*

Adam Wood

Keywords Gappy existence · Marsilius of Inghen · John Buridan · Thomas Aquinas · Nicole Oresme · Origins essentialism

Near the end of *De generatione et corruptione* (DGC) Aristotle remarks that "men and animals do not return upon themselves so that the same individual comes-to-be a second time," and more generally that "things … whose substance is perishable … must return upon themselves specifically, not numerically" (Aristotle 1984, 2.11.338b8–9 and 16–19). These words provided a locus for various medieval scholastic philosophers to weigh in on the issue of whether humans, animals or other entities of various other sorts might, after having ceased to exist, return to existence numerically the same as they were previously. Aristotle's remark appears to deny this possibility in the case of "things whose substance is perishable." But the doctrine of the bodily resurrection gave medieval writers a putative reason for thinking it possible, at least by God's power. Hence in addition to considering the possibility of temporal gaps in a thing's existence ("gappy existence," for short) in commentaries on DGC and in quodlibetal disputations, scholastic theologians frequently raised the issue in their discussions of eschatological issues in commentaries on the last book of Peter Lombard's *Sentences*.

The common medieval view of the matter, as Francisco Toledo tells us in his DGC commentary, was that "God is able to reduce permanent things that were corrupted, but nevertheless this is impossible for any natural agent by its own

A. Wood (✉)
Wheaton College, Wheaton, IL, USA
e-mail: adam.wood@wheaton.edu

J. P. Hochschild et al. (eds.), *Metaphysics Through Semantics: The Philosophical Recovery of the Medieval Mind*, International Archives of the History of Ideas Archives internationales d'histoire des idées 242, https://doi.org/10.1007/978-3-031-15026-5_20

power" (Toledo 1588, 307).[1] The "permanent things" Toledo mentions here stand in contrast to successive things, typical examples of which are times and motions, and which, according to another common view, cannot be brought back numerically the same by any power whatsoever once they are gone. Rejecting the common view in one direction, Toledo notes, are John Duns Scotus and Richard of Mediavilla, who hold that natural agents too are able to bring back things previously corrupted. Rejecting it in the other direction, he says, is Marsilius of Inghen, who holds that restoring things that were corrupted is simply impossible, even for God. Toledo cites question eighteen from Marsilius's commentary on the second book of DGC, which asks "whether something corrupted can be restored the same in number" (Marsilius 1518, 128ra).[2]

The purpose of this article is to examine Marsilius's position on gappy existence in this question, alongside another question which sheds important light on *why* Marsilius adopts the uncommon stance he does, namely the ninth question of book one of his DGC commentary, which asks "whether one and the same generable thing could be generated in any of many given instants?" (ibid., 74rb).[3] Marsilius's answer to this latter question is an emphatic "no." A thing's temporal origins are essential to it, in such a way that it could not have originated before or after the moment it did. As Marsilius sees it, the two questions are intimately related to one another: if a thing's temporal origins are essential to it, then it cannot be restored after being corrupted, and vice versa.

I shall proceed as follows. In the paper's first section I'll examine briefly the views of John Buridan and Nicole Oresme on the issues just mentioned, since the way Oresme diverges from Buridan's position appears to have influenced Marsilius's own reasoning. I'll then consider Marsilius's own view and the arguments he offers on its behalf. Many of these are perplexing. Hence, the third and final section of the paper considers the philosophical plausibility of Marsilius's position, drawing on a recent paper of Gyula Klima's on gappy existence in Aquinas.

20.1   Buridan and Oresme on Gappy Existence and Origins Essentialism

As H.A.G. Braakhuis notes in his study of Buridan's "Parisian school" on the issue of gappy existence, Buridan himself "proceeds rather hesitantly" with regard to the question "whether something that is simply corrupted can be restored the same in number?"—the twenty-fourth and last of his commentary on book one of DGC

---

[1] "Deus potest omnia permanentia corrupta reducere, id tamen impossibile est cuicunque agenti naturali virtute propria, et est haec communis sententia." All translations are my own.

[2] "Utrum corruptum possit reverti idem in numero."

[3] "Utrum in quolibet plurium instantium idem generabile datum possit generari."

(Braakhuis 1997, 129; Buridan 2010, 179).[4] After offering seven opening arguments for the view that simply corrupted things can be restored the same in number, Buridan states that Aristotle himself thinks the opposite, and posits as his own initial conclusion that nothing "substantially and simply corrupted" can *naturally* be restored the same in number (Buridan ibid., 181). This, he says, is hard to prove, but he offers three ways of "persuading" someone of its truth.[5]

First, he reasons, just as an interruption in a motion by an intervening rest or the interruption of a magnitude by an intervening space disrupts the numerical unity of the motion or magnitude, so too an interruption in the continuity of any given thing's existence would disrupt the numerical unity of that thing. Accordingly, if a thing should cease to exist, nothing generated afterwards would be numerically the same as the thing that existed previously then ceased.[6]

Second, if things *could* be restored the same in number, this would be on account of the agents and patients of their coming into being remaining the same and remaining similarly related to one another. Yet these conditions can clearly be met *without* their products being numerically the same. God, the *primum mobile*, and the first mover are all the same and are all related to one another the same way as they were one thousand years ago. Yet today's revolution of the *primum mobile* isn't the same as it was then, or else today's time would be the same as it was then, and those who died one thousand years ago would exist at the same time as those who live now.[7]

Finally, "by mixing theology with natural philosophy" Buridan speculates that after some water is heated by some fire, God might preserve the water's heat apart from the water itself. If the same water is then heated again by the same fire, the second heat will clearly be distinct from the first. Hence, the same would seemingly be true if the first heat were *not* miraculously preserved.[8]

---

[4] "Utrum quod est simpliciter corruptum possit reverti idem in numero."

[5] Buridan 2010, 181: "est difficile probare istam conclusionem. Tamen potest sic persuaderi…"

[6] Ibid.: "interruptionem in motu per quietem mediam provenit quod motus non manet idem in numero … Sic similiter propter interruptionem continuitatis in magnitudine provenit quod illud quod ante erat unum in numero, non amplius in numero … Sic simili modo, cum aliquid desinit esse, propter interruptionem continuitatis in essendo numquam postea genitum erit sibi idem numero."

[7] Ibid., 182: "Si corruptum posset reverti idem numero, hoc esset propter esse idem agens et idem passum et ea. similiter se habere ad invicem; non enim alia causa quare debeat reverti idem numero. Sed constat quod haec omnia non sufficiunt, quia primum mobile, scilicet ultima sphaera, et primus motor, scilicet Deus, manent idem et similiter se ad invicem habentes, et tamen non est eadem revolutio hodierna quae fuit hesterna, nisi tu dicas idem tempus esse hodie quod heri et hodie quod a mille annis, cum ille motus primus sit tempus; modo hoc dicere videtur absurdam, quia tunc tempore essent qui nunc sunt et a mille annis mortui sunt."

[8] Ibid.: "Miscendo theologiam cum naturali philosophia … pono quod modo in illa aqua fiat caliditas ab illo igne et istam caliditatem factam removeat Deus ab hac aqua et reservet eam seorsum. Deinde iterum haec eadem aqua ab illo eodem igne calefiat. … constat quod haec caliditas secundo genita non est eadem cum illa reservata, quia distant loco et subiecto. Ideo etiam manifestum est quod si prima fuisset corrupta et non reservata, tamen illa secundo genita non fuisset sibi eadem, sed alia."

Despite the persuasiveness of these arguments, Buridan follows them by positing as a second conclusion that "through the absolute power of God," it is indeed possible for things simply corrupted to be restored the same in number.[9] Suppose God were to annihilate the entire created order. In that case God would stand in precisely the same relation toward the world as he did before the beginning of creation. And hence if he created anew, there is no reason for supposing that the second creation wouldn't be numerically the same as the first.

Buridan nowhere addresses directly the relationship between his conclusion and arguments regarding the natural impossibility of restoring things that were corrupted and the supernatural possibility of the same. He does, however, end his discussion with some reflections on the ultimate source of numerical identity and diversity that shed some light on his view. It is "often" the case, Buridan says, that forms are numerically diversified by matter, or by their agents, when they are in the same matter.[10] Hence, a form brought about in just one subject by just one agent is thought to remain the same so long as its existence is uninterrupted; for instance "if heat doesn't cease in this water, it is said to be the same [heat]."[11] Nevertheless, Buridan adds, even if the water is continuously heated such that "the whole heat is the same in number," still "the grade of heat first acquired isn't the same as the second grade acquired."[12] And if we ask "whence it originally comes about that the former grade is diverse from the latter," Buridan's response is "that every thing in the world is intrinsically itself and no other, and all diverse things in the world are diverse intrinsically by themselves and nothing other, and so whenever they will be diverse they will be diverse by themselves and nothing other."[13] So the two grades of heat "don't have their diversity from anywhere else, but from themselves, unless because we are finally able to come back to the principle of every diversity or identity, which is God himself."[14] Ultimately, Buridan says, whatever God understands to be distinct is distinct, and whatever God understands to be the same is the same. Buridan's claim that things in the world are intrinsically diverse from one another

---

[9] Ibid., 182–83: "nihil prohibet quod simpliciter corruptum possit reverti idem numero supernaturaliter, scilicet per absolutam Dei potentiam, quia, ... si omnia essent nunc annihilata praeter Deum, totaliter esset ita sicut erat ante creationem mundi, et ... nihil videtur prohibere quin potest omnia facere ea. quae fecit, et non solum similia, sed eadem."

[10] Ibid., 183: "saepe ex diversitate materiae est diversitas numeralis formarum, si sint ab eodem agente, et quandoque est ex diversitate agentium, si sint in eadem materia.

[11] Ibid., "si in hac aqua non desinit caliditas esse, ipsa dicitur eadem."

[12] Ibid., "si aqua continue calefiat, tamen gradus caliditatis primo acquisitus non est illud idem quod est gradus secundo acquisitus."

[13] Ibid., 183–84: "Tunc igitur quaeritur unde est originaliter quod ille gradus est diversus ab illo. Respondetur quod intrinsice omnis res de mundo est se ipsa sibi eadem et nullo alio; et omnes res de mundo diversae sunt intrinsece ipsis diversae et nullo alio."

[14] Ibid.: "illi gradus non haberent aliunde diversitatem, sed ex se ipsis, nisi quod finaliter possemus recurrere ad ipsum principium omnium diversitatum et identitatem, quod est ipse Deus. ... Ideo quaecumque Deus intelligit sic distincte, impossibile est quod hoc fiat idem illi sive in eodem subiecto sive ab eodem agente sive etiam in eodem tempore. Et omne illud quod Deus intelligit idem sibi, impossibile est quod fiat diversum a se."

just by themselves is unsurprising; as Peter King puts it, "Buridan holds that no principle or cause accounts for the individuality of the individual, or at least no principle or cause other than the very individual itself, and thus there is no 'metaphysical' problem of individuation at all—individuality, unlike generality, is primitive and needs no explanation" (King 1994, 397). Nevertheless, what Buridan adds about God as the ultimate source of all numerical identity and distinctness is striking. Braakhuis says he has "been unable to find other passages by Buridan which could form a parallel to this consideration on the ultimate origin of individuality" (Braakhuis 1997, 131).

Braakhuis also says he finds it "remarkable" that Buridan doesn't bring up the bodily resurrection in order to defend this conclusion that God can restore things that were previously corrupted (ibid., 129). He notes that several of the theses condemned in 1277 by Etienne Tempier bore on the question of whether corrupted things could be restored numerically the same, and what philosophers should say about the resurrection (ibid., 111). Perhaps Buridan wished in this case to avoid theological controversy.

His younger contemporary Nicole Oresme is, however, willing to bring up the case of the resurrection while discussing related issues in his DGC commentary. Oresme's commentary does not make the issue of gappy existence the central focus of any question, but he discusses it in the course of considering the relationship between a thing's origins and its identity in two questions which investigate, respectively, whether a given generable can be generated "by any of many agents" —book one, question nine—and "at any of many instants"—question ten (Oresme 1996, 70 and 78).[15] In a careful study of these questions Stefano Caroti writes that while Buridan follows a thirteenth-century tradition of commentators in discussing individuation in the context of cycles of generation and corruption, Oresme initiated a trend of discussing it in the first book, and that "[v]ery likely, his move was provoked by Buridan's discussion, with which he disagrees" (Caroti 1999, 184–85).

How so? Unlike Buridan, who as we've seen claims both that numerical identity and distinctness are both primitive and also ultimately dependent on God, Oresme thinks they are essentially tied to the origins of the things in question. In question nine Oresme argues that a thing's identity depends essentially on its material and agent causes. As he puts it, "an effect whose cause is *that* matter could not have a different material cause" and "it is impossible that a given generable thing be produced by whichever of many principle agents" (Oresme 1996, 73).[16] As a result, he says, Socrates could not have been generated any other mother or any other father than the parents he had—a conclusion that may remind contemporary readers of Saul Kripke's reflections in *Naming and Necessity* on whether Queen Elizabeth could have been born to different parents, and his denial that she could have been the result of a different sperm and egg (Oresme ibid., 73 and 75; Kripke 1980,

---

[15] "Queritur nono utrum dato aliquo generabili possit a quolibet plurium agentium generari" and "decimo utrum dato aliquo generabili illud in quolibet plurium instantium possit generari."

[16] "ille effectus cuius illa materia est causa non potuit habere aliam causam materialem" and "impossibile est quod a quolibet plurium agentium principalium producatur."

112–13). Question ten extends these reflections on the necessity of a thing's material and agential origins to its temporal origins. Oresme posits that "given some generable thing it is impossible that it be produced in just whichever of many instants" (Oresme ibid., 83).[17] His reasoning is that anything that comes about through a given productive process could not possibly have come about through any other numerically different process, whereas no productive process or motion can possibly occur at a different time than it does.[18] Clearly, the conclusions Oresme reaches in the two questions are closely related to one another. According to the first question, varying the matter or agent responsible for a thing's production must necessarily vary thing produced. But similarly, according to the second question, varying the time at which the agent acts on the matter so as to bring the thing in question about must also necessarily result in a numerically different thing being produced.

Caroti's discussion of these conclusions focuses mainly on the way Oresme tries to evade the worry that they entail determinism, with each and every event in creation happening just exactly when and as it must. For present purposes, however, what is especially important to note is the way Oresme links the essentiality of a thing's causal and temporal origins with the question of gappy existence. In the question regarding temporal origins, immediately after six opening arguments each purporting to show that the time a thing comes about is *not* essential to its identity, Oresme writes that: "the opposite is argued, since if it were so, it would follow that something corrupted could be generated again, for example Caesar" (Oresme ibid., 79).[19] The unstated assumption is that it is *not* possible for Caesar to be regenerated. He doesn't explain immediately why we should rule out this possibility, but returns to the issue near the end of the question, reiterating that "it is impossible for the same thing in number be able to be regenerated," and claiming that the "foundation of this conclusion is from the preceding, and is easily proved, since then that thing could be produced twice, and thus could be produced in whichever of many instants of time, which is against the first conclusion" (ibid., 84).[20] The conclusion he refers to is that "it is impossible for any motion made in a given time to be made in a different time while remaining the same in number" (ibid., 80).[21] Oresme's reasoning isn't entirely clear (to me at least), but it seems possible that he has something like this is mind: if a thing's temporal origins are essential to its identity, then the process leading to its production cannot be repeated, and hence the thing itself cannot be

---

[17] "dato aliquo generabili in quolibet plurium instantium impossibile est illud produci."

[18] Oresme 1996, 83: "sit *a* aliquod producibile in *b* instanti sicut prius, tunc producatur productione, que sit *c*. Et arguitur sic: impossibile est *c* productionem alias ante fuisse, ergo impossibile fuit *a* produci ante."

[19] "Oppositum arguitur, quia si ita esset, sequitur quod corruptum iterum posset generari, verbi gratia Cesar."

[20] "impossibile est idem numero posse regenerari, et sic tam probatio et fundamentum huius conclusionis est ex precedentibus et probatur faciliter, quia tunc posset illud bis produci, et sic in quolibet plurium instantium posset produci, quod est contra primam conclusionem."

[21] "omnem motum factum in aliquop tempore impossibile est fieri in alio tempore idem numero."

brought back by any process subsequent to its demise. I'll discuss this reasoning further in the last section of this paper below.

What about God's ability to regenerate a corrupted body on the day of resurrection? Oresme raises this question as a potential objection against his view, responding as follows:

> Some say that God cannot regenerate the same thing in number and that it implies a contradiction, just like repeating a past time. And when it comes to the resurrection, this won't take place because of a new production or new creation, but because of the reunion of separated things, namely the soul and body. Nevertheless, it is possible supernaturally, and therefore the question should be understood naturally speaking (ibid.).[22]

The last bit of Oresme's response appears to indicate that everything he has said in the question so far applies only to the course of nature. God, he seems to say, can indeed bring the same things in number. It isn't clear whether he thinks this is because God can indeed repeat past times, or that he thinks temporal origins are not essential in cases of divine production. It is also curious that while Oresme suggests a way of handling the issue of the bodily resurrection without endorsing the possibility of gappy existence—namely by appealing to the continued existence of souls separated from bodies after death—he doesn't ultimately endorse this solution. The same is not true, however, of Marsilius, as I'll explain in the following section.

20.2 Marsilius on Origins Essentialism and Gappy Existence

Marsilius's DGC commentary shows clear signs of having been influenced both by Buridan's and Oresme's treatments of the questions discussed in the previous section. Like Oresme, Marsilius devotes two questions in the first book of his commentary to the connection between a thing's causal and temporal origins and its identity. Like Buridan, however, Marsilius also addresses a separate question directly to the question of gappy existence.

In fact, the two questions Marsilius poses concerning origins essentialism are almost exactly the same as Oresme's: "whether an effect can be generated the same in number by whichever of many agents?"—book one, question eight—and "whether in whichever of many instants the same given generable thing could be generated"—question nine (Marsilius 1518, 73ra and 74rb).[23] In responding to the first of these, while some of the opening arguments Marsilius considers are quite similar to those in Oresme's commentary, Marsilius devotes time rejecting a distinction his older contemporary had drawn between different kinds of agent causes that

---

[22] "dicunt aliqui quod Deus non potest regenerare idem numero et quod implicat contradictionem, sicut quod reiteraret tempus preteritum. Et quando erit resurrectio, non erit propter hoc nova productio aut nov creatio, sed separatorum, scilicet anime et corporis, reunio. Tamen possibile est supernaturaliter, et ideo questio debet intelligi naturaliter loquendo."

[23] "Utrum idem effectus numero posset a quolibet plurium agentium generari" and "Utrum in quolibet plurium instantium idem generabile possit generari."

somehow flow into their effects (*influentes aliquid in effectum*) and those that do not (*non influentes*) (Marsilius 1518, 73va–b and Oresme 1996, 72–73; see Caroti 1999, 187). This departure notwithstanding, Marsilius's response to the main question itself is quite similar to Oresme's. He agrees, for instance, that "variation of the matter and form that cause a substantial composite varies the substantial composite itself," with the result that "a given donkey couldn't be generated by a different donkey" and that "the same must be understood about a human and a horse and all other animals" (Marsilius 1518, 73va).[24] Likewise when it comes to agent causes Marsilius holds that "the same effect in number cannot be generated by many different agents producing that effect *per se*" (ibid., 73vb–74ra).[25] If it were possible for the different *per se* agent causes to bring about a given effect, he adds, then the same effect could be produced twice. But this is impossible, he tells us—clearly connecting here the issues of a thing's causal origins and the possibility of its being restored the same in number after ceasing to exist.[26] The same is true in question nine, where after a series of opening arguments for the conclusion that "the same given generable thing can be generated in whichever of many instants," Marsilius follows Oresme closely in writing that "the opposite is argued, first since it would follow that the same effect could be generated twice: an impossible result" (ibid., 74va).[27] Marsilius's reasoning for his principle conclusion in this question is quite similar to Oresme's as well. It is impossible for the time at which a given thing is generated to vary because it is impossible for the process of mutation through which the thing is produced to vary, and varying the time of the process must vary the process itself.[28] It follows from this, Marsilius agrees, that "the same thing in number cannot be regenerated" (ibid., 75ra).[29] If one should object that surely God is able to regenerate things that have previously ceased to exist, Marsilius says here that "the power of God acting supernaturally or miraculously doesn't concern us at present, since we are speaking physically here" (ibid.).[30] Still, he adds in conclusion:

---

[24] "variationem materie et forme effectus substantialis compositi variatur ipsum compositum"; "correlarium asinus non potuit generari ab alia asina" and "sicut haec correlaria dicta sunt de asino, ita intelligantur de homine et de equo et de aliis animalibus."

[25] "a quolibet plurium agentium per se ipsum effectum producentium non potest idem effectus numero generari."

[26] Marsilius 1518, 74ra: "probatur, quia si sic sequeretur quod idem effectus posset bis produci. Consequens est impossibile."

[27] "Oppositum arguit primo quia sequeretur quod idem effectus posset bis generari, consequens impossibile."

[28] Marsilius 1518, 74vb: "generabile datum impossibile est in quolibet plurium instantium produci. Probatur sic sit *a* generabile datum quod potuit produci in *c* instanti per mutationem *b*. Tunc arguit sic: *b* mutationem non potuit eadem in alio instanti, ergo *a* non potuit in alio intanti generari, ergo etc."

[29] "non est posse idem numero regenerari. Probatum, quia quod semel est corruptum amplius redire non potest, et ideo semel genitum non generatur idem numero."

[30] "de potentia Dei supernaturaliter aut miraculose agente nihil curatur ad praesens, sed loquimur hic physice."

It is probable to say that God couldn't bring it about that the same corrupted thing should
return or that the same thing in number should be regenerated, speaking about those things
that are truly corrupted, like a donkey or cow, for a human isn't properly corrupted, but their
form is separated from their matter (ibid.).[31]

In this question, then, like Oresme, Marsilius doesn't commit himself wholeheart-
edly to the impossibility of God's bringing things back from having ceased to exist.

What Marsilius leaves merely "probable" in book one, question nine of his commentary, however, he argues for explicitly in book two, question eighteen, which
poses the same question about gappy existence that we saw Buridan discussing in
the previous section. Of the nine opening arguments Marsilius considers for thinking that corrupted things could be restored the same in number, at least five of them
closely resemble arguments that Buridan had also introduced.[32] Marsilius's response
to the question begins, however, by drawing some distinctions that Buridan doesn't
make explicit. First, things can be generated or corrupted either subjectively (like
matter), terminatively (like form) or completively (like the composite).[33] Second,
composites can be generable either *simpliciter* by coming to exist *de novo*, or else
secundum quid, "as when the sun is called generable above our horizon" (ibid.,
128va).[34] Making use of these distinctions, Marsilius argues that something "subjectively corruptible" can indeed be "restored to the same generable form as its
substantial subject" (ibid.).[35] This is what happens, for example, when someone
knows Euclid's first proposition, then forgets it, and later remembers it. The knowledge reacquired is the same only in species, Marsilius makes clear. Furthermore,
something generable merely *secundum quid* can be generated *secundum quid* many
times numerically the same. This is what happens when the sun is many times "generated" above our horizon.[36] Lastly, however, and most importantly for present purposes, Marsilius argues that something "completively or terminatively generable"

---

[31] "probabile est dicere Deus non posse facere idem corruptum redire, aut idem numero regenerari,
loquendo de eis que vere corrumpuntur, sicut asinus et bos. Homo enim non proprie corrumpitur,
sed forma eius a materia eius separatur."

[32] Marsilius's first and second arguments incorporate points Buridan makes in his second argument,
while his third argument closely resembles Buridan's first, and Marsilius's fourth and fifth arguments correspond closely to Buridan's fourth and fifth.

[33] Marsilius 1518, 128va: "est aliquod generabile subiective ut materia, et aliquod terminative sicut
forma, et aliquod completive ut totum compositum ... similiter aliquod dicitur corruptibile subiective, puta subiectum in quo sit corruptio, aliquod terminative ut forma, et aliquod completive ut
compositum."

[34] "generabile dicitur de composito dupliciter. Uno modo simpliciter, ut homo dicitur generabilis,
quia potest fieri de novo ens. Alio modo secundum quid, ut solum dicitur generabilis super nostum
horizontem."

[35] "Idem corruptibile subiective pluries potest reverti ad eandem formam generabilem subiective
substantialiter ... similiter eadem anima potest pluries generari sub eadem scientia in species, et est
corruptibile subiective."

[36] Marsilius 1518, ibid.: "generabile secundum quid potest idem numero pluries generari secundum
quid. Probatum: quia idem sol pluries generatur super nostrum horizontem."

cannot be generated many times, either at once or successively.[37] Since he understands "being generated twice" and "being restored from corruption" as convertible turns of phrase, Marsilius's claim should be understood as denying that forms or composites of form and matter, having been corrupted, can be restored the same in number as they were before.[38] For this conclusion Marsilius offers four arguments.

The first appears to combine points from two of the arguments we saw Buridan offer above in support of a similar conclusion.[39] Marsilius claims that *if* a corrupted thing were able to return the same in number, this would have to be because the same causes that initially generated it concurred in regenerating it. As we saw above, Buridan had claimed something similar: "if something corrupted can be restored the same in number this would be on account of the agent and patient being the same and being similarly related to one another" (Buridan 2010, 182). But Marsilius goes on to argue that "the powers of purely natural agents" could never combine to produce exactly the same set of causal influences as were present at some previous time, since the exact same "celestial motions and heavens" that existed previously can never return. Nor could God bring about the restoration of a corrupted thing through a miracle. Marsilius's defense of this crucial point is unfortunately obscure. Like Buridan's reasoning about the miraculously preserved heat above, Marsilius appeals to God's ability to preserve a thing's form without the form itself. If God does this, then he clearly couldn't generate the thing anew, for cases of generation are cases of coming-to-be *de novo*, whereas in this case the thing's form would already existed. But no more could God generate a thing that had been totally corrupted, for, Marsilius says, "no reason can be found why God should be more capable of generating *b* itself with *b* having been corrupted than with it existing." Just

---

[37] Ibid.: "generabile completive seu terminative idem numero pluries generari est simpliciter impossibile sive simul sive successive."

[38] See ibid., "et quasi pro eodem accipitur corruptum posse reverti et idem bis generari."

[39] Marsilius 1518, 128va–b: "corruptum non potest idem in numero redire. Igitur non potest idem simpliciter generari bis. Consequentia tenendum: quia si bis genaretur primo corruptum posset redire. Antecedens probatur sic: quia si corruptum posset redire idem in numero hoc maxime esset propter identitatem causarum concurrentium ad suam generationem, sed propter hoc nequit redire, igitur et cetera. Maior patet: quia non videtur propter quid rediret nisi forte quia possunt omnes cause eedem reverti. Et minor declaratur. Primo in potentiis pure naturaliter agentibus constat quod non possunt omnes eedem cause redire et esse eo quod influentie et motus celestes vel celi idem in numero qui prius fuerunt nunquam redibunt per naturam. Sed quod nec per miraculum declaratur sic: quia si deus ex materia *a* generasset generabile *b* tunc isto *b* manente nunquam ipsum ex materia *a* iterum ipsum generare posset. Sed non plus posset ipsum generare si corruptum esset *b* ex iste materia. Ergo deus non potest regenerare corruptum. Ergo corrumptum nequit redire. Maior patet: quia quamvis deus formam ipsius *b* conservaret sine *b* nunquam ea. manente secundo eam generaret. Ratio quia quod generatur ante non fuit modo forma ipsius *b* ante fuit. Ergo non producitur de novo in esse. Ergo non generatur *b*. Patet: quia non est aliqua potentia ad generandum *b* de novo, quia non per hoc quod *b* est corruptum, prout notum est, nec in materia, prout manifestus est, nec in aliquo alio, quia non posset assignari ubi esset. Ergo non magis posset deus producere *b* de novo eo corrupto quam eo existente. Item propter quid esset deus potentior ad generandum *b* ipso *b* corrupto quam ipso existente non potest assignari causa igitur minor est vera."

why Marsilius takes this to be obvious is unclear, however, at least to me; I'll return to this point in the final section of this paper.

Marsilius's second argument hinges on the claim that once a form is corrupted, there is no matter that remains any longer in potency to receiving it.[40] Marsilius takes this to follow straightforwardly from the fact that "there is no power over the past." But he also defends it with a more elaborate bit of reasoning designed to show that the ability of a given portion of matter to receive a given form is entirely exhausted by its having received that form once, and hence cannot receive it any longer so as to regenerate a given composite once it has been corrupted.

His third and fourth arguments also incorporate elements reminiscent of arguments we saw from Buridan. The third argument points out simply that if discontinuity in the magnitude of an extended thing such as a piece of wood results in two pieces of wood, not one, then interruption in the existence of a given generable thing by its ceasing to exist must surely entail that any future thing coming to exist is numerically distinct from what had previously ceased.[41] Buridan had likewise argued from the impossibility of discontinuity in a thing's magnitude to the impossibility of gaps in its existence. Marsilius's fourth argument relies on a different parallel, between the impossibility of restoring a past year to the impossibility of restoring anything from the past.[42] As Marsilius puts it, "there is no more potent reason about one generable thing than about another," hence if a period of time from the past cannot be restored, then neither can any form or composite that has ceased to exist. Buridan had argued something similar, reasoning that if a given revolution of the *primum mobile* could be the same as one that had previously taken place a thousand years ago, then things existing in the world now would exist simultaneously with things that had existed in the previous millennium, given that "to exist at the same time is nothing other than to exist with the same time measuring" (Buridan 2010, 182).

Despite the parallels I have noted between Buridan's and Marsilius's arguments for the impossibility of restoring things from corruption, the two ultimately disagree about whether this feat is possible for God. Their disagreement is evident in their

---

[40] Marsilius 1518, 128b: "Forma corrupta nulla materia est amodo in potentia ad eam. Ergo non potest generari. Ergo idem nequit bis generari simpliciter. Tenent consequentiae. Antecedens probatur primo quia nulla potentia est ad preteritum. Secundo, quia tota potentia quam habet materia ad formam reducitur ad actum in generatione ipsius forme ex materia. Ergo ammodo non manet materia in potentia ad istam formam. Ergo corrupta ista forma non est materia ista plus in potentia ad eam."

[41] Ibid.: "Tertio probatur sic conclusio. Maior est interruptio in esse quam in magnitudine, sed interruptio in magnitudine impedit identitatem numeralem, ergo a fortiori in esse. Ergo si aliquid non est et prius fuit hoc nequit reverti. Ergo idem non potest bis simpliciter generari. Maior patet de se, et minor patet, quia si lignum continuum dividatur post divisionem non est idem lignum numero quod fuit ante, quia non est idem, cum non sit ens."

[42] Ibid., "Quarto sic. Iste annus nequit reverti, ergo nullum corruptum potest reverti, ergo idem bis simpliciter non potest generari. Consequentia prima tenet: quia non est potior ratio de uno generabili quam de alio."

responses to one of the opening arguments that both consider.[43] If God couldn't restore things from corruption, the argument runs, then his power diminishes every day, since yesterday he could create many things that are now corrupted and cannot be brought back. But surely God's power stays the same. Hence he must be capable of restoring things from corruption. Buridan responds to this simply that God *is* able recreate and regenerate corrupted things.[44] Marsilius, however, points out that God's power "is not less due to his inability to do what cannot be done," and that even if he cannot restore things that were corrupted, he can nevertheless make things *like* them, utilizing power equal to what it had taken to make the corrupted things.[45]

Unlike Buridan but like Oresme, Marsilius brings up the doctrine of the bodily resurrection as a potential objection against his view that it is categorically impossible for corrupted forms or composites to be restored the same in number. He declares that:

> It is easy to respond, because the generation of a human being isn't properly speaking a generation, the reason being that in a generation properly speaking there is a form that is generated, and not a form that is caused miraculously, whereas in the generation of a human there is the creation of the human form in matter. Therefore it isn't properly a generation. Similarly the corruption of a human isn't properly a corruption, since in corruption properly speaking the same form that is corrupted ceases to exist, and the substance is corrupted with the corruption of its substantial form. But in the corruption of a human no form is corrupted, but the intellective soul is just separated from its subject. And therefore the thing that is the form is not corrupted, since it remains, nor is the composite properly [corrupted], since both of its parts remain, although it truly dies because of the separation of the form from the matter (ibid., 129ra).[46]

---

[43] Buridan 2010, 180: "Si non posset idem numero reverti, sequeretur quod potentia Dei quolibet die diminueretur. Consequens falsum. Et consequentia probatur quia: Deus heri poterat multa creare quae creavit et iam corrupta sunt; et si non potest amplius ea. creare (si non possunt reverti eadem numero), ideo multa poterat quae nunc non potest; et sic potentia sua in hoc est diminuta." Marsilius 1518, 128rb: "nisi sic sequitur quod virtus Dei continue minor fieret. Consequens est falsum. Probatur consequentia, quia quodlibet generabile non genitum prius Deus potest facere, et postquam ipsum fecisset non posset ipsum iterum facere, ergo minoris virtutis esset quam ante fuisset."

[44] Buridan 2010, 185: "Ad quintam, quando dicitur quod potentia Dei esset diminuta, dico quod non, quia posset recreare et regenerare corrupta."

[45] Marsilius 1518, 129rb: "Ad quintum dicitur quod virtus Dei non redditur minor quia non potest facere corruptum reverti, quia tale non potest reverti, modo non est virtus eius minor eo quod impossibile fieri non potest facere. Et ad probationem istius dicitur quod licet Deus ante potest facere *a* et non potest postea, tamen postea potest facere simile ipsi *a* quid facere includit tantam potentiam sicut facere *a*, et ideo ratio non procedit."

[46] "Respondetur faciliter quod hominis generatio non est proprie generatio. Et est ratio, quia: in generatione proprie dicta est forma que generatur et non forma que causatur miraculose; modo hominis generatio est creatio forme humane in materia; igitur non est proprie generatio. Similiter corruptio hominis non est proprie corruptio, quia in corruptione proprie dicta desinit ess forma que corrumpitur, et corrumpitur substantia in corruptione sue forme substantialis. Modo in corruptione hominis nulla forma corrumpitur, sed solum anima intellectiva a suo subiectio separatur. Et ideo non corrumpitur res que est forma, cum ipsa maneat, nec compositum proprie, cum ambe eius partes maneant, licet bene moriatur propter separationem forme a materia."

Oresme had suggested a response along these lines, but backed away from endorsing it fully. Marsilius, however, appears willing to accept that the possibility of the bodily resurrection depends upon the immortality of the human soul.

20.3 How Plausible Is Marsilius's Position?

Having seen how Marsilius connects the issues of temporal origins essentialism and gappy existence, building on the work of his predecessors Buridan and Oresme, I turn in this section to the philosophical plausibility of Marsilius's views and arguments. Is there really such a strong connection between the two issues as all three authors seem to believe there is? If so, is it strong enough to uphold Marsilius's unusual position with respect to God's inability to restore things that have ceased to exist? To address these questions it will be helpful to consider briefly an article of Gyula Klima's on gappy existence in the thought of Thomas Aquinas (Klima 2016).

The article focuses on a question from Aquinas's fourth quodlibetal session (q. 3, a. 2), held probably in Lent of 1271, which asks "whether God can restore numerically the same thing which was reduced to nothing?" (Aquinas 1996, 325).[47] Aquinas responds that even God cannot restore certain "successive" entities to existence once they are gone, since the notion of continuity is built into their very essences, and interruption in this continuity is repugnant to it, destroying them forever. Motions and times are things of this sort. But the essences of "permanent" entities do not include continuity of duration, and hence Aquinas says that God can indeed restore these entities, although natural agents cannot. Why this distinction between what God and natural agents can do? Because natural agents can only bring things about by means of some motion—a process of generation, presumably. So because motions, being successive entities, cannot be restored, natural agents cannot employ the numerically same motions so as to restore numerically the same permanent entities once they have ceased to exist. God, however, can "produce an effect without the intermediate causes," and hence can bring beings into existence without any

---

[47] "Si aliquid esset in nihilum redactum, utrum Deus possit illud reparare idem numero?" Here is Aquinas's reply in full: "Respondeo. Dicendum, quod in his quae in nihilum redigi possunt, est quaedam differentia attendenda. Quaedam enim sunt quorum unitas in sui ratione habet durationis continuitatem, sicut patet in motu et tempore; et ideo interruptio talium indirecte contrariatur unitati eorum secundum numerum. Ea vero quae contradictionem implicant, non continentur sub numero Deo possibilium, quia deficiunt a ratione entis: et ideo, si huiusmodi in nihilum redigantur, Deus ea. non potest eadem numero reparare. Hoc enim esset facere contradictoria simul esse vera; puta si motus interruptus esset unus. Alia vero sunt quorum unitas non habet in sui ratione continuitatem durationis, sicut unitas rerum permanentium, nisi per accidens, in quantum eorum esse subiectum est motui: sic enim et mensurantur huiusmodi tempore, et eorum esse est unum et continuum, secundum unitatem et continuitatem temporis. Et quia natura agens non potest ista producere sine motu, inde est quod naturale agens non potest huiusmodi reparare eadem numero, si in nihilum redacta fuerit, vel si fuerint secundum substantiam corrupta. Sed Deus potest reparare huiusmodi et sine motu, quia in eius potestate est quod producat effectus sine causis mediis; et ideo potest eadem numero reparare, etiamsi in nihilum elapsa fuerint."

motion—any process of generation. Accordingly, he can indeed restore permanent beings that have previously ceased to exist.

So much is agreed upon by all readers of Aquinas's quodlibetal question, but at this point Klima's interpretation diverges from the medieval consensus by suggesting that Aquinas's reply introduces a further distinction between two different kinds of permanent things, some of which have an act of being "subject to motion," other of which do not. Klima's reading is that the former sort of permanent beings includes all sublunary material substances, along with their permanent material accidents, such as qualities and quantities. It includes humans too. Hence, Klima writes:

> Our being, our existence, that is, our life, is clearly measured by the years (months, weeks, days, minutes, seconds, etc.) we have lived, and it is equally clear that we cannot have our entire life all together at once, but only in a temporal sequence, one part after another. So, our existence is successive, just like motions or processes are. ... Therefore, even if in the case of permanent things such as sublunary material substances there is nothing to prevent their re-creation on account of *what* they are, that is, their essence, they cannot be re-created on account of *how* they are, that is, on account of the kind of existence that this sort of essence determines for them, which is temporal, and hence successive, because it is divisible *secundum prius et posteriorius*, which requires continuity for its unity (Klima 2016, 124 and 129).

On Klima's interpretation Aquinas agrees with Marsilius about sublunary material substances and forms that once they are gone, they are gone forever. He agrees too with Marsilius's explanation how the bodily resurrection remains a supernatural possibility:

> Even if our death is the end of our existence absolutely speaking, our existence is continued in the same, uninterrupted act of existence of our immortal soul. Therefore, we *can* be resurrected to the same life that ceased to be ours when we ceased to be, but which itself never ceased to be, and will be ours again forever, once our immortal souls are reunited with our bodies in the supernatural act of resurrection (Klima 2016, 129).

As mentioned, Klima's interpretation of Aquinas was a minority view in the Middle Ages. Toledo, to name just one example, cites Aquinas along with Giles of Rome as holding that God, though not natural agents, is able to restore any and all permanent beings that have ceased to exist (Toledo 1588, 307). Scotus appears to read Aquinas in Klima's way only to criticize his view, whereas Durand of St. Pourçain appears to agree with both the interpretation and the view itself.[48]

I bring up Klima's reading of Aquinas, however, not to reconsider its feasibility as an interpretation, but rather for the light it sheds on the arguments from Marsilius and the others discussed above. Why do Oresme and Marsilius consider the necessity of a thing's origins and the impossibility of its regeneration (at least naturally speaking) to follow from one another? They do not spell it out for us very clearly. But one possibility is that their basic line of thought resembles the reasoning Aquinas gives for denying that natural agents can restore permanent things after

---

[48] See Scotus 1894, 5–6, discussed in Wood 2015, 122–23 and Durand 2012, 45–46. Wood 2015 defends an interpretation of Aquinas much like Klima's, as does Toner 2015, while Nevitt 2016a, b criticizes it, interpreting Aquinas in line with Toledo and the medieval consensus.

they have ceased to exist. A permanent thing could only be restored through some process of generation. But the numerical identity of processes of generation are individuated by the times at which they occur, and hence no two such processes occurring at different times could be numerically identical to one another. Accordingly, the results of two such processes must differ numerically as well.

So far, so good, it might be thought, but why couldn't God bring permanent things back *without* any process of generation, as Aquinas suggests he might? Two possibilities suggest themselves.

Above I noted that in his first argument against the possibility of things being restored Marsilius rather disappointingly rules out the possibility of this happening by a miracle simply by saying that "no reason can be found why God should be more capable of generating [a given thing] *b* itself with *b* having been corrupted than with it existing."[49] He doesn't explain why this is so. Perhaps, however, Marsilius simply assumes that God would require *some* process of generation to restore any natural thing to existence, even it is a miraculous one.

Another possibility, however, is that Marsilius agrees with Klima's Aquinas that sublunary material substances and their forms must exist continuously, just as motions or times or spatial magnitudes must be continuous. That would explain why Marsilius thinks we can argue successfully from what is true of times or spatial magnitudes to what is true of all composites or forms in nature. If it is true that natural composites and forms, because their acts of being are subject to time and motion, must exist continuously, then it doesn't really matter by what sort of process they come about. Their numerical identity is still going to be traceable to the time at which they come about. So whether we call the putative miraculous process regeneration or recreation, it is necessarily going to be temporally distinct from the process that brought about the natural thing in the first place. And given the necessary distinctness of temporally distinct processes, and the corresponding necessary distinct of their product, perhaps Marsilius takes it to be obvious that God incapable of generating natural things after they have been corrupted.

Is this reasoning sound? Buridan's comments on individuation suggest one way of challenging it. As Buridan explains matters in the question I considered above, while it might be true that we commonly rely on a thing's temporal origins in our thinking about numerical identity and distinctness, things are identical or distinct from one another primitively, and ultimately by divine fiat. God chooses to make the world a certain way, and by that choice things simply are the individuals they are, end of story. Now, if this view is correct, then one might object to Marsilius and Klima's Aquinas alike when they reject the possibility of gappy existence in sublunary material entities. It might be true that a thing's identity is originally tied to its temporal origins. But if a thing should exist for a while, then cease to exist, whether or not something coming into existence in the future is numerically identical to it or not is ultimately up to God. He is the one who settles the question whether the future event is genuinely an act of coming into being or whether it is merely an act of

---

[49] See n. 39 above.

resuming an interrupted existence. In contrast, if Marsilius is correct, then anything coming into existence in time is marked by its temporal origins as necessarily distinct from anything that has existed before or might come into being afterwards. It is worth noting that some contemporary philosophers continue to follow Kripke in defending versions of origins essentialism related to Marsilius and Oresme's.[50] But I won't attempt to defend their view against Buridan's here. Nor, unfortunately, have I had the opportunity to consult in detail Marsilius's discussion of the resurrection in his *Sentences* commentary, an edition of which is currently under preparation. It is to be hoped that examination of that text, along with further study of his DGC commentary, may help us further to understand Marsilius's origins essentialism and his uncommon stance on gappy existence are related.

Bibliography

Aquinas, Thomas. 1996. *Quaestiones de quolibet*. In *Opera omnia jussu Leonis XIII P. M. edita, t. 25/2*. Rome: Leonine Commission.

Aristotle. 1984. On generation and corruption. Trans. H.H. Joachim in *The complete works of Aristotle*, ed. Jonathan Barnes. Princeton: Princeton University Press.

Braakhuis, H.A.G. 1997. John Buridan and the "Parisian school" on the possibility of returning numerically the same. A note on a chapter in the history of the relationship between faith and natural science. In *La nouvelle physique du XIVe siècle*, ed. S. Caroti and P. Souffrin, 111–140. Florence: Olschki.

Buridan, John. 2010. Quaestiones super libros De generatione et corruptione Aristotelis, ed. Michiel Streijger, Paul J.J.M. Bakker and Johannes M.M.H. Thijssen. Leiden: Brill.

Caroti, Stefano. 1999. "Generatio potest auferri, non differri." Causal order and natural necessity in Nicole Oresme's *Questiones super De generatione et corruptione*. In *The Commentary Tradition on Aristotle's "De generatione et corruptione,"* ed. J.M.M.H. Thijssen and H.A.G. Braakhuis, 183–205. Turnhout: Brepols.

Durand of St. Pourçain. 2012. Scriptum super IV libros Sententiarum. In *Distinctiones 43–50 libri quarti*, ed. Thomas Jeschke. Leuven: Peeters.

King, Peter O. 1994. Jean Buridan (b. ca. 1295/1300; d. after 1358). In *Individuation in scholasticism. The later middle ages and the counter-reformation, 1150–1650*, ed. Jorge J.E. Gracia, 397–430. Buffalo: State University of New York Press.

Klima, Gyula. 2016. The problem of "gappy existence" in Aquinas's metaphysics and theology. In *The metaphysics of personal identity*, ed. G. Klima, Alexander Hall, and Stephen Ogden, 119–134. Newcastle upon Tyne: Cambridge Scholars Publishing.

Kripke, Saul. 1980. *Naming and necessity*. Cambridge, MA: Harvard University Press.

Marsilius of Inghen. 1518. *Quaestiones in libros De generatione et corruptione*. In *Egidius cum Marsilio et Alberto de generatione*. Venice.

Nevitt, Turner. 2016a. Annihilation, re-creation and intermittent existence in Aquinas. In *The metaphysics of personal identity*, ed. G. Klima, Alexander Hall, and Stephen Ogden, 101–118. Newcastle upon Tyne: Cambridge Scholars Publishing.

———. 2016b. Don't mind the gap: A reply to Adam Wood. *Oxford Studies in Medieval Philosophy* 4: 198–2013.

Oresme, Nicole. 1996. In *Quaestiones super De generatione et corruptione*, ed. Stefano Caroti. Munich: Bayerische Akademie der Wissenschaften.

---

[50] See, for example, Rohrbaugh and DeRosset 2004.

Rohrbaugh, Guy, and Louis DeRosset. 2004. A new route to the necessity of origin. *Mind* 113 (452): 705–725.

Scotus, John Duns. 1894. *Ordinatio*. In *Joannis Duns Scoti Opera omnia, t. 20*, ed. L. Wadding. Paris: Vives.

Toledo, Francisco. 1588. *Commentaria in librum De generatione et corruptione Aristotelis*. London: Sib. á Porta.

Toner, Patrick. 2015. St. Thomas Aquinas on gappy existence. *Analytic Philosophy* 56 (1): 94–110.

Wood, Adam. 2015. Mind the gap? The principle of non-repeatability and Aquinas's account of the resurrection. *Oxford Studies in Medieval Philosophy* 3: 99–127.

Chapter 21
John of Ripa and the Metaphysics of Christology

Richard Cross

Keywords John of Ripa · *homo assumptus* · Christology · Deification

In 1959, Paul Vignaux wrote a short piece on the Christology of John of Ripa for the *mélanges* offered to Étienne Gilson (Vignaux 1959). Apart from that short article, Ripa's Christology—which, it turns out, is quite unusual—has received scant attention from commentators. So, much as Vignaux thought it an appropriate topic with which to honor Gilson, I chose it to honor another great medievalist and philosopher, albeit one about as different from Gilson as could be imagined: Gyula Klima. And I do so too to recall the memory of the two French scholars just mentioned.

Now, one thing that unites Gilson and Klima, of course, is an overarching—one might almost say unholy—interest in the thought of Thomas Aquinas. Doubtless another such thing would be deep suspicion of John of Ripa, the super-subtle doctor excoriated by Jean Gerson because he was too dependent on the already-subtle doctor Duns Scotus: the latter himself rendered rather suspect in Gerson's mind by (among other things) association with the realism of the recently-condemned John Wyclif.

As it turns out, the aspect of Ripa's thought that I shall consider here does have some relation to Aquinas. As the title of Vignaux's piece suggests ("The dogma of the Incarnation and the metaphysics of form in John of Ripa"), the idea that God might be in some sense the form of a creature is central to Ripa's Christology. Vignaux, in his piece, does not pick out the all-important motivation for this in Ripa's account of the Savior—something I shall return to below. But it is hard not to be reminded of Aquinas's view that in the beatific vision the divine essence comes to be in some manner a *form* of the intellect: not an inherent form, but some kind of intellectual form, playing a role akin to that played in standard cases by the

R. Cross (✉)
University of Notre Dame, Notre Dame, IN, USA
e-mail: richard.cross@nd.edu

J. P. Hochschild et al. (eds.), *Metaphysics Through Semantics: The Philosophical Recovery of the Medieval Mind*, International Archives of the History of Ideas Archives internationales d'histoire des idées 242,
https://doi.org/10.1007/978-3-031-15026-5_21

377

intelligible species. This idea, of course, is one that Aquinas has borrowed from Averroes.[1] Ripa himself credits it to Hugh of St Victor, as we shall see; and doubt-less underlying that is Pseudo-Dionysius. So, there is a complex genealogy or gene-alogies underlying Ripa's view. But that is not what I am concerned with here, though doubtless tracing the links between Ripa's Christology and his theory of cognition would be a task well worth undertaking.

Ripa's Christology has two distinctive features. The first is an attempt to under-stand the basic metaphysical structure of the union of divine person and human nature in terms of the formal actualization of the human nature by the divine person. The second distinctive feature is Ripa's acceptance of a *homo assumptus* Christology: the view that the assumption of a human *nature* consists fundamentally in the assumption of a human *being*, an assumed man (*homo assumptus*). It is highly unusual to find this view in the developed Christologies of the later Middle Ages, since talk of an assumed man was associated with the (heretical) view that there are two *persons* in Christ, a divine one (a God) and a human one (a man or human being). Indeed, the only other late medieval thinker known to me who accepts such a view is none other than Wyclif himself.

There is a further difficulty too. If "man" here refers not to the divine person (as in Chalcedonian orthodoxy) but to the assumed human nature, it looks as though predications such as "this human being is God" or "this human being is impassible" will require the human nature to bear the relevant divine attributes—which looks as though it will simply obliterate the human nature. So, not only are such Christologies in danger of Nestorianism; they seem to be in danger of the opposite worry too: monophysitism. *Homo assumptus* Christologies can be found in the earlier Western tradition from Augustine to Hugh of St. Victor, but after the translation of John of Damascus's *De fide orthodoxa* in the 1250s they were generally rejected.

The two positions that Ripa accepts—that the divine person is something like a form of the human nature, and that the assumed nature is an assumed human being—are in principle independent of each other. Thus, it would be possible to accept an actualization model of the union without accepting the *homo assumptus*; and it would be possible to accept a *homo assumptus* Christology without accepting an actualization model. In what follows, I first of all outline the basic structure of Ripa's actualization model, and then show how it applies specifically to a *homo assumptus* Christology. We shall see that Ripa blocks the Nestorian worry by argu-ing that being the same as a person does not entail being a person; and that being God does not entail being the divine essence. What remains unclear to me is what prompted Ripa to accept such a difficult and unfashionable view in the first place.

---

[1] The *locus classicus* here is Aquinas, *In Sent.* IV, d. 49, q. 2, a. 1 c. (Aquinas 2000).

21.1   God as Formal Cause

The eleventh and final conclusion in Ripa's extended discussion of the question of whether or not the Word "can be united [to the human nature] in essential *esse* (*esse essentiali*)"[2] is the following: "it is not possible for the divine essence, from the power of the union—be it essential or supposital—to be united to a creature intrinsically and informatively."[3] In his discussion of this conclusion, Ripa distinguishes two kinds of form: "subsistent, not apt to inhere," and "inherent, or apt to inhere."[4] The first kind includes the divine essence and separated substances; the second, substantial forms (including the human soul) and accidents.[5] According to Ripa, both kinds of form "are communicable": the first "are subsistent forms, [and], if they are communicated, actuate in a subsistent way (*subsistenter*)"; the second "actuate inherently and in an in-existent way."[6] The second of these involves both perfection (actuating) and imperfection (natural aptitude for being part of a composite).[7] Now, Ripa takes it to be a feature of the technical term "information" that it is restricted to the second kind of communication. So, the divine essence cannot be communicated "informatively."[8] But it can be "subsistently and terminatively the form of a creature,"[9] and thus "God can be the form of a creature, or is able to have formal causality in relation to a creature"[10]: "In such a union the divine essence was the form of a creature, not in-existently and informatively, but subsistently and terminatively."[11]

The gist of this is that the divine essence can be the form of a creature, but without informing the creature. (Admittedly, Ripa acknowledges that "names are conventional, and if someone wants to use ['information' for any type of communication] here, they can."[12]) In the earlier part of the discussion, Ripa rejects the view that the divine essence could be a "constitutive" form,[13] or an "intrinsically perfective form."[14] But he then proposes a sequence of conclusions that culminates in the eleventh, just discussed, in which he nevertheless finds ways in which the divine essence can in some sense be the form of a created nature. There is a theological assumption here, which is that the "divine essence, as personal subsistence, is communicable to

---

[2] Ripa, *Determinationes* [= *Det.*], q. 1, a. 3 (Ripa 1957, 88.82).

[3] *Det.*, q. 1, a. 3 (Ripa 1957, 102.4–6).

[4] *Det.*, q. 1, a. 3 (Ripa 1957, 102.7–8).

[5] See *Det.*, q. 1, a. 3 (Ripa 1957, 102.8–18).

[6] *Det.*, q. 1, a. 3 (Ripa 1957, 102.20–22).

[7] See *Det.*, q. 1, a. 3 (Ripa 1957, 102.36–103.42).

[8] See *Det.*, q. 1, a. 3 (Ripa 1957, 102.22–6).

[9] *Det.*, q. 1, a. 3 (Ripa 1957, 105.2–3).

[10] *Det.*, q. 1, a. 3 (Ripa 1957, 105.11–13).

[11] *Det.*, q. 1, a. 3 (Ripa 1957, 103.67–9).

[12] *Det.*, q. 1, a. 3 (Ripa 1957, 102.29–30).

[13] See *Det.*, q. 1, a. 3 (Ripa 1957, 80.4–82.93).

[14] *Det.*, q. 1, a. 3 (Ripa 1957, 82.95; see too 88.80).

a creature."[15] This union cannot be explained by the divine person's personal property, since "in God no supposital feature (*ratio*) is, as opposed to an essential feature, formally act or form; therefore the communication of no such [feature] is communication in the *esse* of act and form."[16] But the point, as we shall see shortly, is that the divine essence can be communicated along with a divine subsistence or personal property.

If the hypostatic union is to be possible, then it must be explained in some sense by the communication of the divine essence, as a form. So, first, "the formal [component] of each essential divine notion (*rationis*) is really communicable *ad extra* by union with a creature."[17] Secondly, this is necessarily "through fullness as to degree."[18] Given divine simplicity, it is not possible that the divine essence is united "according to some essential notion and not according to the fullness of deity,"[19] and thus it is "possible for the divine essence to be really united to a creature according to the whole essential fullness of divine *esse*."[20] In favor of this last conclusion, Ripa mentions the view of "Bonaventure" and "Scotus" that "the divine essence can be the *per se* end term of the union of the created nature, discounting any relative personality."[21]

From all of this, Ripa concludes that "from the force both of the personal union and of the essential [union], the divine essence is made intrinsic to the thing united."[22] He explains his terms with considerable care:

> Here I call 'essential union' that which is to the divine essence, in essential *esse*, such that essential *esse* is *per se* firstly the end term of the union; 'personal', that which [is] to the *suppositum* as such; and here I call something 'intrinsic to another' from whose union or real communication that to which it is united is really changed.[23]

For reasons we shall see below, Ripa regards both unions—that to essential *esse* and that to personal *esse*—as necessary for the hypostatic union. Here he states that the essential union is prior to the personal union. It follows from the essential union that the union is "formal," because the divine essence is a form.[24] And this in turn entails that "it is the divine essence's union of formal causality with respect to the creature,"[25] and that it is thus "possible for the divine essence to be united to a

---

[15] *Det.*, q. 1, a. 3 (Ripa 1957, 86.94–5).

[16] *Det.*, q. 1, a. 3 (Ripa 1957, 87.22–4).

[17] *Det.*, q. 1, a. 3 (Ripa 1957, 88.84–5).

[18] *Det.*, q. 1, a. 3 (Ripa 1957, 92.39).

[19] *Det.*, q. 1, a. 3 (Ripa 1957, 94.81–3).

[20] *Det.*, q. 1, a. 3 (Ripa 1957, 95.94–5).

[21] *Det.*, q. 1, a. 3 (Ripa 1957, 95.3–6).

[22] *Det.*, q. 1, a. 3 (Ripa 1957, 96.35–6).

[23] *Det.*, q. 1, a. 3 (Ripa 1957, 96.37–41).

[24] See *Det.*, q. 1, a. 3 (Ripa 1957, 100.73–101.92).

[25] *Det.*, q. 1, a. 3 (Ripa 1957, 101.93–4).

creature as an intrinsic formal cause."[26] From this Ripa infers the eleventh conclusion with which I started this section.

21.2   Ripa's Christology

My discussion up to this point has left it perhaps mysterious why Ripa would want to defend the view that the divine essence can be, after a fashion, the form of the human nature—something that Vignaux does not make clear in his discussion either. But two conclusions that I have not thus far discussed, the fifth and the sixth, make the motivation quite plain:

> It is not possible for something to be united to the deity, really, through its fullness, and not be really God, that is, through the *communicatio idiomatum*.[27]
>
> It is absolutely possible for something to be God and really distinct from the deity.[28]

So, while Ripa denies that the divine essence informs the human nature such as to make a composite, he ascribes to it the full truth-making function ascribed to informing forms. As the two conclusions just quoted make plain, the communication of the divine essence to the human nature grounds the predication "this man—this human nature—is God." The same goes for all divine attributes:

> Whatever is united really to the deity according to every essential notion really communicates with the deity according to every perfection unqualifiedly. Therefore it is concretely a universally perfect being. Therefore it is God. Furthermore, if the divine essence were united informatively to some thing, that thing would be God concretely. But any real union with the divine *esse* is no less perfect and intimate, provided that it is through essential fullness. Therefore what is united is, from the force of the union, really God.[29]

Talk of something being "concretely" God is intended to exclude the identity of the item—in this case, the human nature—with the deity as such: the human nature is God, and has divine attributes, but it is not the deity, or the divine goodness, or wisdom. It is divine without being the deity. And the divine essence achieves this for the human nature in much the way that an inherent form grounds predication: my wisdom, such as it is, is the formal explanation for my being finitely wise; the divine wisdom is the formal explanation for the united item's being infinitely wise.

This is on any showing a remarkable doctrine. The assumed human nature is God, and is infinitely wise, and so on: "something is in fact God that is not the deity—that is, the individual man assumed by the Word."[30] Now, the human nature and the divine nature are distinct natures: "no union to the deity destroys the essential distinction of the natures, otherwise there would be through that union a confu-

---

[26] *Det.*, q. 1, a. 3 (Ripa 1957, 101.99–100).

[27] *Det.*, q. 1, a. 3 (Ripa 1957, 95.7–9).

[28] *Det.*, q. 1, a. 3 (Ripa 1957, 96.22–3).

[29] *Det.*, q. 1, a. 3 (Ripa 1957, 96.10–17).

[30] *Det.*, q. 1, a. 3 (Ripa 1957, 96.32–3).

sion or substantial conversion of the natures; therefore whatever is essentially God through the union is distinguished from the deity."[31] But the human nature and the divine person are not distinct Gods or distinct persons. As Ripa puts it elsewhere, "wherever deity were communicated formally to diverse things, such diverse things would be one God, since they communicate in the same *esse* of the deity both formally and subsistently."[32]

To correspond to the two kinds of formal communication he outlines, Ripa develops distinctive semantic analyses. He starts from the case of denominative predication (e.g. "this is white"—to use Ripa's example). "Denominatives," he claims, "can be taken adjectivally or substantivally." The point is merely grammatical: adjectives ("denominatives") can have substantival uses too in Latin. Now, suppose that the same whiteness belongs to two subjects. Taking "white" adjectivally, we count *whites* in terms of the number of the accident: so, "they are one in white, adjectivally (that is, one *esse* of white)"; taking "white" substantivally, we count *whites* in terms of the number of subjects: so, they are "two whites (that is, two subjects of white)."[33] The case in which the relevant form comes to be in some way the same as the item to which it is communicated—the same *God*, for instance—seems to exemplify the opposite principle, as in the last sentence of the previous paragraph: there is one form—the divine essence along with the Son's subsistence—in virtue of which the natures, divine and human, are one person. So, we count one. The human nature is in some sense identical with an item that is both God and the divinity. The contrast with standard views is this. In standard accounts, going right back to Cyril of Alexandria, the referents of both "God" and "man" are the divine person; neither can refer to the human nature; and what makes it true that God is man is that the divine person bears the human nature in a way akin to that in which a substance bears an accident.

The expressly Christological part of the *Determinationes* develops in a little more detail the basic line of thinking just sketched. Again, Ripa develops his argument in a series of conclusions. The first is that "it is not possible for the divine essence to be united to a creature in the *esse* of essence (*esse essentiae*) and not in the *esse* of personal subsistence (*esse personalis subsistentiae*)."[34] The reason is that essence and personal subsistence are inseparable, and thus that union with essence brings along with it union in personal subsistence.[35] And union with essence is prior because essence is metaphysically prior to personal property.[36]

Secondly, while union with personal subsistence is necessary given union with divine essence, it is nevertheless a contingent matter which of the three divine

---

[31] *Det.*, q. 1, a. 3 (Ripa 1957, 96.28–31).

[32] *Det.*, q, 1, a. 3 (Ripa 1957, 142.93–6).

[33] *Det.*, q. 1, a. 3 (Ripa 1957, 141.85–7).

[34] *Det.*, q. 1, a. 4 (Ripa 1957, 154.14–15).

[35] See *Det.*, q. 1, a. 4 (Ripa 1957, 154.16–19).

[36] See *Det.*, q. 1, a. 4 (Ripa 1957, 154.20–3).

personal subsistences is united.[37] The intra-Trinitarian productions show that the communication of the divine essence does not involve the communication of any given personal property.[38]

So, the communication of the divine essence requires the communication of a divine subsistence. Ripa next considers whether the communication of the divine essence is necessary for the communication of the divine subsistence. He claims that it is indeed necessary, though with the qualification that he posits the conclusion "as probable,"[39] as being supported by positive arguments:

> If such a [personal] union is possible without the essential [union], it follows that it is possible for something to be the divine Word and yet not be God by the *communicatio idiomatum*. The consequent is impossible. And I prove the consequence, for the divine Word is denominated 'God' not by the supposital character (*rationem*) but by the essential [character]: for being God is an essential denomination. Therefore, if *per impossibile* the Word existed according to supposital *esse* and not according to essenital [*esse*], the Word would not be God. Therefore if the Word is united according to supposital *esse* and not according to essential [*esse*], the thing [united] would not have, from the force of the union, that it is God.[40]

The (counterfactual) proposal is that the human nature is united (in the way described above) to the supposital property but not the divine essence. Note that, as we saw in the previous section, Ripa has already rejected the view that the supposital property could be a form; but here he seems to be countenancing this possibility by way of defending his stated conclusion. In the counterfactual case considered here, the human nature would be the Word without being God, in much the same way as the Word would (*per impossibile*) fail to be God if the Father conferred the Word's personal property without conferring the divine essence.

Ripa offers two further arguments. One is that if essential *esse* cannot be united without personal *esse*, then, given the priority of essence over personal property, it follows "much more" that personal *esse* cannot be united without essential *esse*.[41] The other is that union merely to personal property would not render the nature more perfect, given the (Scotist) assumption that personal properties are not perfections. This would mean that hypostatic union would be a less perfect condition than the possession of any created form: a possibility that Ripa "will not freely concede."[42]

Given this, Ripa's fourth conclusion is that the divine essence is indeed united "according to essential *esse*" to the human nature.[43] The basic reason is that "by this union of the human nature to the Word, man is God; therefore the humanity is united not only to the deity in supposital *esse*, but also in *esse essentiae*."[44] In support, Ripa

---

[37] See *Det.*, q. 1, a. 4 (Ripa 1957, 155.35–6).

[38] See *Det.*, q. 1, a. 4 (Ripa 1957, 155.37–44).

[39] See *Det.*, q. 1, a. 4 (Ripa 1957, 156.79–80).

[40] *Det.*, q. 1, a. 4 (Ripa 1957, 157.99–7).

[41] See *Det.*, q. 1, a. 4 (Ripa 1957, 156.81–4).

[42] See *Det.*, q. 1, a. 4 (Ripa 1957, 157.89–95).

[43] See *Det.*, q. 1, a. 4 (Ripa 1957, 158.28–30).

[44] *Det.*, q. 1, a. 4 (Ripa 1957, 159.49–51).

quotes a series of texts from Augustine asserting the conferral of divine properties on the "assumed man."[45]

The final two conclusions seem to state much the same thesis again, making explicit some things that follow from the discussion in the previous article: "the divine essence according to the whole essential fullness of the deity is united to the human nature in unity of the Word's *suppositum*,"[46] and "the divine essence, even if it is not really united in the *esse* of an informative form, [is] nevertheless [united] in the *esse* of a subsistent form terminating the human nature and each part [of it]."[47] In support of the first of these, Ripa first of all quotes a Christological text classically understood as demonstrating the union of the divine subsistence *and essence* to the assumed man: "In Christ… inhabits the whole fullness of the divinity corporeally" (Col. 2:9).[48] And, again, both conclusions are supported by a catena of relevant texts from Augustine, Hugh of St. Victor, and Peter Lombard—the former two authorities in support of the *homo assumptus*, and the latter in support of the view that God could be something like a form.

One objection to Ripa's position is that, if Ripa is correct, it will follow that the communication, to Christ's body in the tomb, of the divine essence—which includes the divine life—will mean that the body is alive. Ripa's replies give some clues as to how he analyses locutions in which the divine essence and attributes are predicated of the assumed man. He offers three possible alternative responses. The first two accept the objector's conclusion that there is a sense in which the body in the tomb is alive; the third rejects it. I examine all three in turn.

The first is that "in the triduum God was flesh and flesh God; and in this way that flesh of Christ was alive in the triduum—not formally informatively, but terminatively and subsistently, for it was united to immense subsistent life, immensely, and for this reason subsistently alive."[49] So the predication is grounded not in the divine person's informing the flesh, but in the divine person's being united as a terminating subsistent form: precisely the analysis noted above. Ripa gives an example: "a stone can be called 'rational' and 'alive' by the *communicatio idiomatum*—for example, if God united [to God] the nature of a stone—for then the stone would be God."[50] In effect, Ripa simply bites the bullet, and presumably deals with potential contradictions by claiming that in cases in which one form informs and another apparently inconsistent form merely terminates, formal contradiction is avoided.

The second response is similarly bullet-biting. Ripa draws on his distinction between taking denominative terms such as "alive" adjectivally and substantively. The first is based on the essential or accidental possession of life; the second is based on identity (of some sort) with something that is alive. In the first way, it is not

---

[45] *Det.*, q. 1, a. 4 (Ripa 1957, 158–9).

[46] *Det.*, q. 1, a. 4 (Ripa 1957, 160.61–2).

[47] *Det.*, q. 1, a. 4 (Ripa 1957, 164.79–81).

[48] *Det.*, q. 1, a. 4 (Ripa 1957, 160.64–5).

[49] *Det.*, q. 1, a. 3 (Ripa 1957, 128.36–129.39).

[50] *Det.*, q. 1, a. 3 (Ripa 1957, 128.34–5).

true that the body is alive; in the second way, it is true.[51] (Note that Ripa does not appear to assent to the view that the body was dead.)

The third possible response denies that the body was alive. For a body to be alive, it must be used by a created soul in sensory activity. God cannot use a body such that "some vital act of divine life… is exercised through the body as an instrument."[52] I must say, this response seems to concede too much. If God cannot communicate life to the body since the body is not appropriately receptive of such life, then one might be forgiven for wondering whether the same kinds of consideration might lead one to conclude that God cannot communicate any divine attribute to the body.

A more severe objection along the same lines is that positing that the assumed humanity is a divine person without being the divinity compromises the doctrine of the Trinity, namely that there are just three divine persons:

> When it is said that the soul of Christ is God, or that the flesh is God, 'God' supposits [either] for the deity (and then it is false), or for the subsistence of the deity (and thus it is denominated that the soul of Christ is suppositally God), and thus it is true according to all Catholics: for it is united to God in unity of person, and consequently has the same *per se esse* as the deity. Thus it is God personally.[53]

The nature is non-identically the same as the divine person, and in this sense is God. How many divine persons does that make? One, according to Ripa, presumably because he supposes that we count persons by some kind of numerical sameness falling short of strict identity. But note that this is not at all how most "Catholics" understood the matter: what makes personal predications true is that the divine person sustains a human nature, not that the divine person is non-identically the same as a human nature.

Again, as we shall see in a moment, a series of objections claims that Ripa's position is incompatible with certain divine attributes. I consider first Ripa's replies to two of these: that God cannot be created, and that God cannot be communicated to a creature. Against the first, Ripa reasons as follows:

> The argument concludes against every Catholic, for whether the deity is communicated to the flesh of Christ informatively or merely subsistently and personally, provided that it is really communicated, this cannot be other than through a divine action; therefore through creation; therefore God is created. For just as anything that has the deity informatively is formally God, thus whatever has the deity subsistently and terminatively is really God, on account of the greater unity with divine *esse*.[54]

I take it that the "greater unity" referred to in the final sentence here is unity with the divine essence possessed "terminatively," relative to unity with a form possessed "informatively."

---

[51] See *Det.*, q. 1, a. 3 (Ripa 1957, 129.40–8).

[52] See *Det.*, q. 1, a. 3 (Ripa 1957, 129.49–64).

[53] *Det.*, q. 1, a. 3 (Ripa 1957, 130.81–6).

[54] *Det.*, q. 1, a. 3 (Ripa 1957, 148.73–8).

The reply to the second of these objections illustrates very nicely Ripa's bullet-biting propensities: *all* divine attributes are predicated of the human nature. As Ripa reasons:

> Whatever has, through communication, immense *esse* is God from the force of the union. And for this reason it consequently has, from the *communicatio idiomatum*, immense power and activity. And this is conceded, by every Catholic, of the man assumed by the Word. For if that man is God, he is omnipotent, etc. And it would be in the same way for a stone, if it were united to [God]. And through this communication it can be conceded that the flesh of God is immensely wise, knowledgeable, and willing.[55]

In response to the objection that nothing temporal (such as a human nature) can be God, he argues: "this man is the eternal God, although not eternally God."[56] He borrows an argument from the *Summa halensis* in defense of the legitimacy of the first of the three Christological opinions outlined by Lombard (that is to say, the *homo assumptus* theory). The context is an objection, quoted from the *Summa*, to the effect that if the assumed "man began to be God... then he is newly God, which is against Augustine, who says that... Christ... is not a new God."[57] "He [the author of the *Summa halensis*] responds thus: this does not follow, 'He is newly God, therefore he is a new God', just as it this does not follow, 'He is newly an old man, therefore he is a new old man'."[58] The *Summa* goes on to explain: "an adverb, since it is the adjective of a verb, posits its signification not in relation to the *suppositum*, but in relation to the copula, whereas 'new', since it is an adjective term, posits its thing in relation to the *suppositum*."[59] So it does not follow from being newly something that the item so qualified is new. The example of the old person makes the point vividly: being newly old is not the same as being a new thing—being *young*.

All in all, then, Ripa attempts to show that his *homo assumptus* can be shown to conform to the formal requirements of Chalcedonian orthodoxy. He does so by relying extensively on an inchoate account of relative identity. To make plausible his claim that God can be the form of Christ's human nature, he appeals expressly to the claim that God can be the form of the intellect in the beatific vision. In response to an opponent (the Franciscan Astenius of St. Colombe), he argues as follows:

> His position is firstly said to be defective (and this is *ad hominem*) since he has elsewhere expressly posited, publicly in this university and elsewhere, in my hearing, that God is the formal beatitude, informative of each blessed creature, and he said that this is the express intention of Hugh in the booklet *De sapientia animae Christi*. Consequently he posited not

---

[55] *Det.*, q. 1, a. 3 (Ripa 1957, 147.54–61).

[56] *Det.*, q. 1, a. 3 (Ripa 1957, 146.7–8).

[57] *Det.*, q. 1, a. 3 (Ripa 1957, 145.100–3), quoting *Summa halensis* III, tr. 1, q. 4, d. 3, m. 4, c. 2, a. 1 (IV, 70).

[58] *Det.*, q. 1, a. 3 (Ripa 1957, 145.3–5), quoting *Summa halensis* III, tr. 1, q. 4, d. 3, m. 4, c. 2, a. 1 (IV, 71).

[59] *Summa halensis* III, tr. 1, q. 4, d. 3, m. 4, c. 2, a. 1 (IV, 71).

only that God is able to be a form informative of each blessed creature, but also now *de facto* is [such a form].[60]

In late medieval theology, a *homo assumptus* Christology was not at all fashionable; but thinking of God as in some sense a form of a human being was not so outlandish.

Bibliography

Aquinas, Thomas. 2000–. *Opera omnia*. Recognovit et instruxit Enrique Alarcón automato electronico. Pompaelone: Universitatis Studiorum Navarrensis. https://www.corpusthomisticum.org/iopera.html

Hugh of St Victor. 1854. *De sapientia animae Christi*. ed. J. P. Migne, Patrologiae cursus completus, Series Latina, vol. 176. Paris.

John of Ripa. 1957. *Determinationes*. ed. André Combes, Textes philosophiques du Moyen Age, vol. 4. Paris: J. Vrin.

Summa halensis. 1924–1948. 4 vols. Quaracchi: Collegii S. Bonaventurae.

Vignaux, P. 1959. Dogme de l'Incarnation et métaphysique de la forme chez Jean de Ripa. In *Mélanges offerts à Étienne Gilson de l'Académie française*, Etudes de philosophie médiévale, Hors série, 661–672. Paris: J. Vrin.

---

[60] *Det.*, q. 1, a. 3 (Ripa 1957, 135.99–5); see Hugh, *De sap. an. Christi*, c. 10 (Hugh of St Victor. 1854, col. 851B).

Afterword
Gyula Klima as Medievalist:
A Select Bibliographical Essay

Jacob Archambault

1 Introduction

This essay provides a broad overview of Gyula Klima's published work as a philosopher, logician, translator and historian of medieval thought. I begin with an account of Klima's pioneering contributions in the field of medieval semantics. From there, I examine his work editing, translating, and engaging with the Parisian arts master and logician John Buridan. I close with some remarks on the unique character and import of Klima's work as a historian of medieval philosophy within today's philosophical landscape.

2 Gyula Klima's Contributions in the History of Semantics

Klima's scholarship stretches historically from some of philosophy's best-known figures in Anselm, Aquinas, Ockham and Descartes and lesser-known figures including Thomas of Sutton and Henry of Ghent, to Frege, Geach, Kenny, and others who have produced some of the most impactful scholarship in the analytic tradition; and thematically from debates on identity, categories, and causation in metaphysics, on skepticism in epistemology and theories of mental content in philosophy of mind, to others too numerous to mention.

Klima's influence to date is most felt in the history of semantics. From his earliest contributions to the field, Klima recognized that on account of its limited interest

J. Archambault
C# .NET developer, Louisville, KY, USA
e-mail: jacobarchambault@gmail.com

© The Editor(s) (if applicable) and The Author(s), under exclusive license to
Springer Nature Switzerland AG 2023
J. P. Hochschild et al. (eds.), *Metaphysics Through Semantics: The Philosophical Recovery of the Medieval Mind*, International Archives of the History of Ideas Archives internationales d'histoire des idées 242,
https://doi.org/10.1007/978-3-031-15026-5

389

in developing the semantics of propositions as a precondition for the development of a theory of consequence, the traditional apparatus of classical semantics affords less attention to the components of propositions themselves. Klima fills this lacuna by providing some of the earliest and most ambitious applications of restricted quantification in the history and philosophy of logic, using it both to formalize the medieval theory of *supposition*[1] and to provide a general account of quantitatively ambiguous natural language sentences.[2] Elsewhere, Klima's formalizations of supposition theory specifically and medieval semantics more broadly provide us with an account of abstract and connotative terms (Klima 1991b), a semantic foundation for Aquinas's theory of the analogy of being (Klima 1996, 2002a), and a clean resolution of the problem of existential import in the Aristotelian square of opposition.[3]

2.1 *Decoupling* via antiqua *and* via moderna *Semantics from Metaphysics*

In one sustained thread of that work, Klima decouples *via antiqua* and *via moderna* semantics from the realist and anti-realist metaphysics with which they are most commonly paired, contending that neither semantics by itself strictly entails its associated metaphysics (Klima 1999, 2011b). Rather, archetypical realists were required to adopt non-straightforward semantic accounts of the meanings of terms in at least some cases by their antecedent metaphysical commitments, e.g. to divine simplicity (Klima 2002b), while some of the best known nominalist logicians incorporated what today would be regarded as realist elements in their logic (Klima 2005). For Klima, the *via antiqua* and *via moderna* traditions of medieval logic differ not in their *quantity* of ontological commitments, but in the tools they provide for *handling* ontological commitments, which in turn differ from those of the model-theoretic framework dominant today.

Via antiqua semantics takes an affirmative statement to be true when what is signified by its predicate inheres in what is signified by its subject—sometimes called the *inherence theory of predication*. Within this framework, terms predicating common natures or accidental features of a subject are taken to ultimately refer to exactly the categorical entities one might expect. But the framework avoids full, immediate, fundamental commitment to entities that today's nominalists might find objectionable by providing a rich theory according to which being is predicated in different degrees.[4]

Conversely, the *via moderna* framework that became ascendant after William of Ockham, takes an affirmative statement to be true when its subject and predicate

---

[1] See Read 2019 for an overview.

[2] Klima 1988, 1990, 1991a; Klima and Sandu 1990. Cf. Parsons 2014.

[3] Klima 2001. Cf Read 2015.

[4] See Klima 2002a.

term refer to the same object—sometimes called the *identity theory of predication*. Within this framework, terms predicating common natures or accidental features of a subject need not be taken to ultimately refer to different types of objects such as abstract genera or relations, but instead refer to familiar objects *differently*. For example, the truth of "Socrates is a father" does not require commitment to a distinct entity that is Socrates' fatherhood. Instead, the sentence's predicate may (non-rigidly) refer to Socrates himself, albeit connoting his being a father, and hence refer to the same object as that rigidly referred to by the proper name "Socrates.' Granting some license for intensional contexts,[5] the verb "is" or "exists" in *via moderna* semantics is equally ontologically committing in its various uses, but *what* one is committed to by its uses need not be immediately apparent (Klima 2008b, 427–30).

Both medieval frameworks would reject the object-language metalanguage distinction taken for granted since Tarski in their theory of truth; and in their use of ampliation for tensed, modal, and intensional contexts, both provide ample tools for rejecting a naïve application of Quine's account of ontological commitment in terms of existential quantification.[6]

2.2 Ontological Neutrality and Independence

None of this means that there is *no* relationship between an author's positions in metaphysics and his semantics: rather, the semantic framework an author adopts conditions what options that author has in metaphysics without fully determining them. For example, extreme realism in metaphysics doesn't follow strictly from the *via antiqua*'s inherence theory of predication, but it is the most natural fit for that theory if one accepts the view that terms signifying accidental being denote their referents rigidly while rejecting that framework's insistence on multiple, analogically related senses of "being" (Klima 1999, 125). Conversely, the broad outlines of Ockham's account of the relation between language, thought, and reality serve not only as a foundation for Ockham's own metaphysical reductionism, but also for the realism of a Descartes, Malebranche, Putnam or a Leibniz (Klima 1991b).

There is, however, no relationship of *entailment* from purely semantic principles to metaphysical truths. Klima writes:

> To be sure, this is not to say that metaphysical principles are to be derived from, or somehow justified in a weaker sense on the basis of, semantic principles. Metaphysical principles, being first principles using the most general terms, such as the transcendentals and the categories, cannot be derived from prior principles, and their terms cannot be defined on the basis of more general terms. What semantics can do, however, is that it can provide the principles of interpretation of metaphysical principles. On the basis of these principles of interpretation the implications of metaphysical principles are more clearly delineated, which then can be used in their evaluation in dialectical disputations concerning their

---

[5] See Klima 2005.
[6] Cf. Klima 2004; Klima 2009b, 171–74.

acceptability in the interpretations thus clarified. Furthermore, if the semantic principles of interpretation are made explicit, they can also be subject to further evaluation, in a disputation on a different level, the sort appropriate to the comparison of different logical theories (Klima 2011a, 49).

Modern mathematics names a relation quite close to this in its notion of *independence*, though as the name implies, the fundamental notion itself is by no means a recent one. Just as Cantor's continuum hypothesis is neither provable nor refutable from the principles of Zermelo-Fraenkel set theory alone, or—to provide a more medieval example—truths of revealed theology are neither provable nor refutable from the principles of natural philosophy, neither on Klima's account are metaphysical principles provable or refutable from those of semantics alone.

2.3 Pluralism, Linguistic Imperialism, and the Problem of Cross-Cultural Communication

Two complications distinguish the semantic case from those mentioned. The first is that while both the set-theoretic and theological case mentioned above concern provability and refutability in a single system, the sheer multiplicity of semantic frameworks itself may provide a barrier to a broadly acceptable account of provability across those frameworks. The second complication generalizes a problem nearly the opposite of that established by Gödel in his first incompleteness theorem (Gödel 1931): where that theorem established the expressibility of unprovable claims of number theory in any sufficiently robust system, the semantic problem we face here is that a claim of metaphysics may be taken to be established or refuted merely on account of the lack of expressibility of the particular semantic framework one occupies.

Klima's response to these problems is anti-pluralist without thereby being dogmatically classical. While it would be easy enough to, for instance, construct a metalogical account of validity by quantifying over distinct logical systems on the model of possible world semantics and regarding as valid all and only those theorems valid in every system, Klima instead recognizes the known limitations of classical semantics while also taking the provable equivalence of systems containing distinct logical primitives as *prima facie* evidence for the possibility of a fundamental diversity at the *conceptual* level that nevertheless does not entail a despairing or indifferent anti-realism at the *metaphysical* level (Klima 2012). Instead, Klima's response, both technically and philosophically, is to *extend the framework*. Meeting the tradition where it is, he extends classical semantics to allow for treatment of donkey anaphora (Klima 1988, 2010), non-existent entities (Klima 2001), and quantificational phenomena (Klima and Sandu 1990), while more broadly appealing (in a rare quote of a "continental" philosopher that shows up in multiple places throughout his *œuvre*) to the possibility of a Gadamerian "fusion of horizons" as a solution to the impasse of communication across distinct semantic frameworks, cultures, or philosophical traditions and the attitude of metaphysical anti-realism it encourages (Klima 2000, 2009a).

3 John Buridan

Nowhere has this effort been more sustained than in Klima's scholarship on John Buridan, which has helped elevate the 14th-century arts master from a lesser-known figure to one whose stature is closer to that of an Ockham, arguably surpassing the Franciscan in his logic.

Like the study of medieval contributions to logic and philosophy of science in the early 20th century more broadly, the resurgence of interest in Buridan's writings at that time was stimulated by both their promise as a resource for solving contemporary problems in those disciplines and the way in which they seemed to herald contemporary developments: Duhem, for instance, held out Buridan's theory of impetus as a precursor to Galileo's account of projectile motion; Boehner took the logical systems of Buridan and his contemporaries to be closer to the formal work of the Lvov-Warsaw school than to the anti-formalist tendencies in neo-scholastic textbooks of the day (Boehner 1952), and Louise Nisbet Roberts took Buridan's solution to the Liar paradox to anticipate that of Tarski (Roberts 1953, 100). This interest paved the way for critical editions of Buridan's writing, beginning with Hubien's edition of his *Tractatus de consequentiis* in 1976 and later extending to his output in logic, philosophy of mind, physics and metaphysics.[7]

Klima has built on these contributions both straightforwardly as an editor and translator as well as critically across his articles, books, and various other scholarly contributions. The subtlety of Klima's work as a translator is apparent throughout his translation of Buridan's massive *Summulae de dialectica*, whose footnotes provide an interesting window not only into the text itself, but also into Klima's own decisions on how to translate a text whose parts are frequently concerned with linguistic imprecision and ambiguity. Take, for instance, the following footnote text introducing his translation of the Latin *passio* as "attribute" early on in treatise 1:

> The term *passio*, deriving from the verb *pati* (to suffer, to be affected/acted on, to undergo change), has the primary sense of something affecting a subject (which receives the action of an agent). But since the relation between the term signifying such an affection and the term that signifies the subject is analogous to the relation between the affection itself and the subject itself, the term signifying the affection is also called a *passio* (and the term signifying the subject is also called *subiectum*). Therefore, in this technical sense, whenever a *passio* is correlated with a *subiectum*, referring to a term that is attributed to a subject term in an act of predication, I will translate *passio* as 'attribute.' Whenever *passio* is used to refer to the correlative of some action, however, as is normally the case in the context of Aristotelian physics, or to the correlative category of the category of action, or to the third species of the category of quality discussed below (3.5.4), as is usually the case in the context of the theory of categories, I will use the customary English transcription 'passion.' To

---

[7] See the extensive bibliography provided in Zupko 2018.

be sure, even despite existing translational traditions to this effect, this may occasionally sound odd, given the primary contemporary meaning of the term indicating some strong emotion (which is actually quite fitting in the case of the third species of quality, especially in 3.5.4(2)). But this will be very useful when Buridan exploits some of the conceptual relations between the notions of 'passion' in the technical senses intended here and those of being affected, being acted on, undergoing change, suffering (as the Passion, i.e., the suffering of Christ), and passion in the emotional sense, all of which are conveyed by the Latin *passio* (John Buridan 2001, 5).

In this example (which apart from its discussion of present-day English idiom could well pass for a translation of one among the better specimens of scholastic Latin), Klima's parsing out the different significations of the term *passio*, relating its meaning to that of its English derivative, then justifying different translations for different contexts provides a worthy example of how Klima's long study of Buridan's logic and semantics itself informs his translation of the very Latin texts conveying them.

Klima's Buridan scholarship contrasts with that of preceding generations, however, in three main respects. The first is its breadth: the arc of Klima's scholarship—first gaining notoriety in the fields of logic and semantics, extending from there into medieval natural philosophy and metaphysics, and with an increased focus in recent decades on philosophy of mind and epistemology, culminating in a critical edition of and companion volume to Buridan's *Quaestiones De Anima*—has over time expanded to cover the whole territory of Aristotle's "semantic triangle" mapping out the relations between word and thing through the mediation of concepts. Because of this, Klima's body of work provides what is arguably the most integrated and complete account of John Buridan's philosophy to date.

The second respect in which Klima's Buridan scholarship is distinctive is its stance vis-a-vis contemporary analytic philosophy. Where much earlier scholarship on Buridan's thought stressed its proximity to recent discoveries to lend it greater credibility, Klima has more often used this proximity to challenge contemporary positions on their own terms. For example, where every well-known model theory since Tarski both identifies truth in a model with satisfaction and grounds its account of logical consequence on that of truth, leading Tarski himself to regard all semantically closed languages as inconsistent (Tarski 1943, 348–49), Klima shows how Buridan both rejects the Tarskian identification and inverts the above grounding relation between consequence and truth. Reason for rejecting the first can be found without recourse to semantic paradoxes, merely by considering statements like "no sentence is negative," whose satisfaction conditions preclude them from being true at their time of utterance (Klima 2004, 96–100). Furthermore, not only is there no need for an account of satisfaction grounding that of consequence to do double duty as an account of truth, but because statements may fail to be true by being inherently inconsistent with what they posit (as occurs with "no sentence is negative"), or merely contingently so (as occurs with reciprocal liar sentences that in other contexts would be merely true or false), the semantics for terms like "true" and "false" themselves presuppose a notion of entailment like that hinted at in Buridan's idea of a sentence virtually implying its own truth.[8] Consequently, a sentence meeting its satisfaction conditions constitutes a necessary, but not a sufficient condition for its truth, and the T-Schema for truth is simply mistaken. In another example, Klima inserts Buridan into the dispute between Quine and his fictional interlocutor Wyman over what exists, to argue that both are mistaken not in the particularities of their approach to ontological commitment, but more broadly in accepting a context-insensitive quantifier with its tacit assumption of the availability of a metalinguistic "view from nowhere" as a criterion for ontological commitment at all: "the solution Buridan offers is not an overall split between object-language and meta-language but a more careful regulation of the reflective uses of the same language" (Klima 2009b, 174). More recently, Klima has expanded the differences expressed arche-typically here in different attitudes towards the object-metalanguage distinction into a concise summary of the different orientations of the medieval project Buridan engaged in and that which animated Quine, Tarski and the tradition after them:

1. The "modern project": to "cannibalize" ever greater portions of all possible forms of natural language reasoning, expand the expressive resources of our formal language(s) for which we can have a uniform definition of validity, grounding the construction of a universal method for checking validity either in terms of deduction rules or a composi-tional semantics.
2. The "medieval project": to "regulate" ever greater portions of all possible forms of natu-ral language reasoning, regiment the syntax of our natural language as much as ordinary usage would tolerate, so as to be able to accommodate as many forms of natural lan-guage reasoning as possible, and thus to be able to separate valid from invalid conse-quences in accordance with a range of different criteria of validity.[9]

This depth of critical engagement with both medieval and modern philosophy has often led to a certain prescience in the themes and positions advanced in Klima's work: his use of restricted quantifiers in formalizing Buridan's logic predates revived interest in these in work on relevant logic and semantic paradox by roughly twenty years;[10] his formalization of the medieval square of opposition, on which the existential import of categorical sentences is determined by their quality (affirmative or negative) rather than their quantity (universal or particular), significantly predates comparable formal treatments in ancient and medieval logic,[11] and his early analysis of suppositional descents is echoed in articles on pronouns and donkey anaphora being published as this paper is being written.[12]

---

[8] Klima 2004, 101–7. Cf. Klima 2009b, 221–25; Hughes 1982, 22–27.

[9] Klima 2016, 341. Cf. Klima 2008b, 429–30.

[10] Cf. Klima 1988, Beall et al. 2006, Field 2014. For earlier work, see Hailperin 1957a, b.

[11] Cf. Klima 1988, 18–43; Chatti and Schang 2013, Read 2015.

[12] Cf. Klima 1990, Blumberg 2021.

4   Klima as Historian

The third respect in which Klima's Buridan scholarship, and indeed his work as a medievalist as a whole, has distinguished itself is in its orientation towards its source material. While the above shows Klima amply capable of both "pure" historical scholarship and bringing medievals into engagement with his contemporaries, much of his work goes beyond that to broader questions of how historical shifts in medieval thought have occasioned the adoption of beliefs widely held today, and by extension the impasses they lead to. In this way, Klima's reading of Buridan, Ockham, Aquinas and others does not so much mine them as resources for arguments and positions as it takes their study as part of a kind of philosophical recovery program. In various places his writings begin with one question only to lead their reader to a higher one: moving, for instance, in his Stanford Encyclopedia article on medieval theories of universals from the various questions arising out of Plato's theory of forms that the medievals inherited from Porphyry via Boethius to a consideration of how the debate factored into the disintegration of scholastic discourse (Klima 2017); or from considering changes to the notion of an efficient cause in the late medieval period to the impact of those changes on how we continue to think about knowledge and certainty today (Klima 2013). In a review of Anthony Kenny's *Aquinas on Mind*, Klima contrasts that book's approach of making Aquinas's ideas "accessible to the philosophically interested contemporary reader in terms of such philosophical, scientific and everyday concepts with which the reader can safely be assumed to be familiar" (Klima 1998, 113) with his own approach as follows:

> First, as should be obvious, we shall never understand properly any of Aquinas's theories without first "learning his language." However, "learning his language" does not mean just learning Latin, but rather acquiring the radically different conceptual apparatus encoded in his language, constantly reflecting on how this different apparatus constitutes its own self-evident truths, while questioning the validity of what we take to be self-evident truths on account of the conceptual apparatus encoded in our philosophical language. Second, we shall never be able to communicate our understanding of Aquinas authentically unless we learn how to "teach his language" (Klima 1998, 115).

For the kind of teaching that Klima is demanding here, let us consider an example from elsewhere in his *corpus*, where he leverages a comparison to modern thermodynamics into a defense of a claim from Aristotle's *Physics*, oft-quoted by Aquinas, that "man is generated by man and the sun":

> [A] universal cause as Aquinas thinks about it, is certainly not a universal in its being (given that Aquinas rejects Platonic universals), but in its causality: a particular cause is the cause of only this particular effect, whereas a universal cause is a cause of several particulars of a given kind. However, an immediate consequence of this interpretation and the above-demonstrated irreflexivity of per se efficient causality is that a universal cause of a given kind of particulars itself cannot be of the same kind; for otherwise, being the cause of all particulars of the same kind, it would have to be a cause of itself, which is impossible. Therefore, the universal cause of a species cannot be a member of the same species: it has to be a non-univocal cause, that is to say, the form by virtue of which it acts and produces and/or sustains its effects is not the same form that it brings about in its effects. This is the reason that talking about more or less universal causes, which Aquinas also explicitly iden-

tifies with more or less remote causes, he means not only that the causality of a more universal cause extends to more kinds, but also that the reason why its causality covers more kinds of effects is that it is causing them in a more universal respect: it has a power and a corresponding activity that can be received in so many different ways by different kinds of recipients, as the radiation of the sun received as heat in water powers the water cycle around the globe, while received in the chloroplasts of plants, it powers (most of) the biosphere (Klima 2013, 41).

The unintuitiveness of this claim itself provides a solid test case for the kind of work that Klima takes to be necessary for understanding medieval philosophy, and with it for understanding how its developments both presage and hint at ways out of our own persistent philosophical impasses. Within the pages preceding this selection, Klima outlines the notion of efficient causality largely taken for granted today as a diachronic relation holding between events, contrasts it with the medieval notion as a synchronic relation between individual things, and lays the groundwork for showing how the medieval notion is in certain ways closer to the scientific accounts used today in thermodynamics and information theory. The charity Klima aims for here is fundamentally higher than that typically afforded to this and other historically discarded theories—not merely to explain how it could have been believed given the information available and/or the psychological makeup of the inhabitants at the time, but to explain how such claims *understood on their own terms* could themselves approximate the truth.[13]

5 Conclusion

Despite the depth and breadth of his work, the amount of space Klima devotes to advancing positions that are unambiguously his own, rather than to steel-manning positions of historical or contemporary figures he may or may not agree with, is comparatively little.[14] Still, Klima's analysis here provides a window into the answer to a more personal question that his scholarship solicits: namely, of all the intellectual pursuits to devote oneself to, why study medieval philosophy, and specifically medieval semantics?

In one uncommonly autobiographical passage, Klima writes:

I remember that when I was at Notre Dame (so this happened in the second half of the nineties), I asked several of my colleagues, and even the then visiting David Armstrong, to provide metaphysically non-committal clarifications of the semantics of the language they were using in describing their metaphysical theories. In response, I was given puzzled looks and declarations strongly reminiscent of the way medieval nominalists characterized the attitude of their realist opponents: we don't care about names; we go right to the things

---

[13] Cf. Rovelli 2015.

[14] Exceptions include his acceptance of both Anselm's proof of God's existence and Aquinas's proof of the immateriality of the intellect as sound (Klima 2000, 2009a) and his advancing, based on an examination of Buridan's treatment of reciprocal liar paradoxes, that any adequate semantics for natural language must be semantically closed and token-based (Klima 2004, 2008a).

themselves!—Well, just look at the history of late-scholasticism and early modern philosophy to see what good that attitude did for them.

So, what can we do to avoid the late-scholastic scenario, going on another cycle of end-
less and more and more meaningless metaphysical debates until the arrival of another Kant
declaring the whole enterprise ill-founded and another Carnap declaring it to be meaningless, to launch another anti-metaphysical cycle of meaningless search for meaning to be
abandoned yet again for metaphysics, etc., etc.? Why don't we try both in tandem, i.e.,
analysis and metaphysics at the same time, as the very designation "analytic metaphysics"
would seem to demand? For then we could start by laying down our clearly defined semantic principles (instead of making them up and twisting them around as we go) and engage
each other in our metaphysical debates according to the same principles, instead of talking
past each other, making clear that whoever is talking according to different semantic principles is just playing a different game (Klima 2014, 86–87).

Here, the difficulty that Klima's apology for analysis aims to alleviate remains—
namely, that in much debate in the core disciplines of analytic philosophy and in
metaphysics in particular, rival participants are often unable or unwilling to state
their positions in a linguistic context their opponents would be able to agree to, leaving such debates unfruitful from the start. Without the opportunity for common
ground that semantics provides, not only shared understanding, but even proof,
refutation, and disagreement itself become unattainable.

With this problem in mind, Klima's study of medieval semantics, as a study of
frameworks of meaning remarkably foreign to that of our own time, provides an
example *par excellence* of the kind of interpretive charity needed to surmount our
own crises of meaning and communication.

Bibliography

Beall, J.C., Ross T. Brady, A.P. Hazen, Graham Priest, and Greg Restall. 2006. Relevant restricted
    quantification. *Journal of Philosophical Logic* 35 (6): 587–598. https://doi.org/10.1007/
    s10992-005-9008-5.
Blumberg, Kyle. 2021. Pronouns as demonstratives. *Philosophers' Imprint* 21 (35): 1–22.
Boehner, Philotheus. 1952. *Medieval logic: An outline of its development from 1250 to c.1400*.
    Manchester: Manchester University Press.
Chatti, Saloua, and Fabien Schang. 2013. The cube, the square and the problem of existential
    import. *History and Philosophy of Logic* 34 (2): 101–132. https://doi.org/10.1080/01445340.
    2013.764962.
Field, Hartry. 2014. Naive truth and restricted quantification: Saving truth a whole lot better.
    Review of Symbolic Logic 7 (1): 1–45. https://doi.org/10.1017/s1755020313000312.
Gödel, Kurt. 1931. Über Formal Unentscheidbare Sätze Der Principia Mathematica Und
    Verwandter Systeme i. *Monatshefte Für Mathematik Und Physik* 38 (1): 173–198.
Hailperin, Theodore. 1957a. A theory of restricted quantification I. *Journal of Symbolic Logic* 22
    (1): 19–35. https://doi.org/10.2307/2964055.
———. 1957b. A theory of restricted quantification II. *Journal of Symbolic Logic* 22 (2): 113–129.
Hughes, G.E. 1982. *John Buridan on self-reference*. Cambridge: Cambridge University Press.
John Buridan. 2001. *Summulae de Dialectica*. Translated by Gyula Klima. Yale Library of
    Medieval Philosophy. New Haven: Yale University Press.
Klima, Gyula. 1988. *Ars artium: Essays in philosophical semantics, medieval and modern*.
    Budapest: Institute of Philosophy, Hungarian Academy of Sciences.

————. 1990. Approaching natural language *via* mediaeval logic. In *Zeichen, Denken, Praxis*, ed. J. Bernard and J. Kelemen, 249–267. Vienna: Institut für Sozio-Semiotische Studien.

————. 1991a. Latin as a formal language: Outlines of a Buridanian semantics. *Cahiers de l'Institut Du Moyen-Âge Grec Et Latin* 61: 78–106.

————. 1991b. Ontological alternatives vs. alternative semantics in mediaeval philosophy. *S: European Journal for Semiotic Studies* 3 (4): 587–618.

————. 1996. The semantic principles underlying Saint Thomas Aquinas's metaphysics of being. *Medieval Philosophy and Theology* 5 (1): 87–141.

————. 1998. Anthony Kenny, *Aquinas on mind. Faith and Philosophy* 15 (1): 113–117.

————. 1999. Ockham's semantics and ontology of the categories. In *The Cambridge Companion to Ockham*, ed. Paul Vincent Spade, 118–142. Cambridge: Cambridge University Press.

————. 2000. Saint Anselm's proof: A problem of reference, intentional identity and mutual understanding. In *Medieval Philosophy and Modern Times*, edited by Ghita Holström-Hintikka, 69–87. Synthese Library 288. Dordrecht: Kluwer.

————. 2001. Existence and reference in medieval logic. In *New essays in free logic*, ed. Alexander Hieke and Edgar Morscher, 197–226. Dordrecht: Kluwer.

————. 2002a. Aquinas' theory of the copula and the analogy of being. *History of Philosophy & Logical Analysis* 5: 159–176.

————. 2002b. Contemporary 'essentialism' vs. Aristotelian essentialism. In *Mind, metaphysics, and value in the Thomistic and analytic traditions*, ed. John Haldane, 175–194. Notre Dame, IN: University of Notre Dame Press.

————. 2004. Consequences of a closed, token-based semantics: The case of John Buridan. *History and Philosophy of Logic* 25 (2): 95–110.

————. 2005. The essentialist nominalism of John Buridan. *Review of Metaphysics* 58 (4): 739–754.

————. 2008a. Logic without truth: Buridan on the liar. In *Unity, truth and the liar: The modern relevance of medieval solutions to the liar paradox*, ed. S. Rahman, T. Tulenheimo, and E. Genot, 87–112. Berlin: Springer.

————. 2008b. The nominalist semantics of Ockham and Buridan: A rational reconstruction. In *Handbook of the history of logic, Volume 2: Mediaeval and renaissance logic*, ed. Dov M. Gabbay and John Woods, 389–432. Amsterdam: Elsevier.

————. 2009a. Aquinas on the materiality of the human soul and the immateriality of the human intellect. *Philosophical Investigations* 32: 163–182.

————. 2009b. *John Buridan*. Great Medieval Thinkers. Oxford: Oxford University Press.

————. 2010. Natural logic, medieval logic and formal semantics. *Magyar Filozófiai Szemle* 54: 58–75.

————. 2011a. Thomas of Sutton and Henry of Ghent on the analogy of being. In *Categories and what is beyond*, edited by Gyula Klima and Alexander W. Hall, 49–64. Proceedings of the Society for Medieval Logic and Metaphysics 2. Newcastle upon Tyne: Cambridge Scholars Publishing.

————. 2011b. Two *Summulae*, two ways of doing logic: Peter of Spain's 'realism' and John Buridan's 'nominalism'. In *Methods and methodologies: Aristotelian logic east and west 500–1500*, ed. Margaret Cameron and John Marenbon, 109–126. Leiden: Brill.

————. 2012. Ontological reduction by logical analysis and the primitive vocabulary of mentalese. *American Catholic Philosophical Quarterly* 86 (3): 403–414.

————. 2013. Whatever happened to efficient causes? In *Skepticism, causality, and skepticism about causality*, edited by Gyula Klima and Alexander W. Hall, 31–42. Proceedings of the Society for Medieval Logic and Metaphysics 10. Newcastle upon Tyne: Cambridge Scholars.

————. 2014. "The rises and falls of analysis and metaphysics." In *Metaphysical themes, medieval and modern*, edited by Gyula Klima and Alexander W. Hall, 85–88. Proceedings for the Society of Medieval Logic and Metaphysics 11. Newcastle upon Tyne: Cambridge Scholars Publishing.

————. 2016. Consequence. In *The Cambridge companion to medieval logic*, ed. Catarina Dutilh Novaes and Stephen Read, 316–341. Cambridge: Cambridge University Press.

————. 2017. The medieval problem of universals. In *The Stanford encyclopedia of philosophy*, edited by Edward N. Zalta, Winter 2017. https://plato.stanford.edu/archives/win2017/entries/universals-medieval/

Klima, Gyula, and Gabriel Sandu. 1990. Numerical quantifiers in game-theoretical semantics. *Theoria* 56 (3): 173–192. https://doi.org/10.1111/j.1755-2567.1990.tb00181.x.

Parsons, Terence. 2014. *Articulating medieval logic*. Oxford: Oxford University Press.

Read, Stephen. 2015. Aristotle and Łukasciewicz on existential import. *Journal of the American Philosophical Association* 1 (3): 535–544.

————. 2019. Medieval theories: Properties of terms." In *The Stanford encyclopedia of philosophy*, edited by Edward N. Zalta, Spring 2019. https://plato.stanford.edu/archives/spr2019/entries/medieval-terms/

Roberts, Louise Nisbet. 1953. Every proposition is false – A medieval paradox. *Tulane Studies in Philosophy* 2: 95–102.

Rovelli, Carlo. 2015. Aristotle's physics: A physicist's look. *Journal of the American Philosophical Association* 1 (1): 23–40. https://doi.org/10.1017/apa.2014.11.

Tarski, Alfred. 1943. The semantic conception of truth and the foundations of semantics. *Philosophy and Phenomenological Research* 4 (3): 341–376. https://doi.org/10.2307/2102968.

Zupko, Jack. 2018. John Buridan. In *The Stanford encyclopedia of philosophy*, edited by Edward N. Zalta, Fall 2018. https://plato.stanford.edu/archives/fall2018/entries/buridan/

Abstracts

Introduction: In Appreciation of Gyula Klima, by Joshua P. Hochschild

To help frame the Festschrift for Gyula Klima, this appreciation offers perspective on the scholar's person and project. Drawing on biographical details and reflecting on signal contributions, it seeks to honor a distinguished philosopher who deserves to be celebrated by friends and introduced to a new generation of readers.

Chapter 1: Pythagoras, the Philosopher and Grammar Teacher (Br. Lib. Add. MS 37516 *recto*), by István Bodnár

The chapter is about a *chreia*—a one-liner used as a grammatical exercise sentence—that presents Pythagoras as proscribing an expression from admissible linguistic usage. This injunction is funny because it can be construed as Pythagoras railing against the use of a particular variant form of an adjective—and also as against the use of items denoted by that adjective. In the chapter I add to this line of interpretation the further point that the *chreia* also claims that in this latter construal the injunction was Pythagoras's signature insight, making him the philosopher that he was.

© The Editor(s) (if applicable) and The Author(s), under exclusive license to
Springer Nature Switzerland AG 2023
J. P. Hochschild et al. (eds.), *Metaphysics Through Semantics: The Philosophical Recovery of the Medieval Mind*, International Archives of the History of Ideas Archives internationales d'histoire des idées 242,
https://doi.org/10.1007/978-3-031-15026-5

Chapter 2: Abelard on Existential Inference, by Peter King

Peter Abelard is nowadays credited as the first philosopher to recognize the problem of existential import. I argue that he does not recognize our modern problem, and that his own take on the logical issues that are said to give rise to the problem is much more interesting and subtle than has usually been acknowledged, depending on claims in the philosophy of language that are worthy of investigation in their own right—in the end, vindicating Abelard's claims about the traditional Square of Opposition.

Chapter 3: Rereading "Saint Anselm's Proof", by Daniel Patrick Moloney

Gyula Klima's paper "Saint Anselm's Proof" is only secondarily about St. Anselm and his *Proslogion* argument for the existence of God; it is primarily an interpretation of Aquinas's criticisms of attempts to argue that the existence (and other attributes) of God can be *per se notum*, such that no "cosmological" argument (*demonstration quia*) is necessary for "God" to serve as the central concept in *sacra doctrina*. Klima's criticism of Anselm appears to be misplaced, since Anselm does not claim that his argument is *a priori* or *per se notum*, nor does he fail to appreciate the importance of what Klima calls constitutive reference to the success of his argument. Nevertheless, Klima's paper is brilliant and needed. It presents a subtle and insightful exegesis of a neglected article in the *Summa Theologiae*, with ramifications for understanding the project of the *Summa* as a whole, and other debates among Thomists and their critics (e.g., about the New Natural Law). Equally as important, it presents an inspiring vision of the philosophical life as capable of bringing people together across conceptual differences

Chapter 4: Albert the Great Among the Pygmies: Explaining Animal Intelligence in the Thirteenth Century, by Peter G. Sobol

Aristotle's restriction of intellect to humans raised the problem of how animals are able to react to and learn from their environment if they lack the ability to recognize classes of objects, an ability supposedly conferred by intellect. Aristotle's delineation of the internal senses into the common sense, imagination, and memory did not include a locus for the cleverness or prudence that he found animals to possess in varying degrees. Avicenna supplemented Aristotle's internal senses by adding the estimative power, which allowed animals to recognize the value of a perceived object in terms of its potential benefit or harm. Albert the Great, who showed more interest than most medieval philosophers in the problem of animal behavior, adopted the estimative power and began his inquiry by considering pygmies, which he judged to be the highest form of animal. This inquiry led Albert to weaken but in the end to retain the distinction based on intellectual abilities between animals and humans.

Chapter 5: "The Essential Differentiae of Things are Unknown to Us": Thomas Aquinas on the Limits of the Knowability of Natural Substances, by Fabrizio Amerini

Thomas Aquinas is often presented as a philosopher with a realist and optimistic attitude toward human knowledge. This is essentially true. Nevertheless, there are texts where Aquinas underscores the limits of our knowledge of natural things. For example, he states that we arrive at knowing and naming the substance of a thing only through knowing its accidents. Aquinas makes three main claims about this process: first, the essential principles of natural things are unknown to us; second, the accidents of a thing give a great contribution to the knowledge of what a thing is; third, we impose names on things moving from their accidents. Such claims may be read as introducing a skeptical concern. On the contrary, they express a form of phenomenal realism, which Aquinas reconciles with representationalism in knowledge.

Chapter 6: Aquinas, *perversor philosophiae suae*, by Gábor Borbély

In the closing passages of his *De unitate intellectus*, Thomas Aquinas makes some indignant remarks about the use of language and the philosophical views of one of his unnamed opponents, whom I call Athaq in this paper. I will argue that Aquinas does not intend to accommodate Athaq's claims in his own system of beliefs. Quite the contrary, he tries to render these claims as outlandish as possible in an attempt to expose what he supposes to be Athaq's true intention. Aquinas's theoretical unkindness, however, comes at a price, as it makes himself less rational and coherent, at least with respect to the issues concerned. Put differently, his uncharitable interpretation has a destructive effect on his own philosophy and theology.

Chapter 7: Knowing Non-existent Natures: A Problem for Aquinas's Semantics of Essence, by Turner C. Nevitt

Aquinas considers the questions "Does it exist?" and "What is it?" basic to any science in Aristotle's sense. In his early works, Aquinas claims that we can answer the second question without answering the first, knowing a thing's essence without knowing whether it exists. This claim is part of a famous argument for the real distinction between essence and existence in creatures, and for the existence of God. But in his later commentaries on Aristotle, Aquinas appears to abandon the claim, insisting that it is impossible to know what something is without knowing whether it exists. What should we make of this apparent contradiction? It is possible that Aquinas simply changed his mind, or that in his later commentaries he is only explaining Aristotle's view, with which he disagrees. In this chapter, however, I defend a third solution based upon Aquinas's distinction between two ways of knowing what something is—"by means of a definition" and "by means of a proposition." For Aquinas explains that in one way we can know a thing's essence without knowing its existence, and in the other way, we cannot. Thus, the apparent contradiction can be resolved by making just such a distinction. Yet understanding this third solution requires an examination of the semantics of definitions and propositions informing Aquinas's logical approach to essence. Such an examination not only allows us to resolve the apparent contradiction between his works but also gives us a better understanding of his logical approach to essence.

Chapter 8: Metaphors, Dead and Alive, by Martin Klein

This chapter examines how the medieval distinction between proper and improper signification can give a plausible explanation of both metaphorical use and the usual transformations a language can undergo. I will show how Thomas Aquinas distinguishes between ordinary ambiguous terms and metaphors, whereas William of Ockham and Walter Burley do not leave room for this distinction. I will argue that Ockham's conception of transfer of sense through the subsequent institution of words is best thought of as an explanation of how ordinary usage can contain ambiguities, whereas Burley's conception of transfer of sense without new imposition is more plausible when it comes to explaining metaphors. If metaphorical use is lumped together with equivocation, the account of how they work cannot do full justice to either, an insight that we already find in Peter Abelard, if not in Boethius.

Chapter 9: Truth and Person in Aquinas's *De veritate*, by Robert J. Dobie

Aquinas's *Disputed Questions on Truth* (*De veritate*) are perhaps his most sustained examination of the implication that being is fundamentally and intrinsically intelligible and desirable, i.e., that "true" and "good" are transcendental terms convertible with "being." I argue that the primary implication that Aquinas draws from this principle is that material creatures are not only intrinsically true and good, but that, in being so, they mediate a personal reality insofar as material creatures mediate the ideas and desires of a divine, creative mind and will to created minds and wills, for an infinite and perfect mind must be the *transcendent ground* or cause of the transcendental properties of being. So, just as creatures are inherently true and good, the created world is inherently interpersonal: all creatures, insofar as they exist, are inherently oriented toward communicating the mind and will of their Creator—not in actuality, but in potentiality, for the world becomes actually interpersonal only to the degree that the truth of its Creator is known by faith. This is so because the virtue of faith orients our minds and wills to Christ as the ground of the interpersonal nature of the world, but it also actualizes and perfects our intellects and wills by revealing that the mystery of the transcendent ground of truth and goodness is analogous to the mystery of the incarnate person.

Chapter 10: Transcendentals Explained Through Syncategoremata: Is Being as Truth a Transcendental According to Thomas Aquinas?, by Giovanni Ventimiglia

Being as truth has a greater extension and universality than being as an act of being in Aquinas's metaphysics, because it also includes privations and negations. In order to better understand this aspect, it is necessary to examine the role played by logic and, in particular, by the syncategoremata "est" and "non" in the definition of being as truth. This analysis leads to the discovery that being as truth is expressed in terms of an *est* as a *passio enuntiationis* and corresponds to the *affirmatio* or *actus compositionis* of which contemporary treatises on logic spoke. Can such a *passio enuntiationis* be a *passio entis*? In Aquinas's works, there are arguments for and against.

Chapter 11: Truth as a Transcendental, by Edward Feser

This chapter examines the Scholastic thesis that truth is a transcendental property of being, and its relevance to debates in contemporary analytics philosophy. The chapter begins with a brief survey of analytic views about truth. Then, after setting out the Scholastic doctrine of the transcendentals in general, it explains how truth in particular fits into it, with special attention to the Scholastic distinction between logical truth and ontological truth. The chapter then considers the light these Scholastic ideas shed on debates about realism and anti-realism, skepticism and conceptual relativism, the Principle of Sufficient Reason, the Augustinian theistic argument from eternal truths, Trinitarian theology, and other controversies.

Chapter 12: Four Notes on the Grammar of Ockham's Mental Language, by Claude Panaccio

William of Ockham's discussion of which grammatical categories are relevant for describing the syntax of mental language occurs in two short and closely related passages: *Quodlibeta* V, 8 and *Summa logicae* I, 3. In the present chapter, I discuss four riddles that are raised by these two texts: (1) I point to an apparent anomaly in the structure of *Summa logicae* I, 3, and I propose an amendment to the St. Bonaventure edition in this regard; (2) I argue that Ockham's main grammatical source in the two passages is the Latin grammarian Donatus rather than Priscian (as might have been thought), and I show why this is relevant; (3) I clarify what problem Ockham has in mind when saying that there is a special difficulty about whether distinctions of "quality" (*qualitas*) are found among mental names as they are among spoken names; (4) I explain what Ockham means by the "figure" (*figura*) of names and verbs and why he thinks that this grammatical category is of no relevance for the analysis of mental language.

Chapter 13: Thoughts About Things: Aquinas, Buridan and Late Medieval Nominalism, by Calvin G. Normore

Gyula Klima has argued that the disagreements between Nominalists and Realists in the Middle Ages, as exemplified in the views of John Buridan and Thomas Aquinas, centered less in semantics and metaphysics than in epistemology and philosophy of mind. This chapter suggests that in the light of Prof. Klima's arguments, the disagreements in these areas cannot easily be separated and raise a number of issues that remain of philosophical importance.

Chapter 14: Buridan's Reinterpretation of Natural Possibility and Necessity, by Guido Alt

In his natural philosophy, John Buridan reinterprets Aristotelian conceptions of necessity using a framework derived from his logical writings. After a discussion of Buridan's account of varieties of necessity, in this chapter I shall approach some interpretative uses of that account where two natural philosophical concerns are involved. The first is connected with the relationship of modality and time in a question from the first book of his commentary to *De Generatione et Corruptione* addressing a consequence from possibilities of alteration to possibilities of generation. The content of that question hinges on the metaphysical connection between alteration and substantial changes. In the third section, I shall explore a quasi-definition of causal necessity and contingency Buridan discusses in the second book of his commentary to the *Physics*. Buridan's discussion of alternative descriptions of causal necessity and contingency in that context reveals competing pictures of the role of essences in causal explanation associated with Avicenna and Averroes, respectively.

Chapter 15: The Semantic Account of Formal Consequence, from Alfred Tarski Back to John Buridan,
by Jacob Archambault

The resemblance of the theory of formal consequence first offered by the fourteenth-century logician John Buridan to that later offered by Alfred Tarski has long been remarked upon. But it has not yet been subjected to sustained analysis. In this chapter, I provide just such an analysis. I begin by reviewing today's classical understanding of formal consequence, then highlighting its differences from Tarski's 1936 account. Following this, I introduce Buridan's account, detailing its philosophical underpinnings, then its content. This then allows us to separate those aspects of Tarski's account representing genuine historical advances, unavailable to Buridan, from others merely differing from—and occasionally explicitly rejected by—Buridan's account.

Chapter 16: Skeptical Motivators in Buridan's Philosophy of Science, by Ariane Economos

The resemblance of the theory of formal consequence first offered by the fourteenth-century logician John Buridan to that later offered by Alfred Tarski has long been remarked upon. But it has not yet been subjected to sustained analysis. In this chapter, I provide just such an analysis. I begin by reviewing today's classical understanding of formal consequence, then highlighting its differences from Tarski's 1936 account. Following this, I introduce Buridan's account, detailing its philosophical underpinnings, then its content. This then allows us to separate those aspects of Tarski's account representing genuine historical advances, unavailable to Buridan, from others merely differing from—and occasionally explicitly rejected by—Buridan's account.

Chapter 17: Parody or Touch-Up? Duns Scotus's Engagement with Anselm's *Proslogion* Argument, by Giorgio Pini

Can the *Proslogion* argument for God's existence be parodied to demonstrate the existence of the worst evil? This is what Duns Scotus contends in one of his works, where he presents such a parody as evidence for the argument's unsoundness. Elsewhere, however, Scotus defends a "touched-up" version (*coloratio*) of Anselm's argument. In my reconstruction, Scotus's touched-up argument includes three stages: first, a demonstration that that than which a greater cannot be thought is a possible object of thought; second, a demonstration that that than which a greater cannot be thought can be thought to exist and so can exist; third, a demonstration that that than which a greater cannot be thought actually exists. Contrary to what has sometimes been maintained, I argue that Scotus's argument does not make any illegitimate shift from logical to real possibility. I also contend that one of the most characteristic aspects of Scotus's touched-up argument is that the comparison between existing in the intellect and existing in reality (arguably the weakest point in standard reconstructions of Anselm's argument) plays no role in it, and that accordingly Scotus's argument is immune from his own parody of Anselm's argument.

Chapter 18: *De se* vs. *de facto* Ontology in Late-Medieval Realism, by Laurent Cesalli

This chapter considers medieval moderate realism with respect to universals. In the first part, I present and discuss the reasons why some late medieval philosophers— for example, Pseudo-Richard of Campsall and Richard Brinkley—hold the following conjunction of claims: whatever exists is particular *and* universals exist. The short answer is that such a conjunction is possible provided one distinguishes between what is *de se* and what is *de facto*. In the second part, I compare such a philosophical stance with other forms of medieval realism and trace the *de se/de facto* distinction back to (at least) Albert the Great's definition of universals. As a whole, the chapter is an attempt to shed some light on what appears to be the magic formula of medieval moderate realism, namely: be a realist with respect to universals *and* stick to particularist ontology.

Chapter 19: Connotation vs. Extrinsic Denomination: Peter Auriol on Intentions and Intellectual Cognition, by Giacomo Fornasieri

In this chapter, I examine Peter Auriol's contribution regarding (i) what it is for a thing to be an intention or a concept and (ii) what kind of relation connects the object cognized to the cognizing mind as soon as intellectual cognition is occurring. First, I consider Auriol's criticism of Brito's thesis, according to which intentions are the same as cognitive acts, and "being cognized," or for a thing to be objectively in the mind, is just for there to be a cognitive act directed at that thing. Then, I discuss Auriol's thesis, according to which each and every act of thinking must be thought of as a connotative notion, that is, as something implying or connoting an intentional object appearing to the cognizer. In this regard, Auriol's view, as opposed to Brito's, allows him to think of "being cognized" as more than an extrinsic denomination of the object cognized, as well as to incorporate into intellectual cognition a phenomenon that proves to be unique to our cognitive life, viz. the fact that we consciously experience what we cognize while we cognize it. Finally, I offer some concluding remarks on Auriol's doctrine, as well as a brief evaluation of his theory.

Chapter 20: Temporal Origins Essentialism and Gappy Existence in Marsilius of Inghen's *Quaestiones super libros De generatione et corruptione*, by Adam Wood

In his commentary on Aristotle's *De generatione et corruptione* Marsilius of Inghen defends the view—unusual in the Middle Ages—that there is no such thing as intermittent or "gappy" existence. Even God cannot restore things that have been corrupted. This chapter examines Marsilius's unusual position, connecting them to another view he defends, namely that a thing's origins—and in particular the time at which it comes about—are essential to its numerical identity as the particular individual it is. I consider John Buridan and Nicole Oresme's influence upon Marsilius's views, and ultimately evaluate their plausibility, drawing on some recent work of Gyula Klima's on gappy existence in Thomas Aquinas.

Chapter 21: John of Ripa and the Metaphysics of Christology, by Richard Cross

John of Ripa's (fl. 1350s) Christology is highly unusual in the context of late medieval theology, since it is a form of the old *"homo assumptus* (assumed man)" Christology found in St. Augustine and the Victorines, but not generally in later theologians. Ripa explains the incarnation by supposing that the divine essence is in some sense the form of the human nature, such that both "God" and the whole panoply of divine properties can be predicated of it. This move allows Ripa to secure the truth of claims mandated by the authoritative Council of Chalcedon, such as "this human being is eternal." Ripa appeals to a kind of relative identity to argue that the human being is (non-classically) identical with the divine person, such that positing something that "is God, but not the deity" does not result in an additional God or additional divine person.

Afterword: Gyula Klima as Medievalist: A Select Bibliographical Essay, by Jacob Archambault

This essay provides a broad introduction to Gyula Klima's contributions in the field of medieval philosophy, with special attention to his pioneering work in semantics and on the 14th-century arts master and rector at the University of Paris John Buridan. Klima's scholarship provides one of the best examples available among philosophers living today not only of how to read thinkers in the medieval tradition, but also of how the effort to understand a radically different paradigm embodied in that reading provides the first steps to resolving broader problems of communication across distinct traditions and subdisciplines in philosophy at large.